THE THEOLOGICAL ORIGINS OF MODERNITY

The Theological Origins of Modernity

MICHAEL ALLEN GILLESPIE

The University of Chicago Press   *Chicago and London*

Michael Allen Gillespie is professor of philosophy and
the Jerry G. and Patricia Crawford Hubbard Professor
of Political Science at Duke University and the author
of *Hegel, Heidegger, and the Ground of History* and
Nihilism before Nietzsche, both published by the
University of Chicago Press.

The University of Chicago Press, Chicago 60637
The University of Chicago Press, Ltd., London
© 2008 by The University of Chicago
All rights reserved. Published 2008
Printed in the United States of America

17 16 15 14 13 12 11 10 09 08   2 3 4 5

ISBN-13: 978-0-226-29345-5 (cloth)
ISBN-10: 0-226-29345-9 (cloth)

Library of Congress Cataloging-in-Publication Data
Gillespie, Michael Allen.
    The theological origins of modernity / Michael Allen
Gillespie.
        p. cm.
    Includes bibliographical references and index.
    ISBN-13: 978-0-226-29345-5 (cloth : alk. paper)
    ISBN-10: 0-226-29345-9 (cloth : alk. paper)
1. Philosophy, Modern. 2. Philosophy and religion.
I. Title.
    B791.G55 2008
    190—dc22

                                    2007041303

♾ The paper used in this publication meets the
minimum requirements of the American National
Standard for Information Sciences—Permanence of
Paper for Printed Library Materials, ANSI Z39.48-1992.

Is this the Region, this the Soil, the Clime,
Said then the lost Arch-Angel, this the seat
That we must change for Heav'n, this mournful gloom
For that celestial light? Be it so, since he
Who now is Sovran can dispose and bid
What shall be right: fardest from him is best
Whom reason hath equall'd, force hath made supreme
Above his equals. Farewell happy Fields
Where Joy for ever dwells: Hail horrors, hail
Infernal world, and thou profoundest Hell
Receive thy new Possessor: One who brings
A mind not to be chang'd by Place or Time.
The mind is its own place, and in itself
Can make a Heav'n of Hell, a Hell of Heav'n.
What matter where, if I be still the same,
And what I should be, all but less than hee
Whom Thunder hath made greater? Here at least
We shall be free; th'Almighty hath not built
Here for his envy, will not drive us hence:
Here we may reign secure, and in my choice
To reign is worth ambition though in Hell:
Better to reign in Hell, than serve in Heav'n.

MILTON, *Paradise Lost,* 1.242–63

CONTENTS

Preface *ix*
Introduction *1*

1 The Nominalist Revolution and the Origin of Modernity *19*

2 Petrarch and the Invention of Individuality *44*

3 Humanism and the Apotheosis of Man *69*

4 Luther and the Storm of Faith *101*

5 The Contradictions of Premodernity *129*

6 Descartes' Path to Truth *170*

7 Hobbes' Fearful Wisdom *207*

8 The Contradictions of Enlightenment and the Crisis
   of Modernity *255*

Epilogue *289*
Notes *295*
Index *363*

Ours is a visual age, and in the last twenty years two images have shaped our understanding of the times in which we live. The first was the fall of the Berlin Wall and the second the collapse of the World Trade Center towers. These structures were not mere artifacts; they were also symbols deeply embedded in the public psyche. The first was the symbol of totalitarianism and the Cold War confrontation between a free and an enslaved world; the second the symbol of a liberal world unified by the forces of globalization. The fall of the Berlin Wall gave rise to a belief in a liberal future of peace and prosperity that revived a faith in human progress that the catastrophic events of the first part of the twentieth century had almost extinguished. The collapse of the Twin Towers, by contrast, kindled the fear of a rampant new fanaticism that threatened our lives and civilization in an especially insidious way. When the Wall came down, the future seemed to stretch out before us like a broad highway leading to a modern world united by commerce, the free exchange of ideas, and the proliferation of liberal government. This was to be the age of globalization, but a globalization that was conceived as the spread of Western values and institutions to the rest of the world. Science and technology would establish a realm of peace and prosperity in which human freedom could be finally and fully realized. With the destruction of the World Trade Center, globalization suddenly appeared in a new light, not as a one-way street to modernity but as a complex and confusing intersection of paved roads, dark alleys, and mountain pathways. As a result, we ceased to look forward to a new golden age and glanced instead over our shoulders and sideways into the out-of-the-way places we imagined to be filled with dark figures waiting to attack us.[1]

The attack on the World Trade Center thus called the modern project into question, and it did so in a new and unsettling way. The perpetrators seemed to be opposed to modernity not because it had failed to live up to its aspirations or because its obvious benefits had not been equally distributed, but because those aspirations and benefits were themselves defective and even evil. The events of 9/11 thrust these claims in front of us in a particularly trenchant way, and they left many liberal proponents of modernity incredulous. It was easy to understand how someone could be morally outraged by the failure to distribute the benefits of modernity more fairly or widely, or aghast at the environmental impact of modern industrial society, or even distressed by the way in which modernity has ridden roughshod over traditional culture, but how could anyone be opposed to the manifest goods that modernity had to offer, to equality, liberty, prosperity, toleration, pluralism, representative government, and the like? The answer for many was simple and predictable: these new antimodernists were religious fanatics seeking martyrdom, true believers, unenlightened zealots. However, while such answers may relieve the immediate anxiety that we feel in the face of these events, they cannot finally be satisfying, for they simply conceal a deeper perplexity. They name (or brand) the enemies of modernity fanatics, but they leave the source and nature of their fanaticism unexplained. We thus still face an unsettling perplexity. This perplexity in part is the consequence of our profound ignorance and consequent misperception of these new opponents of modernity, and we undoubtedly need to understand them more fully. The problem, however, lies deeper than this, not merely in our failure to understand these others but in our failure to understand ourselves.[2] This challenge to modernity has been particularly hard for us to understand because it forces us to confront an issue that is buried at the bottom of the modern psyche, since it was at the heart of the very decision that gave birth to the modern psyche and to the modern world. I am of course referring to the decision about the place of religious belief in the modern world. Modernity came to be as a result of the displacement of religious belief from its position of prominence at the center of public life into a private realm where it could be freely practiced as long as it did not challenge secular authority, science, or reason. The authority of religion to shape private and public life thus was replaced by a notion of private belief and ultimately personal "values." The current attack upon modernity that is exemplified by the attack on the World Trade Center is particularly unsettling because it has violently reopened this unsettling question. In order to begin to come to terms with the current challenge to modernity, we thus must return to the question of the origin of the modern project.[3]

What then is modernity, and where did it come from? The conventional wisdom on this matter is quite clear: modernity is a secular realm in which man replaces God as the center of existence and seeks to become the master and possessor of nature by the application of a new science and its attendant technology. The modern world is conceived as the realm of individualism, of representation and subjectivity, of exploration and discovery, of freedom, rights, equality, toleration, liberalism, and the nation state. Conventional wisdom also has a fairly clear story of the origin of this modern age. It was a product of seventeenth-century thinkers who rejected scholasticism in favor of science and religious belief and enthusiasm in favor of a secular world. It was rooted in the philosophy of Descartes and Hobbes and the science of Copernicus and Galileo.[4]

Can we still be satisfied with these answers? There are a number of reasons to doubt the adequacy of such accounts. This account is after all the self-congratulatory story that modernity tells about itself and its own origins.[5] Moreover, recent scholarship, following the seminal work of Hans Blumenberg and Amos Funkenstein, has begun to reveal the enormous complexity of the question about the origins of the modern age.[6] As a result, previous attempts to identify modernity as subjectivity, or the conquest of nature, or secularization have begun to look one-sided and inadequate.

This book is an examination of the origins of modernity that is informed by this new scholarship and that seeks to demonstrate the importance of understanding the origins of modernity for coming to terms with the problems we now confront in our globalizing world. It is especially concerned to demonstrate the central role that religion and theology played in the formation of the idea of modernity. This view, of course, is not typically a part of the modern story. Indeed, since the time of the Enlightenment modernity has thought of itself as an effort to suppress religious superstition and authority, encapsulated in Voltaire's famous imperative: "Écrasez l'infame!" In Europe this has meant a continual diminution of the importance of religion, confining it first "within the bounds of reason alone," as Kant put it, then attempting to put it out of its misery by declaring God was dead, and culminating in the exceptional decline in religious belief and practice in the latter half of the twentieth century. Even in America, where religion continues to play a much more important role than in Europe, the attachment to religion is often perceived, especially by intellectuals and academics, as atavistic and unseemly, especially when it takes on a fundamentalist or evangelical tone. And even in America, the idea that religion should guide public life continues to meet widespread opposition.

This opposition to religion in the modern age, however, should not be taken as a proof that at its core modernity is antireligious. It is certainly true that modernity has consistently struggled against certain forms of religious doctrine and practice, including the cult of the saints, teleology, the natural law teachings of scholasticism, the geocentric vision of the natural world, and creationism, but I want to suggest that this does not mean that it was therefore a rejection of religion as such. The argument presented in this book suggests that it is a mistake to imagine that modernity is in its origins and at its core atheistic, antireligious, or even agnostic. Indeed, I will show in what follows that from the very beginning modernity sought not to eliminate religion but to support and develop a new view of religion and its place in human life, and that it did so not out of hostility to religion but in order to sustain certain religious beliefs. As we shall see, modernity is better understood as an attempt to find a new metaphysical/theological answer to the question of the nature and relation of God, man, and the natural world that arose in the late medieval world as a result of a titanic struggle between contradictory elements within Christianity itself. Modernity, as we understand and experience it, came to be as a series of attempts to constitute a new and coherent metaphysics/theology. I will argue further that while this metaphysical/theological core of the modern project was concealed over time by the very sciences it produced, it was never far from the surface, and it continues to guide our thinking and action, often in ways we do not perceive or understand. I will argue that the attempt to read the questions of theology and metaphysics out of modernity has in fact blinded us to the continuing importance of theological issues in modern thought in ways that make it very difficult to come to terms with our current situation. Unless and until we understand the metaphysical/theological core of modernity, we will remain unable to understand religiously motivated antimodernism and our response to it. The current confrontation thus demands of us a greater understanding of our own religious and theological beginnings, not because ours is the only way, but in order to help us understand the concealed wellsprings of our own passions as well as the possibilities and dangers that confront us.

I have many people to thank for their assistance in completing this book. The generous support from the Duke Endowment, the Earhart Foundation, and the National Humanities Center, where I spent a wonderful year working on the last sections of the manuscript, allowed me to complete the manuscript in a reasonably timely fashion. An earlier version of chapter 1 appeared in *The Critical Review* 13, nos. 1–2 (1999): 1–30. I have delivered many of the other chapters in a variety of different contexts, and I want to thank the members of those audiences for their questions and suggestions that pointed me in new and often fruitful directions. Many colleagues, friends, and students have also stimulated new ideas and helped me to sharpen my argument. I would like to thank them all for their inspiration, encouragement, and criticism at various points in the unfolding of this project. Special thanks are due to Douglas Casson, Jean Elshtain, Peter Euben, David Fink, Timothy Fuller, Ruth Grant, Geoffrey Harpham, Stanley Hauerwas, Thomas Heilke, Reinhard Huetter, Alasdair MacIntyre, Nelson Minnich, Joshua Mitchell, Ebrahim Moosa, Seymour Mauskopf, Luc Perkins, Robert Pippin, Noel Reynolds, David Rice, Arlene Saxonhouse, Thomas Spragens, Tracy Strong, Richard Watson, Ronald Witt, and Michael and Catherine Zuckert. I would also like to thank Richard Allen, who edited the text for the University of Chicago Press. His care with details and his many substantive suggestions were invaluable. I would especially like to acknowledge my debt to the teachers who first inspired my interest in the questions I address here including James Friday, Samuel Beer, Patrick Riley, Judith Shklar, and Joseph Cropsey. Finally, I would be remiss if I did not thank the two people who have had to put up with me over the many years that brought this project to fruition, my wife Nancy Henley and my son Tom. Tom in particular has literally grown up with this book and is entangled in it in ways that are not always visible. In many respects his energy, stubbornness, and enthusiasm have provoked and sustained me as I followed the odd paths and forgotten byways that led to its conclusion. Like this book he too has recently left my care to find his own way in the world, and I want to dedicate this book to him in the hope that both of my "children" will prove stronger than their father.

On a gray day in 1326 three men were standing amid a crowd of worshippers in the Cathédrale Notre-Dame des Doms in Avignon. The Romanesque structure was clearly in need of repair, but it had long been the center of the spiritual life of what only a decade before had been a small provincial town. But how all that had changed! The town had become the new seat of the papacy and as a result was undergoing a remarkable transformation. A *palais* was being built; money was flowing in; knights and bureaucrats, courtiers and ambassadors were everywhere. The market was filled with products from all over Europe and the Levant. Scholars, poets, and church officials from near and far came and went on a regular basis. The small town was becoming a city of real importance. That these three men were at the mass was an indication of the changing times. The first was English, the second Italian, and the third German. All spoke fluent Latin. The first, a Franciscan, was nervous and clearly under some stress; the second, a young man, was foppishly dressed and appeared to be a *bon vivant*; the third, an older Dominican, seemed lost in contemplation. When the mass ended they departed and went their separate ways. Little did they or their contemporaries know that the different paths they followed from that mass and from Avignon would lead humanity into the modern age.

Many today think that modernity is passé, but in 1326 it was not yet even a gleam in anyone's eye. The inhabitants of that world did not await a bright and shining tomorrow but the end of days. They did not look forward to the future or backward to the past, but upward to heaven and downward to hell. There is little doubt that they would have regarded our modern world with astonishment. We do not. Familiarity has bred contempt. We take modernity for granted, and we often are bored with it. We also think we know quite clearly what it is. But do we understand modernity? Do we even understand what it means to be modern? The premise of this book is that we do not and that the impact of recent events is driving that fact home to us in a powerful way.

What then does it mean to be modern? As the term is used in everyday discourse, being modern means being fashionable, up to date, contemporary. This common usage actually captures a great deal of the truth of the matter, even if the deeper meaning and significance of this definition are seldom understood. In fact, it is one of the salient characteristics of modernity to focus on what is right in front of us and thus to overlook the deeper significance of our origins. What the common understanding points to, however, is the uncommon fact that, at its core, to think of oneself as modern is to define one's being in terms of time. This is remarkable. In previous ages and other places, people have defined themselves in terms of their land or place, their race or ethnic group, their traditions or their gods, but not explicitly in terms of time. Of course, any self-understanding assumes some notion of time, but in all other cases the temporal moment has remained implicit. Ancient peoples located themselves in terms of a seminal event, the creation of the world, an exodus from bondage, a memorable victory, or the first Olympiad, to take only a few examples, but locating oneself temporally in any of these ways is different than defining oneself in terms of time. To be modern means to be "new," to be an unprecedented event in the flow of time, a first beginning, something different than anything that has come before, a novel way of being in the world, ultimately not even a form of being but a form of becoming. To understand oneself as new is also to understand oneself as self-originating, as free and creative in a radical sense, not merely as determined by a tradition or governed by fate or providence. To be modern is to be self-liberating and self-making, and thus not merely to be *in* a history or tradition but to *make* history. To be modern consequently means not merely to define one's being in terms of time but also to define time in terms of one's being, to understand time as the product of human freedom in interaction with the natural world. Being modern at its core is thus something titanic, something Promethean. But what can possibly justify such an astonishing, such a hubristic claim?

This question is not easily answered, but an examination of the genealogy of the concept of modernity can help us begin to see how we came to think of ourselves in this remarkable way and in what sense it can be justified. The term 'modern' and its derivatives come from the Latin *modus* which means 'measure,' and, as a measure of time, 'just now' with the late Latin derivative *modernus,* from which all later forms derive. Cassiodorus used the term in the sixth century to distinguish his time from that of the earlier Roman and patristic authors. The term *modernitas* was used in the twelfth century to distinguish contemporary times from those of the past.[1] Shortly thereafter, the term began to appear in the vernacular. Dante used the Italian *moderno* around 1300, and in 1361 Nicholas of Oresme used the French *moderne*. However, the term was not used to distinguish 'ancient' and 'modern' until 1460 and was not used in its contemporary sense to distinguish a particular historical period until the sixteenth century. The English term 'modern' referring to modern times first appeared in 1585, and the term 'modernity' was not used until 1627. The concept of modernity as a historical epoch was originally and often since understood in opposition to antiquity. The term 'middle ages' does not appear in English until 1753, although the term 'Gothic' was used in the same sense in the sixteenth century and Latin equivalents even earlier.

While the distinction of old and new was already present in antiquity, it was never used in its modern sense, in large measure because the terms were deployed in the context of a cyclical view of time that was present in ancient mythological accounts of the nature and origin of the cosmos, which were later adopted by ancient philosophers and historians as well.[2] "New" in this context was almost invariably equated with degeneration and decline, as in Aristophanes' *Clouds,* where the newfangled ways of the Athenians are contrasted with the superior mores of the generation that fought at Marathon.

Medieval Christianity worked within this cyclical framework, reshaping it to fit its own theological notion of the world as the unfolding of God's will. From this point of view, the world had a specific beginning, course of development, and end that was prefigured and revealed allegorically in Scripture. In framing this account, Christian thinkers drew heavily on the prophecy in Daniel that described the world as a series of four empires, which they identified as the Babylonian, Persian, Macedonian, and Roman Empires.[3] In their eschatology, Christ appears at the moment the last empire came into being, and he will return to establish his golden age when it comes to an end. For Christianity time thus did not turn in an unending circle but began with the loss of paradise and will end with paradise regained.[4] The medieval Christian thus imagined himself not as a competitor for power or fame in this world but as a sojourner *(viator)* whose actions on earth would determine his salvation or damnation. Piety was thus more important than courage or wisdom.

The concept of the 'modern' arose in the context of the twelfth-century reform of the church, although it had a different signification than it has today. In the belief that they stood at the beginning of a new age, these reformers or *moderni* saw themselves, in the words of Bernhard of Chartres

(1080–1167), as dwarfs standing on the shoulders of giants, lesser men than their predecessors but able to see farther. What they saw from their height, however, was not the way into a shining future of progress and increasing prosperity but the approaching end of time. This understanding was exemplified in the work of Joachim of Fiore (1130/35–1201/02) who preached the imminence of the final age in which the entire world would become a vast monastery.[5] To be modern for them was thus to stand at the end of time, on the threshold of eternity. While this Joachimist vision of the coming spiritual age may seem to anticipate the Renaissance vision of a new golden age or modernity's idea of an age of reason, this medieval notion of the modern was still deeply embedded in the eschatological and allegorical conception of time. There was thus an enormous chasm dividing this view from later conceptions.

The idea of modernity, as we understand it, is closely tied to the idea of antiquity. The distinction of 'ancient' and 'modern' derives from the tenth-century distinction of a *via antiqua* and a *via moderna*. Originally, this was not a historical but a philosophical distinction between two different positions on universals, connected to two different ways of reading Aristotle. The *via antiqua* was the older realist path that saw universals as ultimately real, while the *via moderna* was the newer nominalist path that saw individual things as real and universals as mere names. These logical distinctions provided the schema for a new understanding of time and being.

While the concept of modernity was formulated in connection with the concept of antiquity, the two terms were initially used in a sense different than our own. Petrarch provided the foundation for the idea of a "new" time when he described a dark time that separated antiquity from his own age.[6] However, he did not aim at something "new" or "modern," but at a restoration of the ancient golden age. This view was widely shared by the humanists. Lorenzo Valla, for example, argued in the mid-fifteenth century that his own age had turned away from the wretched modern age in which human beings had lived until recently.[7] Modern to this way of thinking was not the world that was coming into being but the medieval world that was passing away.[8] Valla understood his own time not as something new and unprecedented but as a recovery of what had been lost, a return to an older way of being.

The term 'modern' was actually not used in its current sense until the sixteenth century, and then only to define an artistic style.[9] In fact, it was really only in the seventeenth century that first Georg Horn (1666) and then more importantly Christophus Cellarius (1696) described a three-part schema of world history, with antiquity lasting until the time of Constantine, the Middle Ages until the end of Eastern Roman Empire, and *historia nova* beginning in the sixteenth century.[10]

[The idea of a modern age or, as it was later called, modernity, was part of the self-understanding that characterized European thought from the time of Bacon and Descartes. This idea differed decisively from that used earlier because it rested on a revolutionary notion of freedom and progress.[11] Alluding to the discoveries of Columbus and Copernicus, Bacon, for example, argued that modernity was superior to antiquity and laid out a methodology for attaining knowledge of the world that would carry humanity to even greater heights.[12] He knew that this idea was deeply at odds with the prevailing prejudices of his age that looked to the ancients as unsurpassable models of perfection, and he confronted this problem directly, asserting that while the Greeks were "ancients," this actually was not a reason to grant them authority. In his view they were mere boys in comparison to the men of his own time because they lacked the maturity produced by the intervening centuries of human experience.[13] What underlay this changed evaluation of antiquity was not merely a new notion of knowledge but also a new notion of time not as circular and finite but as linear and infinite. Change was pictured as a continuous natural process that free human beings could master and control through the application of the proper scientific method. In this way they could become masters and possessors of nature and thereby produce a more hospitable world for themselves.

THE QUARREL OF THE ANCIENTS AND THE MODERNS

[This concept of modernity was controversial from the very beginning. The rise of a new science and the corresponding notion of progress in the context of an intellectual milieu dominated by an unrestrained admiration for antiquity led to the famous "querelle des anciens et des modernes" that captured the attention of French thinkers at the end of the seventeenth century. The French Cartesians initiated the debate with the suggestion that the reality of scientific progress was an indication of the possibility of a modern art and literature superior to that of the ancients. In response, Nicholas Boileau and others defended the superiority of ancient art and literature. They, in turn, were attacked by Charles Perrault, Fontenelle, and other French *modernes*. However, these thinkers were not critical of the actual ancients but of those of their contemporaries who favored the Renaissance idealization of antiquity that transformed the ancients into classics.[14]

The quarrel was thus really a debate between the humanists and the Cartesians, and it ended in France with the recognition that while there was progress in the natural sciences, this was not true in the arts. Each age was imagined to have its own standards of artistic perfection.

The differences that came to light in this debate, however, were not so easily resolved or set aside. In the years that followed, for example, Voltaire claimed in support of the moderns that the student leaving the lycée in his day was wiser than any of the philosophers of antiquity. Rousseau, by contrast, argued in the *Discourse on the Arts and Sciences* that modern arts and sciences had served only to undermine human virtue and happiness, which had flowered so magnificently in Sparta and the Roman Republic.

While this quarrel began in France, it was also fought out in England and Germany. In England, where it was called the Battle of the Books, the quarrel extended into the first decades of the eighteenth century. It covered much of the same ground. Thomas Burnet and Richard Bentley among others argued for the superiority of the moderns, and Sir William Temple, Swift, and Dryden defended the ancients. William Wotten sought a middle position, arguing that it was necessary to divide the arts and sciences and judge them by different standards. The debate ended with the triumph of Pope's classicism, but this literary triumph was almost immediately called into question by Newton's remarkable discoveries that seemed to establish the preeminence of the moderns.[15]

In Germany, many of the same issues arose in the latter half of the eighteenth century. In this case, there was perhaps stronger initial support for the precedence of antiquity as a result of the broad influence of Winckelmann's *History of Ancient Art*. In opposition to this position, Herder, Friedrich Schlegel, and Schiller argued that it was necessary to distinguish two different kinds of art and to recognize that modern art had a different ground from that of the ancients. While Hegel seemed to adopt a middle position that viewed different ages as governed by their own standards, he too finally supported the superiority of the moderns, although clearly not without a deep sympathy for the lost glories of antiquity.[16]

This entire debate points to the great importance modernity places upon distinguishing itself from what came before it. Robert Pippin has argued that modernity's need to demonstrate its originality is a reflection of its deep-seated belief in autonomy.[17] One could go even further—modernity needs to demonstrate not merely its originality but also its superiority to its predecessors.[18] The idea of progress in this sense is a corollary to or extension of the idea of autonomy at the heart of the modern project.

The importance of these two ideas is attested by the fact that they were central to the intellectual crisis that called the modern project into question. While the earlier separation of a scientific and an aesthetic/moral realm governed by different standards and laws clearly called into question the initial global claims of modernity, it was really Kant's codification of this separation in his antinomy doctrine that cut the ground out from under the modern project as a whole. He demonstrated that nature and freedom as modernity had conceived them could not coexist, that their relationship was necessarily antinomious. The original modern vision of a unified theory that could explain the motions of God, man, and the natural world thus in his view had to be abandoned. The French Revolution, with its extravagant claims for the rule of reason and its abysmal realization of these claims in the Terror, only made these limitations of the modern project publicly apparent.

Despite the philosophic efforts of many profound thinkers to resolve this antinomy, the nineteenth and twentieth centuries were characterized by an ever-widening gap between these two central components of the modern project. Many Romantics and post-Kantian Idealists, for example, emphasized the role of human freedom but rejected the notion that nature could be explained as the mechanical motion of unthinking matter or the interplay of purely natural forces. However, all of the questions that were raised about modernity were overshadowed by contemporaneous advances in the natural sciences and the rapid development of an industrial civilization that emphasized the benefits of increased human power but was more or less indifferent to the ways in which this power compromised human autonomy. As a practical matter, while the philosophical and aesthetic qualms of a few had some impact on intellectual life, little could shake the general public's growing faith in a modern scientific enterprise that seemed to promise such widespread benefits to humanity. This faith in progress reached its apogee in the latter half of the nineteenth century and found its most lasting expression in futurist art and literature and in great public monuments to technology such as the Eiffel Tower. Even vehement critics of nineteenth-century industrial society such as Marx remained wedded to the underlying aspirations of modernity, arguing only that further steps were necessary to guarantee that the fruits of progress were shared by all.[19]

THE CRISIS OF MODERNITY

Faith in the modern project and the idea of progress was shattered by the events of the first half of the twentieth century. The First World War in particular revealed that the progressive development of human power was not simply constructive but could also be hideously destructive, and that technical progress was not identical with moral progress or with increasing human well-being. The interwar period saw the growth of this pessimism about modernity in philosophical works such as Spengler's *The Decline of the West,* Husserl's *Crisis of the European Sciences,* and Heidegger's *Being and Time,* as well as in the literary works of those who came to be called "the lost generation."[20] However, in light of what at the time was seen as the remarkable social and economic development of the USSR, and the recovery of the world economy in the 1920s, the horrible events of the Great War seemed to be merely a momentary aberration in the progressive development of human power and well-being. However, with the onset of the Great Depression, the rise of National Socialism, and the outbreak of World War II, new and more profound doubts arose about progress and the modern project. These doubts seemed to be all too fully borne out by the Holocaust, after which it appeared to be impossible for even the most ardent modernists ever again to speak of progress. The advent of the Cold War with the Soviet occupation of Eastern Europe in 1948 and the emergence of the threat of nuclear annihilation seemed to put the final nail into the coffin of modernity. The modern project, first conceived in the seventeenth century, had in fact enormously increased human power in precisely the ways Bacon, Descartes, and Hobbes had imagined, but it had not produced the peace, freedom, and prosperity they had predicted. In fact, it seemed to a number of postwar thinkers to have brought out the worst in humanity and in surprising fashion to have demonstrated the truth of Rousseau's claim that progress in the arts and sciences was increasing human power but also and simultaneously undermining virtue and morality.

The critique of the modern project in the aftermath of the Second World War took a variety of forms, building in many ways on the earlier critiques of Spengler, Husserl, and Heidegger. Some, following Husserl, saw the disasters of the twentieth century as the consequence of a defective notion of rationality that had been introduced by Galileo and Descartes. In this vein, Leo Strauss argued that the current crisis was only the final consequence of three successive waves of modern thought that had overwhelmed ancient rationalism and natural law, replacing them with a new technology of power and a doctrine of natural rights. The solution to the crisis of modernity in his view thus lay not in an intensification of modernity but in a recovery of ancient rationalism. In a similar vein, Hannah Arendt also saw hope for renewal in a return to the ancient world, although she drew more on the aesthetic politics and public life of Athenian democracy than on ancient philosophy. Equally critical of modernity, Eric Voegelin saw a revival of Platonic Christianity as the best hope for renewal.

Another strand of critique saw the crisis of modernity not as the result of the defects of modern rationality but as a consequence of the failure of the Western tradition itself that began with Plato and that found its culmination in the thought of Hegel and his progeny. These thinkers did not believe that the solution to the crisis of modernity was a return to an earlier form of reason. Following Heidegger rather than Husserl, they argued that an ontological deconstruction of Western rationalism as a whole was the prerequisite for a new beginning. They thus saw the solution to the crisis of modernity not in a return to a premodern world but in the exploration of postmodern seas. For thinkers such as Adorno, Derrida, and Deleuze it was not a Platonist philosophy of identity but a post-structuralist philosophy of difference that was necessary to free us from the ills of modernity.

In contrast to both the premodernists and the postmodernists, supporters of the modern project have tried to show that the so-called crisis of modernity is not in itself something modern. Rather, in their view it is due to something atavistic that had been reborn within but in opposition to modernity. National Socialism, from this point of view, was not something modern but a remnant of a Teutonic past, or the product of a romantic reaction against modernity, or the consequence of a Lutheran fanaticism that was fundamentally antimodern. Similarly, the totalitarian character of socialism in Russia was not the result of the impossible modern hope of making man the master and possessor on nature but the product of the long spiritual authoritarianism of Russian Orthodoxy that was antimodern through and through. The solution to the crisis of modernity, as these supporters of modernity see it, thus does not require a turn away from modernity and a subsequent revival of previous forms of life or a turn to postmodern alternatives, but a purification of modernity itself and a purgation of these atavistic or alien (and predominantly religious) elements within it. They thus see the triumph over fascism, the growth of secularism, the economic development of Asia and Latin America, and above all the collapse of the Soviet Union as evidence of the continuing vitality and power of the modern project.

The fall of the Berlin Wall marked the end of the era characterized by the confrontation of an individualistic liberalism and collectivist totalitarianism. This confrontation not only dominated the politics of the latter half of the twentieth century, it also dominated intellectual life. The fall of the Wall thus seemed to modernity's supporters to be an indication of the innate and irresistible power of the modern project. All that remained for the future was the transformation of the formerly socialist countries into liberal capitalist societies, and the continued modernization of the developing world. Some commentators, perhaps carried away by the excitement of the time, saw this moment as unique and decisive, proclaiming it the end of history and the realization of humanity's ultimate destiny.[21] In this same vein but in a more modest manner, others recognized that a great deal remained to be done to establish universal prosperity and perpetual peace, but they believed that this could be achieved by a gradual process of globalization and liberalization that relied on incentives rather than force. Others, and particularly those who were wedded to a postmodern future, saw the end of the Cold War as the triumph of an imperialistic liberalism but believed that this could be overcome by an aesthetic politics that sought to establish a multicultural society that was not hegemonic but agonistic and that moved forward by mutual learning and accommodation rather than war or conquest. Differences would thus not disappear and struggle would continue, but the future would be one of productive encounter.

The attack on the World Trade Center called all such optimism into question. In the aftermath of 9/11, the idea of a fruitfully agonistic multicultural world has receded and been replaced by the fear of an impending clash of civilizations. Insofar as this clash at its core is a confrontation between reason and revelation, it calls into question our easy Enlightenment conviction that reason is clearly and unarguably superior to revelation, and that while religion may have a place in modern life, it is clearly an inferior one. It is thus countenanced as a private good and is not seen as a force that ought to shape our public life.

What the events of 9/11 most powerfully call into question is the widespread Western assumption that civilization is grounded in rational self-interest and not in religious faith. While there is a general consensus that this is true, it is not clear in what sense it is true. The fact that others believe so vehemently that it is not has given us little choice in the short run but to defend our modern world and way of life, but at the same time we are impelled by this very challenge to reconsider the origins of modernity itself, and the decisions, now in many cases forgotten, that shaped and continue to shape our way of life.

THE ORIGIN OF MODERNITY

The conventional story that stretches back at least to Hegel sees the modern age as the product of exceptional human beings, of brilliant scientists, philosophers, writers, and explorers who overcame the religious supersti-

tions of their time and established a new world based on reason. Modernity in this way is portrayed as a radical break with the past. This vision of the origin of modernity was already called into question in the early twentieth century by scholars such as Etienne Gilson, who demonstrated that these supposed founders of the new age had in fact borrowed many of their essential ideas from their medieval predecessors.[22] Neither they nor the age they founded was thus as original as they maintained. Building on this beginning, succeeding historians, often focusing on social history and the history of science, have tried to show that the transition from the medieval to the modern world was much more gradual than was hitherto believed. In fact, when examined closely, these historians argue, we see that there were many more similarities and continuities between the two epochs than the traditional view suggests.[23]

Reflecting on these similarities and differences, Karl Löwith argued in *Meaning in History* (1949) that modernity was the result of the secularization of Christian ideals and that it was thus not ultimately distinct from the Middle Ages.[24] For example, from this perspective the notion of progress, which is so essential to the modern self-understanding, appears to have been the secularization of Christian millennarianism. Seen in this way, the traditional account of the emergence of modernity as the triumph of reason over superstition seems to be seriously flawed.

This secularization thesis, which gained many adherents during the 1950s and 1960s, was challenged by Hans Blumenberg, who argued that the modern age is not a secularized medieval world but something new and unique.[25] On the surface, Blumenberg's position seems to be a revival of the conventional view that equates modernity with the triumph of reason, but in fact he adopts a more Nietzschean view that identifies modernity not with reason but with self-assertion. The self-assertion that characterizes the modern world in his view, however, is not merely a random will to power. Rather, it is directed at solving the problem or question left by the collapse of the medieval world. Blumenberg thus sees modernity as the second overcoming of the problem that gave birth to Christianity as we know it, the problem of Gnosticism. Such a second overcoming was necessary, Blumenberg argues, because the Christian attempt to overcome it was defective from the very beginning. Gnosticism in his view reappeared at the end of the Middle Ages in the form of nominalism, which destroyed scholasticism and gave birth to the view of a voluntaristic as opposed to a rational God. In opposition to this new Gnosticism, modernity attempted to establish a ground for human well-being in the notion of human self-assertion. Modernity in this way was not merely the secularization of

Christianity but something new and legitimate in its own right. Phenomena that look like secularized elements of the Christian view of the world are thus in fact only "reoccupations" of now empty Christian positions, that is, attempts to answer outmoded Christian questions in modern ways. The idea of progress, from this point of view, is not a secularized form of Christian millennarianism but rather the "reoccupation" of the medieval need to show God's hidden hand in all events. According to Blumenberg, the misperceived need to answer such now meaningless questions has blurred our understanding of modernity and led us incorrectly to question the legitimacy of the modern enterprise.

Blumenberg's account points us in the right direction, but he does not understand the metaphysical significance of his own argument and thus does not appreciate the way in which modernity takes form within the metaphysical and theological structures of the tradition. Modernity, as he correctly points out, arose not in opposition to or as a continuation of the medieval world but out of its rubble. Superior or more powerful modern ideas did not drive out or overcome medieval ideas; rather, they pushed over the remnants of a medieval world after the internecine struggle between scholasticism and nominalism had reduced it to rubble. Modern "reason" was able to overcome medieval "superstition" or "dogma" only because that "dogma" was fatally weakened by the great metaphysical/theological crisis that brought the world in which it made sense to an end. Blumenberg is also correct in his assertion that the destruction of the medieval world did not merely open up space for new ideas and new ways of life but presented humanity with a new "epochal" question that has guided human thought in important ways ever since. What is missing in his account is the recognition that the shapes that modern thought subsequently assumed were not arbitrary reoccupations of medieval positions but a realization of the metaphysical and theological possibilities left by the antecedent tradition. To understand the shape of modernity as it has come down to us, we thus need to examine carefully the origins of modernity, to look behind the veil that modernity itself has drawn to conceal its origins. The origins of modernity therefore lie not in human self-assertion or in reason but in the great metaphysical and theological struggle that marked the end of the medieval world and that transformed Europe in the three hundred years that separate the medieval and the modern worlds. This book is the account of the hidden origins of modernity in those forgotten centuries.

In his inaugural lecture at the University of Freiburg in 1929, Martin Heidegger argued that human thought and action are propelled and guided by

the experience of fundamental questions, that is, by the experience of profound aporia that call into question the meaning and nature of everything
including the being of the questioner himself. These questions arise in moments in which the meaningfulness and legitimacy of all existing ways of
thinking and being dissolve and the world seems to be transformed into
chaos or nothingness. The experience of this abyss generates a profound
anxiety that impels human beings to search for answers, to formulate new
ways of thinking and being, and thus to radically reshape the world in
which they live. Real historical change in Heidegger's view occurs in these
moments as the result of a confrontation with such epochal questions. Everything else follows from them. These questions do not merely liberate us
from the past but direct us toward a new future. Heidegger believed that
the pre-Socratic Greeks had faced such a fundamental question and that
the history of the West since that time had been nothing other than a series
of attempts to answer it. Nihilism, in his view, was the recognition that all
of the answers to this question were inadequate. It was simultaneously the
experience of the question itself. Humanity in his opinion once again had
come face to face with such a question that shattered existing ontology and
consequently opened up the possibility of a new beginning, a new world
order, and a new history.

[In developing this argument, Heidegger drew heavily on Nietzsche,
who also saw the advent of nihilism as a moment of epochal openness.
Nietzsche believed that while the death of God and the consequent collapse of European values would throw humanity into an abyss of war and
destruction, this event would also open up the world in a way unknown
since the tragic age of the Greeks. While he recognized that God's death
would produce "a monstrous logic of terror," he also believed that "at long
last, the horizon appears free to us again."[26] If God is dead and nothing is
true, then, he concluded "everything is permitted."[27] The abyss of nihilism is thus intimately connected with a radical, epochal openness. While
Nietzsche and Heidegger were correct in seeing the decisive nature of such
questions, they exaggerated the openness that they produced. In fact, the
experience of these questions may propel humanity in new directions and
toward new answers, but human beings always formulate these answers
within prevailing conceptual structures that thus continue in many ways
to shape our ways of thinking about things. We see this clearly in the development of modern thought.

Modernity comes into being as the result of the confrontation with an
epochal question. The real "world-midnight" that has shaped our thinking, however, lies not at the end of modernity but at its beginning. In fact,

the "nihilistic" end of modernity is only the pale image of this beginning, and if we want to understand ourselves, where we have come from, what has impelled us, and what continues to impel us we need to come to terms with this beginning. This is a book about that beginning, about the "nihilistic" crisis in late medieval thought that gave birth to the epochal question that stands behind and guides modernity. I will argue in what follows that modernity, as we understand it, came into being through a series of answers to this question that constructed new ways of thinking, being, and acting for a world that seemed to be slipping into an abyss. I will also try to show that while these "answers" all share certain ontological assumptions, they lay out radically different and at times mutually antagonistic visions of the nature and relationship of man, God, nature, and reason. An understanding of the *question* of modernity in this sense opens up a view into the conflictual essence of modernity.

The epochal question that gave birth to the modern age arose out of a metaphysical/theological crisis within Christianity about the nature of God and thus the nature of being. This crisis was most evident as the nominalist revolution against scholasticism. This revolution in thought, however, was itself a reflection of a deeper transformation in the experience of existence as such. Scholastics in the High Middle Ages were ontologically realist, that is to say, they believed in the real existence of universals, or to put the matter another way, they experienced the world as the instantiation of the categories of divine reason. They experienced, believed in, and asserted the ultimate reality not of particular things but of universals, and they articulated this experience in a syllogistic logic that was perceived to correspond to or reflect divine reason. Creation itself was the embodiment of this reason, and man, as the rational animal and *imago dei*, stood at the pinnacle of this creation, guided by a natural *telos* and a divinely revealed supernatural goal.

Nominalism turned this world on its head. For the nominalists, all real being was individual or particular and universals were thus mere fictions. Words did not point to real universal entities but were merely signs useful for human understanding. Creation was radically particular and thus not teleological. As a result, God could not be understood by human reason but only by biblical revelation or mystical experience. Human beings thus had no natural or supernatural end or *telos*. In this way the nominalist revolution against scholasticism shattered every aspect of the medieval world. It brought to an end the great effort that had begun with the church fathers to combine reason and revelation by uniting the natural and ethical teachings of the Greeks with the Christian notion of an omnipotent creator.[28]

[Until recently, the importance of this debate and the nominalist revolution that it engendered were not recognized. This was certainly due in part to the decision of the Catholic Church in the late nineteenth century to unify church doctrine around Thomism, which led to the neglect and belittlement of the fourteenth- and fifteenth-century critics of Aquinas. This emphasis on Aquinas was motivated by a reasonable desire to clarify Catholic doctrine, but it also rested on the recognition that these nominalist critics had played an important role in laying the intellectual groundwork for the Reformation. A second and perhaps more important reason for the failure to recognize the importance of this epochal revolution is the fact that the God of nominalism was so unsettling. The God that Aquinas and Dante described was infinite, but the glory of his works and the certainty of his goodness were manifest everywhere. The nominalist God, by contrast, was frighteningly omnipotent, utterly beyond human ken, and a continual threat to human well-being. Moreover, this God could never be captured in words and consequently could be experienced only as a titanic question that evoked awe and dread. It was this question, I want to suggest, that stands at the beginning of modernity.

[The new vision of God that rose to prominence in the fourteenth century emphasized divine power and unpredictability rather than divine love and reason, but this new God only made sense because of the tremendous changes in the world itself. The Great Schism, the Hundred Years War, the Black Death, the development of gunpowder, the dire economic circumstances brought on throughout Europe by the advent of the Little Ice Age, and the dislocations wrought by urban development, social mobility, and the Crusades, were all of crucial importance to the formation of the anxiety and insecurity that made the nominalist vision of the world believable.

THE METAPHYSICAL PATH TO MODERNITY

[Modernity came into being as the result of a series of attempts to find a way out of the crisis engendered by the nominalist revolution. These attempts were neither arbitrary nor accidental but reflected the philosophical choices from among the available metaphysical possibilities. As we will see in what follows, each effort to find a way out of the abyss that nominalism seemed to open up was an attempt to construct the world on a specific metaphysical foundation. To understand what this means, however, we must briefly discuss the nature of metaphysics.

[We understand metaphysics today as a specific branch of philosophy, a branch that in our secular and generally positivistic age is often denigrated for its concern with those things that transcend the senses and for its connection with religion. Metaphysics in the period we are investigating, however, had a broader meaning. It was divided into *metaphysica generalis,* which included ontology and logic, and *metaphysica specialis,* which included rational theology, rational cosmology, and rational anthropology. Metaphysics was thus not a part of philosophy but the broadest kind of knowing, including the study of being, reason, God, man, and the natural world. To put this in more contemporary terms, general metaphysics involved the investigation of the nature of being and the nature of reason, while special metaphysics involved the investigation of three specific realms of being: the human, the natural, and the divine. To use the language that Heidegger later made famous, general metaphysics was concerned with ontological questions, while special metaphysics was concerned with ontic questions.

The nominalist revolution was an ontological revolution that called being itself into question. As we saw above, it thus gave rise to a new ontology, a new logic, and a new conception of man, God, and nature. All succeeding European thought has been shaped by this transformation. While nominalism undermined scholasticism, it was unable to provide a broadly acceptable alternative to the comprehensive view of the world it had destroyed. Some retreat from radical nominalism was thus probably inevitable. On the basic ontological point, however, there was no turning back—all or almost all succeeding forms of thought accepted the ontological individualism that nominalism had so forcefully asserted. With respect to the other elements of metaphysics, however, there was considerable variation, although these variations themselves were constrained by the structure of metaphysics itself. In fact, as we will see, succeeding thinkers focused not on the fundamental ontological question but on the ontic question of the priority or primacy of particular realms of being within *metaphysica specialis.* The deepest disagreements in the period between the fourteenth and the seventeenth centuries were thus not ontological but ontic, disagreements not about the nature of being but about which of the three realms of being—the human, the divine, or the natural—had priority. To put it simply, post-scholastic thinkers disagreed not about being itself but about the hierarchy among the realms of being.

This is immediately apparent from even a superficial examination of humanism and the Reformation, the two great movements of thought that stand between nominalism and the modern world. Both accepted the ontological individualism that nominalism proclaimed, but they differed fundamentally about whether man or God was ontically primary. Humanism, for example, put man first and interpreted both God and nature on this basis. The Reformation, by contrast, began with God and viewed man and nature only from this perspective. Despite their agreement on ontological matters, the differences that resulted from their ontic disagreements were irremediable, and they played an important role in the cataclysmic wars of religion that shattered European life in the sixteenth and seventeenth centuries. Modernity, as we more narrowly understand it, was the consequence of the attempt to resolve this conflict by asserting the ontic priority not of man or God but of nature. As we will see, while this new naturalistic beginning helped to ameliorate the conflict, it could not eliminate the antagonism at its heart without eliminating either God or man. However, one cannot abandon God without turning man into a beast, and one cannot abandon man without falling into theological fanaticism.

The two great strains of modern thought that begin respectively with Descartes and Hobbes seek to reconstruct the world not as a human artifact or a divine miracle but as a natural object. They disagree, however, about the nature and place of God and man in the world as they open it up. For Descartes, man is in part a natural being, but he is also in part divine and is thus distinguished from nature and free from its laws. For Hobbes, man is thoroughly natural and thus free only in a sense compatible with universal natural causality. These two poles of modern thought are thus rent by the same contradiction that set humanism and the Reformation at odds with one another.

This contradiction posed a profound problem for modern thought, and successive modern thinkers dedicated to the process of enlightenment sought to resolve it, but in the end these efforts were to no avail, for this contradiction could not be resolved on modern metaphysical grounds. The recognition of this fact, which found its first and foremost expression in Kant's antinomy doctrine, brought about the crisis of modernity, in whose shadow we still live. To speak of the crisis of modernity is not to assert that modern thinkers gave up on the modern project. German idealism in particular was at its core nothing other than the attempt to find a solution to this problem. With the failure of this idealist project to reconcile modern reason, modernity has been increasingly characterized by a deep cleft between a radical voluntarism and a radical determinism. The persistence of this division and the seeming incapacity of modern thinkers to find a way to heal this wound has led many to abandon modernity in favor of either premodern or postmodern alternatives.

Whether and to what extent we can find an answer to this contradiction depends upon our coming to terms with the question that gave birth to modernity. Confronting this question, however, means considering again the question of the relation of reason and revelation. If modernity is the age in which we define our own being in terms of time, and time in terms of our own being as historicity, we can only come to terms with ourselves by coming to terms with our temporality. Temporality, however, becomes meaningful for us against the background of eternity. To understand the question that modernity thus poses for us, we must consequently consider the question of the theological origins of modernity. This book is an attempt to raise that question.

1 | *The Nominalist Revolution and the Origin of Modernity*

THE THEOLOGICAL CRISIS OF LATE MEDIEVAL THOUGHT

While the modern world became conscious of itself in the sixteenth and seventeenth centuries, it would be as much a mistake to believe that modernity began at that time as it would be to believe that human life begins when one first becomes self-conscious. Modernity did not spring forth full-grown from the head of Galileo, Bacon, Descartes, or Hobbes but arose over a long period of time and as a result of the efforts of many different people in a variety of contexts. As we discussed above, it is one of the chief characteristics of modernity to conceive of itself as radically new and unprecedented. This is the consequence of a peculiarly modern understanding of human capacities and of the way in which human being unfolds in time. However, there are good reasons to doubt that this modern self-understanding is correct. As Oedipus tragically discovered, no one is "fortune's child"; everyone and everything has an origin and is shaped in decisive ways by that origin. To begin to understand the nature of the modern world, it is thus crucial that we examine its early, "preconscious" development in the three hundred years between the collapse of the medieval world and the rise of modernity.

The origins of the medieval world can be traced to the synthesis of Christianity and pagan philosophy in the Hellenistic world of late antiquity. This began in Alexandria in the first and second centuries. Here various strains of Christian thought, eastern religious beliefs, Neoplatonism, and a variety of other ancient philosophical views were amalgamated in different and at times conflicting ways, reflecting the intellectual and spiritual ferment of the times. This process of amalgamation was clarified and institutionalized when Christianity was adopted as the official religion of the Roman Empire under Constantine. The various conflicting strains of Christianity were fused into a formalized doctrine in the series of councils beginning with the Council of Nicea (323). However, despite this doctrinal consolidation enforced by imperial authority, the tensions within Christianity between revelation with its emphasis on divine omnipotence and incarnation, on one hand, and philosophy with its emphasis on rationalism and the notion of a rational cosmos, on the other, were not so easily resolved and remained a continuing problem for Christianity throughout its long history. Indeed, much if not all of the succeeding development of Christian theology was made necessary by the continual and periodically deepening antagonism between these two elements of Christianity.

⟨During the early medieval period, the knowledge of the impact of Greek philosophy on Christianity was largely lost in Western Europe, although Boethius provided a slim connection to this earlier intellectual tradition. The decisive event in medieval Christianity was the rediscovery of Aristotle, largely through contact with the Arab world in Spain and the Levant. This led, shortly after the millennium, to the rise of scholasticism, which was the greatest and most comprehensive theological attempt to reconcile the philosophical and scriptural elements in Christianity.

⟨While there was considerable variety within scholasticism, its classic form was realism. Realism, as the scholastics understood it, was a belief in the extra-mental existence of universals. Drawing heavily on a Neoplatonic reading of Aristotle, scholastic realists argued that universals such as species and genera were the ultimately real things and that individual beings were merely particular instances of these universals. Moreover, these universals were thought to be nothing other than divine reason made known to man either by illumination, as Augustine had suggested, or through the investigation of nature, as Aquinas and others argued. Within this realist ontology, nature and reason reflected one another. Nature could consequently be described by a syllogistic logic that defined the rational structure of the relationships of all species to one another. Moreover, while God transcended his creation, he was reflected in it and by analogy could be understood through it. Thus, logic and natural theology could supplement or, in the minds of some, even replace revelation. For similar reasons, man did not need Scripture to inform him of his earthly moral and political duties. He was a natural being with a natural end and was governed by the laws of nature. Scripture, of course, was necessary in order to understand everything that transcended nature, including man's supernatural destiny, but earthly life could be grasped philosophically.

⟨For all of its magnificence, the cathedral of scholastic thought depended on the delicate counterbalancing of Christian belief and pagan rationalism, and it was the instability of this relationship that brought it down.[1]

This balance was threatened both by the growing influence of reason and secularism within the church, which fostered a falling away from Christian practices, and by the ever recurring and ever more urgent demands for a more original Christianity, based on revelation and/or an imitation of the life of Christ. The preservation of medieval Christianity depended upon a reconciliation of these two powerful and opposing impulses. Such a synthesis, however, could only be maintained in theory by the creation of an ever more elaborate theology and in practice by the ever increasing use of papal and princely power.

The immediate cause of the dispute that shattered this synthesis was the growth of Aristotelianism both within and outside the church. The increasing interest in Aristotle was in part an inevitable consequence of the growth of scholasticism itself, but it was decisively accelerated by the reintroduction of many Aristotelian texts to Christian Europe through the commentaries of the great Islamic philosophers Avicenna and Averroës. The most visible manifestation of this new interest in Aristotle was the development of an independent system of philosophy alongside theology and a new kind of secular Christian intellectual.[2] This phenomenon was viewed with deep suspicion by the pious defenders of a more "original" Christianity not merely because of its pagan roots but also and perhaps more importantly because of its connection to Islam. Paganism was a known and tolerable evil; Islam, by contrast, was an ominous theological and political threat. This was especially true after the failure of the Crusades. For almost two hundred years Christianity had seemed to gain ground against Islam, especially in the East, but after the loss of all the Christian colonies in the Levant in the later thirteenth century and the rise of Islamic military power, this optimism dimmed and the suspicion of Islamic influences on Christian thought became more intense. The growth of Aristotelianism in this context was often seen by suspicious defenders of the faith as the growth of Averroism.[3]

The church attempted to limit what it saw as a theologically subversive development by fiat. Aristotelianism was condemned first in 1270 and then more fully in 1277 by the Bishop of Paris Etienne Tempier and by Archbishop of Canterbury Robert Kilwardby.[4] The position staked out in this Condemnation laid great emphasis on omnipotence as the cardinal characteristic of God, and in the succeeding years, this notion of omnipotent freedom came to constitute the core of a new anti-Aristotelian notion of God. This view of God was reflected in part in the work of Duns Scotus but more clearly and decisively in the work of William of Ockham and the nominalist movement his thought engendered.

Ockham was born in England between 1280 and 1285. After entering the Franciscan order at an early age, he completed his studies at Oxford. He was probably not the student of his famous successor, Duns Scotus, but was certainly deeply influenced by his thought, which remained strong at Oxford. Most of Ockham's philosophical and theological work was completed between 1317 and 1324, when he was summoned to Avignon to answer charges of heresy. In 1326, fifty-one of his assertions were declared open to censure although none was actually condemned.

Drawing on the work of earlier proto-nominalist thinkers such as Roscelin and Abelard, and the work of Henry of Ghent and Scotus, Ockham laid out in great detail the foundations for a new metaphysics and theology that were radically at odds with scholasticism.[5] Faith alone, Ockham argues, teaches us that God is omnipotent and that he can do everything that is possible, that is to say, everything that is not contradictory.[6] Thus, every being exists only as a result of his willing it and it exists as it does and as long as it does only because he so wills it. Creation is thus an act of sheer grace and is comprehensible only through revelation.[7] God creates the world and continues to act within it, bound neither by its laws nor by his previous determinations. He acts simply and solely as he pleases and, and as Ockham often repeats, he is no man's debtor. There is thus no immutable order of nature or reason that man can understand and no knowledge of God except through revelation. Ockham thus rejected the scholastic synthesis of reason and revelation and in this way undermined the metaphysical/theological foundation of the medieval world.

This notion of divine omnipotence was responsible for the demise of realism. God, Ockham argued, could not create universals because to do so would constrain his omnipotence.[8] If a universal did exist, God would be unable to destroy any instance of it without destroying the universal itself. Thus, for example, God could not damn any one human being without damning all of humanity. If there are no real universals, every being must be radically individual, a unique creation of God himself, called forth out of nothing by his infinite power and sustained by that power alone. To be sure, God might employ secondary causes to produce or sustain an entity, but they were not necessary and were not ultimately responsible for the creation or the continued existence of the entity in question.[9]

The only necessary being for Ockham was God himself.[10] All other beings were contingent creations of his will. In a technical sense, the things God chooses to bring into existence already have a nature, but these natures are not themselves universal but apply only to each individual thing. Moreover, they are infinite in number and chosen freely by divine will.

These "natures" thus do not in any real sense constrain divine will except insofar as they exclude the impossible, that is, the logically contradictory. They are neither implied by nor are they the presupposition of anything else. In this way, Ockham's assertion of ontological individualism undermines not only ontological realism but also syllogistic logic and science, for in the absence of real universals, names become mere signs or signs of signs. Language thus does not reveal being but in practice often conceals the truth about being by fostering a belief in the reality of universals. In fact, all so-called universals are merely second or higher order signs that we as finite beings use to aggregate individual beings into categories. These categories, however, do not denote real things. They are only useful fictions that help us make sense out of the radically individualized world.[11] However, they also distort reality. Thus, the guiding principle of nominalist logic for Ockham was his famous razor: do not multiply universals needlessly.[12] While we cannot, as finite beings, make sense of the world without universals, every generalization takes us one more step away from the real. Hence, the fewer we employ the closer we remain to the truth.

Since each individual being for Ockham is contingent upon God's free will, there can be no knowledge of created beings prior to investigation.[13] As a result, humans cannot understand nature without an investigation of the phenomena themselves. Syllogism is thus replaced by hypothesis as the foundation of science. Moreover, human knowledge can never move beyond hypothesis, for God is free in the fullest sense, that is, free even from his previous decisions. He can thus overturn anything he has established, interrupt any chain of causes, or create the world again from the beginning if he wants to. There is therefore no absolute necessity except for God's will. God, according to Ockham, did not even have to send his son in the form of a man; the savior might have been a donkey or a rock.[14]

In defending such a radical notion of omnipotence, Ockham and his followers came very close to denying the truth of revelation. They sought to avoid this heretical conclusion by distinguishing between God's *potentia absoluta* and his *potentia ordinata,* between his absolute and his ordained power, between what God could do and what he determined that he would do. This distinction, however, was difficult to maintain because God was under no obligation to keep his promises or to act consistently. For nominalism God is, to use a technical term, "indifferent," that is, he recognizes no natural or rational standards of good and evil that guide or constrain his will. What is good is good not in itself but simply because he wills it. Thus, while today God may save the saints and damn the sinners, tomorrow he may do the reverse, recreating the world from its very

beginning if necessary. To be fair, neither Ockham nor most of his followers believed that God was likely to do this. They were for the most part
probabilists, that is to say, they believed that in all likelihood God could
be relied upon to keep his promises. They thus did not really believe that
God would damn the saints or save the sinners, but they insisted that such
a possibility could not be dismissed without denying God's divinity.

Most nominalists were convinced that human beings could know little
about God and his intentions beyond what he reveals to them in Scripture.
Natural theology, for example, can prove God's existence, infinity, and supremacy, according to Ockham, but it cannot even demonstrate that there
is only one God.[15] Such a radical rejection of scholastic theology clearly
grew out of a deep distrust not merely of Aristotle and his Islamic interpreters but of philosophic reason itself. In this sense, Ockham's thought
strengthened the role of revelation in Christian life.

Ockham also rejected the scholastic understanding of nature. Scholasticism imagined nature to be teleological, a realm in which divine purposes were repeatedly realized. Particular entities became what they already potentially were in attaining their special end. They thus saw motion
as directed toward the good. The nominalist rejection of universals was
thus a rejection not merely of formal but also of final causes. If there were
no universals, there could be no universal ends to be actualized. Nature,
thus, does not direct human beings to the good. Or to put the matter more
positively, nominalism opens up the possibility of a radically new understanding of human freedom.

The fact that human beings have no defined natural ends does not mean
that they have no moral duties. The moral law continues to set limits on
human action. However, the nominalists believe that this law is known
only by revelation. Moreover, there is no natural or soteriological motive
to obey the moral law. God is no man's debtor and does not respond to
man. Therefore, he does not save or damn them because of what they do or
don't do. There is no utilitarian motive to act morally; the only reason for
moral action is gratitude. For nominalism, human beings owe their existence solely and simply to God. He has already given them the gift of life,
and for this humans should be grateful. To some few he will give a second
good, eternal life, but he is neither just nor unjust in his choice since his
giving is solely an act of grace.[16] To complain about one's fate would be irrational because no one deserves existence, let alone eternal existence.

As this short sketch makes clear, the God that nominalism revealed was
no longer the beneficent and reasonably predictable God of scholasticism.
The gap between man and God had been greatly increased. God could no

longer be understood or influenced by human beings—he acted simply out of freedom and was indifferent to the consequences of his acts. He laid down rules for human conduct, but he might change them at any moment. Some were saved and some were damned, but there was only an accidental relation between salvation and saintliness, and damnation and sin. It is not even clear that this God loves man.[17] The world this God created was thus a radical chaos of utterly diverse things in which humans could find no point of certainty or security.[18]

[How could anyone love or venerate such an unsettling God? This was not a new question. The author of Job had posed it many centuries earlier in confronting a similar possibility, and Calvin was later so troubled by the injustice of such a God that he could only imagine him to be the devil in disguise.[19] It is perhaps no accident that this view of God originated among the Franciscans, who stood at the opposite extreme on the theological spectrum from the Aristotelians. During the late medieval period, they were the preeminent voice calling for a more original or "primitive" Christianity that took its bearings not from the philosophical ideas of the Greeks and the corrupt political structures of the Roman state but from the example of Christ. The Christian life, they argued, was not to be found in papal palaces and curial power but in poverty and asceticism.[20] The most radical Franciscans found even revelation insufficient and believed that one could only live a Christian life if one imitated the life of Christ and his disciples. They were not alone in their pursuit of this alternative. In fact, they were only the most famous of the "primitivist" movements within the church that included the earlier Cathari, Waldensians, and Humiliati. Francis, however, spoke for all of these radicals when he argued that to be a Christian one must walk with Christ, retracing the *via dolorosa*. Only in this way could one appreciate the meaning of the Incarnation and God's love for man. Francis embodied this dedication to suffering in his own asceticism (and stigmata) and enshrined it in his famous Rule that imposed austerity and poverty upon his followers.

[After his death in 1226, the Franciscan order split between the zealots who demanded strict obedience of the Rule and the moderates who sought a papal dispensation from its more extreme strictures.[21] Given the broad appeal of this movement among the common people and the consequent threat that it represented to the well-heeled clerical hierarchy, Pope John XXII (1249–1334) not only granted such a dispensation, he also condemned and hunted down the most zealous Franciscans, the so-called Fraticelli. While this satisfied the more pragmatic members of the order, John did not stop there. Drawn into a dispute with the Franciscan order and their governor general Michael of Cesena over the issue of poverty (the so-called Poverty Dispute), he ultimately condemned the Franciscan belief in the moral superiority of the ascetic life in 1326, arguing that this opinion contradicted Scripture.

[John recognized that the doctrine of poverty not only threatened his power within the church but also threatened to transform Christianity as a whole. The medieval church understood itself as the embodiment of the Holy Spirit and thus as exercising God's dominion or kingship on earth. Churchmen thus imagined that they should live in a manner befitting their status. The Franciscan doctrine of poverty challenged this view. Man, as Francis understood him, is not by nature an exalted being. His joy comes not from his place or possessions in the world but from his nearness to God. The Kingdom of God is thus not a literal kingdom here on earth represented by the church, but a spiritual kingdom in which individuals are related to one another only in and through God. Taken to its extreme, such a doctrine was thus not merely an attack on priestly wealth and power; it was also an attack on clerical hierarchy and on the church itself.

[One of the leading spokesmen for the Franciscan side in this debate was William of Ockham, who was then in Avignon to defend himself against charges of heresy leveled by his Thomistic opponents. The pope based his argument against the superiority of poverty on the natural necessity of property to the preservation of human life, asserting that property existed even before the Fall. The Franciscans by contrast rested their case on revelation, arguing that property existed not by nature but only as a result of sin and therefore only after the Fall. They also asserted that through God's absolute power Christ and his disciples were able to return to this prelapsarian state, living a pious life without property. Francis in their view had opened up this possibility anew and thus had laid out the grounds for a genuine Christian practice. When John rejected this view on the grounds of the invariance of the ordained order of nature, Ockham and the Franciscans were horrified. They were convinced that God could not be bound by the "laws" of nature that he himself had previously made. Christ's life was a demonstration of this fact. Thus, in their view the pope's declaration was a revival of Abelard's heretical position that God is bound to save some from all eternity by his previous will.[22] God, they argued, is not bound by such laws and is subject only to the principle of noncontradiction. Otherwise, he is free and sovereign. To deny this fact is to deny God. They consequently proclaimed the pope a heretic and fled Avignon, seeking the protection of the emperor. Ockham in fact became a member of the imperial court and along with Marsilius of Padua (1270–1342) was instrumental in formulating the intellectual defense for the emperor in his dispute with the papacy.

⟨Nominalism in this sense was Franciscan theology.[23] It destroyed the order of the world that scholasticism had imagined to mediate between God and man and replaced it with a chaos of radically individual beings. However, it united each of these beings directly to God. From the Franciscan point of view, life in a radically individualized world seemed chaotic only to those who did not see the unity of creation in God. For those such as Francis who shared in this mystical unity, all other beings were their brothers and sisters, since all animate and inanimate beings were equally the creatures and creations of God.

⟨The church attempted to suppress nominalism, but these efforts had little impact. Ockham's thought was censured in 1326 and repeatedly condemned from 1339 to 1347, but his influence continued to grow, and in the one hundred and fifty years after his death nominalism became one of the most powerful intellectual movements in Europe. There was a strong Ockhamist tradition in England that began in the first half of the fourteenth century under the leadership of Thomas Bradwardine (the archbishop of Canterbury), Robert Holcot, and Adam Woodham. The Ockhamists in Paris during the fourteenth century were also strong and included Nicholas of Autrecourt, John Buridan, John of Mirecourt, and later Peter D'Ailly, Jean Gerson, and Marsilius of Inghen (who was also active in Heidelberg). In Germany there was a powerful nominalist tradition, especially in the later fourteen and fifteenth centuries that culminated in Gabriel Biel. In fact, outside of Spain and Italy the influence of nominalist thought grew to such an extent that by the time of Luther there was only one university in Germany that was not dominated by the nominalists.

⟨While nominalism undermined the view of a harmonious Christian world that scholasticism had developed (often in the face of the less than harmonious political and religious realities) and thus worked a revolution in Christianity, it was not merely destructive. Nominalism presented not only a new vision of God but also a new view of what it meant to be human that placed much greater emphasis on the importance of human will. As Antony Levi has pointed out, scholasticism from the thirteenth century on never had at its disposal a psychology that could explain action as both rational and willful.[24] For scholasticism the will both in God and man could therefore either do everything or nothing. Aquinas effectively argued for the latter. Scotus (building on Bonaventure's emphasis on God's independence of his contingent creation) and then Ockham asserted the radical freedom of divine will. In emphasizing the centrality of divine will, however, they both also gave a new prominence to and justification of the human will. Humans were made in the image of God, and like God were principally willful rather than rational beings. Such a capacity for free choice had always been imagined to play a role in mundane matters, but orthodox Christianity had denied that humans were free to accept or reject justificatory grace. Still, if humans were truly free, as many nominalists believed, then it was at least conceivable that they could choose to act in ways that would increase their chances of salvation.

While this position is reasonable, by the standards of the time such a view was highly questionable since it came perilously close to the Pelagianism that had been condemned by Augustine and by almost every orthodox theologian after him.[25] Despite the repeated claims by Ockham and many of his followers that God did not in any way respond to man and thus could not be influenced by any act of the human will, however free, nominalists were thus continually attacked as Pelagians. In part this had to do with their interpretation of man as a willing rather than a rational being, but it was also certainly due to the fact that a number of nominalists simply found it difficult to countenance a God who was so terrifying and merciless, arguing not on the basis of theology but simply as a practical matter that God would not deny salvation to anyone who gave his all or did everything that was in him to do: "Facientibus quod in se est, deus non denegat gratiam" ("If you do what is in you, God will not deny grace"). This was the so-called *Facientibus* principle. Such a view seemed to imply that there were standards for salvation, but that the standards were completely idiosyncratic to each individual. One man's all might be quite different than that of another. The determination of sanctity and sinfulness was thus taken out of the hands of the church. No habit of charity was necessity for salvation, for God in his absolute power could recognize any meretricious act as sufficient, and more importantly could recognize any act *as* meretricious.[26] The *Facientibus* principle thus not only undermined the spiritual (and moral) authority of the church, it defended a notion of salvation that was perilously close to Pelagianism.

Appearances notwithstanding, this view of nominalism as thoroughly Pelagian is mistaken. While later nominalists such as Gabriel Biel did in fact promote at least a semi-Pelagian idea of salvation, Ockham and his fourteenth- and fifteenth-century followers did not. Their emphasis on divine omnipotence simply left too little room to attribute any efficacy to the human will. It is true that their recognition of the importance of the human will seemed to suggest that human beings could win their own salvation, but this was mitigated by their assertion that all events and choices were absolutely predestined by God. While their doctrine seemed to open up space for human freedom, this was negated by their commitment to a divine power that determined everything absolutely but did so in an utterly arbitrary and therefore unpredictable way.

With this emphasis on divine determinism, nominalism was able to avoid Pelagianism, but the price was high, for the notion of predestination not only relieved humans of all moral responsibility, it also made God responsible for all evil. John of Mirecourt saw this conclusion as the unavoidable consequence of his own nominalism, admitting that God determined what would count as sin and who would act sinfully. Nicholas d'Autrecourt went even further, declaring that God himself was the cause of sin.[27] While this conclusion for good reason was not emphasized by most nominalists, it was too important to remain submerged for long, and it emerged in all of its distinctive power in the period of the Reformation.

Nominalism sought to tear the rationalistic veil from the face of God in order to found a true Christianity, but in doing so it revealed a capricious God, fearsome in his power, unknowable, unpredictable, unconstrained by nature and reason, and indifferent to good and evil. This vision of God turned the order of nature into a chaos of individual beings and the order of logic into a mere concatenation of names. Man himself was dethroned from his exalted place in the natural order of things and cast adrift in an infinite universe with no natural law to guide him and no certain path to salvation. It is thus not surprising that for all but the most extreme ascetics and mystics, this dark God of nominalism proved to be a profound source of anxiety and insecurity.

While the influence of this new vision of God derived much of its force from the power of the idea itself and from its scriptural foundation, the concrete conditions of life in the second half of the fourteenth century and early fifteenth centuries played an essential role in its success. During this period, three momentous events, the Black Death, the Great Schism, and the Hundred Years War, shook the foundations of medieval civilization that had been weakened by the failure of the Crusades, the invention of gunpowder, and the severe blow that the Little Ice Age dealt to the agrarian economy that was the foundation of feudal life.[28] While such a vision of God might have been regarded as an absurdity in the twelfth and thirteenth centuries, the catastrophes of the succeeding period helped make such a God believable.[29]

While the Middle Ages ended with the triumph of this nominalist vision of God, the scholastic enterprise did not simply vanish. In fact, it was revived a number of times but never with the same global aspirations. Even

Francisco Suarez, Aquinas's greatest defender and the last great scholastic, was ontologically a nominalist. On one level, he supported Thomistic realism, arguing for the extra-mental existence of universals, but at a deeper level he twisted this argument in a nominalistic fashion, asserting that every individual being was a universal. The world in which modernity came to be was thus not the world of scholasticism but the world of scholasticism overturned. This collapse of scholasticism did not, of course, occur all at once or in a short space of time, but it was well underway by the end of the fourteenth century.

FROM AVIGNON TO THE MODERN WORLD

(In 1305, the seat of the papacy was relocated to Avignon in part because the new French pope was beholden to the French king, but also because violence had become so endemic in Rome that the pope was no longer safe there. It remained there until 1378. During this time Avignon became the locus for European intellectual life. Although it was far from centrally located, the city was on a major trade route and had relatively easy communication with France, Spain, Italy, Germany, and England. Intellectuals were drawn there for many different reasons. Conservative theologians sought to use the power of the curia to win intellectual battles they were losing in Paris, Oxford, and other university towns, while their opponents came to defend their radical views. As we have seen, it was for this reason that Ockham came to Avignon, but it was the defense of his order that kept him there and that catapulted him into his struggle with the pope. However, he was only one of the important thinkers who came to Avignon during this period.

[In fact, as Ockham and the pope were fighting the final theological battle of the Middle Ages in the convents and courts of Avignon, a few blocks away the son of a Florentine exile was just beginning a lifelong project that would help to define the modern age. He was Francesco Petrarch. Like Ockham, Petrarch rejected scholasticism as overly rationalized, but he was also repulsed by the nominalists' endless arguments about terms and what he saw as vapid speculation about divine power.[30] Like the nominalists he too was aware of the corruption of the church and hoped for purification and renewal, but he sought such a renewal not through faith and a new scriptural theology but through an amalgamation of Christian practice and ancient moral virtue.[31]

[Petrarch believed that a Christian life required not merely faith and ceremonies but moral practice as well, and that such morality could only be achieved by a richer understanding of what it meant to be human that drew not merely on Scripture but on the moral models of antiquity. In sharp contrast to the asceticism of late medieval Christianity, he thus sought to revivify the love of honor and beauty as preeminent human motives. While his thought remained generally Christian, he envisioned a new kind of man with new virtues, not a citizen of a city-state or a republic but an autarchic individual being who was whole and complete in himself. Petrarch recognized that such individuals might surround themselves with friends or join with others as citizens, but he was convinced that they could only do so effectively if they were autonomous individuals first. It was this ideal of human individuality that inspired the humanist movement.

Such a focus on the individual was unknown in the ancient world. The ideal for the Greek artist and citizen was not the formation of individual character or personality but assimilation to an ideal model. Petrarch and his humanist followers did not put the human per se at the center of things but the *individual* human being, and in this respect they owed a deeper ontological debt to nominalism than to antiquity. For humanism, the individual is not a rational animal standing at the peak of creation. Like Ockham the humanists were convinced that human beings have no natural form or end. They also thus concluded that humans are characterized by their free will. This will, as humanism understood it, however, differs in one decisive respect from the will that Ockham and nominalism attribute to humans. It is not simply a created will but also a self-creating will. God grants humans the capacity to will, and they then make themselves into what they want to be. This notion of a self-willing being has clear affinities to the model of the nominalist God. Like the God who creates him, this man is an artisan, but an artisan whose greatest work of art is himself, a poet in the literal sense of the term, able to identify with every being and make himself into any one of them.

[Such an individual, however, is not God. He is limited by his own mortality and by the chaotic motions of matter or by what humanists following the Romans dubbed *fortuna*.[32] Artists can give form to things, paint pictures, shape marble, build palaces, and even create states, but fortune will eventually bring all to ruin.[33] Even the greatest of princes, as Machiavelli, for example, argues, will only be able to succeed half the time. While the individual for humanism is free and in some sense divine, he is not omnipotent, for he has both a childhood and a dotage in which he is dependent on others, and a death that inevitably brings his mastery to an end.

This humanist idea of fortune reflects an underlying notion of time as degeneration. Form and purpose do not inhere in nature but are the products of an artistic will that builds dikes against the floods of fortune, dikes, however, that fortune ultimately overflows. This humanist pessimism about the capacity of art to master nature was reflected in their understanding of their own place in time. They knew that the magnificent world of the ancients that they so admired had perished and been superseded by a dark, Gothic age. They hoped to establish a new golden age but they never imagined it would last forever and never dreamed that it might be successively improved for all time.

Humanism grew alongside and also out of nominalism.[34] It offered a solution to many of the problems posed by divine omnipotence. This solution was itself constructed on nominalist grounds, that is, on the understanding of man as an individual and willful being, although it is only successful because it vastly narrowed the ontological difference that nominalism saw separating man and God. The consequent vision of the magnificent individual, towering, as Shakespeare's Cassius puts it, "like a colossus," was thus something distinctively new and a clear step beyond the Middle Ages. Glory not humility was this man's goal, and to this end he employed art rather than philosophy and rhetoric rather than dialectic. Humanism thus sought to answer the problem posed by divine omnipotence by imagining a new kind of human being who could secure himself by his own powers in the chaotic world nominalism had posited.

We today imagine humanism to be antagonistic to religion or even a form of atheism. Renaissance humanism, however, was almost always Christian humanism. In formulating their particular brand of Christianity, however, humanists drew heavily on Cicero and Neoplatonism and laid out a vision of Christianity that placed much greater weight on moral practice than on faith or ceremonies. This transformation, which was evident even among the more moderate northern humanists, pushed Christianity in a Pelagian direction that was deeply offensive to many ardent Christians. In this respect, the humanist impact upon Christian belief and practice was very important in fomenting the second great intellectual movement in answer to the problem posed by the nominalist revolution, the Reformation.

Luther was the father of the Reformation, and his life and thought were in many ways a reaction to the problems posed by nominalism. However, in his response to nominalism, he followed a path that was radically different than that of the humanists, not away from God toward man but from man back to God. The humanists had sought to reform Christianity, but Luther's idea of reformation was more radical and all-encompassing.

The Reformation has been described as the last great upsurge of medieval religiosity, and while not entirely false, this claim conceals the astonishing extent to which Reformation Christianity rejects medieval Christianity on essentially nominalist grounds. Luther's example makes this clear. As a young man, Luther became an Ockhamist, but he was troubled by the impenetrability of the God nominalism described, and tormented by the consequent uncertainty of his own personal salvation. Luther's concern with personal salvation could hardly be stilled by a God who was unstillness itself, who today might save the saints and damn the sinners but tomorrow do exactly the reverse.

Luther's personal quest for certainty vis-à-vis this God was intertwined with his struggle against corruption in the church. The corruption of the church in Luther's mind was bound up with the doctrine of works and the sale of indulgences in particular. Luther rejected the redemptive power of works on nominalistic grounds. If what was preeminent in God and by extension in man was the will, then sin could only be remitted through right willing, regardless of the result.[35] But right willing depended not on man but on God. Luther's answer to the question of indulgences was thus his answer to the problem of the nominalist God: "faith alone saves." Luther accepted the nominalist notion of man as a willing being but transformed this notion by reconfiguring the relationship of divine and human will. Faith, according to Luther, is the will to union with God, but faith can come only from God through Scripture.[36] Faith in Scripture, in other words, guarantees salvation.

At first glance, it is difficult to see how Scripture solves the problem posed by nominalism, since the reliance on Scripture seems to assume the invariance of what God has ordained, an invariance that nominalism explicitly denies. Luther, however, gives Scripture a different status. In his view, it is not simply a text, but a means by which God speaks directly to man.[37] Faith arises from hearing the voice of God. God's power is thus not something abstract and distant but acts always in and through us. In this way, Luther was able to transform the terrifying God of nominalism into a power within individual human beings. The Christian is reborn in God because God is born in him.

Ockham proclaimed the individuality of every being as a unique creation of God, but he saw the radical separation of God and man as an impenetrable barrier to human understanding and an insuperable barrier to the human will. He thus turned to Scripture, but even Scripture only revealed the momentary determination of a distant God's will, which might at any moment be otherwise. Luther too saw God as a *deus absconditus*

who could not be philosophically analyzed or understood. He too turned
to Scripture as the sole source of guidance. In contrast to the nominalists,
however, he recognized that the difference between God and man could be
bridged by the scriptural infusion of divine will that banishes all doubts.
In contrast to the humanists, however, this was not because man willed in
the same way that God wills, that is, creatively, but because he willed *what*
God willed, that is, morally and piously. Man does not become a demi-
god but becomes the dwelling place of God; God becomes the interior and
guiding principle of his life, or what Luther calls conscience.

Neither the humanists nor the reformers saw themselves as founding a
new age or initiating something distinctively new. Rather, they understood
their task as restoring something ancient and traditional. In doing so, however, they found themselves entwined in the conflict about the relationship
of the divine and the human that had bedeviled Christianity from the very
beginning. Italian humanism suggested in a Promethean fashion that man
could lift himself to the level of God or even in some respects become God.
In this sense it was clearly Pelagian, or at least semi-Pelagian. Humanism's
vision of man was thus incompatible with divine omnipotence and with
the notion that God was God. Without such a God, however, it was difficult to see how man could be more than an animal. The Reformation was
directed not merely against the abuses in the church but also against this
Pelagian humanism. God for the Reformers was omnipotent, and man was
nothing without God. The idea of a free human will was thus an illusion.
This anti-Pelagian and antihumanist position, however, was equally unsatisfying, for if the human will is utterly impotent, then God and not man
is the source of evil, and humans cannot be held morally responsible for
their actions. While humanism thus could not sustain a notion of divine
omnipotence, it also could not exist without it. Similarly, Reformation theology could not countenance a free human will and yet could not sustain
the notion of a good God in its absence. The humanists and the Reformers
were thus entwined in an antinomy from which there was no escape. They
were thus inevitably brought into conflict. This disagreement appears in its
clearest light in the debate between Erasmus and Luther over the freedom
or bondage of the will, but also in the disastrous Wars of Religion that
raged across Europe for more than a hundred years.

Humanism and the Reformation founded their views of the world on
man and God respectively. These choices were rooted in the long history
of Christianity, and the conflict that arose between them was in many
ways a reflection of the contradictions that had been present in Christianity since the beginning. In the midst of this conflict, a small group of

thinkers sought a new path, abandoning both God and man as the foundation of their investigations, turning instead to the natural world. Modernity proper in this way begins with the goal of developing a science that will make man master and possessor of nature. This project was deeply indebted to nominalism in many different and important ways.

Nominalism destroyed the ontological ground of medieval science by positing a chaotic world of radically individual beings. Indeed, for the nominalists, the world itself is only a higher order sign, an aid to the understanding that does not correspond to any reality. Nominalism thus seems to make science impossible. In fact, however, modern science develops out of nominalism as the result of a reconsideration of the meaning of nominalist ontology.

Scholastic metaphysics understood God as the highest being and creation as a rational order of beings stretching up to God. From the nominalist perspective, however, such an order is untenable not only because each being is radically individual but also and perhaps more importantly because God himself is not a being in the same sense as all created beings. While Ockham points to this gulf between God and his creation, he does not extensively explore it. This task was undertaken by the great thinker whose path crossed that of Ockham and Petrarch in Avignon, the German mystic Meister Eckhart (1260–1328).

Eckhart was deeply influenced by Neoplatonism, although his Neoplatonism was transfigured by his mysticism. Like Ockham, Eckhart saw an infinite distance between God and the world. From the perspective of the beings we encounter in everyday life, God thus seems to be nothing. In Eckhart's view, however, this issue must be examined from a divine rather than a human perspective, not logically but mystically. From this perspective, it is not God but the beings of the world that are nothing, or at least they are nothing without God. Since, however, these beings in some sense "are," they must "be" God, that is, God must be "in" beings in some way. Without him, they would be pure nothingness. However, the infinite difference between God and his creation means that God cannot be in things as their whatness or essence. God, Eckhart suggests, is in them in a different sense, as their how, the operative force that determines their becoming. In nominalistic terms, God is pure willing, pure activity, or pure power, and the world in its becoming is divine will, is this God. Or in more modern terms, the world is the ceaseless motion that is determined by divine will understood as efficient or mechanical causality. The world is the incarnation, the body of God, and he is in the world as the soul is in the body, omnipresent as the motive principle.[38]

Creation is thus not simply disorder. God is in the world in a new and different sense than scholasticism and traditional metaphysics imagined. He is not the ultimate whatness or quiddity of all beings but their howness or becoming. To discover the divinely ordered character of the world, it is thus necessary to investigate becoming, which is to say, it is necessary to discover the laws governing the motion of all beings. Theology and natural science thereby become one and the same.

Rationalism and materialism both work within this general understanding of the relationship of God and his creation, but they differ considerably in their understanding of the meaning of this relationship. Rationalism, for the most part, understands this identification of God and his creation pantheistically. The motion of nature therefore is the motion of God, and nature's laws are the forms and structures of divine will. Rationalist science thus is theologically grounded not in Scripture but in the deduction of the laws of motion from transcendental will or freedom.

Materialism, by contrast, understands the meaning of the identification of God and creation atheistically.[39] To say that the God of nominalism as Ockham understood him is in everything in the way Eckhart (and later Nicholas of Cusa) suggested is to say that everything is willfulness, motion without purpose or end, and without any necessary regularity. Viewed in this manner, there is no effective difference between the nominalist cosmos and a godless universe of matter in motion. The existence or nonexistence of God is irrelevant for the understanding of nature, since he can neither increase nor decrease the chaos of radical individuality that characterizes existence. Science thus does not need to take this God or Scripture into account in its efforts to come to terms with the natural world and can rely instead on experience alone. "Atheistic" materialism thus has a theological origin in the nominalist revolution. Materialism, it is true, also draws upon ancient atomism and Epicureanism, but both of these are received and understood within what was already an essentially nominalist view of the world.

This new understanding of becoming or change as a manifestation of divine will is the ontological foundation for the self-consciousness of modernity. Since Plato, being had been understood as timeless, unchanging presence. Change was always a falling away from being, degeneration. Nominalism called this notion into question with its assertion that God himself was not only subject to change but was perhaps even change itself. The changeable cosmos was no longer seen as a falling away from perfection, no longer merely "the moving image of eternity," as Plato put it in the *Timaeus*. Change was not simply degeneration. While this new view of becoming was never entirely spelled out and was constantly troubling to modern thinkers who strove repeatedly to discover an unchanging "ontological" ground of becoming, it was a crucial step away from both ancient and medieval notions of time and change.

If change is not simply degeneration, then some change may be progressive. Change guided by an enlightened humanity may produce good. Progress in this way is opened up as a human possibility. The ability of the will to master the world was already clear to the Renaissance humanists such as Machiavelli, but their reliance on *individual* prowess and willing made a thorough mastery of nature inconceivable to them. Human finitude meant that even the greatest individuals would inevitably succumb to all-conquering time. Mastering nature thus would require something more than a merely individual will. Early modern thinkers argued that this problem could be solved only if human beings came to understand that science is not an individual accomplishment but a broadly based social or political enterprise. In this way, it was possible to imagine a human will of unlimited longevity that might finally master the natural world.

Francis Bacon (1561–1626) is often characterized as the father of modern science. Like his nominalist predecessors, Bacon rejected realism both in its scholastic and in its classical form. He agreed with the nominalists that "in nature nothing really exists besides individual bodies, performing purely individual acts."[40] As a result, the universe is a labyrinth that is impenetrable to unaided human reason.[41] Previous thinkers in Bacon's view did not make any progress through this labyrinth because they did not use the powers available to them to attain this end, relying instead on mere observation and overhasty generalization.[42] There are various reasons for such ineptitude, and Bacon describes them in great detail in *The New Organon* in his famous discussion of the four idols or false notions that have become rooted in the mind.[43] Human beings have come to believe that all they need to know comes from their immediate experience. Consequently, they have been unwilling or unable to verify their generalizations by the examination of particulars. They have thus been content to guess rather than know and have put the dreams of the imagination in place of real knowledge.[44] Even in his own time, when realism had been called into question, Bacon believed that men were still deterred from such an investigation by an undue reverence for antiquity and by the belief that scientific progress was impossible because of the obscurity of nature, the shortness of life, the deceitfulness of the senses, the weakness of the judgment, the difficulty of experiment, and the like.[45] What is needed, he argued, is a total reconstruction of science, the arts, and human knowledge on a proper foundation.[46]

The knowledge that Bacon seeks differs profoundly from that of scholasticism. He is not concerned with what nature is and what it tends toward, that is, with the formal or final cause of things, but with the particular character and motion of matter, that is, with material and efficient causality. In other words, he wants to know not *what* nature is but *how* it works, and his goal is thus not theory or speculation but the practical betterment of the human condition.[47] When nature is comprehended in this manner, it can be made to produce works that are useful for human life, for when we understand the properties of particulars we will be able to bring them together in ways that will produce the effects we desire. Bacon's ultimate aim is to produce a model of nature not as a static system of categories but as a dynamic whole, as the interacting operation of all particulars.[48] To understand nature in this way is to comprehend nature as power.

Bacon believed that the power that arose from the knowledge of nature could carry humanity to hitherto unimaginable heights. However, in his view such knowledge can only be gained by first lowering oneself, by subordinating oneself to nature and limiting the exercise of one's own will. To master and command nature, it is necessary first to be the servant and interpreter of nature. For Bacon, the goal of science is thus not the mere

> felicity of speculation, but the real business and fortunes of the human race, and all power of operation. For man is but the servant and interpreter of nature: what he does and what he knows is only what he has observed of nature's order in fact or in thought; beyond this he knows nothing and can do nothing. For the chain of causes cannot by any force be loosened or broken, nor can nature be commanded except by being obeyed. And so these twin objects, human Knowledge and human Power, do really meet in one; and it is from ignorance of causes that operation fails.[49]

The presupposition of such knowledge is the humiliation of the human spirit, since success depends upon abandoning our proud belief that we occupy a superior place in the order of creation. Instead of acting as lords of creation, in the way that humanism suggested, we must become apprentices in nature's workshop.[50] We do not need great wit or individual excellence, but a dogged persistence and obedience to the surest rules and demonstrations.[51]

While *humility* gains us entrance to the study of nature, *cruelty* is the means by which we reach our end. Mere experience will take us only into nature's outer courts. To come to nature's inner chambers, we must tear it to pieces, constraining, vexing, dissecting, and torturing nature in order to force it to reveal the secret entrances to its treasure chambers.[52] Only as merciless servants who bind and torture their master to learn the source of his power can we win from nature the knowledge of its hidden forces and operation. On the basis of this knowledge, we can then produce "a line and race of inventions that may in some degree subdue and overcome the necessities and miseries of humanity."[53]

Bacon thus offers a new and revolutionary answer to the problem posed by nominalism and the nominalist God. He confronts and accepts the nominalist vision of the world and attempts to find a solution to its fundamental problems. He seeks neither a poetic transfiguration of this world nor a new covenant with its God. Instead, he strives to discover the hidden powers by which nature moves in order to gain mastery over it. For Bacon as for Ockham and Petrarch, man is a willing being who seeks to secure himself in the world. In contrast to both Franciscan asceticism and the humanist notion of godlike individuality, however, Bacon imagines man to be a relatively weak and fearful being who can only succeed by consistently working with his fellow human beings over many years to learn nature's laws and turn this knowledge to human use. It is the very democratic character of Bacon's project that makes its success conceivable. It does not depend upon the exercise of great and thus rare genius, but upon the consistent application of ordinary intelligence to a series of small problems that can be easily analyzed. Bacon in this way differs considerably from his humanist predecessors. The hero of knowledge that Bacon imagines in his *New Atlantis,* for example, is not a sparkling "great-souled man," but a solemn, priestlike, and unheroic scientist who is willing to investigate not merely the beautiful and noble but the low and foul, for like Bacon he knows that "whatever deserves to exist deserves also to be known."[54]

While Bacon laid the first bricks of the new science on a nominalistic foundation, it was Galileo, Descartes, and Hobbes who raised its walls. Bacon's method, in fact, was ill-suited to the comprehension of nature understood as matter in motion. Its unmitigated nominalistic focus on individual beings and its inductive method rendered it incapable of grasping motion as such. Galileo's transposition of motion into the abstract world of geometry and his new understanding of inertia were crucial steps that made modern mathematical science possible.[55] On this foundation, Descartes and Hobbes developed alternative visions of the modern scientific enterprise.

The differences between Descartes and Hobbes are crucial and central to the bifurcation of modernity. There is one strain of modern thought that begins with Descartes and includes Leibniz, Malebranche, Spinoza, Kant, Fichte, Hegel, Schopenhauer, and most contemporary continental philosophers. There is a second beginning with Hobbes, Locke, Hume, and Mill, and that includes many contemporary Anglo-American thinkers. These two strains of thought represent alternative answers to the fundamental problem posed by the nominalist God within the framework of modern science. The differences between them turn on a number of issues, but the question of the nature and relationship of man and God is of central importance.

Man for Bacon is a part of nature. He thus "can do so much and so much only as he has observed in fact or in thought of the course of nature. Beyond this he neither knows anything nor can do anything."[56] Man is a natural being subject to all of the constraints of nature. While he can ameliorate his condition and in a limited sense master the natural world, he remains a part of nature and is not its creator.

Descartes offers us a different vision of the modern project. His thinking too was deeply influenced by the problem of the nominalist God, but his solution to this problem was different in decisive respects from that of Bacon. In particular, he has a radically different notion of man's position with respect to both God and nature. In his early thought, Descartes was convinced that he could construct an apodictic science on the basis of mathematics. Such a science, he believed, could produce a mathematical representation of all motion that would allow human beings to truly master nature, make them able not merely to ameliorate human misery as Bacon had hoped but actually to make man the immortal lord of all creation.[57] This initial project was called into question by Descartes' realization that the idea of a truly omnipotent God undermined the certainty of mathematics. This realization led to the spiritual quest that ended with Descartes' articulation of his famous principle, *cogito ergo sum,* as the foundation for all human knowledge. The scientific project as Descartes lays it out in his mature thought is thus a clear response to the problem posed by nominalism.

What distinguishes the Cartesian solution to this problem from that of Bacon is evident in his fundamental principle, for it grounds all of modern science on an autonomous subject who not only transcends nature but is also able to resist and ultimately challenge (or even replace) God himself. Man for Descartes becomes master and possessor of nature by dispossessing its current owner, that is, by taking it away from God. This is possible because man in some sense already is God, or at least is the same infinite will that constitutes God.[58]

The Cartesian notion of science thus rests upon a new notion of man as a willing being, modeled on the omnipotent God of nominalism and able like him to master nature through the exercise of his infinite will. Descartes draws here not merely upon nominalism but upon the humanist ideal of a self-creating and self-sufficient individual, and upon Luther's idea of the conjunction of the human and divine will. It is this potent combination that gives rise to the notion of subjectivity that plays a central role in rationalism, idealism, and later continental thought as well.

Insofar as Descartes both leaves man within nature as a body in motion and elevates him above it into a quasi-omnipotence, he lays the groundwork for an inevitable and irremediable dissatisfaction that poses tremendous moral and political dangers for modernity. The infinite human will constantly strives to master and transcend the body but is itself at the same time always bodily. In its striving to realize its infinite essence, it must always negate the finite. Such a negation, however, is impossible. As idealistic and noble as its aspirations may be, idealism in its practical form thus constantly faces a millenarian temptation to use ever more extreme means of control to achieve its unachievable ends.

Hobbes has a more limited view of human capacities than Descartes. Man for Hobbes is a piece of nature, a body in motion. Like the nominalists, Hobbes believes that this motion is not teleologically determined, but in contrast to them he sees it not as random but as mechanical. It neither realizes its essence in Aristotelian fashion, nor is it attracted to a natural end by love or beauty, but is pushed ever onward by collisions with other individual objects. Man is therefore moved not by his intrinsic natural impulses, nor by divine inspiration or free will, but by a succession of causal motions. In contrast to Descartes, Hobbes does not see human beings rising above nature. Humans are rather thoroughly natural objects that obey the laws of nature. According to these laws that govern all matter, each of these (human) objects will remain in its given motion unless this motion is contravened by collision with another body. Such a collision of human objects is conflict, since it limits the continuous (and therefore in Hobbes' view free) motion of the individual. In a densely packed world, the natural state of man is thus the state of war. The purpose of science, as Hobbes understands it, is to organize the motion of both human and non-human bodies to maximize the unimpeded (and therefore free) motion of human beings.

The importance of free will is vastly diminished in Hobbes' thought. In fact, Hobbes denies that human beings have a free will, characterizing the will as simply the last appetite before action.[59] For Hobbes, human life is lived within nature and is always constrained by the natural world. Man is more a creature than a creator, more governed by laws than law-giving.

He is not a transcendent being who might imagine himself a god but an impelled object whose chief desire is to continue on his prescribed course with the least interference from others.

(Most human beings in Hobbes' view fear death and consent to be ruled in a state to achieve peace and maximize their free motion. The chief dangers to such rule and the peace it makes possible are the desire for glory (that characterized humanism) and the belief that our actions in this life can affect the life to come (that was central to the Reformation). The impact of the desire for glory is mitigated by the Leviathan, who Hobbes characterizes as a "mortal god," since no one can compete with him for honor. The impact of religious passion is reduced by a correct understanding of predestination. Hobbes agrees with Luther and Calvin that everything is predestined but argues that it is precisely this fact that demonstrates that the things we do in this world have no impact on our salvation. If everything is already determined, then there is nothing anyone can do to either gain or lose salvation.

With the elimination of glory and beatitude as motives for human action, Hobbes believes human beings will be naturally inclined to pursue preservation and prosperity. These are lesser goods than earthy or supernatural glory, but they are also less likely to be the source of violent conflict. Hobbes thus seeks to make man master and possessor of nature not in order to achieve his apotheosis but in order to satisfy his natural, bodily desires.

Modernity has two goals—to make man master and possessor of nature and to make human freedom possible. The question that remains is whether these two are compatible with one another. The debate between Hobbes and Descartes in the Objections and Replies to the *Meditations* would suggest that they are not. Indeed, what we see in this debate is the reemergence of the issues at the heart of the debate between Luther and Erasmus. For Descartes as for Erasmus, there is human freedom in addition to the causality through nature. For Hobbes as for Luther there is only the absolute power of God as the ultimate cause behind the motion of all matter. In this way we see the reemergence at the very heart of modernity of the problematic relationship of the human and the divine that bedeviled Christianity from its beginning. The modern ontic turn away from man and God to nature thus in the end still assumes a continuing metaphysical and structural importance for the very categories it seeks to transcend. The successors to Hobbes and Descartes in the modern tradition struggle with this question. The Enlightenment in particular is characterized by a series of unsuccessful attempts to solve this problem. The centrality of this problem to the modern enterprise becomes apparent in Kant's antinomy doctrine and in the French Revolution. At the end of modernity, we are thus left to confront the question whether there is any solution to this problem within the ontological horizon that modernity opens up, and thus whether modernity even in its most secular form can escape from the metaphysical/theological problem with which it began.

In his *Parmenides* Plato explores the primordial question of the one and the many. This question is primordial because it cannot be answered, and it cannot be answered because it is itself the presupposition of all thinking, and therefore of all questioning and answering. We cannot think about things without thinking those things as being *both* one and many. There are different explanations for this dilemma, some rooted in the contradictory nature of existence and others in the inadequacy of language to grasp being, but we need not go into those matters here. It is sufficient for our purposes to recognize that there is no unequivocal answer to this question. As a result, there can be no final theoretical vision of the whole that can serve as the absolute, fundamental, and unshakable truth. Neither a Parmenidean dwelling in the one nor a radical individualism or nominalism can dissolve this contradiction. Nor can it be eliminated by means of a linguistic turn that imagines everything to be the play of mere words or signs, a language game or games that create the world anew every time we speak. This question thus underlies and shapes all philosophizing. Plato's Parmenides argues there that the attempt to explain the world either through the one without reference to the many or through the many without reference to the one is doomed to failure. Nominalism rejects realism because it goes too far in the direction of the one, positing an identity between God and his creation. Nominalism by contrast draws a sharp distinction between the two and as a result puts great emphasis on manyness and particularity.

The three men who left the Cathédrale Notre-Dame des Doms that day in 1326 in—William of Ockham, Francesco Petrarch, and Meister Eckhart—faced this question and sought to answer it. Their answers and those of their successors in various and often contradictory ways have shaped the modern world, redefining the nature and relation of man, God, and the cosmos. In the struggles that we now face and in those that the future holds in store over the nature of modernization and globalization, it is imperative that we understand the ways in which not only our opponents but we ourselves continue to be shaped and motivated by beliefs and ideas that are themselves not modern, that are in fact the reappearance of the very questions that gave birth to the modern age.

2 | Petrarch and the Invention of Individuality

On a beautiful day in 399 B.C., one of the most clear-minded human beings who ever lived chose to die rather than to go into exile from his native city. This man was, of course, Socrates. Why he finally came to this decision we will never know, but apparently it occurred at some point after the deliberative phase of his trial had concluded and before the determination of his sentence. He was standig with his friends in the agora, the marketplace where he had spent his life pestering his fellow citizens and philosophizing with his friends and followers. Towering above him was the acropolis and the temples to the gods whose nature if not existence he had called into question. Great Athena herself, emblazoned with gold, holding her great spear and gleaming in the brilliant Attic sunlight, stared down at him unspeakingly. He knew the vote would be close, and he almost certainly hoped that a majority of the five hundred jurors would vote in his favor. But if not, he would have to propose a punishment, and his accusers would certainly demand his death. He knew that most of the jurors would prefer simply to be rid of him. If he were convicted, he could thus choose to go into exile and live elsewhere with some of his friends. But this was apparently unacceptable to him. We do not know why he rejected this possibility, but it led directly to his death. From the later accounts of his friends and followers, we know that they believed he had concluded that he could not be the same person anywhere else, that his identity in a decisive way was bound up with Athens.

Socrates' choice came to exemplify the essentially political character of being human. As Aristotle later argued, to be human is to be a *zōon logon echon*, literally "life that has speech," or, as it was later translated a "rational animal." Speech, however, only exists in community with others. Therefore, to be a *zōon logon echon*, one must also be a *zōon politikon*, a "political animal." Those who live outside the city in Aristotle's view are thus either beasts or gods, and even the most autarchic human being, the philosopher, is not capable of such an extrapolitical existence.

This vision of human identity as essentially political was called into question by later Stoic philosophers who insisted that the wise man was a citizen not of a particular city but of the cosmos, and that he participated not merely in the *logos* of one city but in the divine *logos* that coursed through all things. It was never clear to them, however, that anyone other than perhaps Socrates had ever attained such independence, and even he, of course, had chosen not to follow such a path. Moreover, in their account the supremely wise man is not beyond the city in the larger sense of the term, for the cosmos itself in their view is a titanic city with natural laws of its own. The Stoic wise man is thus not a-political but cosmo-political, not an independent individual but a citizen of the cosmic city.

Christianity also posed a challenge to the hegemonic role of the political in the constitution of identity in the ancient world. However, while Christians rejected citizenship in the cities of the pagans, they did so only because they imagined themselves to be citizens of a higher and more exalted city, the city of God. They thus gathered together in small and large communities in this world to worship God, always living in anticipation of his return and the transformation of the entire world into one righteous city ruled over by God himself. This eschatological vision animated ancient Christians from Paul to Augustine and continued to exercise a powerful influence down to the time of Dante (1265–1321) nearly a thousand years later. Exiled from his beloved Florence by internecine political conflict, he spent the last two decades of his life constructing in his imagination the world to come, a final "city" with a divinely ordained place for the blessed, the damned, and everyone in between.

The transition to the modern world begins with the rejection of this political, cosmological, and theological vision of human identity. In part this is rooted in the nominalist rejection of the orderly cosmos and the orderly God portrayed by scholasticism. As we have seen, according to the nominalists there is no divine logos or reason that can serve as the foundation for a political, cosmopolitan, or theological identity. Moreover, the idea of an orderly political and theological world in which Dante and his predecessors grew up was falling to pieces. The struggles between the pope and the emperor, between the forces of localism and nationalism, and between town and country were a reflection of the disintegration of medieval life that had begun with the failure of the Crusades. How would it be possible to find a ground for identity in a world in which God, man, and nature were all in motion, all incomprehensible, and all at war with one another?

The first to face this question and attempt to answer it was Francesco Petrarch (1304–74), who looked not to the city, God, or the cosmos for support but into himself, finding an island of stability and hope not in citizenship but in human individuality. Petrarch grew up in a world that was shaped by the collapse of an idea of political and cultural order that had sustained Europe for centuries. Although only forty years younger than Dante, he was separated from him and the entire tradition stretching back to Socrates by a gulf that is immediately evident at the beginning of his autobiographical *Familiar Letters:*

> I have spent all of my life, to this moment, in almost constant travel. . . . I, begotten in exile, was born in exile, with so much labor undergone by my mother, and with so much danger, that she was considered dead for a long time not only by the midwives but by the doctors. Thus I experienced danger even before being born and I approached the very threshold of life under the auspices of death. . . . Since that time to the present I have had no opportunity or only a very rare one to abide anywhere or catch my breath.[1]

A man without a home, driven continuously about in the world, prey to fortune, and surrounded by a perplexing multitude of human beings, Petrarch struggled to find some connection to others that would provide stability in his life. In his earlier years, his friends seem to have played this role. Unfortunately, friendship proved inadequate, for in 1348 the Black Death arrived and "all these friends . . . in no time at all were destroyed in almost one stroke."[2] The consequences were awesome: "The year 1348 left us alone and helpless. . . . It subjected us to irreparable losses."[3] In the face of these difficulties Petrarch neither turned to religion nor succumbed to despair. "In fact, I have become stronger out of that very state of despair. After all, what can frighten someone who has struggled with death so many times?" In the midst of these troubles, without a home, his friends ripped away from him, he found a new way of life that gave him such strength that he was convinced that "I shall never succumb to anything further. 'If the world slips into destruction, the crumbling ruins will find me fearless.'"[4] Beyond the community and beyond religion, amidst war, collapse, and destruction, Petrarch discovered a new foundation for human life, a foundation for what was to become the modern age.

This chapter examines the very beginnings of modernity in Petrarch's conception of individuality. Petrarch's thought is a response to the crisis of late medieval civilization. He finds an answer to this crisis in a vision of man as a finite individual capable of self-mastery and self-perfection. However, for Petrarch such self-mastery is only possible outside of political life. At its foundations, the modern notion of the individual and thus the modern age is intensely private and apolitical.

PETRARCH'S LIFE

Petrarch's father, grandfather, and great-grandfather were all Florentine notaries. Like Dante, his father was forced to leave the city as a result of political conflict. He went first to Pisa and then in 1312 to Avignon, where he obtained work at the papal court. Petrarch was brought up in Carpentras, a small town near Avignon. As a boy, he studied grammar and rhetoric, and like his father demonstrated great enthusiasm for Cicero.[5] In 1316, at the age of twelve he was sent to study law at Montpelier, where he remained until 1320 when he went with his younger brother, Gherardo, to continue his studies at the University of Bologna. During this time he broadened his knowledge of Cicero and Virgil as well as the other traditional authors within the legal curriculum.[6] He also came in contact with those writing vernacular poetry and began his lifelong study of Augustine. With the death of his father, he and his brother returned to Avignon early in 1326.

This was a tumultuous year in the papal city, which was then the intellectual center of the Christian world. Pope John XXII was in the midst of his struggle with the Franciscans over the question of poverty. As we saw in the last chapter, Michael of Cesena and William of Ockham defended the Franciscan position. The conflict that grew increasingly heated pitted the pope and the curia against the most popular and fastest growing spiritual order in the church on an issue that cut to the heart not only of the meaning of Christianity but to question of the appropriate manner of life for the clergy. While there is no direct evidence that the young Petrarch followed this debate, it is hard to believe that he was not reasonably well acquainted with the positions of both parties. He was on friendly terms with the powerful Colonna family, who exercised great power within the curia during this period. We also know from his later recollections that he was immersed in the intellectual life of Avignon at this time.[7] It thus seems likely that Petrarch was well acquainted with this debate.

Whatever the impact this dispute and the nominalist position that Ockham defended had upon Petrarch's view of the world, it was all soon superseded by the signal event of Petrarch's life, his encounter in 1327 with a young woman with whom he fell immediately in love. As his affection was not returned, his love was both hopeless and tragic. His entire lyric outpouring was occasioned by his love for this woman, whom he called Laura in his poems. Her subsequent death during the plague did little to settle his soul, and he struggled throughout his life to master this passion.[8]

(Having run through his inheritance, Petrarch found himself in need of money and decided to pursue a clerical career, taking up minor orders and entering the service of Cardinal Colonna in 1330.[9] Colonna was more a patron than an employer and allowed Petrarch considerable time for traveling, book collecting, reading, and especially writing. He remained nominally in Colonna's service until 1347, although during this period he traveled a great deal and spent much of his time in a small house he had purchased in a beautiful valley not far from Avignon, known as the Vaucluse. After leaving Colonna's service, Petrarch derived support from various benefices he had obtained over the years and from several other patrons, including the infamous Visconti, a family of Milanese tyrants. He lived chiefly in Parma, Milan, Padua, and Venice. His literary production was voluminous, although due to his habit of repeated revision it was not all published during his lifetime. Early in his service to Cardinal Colonna, he produced the first scholarly edition of Livy. A series of important works followed: his great collection of lyric poems generally known as the *Songbook (Canzoniere)*; a collection of exemplary lives entitled *Illustrative Lives (De viris illustribus)*; an epic poem on Scipio Africanus's triumph over Hannibal called *Africa*; an intensely introspective and self-critical dialogue between himself and Augustine called *My Secret (Secretum meum)*; a great work extolling the private over the public life called *On the Solitary Life (De vita solitario)*; and his most popular work, *Remedies for Fortune Fair and Foul (De remediis utriusque fortunae)*, which was widely read throughout Europe for well over three hundred years. In addition, on the model of Cicero's quasi-autobiographical *Letters to Atticus,* Petrarch published four different collections of his letters, including a number of letters to ancient authors.[10] He received the laurel crown for poetry in Rome in 1341 and was compared favorably both while alive and after his death to Cicero and Virgil.

(While Petrarch's literary production had a profound impact upon his contemporaries and successors, his lifelong attempt to resurrect and popularize the great literary and philosophical works of the ancient world was equally important to the humanist enterprise and to the Renaissance itself. By the time of his death Petrarch possessed the largest private library in Europe, and it was this collection that served as the foundation for the *studia humanitatis*.[11] Petrarch was also a lifelong supporter not merely of the resurrection of Roman literature but of the reinstitution of the Roman state and the return of the papacy to Rome. He supported the attempts of

Cola di Rienzo to revive the Roman Republic, and when this effort failed, he repeatedly sought to convince the emperors Ludwig IV and Charles IV to return to Rome. He also urged a series of popes to reestablish the papacy in Rome. Because of his intellectual standing, he also served on a number of diplomatic missions aimed at mediating between warring states in keeping with his larger goal of Italian reunification and an elimination of foreign intervention in Italian affairs. Already by the 1340s, he had become the most famous private man in Europe and was sought after by popes, emperors, and various princes and tyrants. Petrarch, however, was determined to maintain his freedom and privacy, declining all offers of courtly life. In this way he set the model for the independent intellectual life that became central to the humanist tradition and that continues to play an important role today.

PETRARCH'S VIEW OF THE WORLD
AND THE HUMAN CONDITION

Petrarch remarks at the beginning of the second volume of the *Remedies* that there is nothing more deeply imprinted in his mind than Heraclitus's saying that everything exists by strife. Everything, he continues, attests to it, for *"Mother Nature has created nothing without strife and hatred."* [12] Petrarch sees continual change everywhere, beginning with inanimate things and extending through the entire spiritual sphere.[13] War, he asserts, is universal: "From the firstmost of the angels to the smallest and least of the worms—the battle is unceasing and relentless."[14]

Human life is particularly beset by strife.[15] One cause of this lies in the nature of things, according to Petrarch, but far greater is the war that takes place within our souls.[16] It is thus not only nature or fortune that threatens man but man himself. In the first instance, this is the result of the struggle for preeminence that characterizes human life, driven by a desire for fame and the contrary workings of envy and resentment.[17] As a result, "the affairs of man never stand still and . . . the one who sits highest on the slippery wheel is closest to his downfall."[18] Indeed, "no power on this earth is stable," for war hides under the guise of peace.[19] And even in times of peace, we are still beset by our own passions, by "invisible masters in [our] mind," born of "a hidden poison [that] lurks in the very origin of man."[20] The companions of peace are thus license and lust.[21] In order to attain and maintain his freedom, man thus must forever battle temptation.[22]

Petrarch was convinced that the religious institutions of his time were not only incapable of resolving this problem but actually exacerbated it.

The church hierarchy in his view was corrupt.[23] He reproved the notoriously greedy Cardinal Annibaldo, on one occasion, suggesting that it was important for the church to possess gold but not be possessed by it.[24] In Petrarch's view this corruption was due in part to the subjection of Rome to Avignon and the French, but it was also the manifestation of a deeper spiritual failure that lay at the heart of medieval Christianity.

Petrarch believed that European history fell into four periods. The first two periods were guided by reason.[25] The first of these was dominated by Platonic metaphysics, and the second by the moral wisdom of Seneca and the Stoics. In both of these reason aided human virtue. The third period, which began with the Incarnation and ended in the fifth century, was supernaturally guided. The fourth period, which drew on Aristotle's attack on Plato, was dominated by scholasticism and Averroism in particular.[26] Reason rather than revelation guided human life in this period as well, but in this case it served to undermine rather than promote virtue.

Petrarch was dissatisfied with both realist scholasticism and nominalism but for different reasons. He was unequivocal in his attack on Averroism, which he considered the most extreme form of realism. The basic principle of Averroism places the intellect above every form of individuation, considering it not as divided but as a unity. It is thus not the individual self but being that is the object of thought.[27] Petrarch, like the nominalists, saw this position as heretical.[28] Like the nominalists he also thought that realist scholasticism was lost in Aristotelian categories and thus did not encounter the ultimate reality of individual things.[29] While he may have agreed with the nominalists on these matters, he detested their dialectical approach, which seemed to him too often to be a mere fighting with words with little concern for the truth. Here he was particularly irritated with the "Brittani," among whom he apparently included Scotus, Ockham, and their followers.[30] Like many of his time he was fed up with what seemed to be an interminable squabbling about matters distant from reality in terminology that was impossible to understand. Theology, he felt, was becoming increasingly distinct from piety, and, with its abstract language and technical terms, it had moved as far as possible from anything that might actually persuade or inspire ordinary human beings.[31]

Petrarch's relations with the Franciscans were also ambivalent. He discussed Francis of Assisi in *The Solitary Life*, although only briefly, and while he seems to have admired the general goals of the Franciscan order, he vacillated between a view that their austerity was overly severe and his suspicion that it was often insincere.[32] Moreover, it is doubtful that Petrarch wished to see all Christians living according to Franciscan standards. In

The Solitary Life, Petrarch praises the religiosity of Francis and the other ascetics but finds their lives barbarous and inhuman.[33] They may avoid corruption, but they do so only by lurching to the opposite extreme. In Petrarch's view, the life of excess could not be cured by a life of deprivation. A middle way was necessary, and he believed this was the life of virtue.

(According to Petrarch, only virtue can make us victorious in our never-ending war with fortune.[34] Fortune batters us continually with its two weapons, prosperity and adversity, and the wounds these weapons inflict are the passions or affects.[35] Struck by the passions, we cease to be masters of ourselves and are pulled this way and that. Humans can avoid this fate only by early training and habituation. Such a system of training characterized the Roman world and gave it its great strength and nobility. In his own corrupt times Petrarch believed the institutions of education and training actually exacerbated the problem. He thus felt that the only way to bring about moral reform was to transform human values, for the fallenness of his time was not a political problem but a cultural one. He hoped to persuade the aristocracy to honor not wealth and luxury but virtue and wisdom, and they in turn would serve as models for the rest of humanity.[36] Such a change, however, would require a thorough reformation of culture. Petrarch's immediate task, as he understood it, was thus to bring about such a reformation by laying out a more noble and beautiful vision of the good life.

Petrarch's project from beginning to end was thus cultural renewal.[37] The means to such a renewal, however, are not given or fixed. Petrarch believed that in all ages humans are capable of attaining a high level of culture and virtue, but that they could do so only if they received appropriate nourishment. Unfortunately, for the last thousand years, they have been starved. Petrarch felt that the first step in remedying this problem was to make clear what a virtuous life was and then convince his fellow human beings of its beauty and nobility. To answer this question and provide convincing images of such a life, he returned to the ancients.[38] Petrarch thus was not interested simply in imitating antiquity but in improving human beings.[39] He looked to the ancients and hoped to restore the great position that culture had enjoyed in Rome, but only because he was convinced that this was the only way to produce virtue in a world of continual strife and change.[40] Petrarch's project had a political component but was not essentially political—political life, as he understood it, was a means to morality and not an end in itself. He recognized the importance of political support for culture but put culture finally above the state. Moreover, Petrarch, for reasons that we will examine below, had sincere doubts that cultural and moral standards could be set by the community. He imagined a world in which human beings were held together not by natural political bonds but by the voluntary bonds of friendship. The community he imagined was thus to be more a fellowship of private men in friendly intercourse with one another, communicating through speech, letters, books, etc., than a republic or principality.[41]

Petrarch was convinced by his encounter with scholasticism that morality could not rest merely on true knowledge. Human beings had to will moral action. Humans thus had to have a moral purpose and want to attain it.[42] Thinking in this sense is the pursuit of the good. The moral problem that thought confronts in a world that is characterized by strife rather than order, however, is that there are no natural ends for humans to pursue. Here Petrarch shares the nominalist premise that there are no substantial forms, no real species, and thus no natural ends. In order to understand what ends I ought to pursue it is thus necessary for me to understand what I am, for I am not just another member of the human species who has certain essential defining characteristics and a certain set of moral duties but an absolute particular, an individual created immediately and uniquely by God. To understand what I ought to do, I thus have to understand what I am in and for myself. For Petrarch, all moral questions thus go back to self-knowledge, and all human history is a study of human biography.[43]

LOVE AND VIRTUE

This new vision of the individual first begins to emerge in the context of Petrarch's lyric poetry. The story of Petrarch's poetry is the story of his struggle to overcome love, to free himself from the tyranny of this passion, and master himself.[44] His poetry is thus extremely introspective.[45] His famous collection of poems, the *Songbook,* recounts this psychological struggle and reveals Petrarch's defeat. It is a lament for his servitude, a proclamation of his shame, and a moral example for others.[46] Petrarch's poetry, however, is also the means by which he fights against this passion, bringing himself back to himself, and revealing love as a kind of subjection that must be overcome through the contemplation of death and the brevity of life, which reveal the hollowness of this passion for an earthly object.[47]

Love for Petrarch, in contrast to Dante, is not the solution to the human problem but a great danger, for unless we are attracted to the appropriate object love enslaves us and distracts us from both virtue and God.[48] Thinking is motivated by love, but love must have the right object. Love for earthly things can be overcome, as Petrarch tries to demonstrate with his own example, only when it contemplates death and the transience of all the earthly objects of passion. The disdain for created forms that the constant thought of death engenders is thus the first step on the path to virtue. Virtue can only be attained, however, if we are also attracted to the proper object, if we come to love what is truly worthy of love. In Petrarch's mind the only earthly object so worthy is virtue, and the strongest spur to virtue is the love of fame.[49] It is this idea that draws Petrarch to the ancients.

Petrarch knew from his study of Aristotle that virtue was attained through habituation and the imitation of the good man. The problem for his world, however, was that there were no institutions that fostered virtue and too few good men to emulate. Contemporary humanity thus could be moved to pursue virtue only if it was confronted with inspiring images of the virtuous life. In Petrarch's view, the creation of such images was the job of poetry. Thus, he felt that only the poetic presentation of exemplary lives could promote the will to act virtuously, and he believed he had found such models in the ancient world.[50]

In 1337, Petrarch began work on his *Illustrative Lives,* a treatise that he hoped would encourage virtue by presenting a series of exemplary heroic lives.[51] Like Livy and Plutarch, Petrarch uses history as a pool of moral examples.[52] He tries to show in this work that the achievements of illustrious men are not the result of good luck but the product of virtue and a desire for glory.[53] The examples, however, are quite different from one another. There is no single path to virtue. In fact, the lesson of the work is that virtue is not the assimilation of each individual to an ideal but the attainment of what is essential to each individual's character and capacities.

Petrarch constructs his project on Roman models, drawing on Livy, Virgil, Horace, Cicero, and Seneca. In Petrarch's view, Aristotle may well have had a more profound understanding of virtue, but he did not provide the means to make men good. The Roman moralists by contrast were concerned with what morality was and with inspiring men to act morally. Petrarch cast himself in a similar role as a lay moral counselor to his contemporaries, showing them magnificent examples of moral action and calling on them to raise themselves to a higher level, to emulate and compete with these glorious men of the past.[54]

While working on his *Illustrative Lives,* Petrarch was struck with the idea of composing an epic poem in Latin that would provide the supreme example of the virtuous life. Two possibilities presented themselves to him, Julius Caesar, the medieval hero who founded the universal and divinely ordained empire, and Scipio Africanus, who saved the Roman republic by defeating Hannibal and the Carthaginians. Petrarch chose to focus on Scipio and titled his poem *Africa*. In this work, Scipio's triumph over Carthage and the virtues of republican Rome come in large measure to replace Caesar's more problematic virtues and his foundation of the Roman empire as the supreme model of the virtuous life.[55] In part this choice is a reflection of Petrarch's underlying republican sympathies, which were also evident in his friendship and support for Cola di Rienzo's republican revolution in Rome in 1347.[56] Scipio, however, was also a better example for Petrarch because he was more reflective and introspective than Caesar.

Petrarch's Scipio is beautiful, tall, barrel-chested, muscular, chaste, and tranquil; he possesses great gravity and grace; he is a harsh foe, a sweet friend, immune to fortune's boons and blows, and indifferent to wealth. He venerates true glory, is pious, filled with rectitude, confident in battle, and courageous. He is also a lover of solitude, beauty, justice, and his fatherland.[57] It is hard to imagine a more perfect man. Scipio for Petrarch is exemplary not merely because he conquers Carthage but because he conquers himself. It is this that makes him a true paragon of virtue.[58] He not only is virtuous, virtue is the *only* thing that delights him.[59] Virtue, as he sees it, is the only truly lovable thing because it conquers death and insures one's fame, which stands fast against everything except time that undoes everything.[60]

Petrarch's Hannibal, by contrast, is a man without virtue. His martial skills are easily equal to those of Scipio, but he is faithless and untrustworthy, resentful of the world and the gods, cruel of heart, insatiate for blood, in league with infernal powers, given to savage wrath, impious, and overconfident.[61] All of his victories are thus hollow and empty because he is not master of himself but a slave to his passions. For similar reasons, he is incapable of true friendship and unable to endure solitude.

Africa thus presents two supreme moral examples: the virtuous and heroic man who can disdain fortune because of the strength of his character, and the "Machiavellian" man who is willing to do anything to secure victory but who is never master of himself and his own desires.[62] Both dramatically and philosophically, however, the work is flawed. Dramatically, its hero is simply too good. He combines all of the pagan social virtues and a kind of Christian otherworldliness.[63] He has nothing to overcome, no internal struggle, no flaws with which we can sympathize. He is a statue placed on a pedestal so high above the reader's head that it is scarcely possible to behold him, let alone emulate him.

Philosophically, the work fails because it vacillates between the praise of fame and the praise of virtue. Petrarch knew that most great men are motivated by a desire for fame and wished that only the virtuous would attain glory, but he knew this is not the case. Scipio's virtue inspires virtue in his fellow Romans and they conquer the vicious Hannibal and his money-loving Carthaginians, but they were also fortunate, for except for a moment of overconfidence after the battle of Cannae, Hannibal would have sacked Rome itself. Scipio's victory and fame thus seem to owe as much to fortune as they do to virtue. This point is evident at the beginning of the work, when the ghost of Scipio's father tells him that while his victory will win great fame for him and great longevity for Rome, both will fade. Over time he and Hannibal will even win equal praise because "the vulgar multitude cannot discern the gap that yawns between magnificence and deeds of foul enormity." [64] Moreover, even Rome shall fade and become merely a corrupt and pale image of its former self: "All that is born must die and after ripeness comes decay; no thing of earth endures." [65] Time thus triumphs over fame. Thus it is not glory that one should pursue but virtue, for "virtue alone, that heeds not death, endures. Virtue alone prepares the way to Heaven." [66] Fame is a reward that others give to greatness whether for good or ill; virtue is often unrecognized by others but is good in itself because it secures a victory over the passions and thus guarantees self-mastery.

In the public sphere, virtue is thus inevitably entangled with the desire for glory. The desire for glory, however, does not necessarily produce virtue and may produce the most monstrous vices. The ground for true virtue thus cannot lie in the love of fame. Hence Petrarch recognized that the magnificent examples of greatness from the ancient world that he had sought to portray in his *Illustrative Lives* and *Africa* were inadequate as grounds for the inculcation of moral virtue. As a result, he discontinued work on these texts and on a third book, *Memorable Things (Rerum memorandum)*, in which he planned a systematic indoctrination through examples in the four cardinal virtues as defined by Cicero, drawing on secular rather than sacred sources. Instead, he turned in a new direction that was to have immense importance for modern thought, to an introspective examination and critique of himself.[67]

PETRARCH'S CHRISTIANITY

In order to understand this inward turn, we need to examine briefly the impact of Christianity on Petrarch's thought. As we saw above, human beings for Petrarch live in a chaotic world and are constantly pulled by their passions or loves in multiple directions. Such loves, however, fade in the face of death. Death itself, in turn, can be overcome by fame. And fame falls prey to time. But is there anything that overcomes time? Within the context of the ancient world with which Petrarch was primarily concerned, only virtue seems to offer such a possibility, for virtue, at least as it was understood by Plato and the Stoics, touches the eternal. Virtue, in the end, however, is insufficient, for it is not clearly superior to time. The triumph over time is thus made possible only by Christianity, and we can come to terms with Petrarch's thought at the deepest level only when we understand what Christianity meant for him.[68]

(It is often assumed that Petrarch was devoutly Christian, but this position is difficult to reconcile with his classicism. Many scholars see a distinctive turn towards Christianity in Petrarch's life after 1343, when his brother Gherardo became a Carthusian monk. This event supposedly evoked a spiritual crisis in Petrarch that changed his whole outlook. There is, however, little evidence to support such a contention. In fact, there are many indications that his growing concern with sacred writings and his waning attention to the examples of antiquity had more to do with his reflections on the limitations of fame than with any spiritual crisis.[69]

(There are, moreover, good reasons to be suspicious of Petrarch's Christianity. It is doubtful, for example, that he ever took any interest in the Christian virtues of faith, hope, and charity.[70] Or as Voigt points out: "It is truly unique that Petrarch, in his writings, speaks so rarely of saints and of heresies, of miracles and of relics, of visions and of revelations. . . . For all of what the church had made, from the time of the first fathers, for all of that mélange which is in it of paganism and superstition, for that final hierarchy, he has nothing but indifference."[71] To tell the truth, Petrarch has so little connection to the Christianity of the Middles Ages that he seems to be oblivious to the problem of damnation.[72] In contrast to Dante, whose work he knew and admired, he ignores the Christian view that hell and damnation are a completion of divine justice and an element in beatitude.[73] There is similarly no allusion to the importance or even the need for prayer, and divine grace itself is virtually ignored in favor of a quasi-Pelagian preference for virtue.[74] Finally, Petrarch suggests that even if the soul were mortal, it would be better to think of it as immortal, for doing so would inspire love of virtue, which is a thing to be desired for its own sake.[75] Petrarch's concern with religion thus seems to be more a concern with the subjectivity of belief and the sense of salvation, with how the individual in this world regards himself in relationship to divine promises.[76]

(In this respect, Petrarch like the nominalists sees Christianity through the lens of Augustine, and in his case through an Augustine who was deeply influenced by pagan thinkers such as Plato and Cicero.[77] We today often assume that Augustine was the bedrock of medieval Christianity, but in fact his work was generally known only from the excerpts presented in Peter Lombard's famous *Sentences*. Moreover, with the revival of Aristotle in the thirteenth century, Augustine suffered a marked decline, although the Franciscans and Augustinian Hermits remained loyal to him.[78] It was thus only with the nominalist revolution and the rise of humanism that Augustine returned to the center of theological and philosophical speculation.[79]

Petrarch sees Augustine philosophically as a Platonist. Petrarch, however, did not know Plato well. He believed, for example, that for Plato the final good is virtue, which can only be attained by imitating God. Therefore, he was convinced that for Plato to philosophize was to love God. This is a point, he argued, with which Augustine agreed.[80] Furthermore, since "there can be no doubt that the only true knowledge is to know and to honor God, [it follows that]: 'Piety is wisdom.'"[81] To know God, however, one must know oneself. The supreme philosophical/theological work is thus Augustine's *Confessions,* and it was this work, above all others, that shaped Petrarch's Christianity.

The importance of Augustine for Petrarch becomes apparent in his famous account of his ascent of Mount Ventoux.[82] Allegorizing his brother's direct ascent up the mountain and his wayward course to their different approaches to the divine, he writes that when he reached the summit, he sat down and opened his copy of the *Confessions* and his eyes immediately fell upon the following passage: "And men admire the high mountains, the vast floods of the sea, the huge streams of the rivers, the circumference of the ocean, and the revolutions of the stars—and desert themselves."[83] He says that he was stunned and angry with himself that he still admired earthly things. He concludes, citing Seneca, that "long since I ought to have learned, even from pagan philosophers, that 'nothing is admirable besides the mind; compared to its greatness nothing is great.'"[84] What he learned from Augustine and what he feels he ought to have learned already from Seneca was the comparative unimportance of earthly goods (including fame) and the crucial need for self-examination, for it is only by knowing oneself that it is possible to come to know the eternal.[85] It was this insight that was at the heart of the great transformation in Petrarch's thought that produced his most introspective and penetrating work, *My Secret,* or *The Soul's Conflict with Passion.*

PETRARCH'S SEARCH FOR HIMSELF

My Secret has been called the "most scathing self-examination that any man ever made."[86] It is written as three confessional dialogues between

Petrarch and Augustine. The first dialogue begins with Augustine's assertion that Petrarch needs to remember above all else that he is a mortal being, for "there can be no doubt that to recollect one's misery and to practice
frequent meditation on death is the surest aid in scorning the seductions of
this world, and in ordering the soul amid its storms and tempests."[87] This
is the triumph of death over the passions that we discussed above. He asserts, however, that Petrarch like most men fails to confront death with the
needed seriousness and deceives himself continually about himself, cling-
ing willingly to his own miseries.[88] The rest of the first dialogue lays great
stress on the self-redressing power of will.[89] Knowledge, Augustine repeatedly asserts, is insufficient to bring about Petrarch's moral reformation:
"There must be will, and that will must be so strong and earnest that it can
deserve the name purpose."[90] The good can only be truly loved if Petrarch
thrusts out every lower desire, and it is only the profound meditation on
death that makes such purgation possible.[91]

In the second dialogue, Petrarch's morals are evaluated in terms of the
traditional seven mortal sins. While he is acquitted of envy, anger, and
gluttony, he is charged to his surprise with pride and avarice and not to
his surprise with lust and melancholia (accidia).[92] In contrast to the first
dialogue, however, the second focuses on failures of the mind rather than
the will. But in this dialogue Augustine relaxes his moral strictures and
says he never meant to urge Stoic abnegation on Petrarch but only a kind of
Peripatetic moderation.[93] That said, the dialogue closes with a characteristic Stoic claim that a soul serene and tranquil in itself will not be affected
by cares of the world.[94]

The third dialogue is a discussion of Petrarch's two most profoundly
moving passions, love and fame. His love of Laura is characterized as a
form of idolatry that robs him of dignity and liberty, intensifies his melancholia, undermines his morals, and turns his desires from the creator
to the creature.[95] As we saw in our discussion of the *Songbook,* both the
human self and God are forgotten in such love.[96] Glory is also accounted
a false form of immortality, but Petrarch is unable or at least unwilling to
renounce it.[97] He does agree, however, to take Augustine's advice to aim at
virtue and let glory take care of itself.[98]

This pathway to virtue, however, lies not in a scholastic investigation
of man's place in the natural order of things but in an introspective examination of the individual self. This examination, at least in *My Secret,*
is achieved through an inner, imaginary dialogue with a spiritual mentor,
in this case a friend that Petrarch knew only from books but in Petrarch's
mind a friend nonetheless. The self is thus understood not immediately but

through dialogue or discussion. Self-knowledge thus comes about through seeing oneself through the eyes of another, but another who is also in some sense another self.[99] As Petrarch later remarks in the *Remedies,* such talk "will discover you unto yourself, who seeing all things, sees not yourself."[100] The purpose of such a discovery is not merely self-understanding but self-improvement and self-perfection.

This becomes clear if we compare *My Secret* to its obvious model, Augustine's *Confessions.* In the *Confessions,* Augustine speaks directly to God, lays bare his soul to one who already knows it thoroughly in the hope of forgiveness and the redemption of his sins. In *My Secret,* Petrarch speaks to a human being long dead, who of course does not know anything about him, with the goal not of gaining forgiveness but of curing himself.[101] He does not throw himself on God's mercy but hopes through his imaginary therapeutic conversation to free himself from the passions that have distracted and enslaved him. His goal is thus not redemption but self-perfection, and he hopes to achieve this not by grace but by the human will.[102] At the center of *My Secret* is thus not God but the ideal of undifferentiated moral perfection, ontologically Platonist and morally Stoic.[103] Moreover, the Augustine who appears in *My Secret* is more akin to Seneca than to the Augustine who actually wrote the *Confessions* or the *City of God.*[104]

THE SUPERIORITY OF THE PRIVATE LIFE

At the end of the *My Secret,* Petrarch promises Augustine: "I will be true to myself, so far as in me lies. I will pull myself together and collect my scattered wits, and make a great endeavor to possess my soul in patience."[105] He foresees, however, that he will be distracted from this goal by a crowd of important worldly affairs. A life of virtue in which one remains true to oneself requires removal from the press of daily life. Petrarch explains and justifies this retreat in *The Solitary Life* (1346–56). In this work, written during the plague years, he lays out a path between the *vita activa* of classic virtue that he portrayed in his *Africa* and the *vita contemplativa* of monasticism that withdraws itself from any engagement with others.[106] This path is in fact a conception of what we have come to think of as the private life that frees itself from the burden of public affairs not out of any hatred of man or love of God but in order to enter into a life of study, of reading and writing surrounded by friends and devoid of the distracting passions engendered by the world.[107]

Petrarch asserts unequivocally in *The Solitary Life* that public life is incompatible with virtue. At the heart of this claim is his conviction that social life is dominated by the opinions and values of the multitude, who are invariably slaves to their passions. Man in society is thus not a free being who seeks his own good but a slave who desires the praise and fears the blame of others and who consequently wants only what others want. Those engaged in public affairs,

> are ruled by the power of another man's nod and learn what they must do from another man's look. They claim nothing as their own. Their house, their sleep, their food, is not their own, and what is even more serious, their mind is not their own, their countenance not their own. They do not weep and laugh at the promptings of their own nature but discard their own emotions to put on those of another. In sum, they transact another man's business, think another man's thoughts, live by another man's grace.[108]

The multitude thus merely follow one another, which is to say, they are dominated by the lowest desires and turn the satisfaction of these desires into objects of praise.[109] Under such circumstances, virtue is impossible and man necessarily becomes vicious, prey to envy and resentment. The busy man's heart is wholly fixed on treachery, and he becomes pernicious, unstable, faithless, inconstant, fierce, and bloody.[110]

The intellectual life also disappears in the public sphere, for public life is devoted to the cultivation of estates and not minds.[111] In fact, minds are deadened under such circumstances by the mania for talk, noise, and disturbance.[112] Petrarch admits that there are some saintly active men (such as Scipio), but he believes that they are very few and that they are not happy.[113] In his view a noble spirit will never find repose save in God or in himself and his private thoughts, or in some intellect united by a close sympathy with his own.[114]

It is only in private life, only in what Petrarch calls solitude or retirement, that man can be true to himself and enjoy his own individuality. This idea is a fundamental departure from the medieval tradition. Scholasticism had understood man not in his particularity and uniqueness but as a species, as the rational animal. Human happiness for scholasticism consisted in actualizing one's natural potentialities and fulfilling one's supernatural duties. Ockham and the nominalist movement rejected this view, arguing that all beings are radically individual, created directly by God. Thus, there are no universals or species, and all supposed species are merely names or signs. Petrarch had similar doubts that humans could be understood as a species. In a letter to his brother Gherardo, he argued that "human inclinations conflict not only for man in general but also for the individual: this I confess and cannot deny, since I know others and myself as well, and since I contemplate the human species in groups and singly. What in truth can I say about all men, or who could enumerate the infinite differences which so mark mortals that they seem to belong neither to a single species nor to a single type?" [115]

[This insight into the radical individuality of human beings shapes Petrarch's thought. We have already examined his attempts in the *Songbook* and *My Secret* to portray himself as a particular individual with all of his idiosyncrasies. Gustav Körting argues that this emphasis on personality marks a definite break with the Middle Ages.[116] Erich Loos suggests that Petrarch is a witness for a new understanding of the meaning of the individual as an irreplaceable personality.[117] His own self-presentation in his written work is an example of the unfolding and expression of character that Petrarch has in mind.[118] To know how one ought to live, it is essential to know who one is. He thus does not seek to lay down a rule for others but only to expose the principles of his own mind. His life appeals to him as supremely desirable, but he does not therefore recommended it for general imitation.[119] It is crucial that each man decide according to his own preferences, for it is impossible that a single road should suit all men.[120]

[Petrarch does not mean that everyone should simply follow his whims: "Each man must seriously take into account the disposition with which nature has endowed him and the best which by habit or training he has developed." [121] In the plan to reform our lives, we should be guided not by idle wishes but by our character and predisposition. It is thus necessary for man to be particularly honest and exacting in passing judgment on himself and to avoid temptations of eye and ear.[122] This is only to say that each man should undergo the kind of self-examination undertaken in the *My Secret*. Once one has come to the bottom of oneself and grasped one's peculiar nature, warts and all, he or she should follow the path that this nature demands. As Petrarch puts it, "Each person, whether saint, soldier, or philosopher, follows some irresistible call of his nature." [123]

⟨In his view, however, we generally do not do this because we are guided not by our own judgment but by the opinions of the crowd.[124] This distortion of judgment is the great danger that makes the private life, or the life of solitude, necessary. Independence of mind is possible only in solitude, in private away from the crowd, away from politics. Only there is it possible "to live according to your pleasure, to go where you will, to stay where you will . . . to belong to yourself in all seasons and wherever you are to be ever with yourself, far from evil, far from examples of wickedness!" [125]

[Petrarch's previous thought (and his later thought in *Remedies*) clearly owes a great deal to Stoicism. The tremendous emphasis on virtue and the general denigration of pleasure is deeply indebted to Cicero and Seneca. The position that Petrarch lays out in *The Solitary Life,* however, owes at least as much to Epicurus. Petrarch even employs the famous Epicurean image of the tower to describe the relation that the wise man adopts toward the world.[126] This Epicurean ideal of withdrawal from society into the philosophic garden, however, is combined with the emphasis on moral autonomy and virtue drawn from Roman Stoicism. This notion of psychic and moral self-sufficiency, however, is not identical to the Stoic notion.[127] Stoicism never recognized such a notion of radical individuality. For Stoicism the supreme model for human life is the sage. Everyone else has their duty commensurate with their place in society. Petrarch, however, sees the private man affirming and living in accordance with his own idiosyncratic being. Thus, not only does Petrarch value individuality, he asserts, as Zeitlin puts it, that we have a right to the expression of our individuality, the right of the human personality to express and realize itself according to its individual qualities, the right of a particular individual to regulate his life according to the disposition and humor with which nature has endowed him and without any reference to the claims of his fellow men upon him.[128] Thus, Petrarch tells us that, while he admires Cicero more than any other thinker, he does not imitate him, since he does not want to be an imitator of anyone.[129] Petrarch wants to be himself and enjoy his own being, and the legitimation of this desire—Petrarch's protestations notwithstanding— owes more to Epicureanism than to Stoicism.

[Moreover, this notion of individuality has important implications for the realization of virtue that call into question Petrarch's attachment to Stoicism.[First, it is fairly clear that virtue, as it is understood in this work, cannot be produced by political institutions or by a system of education or training, because each person's unique potentialities and the virtues pertaining to them can only be known by means of an introspective self-examination.\Second, for those who live within society it is impossible to overcome their lower impulses because they are constantly distracted from their ownmost goals by the praise and blame of others. Thus, the immoderate desire for fame (the unresolved problem of the *My Secret*) can be satisfied only by withdrawal from active life and the proper use of leisure.[130] Only in private will it be possible to win the war over our passions, "to expel vice from our borders, put our lusts to flight, restrain our illicit propensities, chastise our wantonness, and elevate our mind toward higher objects."[131] "Let some govern the populous city and others rule the army. Our city is that of our mind, our army that of our thoughts."[132]

Humans in this way remain political but only because they become autarchic cities with laws and customs peculiarly their own.

The solitude that Petrarch recommends is not a form of idleness but of spiritual activity. Here again Scipio serves as a model, Scipio who claimed "that he was never less idle than when at leisure, and never less lonely than when alone."[133] As Petrarch puts it: "The holiday I ordain is for the body, not for the mind; I do not allow the intellect to lie fallow except that it may revive and become more fertile by a period of rest. . . . I not only entertain but take pains to summon noble thoughts."[134] This life is above all else devoted to study, with a view not to fame or a reputation for learning but to self-improvement and self-perfection. Petrarch thus admits that he could not endure his solitude without reading: "Isolation without literature is exile, prison, and torture; supply literature, and it becomes your country, freedom, and delight."[135] Not only is solitude conducive to reading, it also promotes composition, for "literature can be carried on no where more successfully or freely than in solitude."[136] Indeed, such leisure or freedom has always been the source of the arts.[137] The solitary life is thus ideally suited to the most truly human lives, those of the philosopher, the poet, the saint, and the prophet.[138]

The goal of this life is to spend time in the company of noble thoughts, inspiring books, and loving friends.[139] The solitary life that Petrarch lauds is thus not an isolated life like that of a monk or a hermit, but a private life lived among friends.[140] "No solitude is so profound, no house so small, no door so narrow but it may open to a friend."[141] Indeed, solitude for Petrarch is enriched by the presence of a friend. He even asserts that he would prefer to be deprived of solitude rather than his friends.[142] The solitary life for Petrarch is not so solitary. In fact, it is much more a private fellowship of like-minded spirits. All of this is again very reminiscent of Epicurus's garden.[143] It is also deeply rooted in Petrarch's own life experience, for he worked very hard throughout his life to cultivate and maintain a large circle of friends. Friendship for Petrarch, however, always meant conversation whether in person or in writing. Indeed, in this way Petrarch could repeatedly refer to thinkers long dead as his friends.[144] They spoke to him through their books. The solitary life for Petrarch is thus not the silence of the Carthusian monastery (which his brother chose and which Petrarch praised in his *Religious Leisure*) but a continual conversation, with friends, through books, in letters, and in the imagination.[145]

Solitude, for Petrarch, "is indeed something holy, innocent, incorruptible, and the purest of all human possessions."[146] "Therefore, whether our desire is to serve God, which is the only freedom and the only felicity, or by virtuous practices to develop our mind, which is the next best application of our labor, or through reflection and writing to leave our remembrance to posterity and so arrest the flight of days and extend the all too brief duration of life, or whether it is our aim to achieve all these things together, let us, I pray you, make our escape at length and spend in solitude what little time remains."[147] Petrarch clearly knows, however, that solitude is not for everyone. Indeed, the disposition of most men is not favorable to such a life. Petrarch claims he will thus be happy if he can persuade a few to follow this path and the rest simply to view solitude in a more friendly fashion.[148]

BETWEEN ADAM AND PROMETHEUS

The question of human dignity was shaped, for medieval Christianity, by the nearly unanimous opinion that Adam's fall had cost man dearly.[149] From this perspective, man had no intrinsic worth or dignity. He had once occupied an elevated position as the *imago dei* but lost it as a result of his original sin. Humans thus could only be redeemed from their fundamental sinfulness by divine grace. Astoundingly, the question of sin seldom arises for Petrarch. He certainly believes that we are often misguided by our various passions, but he seems equally certain that we can overcome them if we try. Here Petrarch is quite distant from his medieval predecessors. Public virtue, which in his view is generally a byproduct of the desire for fame, may be tainted by the corrupt desire for the praise of the mob, but private virtue, such as that described in *The Solitary Life*, is the product of an individual will that attains its dignity through self-mastery. The individual's dignity, however, is thus not a consequence of what he *is,* that is, the rational animal occupying the highest rung in creation, but of what he *does,* of the fact that he employs his will to liberate himself from the mastery of his passions.[150] What on the surface looks like the renunciation of the world in *The Solitary Life* is thus in reality an affirmation of human individuality that simultaneously sanctions the virtuous individual's enjoyment of his own being.[151]

While Petrarch does not thereby abandon Christianity, he does at least seem to adopt a quasi-Pelagian view that man renders himself worthy of salvation or damnation by his own actions. If man is capable of lifting himself, he has little practical need of divine grace. It is precisely on grounds such as these that J. H. Whitfield has suggested that Petrarch's thought leads to Epicureanism. He recognizes that Petrarch is generally quite critical of Epicurus but believes that there is much the two have in common.[152] Petrarch sees the *summum bonum* as *honestas* in contrast to Epicurus's view that it is *voluptas,* but if virtue is always idiosyncratic to an individual's own being, then it does not differ from one doing whatever gives one pleasure, or to put it in other terms, *honestas* is indistinguishable in practice from *voluptas.*[153] Petrarch, of course, wants to deny such a conclusion, but it is clear that this possibility is present in Petrarch's thought.[154] Whitfield quite plausibly suggests that modernity has subsequently never been wholly able to deny Epicurus his place. Whitfield admits that this turn to hedonism looks like a turn away from Petrarch, but he suggests it is rather a rejection of the negative elements in Petrarch's thought in the context of a broader affirmation of Petrarch's essentially Epicurean position.[155]

In contradistinction to the charge that Petrarch betrays man's humanity by denying his nature as the rational animal and the *imago dei,* critics have accused him of vastly exaggerating human potentialities by attributing a superhuman power to the human will. Petrarch's notion of individuality seems particularly open to such a charge. He argues in the *Remedies* that God has demonstrated man's superiority over all other creatures.[156] Indeed, in reflecting on Christ, he asserts that "so being made a man He might make man a god. . . . Does not this alone seem to ennoble somewhat the condition of man and to relieve a little of its misery? What more, pray, could man, I do not say hope for, but aim at, and think of, than to be God? . . . He did not assume any other body and soul than that of a man (although He could have done so)."[157] In this way Petrarch seems to magnify the capacities of the individual beyond human limits.

While it is certainly the case that both of these charges can be plausibly leveled against Petrarch, I do not believe that either of them finally strikes to the core of his thought. Petrarch does not seek either to confine human being to the finite realm of mere matter in motion or to promote a striving to challenge God but pursues instead a middle course between Epicurus and Prometheus. He has a deep appreciation of the need for a sense of the infinite (and eternal) in human life and is equally sure that man himself cannot supply or even ultimately comprehend it. Plotinus, according to Petrarch, recognized four kinds of virtue: political, purgatorial, purified, and godly virtue.[158] The first are the virtues of a Caesar or a Scipio. The second are the virtues of those private men who become followers of philosophy and successfully eradicate the passions that are only moderated in the case of the former. Petrarch puts himself in this group. The third are the virtues of the (Stoic) sage. As admirable as these may be, Petrarch doubts that any such human beings ever existed. Finally, the virtues of the fourth category pertain to God alone and are utterly beyond human beings. The highest form of life possible for actual human beings, in Petrarch's view, is thus the life of the man who truly masters his passions by eliminating rather than merely moderating them. For Petrarch such a life is only possible if it is led in private to please oneself and not in public for the praise of the multitude.

The ability to succeed in such a life depends in good measure upon individual human capacities, and particularly the strength of one's will, but Petrarch never claims that such capacities are all that is needed. Without Christ and his help, he asserts, no one can become wise and good.[159] Petrarch thus seems to reject Pelagianism. For Petrarch, God as the Trinity is the highest power, the highest wisdom, and the highest good.[160] This claim tells us a good deal about Petrarch's theological views. Ancient thinkers such as Cicero, according to Petrarch, understood that the divine must be rational and good, but they did not and could not comprehend divine power because they were unable to grasp the divine capacity for *creatio ex nihilo*. This was the great breakthrough that Christ and Christianity made possible.[161] It is this crucial fact that "Epicurus and his followers could not know and our Aristotelian philosophers do not deign to know."[162] They did not understand that the world is created through the word as an expression of divine will, that is, that the articulation of the word creates the world because it is the expression of divine will and power. The ancients were unable to understand such a God because they continued to measure all gods by human capacities. Omnipotence, however, is not possible for man. Like the nominalists Petrarch lays great emphasis on the omnipotence of the divine will and the radical separation of God and man.

In contrast to the nominalists, however, Petrarch sees a God who is willful but not unsettling. For nominalism, the idea of absolute divine power had as its corollary divine unpredictability. For Petrarch, by contrast, God is "the one, the Good, the True, the stably abiding."[163] As such, he is a lodestone for human beings: "Human longing is boundless and insatiable until it comes to rest in thee, above whom there is no place to which it could still rise."[164] In his omnipotence, such a God, in Petrarch's view, is both unreachable and yet infinitely lovable. Petrarch ties together this view of the divine and the role of religion in human life with his concern for virtue in his late treatise, "Of Our Own Ignorance and That of Many Others":

Though our ultimate goal does not lie in virtue, where the philosophers locate it, it is through the virtues that the direct way leads to the place where it
does lie; and these virtues, I must add, must be not merely known but loved.
Therefore, the true moral philosophers and useful teachers of the virtues are
those whose first and last intention is to make hearer and reader good, those
who do not merely teach what virtue and vice are . . . but sow into our hearts
love of the best and eager desire for it and at the same time hatred of the
worst and how to flee it. It is safer to strive for a good and pious will than for
a capable and clear intellect. The object of the will . . . is to be good; that of
the intellect is truth. It is better to will the good than to know the truth. . . .
In this life it is impossible to know God in His fullness; piously and ardently
to love Him is possible . . . [as it is] to know that virtue is the next best thing
to God himself. When we know this, we shall love him for his sake with our
heart and marrows, and virtue we shall love for His sake too.[165]

On its surface, this view seems very pious, but it does not live up to Jesus' two commandments. Petrarch does not suggest that we follow divine
commands, that we love our neighbor, or that we lead a life of poverty and
ascetic denial. Still, he also does not fall into either an Epicureanism or
Stoicism that is centered completely on man.[166] He continues to praise the
classical life of virtue, the value of friends, and the necessity of leisure, but
he praises them not in their own right but because it is pleasing to God
and is the road to our immortality. The highest Christian possibility, for
Petrarch, thus looks remarkably like the life of the philosophic sage and
decidedly unlike that of the saint or the martyr. Petrarch mentions the
example of Socrates only rarely, but it is clearly something like the life of
Socrates that he has in mind. Thus, in his view we come to understand our
duty not through Scripture or the works of the Fathers, but through an
introspective self-examination. "Conscience," Petrarch tells us, "is the best
judge of virtue."[167] It is the witness that tells us what is right.[168] Coming
to terms with this voice may include the reading of Scripture (along with
Cicero, Seneca, et al.), but it ultimately depends upon the kind of critical self-examination Petrarch undertook in *My Secret* and the withdrawal
from public life that he described in *The Solitary Life*.

Petrarch thus neither sets man up to rival God nor deprives man of God.
Rather, he seeks to combine Christianity with the notion of virtue he finds
in Cicero and Seneca. All of this is enclosed within a notion of individuality that is prefigured in if not derived from nominalism. To put the matter
more generally, Petrarch seeks a synthesis of Augustinianism that emphasizes man's dependence on his creator with a Stoicism that emphasizes his

independence.[169] These two positions, however, seem on the surface to be contradictory. The concept of individuality that he deploys is intended to resolve this contraction. These two can be held together within the individual if the individual is properly (and extensively) educated, chooses to live a private rather than a public life, has the wherewithal to live a life of leisure, has the will to master his passions, and is able to surround himself with true friends.

The good life for Petrarch is thus possible only for exceptional individuals. Consequently, there is unquestionably a fundamental elitism to Petrarch's position. Late in life, Petrarch remarked that he aimed to combine Platonic wisdom, Christian dogma, and Ciceronian eloquence.[170] This was of course a titanic task and he realized he had not been able to complete it, but his magnificent example was a beginning that inspired successive generations of humanists to follow this path. It is to an examination of this humanist project that we now turn.

3 | *Humanism and the Apotheosis of Man*

It is difficult today to appreciate the impact Petrarch had on his contemporaries in part because we find it so difficult to appreciate his impact on us. Petrarch is scarcely remembered in our time. There are very few humanists or academics who can name even one of his works; and none of his Latin works makes it on to a list of great books. And yet, without Petrarch, there would be no humanists or academics, no great books, no book culture at all, no humanism, no Renaissance, and no modern world as we have come to understand it. Why then have we forgotten him? Several factors contribute to his oblivion: the neglect of Latin literature as literary scholars have increasingly focused on national literatures, changing scholarly tastes and fashions, and the fact that many of his works fall outside familiar genres. But the real cause lies deeper. Petrarch seldom tells us anything that we don't already know, and as a result he seems superfluous to us. But this is the measure of his importance, for what he achieved is now so universally taken for granted that we find it difficult to imagine things could have been otherwise.

At the time of his death, Petrarch was the most famous private man in Europe, and during the next 150 years his fame and influence continued to grow and spread.[1] In part this was certainly the result of his masterful command of language and his ability to move the human heart, but this cannot be the whole story. Dante had written vernacular poetry a generation before that was widely admired, but he did not inspire generations of imitators. Petrarch's impact was more the result of the fact that he offered a new vision of how to live to a Christian world caught in the tremendous spiritual crisis brought about by the nominalist revolution and the cataclysmic events of the fourteenth century, a Christian world turned inward by the failure of the Crusades and the looming threat of a rejuvenated

Islam in both the east and the west. This Petrarchian project rested on the assertion of the ontic priority of individual human beings and the assertion that the search for a meaningful human life began with an examination of human individuality. Petrarch was able to make this vision concrete and attractive by displaying to the public his own inner life as well as those of an astonishing array of ancient personalities quite different from the saints and martyrs who guarded all of the entryways into the cathedral of Gothic Christianity. In this way Petrarch set his contemporaries on a two-fold journey. The first phase of this journey led inward to the unexplored territory of a self filled with passions and desires that were no longer something mundane and unspiritual that had to be extirpated or constrained but that were instead a reflection of each person's individuality and that consequently deserved to be expressed, cultivated, and enjoyed. The second phase of the journey led backwards to an ancient but now suddenly relevant past filled with courageous and high-minded individuals who had won fame and a kind of immortality by cultivating their own individuality. Moreover, these two journeys were connected, for it was through the exploration and appreciation of the biographies of the great men of antiquity that one could begin to understand how to give shape to one's own individuality and thereby lead not merely a pious but a noble life, a life worthy of being remembered. He showed that immortality did not merely belong to the saints and martyrs but also to all those who emulated men like Scipio, Cicero, Homer, Virgil, Socrates, and Plato, the warriors, statesmen, artists, and philosophers who had created and sustained the Greek and Roman worlds. What lies concealed behind these fabulous examples is the idea that individual human beings and their goals matter, that they have an inherent dignity and worth. This assertion was revolutionary and stood in stark opposition to the regnant doctrine of original sin and the Fall, which denied that individuals had either an intrinsic value or a capacity for self-perfection. It was this Petrarchian notion of the ontic priority and value of the individual human being that became the guiding light of the humanist project and that made the Renaissance and the modern world possible.

The humanist project was prefigured in Petrarch's aspiration to combine Christian piety with Roman virtue under the rubric of Platonism. While Petrarch himself was never able to achieve this goal, those who followed in his wake redoubled their efforts to bring it to completion. As we will see, however, synthesizing such disparate elements was a difficult task and required humanists to rethink not merely what it meant to be moral but also what it meant to be Christian. Italian humanists focused more on

Roman models, and they were pulled increasingly toward a heroic and ultimately Promethean individualism that required an ever-greater emphasis on a Neoplatonic interpretation of Christianity that deemphasized the Fall in favor of the view of man as the *imago dei*. As a result, Italian humanists found it increasingly difficult to maintain the separation of God and man. Northern humanists had a less exalted view of human capacities, but they too emphasized the importance of the moral life. Their model for such a life, however, was not Scipio, Cicero, or Caesar but Christ. They thus did not seek greatness or glory but decency and dignity through the practice of simple Christian charity. In contrast to their Italian compatriots, northern humanists did not imagine that man could thereby become God, but they did imagine that man's free will could play an important role in determining whether or not he would be saved. While they thus did not fall into Prometheanism, they did often come very close to Pelagianism. However, neither of these forms of humanism was able to achieve a synthesis that could fully relieve the immense anxiety generated by the notion of divine omnipotence. Neither was thus able to forestall the rise of a more ardent evangelical Christianity that turned away from the humanist synthesis of Christian piety, Roman morality, and Platonism to an apocalyptic theology that shook Europe to its core.

The term 'humanism' was first used by nineteenth-century scholars to name the Renaissance system of education based on the classics. They drew on the fifteenth-century term *umanista,* referring to those who studied classical literature and philosophy in the *studia humanista* or *studia humanitatis* not with a view to understanding God or generating a theology but in order to understand what it meant to be human and how human beings ought to live.[2] Humanism thus was understood as a comprehensive system of education and training that put great emphasis on human individuality, human dignity, and the privileged place of humans in the universe.[3] "Humanism" was thus not simply a philosophy but was a comprehensive cultural movement that included poetry, art, literature, history, and moral philosophy.[4]

While everyone agrees that humanism drew its inspiration from Petrarch, many believe that it also owed a great deal to an older Italian tradition of letter writing and public oratory. Medieval civilization had never penetrated Italy as deeply as it had the rest of Europe. There was a persistent and idiosyncratic Italian tradition that went back to late Roman times, expressed in arts and poetry, lay education, legal customs, grammar, and rhetoric.[5] The masters of this kind of public speaking and writing were called *dictatores.*[6] Petrarch's father was brought up in this tradition and gave his son a similar education. It is also clear that many of the other early humanists were trained in this tradition. While no one really doubts that this earlier tradition played some role in the development of humanism, there is considerable debate about how important it actually was, since in contrast to the humanists the *dictatores* had little concern for antiquity. Those who see humanism as a mere extension of this *dictatores* tradition view the humanist concern with the ancients as merely a means of improving their own rhetorical art and not as a fundamental reorientation of their goals and activities.[7] They argue that humanists such as Salutati occupied positions identical to those of the *dictatores* 150 years before. They also point to the fact that humanists typically held chairs in rhetoric or grammar rather than moral philosophy at universities before the fifteenth century and that they did not develop a metaphysics of their own.[8] However, such arguments are not very convincing. While the humanist project may have grown out of the *dictatores* tradition, it also clearly outgrew it not merely in the humanists' return to the ancients but also in their goals and aspirations. Petrarch, for example, never called himself an orator but referred to himself as either a moral philosopher or a poet.[9] Furthermore, while the humanists did not occupy positions of moral philosophy at the universities during the first part of the fourteenth century, this was almost certainly due to their rivals' monopolistic hold on such positions. Similarly, while early humanists did not develop a metaphysics, this had less to do with their disinterest in philosophy than in their preference for moral philosophy and their distaste for the interminable metaphysical disputes that characterized scholasticism. Thus, while humanism was indebted to the *dictatores* tradition, it clearly transcended it, and after Petrarch there can be no question that humanists had a goal different from that of their predecessors.

Scholars have questioned not only the origins of humanism but also its meaning and significance. Since at least the time of Burckhardt and Nietzsche, humanism has been understood by one school as an anti-Christian revival of pagan antiquity, a turn from what Nietzsche called slave morality to the master morality of the Greeks and the Romans. This view of humanism as anti-Christian came to be more broadly accepted in the twentieth century as 'humanism' was increasingly identified as 'secular humanism.' Seen in this light, humanism was widely attacked by both Catholics and Protestants as the harbinger of a secular and ultimately atheistic modernity. The Thomist Etienne Gilson, for example, argued that humanism was in fact a rebirth of Epicureanism that was largely responsible for the rampant hedonism that he believed was undermining modern life.[10] The Protestant theologian Reinhold Niebuhr in a similar fashion saw humanism as an attempt to put man rather than God at the center of things, exaggerating human capacities and particularly the power of the human will to achieve its own salvation.[11] These opinions were broadly shared in the religious community.

As humanism was increasingly criticized by the religious, it became increasingly attractive to a secularizing society as a possible foundation for moral and political life. Perhaps the dominant secular interpretation of humanism, first formulated by Hans Baron, associates humanism with civic republicanism. This interpretation accepts the Nietzschean reading of humanism as essentially pagan, skeptical, secularizing, and antireligious but rejects his elitist conclusion that humanism is coterminous with tyranny. Instead Baron and his many followers see humanism and particularly its emphasis on Roman virtue and civic life as the foundation for the civic republicanism of Florence and other Italian states.[12] The supporters of this interpretation see the humanists not as thinkers and artists living the *vita contemplativa* but as political actors focused on the *vita activa*. They point to Salutati, Bruni, and Bracciolini, all of whom were chancellors in the Florentine Republic, as well as to later humanists such as Guicciardini and, above all, Machiavelli, who not only served as (second) Chancellor in Florence but also developed a theory of republicanism on the Roman model and was responsible for the organization of the first Florentine republican army. This view of humanism is particularly pronounced in Anglo-American scholarship that focuses on the humanists' imitation and revival of ancient civic and republican structures and virtues and on the impact of this republicanism on English and American institutions and practices.[13]

The idea that humanism is preeminently civic humanism, however, is mistaken and misleading. Civic humanism or civic republicanism did play a role in a number of Italian cities during this period, but it did not constitute the whole or even the principal part of the humanist movement. To see it as central is to accept a historical myth propagated by the humanists themselves, who clearly knew that they were not pagans but Christians and as much members of the *republica christiana* as of their secular regimes.[14] And even if one is willing to grant that this civic element may have played an important role in Italian (or at least Florentine) humanism and a derivative but still important role in the development of seventeenth- and eighteenth-century Anglo-American liberalism, in the fifteenth and sixteenth centuries civic humanism was much less important in the rest of Europe, and almost certainly in Italy as well, than was Christian humanism. Those like Baron who wanted to find a secular foundation for republican government that was not associated with a Lockean notion of rights and with what they saw as a capitalist political economy read too much into the earlier humanist tradition. They thus overlooked the deep connection of humanism and Christianity.

Christian humanism is typically associated with the northern humanism and with Erasmus and Thomas More in particular. While they were indisputably Christian, it would be a mistake to believe that the earlier Italian humanists were not. The humanist vision of Christianity that developed in Italy was radically at odds with medieval and scholastic Christianity and had little in common with either the Protestant or Catholic theology that developed in the struggles of the Reformation, but it was unquestionably Christian in its intentions, and, as we shall see, it played an important if often concealed role in the development of Christianity from the seventeenth century onward. How then ought we to understand the connection of humanism and Christianity?

Although humanists almost universally rejected scholasticism, they were more equivocal about nominalism. Indeed, while they abandoned the nominalistic method and language, they held surprisingly similar views on a number of matters. Building on the earlier work of Ernst Cassirer, scholars such as Jerrold Seigel and Charles Trinkaus have argued quite cogently that the humanist enterprise was indebted to nominalism.[15] While this is obvious in the case of Salutati and later thinkers such as Nicholas of Cusa, it is less evident in the case of Petrarch, whose thought was more or less contemporaneous with that of Ockham and his immediate followers.

Untangling this connection is made difficult by the fact that scholasticism was not nearly as strong and widespread in Italy as it was in northern Europe in the thirteenth century. Indeed, scholasticism became prominent in Italy at about the same time as humanism.[16] The Italian experience of scholasticism was thus markedly different from that of the rest of Europe.[17] However, Trinkaus and others have demonstrated that Italians were involved in the tense nominalist controversies of the early fourteenth century.[18] They also suggest that Petrarch, Salutati, Braccolini, Ficino, etc. were responding to the philosophical and psychological dilemma that arose in the great debate between the realist scholastics and their nominalist opponents.[19] We know that Petrarch was cognizant of the terminological arguments of the nominalists.[20] Moreover, while he was Italian by birth and studied for a time in Bologna, he also spent a great deal of his early life in Avignon and had contact with the scholastic community there. Finally, he and Salutati both were close to many Augustinians such as

Dioigi of Borgo San Sepolcro and Luigi Marsili who were well acquainted with nominalism.[21]

Even if one rejects the notion that Petrarch was shaped by or was responding to nominalist thought, there is no question about the influence of nominalism on later humanist thought. The parallels are obvious.[22] Ontologically, both nominalism and humanism reject realism in favor of individualism. Both also reject syllogistic logic. The nominalists seek to replace it with a logic of names or terms. Humanists turn to rhetoric.[23] Theologically, both portray God as radically omnipotent and consequently reject rational theology in favor of Scripture.[24] Both also draw heavily on Augustine. Cosmologically, both see the world not as an immutable natural order but as a chaos of individual bodies in motion. Finally, both see human beings not as rational animals but as individual willing beings.[25] In the political realm, they both also sought to develop more republican theories of authority.[26] All of these similarities, however, might be simply accidental. Moreover, there are real and important differences between humanism and nominalism in all of their different forms and permutations. To understand the connection of humanism and Christianity we thus need to examine the development of humanism more carefully.

Humanism from the beginning was a strange construction of what at times seemed to be incommensurable parts. The admiration of pagan antiquity, of its moral and political heroes, its art and philosophy, its tragic literature and rhetorical practices was not easily compatible with original sin, the adoration of martyrs, monastic withdrawal, Christian charity, the preeminence of Scripture, or asceticism, and it was always a struggle to hold the two together. As we saw in the last chapter, Petrarch admired and praised the *vita activa* and the virtues needed to sustain it, but he also recognized the virtues of the *vita contemplativa* practiced by the monks and developed a new vision of a *secular* private life with its own leisure for contemplation and creation. He thus sought to combine the active political life of the heroic Romans he so admired with the Augustinian Christianity he found so compelling. He was critical of corruption in the church, but he saw the source of this corruption not in Christian doctrine or in the institutional structures of the church but in the weakness of human nature. He also doubted that human beings could live entirely secular lives. While he asserted in his most secular work, *Remedies for Fortune Fair and Foul,* that reason could play an important role in ameliorating human difficulties, he also recognized that the solution to earthly problems could not be separated from the question of salvation. Finally, although he admired noble men such as Scipio and Cato, he never forgot that they were pagans, rejecting, for example, Cicero's teaching that virtue was in one's power while fortune was in the hands of others.[27]

While Petrarch saw the necessity of reconciling *pietas* and *humanitas,* he was never able to bring them into a coherent synthesis. He did, however, set a goal that his successors in different ways tried to attain. As we noted above, the key to such a combination in his view was Platonism. What he actually imagined Platonism to be, however, is not entirely clear. Most of what he knew about Plato he knew at second hand, principally from Cicero and Augustine. The fact that both of his spiritual mentors admired and drew on Plato apparently convinced him that a reconciliation of Christianity and paganism on a Platonic basis was possible. His actual knowledge of Plato, however, was quite limited and his knowledge of the later developments of Platonism more limited still. All this notwithstanding, his humanist successors followed his lead in turning to Plato and Platonism in their efforts to reconcile Christian piety and Roman virtue.

Humanists after Petrarch were less willing to praise or even accept monasticism and a number of other medieval religious practices, but they were not antireligious or anti-Christian. They too sought to reconcile morality and piety. In attempting to balance these two elements, they typically relied upon a Neoplatonic reading of Christianity that saw man not as an irremediably fallen creature but as the *imago dei* in order to justify their vision of heroic individuality. However, this decision required them to so deemphasize original sin and the Fall that they were constantly in danger of falling into Pelagianism. But still, even at their most extreme, the humanists did not think of themselves as un-Christian. This is surprising to us, because we find it difficult to imagine that anyone could believe that such heroic or Promethean individuals could be good Christians, in large part because we associate Christianity with humility. We are thus prone to conclude that the Christianity of the Italian humanists was merely camouflage for fundamentally anti-Christian goals. This conclusion, however, is mistaken. The humanists themselves were aware of this tension in their thought, but they thought that these different elements could be reconciled with one another and thus did not believe they had to choose between Athens and Jerusalem or between the city of God and the city of the pagans.

It is certainly true that the religious views of most humanists were quite different than those of their medieval predecessors, but that does not mean that they were any less Christian. Indeed, in many instances they developed their beliefs and practices as a result of their disgust with medieval Christianity and as part of their effort to recover a more original and authentic Christian practice. The humanists were convinced that the religious practices of their contemporaries were at best distorted images of the genuine Christianity of Augustine and the other church fathers, and they blamed this distortion on the scholastic reliance on the pagan Aristotle and the Islamic Averroës. They believed that the key to reawakening genuine religiosity was to locate and root out those beliefs and practices that their historical and linguistic scholarship increasingly revealed to be later additions to Christianity. This reformatory impulse was strengthened by the recovery of the works of Cicero, Seneca, and other Roman writers as well as the dialogues of Plato and the works of the later Neoplatonists.[28] These works gave them an increasingly accurate picture of the intellectual environment within which Christianity first developed and the ways in which ancient moral and metaphysical teachings had informed Christian belief and practice.

ITALIAN HUMANISM

From the very beginning Italian humanism sought to reconcile Christian piety and ancient virtue. The leading humanist of the generation after Petrarch was Coluccio Salutati (1341–1406). As a young man, he was taught by Moglio, a friend of Petrarch, and then served as a papal secretary. In 1368 he began a correspondence with Petrarch. He was recalled to Florence in 1375 to serve as the chancellor (or Latin secretary) of the Florentine republic and was one of the leading proponents of civic republicanism. Although he was mostly involved in civic affairs, he wrote two short treatises, *On Fate and Fortune* and *On Religion and Flight from the World.* Strongly influenced by Petrarch and by nominalism, he developed a concept of the individual that laid great emphasis on the power of the will. He drew on pagan models in formulating his idea of the individual and was attacked by Dominicans such as Giovanni Dominici (1357–1419) for doing so, but the notion of the dignity of the individual that he developed in *On Fate and Fortune,* for example, was clearly rooted in the idea of the free will he derived from Augustine.[29] He also condemned the Stoic belief that virtue was the only good and that emotions were un-Christian and harmful. He rejected Aristotelianism on essentially nominalist grounds, but he also rejected the nominalist contention that God's omnipotence made all human freedom impossible.[30] It is not surprising then that opponents on both sides of the realist/nominalist debate considered him anti-Christian, but it would be a mistake to assume that their testimony was dispositive. In the fourteenth and fifteenth centuries there was no single monolithic form of Christianity, but various kinds of Christian belief and practice. Christian humanism was certainly never the choice of a majority of Christians, but it was influential especially among the intellectuals and generally accepted as orthodox.

Central to the humanist enterprise was the defense of a notion of human dignity.[31] In order to defend such a notion, it was necessary for humanism to emphasize the fact that man was created in the image of God and to minimize the effects of the Fall and original sin. These points were crucial for most humanists but also problematic. They understood that without a liberal reading of both matters, they would have to conclude that the great moral heroes of antiquity, Socrates, Cicero, and Cato, had been damned. Dante had sought to finesse this problem by putting Socrates in limbo, but this was insufficient for most humanists who needed to believe that morality and piety were more or less identical. If men such as Socrates had been damned, it would be hard to avoid the nominalist conclusion that God was indifferent or even unjust. However, if it was possible for such virtuous men to be saved without knowing Christ, then it was hard to understand why Christ and his sacrifice were necessary.

Humanists employed two different strategies in their efforts to resolve this problem. Following Paul's account in Romans that God's laws were revealed through the order of nature, they argued that pagans who had led virtuous lives according to nature had thus recognized, honored, and perhaps even "worshipped" God even though they did not know of Christ. This was especially true for those pagans like Socrates and Cicero who recognized that there was only one god. Thus, the virtuous pagans could by only some slight stretch of the imagination be counted among the elect. The problem with such a view was that it seemed to propel one toward Pelagianism. The second possibility, which we will discuss below, was to imagine that there was a common origin to both Christianity and pagan thought. Such a common origin could justify the humanists' belief that the moral teachings of pagans were inspired by God and thus essentially identical with the teaching of Christ.

The rapprochement of pagan and Christian thought was facilitated by the work of Leonardo Bruni (1369–1444), who was a student of Salutati and like him served as a papal secretary before returning to Florence in 1415 as his successor in the chancellorship. Among his many contributions, Bruni greatly eased religious suspicions that the humanist reading of secular texts corrupted piety by translating and publishing a letter from Basil, one of the greatest Christian heroes, defending the reading of pagan poets by Christian students.[32] He also popularized a new notion of history, originally formulated by Flavio Biondo (1392–1463), that divided history not according to the four empire theory that had dominated historical thinking for almost a thousand years but according to a tripartite division of ancient, medieval, and modern periods. This new understanding, which was indebted to Petrarch's notion of a dark age separating his time from that of the ancients, was crucial to the development of Christian humanism, for it legitimized humanist efforts to recover a pristine, ancient Christianity much closer to ancient moral thought than the corrupted Christianity that had developed during the dark, middle age. Finally, he was one of the first to translate the Platonic dialogues, although his translations were not very accurate.

Such a belief in the possibility of a rebirth that combined Christian piety with ancient morality was especially clear in the work of one of Bruni's students, Lorenzo Valla (1407–57). Valla was a fierce defender of Christianity but also a convinced Neoplatonist, and he was as opposed to Aristotelianism and Averroism as any of those who had authored the Condemnation of 1277.[33] He was particularly upset by what he saw as Stoic and peripatetic moralism posing as Christian piety. He believed that to be a Christian one had to accept the truth of Scripture. As he saw it, however, this truth had been massively distorted. Fortunately, humanist philological tools enabled scholars to correct many of these distortions. The most famous and certainly the most important of his "corrections" was his sensational demonstration in 1440 that the Donation of Constantine, the foundation for the temporal authority of the papacy, was a forgery. While this demonstration weakened the church's power, it was not anti-Christian, nor was it understood to be so at the time. Indeed, Valla was appointed papal secretary in 1448 in part because of the very linguistic skills that had enabled him to demonstrate the forgery.

As we saw in the last chapter, Petrarch saw humans as willing rather than as rational beings. Indeed, this was intrinsic to their individuality. The consequences of this position, however, were never entirely clear to Petrarch and only gradually became clear to later humanists. Thinking from this perspective is not a form of contemplation but of action. In thinking, humans then do not simply discover an inherent order in the world but will it or give it form. All *logos* or language is thus a form of *poiēsis* or poetry, and knowing is thus always a form of creation.[34] Human creation, however, is not and cannot be a *creatio ex nihilo,* because divine will has already given the world form. Knowing thus is always a remaking, a *mimēsis,* to use Plato's term, of the original divine making, a re-willing of what God has already willed. In this way, art comes to play a central role in the humanist project, although it is not conceived as an exercise of creativity or expression. Rather, drawing on Plato, humanism imagines the artist to recreate the divinely beautiful essence of creation in all of its shapes and forms, up to and including the depiction of God himself.

Valla saw this connection of art and religion quite clearly. Trinkaus writes: "The world of religion, declares Valla, is invented and depicted by man, not because it is not there, for the transcendent conviction of our faith asserts that it is, but because we cannot know it except prophetically and allegorically." [35] God as an infinite being cannot be captured in merely finite forms except in an allegorical fashion. Therefore, religion has to be given form by the human will. However, religion does not differ in this respect from other forms of knowing. Thus, Trinkaus concludes that for Valla, not "only the world of the divine but also the eternal world of nature and man are continually being reinvented and redepicted by the active, creative mind and imagination of man himself. Man operates in this fashion because he has been created in the image and likeness of God, who is thus invented and depicted by holy men themselves." [36] This human power in Valla's view does not set man up against God but is actually an expression of man's own participation in divinity as the *imago dei*. The human will thus operates within the will of God to shape the world, but it always acts within a world that the divine will has already formed.

How these two wills can coexist, however, is puzzling. Valla was mystified by this question. In his work *On the Free Will,* for example, he admits that humans cannot understand how free will can be compatible with divine foreknowledge. While he was convinced that it was, he could only speculate about how that could be the case, suggesting at times that God's will works through the human will (a notion that Luther later developed much more explicitly), albeit in a completely mysterious way that seemed to entangle him simultaneously in both Pelagianism and Manicheanism. [37]

In assigning such a role to human will, Valla drew on the syncretistic Neoplatonism of the later Roman Empire. [38] Petrarch and Salutati had already turned to Plato in their attempts to lay out a theological position independent of both scholasticism and nominalism. This turn was legitimated in their minds by Augustine's avowed Platonism. Thinkers of the fourteenth and even the early fifteenth centuries, however, had only limited access to the works of Plato and the Neoplatonists. Augustine himself was known almost exclusively only from the selective extracts of his work included in Peter Lombard's *Sentences,* which gave a one-sided impression of his thought. The recovery of Platonic and Neoplatonic thought was accelerated by renewed contacts with Eastern Christianity at the Council of Ferrara (1438–45), where for the first time Italian humanists met a living representative of the Neoplatonist tradition, Gemistus Pletho (1355–1464). His impact and that of his disciple John Bessarion (1403–72), especially on the Florentine humanists, was extraordinary, stimulating the study of ancient Greek and ancient Greek philosophical texts. This growing impact of ancient Greek thought on humanism certainly had an impact on secular society, but the impulse behind it was unquestionably religious, and its aim was not to discover a pagan or secular alternative to Christianity but to recover a form of Christianity that would help to reunify the church in the face of the very real Turkish threat.[39] The search for a Christian warrior who combined piety and martial virtue and who could thus stand up to the religiously inspired warriors of Islam was central to the humanist project and found expression in many of the great artworks of humanism, such as Tarquato Tasso's *Jerusalem Delivered* and Dürer's *Knight, Death, and the Devil.*

The receptivity of humanists not merely to Platonism but to Neoplatonism was grounded in the mystical tradition and particularly in the thought of Meister Eckhardt (1260–1327/28) and John of Ruysbroeck (1293–1381), who laid great emphasis on the infinite potentialities of the individual human spirit as the habitation of God. In their thought, however, the ultimate goal of such knowledge was not independence and autonomy but reunion with God through the dissolution of individuality in the infinity of divine being. The similarities of their thought to that of Plotinus are palpable.[40] Humanism followed this same path but emphasized not the dissolution of the individual in God but the indwelling of the divine power in the individual. This ultimately led Italian humanism to a Prometheanism that was incompatible with Christianity, but this was only at the end of a long path that otherwise remained within the relatively broad orthodoxy of pre-Reformation Christianity.

While humanists from Petrarch to Valla had seen Platonism as the principal ground for reconciling Christian piety and Roman morality, they were not sufficiently acquainted with Platonic and Neoplatonic thought to do so effectively. Valla obviously knew more about Platonism than Petrarch, but his knowledge was still limited. It was thus really only beginning with Marsilio Ficino (1433–99) that Platonism became the beating heart of the humanist project.[41] Although Ficino was preeminently a philosopher, he was also a scholar, doctor, musician, and priest. He translated almost all of the works of Plato and many other Platonists into Latin. His villa in Florence was also the gathering spot for a group of humanists interested in Plato, loosely referred to as the Platonic academy. He had a profound and direct impact on many of the greatest figures of the Renaissance including Lorenzo de' Medici, Leone Battista Alberti, Angelo Poliziano, Christoforo Landino, Pico della Mirandola, Botticelli, Michelangelo, Raphael, Titian, and Dürer, as well as an indirect impact on many more. He was convinced that Plato and the Neoplatonists could sustain the synthesis that Petrarch had sought, because they revealed the immortal and divine principle within each human being that Scripture pointed to in characterizing man as the *imago dei*. He had good reasons for this opinion. He knew that the church fathers had drawn heavily on Platonic and Neoplatonic thought, and he was convinced that Christianity and Platonism had a common origin in the more ancient thought of Hermes Trimegistus and Zoroaster.

While contemporary scholars agree that Neoplatonism had a profound impact on early Christianity and even recognize that Greek and Judeo-Christian thought are indebted to Zoroastrian thought in some ways, they reject the idea of a literal Hermetic tradition as the common origin of both.[42] For more than two hundred years, however, the belief in such a common origin was widespread and played a central role in the self-understanding of Christianity and, as we shall see, in the formation of modern thought. Indeed, unless one recognizes the importance of this Hermetic tradition, it is very difficult to make sense of the origins of modernity.

Nearly all of the later church fathers drew heavily on the conceptual resources of Neoplatonism, but the awareness of this fact was lost for a long time, in large part as a result of Justinian's closing the Platonic Academy in A.D. 529 and his general antipagan initiative that helped separate Christian thought from ancient philosophy. The only source of Neoplatonism known in the Middle Ages was Apuleius, who was also the reputed translator of the dialogue *Asclepius,* the only account of Hermeticism available in medieval times.[43] The decisive figure in the revival of Platonic and Neoplatonic thought was Michael Psellos (1018–81), a Byzantine scholar who combined Platonic philosophy, the *Chaldean Oracles* (attributed to Zoroaster), and the *Corpus hermeticum* (attributed to Hermes Trismegistus) with Scripture. He was thus the father of the Byzantine tradition that culminated in Pletho and Bessarion and that was reborn in the West with Ficino.[44]

What then was Hermeticism? Hermes Trimegistus was thought to have been the voice of ancient Egyptian wisdom. He supposedly taught not merely Moses and through him the Jews and the Christians but also Orpheus and thus the Greeks, including Pythagoras and (indirectly) Plato. The work of Hermes and other ancient wisdom texts such as the *Chaldean Oracles,* along with the Jewish Kabbalah, were thought to be the source of Jewish and Christian Scripture. In order to revive a more genuine Christianity, it thus seemed important to understand this origin and to use it in the interpreting the Bible.

Ficino was clearly influenced by the Byzantine Neoplatonist tradition, but there was also something accidental in his encounter with Hermeticism. In 1462 Lorenzo de' Medici gave Ficino some manuscripts to translate. They included many of the Platonic dialogues and the *Corpus hermeticum.* We know now that the latter texts were produced by Alexandrian Neoplatonists between the first and third centuries, but Ficino and his contemporaries had no way of knowing this. They assumed the works were what they claimed to be. Ficino had earlier written a commentary on a text that we know now to be Hermetic, *The Book of Twenty-Four Philosophers.* Even at this time he recognized the similarities to Plato. When he received the *Corpus hermeticum,* he had just finished translating the Orphic Hymns, and he almost immediately noticed the similarities between the earlier Greek accounts of creation, as well as Plato's tale in the *Timaeus,* the story told in Genesis, and the creation story in the *Corpus hermeticum.* Not surprisingly, he came to the conclusion that they shared a common origin.[45] This was the beginning of an error that lasted well into the seventeenth century, and, as we shall see, while it was an error, it was an incredibly productive error that played a tremendous role not merely in the thought of humanism but in the development of modern science from Copernicus and Bruno through Bacon, Galileo, and Kepler, to Descartes and Newton.[46]

While the texts of the *Corpus hermeticum* were not what they purported to be, they did contribute in important ways to the formation of early Christian thought and particularly the idea of God's absolute power and freedom. This strand of Neoplatonism developed in an Egyptian world that was awash in philosophic and religious ideas of many different kinds. The syncretistic impulse was also quite strong. Philo, Plotinus, and Proclus grew up in this milieu, and their thought shares many of these syncretistic tendencies. The Hermetic texts were part of this syncretistic movement and brought together elements from multiple traditions. They had a profound impact on many of the early church fathers, including Victorinus, Athanasius, Clement of Alexandria, and Origen.[47] Thus, while Ficino and his humanist successors were wrong in thinking that Hermetic thought was the source of Jewish and Christian thought, they were right about its importance for Christianity.[48]

As a result of his work on these texts, Ficino became convinced that humanism could recover a more original (and muscular) Christianity if it viewed Scripture through a Platonic lens.[49] Moreover, such a Platonic Christianity could serve as an alternative to scholasticism. In articulating this vision, he drew not merely on Plato but on Augustine, although more on Augustine's earlier anti-Manichean thought that attributed more importance to human free will than his later anti-Pelagian works that called such a free will into question. He also was deeply influenced by his study of later Neoplatonism (he translated Plotinus and Proclus) and especially the work of Pseudo-Dionysus, who Ficino thought was the first of Paul's Athenian followers (mentioned in Acts 17:34) but who we now know to have been a follower of Proclus.[50]

For Ficino, man is above all else the *imago dei,* and as such he has an intrinsic dignity and power. Plato and his followers, according to Ficino, assert such a point with their doctrine of the immortality of the individual soul.[51] This is the basis for man's divinity, and it is through the cultivation of the soul that we become like God. Ficino thereby revived the Neoplatonic doctrine of the world-soul as the center of the universe and gave the human soul a privileged place in the universal hierarchy, as the bond of the universe and the link between the intelligible and corporeal worlds.[52] Cultivating the soul in his view allows humans to "become all things." Ficino even believed that man could "create the heavens and what is in them himself, if he could obtain the tools and the heavenly material."[53] Since he cannot, he must content himself instead with recreating this world mimetically through the use of his skills and his imagination.

At the core of Ficino's theology was a vision of God that was at odds with that of scholasticism but in continuity with the God of his humanist predecessors. This God was a God of will, not of reason, modeled not on Aristotle's prime mover but Plato's artificer. Plotinus had demonstrated and Augustine accepted the notion that a trinitarian God must not merely love but *be* love in order to be at all, since it is only love that can solve the problem of the one and the many within divine being. Reason cannot bring this about. God's creation of the world must thus be an act of loving will. Moreover, if God is essentially love, then all his creatures and human beings as well must be governed and guided by love. Such a view of love, however, is precisely the view that Ficino discovered in Plato's *Symposium* and that he described in great detail first in *On Pleasure* (1457) and then more fully in *On Love* (1466), which has rightly been called the most important literary work of the Renaissance. While Ficino accepted the ontological individualism posited by nominalism, he saw all individual beings filled with and united by sparks of divine love. Motivated by love, they are naturally attracted to the good and thus to God.[54] He thus asserted that behavior based on instinct and natural passions, including sexual desire, draws humans toward the divine. Nature was itself thus a form of grace that Ficino concluded leads humans toward the good and thus to God.

This vision was further spelled out in his *The Christian Religion* (1474), the first work ever published on the topic, and in his *Platonic Theology or the Immortality of Souls* (1482), which brought together the pagan and Christian strands of his thought.[55]

Ficino's views of religion were expansive. Indeed, he was convinced that while Christianity was best, there were many different forms of legitimate religious belief and practice: "Divine providence does not permit any part of the world at any time to be completely without religion, although it does allow rites to differ. . . . God prefers to be worshipped in any manner, however unwittingly . . . than not to be worshipped at all through pride."[56] While Ficino's Christianity is thus obviously influenced by Neoplatonic, Gnostic, and Hermetic sources, it is not anti-Christian. Central to his thought and to the Christian humanist enterprise generally was the notion that nature is a form of grace.[57] This idea is so important because it provides a foundation for the reconciliation of divine and human will. If nature is ordered by God so that humans naturally are attracted to the good, then humans can freely exercise their wills in a manner that is harmonious with divine will. The impediment to such a notion within the Christian tradition is, of course, original sin. The effects of original sin, however, are debatable, and humanists generally argued that it produced only a darkening of our reason that was not insuperable even before the redemption and that was even more easily transcended in its aftermath. While this was contrary in many respects to official church doctrine, it was not un-Christian in its intentions.

While Neoplatonism in this way provided a means of harmonizing humanist individualism with divine omnipotence, it came very near to Pelagianism in doing so, and in some instances clearly stepped over the line. This was certainly true in the case of Ficino's student, Giovanni Pico de la Mirandola (1463–94), who pushed the humanist project to its limits and carried it in many respects beyond where Christianity could go.

Pico was originally trained in the scholastic tradition. He also studied with the Jewish Averroist Elea del Medigo, and learned Hebrew and Arabic in Perugia, after developing a deep interest in the Kabbalah.[58] Through Ficino he came in contact with many other non-Christian sources and like him used them in his efforts to shape a Christianity that could accommodate the spirituality he believed was essential to human thriving. Building on Ficino's arguments in *The Christian Religion,* Pico asserted in his *Oration on the Dignity of Man* (1486), that humans were self-creating beings who could choose their own nature. This power for Pico is not intrinsic to human beings but is a divine gift. Human will and freedom are not a consequence of the fact that man is the highest of the creatures but a result of the fact that as the *imago dei* man is above all creatures, the creature who most fully participates in divine being. This account of the origin of man in the *Oration* was the introduction to Pico's defense of nine hundred theses drawn from almost all of the world's religions. Pico's goal was to make human beings recognize their special dignity and the power of their free will, which, following Ficino, he believed was akin to that of God himself.[59] Whether this titanic project could ever have been completed is an open question, for even in its initial formulation it went so far beyond the bounds of what the church was willing to accept that Pico and his work were condemned. However, he did not abandon his efforts to formulate a comprehensive account of all knowledge.

Pico was convinced that truth was universal and that all philosophies and religions had a part in it.[60] In his later work *Heptaplus,* he argued that in addition to the hierarchy of angelic, celestial, elementary worlds, there is a fourth world constituted by man himself.[61] In this work too, he tried to show that the creation story in Genesis was in accord with the Greek view of nature. In his last work, *Of Being and Unity,* he even argued that Plato and Aristotle—thought by most of his contemporaries to be diametrically opposed—were in essential agreement. His efforts demonstrate both the perceived necessity and the real difficulties of the Neoplatonic effort to reconcile the wisdom of the pagans with Christianity. However, at its core this was still a Christian and not a pagan project. Pico's own example provides us with evidence of this. He was convinced that philosophy could only go so far in penetrating to the truth of the divine, which in his view remained dark. Thus, while philosophy could take man a long way, it was always necessary at some point to rely on religion. In his own case, when it proved impossible to achieve the reconciliation of pagan sources with Christianity, he chose to follow a more fundamentalist notion of Christianity, under the influence of Savonarola. At its most extreme, on the verge of a Promethean rejection of God, humanism thus stepped back from the brink.

While the humanist project thus developed in a direction that over time placed ever more weight on human will and ever less on divine will in its attempt to make sense of the mysterious relationship of God and man, it was never willing to solve the problem by denying the efficacy or authority of God. The humanists were clearly aware of this Epicurean solution to their problem, but they chose not to employ it. Many have argued that the humanists were not actually religious but only feigned belief in order to avoid being burned at the stake as heretics. However, a careful consideration of the lives of most humanists makes it clear that very few could even be plausibly considered atheists during this period.[62] The humanist project at its extreme in the thought of Pico elevates man to a quasi-divine status, but it does not thereby reject God. Indeed, the justification for the elevation of man over other beings is not his own intrinsic excellence or power but his status as the *imago dei*.

The debate within humanism about the nature and relationship of God and man recapitulates in a certain sense the Christian debate between the Arians and the Trinitarians about the relation of the father and son within the Trinity. For humanism this becomes the question whether man is better understood as one of the creatures or as more akin to God himself. The answer to this question, however, depends not merely on how one conceives of man but also on how one conceives of God. If man is merely a creature, an examination of human nature can tell us nothing about God, but if he is godlike, then we can come to understand God and his commandments not merely through Scripture but through an examination of ourselves. Under such circumstances, ancient philosophy, which offers such profound insights into the human soul, can assist us not just in understanding the world but also in understanding God. While this might seem un-Christian to some, it was authorized for the humanists by Augustine's own example.[63]

The problem that humanism increasingly had to face, however, was prefigured in Pico. Humanist scholarship was rapidly discovering and popularizing texts from many different traditions. Confronting this mass of new and often contradictory material, the humanist faith that truth was one became increasingly difficult to sustain. Making sense of the nine hundred theses in Pico's *Conclusions* was a Herculean task even in theory and an impossible one in practice. The notion of a universal wisdom thus began to fade.

Pico attributed to man a quasi-divine capacity for self-making, and many humanists sought to make themselves into such "Renaissance men," striving for glory and a kind of undying fame in politics, literature, and the arts. However, for the humanists, as Machiavelli made clear, even the greatest individuals cannot always succeed. Fortune plays too powerful a role in human affairs, and death establishes the ultimate limit to human striving. God may have given humans godlike freedom, but he did not give them godlike power or wisdom or a godlike lifespan in which to attain their goals. The recognition of this fact led humanism in different directions. On one hand, some humanists focused on producing verbal and visual images that embodied humanist ideals but also concealed many of the vexing contradictions with which they increasingly struggled.

Others, unwilling to abandon the search for a universal truth, persisted in the investigation of both nature and man but fell increasingly under the spell of skepticism, which had returned to modern world with the reappearance of Cicero's *Academica* in 1471. This skepticism grew and spread within the humanist movement. It did not deny the possibility of all knowledge but only suspended judgment about the truth of things and relied on probable rather than absolutely certain or apodictic reasoning. Even so, it helped augment the sense of aimlessness and crisis that played an important role in the period leading up to the Reformation.[64]

In this context, the humanist project as Petrarch had imagined it began to dissolve. Three different paths presented themselves, corresponding to the three elements that Petrarch had emphasized in his late thought. One possibility was to emphasize an Augustinian piety above all else, abandoning both Platonism and martial virtue. A second possibility was to emphasize the martial virtues of the Romans and deemphasize or abandon both Christian piety and Platonism. Or finally, one could take a generally Neoplatonic approach to Christianity and abandon both piety and martial virtue. The first was the path of Savonarola (and later Luther), the second the path of Machiavelli, and the third the path of Erasmus.

Trained in the Aristotelian and Averroist tradition, Savonarola (1452–98) had no love or even tolerance for humanism.[65] Savonarola underwent a sudden religious conversion at the age of twenty-two, joined the Dominicans, and began to live and preach a life of mortification and self-deprivation. He was appalled by the corruption of the Florentine humanists led by the Medici and (rightly) considered the curia under Alexander VI to be simply a den of iniquity. His theology (like that of Luther twenty years later) was apocalyptic and rigorous. He attacked the paganism of the humanists, the corrupting impact of wealth on the ruling classes, and the unconstitutional domination of Florence by the Medici. After the death of Lorenzo the Magnificent and the intervention of the French to drive the Medici from the city, Savonarola became the head of a quasi-theocratic republic that in some ways anticipated Calvin's Geneva. He ruled from 1494 to 1498. While he was a superb orator and preached against irreligion, economic corruption, and the misuse of political power—all popular issues— he was politically inept. His power grew out of his charismatic rhetoric and thus rested almost entirely on the enthusiasm of his followers. Having come to power by these means, he made no effort to secure his position by institutional reform. He then angered Pope Alexander VI with his constant criticism, and the pope consequently deprived him of his authority to preach. Unable to use the pulpit to enthuse and mobilize his supporters, he was overthrown by a coalition of the dominant interest groups he had attacked, hanged, and then burned at the stake. His failure was a lesson well learned by men such as Machiavelli, who saw that mere piety—however intense—was unable to provide a stable basis for human sociality.

With the downfall of Savonarola, Piero Soderini (1450–1513) came to power and the Florentine republic was reestablished. It was in this republic that Machiavelli first came to public attention, serving as second chancellor. Machiavelli's father had been a notary in the tradition of the *Dictatores* and was a friend of the Florentine Chancellor Bartolomeo Scala (1430–97). He did his utmost to see that his son received a humanist education that would prepare him for a similar public career.

The Medicis' support for Florentine humanism had turned it in a more Platonic and less republican direction. They generally favored the production of an educated elite dedicated to the *vita contemplativa,* rather than practically minded republicans who might oppose their rule. Ficino was the preeminent example of such an abstracted "Platonic" humanist. This approach was still regnant in the last years of their rule when Angelo Poliziano (1454–94), a student of Ficino and Christoforo Landino (1424–98), championed a humanism at the Studio that subordinated all other subjects to the study of various sorts of literary works. However, even he turned in a somewhat less Platonic direction, giving precedence to the study of history over poetry and philosophy. After the downfall of the Medici, humanist education took an increasingly practical turn. Polziano's successor at the Studio was Marcello Virgilio. He was an Aristotelian and thus found the flight from political life to the Platonic ideal deplorable.[66] In contrast to Poliziano, he emphasized the importance of the *studia humanitatis* for politics rather than literature, and of the *vita activa* rather than the *vita contemplativa.* He thus saw utility as more important than pure learning and sought to produce men of action rather than men of thought.[67] Under Soderini, he served as first chancellor and was thus Machiavelli's colleague.

Machiavelli was drawn toward a more practical humanism, but he also pursued a life of reading and writing. He considered himself a statesman *and* a poet. In both, however, he was a realist and had little use for Platonism in any form, rejecting out of hand the idealism of Ficino and his followers. His humanism was thus not Platonic or Augustinian but Roman. Even in his admiration for the Romans, however, his thought moves away from the earlier humanist admiration for Roman moralists in favor of Roman statesmen and historians. Livy and Tacitus were thus of much greater importance to him than Cicero or Seneca. He was also less concerned with individual moral purity than with political effectiveness. While Petrarch elevated a morally virtuous Scipio above a clever but immoral Hannibal, Machiavelli clearly preferred the latter, although he recognized that the successful prince must appear to be the former.

His attitude toward religion was complex. The failure of Savonarola convinced him that mere piety could not provide an effective foundation for social life. He also recognized that the corruption of the church was widespread and deeply entrenched. He was thus anticlerical (although not as anticlerical as his friend Guicciardini). He attended mass now and then but never displayed real zeal for any form of religion. Contrary to what we are prone to believe today, he was almost certainly not an atheist, although like many of his fellow humanists his religious beliefs were hardly orthodox by earlier or later standards.

While he apparently believed that God had created the world (about 40,000–50,000 years ago), he was more interested in the creation and organization of human society, which in his mind was clearly not of divine institution. He argued that God gave human beings free choice and did not interfere in human affairs.[68] The success and failure of human society thus rests solely with man. Prayer and religious rituals can do nothing to improve life on earth and nothing to improve our chances of salvation. God judges us according to what we do with our freedom. We are thus saved or damned on the basis of our accomplishments.

This position is certainly Pelagian and thus by our standards heterodox, although such Pelagian notions were not thought to be wildly unorthodox at the time. Machiavelli, however, is actually more authentically Pelagian than many of his fellow humanists, because like Pelagius he imagines that God has a particular preference not merely for virtue but for superhuman virtue. In Machiavelli's view the truly virtuous men are not the saints or martyrs but those who found states and give them their laws. Like Cicero he suggests that these founders achieve apotheosis.[69] God loves and exalts them because they produce the highest good.[70]

For Machiavelli, what is most pleasing to God is thus not spiritual or pastoral work but statesmanship at the highest level.[71] As De Grazia puts it,

> What Niccolò believes in or would like to be true or what runs up in his writings as expressions of belief or of attempts to convince himself or convert others, is a new or reformed redemptive system, a true religion in which the master deity is God, the saints on earth are few, poor, and honest, the beloved of God are makers of states in deed and in writing, great legislators, founders of religion, warriors, and saviors of country who, their entering

and exiting evil divinely comprehended, go postmortem by God's immediate and final judgment directly to the dwelling place of heroes.[72]

Machiavelli imagines that God recognizes that princes must commit evil in order to establish and maintain a well-regulated state, the highest earthly good. God therefore must recognize the essential goodness of the prince. Despite the "evil" the prince does, he thus does not burn in hell and is in fact welcomed into heaven.[73] Machiavelli's humanism is thus Christian in the broadest sense of the term, but it is a Christianity that is subordinated to the very human needs of this world.[74]

In his depiction of such legislators, Machiavelli portrays them as self-making Promethean figures, drawing heavily on Pico, whom he greatly admired. In his view, they exist in a certain sense outside of ordinary human society and develop an independence and resourcefulness that sets them apart from other human beings. Their utter self-reliance better equips them to deal with the exigencies of life and consequently the exigencies of politics. Such independence is manifest in Machiavelli's four great examples of successful founders, Moses, Cyrus, Theseus, and Romulus. All of them were fatherless children and thus had to rely on their own arms almost from birth. This point is reemphasized by Machiavelli's discussion of Cesare Borgia, who was perhaps as great in all other respects as Machiavelli's four heroes but who failed to secure his power because he had and relied upon a father.

In contrast to Pico and Ficino, however, Machiavelli recognized that the powers of even the greatest human beings were finite. From their more aesthetic and theoretical perspective, Pico and Ficino could imagine that the truly creative human being could mimetically re-create the world. Machiavelli's experience of political life convinced him that all human beings were constrained by a whole variety of unpredictable factors. Even at their most proficient, humans in his view can succeed only half the time.

In his pessimistic realism, Machiavelli is closer to Petrarch than to Ficino. As we have seen, Petrarch was convinced that chaos and war were the natural state of things. He hoped that a new Scipio could bring order to this chaos, but short of that he was convinced that happiness could be obtained only by retreating into solitude with a small group of friends. Beginning with Ficino and drawing on Plato, humanists began to believe that there was an innate principle in all things, an order of love that pulled everything toward the good and thus toward God. In Machiavelli we see the ultimate rejection of this idea. At least since the time of Cain, he tells us, the loving harmony of the world has been disrupted by anger and ambition.[75] Human beings are directed not toward the common good and God but toward their own good, and it is a good that is always enjoyed at the expense of others. Pride, envy, sloth, ambition, hate, cruelty, and deceit—Machiavelli's version of the seven deadly sins—run rampant.[76] Under such circumstances, human beings must constantly struggle in order not to be swallowed up by ill fortune. Only a well-founded and well-run state can ameliorate this condition and protect humans from depredation, and those able to found and sustain such states are rare. These founders, however, provide human beings with the highest good and are thus immensely valuable.

While Machiavelli's account of the social world is in many ways similar to that of Petrarch, the consequences that he draws from it are different. For Petrarch, the key to happiness is a kind of equilibrium or balance, and this is achieved by mastering oneself. The greatest danger to such an equilibrium, as he sees it, comes not from adversity but from success, that is, not from bad fortune but from good. This is why he finally believes that only the private life offers the possibility of true happiness. For Machiavelli, good fortune is not a danger, or at least is a danger only insofar as it puts us off our guard. It is crucial that we recognize the unremitting pressure of bad fortune and that we constantly be prepared for it. Machiavelli's world thus may have been created by God but it is not governed by divine love. Indeed, it is governed by sin, and it is only by understanding how to sin in the interest of the common good that we can make any headway and provide any space for human thriving. The world that Machiavelli inhabits is thus very like the world that nominalism uncovered two centuries before, but it is a world in which God does nothing and in which even those with the greatest human strength and ingenuity can only succeed in part and for a short time. Ordinary men, by contrast, may succeed momentarily but only by pure chance. Thus, Machiavelli's humanism is both heroic and tragic. In his thought we see the ultimate apotheosis of the individual in the practical realm, but we also see that even these new titans are not titanic enough to master the dizzying chaotic world that spins about them. His humanism therefore offers a sorry solace to those who seek peace and stability, and only the slightest hope to those who long for glory or hope for wisdom.

NORTHERN HUMANISM: DESIDERIUS ERASMUS

The heroic humanism that played such an important role in Italy was moderated when it moved north across the Alps by the encounter with the *devotio moderna,* a religious movement founded by Gerard Groote (1340–84) of Deventer, who believed that to be a Christian one had to follow Christ's moral example. The movement began in Holland but spread throughout Germany and much of Poland. Its doctrines were laid out in the *Imitatio Christi* attributed to Thomas à Kempis. Institutionally, it produced a new form of monasticism that aimed at spiritual self-perfection and a lay movement known as the Brethren of the Common Life.

The *devotio moderna* offered an answer to many of those who were plagued by philosophical skepticism but who were not attracted to the heroic individualism of Italian humanism or the opportunism of Machiavelli. The Brethren sought relief in a spirituality that emphasized a simple life with religious feeling (rather than reason or will) as the essence of faith. Practically, the *devotio moderna* was a personal and inward religion of love, faith, and humility that deemphasized works and ceremonies. This position was laid out explicitly by Nicholas of Cusa (1401–64), who emphasized the simplicity of faith in contrast to the uncertainty of reason in *On Learned Ignorance* (1440).[77] His work was important in its own right, but it also exercised an important influence on Lefevre, Colet, and Erasmus.[78]

In comparison to the Italians, northern humanists were more moderate in their claims about human capacities, more skeptical, less convinced that love ruled the world, more rooted in Scripture, less concerned with martial virtue and greatness, less reliant on Gnostic, Hermetic, and Neoplatonic sources, and more reliant on those church fathers who focused more on Scripture than on philosophy. They were also concerned with the reformation of the church, the elimination of abuses, and the reduction of ceremonialism. The danger that they posed to the established church thus lay less in their extravagant claims about the abilities of human beings than in the simple appeal of their message to large numbers of common people. Italian humanism had always appealed to the upper classes and intellectuals. Northern humanism had a much more democratic appeal and contributed in powerful ways to the growing protest against the established church that led to the Reformation.

This form of humanism posed a greater danger to the monks and clerics than Italian humanism because it was less extravagant, less pagan, and more rooted in an ideal of Christian charity that the church at least nominally shared. The church recognized this danger from the beginning and sought to suppress it. The most famous example of their efforts was the attempt to condemn Johannes Reuchlin (1455–1522), the humanist who brought the teaching of Hebrew into German academic life.[79] Many humanists came to his defense, and Pope Leo X eventually refused to condemn him, which was a kind of victory for humanism. However, the battle lines had been drawn, and in the next generation, the generation of Erasmus and Luther, the battle would begin.

Erasmus was born in 1466 in Rotterdam. He was the illegitimate son of Roger Gerard, who became a priest, and Margaret, a physician's daughter. He attended a humanistically oriented school in Deventer run by the Brethren of Common Life. When his parents died, he was forced to enter an Augustinian monastery at Steyn near Gouda where he lived from 1485 until 1492. He was treated so harshly there that he developed a lifelong enmity for the monks. During this period, he drew most of his intellectual inspiration from the work of Valla, whose *Eloquence* he paraphrased. He also wrote *On Contempt of the World* (1489) in which he praised the solitary life. He eventually escaped from the monastery through an appointment as secretary to the Bishop of Cambray, took priestly orders, and went to Paris where he studied until 1499.

In Paris he heard Scotist lectures at the Franciscan Studium and taught Latin to private pupils to support himself. In 1494, he criticized the monastic distrust of learning and argued vigorously for secular education and the utility of the pagan classics in *Against the Barbarians*. This work demonstrated his growing acquaintance with the humanist tradition of Petrarch, Boccaccio, and Salutati.[80] In 1499 he visited England and met Thomas More, who remained his friend until More's death in 1535. He lived mostly at Oxford, where he worked with the humanist John Colet. Colet too hated scholasticism and introduced Erasmus to a more historical way of reading the New Testament.[81] Erasmus also adopted Colet's hostility toward the nominalist notion of an absolute and distant God and began to emphasize the humanity of Jesus in the tradition of the *devotio moderna*.[82] He returned to Paris, living there from 1500 to 1506, and during this time he wrote his *Adages* and *Handbook of a Christian Soldier,* which established his reputation as a leading humanist. The latter work was clearly in the tradition of the *devotio moderna* but also expressed sympathies with the humanist tradition that stretched back to Petrarch. It emphasized the importance of sincerity and righteousness over formalism and conformity to public opinion.

After a short visit to England, he moved to Italy where he lived from 1506 to 1509, serving as tutor to the illegitimate son of James IV of Scotland, working with the publisher Aldus Manutius in Venice, and visiting Rome and Florence. In Rome, he was offered a variety of clerical positions but declined them all, like Petrarch more concerned with his independence than wealth or prestige. In Florence he was so involved with his work that he seems not to have met or even known of Leonardo, Michelangelo, Raphael, or Machiavelli, who were resident in the city at the time.[83]

After the accession of Henry VIII, Erasmus returned to England in hopes of securing a stipend that would allow him to devote himself to his literary activities. As he was leaving Italy, he wrote his famous satire *In Praise of Folly,* a biting critique of monasticism as well as ecclesiastical and political institutions. During this stay in England, he lived chiefly in Cambridge and served as professor of Divinity and Greek. During this period he worked on his Greek edition of the *New Testament* (1516), which in its own way was as important for the Reformation as Luther's 95 Theses (1517).[84]

By 1514 Erasmus stood at the pinnacle of his success and was called the prince of the humanists. The widespread admiration for his work was the result of his success at combining *humanitas* and *pietas* into a vital Christian humanism.[85] He had enemies among the clerics and the monks, but he also had a great deal of influence at the highest levels. In 1515 he was appointed councilor to Prince Charles, who in the following year became King of Spain and then in 1519 emperor Charles V. Erasmus moved to Louvain to be close to the royal court in Brussels and wrote *The Education of a Christian Prince* (1516) in order to prepare Charles for his new responsibilities. In 1519 his edition of St. Jerome appeared, as did the first edition of his *Colloquies,* which is usually regarded as his masterpiece.

The Reformation had a profound effect on Erasmus and his role in European political and intellectual life. With the growing agitation against the church, life at Louvain became increasingly difficult for Erasmus because of the suspicion that he was a secret supporter of Luther. As a result, he moved to Basel in 1521, where he remained until 1529, when he moved to Freiburg in Breisgau, where he died in 1536.

Erasmus, like Colet and many other northern humanists, was committed to a religion of interior conversion, pacifism, and moral ideals.[86] He rejected scholasticism as well as nominalism. In his *Paraphrases* he sought to minimize the role of Christ as priest and sacrificial victim and turned instead to what he called the *philosophia Christi,* the philosophy of Christ, arguing for the centrality of inner moral conversion. He believed that interior piety rather than creedal affirmation was the core of true religion. In this respect he combined elements of the humanist tradition with the simplicity and humility of the *devotio moderna,* tempering the Promethean and martial tendencies of Italian humanism and giving moral depth to northern piety. In opposition to the corruption of the existing church, he sought reforms that would make possible a simple ethical Christianity uncomplicated by theological subtleties.[87] He knew from the Reuchlin affair that this path would likely bring him into conflict with the clerics, scholastics, and monks. His approach to reform was thus indirect, relying on rhetoric and irony rather than disputation to lure others onto his path, mimicking Lucian and the Socrates of the *Apology*.[88]

Erasmus did not believe that the sources of corruption in the church were doctrinal. Like More, he was convinced that disorder in human affairs was principally due to the abuse of power and the profit motive. The secular power of the church, the lucrative character of many of its practices, and the widespread influence of wealth in securing clerical positions had more to do with the corruption of the church and consequent anticlericalism than theological doctrines. The fact that the clerics alone were able to conduct the sacramental ceremonies gave them the opportunity for abuse. The sale of indulgences was only one example of such abuses, which were widespread in the church especially during the pontificates of Alexander VI and Clement VII. Current religious practice, as Erasmus saw it, thus did little to improve public morality and was actually more likely to foster corruption.[89] Reform was urgently needed, and Erasmus thought that a reformed church should combine piety and morality, offering support for basic human dignity. He thus did not seek doctrinal or institutional changes in the church but the improvement of moral behavior. This was the goal of his educational reform. He believed that such a project could succeed, however, only if there were a sufficient number of preachers trained in his philosophy of Christ. Therefore, it was crucial that humanistic education have a place within the church itself.

While Erasmus rejected the most heroic forms of humanism, some wondered whether his emphasis on moral life as the key to salvation did not imply that Scripture and faith were unnecessary. In his *Eulogy of Erasmus and Luther* Melanchthon asserted as much, claiming that Erasmus was a moral philosopher like the ancients, not a true theologian.[90] Such a conclusion, however, rested on a narrow view of Christianity. Erasmus was not opposed to piety, but he was dismayed by the use of religious practices as a cover for the grossest forms of immorality. He saw both an inner faith and a moral life as necessary to salvation. He was also worried that if Christians believed that faith alone sufficed to attain salvation, men might try to work God's will in immoral ways or justify their own immorality with pious litanies. The moral lesson of Christ's life in his view supported

Christian pacifism not bellicose dogmatism.[91] He deeply feared that the process of reform would become violent and destructive, throwing the world into war. In place of such revolutionary change, he pinned his hopes on a gradual process of reform through a system of education in humane letters and the study of Scripture, a process that in his mind ended in a moralistic Christian humanism purged of Italian paganism.[92]

As difficult as this project was, Erasmus had good reasons to believe that he and his fellow humanists were on the verge of success. Not only was he an advisor to the emperor, one of his former students had become Pope Adrian VI, and his friend and fellow spirit Thomas More was an advisor to Henry VIII. Given the broad influence of his thought and the very real influence he and his fellow humanists exercised in political affairs, Erasmus was convinced that he lived at the dawn of another golden age.[93] However, within a very few years all of these hopes were dashed, and the future looked bleak, promising not an age of gold but an age of iron, not an age of peace and prosperity but an age of war and destruction in which competing religious parties fought to the death over doctrinal differences. The source of this unexpected reversal was, of course, Luther.

ERASMUS'S PHILOSOPHY OF CHRIST

Erasmus like most humanists had an antipathy to metaphysics, which in his mind was closely connected to scholasticism and to the debates between the scholastics and the nominalists. He famously described these debates as "higher lunacy."[94] However, this rejection of metaphysical speculation and disputation was not a rejection of philosophy per se. In fact, it was part and parcel of a reconceptualization of philosophy on an ancient model as moral philosophy. Like his humanist predecessors, he believed that the purpose of philosophizing was action and not mere speculation. Philosophizing thus was closely linked to rhetoric. Erasmus, however, was a Christian humanist and was interested not only in promoting morality but in reconciling it with Christian piety. The center of his intellectual enterprise was thus the attempt to develop a philosophy of Christ (*philosophia Christi*) that combined the individualism of Italian humanism (devoid of its martial heroism) with the imitation of Christ (*imitatio Christi*) of the *devotio moderna* by means of a humanistic study that combined the study of pagan literature and Scripture within the Neoplatonic horizon of Origen, Jerome, and Augustine as well as Petrarch, Valla, and Pico.

Although Erasmus had little interest in metaphysical speculation, he could not avoid making a number of metaphysical assumptions. Like most

of his humanist predecessors, he accepted a nominalist ontology of individual beings, although without giving it much thought. He was more
deeply concerned with questions of logic or language and the relationship
of words and things. Like Plato and his humanist predecessors, he rejected
the notion of a natural language or a natural relation between words and
things. He agreed generally with the nominalist contention that words
were principally signs but despised the terminological debates that dominated nominalist thought. He saw language more as a historical phenomenon and thus as a medium of communication between human beings.[95]
This medium, however, could be distorted to promote one's self-interest in
opposition to the common good. All language and therefore all thinking
were thus rhetorical.

Rhetoric in his view was central to moral and religious life. This was
especially true for Christianity, which saw language as the means of communication not merely between human beings but between man and God.
Indeed, for Erasmus God communicates with man only through the Word,
and this Word always has to be understood within a human language that
not only reveals but also conceals the truth. Erasmus's theology is thus essentially rhetorical.[96] Consequently, Scripture cannot be read directly but
must always be read analogically.[97] In his relatively early *Handbook of a
Christian Soldier,* Erasmus assumed that it was possible to read Scripture
in a purely allegorical manner, but after his discovery of Valla's *Annota-
tions* he recognized the importance of grammar and literary criticism.[98]
His increasing awareness of the historical differences between his time and
previous ages, however, led him to believe that while all languages may
proclaim God, reading and interpreting Scripture also requires historical
knowledge because terms have their meanings in particular contexts.[99] He
thus came to believe that it was necessary to come to terms with the divine
Word in its original context. Following Ficino and Pico, he also believed
that the study of ancient moral philosophy and particularly Platonic and
Neoplatonic thought could help in the understanding of Scripture.

Historical and linguistic differences were not, in his view, the only bar-
riers to interpreting Scripture. The core difficulty, as Erasmus saw it, lay in
the fact that God's infinity cannot be fully or even adequately portrayed
in his own revelation. Thus, "Christ conceals his divine nature, in order to
pass himself off as humanly weak."[100] It is similarly the case with Scripture, and, as a result, it is necessary to read not merely what is on the lines
but what is between them. Language, grammar, and rhetoric can help us
understand the teachings of Christ, but they cannot suffice on their own.
What seemed to Erasmus crucially necessary was bringing human lan-

guage and divine language into harmony.[101] Consequently, in reading and interpreting Scripture, he believed humans had to participate in a giant process of discourse with one another in which they seek agreement between mutually distinct interpretations of divine discourse. The goal of scriptural interpretation is thus not an immediate encounter with God but the restoration of the unity of Scripture and the Christian community through a discursive and consensual process.[102] The focus of any such study, however, must always be the living Christ as revealed in Scripture and not some abstract concept of God.

This focus on Christ's life and particularly his *charity (caritas)* is central to Erasmus's *philosophia Christi*. Like Ficino, he sees the moral teachings of the Greek and Roman philosophers as identical with Christian charity as exemplified by Christ. Within the humanist context such a synthesis had long been an ideal, but an ideal some Christians looked on with suspicion, because it seemed to veer toward Pelagianism. For Erasmus, this danger could not be overlooked, but he was convinced that a failure to reach such a synthesis would open Christianity up to a Manicheanism that held God responsible for evil and that thus undermined individual moral responsibility.[103]

Erasmus believed he had found a path between these two extremes. While Erasmus was a humanist, he rejected both the martial element of Italian civic humanism and the Promethean vision of later Italian humanists who saw man not merely as an individual willing being but as a self-willing and self-creating being. His dedication to the *devotio moderna* pointed him in the direction of a more humble humanism that bowed before God but still admired and praised moral virtue. While he did not believe a Christian could legitimately seek glory, especially if it involved violence, a Christian could and should seek to emulate Socrates, Cicero, and Christ in order to live a life of righteousness. For such a life to be possible, however, human beings must have some measure of freedom or autonomy.

Humanism, of course, did not come to an end with Erasmus. Indeed, thinkers like Montaigne carried humanism to new heights. In order to understand the further development of humanism, however, it is necessary to take a step back or if not back at least to the side and examine the development of another strain of thought that arose in response to the nominalist revolution and helped shaped modernity. Humanism in all of its forms accepted the nominalist ontology of radically individual beings. In trying to find its way through the chaotic world that nominalism seemed to engender, however, it followed a decidedly unnominalistic path, giving ontic precedence to human being over either divine being or natural being. Beginning with Petrarch and carried through to the thought of Machiavelli and Erasmus, the first of all things for man was man. Such a view does not deny the existence or importance of God, but it does suggest that we can only come to God through man. This view, as we will see in the next chapter, was anathema to that other strain of thought that lies at the origins of modernity, the thought of the Reformation.

4 | *Luther and the Storm of Faith*

As he made his way back to the university after a visit home, the strapping twenty-five year old had good reason to be satisfied with himself. He had completed his master's degree in January, and he had already begun his study of the law. His father was proud of him, and a path to a better life stretched out before him. It was the second day of July, the exact middle of the year 1505, and except for a few clouds on the horizon there was little to trouble the spirits of the vigorous young man. And yet the clouds on the horizon seemed to be growing and the wind was clearly picking up. He looked about for cover but there was none, and he knew he would soon get wet. Little did he suspect that those clouds and the storm they carried with them were bringing not only wind and rain but a storm of such magnitude that it would engulf and transform all of European civilization. Nor did he realize that the bolts of lightning, the rolling waves of thunder, and the torrents of rain that seemed to descend on him and him alone were in fact only precursors of the flashes of cannon, the roars of armies, and the tears of millions that lay just beyond his horizon. What he did see by the end of the day was that he must leave his promising, secular life and turn to God, whose mighty power seemed to him both his greatest torment and his only refuge. He went into that day as a child of humanism; he left it the future father of a reformed Christianity and one of the founders of the modern age.

Luther's attempt to renew what he believed was the central message of Christianity was the second great effort to answer the fundamental problem raised by the nominalist God. Luther was born in an age of immense change. The discovery of the New World and a new order in the heavens, along with the rediscovery of the ancient world, were vastly expanding horizons that previously had seemed quite near. Tied up with these remarkable events was the development of a new secular culture and social

system. The growth of cities and the middle class, the increasing dissatisfaction of the peasantry with their lot, and the consolidation of principalities into states based on ethnic and linguistic similarities were the main
characteristics of this transformation. France, England, and Spain stood
at the forefront of this development and were the strongest states in Europe. Two great medieval institutions remained, the Holy Roman Empire,
cobbled together out of a number of smaller and ethnically quite diverse
principalities, and the Roman Catholic Church, which exercised considerable secular authority not only in Italy but in Germany as well, where
many German bishops and archbishops exercised political power over vast
domains.[1] These institutions, however, clearly rested on shaky ground, due
to rising ethnic and national feeling within the empire and northern resentment of Italian domination in the church.[2]

The spiritual strength of the church was further weakened by its growing wealth and corruption. Corruption in the church was not new. As we
have seen, Petrarch and Boccacio had already castigated the church on this
account. However, corruption had grown greater and more widespread as
manifold abuses from misfeasance and malfeasance to concubinage, gluttony, and political assassination had become more widely practiced within
the church and better known to those outside it. The longing for a more
original and purer Christianity had given rise in preceding centuries to a
series of radical movements that had severely challenged church authority. The Fraticelli, the Cathers (or Albigensians), and the Waldensians had
raised the banner of a more original Christianity. They had been subdued
by force, but the longing for a purer religious practice that had engendered
them was only satisfied when mendicant orders were established *within*
church.[3] However, as we have seen, even this concession to those who
longed for a purer Christianity did not solve the problem but only inter-
nalized it, for it brought the papacy and curia into open conflict with the
Franciscans, the most popular religious order of its day. While an accommodation was reached between them, the resolution of the Poverty Dispute did not put an end to efforts to reform church practice. The Observant
movements that arose in the fourteenth century and the concomitant development of associated lay fraternities such as the Brethren of the Common Life are only one example of the way this movement continued within
the church.[4] They at least could be folded into the larger community of the
church. The more radical attempts at reform by first Wycliff in England
and then Hus in Bohemia could not. Wycliff advocated reading the Bible
in the vernacular, rejected celibacy, and attacked transubstantiation. He
also argued that the state had the right to seize church property because

the church was fallen. In addition to accepting most of Wycliff's suggested reforms, Hus argued that the true Christian had to obey God and not the pope. He was seized and put to death, and his followers were systematically hunted down. Coercion, however, could not expunge these ideas.

LUTHER'S EARLY LIFE AND EDUCATION

(Luther's father came from a peasant family of miners, but as a result of a fortunate marriage he had been able to purchase several foundries and had moved solidly into the middle class. Martin, his second son, was born around 1484. In keeping with his father's new status, the family was able to provide him with an excellent education. They sent him first to school at Magdeburg in 1497 and then in 1501 to University of Erfurt with a view to his following members of his mother's family into the civil service. In Magdeburg, he lived under the care of the Brethren of the Common Life, which had by that time lost some of its original impetus.[5]

The University of Erfurt was at the forefront of educational change. It had long since adopted a more humanist curriculum, but it was also deeply involved in giving shape to the nominalist movement that had made great inroads in Germany. At the center of one of the most dynamic theological faculties in Europe were the nominalists Jodokus Trutfetter and Bartholomaeus Arnoldi.[6] Erfurt had also long been at the forefront of theological reform in Germany. A member of its faculty, Johannes Wesel, for example, had been condemned in 1479 for opposing indulgences, demanding the laity be allowed to drink wine at communion, and insisting Scripture alone was truth.[7]

Unlike Aquinas or Scotus, Ockham had never founded a school. As a result, the nominalist movement had developed in a number of different theological directions in the fourteenth century, many in conflict with one another.[8] We examined these briefly in chapter 1. While Gregory of Rimini, Pierre d'Ailly, Marsilius von Inghen, and Gabriel Biel went their different ways, they all did argue that human freedom was extremely limited, maintaining that the best a sinner could do was recognize his sinfulness and beg God for forgiveness.[9] However, in 1497 Trutfetter and Arnoldi succeeded in formulating a common core of nominalism and developing it into a cohesive system.[10] This was a real breakthrough, and it was based on the notion that all philosophical speculation about the world must be tested by means of experience and reality-based reason regardless of where the authorities stand on the matter, and that all theological speculation must be tested by the authority of the Scriptures as interpreted by church.[11]

Luther was educated in this environment. He clearly admired the work of Cicero and counted Virgil and Lucian as two of his favorite authors, but he considered Ockham his master.[12] Whatever its intellectual merits, and they were many, this education was not spiritually satisfying for Luther. This is probably not surprising. From the time of Petrarch, humanism moved increasingly toward a Neoplatonist view of Christianity that focused on man as the *imago dei* and diminished the importance of the Fall and original sin. During the latter fifteenth century the difficulties of sustaining this position also led to an increasing skepticism not about the existence of God but about the capacity of human wisdom to understand the divine order of the world.[13] Humanism also employed its growing scholarly resources to demonstrate that Scripture was a human and not a divine creation. Nominalism, by contrast, raised questions not about the existence of God but about his goodness. Both rendered problematic the traditional religious answers to the problem of death and salvation. Humanism seemed to suggest that there might be no life after death and nominalism that even if there were an afterlife there was nothing we could do to insure or even improve our chances of salvation. Luther's education thus not only failed to provide him with the spiritual resources to confront the most serious problems of life, it suggested that no such resources were available.

LUTHER AS A MONK AND HIS SPIRITUAL CRISIS

The seminal event of Luther's spiritual life, discussed above, occurred in 1505 when he was caught in a violent thunderstorm. Fearing for his life, he made a vow to St. Anne to enter the monastery if God spared him. His fear of death and the vow he made point to severe religious doubts, for to fear death, as Luther himself later suggested, is to doubt the central tenet of the Christian faith, the salvific power of the resurrection of Jesus Christ, and to doubt this is to doubt that Jesus Christ is God.[14] More telling for Luther than the fear of death and nothingness, however, were his growing doubts about his own salvation in the face of a distant and harshly judging God who, as Ockham often repeated, was no man's debtor. Luther's entry into the monastery was partly a response to his fear of death, but was more fully a manifestation of his desperate search for a means to gain salvation.[15]

His spiritual concerns aside, Luther's decision to enter a monastery of the observant Augustinian Hermits in Erfurt was almost certainly due to the fact that it was a leading center of nominalist theology. There he apparently studied theology under Johannes Nathen, who had spent four or five years in Tübingen as the younger colleague of the nominalist and follower of Ockham, Gabriel Biel.[16] Luther was thus apparently able to continue his studies and satisfy his almost insatiable longing for learning in the context of the monastery. The rituals of monastic life and his continued studies, however, do not seem to have solved or even ameliorated his spiritual problems.

The monastic life was informed by the conviction that only by striving for perfection could one ever hope to exist before God. Earlier nominalism denied human beings the capacity to determine what God demanded of them. Not surprisingly, Luther's doubts about his worthiness for salvation seem to have intensified. Within the *via moderna,* it was assumed that the best that one could do was not good enough to merit salvation, but it could at least constitute an inclination toward God, a desire for grace to which God would then respond.[17] This was the core of the *Facientibus* principle we discussed above, the practical conclusion that God would save anyone who gave his all. Luther, however, was not comforted by this notion. How could one know what one's all was? He thus lived in terror of a wrathful God. At his first mass, for example, he was terrified to hold the living God in his hands, lest he make a mistake in the liturgy or drop some of the host.

This sense of alienation from God and the extreme focus on the uncertainty of salvation was a vexing problem of monastic life that often led exacting monks away from the world into speculative or ecstatic mysticism.[18] That this did not happen in Luther's case was apparently largely due to the intervention of Johannes von Staupitz. Staupitz was the head of the Augustinian monasteries in Saxony and a dedicated reformer. As a leading interpreter of the Bible, he advocated a return to the letter of the text. More importantly, he taught that Christ was the guarantee of a merciful God and that Christ owed the elect succor through grace. Both of these positions grew out of the *via moderna* but were also at odds with the image of a distant and unpredictable God that nominalism had envisioned.[19] He clearly had an enormous impact on Luther. He prohibited Luther from speculating about God's wrath and urged him to turn his mind to Christ, for meditating on Christ's passion, he argued, would inspire true love and make contrition possible, obliging Christ to redeem him.[20] He also assigned Luther the task of memorizing the Bible line by line. He clearly recognized Luther's enormous potential and had larger plans for him in the context of his reformation of monastic life, as became clear in 1512 when he appointed Luther as his successor to the chair of biblical literature at Wittenberg.

An event crucial to Luther's development, however, intervened, for in November of 1510 he was appointed to represent his order in Rome and present its opposition to Staupitz's reforms. To say that Luther was shocked by his visit would be an understatement. He found atheism rampant in Rome and was disgusted by the corruption of even the highest church officials. His disgust reinforced his doubts in the authority of the church as an institution and in its ability to intercede with God on his behalf. It is thus perhaps not surprising that when he was climbing to the top of the holy stairway preserved in the Lateran Palace to try to win the release of his grandfather's soul from purgatory, he was beset by skeptical doubts about the efficacy of existing church practices and the theology of works that underlay them. It was apparently this skeptical crisis that led him to radically rethink the nature of God and man and the relation between them in a way that would not only challenge the authority of the church but also bring about a fundamental transformation of European life.

Luther's crisis was intensified by his rejection of Staupitz's view that God's omnipotence restricted the devil's power.[21] The devil, Luther believed, is the ruler of this world. He rules men not by force, however, but by guile, in a quasi-Machiavellian fashion, appealing to their pride, their desire for fame, their reason, and even their concern for their fellow man. Luther's devil in contrast to the devil of his predecessors is not the corporeality that weighs down an eternal soul and subverts divine and human reason; it is, rather, a wrongly directed will that aims not at God but at its own self-interest. Luther's sense of the urgency of our need to escape from sin and the devil was augmented by his deeply held belief that the last days were upon us. Not only was there little time left for us to prove ourselves worthy of salvation, but the raging of Satan and his efforts to control human action increased as the final struggle dawned. Luther thus believed that time was short, that Satan was strong, and that God judged human beings harshly by standards that were impossible to understand. It is thus not surprising that he felt himself slipping into a spiritual abyss.

LUTHER'S SOLUTION: THE SAVING POWER OF FAITH

The answer to this profound spiritual problem seems to have come to Luther in 1515 as a result of his so-called Tower Experience. Man, according to Luther, cannot save himself through anything he does. He can only be saved by faith alone. Faith, however, arises only through grace and grace only through Scripture. The watchwords of Luther's great insight and ultimately of the Reformation as a whole were thus *sola fides, sola gratia,* and *sola scriptura.* Luther, as we have seen, had struggled for many years with the vision of God inherited from nominalism. This God seemed to him a distant and merciless judge whose standards of justice could never be known. The justice of this God was the justice meted out on the last day that saved a few and consigned the vast majority to eternal damnation. How such a God could be propitiated let alone loved remained a burning question for him. What good works could he perform to please such a God? Must not everything he did be insufficient?

Luther's great insight was that no works can satisfy such a God but also that no works are necessary, for this God is not a harsh and distant judge but a merciful savior who has sacrificed himself to save us, asking not that we do anything other than believe in him, believe in the resurrection, in the forgiveness of sin, and in eternal life. Luther describes this insight in the autobiographical preface to his complete works, published in 1545. Having long been troubled by the justice of God referred to in Romans, Luther asserts, he determined to work through the text again to see whether he had properly understood the passage that caused him so much suffering. In rereading the passage, he had a profound spiritual insight. The "justice of God" did not refer to something abstract and distant, to an attribute of a transcendent God such as nominalism had imagined, but to God's justification of us. Similarly, "the power of God" was not distant and incomprehensible but the power by which God makes us powerful, and "his wisdom" is that by which he makes us wise.[22] In this way, Luther was able to transform the abstract and distant God of nominalism into an inward power that suffused individual human beings. The faith that arises from the encounter with God's word in Scripture thus works in us and transforms us. Through it we are reborn in God because God comes to dwell in us.[23]

In Luther's view God accomplishes this work in us by grace, by infusing himself in us, and possessing us. He comes to dwell in us as through the word. His love that binds him to us is the source of our salvation. The word in this way, according to Luther, comes to dwell in our heart. This gracious infusion of the word has a startling effect, creating a new self and a new kind of being. As Luther describes his own experience: "Here I felt I was altogether born again and had entered paradise itself through open gates."[24]

This great insight is a rejection of both the *via antiqua* and *via moderna*, of both scholasticism and nominalism.[25] Both, in Luther's view, derived their doctrines from a reading of Aristotle and other philosophers and not from the word of God. In this respect, neither lives up to the direct evidence principle laid down by Trutfetter and Arnoldi as the core of nominalism. Luther thus turns one of the fundamental principles of nominalism against its own theology. He admits as much already in 1520, claiming that it is not a question of the authorities but of arguments and firm assertions. "That is why I contradict even my own school of Occamists who follow the modern way, which I have absorbed completely." [26] Nominalism held that God was supremely free and could consequently be merciless in his wrath and that human beings had only enough free will to welcome God into their lives. Luther's recognition that God's righteousness was not an external judgment, but the righteousness or justification that he gave to human beings, reconfigured the supreme force in the universe into a benign being.[27] Luther thus does not deny divine omnipotence—indeed he magnifies it—but suggests that the awesome power of his God (and the terror it generates) is a blessing because it acts in and through human beings and is the basis of their salvation.

LUTHER AND THE REFORMATION

For all of its profundity, Luther's insight would probably have remained unknown to us except for the intersection of Luther's personal crisis and the spiritual and political crisis of his time. This conjunction produced the Reformation.

The central purpose of religious practice for both Luther and the church was salvation, but they disagreed about how it was to be obtained. According to the church, salvation was wrought by divine grace, but behind such grace lay divine justice and divine reason. God thus saved those who merited salvation by their good works and true repentance. The church played a crucial role in evaluating the sinfulness of human actions and in assigning earthly penance. From an early period, however, the church had found it difficult to convince many newly converted Christians (especially among the most powerful) to perform penitential acts and as a result had come to accept a financial payment in lieu of actual service. This was the origin of the idea of an indulgence. The practice of selling indulgences, however, soon became a dependable source of revenue. Moreover, church authorities began to claim that the church was the repository of all the forgiveness earned by the suffering of the martyrs who had fallen on behalf of Christ and that the church had the right to sell this forgiveness to release sinners or their dead relatives from time they would otherwise have to serve in purgatory. In this way, the questionable practice of accepting gold in lieu of penitential acts in this world became the corrupt practice of accepting gold and promising God's forgiveness for the sins of both the living and the dead. The papacy authorized the sale of indulgences for a variety of reasons. In Luther's own time they were authorized by Leo X to defray the costs of completing the Vatican. Since much of this money was collected in Northern Europe and transferred to Italy, the practice created considerable resentment among the German princes due to the outflow of funds. There was also deep suspicion—often well justified—(that the real purpose of this practice was not to further the purported holy purposes but to support the opulent and decadent lifestyles of the pope and the curia.[28]

(Luther saw the practice of selling indulgences not merely as a manifestation of the corruption of the church but as the work of Satan. Indeed, in Luther's view the doctrine that man can be saved by works at all is Satanic, preying upon human pride to convince man that he can save himself. It is precisely such pride, however, that alienates human beings from God, from the fundamental truth that nominalism recognized, that God is no man's debtor, and from the further truth that Luther articulated, that humans are saved by faith alone, that is, that a gracious God saves those who believe in him.[29] In this way, Luther came to see not merely the sale of indulgences but the idea of works that underpinned it as evidence of the fact that the church had fallen under the sway of Satan.

(This determination was merely a suspicion in October 1517, when Luther formulated his famous Ninety-Five Theses, but it was confirmed by the reaction of the church. While the theses were almost certainly not posted on the door of the church at Wittenberg, as is commonly believed, they might just as well have been, for they were an immediate sensation. Quickly printed in multiple editions, they were known throughout Germany in two weeks and throughout Europe in less than two months.[30] As is already clear in the first thesis, they preached a life of repentance and faith and rejected the doctrine of works and the practice of indulgences.

Luther seems perhaps rather naively to have believed that once the matter had been clearly presented the church or at least the pope would end the practice of selling indulgences. The reaction from the church, however, was at first negative and then increasingly hostile. In his examination by Cajetan in 1518 and his disputation with Eck in 1519, it became increasingly clear how distant he was from reigning church views, and how unwilling the church was to argue the case based on Scripture.

Although the many attacks further alienated him from the church, Luther was reluctant to precipitate a final break. However, as matters developed, he began to believe it was not only necessary but really the only right and holy thing to do. Luther viewed history not in a secular but in a profoundly theological fashion. It was not a simple series of events but a divinely determined plan that stretched from creation to the second coming.

His analysis of current events always took place within this eschatological worldview. In this reading of history, he was deeply influenced by Bernard of Clairvaux, who had argued that the history of Christianity was comprised of three periods of increasing danger. The first was the period of the fathers when the church suffered from the violence of the emperors who created numerous martyrs. The second was a period of heretics whose spiritual subversion was even more dangerous than Roman force. The final and most dangerous period would occur with the approach of the last days when the threat to Christianity came from within the church itself. As a result of the indulgence controversy, Luther had already begun to suspect in 1514 that the last days were at hand.[31] His discovery in 1520 that the Donation of Constantine was a forgery further stoked his growing suspicion that the devil ruled in Rome. He had put the true doctrine of the Gospel in front of the church, he told himself, but those in power had not merely failed to accept it, they had resisted and sought to suppress it. They had also now viciously attacked the bringer of these glad tidings. Surely, he thought, the last days were at hand. In such times, how could one not speak out with the greatest urgency and vehemence?

From this point on, relations between Luther and the church deteriorated rapidly. On June 15, 1520, the pope issued the bull *Exsurge Domine* declaring the continued interdependence of Christ and the church and threatening Luther with excommunication. By November 1520, Luther had decided the pope was the Antichrist.[32] On December 10, 1520, he burned the papal bull and canon law in Wittenberg, and on January 3, 1521 he was excommunicated by Leo X. His excommunication, however, was not generally accepted in Germany. Many Germans, and particularly his protector Fredrick the Wise, Elector of Saxony, insisted that he have a hearing in Germany. This led to the famous confrontation at the Diet of Worms in 1521. This event was organized to prevent Luther from having a public forum in which to express his views. Through a series of clever maneuvers, however, he was able to present most of his claims. Nonetheless, when forced to say finally whether he would recant, he responded: "Unless I am convinced by the testimony of Scripture or by an evident reason—for I confide neither in the pope nor in a council alone, since it is certain that they have often erred and contradicted themselves—I am held fast by the Scriptures adduced by me, and my conscience is taken captive by God's Word, and I neither can nor will revoke anything seeing that it is not safe or right to act against conscience. God help me. Amen."[33] A human being can will rightly only when he is taken prisoner by God's word, that is, only when he is directed by God's will, when his will is God's will. Right willing, however, is the source of true freedom. Thus, the subjection of the human will to the divine will liberates the Christian from all other bonds. "A Christian," Luther thus concludes "is a perfectly free lord of all, subject to none" when he is subject to God.[34]

As a result of this confrontation, Luther was condemned by the young Emperor Charles V and forced to go into hiding in Wartburg. His condemnation, however, did little to limit the spread of his ideas; in fact it probably accelerated their dispersion. In any case, the lines had been drawn and Europe would never be the same again.

The extraordinary democratic potential of Luther's teaching was immediately apparent to many of his followers. If faith alone saved, then the various rites and sacraments of the church were not needed for salvation. Moreover, if faith came from an immediate encounter with Scripture, then priestly intercessors were not only not necessary, they were actually obstacles to an encounter with God. The priestly caste that ruled European spiritual life and the tithes to support them were thus unnecessary. In place of such a spiritual elite Luther held up the possibility of a priesthood of all believers. Finally, if God spoke to each man privately through Scripture, then there was no definitive dogma that characterized Christian belief. Individuals might make their own decisions about their religious responsibilities.

Such innovations in religious practice appealed to many different groups. Many of the knights and peasants saw Luther as a messiah, speaking for their interests.[35] Zwingli in Switzerland and Thomas Müntzer were among the first to articulate the meaning of Luther's religious teachings for social and political relations. Zwingli made common cause with the bourgeois revolution in a way that was later taken over by Calvin.[36] In contrast to Luther, he was convinced that religion depended more on private insight into the character of God's will rather than reliance on a more strict interpretation of the Gospel. Even he, however, did not go as far as many of the Anabaptists who at times seemed willing to dispense with Scripture altogether. At the extreme end of this spectrum were Thomas Müntzer and his followers who raised the Peasants' Rebellion. Müntzer was attracted first to Luther, but he soon moved beyond him to mysticism and then to a radical Anabaptism.[37] Müntzer had come to the conclusion that all princes had to heed the call of God or be exterminated, for the ungodly had no right to live.[38] His movement gathered together a hodgepodge of peasants, artisans, etc., many clearly motivated by his charismatic preaching. He saw his struggle in chiliastic fashion as ushering in the end of days and joined battle with a much superior force, certain that God would join him and exterminate his enemies. In fact, it was Müntzer and his "army" that were exterminated.

While Luther's teaching had inspired many of the radicals, he himself saw such radicalism as the work of Satan. Luther was concerned above all else with salvation and not with political reform, especially in light of the approaching end of days. This is the time of the devil's raging because he knows that with the rediscovery of the Gospel, his time is short. It is thus particularly crucial that princes, however bad they might be, rule in order to control the chaos of a fallen and satanically misguided humanity. The Peasants' Rebellion for Luther was a clear example of the devil's handiwork in fomenting chaos. Müntzer and the Anabaptists fell into his clutches so easily in Luther's view because they abandoned the word of God, the Holy Scriptures, and drew their inspiration from private revelation. Their efforts at political reform were fruitless, he believed, for only the coming of God could work such a political reformation. The Anabaptists and the peasants in rebellion therefore had to be suppressed with utmost rigor, lest they draw men away from their real spiritual concerns.

This demonizing of the radical Reformation hardly endeared Luther to his more radical followers. Many had clearly expected him to lead them out of the moral morass of Catholic Christianity and out from under the tyranny of unworthy princes, but this was not to be. Luther might have combined Augustine and Tacitus to form a new German church and spirit, or he might have raised the banner of political revolution, but he did neither, seeking instead to bring men face to face with the theological questions at the heart of their religiosity. While Luther continued to preach and write at an astonishing pace until his death in 1546, he thus ceased to have a larger social impact. However, while the Reformation moved beyond him, all Reformation thinking remained deeply rooted in his thought.

LUTHER'S METAPHYSICS

In order to come to terms with Luther's thought and to begin to appreciate the radical innovation that it represents, it is necessary to consider Luther's metaphysics more systematically. On the surface, it may seem strange to think of Luther as even having a metaphysics. After all, he certainly and unambiguously rejects not merely scholastic doctrines but scholastic methods in favor of a form of argument that rests upon biblical exegesis.[39] While his thought is not explicitly metaphysical, as we will see, it can be illuminated by analyzing it in terms of the scholastic distinction of *metaphysica generalis* and *metaphysica specialis.* Such an analysis lets us systematically explore the structure of his thought and explain how it differs from that of his predecessors.

Luther's views on ontology grew out of his early nominalist education. Like the nominalists, he rejected the belief in the real existence of universals that characterized scholastic realism. He also rejected the notion that God's being could be understood in the way we understand other beings.[40] In his view there is a radical difference between divine being and created being. Because there is no continuum that connects creator and creation, there can be no levels of ontological perfection of the sort Anselm and later scholastics imagined. Because man is a created being, there can also be no divine spark imprisoned in the body striving to return to its own element as Neoplatonists imagined. Divine being is not like human being, and humans cannot rise to God by purging themselves of corporeality. In this respect Luther opposes Jerome, Origen, and even the Neoplatonism of his beloved Augustine. Being, however, is not just difference, not mere brokenness. For Luther the source of the unity of being is Christ, who bridges the great divide between creator and creation in an utterly mysterious and ontologically inexplicable manner. The central ontological truth for Luther is thus the Incarnation, but it remains philosophically incomprehensible.[41] The fundamental truth about being is thus accessible only through faith.

Luther also follows the nominalists in rejecting the syllogistic logic of scholasticism, but he moves beyond the nominalists' arid terminism in his reliance on the ordinary language of the Gospel. In this instance he was deeply influenced by the humanists' focus on rhetoric. Indeed, for Luther language becomes almost purely rhetorical. It does not reveal the truth, for the truth comes about as a result of an inner experience of the divine that cannot be adequately captured in words. Verbal expression of the truth is always only metaphorical or analogical, conveying passion and conviction only when energy is combined with eloquence.[42] Language is more importantly the medium in and through which God comes to dwell in us. It is the mysterious divine word and not the pale human imitation that is thus at the heart of Luther's thought.

While Luther was deeply influenced by nominalism and to a lesser extent by humanism in his conception of *metaphysica generalis,* he is more revolutionary in his treatment of *metaphysica specialis.* This is particularly true of his new understanding of theology. Luther rejects completely the rational theology of scholasticism and also the technical theology of nominalists such as Ockham and Biel. In this respect, however, he goes little further than Christian humanists such as Erasmus. Reason, and particularly syllogistic reason, cannot come to terms with God, for when the mind tries to think its way to God it arrives at a dead end.[43] In the same vein natural theology fails because it assumes an analogical relation between creator and creation that does not exist. Moreover, both act blasphemously in seeking to understand God when he does not vouchsafe knowledge of himself. They are really only forms of sinful human pride.[44] Luther also rejects the two other traditional paths to God, ecstatic mysticism and fideism. Ecstatic mysticism in his view is dangerously subjective and blasphemously imagines a human capacity to climb up to God or to throw oneself into the abyss of divine being. Fideism, by contrast, rests on a skepticism that is ultimately atheistic and a reliance on religious traditions that are often contradictory and mistaken.

Luther's understanding of God rests on the recognition of God's absolute sovereignty, that is, upon the nominalist notion of divine omnipotence. What follows from this? In Luther's view literally everything, that is to say, everything that occurs happens as a result of God's willing it to be so. The purposes of such an all-overpowering God, in Luther's view, are necessarily unfathomable: "For as in His own nature God is immense, incomprehensible, and infinite, so to man's nature He is intolerable."[45] He argues that we thus must abstain even from a search into God's majesty, for as the Scriptures make clear, "No man may see me and live." God's power is so profound and inexplicable that it would destroy the man who sought to comprehend it. God thus conceals his majesty—he is a hidden God, a *deus absconditus.*

This was the God that so terrified the young Luther, the omnipotent and transrational God of nominalism. In Luther's later thought this God is superseded although he is never truly eliminated. Indeed, this hidden God remains the controlling if incomprehensible force behind all things, and in his unpredictable omnipotence generates a vast and irremediable unease that is strengthened by Luther's insistence that it not be considered.[46] Only this God is truly free, and the grounds of his actions are totally beyond human ken. For us, he is thus not a personal God at all but resembles the Greek concept of fate governing and determining all things.[47]

The difficulty with such a notion of divine omnipotence is that it makes God responsible not only for all of the good in the world but for all of the evil as well. Augustine sought to solve this problem by attributing freedom to the human will in order to free God from the imputation of doing or causing evil. Luther's denial of human freedom removes this as a possible explanation for him. The source of evil for Luther is neither man nor God but the devil. Indeed, for Luther, existence is a continual and unceasing war between God and the devil for possession of man. Satan is pictured as the ruler of this world and God the ruler of heaven. While on the surface this notion seems quasi-Manichean, at the heart of things this cannot be the case, since Satan for Luther must ultimately also be in God's service. Behind Satan lies the hidden mystery of absolute divine sovereignty.[48] The question of demonic forces for Luther is thus only the obverse of the question of God. If God is omnipotent, how can he not be the source of evil? How can he also not be the devil?

Luther's solution to this problem is to insist that we focus not on a theology of glory but on a theology of the cross, not on a hidden and inexplicable God who wills all things but on God as he reveals himself to us in Scripture. We must see, in other words, the incarnate God. In Christ, the hidden God conceals his majesty and transforms it into its opposite, weakness on the cross.[49] This revealed God in Luther's view is more familiar to us and we can love him for the suffering he underwent on our behalf. Human beings, according to Luther, are as unable to completely know the concealed God in all his power and glory as to please him. Therefore it is necessary to let God be God and man be man.[50] It is necessary for humans to leave aside all speculation as to the hidden purposes of God and confine their attention to what God has revealed and affirmed in his word, to focus on "God preached" and to leave alone "God not preached," that is, the hidden God or *deus absconditus*.[51] Everything God reveals of himself transcends human comprehension, and humans must therefore humbly accept God's interpretation rather than their own.[52]

The revealed God is thus the center of Luther's theology, and his Incarnation connects heaven and earth. For Luther, Christ functions as a mediator between God and man, replacing the saints, while God himself recedes into darkness.[53] Christ *is* God and Christ *is* man, but it is this connection to man that is decisive. He is not a distant and unfeeling being, as nominalism at times imagined him. Indeed, according to Luther, he understood to the bitter end what it meant to be human.[54] Christ crucified thus becomes the basis of the Reformation. Luther believes that in our pain and suffering, and in the midst of our doubts, we can be comforted by the fact that Christ himself suffered and doubted. Thus, "to contemplate Jesus is to be reminded in the midst of the most radical kind of doubt and fear that God is with us."[55] God is not only with us but he has promised us salvation if we believe in him. Luther's theology in this way grows out of Staupitz's claim that God owed salvation to those who believed in him and is akin to Bernard's mystical contemplation of Jesus. Luther's problem, however, is much more profound than that faced by Staupitz. Staupitz believed that God's omnipotence severely circumscribed the powers of the devil. He consequently did not directly confront the problem of the origin of evil in a world governed by an absolutely omnipotent God. Such a God must be responsible for all of the evil in the world; he must in other words also be the devil. Luther rebuts this charge by focusing on God not in his omnipotence but as he incarnates himself in Christ and reveals himself in the Gospel.

In an account of his life published in 1545, as we saw above, Luther explained that the righteousness of God as portrayed in Romans, that is, the image of God as judge on the final day, remained an obstacle to his belief in his early years. In rereading Romans in 1515–16, however, he came to the recognition that God's righteousness is not the righteousness he exercises in judging man but the grace by which he justifies man, that is, he recognized that man was justified not by anything he does, not by his works, but by grace alone.[56]

This insight was not entirely new. Paul, Augustine, Gottschalk, Bradwardine, and Wycliff all recognized that salvation was brought about solely through grace.[57] What distinguishes Luther from his predecessors is his further insight that grace can be obtained only by faith, trusting in the word of Christ, and after 1518 trusting in the word alone without the necessity of introspective self-examination.[58] The miracle of faith, according to Luther, is that when we believe, God pays no attention to our sins.[59] Thus, as Luther argues in his commentary on Galatians, "a Christian is not someone who has no sin or feels no sin; he is someone to whom, because of his faith in Christ, God does not impute his sin."[60] Faith for Luther is "the lively apprehension of grace made known and received."[61] "Faith," he argues in the preface to Romans, "is a living and unshakable confidence, a belief in the grace of God so assured that a man would die a thousand deaths for its sake."[62] Luther's insight thus unites God's righteousness with Christ received through faith.[63]

What then does a Christian have faith in? In the first instance it is faith in the resurrection of Christ, that is, in the fact that Christ is God. Christ's resurrection is a miraculous demonstration of the righteousness of God and of the power of God to resurrect the dead.[64] For the early, "Catholic" Luther, faith was faith in God's ability and his promise to save the sinner who is truly repentant, but after his Tower Experience faith for him became an identification with the crucified Christ, with the loneliness of his death and the promise of resurrection it contained.[65] To live a life of faith is to live the life of Christ. "Faith here means, basically, not the decision to assent to a proposition, but a fundamental reorientation and redirection of life. The life of faith is the mode of existence which finds its vital source and center in God's forgiving and renewing grace."[66]

Faith is not something chosen; it arises only through grace. Human beings thus cannot come to believe or have faith by their own power. They are incapable of justifying themselves or of obligating God to justify or save them by having faith in him. Rather they come to have faith and thus warrant salvation because God wills it and graciously causes it to occur. Faith alone saves, but humans have faith only because it is infused in them by God, or to put the matter another way, they are saved because they have faith but they only have faith because God has chosen to save them. Faith is thus a mark of selection and predestination, not its cause.

Faith arises through an encounter with Scripture. Scripture is the means by which God communicates with human beings. There is no mystical individual revelation. Faith is always faith in God's word, but God's word is only known through Scripture. Scripture contains the truths about God that are the premises of Christian life. These truths are not based in reason, but if humans live trusting that they are true, they discover a confirmation in themselves that is sufficient to guide their lives and they discover God responding to them in their hearts.[67] As Luther puts it, "Faith alone is the saving and efficacious use of the Word of God."[68] God's overt acts are mysteriously concealed so that humans come face to face with him not in the physical world but only in the inner response of their souls to the word or Gospel.[69]

In keeping with his nominalist training, Luther was convinced that the reception of the word was a personal experience, but he insisted that it was not a private and idiosyncratic revelation. Rather it was the result of an encounter with Scripture within an interpretative community of fellow worshippers. For Luther Scripture is always powerfully present, a voice speaking to us here and now. This is the reason he emphasizes the spoken word as the most powerful manifestation of God—in fact, the word was one of Luther's most powerful metaphors for God himself.[70] The word thus had to be preached and heard, not merely read. In his *Sermons on the Catechism* he prays: "Dear Father, grant thy Word, that it may be purely preached throughout the world, and then grant grace and power that it may also be accepted and the people believe. The first concerns the Word and the second the fruit of the Word. For if the Word is preached but not accepted, the kingdom of God does not come."[71] By preaching the Gospel the devil is overthrown and the prisoner released from the kingdom of darkness to the kingdom of light and liberty.[72] Hearing the word is the source of faith, the means by which God gives us faith, and the means by which he brings us to change our way of life: "And just as he initially gives us faith through the Word, so later on He exercises, increases, strengthens, and perfects it in us by that Word. Therefore the supreme worship of God that a man can offer, the Sabbath of Sabbaths, is to practice true godliness, to hear and read the Word." [73] "He means a Word that you believe when you hear it, so that the Word is not only the sound of my voice but is something that is heard by you, penetrates into your heart, and is believed by you. Then it is truly hearing with faith, through which you receive the Holy Spirit; and after He has been received, you will also mortify your flesh." [74]

Preaching was the vital core of Luther's theology and practice, and it had a central place in his daily life. There were, for example, sermons every day in Wittenberg. Luther could find no justification for a special religious day in Scripture and concluded that the Sabbath was a Jewish and not a Christian notion. He believed that a preacher could persuade others of the truth of faith or, to speak more correctly, that a preacher imbued with the Holy Spirit could fill his listeners with the word of God, which in turn could work a transformation in their hearts. This understanding of the impact of Scripture and the importance of preaching clearly owes a great deal to the rhetorical tradition of humanism. In and through Scripture God speaks directly and personally to every man. Scripture therefore is the greatest act of rhetoric and God is the greatest rhetorician. Through the word he is able to move those to faith whom he wants to move. Grace thus is infused not directly and internally but by and through the word.

All this notwithstanding, Luther knew that Scripture must always be interpreted by readers and by preachers. If it were perfectly clear and straightforward, it could never be used as a tool in the hands of those who work in the service of the devil. But it certainly is, as Luther repeatedly insists. Understanding Scripture correctly is thus essential. How then does Luther believe we can know which interpretations are correct? How are we to distinguish God's word from satanic deceptions? Luther struggles with these questions and deploys a variety of answers. He at times declares that Scripture is so clear that there is no need for mediators. This view is commensurate with his notion of the priesthood of all believers. But Luther's settled opinion seems to be finally that while all men can be priests not all can be ministers of the word. In the first instance, Scripture is only clear to the believer: understanding "is reserved to faith, for an ungodly man has no idea what the words mean." [75] Scriptural interpretation for Luther is a mystical experience, not ecstatic but a warm communion with God in the act of interpreting the sacred text. [76] Not only must the interpreter be a believer, he must also be able to understand the language of the text. This means an attentiveness to linguistic usage (that Luther derives from nominalism) and the use of humanistic training and scholarship to come to terms with the meaning of the text in its original Hebrew and Greek.[77] One might thus describe Luther's method of interpreting Scripture as a combination of nominalism, humanism, and faith. The hermeneutic principle involves being grasped by the biblical word and the spirit conjoined in such a way that one is laid hold of by more than what the text says. "It is being grasped in one's depth, being redirected in one's total being, including heart and mind by the living Word."[78] The touchstone of textual authenticity, according to Luther, is whether the preacher emphasizes Christ or not. Within his theology, the cross of Christ is thus the standard of exegesis, for only through the cross is God's word truly revealed: *"Crux Christi unica est eruditio verborum dei, theologia sincerissima."*[79]

Luther promotes a more literal reading of Scripture in contrast to the tradition of scholastic interpretation within the church. In this respect he was greatly influenced by Valla and Erasmus and by his own recognition that so-called consensus of the Catholic tradition was a fiction. But it would be a mistake to believe that his reading of the Scriptures is strictly literal. He clearly privileges the texts of John and Paul over those of Matthew, Mark and Luke, and his reading and preaching thus owe more to Paul and Augustine than to the Jesus of the Gospels.[80]

LUTHER'S NEW VIEW OF HUMAN BEING

Luther's radical transformation of theology had a decisive impact on his view of man. In nominalistic fashion, Luther sees humans not as a species but as individuals who are "distinguished from the animals by speech and not by shape or form or any other activity."[81] In this respect and to this extent, he remains within the Aristotelian tradition. However, he quickly diverges from this Aristotelian beginning, for he identifies speech not with reason but with a capacity to apprehend the word. Reason in the traditional sense is in fact merely a manifestation of a false human pride that arises out of a fallacious belief in human power. Humans by nature are not free and powerful, as earlier humanists such as Pico, for example, imagined them to be, but the slaves of Satan without any real power of choice or decision. Only through the word, through God's gracious infusion of faith, can they escape their bondage to the devil. This escape, however, does not lead them to freedom but into subjection to God.

While human beings for the most part are enslaved to Satan, they are generally unaware of this fact. Driven by pride and exercising their reason, they believe they are acting in their self-interest when in fact they are only fulfilling Satan's purposes. Evil in Luther's sense is thus not concupiscence or any other form of bodily desire but rather disbelief and fear of death that produce either a desire to live sensuously in the moment or to strive for immortal fame and glory. Both of these misguided forms of willing drive humans away from God and into themselves, that is, into the arms of Satan. They can only be released from the lordship of Satan by hearing and coming to believe in the word. Such faith makes them into new beings. They are reborn in the spirit, according to Luther, and henceforth are dominated not by their fallen, satanic will, but by God's will acting in and through them. Human being in this way becomes God-infused being.

This rebirth does not lead to perfection. The desire for perfection in Luther's view is a reflection of the pride that leads humans to believe they can master their fate. Such pride characterized those ancients and their humanist imitators who sought moral perfection as well as those Jews and Christians who sought to live perfectly according to the law. Luther believes that both of these paths are impossible for imperfect human beings. The law is a standard of perfection but a standard that for that very reason can never be attained. Its principal purpose is to humble the will by revealing the inability of all human beings to live up to the law and thus their unworthiness for salvation. The law is thus God's gift to help us prepare for repentance.[82]

The inability to abide by the law and the guilt and despair that this failure engenders are the first steps on the path to a truly Christian life, in Luther's view. Recognition of sin is the beginning of the search for forgiveness that leads to Christ. Christ, Luther repeatedly argues, is not for the saints or the righteous but for sinners, for those who have recognized their imperfection and unworthiness and thrown themselves upon him and his mercy. The great learning and talents of the ancient philosophers were thus actually impediments to salvation. They came to believe that they could lead perfect lives by their own efforts. They thus did not find their way to Christ, for it is not excellence but despair that leads to salvation. Despair is the precursor to the recognition of the radical difference between God and man and to recognition of God's graciousness in redeeming us from our fallen humanity by the sacrifice of Christ. Christ crucified is thus the basis for salvation.

Faith is belief in the resurrection of Christ, but such a belief can only arise through the infusion of grace. Such an infusion, however, is nothing other than the transformation or transubstantiation of our humanity: "By faith we are in Him, and He is in us (John 6:56). This Bridegroom, Christ, must be alone with His bride in His private chamber, and all the family and household must be shunted away. But later on, when the Bridegroom opens the door and comes out, then let the servants return to take care of them and serve them food and drink."[83] As a result, man becomes one with Christ: "Christian righteousness is . . . that righteousness by which Christ lives in us, not the righteousness that is in our own person. Therefore when it is necessary to discuss Christian righteousness, the person must be completely rejected. For if I pay attention to the person or speak of the person, then, whether intentionally or unintentionally on my part, the person becomes a doer of works who is subject to the Law. But here Christ and my conscience must become one body, so that nothing remains in my sight but Christ, crucified and risen. . . . The person does indeed live, but not in itself or for its own person."[84] This is not a mere conjunction but a true marriage. For Luther, "Christ is my 'form,' which adorns my faith as color or light adorns a wall. This fact has to be expounded in this crude way, for there is no spiritual way for us to grasp the idea that Christ clings and dwells in us as closely and intimately as light or whiteness clings to a wall. 'Christ,' he [Paul] says, 'is fixed and cemented to me and abides in me. The life that I now live, He lives in me. Indeed, Christ Himself is the life that I now live. In this way, therefore, Christ and I are one.'"[85] The human and fallible self remains, but "I," this new "I" is also there and is godlike: "'I do indeed live; and yet not I live, but Christ lives in me. There is a double life: my own, which is natural or animate; and an alien life, that of Christ in me."[86]

As a result of this doubling, the individual who is justified by faith does not thereby transcend his humanity. He remains a sinful human being, but at the same time is much more than this; he is in fact the divine will. On this point Luther was unwilling to follow the path of the more radical reformers, who believed that justification produced perfection and saintliness. Luther was convinced rather that the natural vices (the old Adam) remain in us after we have received faith.[87] The unified work of faith includes not merely justification but the work of putting the old Adam to death and controlling the flesh, what Luther sometimes calls sanctification.[88] This purgation of the old Adam is facilitated by works of charity and penance, for it is necessary to place a burden on the old man to keep him in line.[89] "These works reduce the body to subjection and purify it of its evil lusts," so that the body may join in loving God and serving others.[90]

Serving others for Luther is not as easy as it might first appear. The principal goal of human life is scripturally determined by the first commandment, to love the lord your God with all your heart, with all your mind, and with all your soul. Such love, as we have seen, is only possible for those who are infused with grace. Such people become the dwelling place of the universally loving divine will. Only those who in this way fulfill the first commandment can fulfill the second commandment, loving one's neighbor as oneself. For Luther, there is thus no human love or moral action apart from divine action. If human beings are not under the domination of God, they are under the domination of the devil, and in this state they are capable only of self-love and self-seeking. Without the love of God there is no love of the neighbor, consequently no real charity or service to others. In the absence of such love, humans are driven by pride and self-interest both of which bring them into conflict with others. Thus, for Luther "the natural condition of the world is chaos and upheaval." [91]

This vision of the world as beset by chaos was not unique to Luther. Indeed, as we saw above, it was a prominent trope in Petrarch and in humanism. For the humanists, however, the solution to such upheaval is the application of the human will to master the forces of chaos. This involves the effective joining of knowledge and power in the manner Machiavelli perhaps most clearly delineated. Luther sees this entire line of thought as misguided. At best it produces only peace but not love and certainly not salvation. Indeed, the desire for peace may actually undermine salvation, for the proclamation of the word causes conflict, especially in the last days when Satan rages against the word. Thus, the attempt to establish worldly peace may only be possible by the suppression of the Gospel.

This does not mean of course that government is unnecessary or that we can dispense with it. It is true that for Luther no government would be necessary if everyone were truly Christian. [92] "Now since no one is by nature Christian or righteous, but altogether sinful and wicked, God through the law puts them all under restraint so they dare not willfully implement their wickedness in actual deeds." [93] The law tells men what they ought to do and what governments should permit and disallow. "If this were not so, men would devour one another, seeing that the whole world is evil and that among thousands there is scarcely a single true Christian. No one could support wife and child, feed himself, and serve God. The world would be reduced to chaos." [94]

God establishes rulers "to make a contribution in both family and society to the survival of the world in the struggle against chaos." [95] Princes are appointed by God, and they rule by force because wickedness must be restrained. [96] If someone tried to rule the world by the Gospel alone "he would be loosing the ropes and chains of the savage wild beasts and letting them bite and mangle everyone, meanwhile insisting that they were harmless, tame, and gentle creatures." [97] It is important in Luther's view to be realistic about humanity. In his view there are four kinds of people: the truly religious who do not need law, the falsely confident and lazy who use freedom as an excuse for sin and who consequently must be guided by law, the truly wicked who must be held in check by law, and the immature in faith who can be helped along by the law until they can learn to distinguish right and wrong.[98] Both spiritual and secular government are thus needed for all but the true Christians, and even these Christians, loving their neighbors, recognize the need for government to avert chaos.[99]

The fact that a fallen humanity needs to be ruled legitimates political authority, not tyranny. Subjects and rulers in Luther's view have reciprocal duties. The Christian submits himself to his ruler and laws because he knows it is the will of God.[100] It is his duty to serve the prince in all matters that do not violate his Christian duty. This in Luther's view includes the duty of the subject to serve in a just war, even plundering and devastating the enemy according to the prince's orders.[101] Secular authority, however, can only rule over externals, and consequently no one can legitimately be compelled to believe.[102] In matters of conscience the subject need not obey the prince, but even in these cases he or she cannot act in any way that produces civil unrest. Resistance in such cases is limited to noncompliance.[103] *Not quite True- see Table Talk*

Luther's strong support of secular authority does not mean, as it is often assumed, that he was an uncritical authoritarian. He drew clear distinctions between better and worse princes. Indeed, in *On Secular Authority* he describes most rulers as foolish and malicious tyrants. "For God the Almighty has made our rulers mad; they actually think they can do—and order their subjects to do—whatever they please."[104] They thus presumptuously set themselves in God's place, lording it over others' consciences and faith. Wise princes are very rare and pious ones even rarer. Princes "are generally the biggest fools or the worst scoundrels on earth."[105] This fact notwithstanding, obedience in secular matters is necessary, for "such a world as this deserves such princes, none of whom do their duty."[106] "The world is too wicked, and does not deserve to have many wise and pious princes. Frogs need storks."[107] But "the common man is learning to think, and the scourge of princes (that which God calls *contemptum*) is gathering force among the mob and with the common man. I fear there will be no way to avert it, unless the princes conduct themselves in a princely manner and begin again to rule decently and reasonably. Men will not, men cannot, men refuse to endure your tyranny and wantonness much longer. . . . God will no longer tolerate it. The world is no longer what it once was, when you hunted and drove the people like game." [108] Therefore, a prince must make himself useful to subjects, protect them, secure peace, and not seek his own advantage. [109]

Luther was no revolutionary. He was convinced that human beings were so sinful that God alone could reform government. He also believed that he lived in the last days and that such reforms were unnecessary, since the time until the end was so short. But finally and most importantly, his goals were otherworldly. He aimed at salvation and not at improvement of life on earth. Thus, for Luther religious purposes supersede all political or moral purposes. "Doing," he argues,

> is one thing in nature, another in philosophy, and another in theology. In nature the tree must be first, and then the fruit. In moral philosophy doing means a good will and right reason to do well; this is where the philoso-phers come to a halt. . . . Therefore we have to rise higher in theology with the word 'doing,' so that it becomes altogether new. For just as it becomes something different when it is taken from the natural area into the moral, so it becomes something much more different when it is transferred from philosophy and from the law into theology. Thus it has a completely new meaning; it does indeed require right reason and a good will, but in a theo-logical sense, not in a moral sense, which means that through the word of the Gospel I know and believe that God sent his son into the world to redeem us from sin and death. Here 'doing' is a new thing, unknown to rea-son, to the philosophers, to the legalists, and to all men; for it is a "wisdom hidden in a mystery" (1 Cor. 2:7). [110]

As a result, the church for Luther is much more important than the state. The true church, however, is not the papacy and the curia but the congre-gation of true believers, what Luther called the invisible church. The vis-ible church is always a mixture of saints and hypocrites, of whom only a handful stand fast until the end. [111] In the true church, by contrast, all men are priests and staunch in their belief, even if all of them are not able to minister and interpret Scripture. The true church is thus made up of all those persons in whom God has infused his grace, in whom he has come to dwell.

Even among true Christians, there is need of an institutional church and religious practices. The Old Adam remains strong and must be con-stantly combated. Thus, even if the church only existed for the elect, it would be necessary that it continue to offer services which include not merely preaching but also sacraments, prayer, music, etc., in order to further the sanctification of those who had already been justified. Sacraments, for Luther, play an especially important role in this process. On this question, Luther adopts a middle position between the Catholic tradition and the radical Protestants. He rejects some of the traditional sacraments as lacking a scriptural foundation, but he accepts the most important. By far the most important is the Eucharist. In contrast to the more radical Protestants, Luther argued that actual transubstantiation of the bread and wine took place in the Eucharist and that the ceremony was not merely a symbolic act. The real transubstantiation was decisive in his view as the foundation for the possibility of man's own transformation through grace into a repository of divine will. If the Eucharist were merely symbolic, then our own transformation would not really modify our nature. We would be left as human and therefore as lost as before. Our salvation thus depends crucially upon the capacity for God to transform the host, for Christ to be present in the host as he is present in us, not in a spatial sense but through a mystical union.[112] The miracle of the Eucharist can thus be expressed and ordered but not fathomed just as our own transformation through grace and faith cannot be understood.[113]

The theological content of the divine service is thus a central reenactment of the basic truth of Christianity that Christ is God and that Christ is man, and that human beings can become godlike through Christ's entrance into their souls. The liturgical aspect of the worship service and the sacraments themselves are another manifestation of the word. They like the written and spoken word do not present a rational argument but a rhetorical appeal that is meant to move the heart, to infuse the heart with Christ. For Luther, the same is true of music that in his view is God's greatest gift after theology.[114] It is another form in which the word comes to dwell in the soul, another means of divine persuasion.

LUTHER'S VIEW OF NATURE AS INCARNATION

In keeping with his nominalist beginnings, Luther rejected both the Aristotelian and Neoplatonic understandings of nature. Nature is God's wonderful creation, given by God's grace, and operating under its own rules. These rules, however, do not conform to the categories of Aristotelian logic. There are no orders of perfection in nature, stretching from God down to the least of his creatures. The central religious truth is the Incarnation, and this is an indication that everything bodily comes from God, even the lowest or most despicable of things. All things are therefore sacred.

This becomes graphically clear when we examine Luther's so-called Tower Experience more closely. In describing this experience, Luther actually says that the Holy Spirit came to him while he was on the toilet, performing what Roland Bainton is his famous biography euphemistically and with some embarrassment calls "the daily task." [115] Since this closet was in his tower, scholars have generally assumed he was referring to the tower itself, unable to believe that Luther was in fact speaking of something so mundane as the toilet, especially since the toilet in Luther's time was generally considered an unclean, unholy place, loved by the devil. Since Freud and Erikson, the connection of Luther's insight to the movement of his bowels has been given center stage in order to interpret Luther's great insight as the manifestation of neurosis. However, both the attempt to conceal Luther's explicit language by the conventionally pious and the attempt to highlight it to undermine piety by the antireligious are wrongheaded. The insight underlying Luther's "tower" experience is in fact quite profound, that is, that God is everywhere, even in what are apparently the most unholy places, that he stands by us in even the lost and least pleasing parts of creation. [116] All beings are his creation and thus are worthy of respect. In contrast to the Neoplatonists who see matter as a fallen state of intellect, Luther sees incarnation as the highest moment of the divine, and a moment that the devil cannot emulate or overcome [117] As Marius has argued, at the heart of his religious being Luther believed in the Incarnation, the goodness of creation, the capacity of the physical and spiritual to be joined together, and that Christ was to restore God's work to its original purity. [118]

Within both Neoplatonism and scholastic Aristotelianism, the divine is imagined to transcend the physical. The source of sin is thus conceived as a falling away from God into the material world, which is at best an imperfect image of the divine and at worst a snare of the devil. For Luther, by contrast, God is conceived out of the Incarnation. [119] The corporeal is thus not a falling away from divine reality but the place in which the divine comes to be in and for us. It is the *parousia*. Human entanglement in the corporeal world is therefore not in itself sinful, not a falling away from God. Not only is the material world not connected to the devil, it is the one thing he cannot penetrate. The devil acts not by stoking our carnal desires but by preying on our spirit, our intellect, and our pride. The devil is the demagogue within, the evil Machiavellian rhetorician who speaks to our self-interest and thereby leads us astray.

Indeed, the devil hates all incarnation, all life. Thus, in Luther's view he hates procreation and marriage because he hates God's life-giving power that is vitally present in the attraction of man and woman. [120] Thus, the notion that the celibate life is higher or more holy than the married life in Luther's view is mistaken. Indeed, it is itself the product of the devil's stoking of priestly pride. The carnal life for Luther is thus a divine gift to be enjoyed. Luther himself loved nature and enjoyed eating, drinking, sexuality, etc. During his disputation with Eck, he carried a rose in his hand that he repeatedly gazed upon and smelled to remind himself of the goodness of creation. That we typically associate the Reformation with Puritan asceticism has little to do with Luther and much more to do with a revival of Neoplatonism in the thought of Calvin and the Calvinists, which replaced Luther's cosmology of incarnation with a more arid intellectual spiritualism.[121]

CONCLUSION

Luther's thought originates out of the deep spiritual problems that arise from his encounter with nominalism. His thinking follows a path that is radically different from that of his scholastic predecessors. In part, this new vision owes a great deal to nominalism, but it is crucially formed by his own great insight into the centrality of incarnation. This radical new ontology produces a new view of God, man, and the natural world. This said, Luther's position is beset by deep and intractable problems. The question of divine justice, for example, cannot be as easily disposed of, as Luther would have us believe. Focusing on Christ and the Incarnation and prohibiting speculation about the hidden God will not put such questions to rest. Why should we assume that this hidden God is merciful and loving rather than indifferent or cruel? How do we know that he is not a *genius malignus,* as Descartes would later suggest? In other words, why should we trust God's promises, trust that he will abide by his *potentia ordinata* when in fact he is more truly a *potentia absoluta?*

Luther's answer to this perplexing question comes down to his faith in Scripture. But Luther himself finds it difficult to sustain this claim. Scripture, as he often admits, has to be interpreted, and that means valuing some passages and books above others. How in such circumstances do we know we are choosing correctly? How do we know what we take to be divine inspiration behind our reading is not in fact the subliminal urgings of our passions and desires?

Moreover, a great deal in Luther's thought turns on the notion of grace, but Jesus never uses the word *charis* in this sense in the Bible. It becomes central only in Paul and later in Augustine.[122] Similarly, it is difficult to find any mention of predestination in the synoptic Gospels. Luther's Christianity therefore perhaps depends more on Paul than on Jesus. But why should Paul be taken as definitive? He may be clearer than Jesus, but is clarity closer to truth than ambiguity, or is it only nearer fanaticism?

Luther's religious mission began on that July afternoon in 1505 when he found himself in a storm from which he never actually emerged. In all the tumult of struggle and debate that surrounded him the rest of his life, he held fast to his core doctrine that saw God as everything and man as nothing. This was the point of certainty on which everything else turned. This position, however, was directly at odds with that of humanism. It was thus in a sense inevitable that these two great movements of thought that had arisen in response to nominalism should collide. The resultant collision produced the greatest debate of the sixteenth century, the debate between Erasmus and Luther on the freedom and the bondage of the will. In this debate we can see the great divide between the two, a divide that remains in the heart of modernity. Their debate was a matter of words, but it was a prelude to a debate of a different kind, in which words were replaced by deeds and pens by swords, and what had been written in ink was henceforth written in blood.

5 | *The Contradictions of Premodernity*

(On a spring day in May 1631, Count von Tilly celebrated a mass to thank God for his conquest of Magdeburg, the chief city of the Protestant Reformation, boasting that no such victory had occurred since the destruction of Jerusalem. He was only slightly exaggerating—the cathedral in which the mass was held was one of three buildings that had not been burned to the ground. His Catholic League troops had besieged the city since November, living in muddy trenches through the winter snows, enduring the daily jeers and abuse of the Protestant inhabitants of the city. Once they stormed through the gates their zeal, rapacity, and greed knew no bounds. The slaughter was unstoppable. Fires were set throughout the city, children were thrown into the flames, and women were raped before being butchered. Fifty-three women were beheaded in a church where they sought refuge. No one was spared—twenty-five thousand Protestants were massacred or incinerated, and of the five thousand survivors some few were noblemen held for ransom, but all the rest were women who had been carried off to the imperial camp to be raped and sold from soldier to soldier. News of this atrocity quickly spread throughout Europe, hardening the sectarian lines of a conflict that had begun thirteen years before and that would rage on for another seventeen.[1]

(The modern world, as we think of it today, was born in this time of religious conflict and destruction. Beginning in the early sixteenth century and lasting until the middle of the seventeenth century, the Wars of Religion were conducted with a fervor and brutality that were not seen again until our own times. Indeed, the ferocity of the combatants may even have exceeded our own, for almost all the killing took place at close quarters, often in hand-to-hand combat, and thus without the emotionally insulating distance that modern technologies make possible. The slaughter at Magdeburg, for all its horror, was not the first nor the last such event.

During the Peasants' Rebellion in the 1520s, over one hundred thousand German peasants and impoverished townspeople were slaughtered, many of them when they rushed headlong into battle against heavily armed troops, convinced by their leader Thomas Müntzer that true believers were immune to musket balls. In 1572, seventy thousand French Huguenots were slaughtered in the St. Bartholomew's Day Massacre. The Franciscan monks who had preached that killing heretics was the surest way to salvation were pleased, but apparently not as pleased as Pope Gregory XIII, who was so delighted to receive the head of the slain Huguenot leader Coligny in a box that he had a special medal struck commemorating the event. And finally, lest anyone imagine that the barbarity was one-sided, Cromwell's model army sacked the Irish town of Drogheda in 1649, killing virtually everyone. They burned alive all those who had taken refuge in the St. Mary's Cathedral, butchered the women hiding in the vaults beneath it, used Irish children as human shields, hunted down and killed every priest, and sold the thirty surviving defenders into slavery. Cromwell, without the least sense of irony, thanked God for giving him the opportunity to destroy such barbarous heretics.

While these accounts are shocking, they only give us an inkling of the horror of these wars that raged over Europe for more than five generations. By conservative estimates, the wars claimed the lives of 10 percent of the population in England, 15 percent in France, 30 percent in Germany, and more than 50 percent in Bohemia. By comparison, European dead in World War II exceeded 10 percent of the population only in Germany and the USSR. Within our experience only the Holocaust and the killing fields of Cambodia can begin to rival the levels of destruction that characterized the Wars of Religion.

While we call them Wars of Religion, it would be a mistake to assume that religion alone was responsible for the carnage. Political, dynastic, and nationalistic factors clearly played a role in fomenting, perpetuating, and exacerbating the conflict.[2] Machiavellian political techniques also undoubtedly made the killing more effective, but the fanaticism of the participants and the brutality they displayed were in large measure a manifestation of religious passions. These passions grew out of a fundamental disagreement about the nature of God and the relationship of God and man. In chapter 4 we discussed the basis of this disagreement in our examination of Luther's theology and his critique of Catholic doctrines and practices. For Catholicism, the church was the embodiment of the Holy Spirit, imparted by Christ to Peter and handed down by Peter to his successors. The hierarchically organized clergy thus stood between God and man, a conduit for commands from above and requests from below. Like any such mediating institution, it was prone to corruption. For Luther, however, the problem was not the result of the moral failures of individual human beings. The church as a whole was corrupt; it was a false church, merely a tool used by Satan to enslave and exploit humanity. The true church consisted of the elect, that is, all of those who were filled with faith by the grace of God. It was these faithful few, and not the clergy, who Luther believed embodied the Holy Spirit, and who were thus the vehicle through which God manifested himself and worked his will in the world. The antagonism that erupted in the Wars of Religion grew out of these differences.

The church that Luther opposed blended traditional beliefs and practices with innovations brought about as a result of the nominalist revolution. The longstanding dominance of the curia, the church's continuing entanglement in temporal affairs, the worship of saints, the doctrine of purgatory, and other similar traditional elements had been combined with a *via moderna* theology that gave precedence to works over faith, countenanced the sale of indulgences, and promoted other such innovations to create a church that Luther thought could only be the tool of the devil. Luther's protest itself, however, was rooted in the same nominalist revolution that had produced many of the ideas and practices he so vehemently opposed. How can we explain this apparent contradiction? It is important here to distinguish two different strains of the nominalist movement. What Luther rejected was the soft, semi-Pelagian nominalism of Holcot and Biel, but in doing so he turned toward the harder, less compromising nominalism of Bradwardine, d'Autrecourt, and Gregory of Rimini that emphasized the arbitrariness and unpredictability of God's absolute power. Salvation thus could not be gained by works but only by faith, and faith itself came only through grace. Grace, however, was not imparted by ceremonies or sacraments but, as we saw in the last chapter, by the word of God. For Luther then, the path to salvation lay not through the mediating institutions of the church but in an immediate encounter with Scripture. Reform, for Luther, meant not merely eliminating corruption or improving morals but a reordering of one's being by God himself. It was this notion of conversion and all that it implied that catapulted Luther and his followers into a struggle with the church that convulsed Europe for almost one hundred and fifty years.

While the necessity for reform had been widely apparent since the time of Petrarch, it is reasonably clear that most people did not think that such a radical change was necessary. Moreover, there were other means to reform the church. Christian humanism, which we examined in chapter 3, offered a vision of Christianity that resembled that of Luther. Its Christianity was also less ritualistic and more spiritual, and equally critical of corruption and hypocrisy, but also more circumspect in its opposition, not attacking fundamental beliefs and practices directly, employing instead irony and satire, and relying ultimately not on an ecstatic and rapturous rebirth in the spirit but on a system of moral training and education. Christian humanism thus offered a less disruptive and less violent path to reformation that by all estimates had a good chance of success.

Why then was this path so unacceptable to Luther? What was wrong with humanism? One might imagine that Luther was unhappy with humanism because it was so secular, because it pulled Christians away from their faith. Surprisingly, this was not the case. While some humanists may have followed a more secular path, this did not particularly concern Luther. Indeed, in his opinion secular humanists were clearly preferable to many other secular possibilities. What he found intolerable was not *secular* humanism but *Christian* humanism. Indeed, the more Christian humanism was, the more dangerous it seemed to him, the more likely to mislead Christians and distort religious life. The real and essential differences between Luther's thought and the thought of humanism thus become apparent only when accidental factors are eliminated, that is, only when they most nearly approach another.

As we saw in the last two chapters, both humanist and Reformation thought developed as responses to nominalism. The differences between them were largely the result of their differing perceptions about what nominalism was and what needed to be done to overcome it. On basic issues they were in agreement. Both accepted the nominalist critique of scholastic realism and the ontological individualism that was central to nominalism. Both also rejected the nominalist treatment of words as mere signs in favor of a rhetorical or hermeneutic understanding of language. On matters of *metaphysica generalis,* they were thus on remarkably similar ground. The real differences between them emerged in the realm of *metaphysica specialis,* and particularly in their conflicting views of the ontic priority of man and God and of the relationship between them. These differences led to profound disagreements about how Christians ought to live as individuals, in communities, and with respect to their God; and it was these disagreements that brought them into conflict.

Their differences on these matters are a reflection of a deep tension within Christianity itself. What distinguished Christianity from the very beginning was not its monotheism (which it shared with Judaism and later with Islam) but its notion of divine incarnation that bridged the gap between God and man. This notion was a source of great strength in a Roman world in which the distance between gods and men had grown quite large, but it also posed a real problem for Christians because it was so difficult to explain what this meant. How should one understand the claim that God had become a man, and that man could in turn become a God, or at least come to dwell with God? This question was in fact two different but related questions. What is the relationship between the divine and the human (or the Father and Son) within the Godhead, and what is the relationship of other human beings to this God-man? How could there be multiple beings and multiple wills that were coordinated with one another? The early Christian debates between the Arians, Manicheans, Pelagians, and Trinitarians were at heart disagreements about how to make sense of this fundamental Christian notion. Building on a Neoplatonic foundation, the church fathers developed a Trinitarian answer to these questions that became church doctrine at the Council of Nicea and succeeding councils. This doctrine was more fully elaborated by Augustine and his followers. They understood God, in many ways following Plotinus, as absolute intellect, absolute love, and absolute power. They argued that man was created in the image of God, was endowed with freedom, had fallen by his misuse of this freedom, and was redeemed by God's incarnation and self-sacrifice.

This answer was revived and elaborated within an Aristotelian (or Averroist) framework by scholasticism. Scholastics held that the words 'Father' and 'Son' could be meaningfully used in relation to the Godhead, but that the usage had to be understood in terms of an analogy to human life. To say that Jesus Christ is the Son of the Father is to affirm a truth, but in a special way: it is not simply a poetic metaphor or an emotive expression, but neither is it a claim that Jesus Christ is the biological son of God. The medieval scholastics and their predecessors explored the rationality of analogical reasoning with subtlety and insight. Augustine, for example, works through a series of progressively more adequate analogies in *On the Trinity*. Aquinas argued that we can gain some insight into God by reflecting on things and their qualities or attributes. Since everything is created by God, the ways in which things are must reflect something of his nature. The entire project was based, however, on the conviction that people could, to a degree, comprehend rationally how words such as 'father' and 'son' could appear in true statements about God as well as about human beings because the meaning of words was rooted in the real existence of universals. The prominence and pervasiveness of reason in this account made possible the reconciliation of God and man within the Trinity and the coordination of divine and human will in the world. The will *(voluntas)* of the Father, the Son, and the Holy Spirit (embodied in the church) were all thought to be directed by divine reason *(ratio)* that was the supreme moment of divine being. The human will was coordinated with the divine will when it was dominated by reason and sinned when it was not. Hence, the principal goal of a Christian was to overcome the irrational self-will that led to sin and adopt the universal reason of God embodied in his creation, his word, and his church as the basis for the direction of one's life.

For all of its obvious advantages, this scholastic view of the supremacy of reason seemed to many to call into question God's divinity, since it subordinated divine power to reason. As we saw in chapter 1, this Aristotelian scholasticism was condemned in 1277 and attacked by Scotus, Ockham, and the nominalists in the years thereafter. They all rejected the supremacy of reason in God (and man) in favor of will. God could only be God if he were truly omnipotent. The essence of omnipotence in their view, however, was an absolute freedom that was indifferent to its object. God wills what he wills and wills it only because he wills it. While this position saved and affirmed God's divinity, it also opened up another problem, for if reason was not preeminent in God or in the world, it was not clear how the divine and human wills, both in the Trinity and in the world, could be coordinated with one another. In this way, the nominalist revolution brought Christians face to face with the central question that had plagued Christianity from the beginning, and revealed and empowered the Arian, Manichean, and Pelagian alternatives that the Christianity of late antiquity (often with the help of imperial power) had suppressed.

Christian humanists and Reformation theologians had to face these questions. In struggling with them, they developed radically different answers on roughly the same ontological and logical grounds. Their disagreements on this point were not the result of a disagreement about being itself or about the relationship of words and things, but about the priority of one realm of beings to another. As we noted in chapter 3, their disagreements were thus not ontological but ontic. In order to begin to understand why this was the case and how these differences came to play such a decisive role, we will examine the debate between Luther and Erasmus on the freedom or bondage of the will.

Erasmus was the greatest of the humanists after Petrarch, and the culmination of the humanist movement. Luther set the Reformation in motion and his theology remained its driving force for a century and a half. They were also both clearly aware of their preeminence. Moreover, these two were so similar in so many ways that their disagreement turned on real differences, not on trivial or insubstantial points: differences so profound that no reconciliation was possible, differences that made the larger conflict inevitable and that remained salient in many respects for modernity.

[Coleridge once remarked that "utter unlikes cannot but end in dislikes and so it proved between Erasmus and Luther."[3] While he correctly saw that the debate between the two was a necessary consequence of the difference or "unlikeness" of their competing positions, he erred in assuming they were *utterly* unlike. In fact, their similarities far outnumbered their differences. Both criticized scholasticism and agreed that the corruption of the church was intolerable. Both also opposed realism and shared an ontological commitment to individualism. Both were sincerely interested in reform, and both believed that this required a return to Scripture and a new hermeneutic based on an encounter with Scripture in its original languages and historical context. And finally, both gave great prominence to will over reason in both God and man. In light of all these similarities, what is so surprising is that they ever became entangled in a debate, let alone one so vitriolic. Coleridge should have said, "such likes cannot but end in dislike, if they are unlike in one crucial respect." Rather than mitigating their differences, their many similarities highlighted and intensified the central disagreement so dramatically that no compromise or reconciliation was possible.

ERASMUS V. LUTHER

[As we saw in the last chapter, Luther's revolutionary theology developed over a long time. Still, there were crucial turning points in his thought and in his relationship to the church. The debate with Erasmus was one of these. While it was clear after the publication of *The Babylonian Captivity of the Church* (1520) that there could be no reconciliation with the pope, there was still a real question whether reformation would follow a more humanistic or more evangelical path. The debate between Luther and Erasmus settled this point, and it opened up a chasm between the humanists and the reformers.

[Many at the time were surprised that Luther and Erasmus came into conflict, since they believed Luther was a follower of Erasmus. They were both opposed to clerical tyranny and corruption and both promoted a simpler, more personal form of Christianity. Luther had also clearly been influenced by humanist thought. He had entered the monastery "hugging his Plautus and Virgil," wholeheartedly on the side of Reuchlin and his nephew Melanchthon.[4] He had also clearly accepted the humanist dictum that Scripture had to be read in its original languages and had worked hard to master Greek and Hebrew. Moreover, he had been deeply influenced by Valla, Pico, and the other Italian humanists. In view of this, it is not surprising that Luther was regarded by many of the younger humanists as one of their own.[5] All of this notwithstanding and whatever his earlier views, after 1515 Luther categorically denied the central humanist thesis that man is an independent being, committing himself to a theology that saw God and his grace as the source of everything. This new position, however, only gradually became clear to the larger world. Thus, while someone like Melanchthon, who was intimately acquainted with both Luther and Erasmus, could understand their differences, the artist Albrecht Dürer, for example, could still hope in 1521 that Erasmus would assume leadership of the Wittenberg Reformation after Luther was incarcerated.[6] Their affinities and more importantly their common enemies thus masked the crucial differences between Luther's *vera theologia* and Erasmus's *philosophia Christi.*[7]

Erasmus first heard of Luther in December 1516, when Frederick the Wise's chaplain, Georg Spalatin, informed him that an (unnamed) Augustinian monk had taken issue with his interpretation of law in Romans.[8] His first real knowledge of Luther came in 1518 when he read Luther's *Theses on Indulgences,* with which he wholeheartedly agreed. Because of Luther's friendship with Melanchthon, Erasmus assumed he was a kindred spirit. He thus saw the first attacks on Luther as attacks on his own humanistic program.[9] Luther wrote a friendly letter to Erasmus on March 28, 1519, and Erasmus responded two months later encouraging Luther but urging restraint.

While he and Luther were never on friendly terms, Erasmus did support the younger theologian. In April 1519 he interceded on Luther's behalf with Frederick the Wise, asserting that the attacks on Luther were the consequence of the breakdown in the church brought about by scholastic theologians and the mendicant orders.[10] In November 1520 he defended Luther again, telling Frederick the Wise that Luther "has committed a great sin—he has hit the monks in the belly, and the Pope in his crown!"[11]

Despite his continuing support for Luther, their differences were becoming clearer to Erasmus. He knew that he was the target of Luther's charge in a letter of May 28, 1522 that "truth is mightier than eloquence, the spirit stronger than genius, faith greater than learning. . . . Christ fears neither the gates of hell nor the power of the air."[12] However, Erasmus was still convinced as late as 1523 that the monks were his real enemies: "If Luther is brought low, neither God nor man will be able to stand against the monks."[13] He saw much that he agreed with in Luther's protest, even though he disliked his vehemence.

Erasmus tried unsuccessfully to mediate between Luther and the pope, and he grew increasingly frustrated with Luther's unwillingness to moderate demands that Erasmus saw endangering the humanist program of reform. Part of Erasmus's frustration arose from the fact that he thought that accommodation was a religious principle, and he did not understand Luther's position that earthly peace must not be purchased at the price of God's anger.[14]

With the intensification of the dispute, Erasmus found it increasingly difficult to remain impartial. His enemies openly characterized him as the father of Lutheranism. When Luther's books were burned at Louvain on October 8, 1520, he was criticized from the pulpit. It was said that he had laid the egg that Luther had hatched.[15] Latomus and others even suspected that Erasmus was actually a Lutheran.[16] Others were convinced that he was more dangerous to the church than Luther. Erasmus's attempt to mediate the conflict also angered many Lutherans. Ulrich von Hutten, for example, was furious that Erasmus would not take his place at Luther's side.

The pressure thus grew on Erasmus to declare his true allegiance. Luther and Melanchthon hoped that he would support them or at least not oppose them. In fact, Luther promised not to attack Erasmus if Erasmus did not attack him first. When this became known, however, Erasmus was put at a further disadvantage since it seemed that he had had a secret agreement with Luther.[17] Erasmus's position became even more difficult after appeals from the pope and Henry VIII to write against Luther. Eventually, he saw no other choice than to come out against Luther.

Those urging him to enter the fray expected him to defend papal supremacy. Erasmus, however, decided to focus instead on the question of the freedom of the will, which he believed was more essential to the question of reform and also a less divisive topic. Moreover, he determined to write with such moderation that Luther could not take offense.[18] In fact, his work was not an attack at all but a discussion intended to draw Luther into a debate about the central issues of his new theology, where he could not simply hurl his assertions against orthodoxy. Erasmus thought it might thus be possible to avoid schism.

Erasmus titled his work *On the Freedom of the Will*. It treated a question that had bedeviled Christianity since at least the time of Augustine.[19] The question of spiritual freedom was also central to Christian humanism. As we have seen, humanism rested on the assumption that man is capable of directing his actions and taking responsibility for them, that man in other words is not just a creature determined in everything he does by God or fate but a freely choosing moral being whose actions make a difference for his earthly life and for his salvation.

When Melanchthon read *On the Freedom of the Will,* he recognized Erasmus's moderation and promised him Luther would be moderate as well.[20] Luther, however, was furious from the moment he discovered that Erasmus had written against him, describing this act as a "great refusal."[21] When he received *On the Freedom of the Will,* Luther was reluctant to read it, and when he did, he repeatedly wanted to throw it under the bench. While his response was long in coming, it was hard-hitting and unequivocal.[22]

Luther titled his response *On the Bondage of the Will.* While Luther had sought to avoid the debate, he proved himself so adept in conducting it that Erasmus was convinced his response had been ghostwritten by Melanchthon and Justus Jonas.[23] His suspicions were misguided but understandable. Luther demonstrated a rhetorical skill in the work that was as unexpected as it was striking. Despite its rhetorical and theological brilliance, however, the work is often exasperating because it does not answer many of the questions Erasmus poses and often degenerates into a personal attack on Erasmus.

Erasmus was shocked. He had tried to help Luther and was astounded by his response, which he believed to be the result of a deep-seated fatalism and antinomianism. If Luther could turn against someone so near to him, how could he get along with anyone? And what effect would such a teaching have on the behavior of the masses? For Erasmus, the Peasants' Rebellion (1524–26) was the terrifying answer. He was also convinced from Luther's reply that there was nothing more he could do to save him from the abyss of fanaticism. Under such circumstances further discussion was futile.

Erasmus responded to *Bondage of the Will* with *The Shield Bearer* (*Hyperaspistes*), a work published in two long volumes. This is a work of pure self-defense. Luther had blackened his reputation and he had to respond. He did so at length, considering Luther's charges one by one. The work was thus not really intended for Luther, and there is no evidence that Luther ever read it.[24]

Whatever the merits of the arguments, in a practical sense Luther won the debate. After the publication of *Bondage of the Will,* no reconciliation between evangelicalism and humanism was possible. Luther thereby forced those interested in reform to choose between him and Erasmus, and effectively forced Erasmus into the arms of the church. Faced with this choice, those clamoring for reform could hardly fail to side with Luther. However, while Luther won in the short term, he was less successful thereafter. The polarization that this debate engendered strengthened the radical wing of Luther's own evangelical movement, giving greater weight to the Anabaptists and antinomians who found Luther himself too conservative. Moreover, since Luther had argued that inspiration trumped morality, he was unable to urge moral restraint on these radicals. He thus had to call on the armed force of the princes to maintain order. This, however, was a fatal decision. His resistance to individual revelation rendered him increasingly superfluous to the rapidly radicalizing Reformation movement, and his turn to the princes helped legitimize the use of state violence on behalf of religious truth, which was to prove so disastrous over the next century. Thus, while Luther's victory made it inevitable that the Reformation would proceed along a more evangelical path, it thus also increased the probability that it would move in a more radical and violent direction than he desired.

While Erasmus lost the debate in the context of his times and was unable to prevent the violent struggle he so feared, in the long run his theological position proved more successful. His debate with Luther angered both Lutherans and Catholics. Each side thought that he was dissembling, though for different reasons.[25] In part, their suspicions were simply due to his practiced use of irony, which made it difficult to know what he actually believed. Luther thus remarked that "Erasmus is slippery as an eel" and concluded: "Only Christ can grab him!"[26] Erasmus also angered orthodox Catholics. He had not attacked Luther in the way they had expected. He gradually lost favor in the church, and during the pontificate of Paul IV (1555–59) his works were put on the Index of forbidden books. Erasmus's project, however, was also carried forward by both Catholics and Protestants. In the longer term, it was thus not Luther's theocentric and apocalyptic vision that won out but Erasmus's more moderate and moral Christian humanism. In England, Arminianism, which was deeply indebted to Erasmus, became dominant, and within mainline Protestant churches Luther's apocalyptic vision was gradually replaced by Erasmus's more worldly concerns. On the Catholic side as well, it was not Erasmus's opponents who won out, but the Jesuits whose educational project was modeled on that of Erasmus. Erasmus's "victory," however, was a long time in coming, and it was made possible only by the widespread recognition of the dangers of religious fanaticism as a result of the Wars of Religion.

THE IDEA OF THE FREEDOM OF THE WILL IN WESTERN THOUGHT

The question of the *freedom* of the will was largely unknown in Greek antiquity because there was no Greek concept of *will*. The Greeks thought more characteristically in terms of reason ruling or being overpowered by passion. However, the absence of a concept of will did not mean that they did not understand the difference between voluntary and involuntary actions, as Aristotle's famous discussion in the *Nichomachean Ethics* makes clear.

Hellenistic thought was also deeply concerned with the issue of freedom, even if the will was something largely unknown to them.[27] For the Epicureans the end of human life was happiness, which they understood to be *autarchia* and *apatheia,* self-sufficiency and freedom from disturbance. They believed that the chief impediment to such freedom was the fear of death. Since the sources of death in their view were other men and the gods, freedom and happiness could only be obtained by withdrawing from civic life into private association with friends and by coming to understand that the gods were unconcerned with the lives of men.

The Stoics understood happiness in a surprisingly similar manner, but rather than trying to isolate themselves from the world or deny divine intervention in human life, they sought to become one with the divine *logos* that governs all things. To do so was to become a supremely wise man or sage. The sage in their view unites himself with the divine *logos* by means of indubitable or veridical knowledge, which he obtains as a result of *kataleptic* (clear and evident) sense impressions. In this way he can know rather than merely opine and become free by becoming one with fate. All other humans are governed by this incomprehensible fate and thus remain slaves. The wise man, on this account, is not free from the natural causes that move all things, but has an inner spiritual freedom in his union with the whole.

The Academics (or as they were later called, the skeptics) argued that the apodictic knowledge that the Stoics sought was an illusion because for every *kataleptic* impression one found another equally certain and opposite impression could also be found. They thus sought to draw the Stoics into debate to force them to defend their assertions. They believed that the Stoics in this way would inevitably become entangled in contradictions. The skeptics also denied that the Stoics had rightly understood necessity because they made an error in imagining that whatever did happen had happened by necessity, when in fact much that had happened happened because it was freely chosen. In place of the certainty that the Stoics thought could alone constitute knowledge, the Academic skeptics sought the "plausible" or "probable" *(to pithanon),* which they believed could be obtained by a rigorous consideration of matters from a variety of viewpoints. Freedom as the skeptics understood it was thus not an imaginary union with the divine *logos,* nor was it a retreat from existence; rather, it was freedom from illusion, since they were determined to suspend judgment and not to affirm as true propositions that were uncertain. While all humans are bound to the world and its illusions, and must often act on the basis of probable judgments, they do not have to do so unwillingly if they follow the skeptical path.

The preeminent Christian response to this debate was Augustine's early dialogue *Against the Academics.* Augustine was opposed to Academic skepticism but saw it as a step in the right direction, since the Academics in contrast to the Stoics and Epicureans did not accept the reality of the material world. However, they were unable to find happiness because they believed that happiness was the very knowledge that their own practice showed was impossible. As Augustine saw it, the skeptics needed to take the next logical step and recognize that the mind itself in its activity was the truth. He saw this as a step back toward the Platonic idealism they had abandoned. Only by moving in this direction could they enter on the road to happiness. This road in Augustine's view led first to the Plotinian ascent to unity with the divine mind, and then to Christ who liberated human beings not merely in and with the divine logos but as individuals. The way to Christ, however, did not follow the path of reason but of faith, and faith came only through divine illumination.

While the question of freedom thus was an essential concern of ancient thought, it was not explicitly connected to a concept of the will, although this concept too had its origin in this debate as part of the Epicurean effort to resolve the problem of the "swerve" that beset their cosmology. Lucretius used the term *voluntas* to name the innate power that each atom had to move itself apart from all other motions and collisions.[28] He later used the same term to describe human motion.[29] Will was thus from the beginning understood as a power of self-movement. For Lucretius, however, will was not separate from mind. Cicero shared this view although he gave it a Stoic intonation. Drawing on Chrysippus, he wrote in the *Tusculan Disputations* that "will is that which desires something with reason," while that which is incited by something other than reason is not will but *libido.*[30] Seneca took this one step further, arguing that the will acts irrationally when reason itself becomes enslaved to the passions.[31] This view later became important for Augustine.

As we noted above, the question of the will took on a special importance within Christianity because of the need to reconcile divine and human will. Scripture insists that God is both good and all-powerful. It also insists that all human beings have sinned and deserve to be punished. What is not clear is how these are compatible with one another. If God is omnipotent, how can human beings be responsible for anything at all? And if they are not responsible, how can they be guilty? And if they are not guilty, how can they be justly punished? And if their punishment is not just, how can God be good? Ancient Christianity recognized this problem and struggled to find a solution.

The Greek fathers first raised the question of the free will of individual human beings in their struggles against the Stoics and Gnostics, arguing that the human will is free both before and after the Fall.[32] The notion of the freedom of the will within early Christianity, however, was still essentially rationalist and saw the will as subordinate to either divine or human reason. Reason in this sense points the will in a particular direction and there is no diminution in divine or human freedom from doing what reason dictates. The will wills what reason tells it is good, and it thereby acts freely.

Augustine was the first to assert that the will can supersede reason, arguing that the will can do evil even when reason tells it this is wrong.[33] In making this argument, he built on the idea that reason can become enslaved to libidinous passions first suggested by Cicero and Seneca. Augustine employed this notion of the will in his early struggles against the Manicheans. The Manicheans had suggested that if God were omnipotent, he must be the source not merely of good but of evil. And if he were not the source of evil, then there must not be one God, but two, an evil creator and a good redeemer. Augustine countered this argument by asserting the independence of the human will not as a foundation for human dignity but in order to show that the source of evil lay not in God but in man. God grants humans freedom, and they freely choose to do evil. In this way Augustine was able to make divine unity or simplicity compatible with divine goodness.

The problem with the attribution of such freedom to man is that it might be construed to imply that just as humans chose to sin and therefore merited damnation, so they can choose not to sin and thereby earn salvation. This was precisely the conclusion that Pelagius drew. This idea, however, was anathema to Christians because it implied that Christ and his sacrifice were unnecessary. In his attacks upon this position, Augustine was forced to rethink his earlier notion of freedom. In the earlier debate he used the term *libero arbitrio.* In the later debate he sometimes used the term *servum arbitrium,* but more characteristically employed the phrase *liberum arbitrium captivatum,* the free will that has been taken captive by sin. Augustine thus did not abandon the idea of the freedom of the will that is essential to human responsibility, but asserted that it could not be effective without grace. While he believed that grace was necessary to salvation, he was also clear that once the bonds of sin were removed, the individual will had to will the good in order to merit salvation.

Scholasticism revived and formalized this Augustinian notion of the will and as a result was forced to confront the question that Augustine had papered over, that is, how human will could be free in a world ruled by an omnipotent and omniscient God. This proved difficult. Anselm, for example, denied that divine foreknowledge and predestination deprived humans of free will, while simultaneously asserting that events do happen by necessity. Bernard of Clairvaux denied that human will and divine will could each be a partial cause, asserting instead that each had its proper sphere; but what the natures of these spheres were and how they related to one another remained obscure. Bonaventure too thought that the will remained free even in the face of divine preordination because no *external* force limited it, but this did not answer the question of the necessitating *internal* sources of the will, and he thus solved the problem only by defining it out of existence. Aquinas, by contrast, sought to harmonize divine and human will by imagining they were both subordinate to reason. However, as we have seen, this rationalist solution opened up the question of God's absolute power and thus his divinity.

It was this claim that was so unacceptable to Scotus, Ockham and their followers, for they saw it as a denial of God's power and divinity. Already in 1277 Henry of Ghent condemned any suggestion that the intellect determined the will. Scotus similarly reasserted the primacy of will in both God and man and the impossibility of subordinating God's will to reason. However, he did not explain how in this light the human and divine wills could be compatible with one another. And as we have seen, the nominalists themselves were divided on this crucial point.

Within the nominalist movement, there were clearly those who put greater emphasis on divine omnipotence and preordination and those who left greater space for human initiative. That said, it is often difficult to determine where different thinkers stood on this issue. The one thing that does seem relatively clear is that Biel moved considerably closer to Pelagianism than his predecessors. He argued, for example, that fallen reason and will were sufficient for humans to begin their journey to God.[34] Grace was thus not strictly necessary since God would save all those who did everything that they could to lead a Christian life. Luther's Augustinian teacher Usingen was a member of the Biel school. It was this semi-Pelagianism, practically embodied in the *Facientibus* principle, that shaped and tormented the young Luther and that an older Luther so decisively and vehemently rejected.

THE DEVELOPMENT OF THE NOTION OF
WILL IN LUTHER'S THOUGHT

Until 1515, Luther understood the will within the horizon established by Biel and Usingen.[35] As we saw in the last chapter, the crucial event that led him to abandon this notion and rethink his theology was his work on Romans (1515/1516). This investigation gave him a new insight into the nature of divine omnipotence and its meaning for human will. He previously had imagined God to be a distant and incomprehensible judge whom he could never satisfy, but he came to the conclusion that his efforts could not save or damn him because in his omnipotence God was responsible for everything. Thus, neither he nor anyone else could either gain or lose salvation, because faith alone saved and faith came only through grace. Luther's soteriology or doctrine of salvation thus rested on the omnipotence of divine will and the powerlessness of human will. He concluded in his lectures on Romans that "with God there simply is no contingency, but it is only in our eyes. For not even the leaf of a tree falls to the ground without the will of the Father."[36]

Luther reiterates and expands this claim in Article 13 of the *Heidelberg Disputation* (26 April 1518), claiming that "free will, after the fall, exists in name only, and as long as it does what it is able to do, it commits a mortal sin." Human beings are not able to do anything on their own except sin, and all of their supposedly autonomous acts are really an expression of a prideful self-will that is interested only in its own glory and thus in setting itself against God. However good they may appear to be, such acts are evil. In the debate with Eck at the *Leipzig Disputation* (1519) he admitted in the heat of the argument that he was in general agreement on this issue with the convicted heretic Hus.

The question of the freedom of the will also occupied a central location in Luther's *Assertion Against All Articles Condemned in the Bull of Leo X* (1520/1521), which he wrote in reply to the papal bull of condemnation, *Exsurge Domine* (1520). He asked in the thirty-sixth article, "Where, then, is free will?" And answered: "It is completely fictitious."[37] Where then did such an idea come from? He answered: "The teaching of Satan brought this phrase 'free will' into the church in order to seduce men away from God's path into his own paths."[38] He thus concluded:

I misspoke when I said that free will before grace exists in name only; rather I should have simply said: 'free will is a fiction among real things, a name with no reality.' For no one has it within his control to intend anything, good or evil, but rather, as was rightly taught in the article of Wycliff, which was condemned at Constance, all things occur by absolute necessity. That was what the poet meant when he said, 'all things are settled by a fixed law.' [Virgil *Aeneid* 2.324].[39]

This is a striking claim not merely because it puts Luther in league with the heretical Wycliff but because it puts him outside the previous Christian tradition altogether. It has no basis or support in Scripture, the church fathers, or scholasticism. Luther in fact was able to support his claim only by citing a fatalistic pagan poet.[40]

In his *Assertion* Luther thus left himself open to the charge of necessitarianism or theological determinism.[41] There is considerable scholarly disagreement, however, about whether this charge sticks. The answer to this question depends in large measure on how we weigh Luther's different utterances on this issue. When the issue came up in the 1520s, Luther typically sided with Wycliff and seemed to assert that God causes every last thing to happen. This conclusion in his view was the necessary and unavoidable consequence of the fact that under the doctrine of divine simplicity God's foreknowledge and will are one and the same. McSorley, however, legitimately asks whether Luther means what he says. "While there can be no doubt that Luther *said* that all things happen out of absolute necessity," it is not clear he understood the crucial difference between *necessitas consequentiae* (the historical or temporal necessity) and *necessita consequentis* (compelling or causative necessity).[42] Moreover, at times Luther asserted that the will is only unfree in spiritual matters, that is, that it is bound with respect to everything above it, that is, it is unable to do anything to gain or lose salvation, but that with respect to everything beneath it, it is free. How much weight we should give to this assertion, however, is unclear. Given the purpose of Luther's argument, he only needed to show that *spiritual* freedom did not exist, a more limited claim than he typically makes. The more universal necessitarian claim that there is no human freedom of any sort also puts him in company of Wycliff and Hus, two convicted heretics. The fact that he does make the broader claim when he does not need to and when it clearly is disadvantageous to do so suggests that he really did hold something like that position. If this is correct, then his occasional statements indicating that he is only concerned with spiritual freedom have to be discounted as aberrations or rhetorical ploys. This conclusion is strengthened by the fact that the necessitarian position is completely consistent with Luther's theological commitments and his general understanding of the relationship of God and man. It is difficult to see how an omnipotent and omniscient God of the sort that Luther describes could allow any kind of freedom even if he wanted to. If knowing and willing are one for him, then his perfect foreknowledge entails a perfect forewilling of everything in every respect. If this is the case, the distinction of *necessitas consequentiae* and *necessita consequenis* dissolves. If divine knowing and willing are the same, humans cannot be free and the human will must then be merely an illusion.

Luther is obviously concerned that an omnipotent God may be an arbitrary God, but he resists this conclusion, asserting that while God can do anything, he only wants to do what is in his nature, and that is what he has ordained: "The free will which seems to bear on us and temporal things has no bearing on God, for in him, as James says, there is no variation or shadow of change, but here all things change and vary." [43] God's will in other words is not like ours. While we become, he is always the same. Thus, while he is not governed by anything outside himself, he is not capricious or changeable, but is the source of the order in the coming into being and passing away of all the things that are. To believe that we could do anything that he has not already predetermined is consequently an illusion fostered by our arrogance. To believe in free will is, therefore, to sin and to serve Satan.

THE BACKGROUND OF THE DEBATE BETWEEN LUTHER AND ERASMUS

Both Erasmus and Luther had considerable knowledge of the earlier discussions of this issue, and they drew upon this knowledge in a variety of ways. An examination of their debate reveals that each saw himself and the other against the background of the debate between the Epicureans, Stoics, and Skeptics on the question of human freedom. This debate had already played a role in earlier humanist discussions, and both Luther and Erasmus were acquainted with it through Augustine's *Against the Academics* and *The City of God*, as well as Cicero's *Academica* (published in 1471) and a number of his other works. [44] How each situated himself in the context of this debate and how each tried to situate his opponent gives us an important insight into the argument that is carried on not just in the lines of the debate but between them.

Both Luther and Erasmus portray themselves as Augustinians, but since Augustine is equivocal on the issue of the freedom of the will, their claims leave considerable room for disagreement. Erasmus clearly prefers the earlier anti-Manichean Augustine and Luther the later anti-Pelagian Augustine, but neither stops there. Erasmus, like his humanist predecessors, wants to interpret the earlier Augustine's notion of the free will in a Neoplatonic fashion, drawing on church fathers such as Origen and Jerome. He also adopts a skeptical position on matters open to interpretation and employs a skeptical strategy in his attempts to draw Luther into discussion. Luther, by contrast, does not rely on the other church fathers or on any philosopher for support but turns instead to Scripture, which in his view speaks directly and indubitably to the individual Christian. His experience of Scripture and his assertion of its absolute certainty, however, are essentially Stoic.[45] Similarly, he resists being drawn into a discussion and insists upon a more judicial proceeding because he understands the skeptical trap that Erasmus has set for him. He also recognizes Erasmus's attempt to make use of this earlier debate to portray himself as a moderate, but he is convinced that Erasmus is disingenuous, concealing his true Pelagian position. He seeks to bring this out in his response. In light of the position Luther takes in *Bondage of the Will,* Erasmus comes to believe that Luther is not merely a Stoicizing Augustinian but a Manichean, a fatalist, and an antinomian. Each thus tries to occupy an Augustinian position, modified somewhat in one direction or the other. Each, however, also suspects that the other is disingenuously trying to portray himself as more moderate than he actually is, and in their ripostes each thus portrays the other as more radical than he actually was.

ERASMUS'S *DIATRIBE*

The debate began with the publication of Erasmus's *On the Free Will: Diatribe or Discussion.* As its title suggests, the work is a diatribe, which classically is a form of deliberative and not epidictic rhetoric, thus not a form of attack but of discussion.[46] Erasmus adopts this mode in part to derail the public inquisition of Luther, but also in an effort to turn the matter in a more philosophical direction.[47] Substantively, Erasmus seeks to engage Luther on the issue that lies at the heart of his differences with the humanists and in a very real sense at the heart of Christianity—the question of the relationship of the divine and human wills.[48]

Erasmus begins by stating that he does not want to engage in a debate and prefers instead a friendly discussion about a question that he himself finds very puzzling, the question of free will. This beginning, as Luther and many others have recognized, is disingenuous, an example of the Socratic irony for which Erasmus was famous. Erasmus's questions, like those of Socrates, are anything but innocent. They are rather an attempt to lure others into a discussion in which their deepest beliefs can be shown to be contradictory. This was a style perfected by Academics such as Arcesilaus and Carneades in their debates with the Stoics, and it is a style that Erasmus adopts here, hoping to draw the assertive Luther into a discussion that will leave him suspended in uncertainty. Erasmus, of course, does not mean to promote total skepticism. He accepts the principal tenets of the Christian faith and nowhere calls them into question. However, he does not believe that Scripture can be interpreted with the absolute certainty Luther claims and hopes through a discussion to get Luther to recognize this fact and act more moderately, seeking consensus rather than delivering pronouncements from on high.

Erasmus justifies this approach not as the surest road to absolute truth but as the surest way to avoid error and the internecine conflict that results from the fanatical defense of what are really only probable opinions. In this indirect way, he thus suggests that Luther's assertive position is unjustifiable and that it is likely to promote public confusion and violence rather than piety. The implication is of course that Luther is acting contrary to principles of Christian charity and the pacifistic teachings of Christ.[49]

In opposition to this claim to indubitable knowledge and a monopoly on morality, Erasmus raises the question of a criterion. What is missing in Luther's assertion of his own infallibility, according to Erasmus, is a criterion of the truth.[50] The question of the criterion was not new to Erasmus. It was the club that the ancient skeptics used against the Stoics (and it was the club that Catholic apologists would use against their Protestant rivals for the next one hundred and fifty years). It calls into question the subjective foundation of experience that Luther and his followers rely on. How, Erasmus asks, can you Luther be sure that Wycliff was a holy man and the Arians heretics?[51] Both make claims to know the truth but they do not agree. Moreover, how can the truth you are subjectively certain of be evaluated by others? Why should we trust your subjective impression or for that matter our own more than that of anyone else? One might claim that such certainty is warranted because it comes from God, but this claim is complicated by the fact that others make similar claims that do not agree with your own. Scripture also suggests that God may not want his teachings to be immediately clear to all. Furthermore, how do you know that it is God rather than Satan who fills you with this sense of certainty?[52] And if you do have the truth, why are there so many great men who stand against you and only three who agree with you—Valla, Hus, and Wycliff—the first in trouble and the latter two already condemned as heretics?[53] Here again Erasmus falls back on a skeptical mode of questioning, seeking to draw Luther into discussion. What Luther needs, according to Erasmus, are firm arguments when all that he has are assertions, which themselves rest only on the fundamental claim that "I have the Spirit of Christ, which enables me to judge everyone but no one to judge me; I refuse to be judged, I require compliance."[54]

The crucial issue in the debate, however, is not epistemological and methodological but substantive. It is the question of the relationship of God and man. Luther had argued in his *Assertion* that God was responsible both before and after the Fall for everything, that there never was and never would be free will. Erasmus argues in opposition that "mankind was created so as to have free will; the tyrant Satan took it away as a captive, grace restored and augments it."[55] Before the Fall man was free and after the Fall his natural liberty was vitiated but not extinguished, and a spark of reason and virtue remained although it could not be effective without further grace.[56] The Fall was thus much less severe than Luther claimed. In opposition to Luther's assertion of the utter nullity of man, Erasmus remarks: "You make lost health into death."[57]

Erasmus in this way sees Luther, like the Stoics, relying on an absolute standard of truth in a world in which there is no infallible standard or criterion. He knows that Luther believes that Scripture is such a criterion, but he knows it cannot serve this function. Scripture is filled with contradictions and obscurities. In part this is because God wants some things to remain unknown, but it is also the result of the fact that different people read Scripture differently depending on the goal they have in view.[58] Many of the apparent contradictions in Scripture are thus not in the text but in the exegesis of the text. Coming to terms with Scripture requires not the uncompromising assertion of what one believes Scripture to mean, but a broad, communal discussion that reflectively compares the multiple views of one's contemporaries and one's predecessors. It is on these issues that Erasmus believes we must act like skeptics and suspend judgment, not on basic Christian doctrine.

The core issue for Erasmus is Luther's unequivocal assertion that God is responsible for everything and that anything man does on his own is sin. For Erasmus this unnecessarily denigrates human beings and removes all the traditional religious incentives for moral behavior. Erasmus recognized Luther's concern with Pelagianism, but he believed that Luther's critique so exaggerated the effects of original sin and the Fall that he came close to Manicheanism.[59]

For Erasmus it is crucial not that God be omnipotent but that he be good.[60] He thus tries to counterbalance Luther's argument in order to preserve divine goodness and promote human responsibility. If humans did not have some degree of freedom, it is difficult to see how God could act justly in punishing sinners or what incentives humans could have to act morally. Erasmus was well aware that his position might be seen as Pelagian and tried to show why it was not. In his view there were five different competing positions on this issue. Pelagians believe that extraordinary works of charity or virtue can win salvation without grace. Scotists believe man is able to do morally good works without grace that merit salvation.[61] Augustine believes that salvation requires grace alone but does not abolish the human will, which works in coordination with grace. Karlstadt believes that grace is essential and that the will is only free to do evil. And finally, Luther believes that grace is the source of everything and that the will is free to do neither good nor evil. Erasmus considers the positions of Pelagius, Karlstadt and Luther to be unorthodox, that of Scotus acceptable but incorrect, and that of Augustine best and closest to his own.

Erasmus believed that Christ's sacrifice gave human beings the chance to accept or reject grace when God offered it to them. This sacrifice, however, did not entirely restore them to their prelapsarian state. In contrast to Adam before the Fall, the human will is now biased toward evil.[62] Humans consequently need God's further assistance in completing the project that their free choice begins with its acceptance of grace. Erasmus thus asserts that while human beings owe the beginning and end of their redemption to God, the middle depends chiefly on them. He consequently contends that his position is both Augustinian and orthodox. But is this the case?

There is some reason to doubt that Erasmus sincerely holds the view he describes here. Elsewhere he asserts that free will is "a power of the will, by means of which man is able to apply himself or turn away from the things that lead to eternal salvation."[63] This statement seems to attribute much more to the will than the position outlined above. When discussing this matter, he also at times does not mention grace at all or suggests that nature itself is grace in the Neoplatonic manner we noted in Ficino.[64] This view is certainly problematic for most Christians, and it is hard to find anyone other than Erasmus who defines man's natural freedom in terms of a supernatural goal without mentioning grace.[65] This point is further strengthened by the fact that Erasmus draws no distinction between natural and acquired freedom, which seems to imply that grace is not needed to help man regain his freedom. He thus seems to believe that the fallen will is not enslaved by sin. Given all this, it is difficult to see how Erasmus's position differs from the classical moral doctrine of Plato and his humanist admirers. Erasmus thus seems to be caught between two worlds, clearly recognizing from a religious point of view that grace is essential and that Pelagianism is heterodox, but admiring and promoting a Neoplatonic moral doctrine similar to that of Pico. On the whole, while Erasmus does not deny the efficacy of grace, he does radically deemphasize it.

Erasmus is more concerned with life in this world than in the next. He does not forget the afterlife, but concern with it does not dominate his view of the moral decisions that humans have to make here and now. In this respect he stands in sharp contrast to Luther who, as we saw in the last chapter, lives in anticipation of the final judgment. While Erasmus does not deny the coming end of the world, he also does not believe it is coming anytime soon. In contrast to Luther who believed an immediate reformation was necessary regardless of the cost, Erasmus was convinced that there was time for a program of education in his *philosophia Christi* that would bring about a gradual improvement in both morality and piety.[66]

LUTHER'S *THE BONDAGE OF THE WILL*

Luther's response to Erasmus was entitled *The Bondage of the Will*. The title was derived from one of the phrases Augustine used in his debate with Pelagius. By choosing this phrase, Luther associated himself with Augustine and Erasmus with Pelagius, and thus announced that the goal of the work which was to show that Erasmus was Pelagian whether he admitted it or not.[67] As we discussed above, Erasmus had sought to turn the confrontation with Luther into a discussion rather than a judicial proceeding. Luther not only rejects this opening, he frames his response as a judicial case against Erasmus. Erasmus had presented himself as a man with doubts who hoped to have them resolved by discussion. Luther presents himself as the advocate for God, seeking to convict Erasmus as a sinner.[68] Erasmus thought of himself as an Augustinian fortified by Academic skepticism. Luther thinks of himself as an Augustinian fortified by Stoicism. Erasmus for him is a protean dissembler who hides behind a series of masks, pretending to be an Augustinian, when in fact he is a Pelagian, a skeptic, an Epicurean, and an atheist, all themselves just further masks for the devil who has concealed himself in Erasmus and who must be forced into the open.[69] On the deepest level, Luther thus sees this as a struggle not with Erasmus but with Satan, and seeks to advance the cause of Christ by showing that Erasmus's philosophy of Christ is mere camouflage for the promotion of the cause of Satan.

Luther begins by in effect declaring that Erasmus is not a Christian.[70] In his view this is evident from the very fact that Erasmus wants to initiate a discussion. Any real Christian in his opinion knows that Christians do not discuss but profess their faith by firm assertions. A real Christian stands up for his faith and is willing to fight for it. Erasmus, by contrast, prefers peace above all else and therefore cannot really be pious. The Christian path "is not to collect the world into a harmony but to set it in opposition to itself: not *collatio* but *collisio*."[71]

Luther thus claims that a Christian is defined by faith and not by discursive reason. But what does he mean by this? In a revealing passage he asserts that Christians must avoid the pitfalls of the skeptics and Epicureans, which open them up to atheism, and hope for men who are as inflexible as the Stoics.[72] This passage points to Luther's acceptance of the rhetorical framework that Erasmus employed. If Erasmus wanted to adopt the position of the skeptics, Luther is happy to adopt the position of the Stoics. There are many similarities between their position and his own. For the Stoics there was only a single truth and it was known only by the Stoic sage who had become one with the divine *logos*. Luther makes a surprisingly similar argument, although the *logos* he has in mind is Scripture and not reason. Moreover, for the Stoics only the sage is free while everyone else is a slave. This too is Luther's claim as he spelled it out in *Christian Liberty*, although the Stoic sage is transformed into the Christian who is "free" only because he is seized by God. Similarly, for the Stoics all those who do not know the truth are equally lost in error and do evil even when they think they are doing good. Again this is Luther's teaching: all those who are not infused with grace are equally lost. As for the Stoics, all evils for Luther are equal; there is no distinction between mortal and venial sins. Finally, what especially distinguishes the Stoic sage is the certainty of his knowledge. The truth for him is so overwhelming that nothing can shake it. This is possible, however, only because of the *kataleptic* impressions that gives him clear and distinct knowledge that eliminates even the possibility of doubt.[73] This too is Luther's position, although he sees this impression arising from the experience of Scripture and not sense perception.

The true Christian for Luther is an Augustinian but an Augustinian who is rooted in something very much like Stoicism. Nothing is more troubling in Luther's opinion than uncertainty and the only thing that resolves this uncertainty is faith. For Augustine, faith is a consequence of an inner illumination, and it comes about as a result of following the skeptical path to its end. He stresses the inner moment of self-certainty that results from the performative contradiction in trying to doubt one's own existence.

Luther, by contrast, focuses on the impact of God's word in generating this certainty. In this respect his thought is more Stoic than Augustinian. For the Stoics one was struck by an undeniable and irresistible impression that actually shaped the soul in an irreversible manner. The Stoics called this experience a turning around, a *metabolê*, or *conversio*.[74] For Luther this is the experience in which Scripture takes hold of a man and speaks directly to and through him. In this moment, the Christian like the Stoic is turned around and redirected. He is turned around, however, not by an undeniable sense impression but by the overpowering experience of the word of God. Conversion thus depends not on reason but on divine will that grasps and possesses the Christian. Scripture thus saves, but it saves only when God grasps us with it, that is, only when grace takes such possession of us that nothing can change our conviction, when we "cannot do otherwise," and cannot even want to do otherwise.

Scripture for Luther is thus not a text to be interpreted, or human speech, but the word of God. And the divine words are not mere drops of meaning that fill up the human mind but the irresistible hand of God that takes hold of us and transforms us. The language of Scripture is thus not a form of discourse that has to be interpreted by humanity, as Erasmus had imagined, but God himself working his will in and through us. In Luther's view, to suggest that the truth of Scripture can be revealed only if one abjures judgment and engages in a broad-based discussion with others about its meaning is thus to miss the decisive point of Christian religion. Only someone who has not been grasped by God could believe such a thing. Luther thus rebukes Erasmus with his famous claim that "the Holy Spirit is not a skeptic."[75] God in other words does not reason with Christians but takes possession of them and uses them for his own ends.

Erasmus suggested that a Christian should adopt a skeptical stance because he had doubts about how to interpret Scripture. Luther discounts this view because in his mind a real Christian simply cannot doubt. Moreover, doubts are not something that need or ought to be managed by discussion and consensus; they must be experienced in the depths of one's soul, because they are the prelude to faith. Luther knew this from personal experience: "I myself was offended more than once, and brought to the very depth and abyss of despair, so that I wished I had never been created a man, before I realized how salutary that despair was, and how near to grace."[76] The path to faith for Luther passes through the abyss of despair. To argue that humans must suspend judgment on matters of this sort as Erasmus suggests is thus to abandon Christ.

In his response to Erasmus, Luther emphasizes God's complete freedom and the utter nullity of man. Free will for him is a divine name, and he is unwilling to call anything less freedom. He believes the crucial issue between him and Erasmus is the distinction between God's power and our own. He takes an uncompromising position: "God foreknows nothing contingently. . . . He foresees, purposes, and does all things according to his own immutable, eternal and infallible will. . . . His will is eternal and changeless, because his nature is so. . . . [And as a result] the will of God is effective and cannot be impeded, since power belongs to God's nature; and His wisdom is such that He cannot be deceived." [77] Luther claims here that God is absolute and could in principle will anything but in fact wills what is in his own nature to will. Therefore, God's *potentia absoluta* is in actuality the same as his *potentia ordinata* because what he has ordained is what he is. This does not mean that God is rational or that the world unfolds in a way we can understand. Luther follows Scotus in asserting that "it is not because he is or was obliged so to will that what he wills is right, but on the contrary, because he himself so wills, therefore what happens must be right." [78] He does not, however, change his mind and will something that he has not ordained.

All things other than God are consequently contingent. As contingent, these things are all also subordinate to his will. This dependence is not accidental or avoidable but ontological and inevitable. Luther recognizes that we seem to ourselves to be free because we choose between one thing and another. However, human choice is ultimately an illusion because humans cannot choose what they want to choose. [79] While God may be indifferent in his choices, humans never are, and always choose and will only what they are motivated to choose or will. [80]

That this is an extraordinarily radical position becomes clear in what is certainly one of the most famous passages in the work: "Thus the human will is placed between the two like a beast of burden. If God rides it, it wills and goes where God wills. . . . If Satan rides it, it wills and goes where Satan wills; nor can it choose to run to either of the two riders or to seek him out, but the riders themselves contend for the possession and control of it." [81] This passage lays out in the starkest terms Luther's differences with humanism. In his *Assertion* Luther had argued in Augustinian fashion that free will was responsible for sin even if it was powerless to gain salvation. In his attribution to the will of at least the power to sin, he took a position that was compatible with some forms of humanism. In *The Bondage of the Will,* by contrast, he argues that humans are not even responsible for sin. They are all ridden by Satan. All of those who are not in God's kingdom are the devil's slaves. Humans sin and are damned not from weakness of the understanding or corruption of the will but because of the wickedness of Satan. Satan rules over all non-Christians including the most virtuous pagans, and even the best philosophers are misled by Satan into thinking they are free when in fact they are motivated by the same prideful self-love that Satan aroused in Adam.[82] Human beings without God thus do evil with no hope of escape. They cannot know the good, they cannot will the good, and they cannot even obey the law that God himself promulgated for them.

Salvation in Luther's view is thus only possible when God drives Satan from the saddle and rides in his place. Humans can become free only by becoming slaves to God. This too is an adaptation of a Stoic position—only the sage is free and he is only free by becoming one with the divine *logos* and thereby reconciling himself with fate. The difference in Luther's case is that man himself can do nothing to bring this about. It is the result of sheer grace. As McSorley remarks, in Luther's theology there is thus no divine call to conversion, no admonition to steadfastness in justice or avoidance of sin, no struggle of man with Satan, no personal dialogue which presupposes a free response to what is found in Scripture, but only a struggle of God and Satan.[83] The advantage of this new bondage is that it eliminates uncertainty, for when God comes to ride man

> the spirits are to be tested and proved by two sorts of judgment. One is internal, whereby through the Holy Spirit or a special gift of God, anyone who is enlightened concerning himself and his own salvation, judges and discerns with the greatest certainty the dogmas and opinions of all men. . . . But this judgment helps no one else, and with it we are not here concerned, for no one, I think, doubts its reality. There is therefore another judgment, whereby with the greatest certainty we judge the spirits and the dogmas of all men, not only for ourselves, but also for others and for their salvation.[84]

God's triumph in Luther's view thus eliminates all our doubts, for when he rules in our souls, we cannot err. We also know without any hint of doubt who belongs to God and who to Satan.

Luther's claim here is a clear break with the previous Christian tradition.[85] There is a good chance, however, that Luther did not recognize this fact. The image of man as a beast ridden by God or the devil has been traced by scholars back to Origen and the Manicheans, but Luther apparently knew it from the *Hypognosticon*, which he and many of his contemporaries mistakenly believed to have been written by Augustine.[86] Luther therefore wrongly concluded that this image of God was orthodox. Whether Luther was mistaken on this point, however, is not nearly as important as the question of the meaning of this doctrine for Christianity. Is this actually a Christian position?

While many of Luther's critics have come to the conclusion that it is not Christian but Manichean, there is crucial difference between Luther's position and that of the Manicheans. For the Manicheans there is an actual struggle between good and evil, the outcome of which is in doubt. In Luther's case God triumphs instantly.[87] There are thus not two quasi-equal Gods but one who manages the whole show. Here we see the continuing impact of the nominalist notion of omnipotence. Hans Blumenberg has suggested that divine omnipotence became a problem for late medieval and early modern thought because of the inadequacy of Augustine's solution to the problem of Gnosticism.[88] This conclusion, however, is incorrect. The problem is not the recurrence of divine dualism and a cosmological struggle of good and evil. In fact, there is no cosmological struggle at all. God's absolute power makes that an impossibility. There *appears* to be a conflict only from the perspective of individual human beings. Luther's notion is thus not Manichean but closer to the Stoic notion of a divine *logos* or fate that determines all things. There is nothing that can be done to change this, and the only hope for individual human beings is that God will tear them away from Satan and unite them with this *logos* and this fate, making it their *logos* and their fate, thus liberating them from their slavery.[89]

The absolute supremacy of God, however, opens up a deeper and more disturbing problem, for it turns the conflict of good and evil, of God and Satan, that is so central for Luther, into a sham, for Satan himself is clearly a creature of God and therefore subordinate to his will. God is both good and evil, and Christians therefore cannot become children of the light without also becoming children of darkness. The Christian who like the Stoic sage becomes one with the divine *logos* thus does not simply become good but also evil. This is not, of course, what Luther asserts but it is the concealed corollary of his argument.

As we discussed in the last chapter, divine omnipotence in this way leads Luther to the notion of the *deus absconditus* or hidden God. Luther recognized quite clearly that his understanding of divine power leaves no possibility for any cause except God himself. Hence, while the great struggle of good and evil that is won by Christ on the cross seems quite real, it is also a *deus ex machina,* for as Luther himself recognized there is a divine puppeteer behind the scene who brings the stage and all its characters into being and moves them about as he wills. The source of all good and all evil for Luther is and can only be God himself. Luther, however, believes that it is crucial that this divine puppeteer remain concealed, and that Christians focus not on him but on the speeches presented on his behalf by the puppets on the stage. Thus, he argues:

To the extent, therefore, that God hides himself and wills to be unknown to us, it is no business of ours. . . . God must therefore be left to himself in his own majesty, for in this regard we have nothing to do with him, nor has he willed that we should have anything to do with him. But we have something to do with him insofar as he is clothed and set forth in his Word, through which he offers himself to us. . . . For it is this that God as he is preached is concerned with, namely that sin and death should be taken away and we should be saved. . . . But God hidden in his majesty neither deplores nor takes away death, but works life, death, and all in all. For there he has not bound himself by his word, but has kept himself free over all things. . . . It is our business, however, to pay attention to the word and leave that in-scrutable will alone, for we must be guided by the word and not by that inscrutable will.[90]

For Luther it is crucial that we take Scripture not to be speeches or ac-counts written by men but the living word of God, the method by which God grasps us, possesses us, and enslaves us, folding us into his being, making us one with him. It is this word that saves all Christians and it is by this word that they must be directed. This is not the *logos* of the world in a strict sense since that narrative would have to include all of God's actions in the world. That larger narrative and its author must remain concealed, in Luther's view. What we need to heed is our narrative, the lines that are written for us, so that we can play our part in this cosmo-theological drama.

But how can this satisfy human beings? The Stoic identification with the divine *logos* brings with it true knowledge free from all opinion and error. It submerges us in the truth. For Luther our identification with God's word is only possible if we avert our eyes from the truth, if we accept and live the scriptural story, even though we know that there is a deeper and more all-encompassing story that calls into question the story we live by. There is thus good reason to doubt that this path can satisfy human beings, for it cannot eliminate the uncertainty and anxiety evoked by the monstrously incomprehensible God who stands behind the stage and is responsible for everything that occurs on it. The nominalist God in all of his power and incomprehensibility thus lurks just beneath the surface of Luther's gra-cious redeemer. Reflecting on this hidden God, Wilhelm Dantine thus rightly points to the "vibrating undertone of terror" that runs throughout *The Bondage of the Will*.[91]

The doctrine of the hidden God presents Luther with a problem that is deeply disquieting, for if the concealed God is the real God and the revealed God merely the mask he presents to humans in Scripture, how can Luther know that he will keep his promises, particularly about salvation? How can this God provide the certainty Luther needs? Or to put the matter in other terms, Luther's theology requires the omnipotence of God and the nullity of man in order to relieve man of uncertainty, but this incomprehensible omnipotence itself undermines the very certainty he seeks. Luther admits:

> He is God, and for his will there is no cause or reason that can be laid down as a rule or measure for it, since there is nothing equal or superior to it, but it is itself the rule of all things. For if there were any rule or standard for it, either as cause or reason, it could no longer be the will of God. For it is not because he is or was obliged so to will that what he wills is right, but on the contrary, because he himself so wills, therefore what happens must be right. Cause and reason can be assigned for a creature's will, but not for the will of the Creator, unless you set up over him another creator.[92]

This passage demonstrates the continuing power of the extreme voluntarist position that played such an important role in shaping the nominalist movement. Luther seeks to make this God palatable to human beings by asserting that faith requires us to trust this God's judgments more than our own, for "many things as seen by God are very good, which as seen by us are very bad."[93] This assurance offers an abstract comfort, but this can hardly be convincing to anyone, Luther included. Divine inscrutability in the end is not comforting but terrifying.

Luther like the Stoics believed that happiness and a kind of freedom was to be found in union with the divine *logos*. This union for Luther, however, differed in several respects from that of the Stoics. First, for Luther it did not entail the dissolution of human individuality. Man was not lost in a Neoplatonic or Averroist One; rather God's will became the will of the individual. As Luther put it in his *Lectures on Romans,* "God is all-powerful through me." As we saw in the preceding chapter, the consequences of this unification are quite different than those of Stoicism. It does not lead to *apathia,* to a dispassionate acceptance of fate, but empowers the individual will with a sense of divine mission. What I do becomes God's work, a calling that is subject to no earthly judgment or limits. Already in Luther, but even more clearly in the radicals who followed in his wake, we see the consequence of his position.

Second, when the Christian is grasped by the word, he becomes certain because he cannot doubt that God's promises are true. He thus takes God's *potentia ordinata* to be insuperable. However, this certainty can be sustained only by avoiding reflection on the hidden God, the *deus absconditus,* whose *potentia absoluta* undermines this certainty. And yet, insofar as one's faith rests on God's omnipotence, it is impossible to leave this God concealed, impossible not to speculate on what is possible by means of his absolute power. The believer thus hovers between these two visions of God, and his faith can be sustained only by constantly revivifying the *kataleptic* experience of the word of God by which he was converted into a Christian. Tortured by the doubts that divine omnipotence engenders, he must constantly recur to the Scripture, to preaching and teaching to counteract the corrosive effect of this vision of the hidden God. The Stoic reading of Augustinian Christianity that Luther develops in his response to Erasmus thus can only with great difficulty be combined with the notion of omnipotence that Luther received from nominalism.

Perhaps even more important from a Christian point of view is the fact that Luther leaves open the question of the origin of evil that was so central to the debate between Augustine and the Manicheans. He attributes evil to Satan, but he does not explain Satan's relationship to God or how Satan became evil. As a creature, to use Luther's own analogy, Satan must at some point have been ridden by God. How then did he become a rider?[94] And if Satan was able to become a rider, why shouldn't God's other creatures as well? Why not us? Moreover, what makes Satan evil? The answer for Luther seems to be merely the fact that God wills him to be evil and wills that what he does is evil.[95]

Not only does Luther have no explanation for Satan's evil, he also cannot explain the Fall, which in the absence of human freedom and responsibility is morally meaningless. If God is as omnipotent as Luther contends, no individual can be responsible for his sins and therefore no one can justly be condemned. The fact that God does condemn some people to damnation for the evil that he himself elicits leads inevitably to the conclusion that God is unjust. In trying to make sense of this, Luther occasionally recurs to the scholastic argument that "God cannot act evilly although he does evil through evil men, because one who is himself good cannot act evilly; yet he uses evil instruments that cannot escape the sway and motion of his omnipotence," but this is an unconvincing argument and he is well aware of this fact.[96] More characteristically, however, he simply admits that God "acts even in Satan and the impious."[97] In responding to Erasmus on this point, Luther in the end takes refuge in the notion of divine inscrutability, asserting that while we cannot understand how God can be righteous in causing evil in others and then punishing them for it, we must accept this, because his justice is beyond our comprehension. Indeed, "this is the highest degree of faith, to believe him merciful when he saves so few and damns so many, and to believe him righteous when by his own will he makes us necessarily damnable, so that he seems, according to Erasmus, to delight in the torments of the wretched and to be worthy of hatred rather than of love."[98]

While Luther would like his God to be both omnipotent and good, in the end he is more concerned to preserve divine power than divine justice. Here the contrast with Erasmus is palpable, and it leads Luther to assert that Erasmus's God is Aristotle's God, a God of reason, or as he cleverly puts it, God asleep, entrusting everything to men.[99] His God, by contrast, is active all the time, and his creatures are all merely tools with which this God carries out his hidden purposes. They are "God's 'masks' (*larvae*) *behind which he works in secret.*"[100] Thus, for Luther "everything we do, everything that happens, even if it seems to us to happen mutably and contingently, happens in fact nonetheless necessarily and immutably, if you have regard to the will of God."[101] Luther complains that men of outstanding ability through the ages have wrongly demanded that God should act according to man's idea of right and do what seems proper to them, or else he should cease to be God. That very attitude is wrong-headed in his opinion because it suggests that God should give way before a fragment of his creation.[102] Luther's God, like the God of Job, does not need to justify himself to man.

For Erasmus God created the world, endowed men with freedom, intervened again to pick man up when he fell, and continues to assist him in his efforts to reach maturity. God is thus involved with his creation but more peripherally. For Luther the situation is almost exactly the reverse. God acts continually to bring everything about. Humans do nothing on their own and are therefore merely spectators to their own possession even if they do not generally recognize this fact. He berates Erasmus: "You think of both God and the devil as a long way off, and as if they were only observers of that mutable free will; for you do not believe that they are the movers and inciters of a servile will, and engaged in most bitter conflict with one another."[103]

Luther thus concludes that God is responsible for everything and man for nothing. As distasteful as this may sound, Luther would not have it any other way:

> I frankly confess that, for myself, even if I could be, I should not want 'free-will' to be given me, not anything to be left in my own hands to enable me to endeavor after salvation; not merely because in face of so many dangers, and adversities, and assaults of devils, I could not stand my ground and hold fast my 'free-will' (for one devil is stronger than all men, and on these terms no man could be saved); but because, even were there not dangers, adversities, or devils, I should still be forced to labor with no guarantee of

success, and to beat my fists in the air. If I lived in the world to all eternity, my conscience would never reach comfortable certainty as to how much it must do to satisfy God. Whatever work I had done, there would still be a nagging doubt *(scrupulous)* as to whether it pleased God, or whether He required something more. . . . But now that God has taken my salvation out of the control of my own will, and taken it under the control of his, and promised to save me, not according to my working or running, but according to His own grace and mercy, I have the comfortable certainty that he is faithful and will not lie to me, and that He is also great and powerful so that no devils or opposition can break Him or pluck me from Him. . . .Thus it is that, if not all, yet some, indeed many are saved; whereas by the power of 'free-will' none at all could be saved, but every one of us would perish.[104]

As Erasmus suggested and as Luther admits, the practical consequence of his vision of Christianity is not peace but war. This war unfolds on several fronts. First, there is the struggle between the church of the world and the true church made up of the elect. The former is the tool of Satan, the latter of God. To defend the latter with all one's power and wit is in Luther's view the chief duty of every true Christian. Nor is this an accidental struggle: "This tumult has arisen and is directed from above, and it will not cease till it makes all the adversaries of the Word like the mud on the streets." [105] To insist on peace, as Erasmus did, was for Luther simply to confirm the triumph of Satan. Better to fight and perish, to be driven out and hunted down in this world than to deny God: "Surely it would be preferable to lose the world rather than God the creator of the world, who is able to create innumerable worlds again, and who is better than infinite worlds! For what comparison is there between things temporal and things eternal?" [106] Luther did not try to conceal the practical consequences of this doctrine. In reflecting on the Peasants' Rebellion, he remarked: "I see other great troubles in time to come, by comparison with which these present seem no more than the whisper of a breeze or the murmur of a gentle stream." [107] And in response to Erasmus's concerns that his bellicose dogmatism would allow evil to triumph, he responded: "As to your saying that a window is opened for impiety by these dogmas, let it be so." [108] His wish unfortunately was granted.

ERASMUS'S *HYPERASPISTIS*

Erasmus's response to Luther was entitled *A Warrior Shielding (Hyperaspistes): A Discussion of Free Will Against the Enslaved Will by Martin Luther.* Luther's response to his initial argument convinced Erasmus that schism was unavoidable. He had already recognized the likely result of Luther's teaching in the *Diatribe:* "This seditious wantonness of your pen . . . brings destruction down on all good things." [109] He had been convinced that Luther's agitation would not eliminate corruption, improve morals, or foster real piety but instead would aggravate the "tyranny of princes, bishops, theologians and monks"; liberal studies would be disregarded, and humanists regarded with deep suspicion. [110] Luther would thus shatter "the whole world with strife and destruction." Nor was he willing to accept Luther's assertion that this conflict was inherent in the word, asserting that it was the result rather of how Luther had interpreted and preached the word. [111] All of these concerns after two years seemed to have been only too fully realized, and they scarcely needed to be pointed out in detail.

Erasmus begins by defending his skepticism. He asserts that Luther has mischaracterized him as a skeptic who calls basic Christian doctrine into question when in fact he only suggests suspending judgment about obscure matters of interpretation on more peripheral issues. For Erasmus a skeptic is not someone who does not care what is true or false, but is rather someone who does not leap to conclusions or fight to the death for his own opinion. Luther, by contrast, acts as if he were God himself, asserting as certain what can at best be probable. Erasmus here again draws on the ancient debate and particularly on Carneades' famous concept of the probable as a sensible alternative to Luther's impossible, "Stoic" demand for certainty.

Behind this discussion of the ways and extent to which we can understand Scripture lie radically different and competing notions of what it means to be a human being and a Christian. For Erasmus humans are fallible and a Christian must constantly struggle along with others using every tool available to make sense out of revelation. God does not suddenly give us supernatural insight into the meaning of Scripture, and conversion is not a rapid and radical reversal but a gradual transformation. Here again Erasmus denies the Stoic core of Luther's position. The knowledge that Luther and the Stoics claim to possess is merely an illusion. Even within the limited confines of the Stoic cosmos, such knowledge was scarcely conceivable. The Stoics themselves, for example, repeatedly wondered whether there had ever been a Stoic sage. For Christians the possibility of such knowledge is even more remote because the object of knowledge is not the finite cosmos but the infinite God.

Erasmus thus derides Luther's claim to certain knowledge as hubristic and argues that such claims to divine knowledge put civilization at risk. He believes that Luther's claim to divine inspiration is especially dangerous, because it is also a claim to absolute rectitude. Moreover, since such inspiration is the only source of goodness, it is also a claim, akin to that of the Stoics, that everyone who is not divinely inspired is evil, and that they are all equally evil.[112] Erasmus points out that the absurd consequence of "these Stoic notions [is] that whatever is done apart from grace is equally damnable, so that the tolerance of Socrates is no less grievous an offence in the sight of God than the cruelty of Nero."[113] This view in his opinion can only lead to disaster.

According to Erasmus, Luther's belief in man's utter subordination to God is wrong on several counts. First, man is not ridden by either God or Satan but chooses to follow one or the other. Human beings are clearly pulled by their inclinations and habits in opposite directions, influenced by their desires, their past choices, and the choices of their ancestors, but they are not utterly determined by any or all of these. Luther is thus wrong to equate fallen mankind with Satan. It is true that both turned away from God and are continually concerned with their passions, but Satan cannot will anything good, while there are still seeds of decency in mankind and a certain inclination and striving for what is right. Adam's sin rendered man's will "faint, not extinct, wounded not killed, crippled by an injury, not amputated, left half-alive, not dead."[114] Thus, when God offers man a chance to change his ways he is able to do so, although the capacity to do so varies from person to person.[115]

In *Hyperaspistes* Erasmus minimizes original sin. Indeed, it becomes almost insignificant. The source of evil lies not in man's nature but in his education. Humans are weak rather than evil.[116] There was good even in a fallen and unredeemed humanity. While "reason without grace is overthrown by the passions, it does not follow that there is no propensity for good."[117] Erasmus thus comes close to articulating a faith in natural and almost inextinguishable human goodness. He subsequently asserts the need to see the continued existence of a natural tendency to virtue even in the wickedest human beings.[118]

In his positive evaluation of human nature, Erasmus appears to be more a Christian *humanist* than a *Christian* humanist. Within the framework of the debate that he and Luther have employed this is a step back from skepticism to something like Valla's Epicureanism, but an Epicureanism that is bound up with Ficino's Neoplatonic vision of love running through creation and pulling us continually toward God.

This attenuation of original sin does not mean that grace becomes unimportant for Erasmus, but it does mean that the specific act of justifying grace that is so decisive for Luther is replaced in Erasmus by a larger system of grace that operates at three different levels. At the foundation of things is natural grace that creates us as we are and pulls us toward the good. At a second level is preparatory grace that offers us the chance to lead a Christian life. And finally, there is justifying grace that helps us resist the attractions of sin after we have been justified.[119] Free will for Erasmus is only the capacity to accept or reject preparatory grace, and a practicing Christian thus does not simply immerse himself in the word but works with the assistance of grace to continually improve his moral character.

Central to Erasmus's view here too is the notion that nature is a kind of grace. An individual's natural gifts, Erasmus argues, are his by the grace of God.[120] Erasmus knew that Paul had considered and rejected this idea, but he believed that it was at least arguably orthodox, basing this assumption on material mistakenly attributed to Augustine.[121] Some have argued that this understanding of nature as a form of grace points to a pantheistic current in Erasmus's thought, but Erasmus does not assume that God is present and active in everything. For example, he points out that "according to some, once God has given to the secondary causes, namely nature, the power to reproduce and act, he does nothing unless for special reasons he suspends the common action of nature."[122] God is pictured here not as a prime mover who sets everything in motion but as an artificer who creates a world that moves on its own, and who for the most part does not afterwards interfere in this creation. If that is true, then man's fate in this world and in the next is largely in his own hands. In *Hyperaspistes* Erasmus moves much closer to such a view than in his *Diatribe*. This change also moves him closer to the heroic humanism of the Italians and further from the Augustinian position he claims to defend. This is evident in a crucial passage in which he misquotes Augustine: "God does many good things in man that man does not do; but man does many things that God does not do."[123] What Augustine actually says, however, is that "God does many good things in man which man does not do; but man does none which God does not make him capable of doing."[124] While this may simply be a careless error, it is an error that allows Erasmus to retain the appearance of orthodoxy while actually defending an unorthodox position. Even if his position is unorthodox, however, there is no indication that it is un-Christian. Erasmus may simply want to expand Christianity to include a natural moral life and a sense of being at home in this world in opposition to the alienation and longing for a cataclysmic transformation that he sees in Luther.

Not only does this view of a minimal role for human free will provide a theological foundation for human dignity, it also frees God from the imputation of authoring evil. God, according to Erasmus, does not wish to seem cruel and unjust on one hand and to be believed to be just and merciful on the other.[125] It is thus "simply wicked to say that God damns anyone who does not deserve it."[126] Not only is it wrong, it does little to promote the love of God. Erasmus thus asks: "Who could bear that God who is supremely good hardens the heart of the king in order to make his own glory more illustrious through the king's destruction?"[127] But this is exactly the position Luther takes, for his assertions commit him to the belief that God throws a human being into the fire who has been guilty of nothing except not having any power over himself.[128] Luther's position even entails the condemnation of unbaptised infants who have injured no one.[129] Erasmus understands that the duality of the revealed God and the concealed God is supposed to resolve this problem, but he does not find it satisfying. Luther, in his view, "grants that God works evil deeds but denies that he acts evilly . . . such reasoning . . . makes God, who is supremely good, and the devil, who is supremely evil, work together to make the same person perform the same work."[130] Erasmus cannot believe that the actions of such a God could ever be justified.[131] Moreover, the reliance on divine inscrutability is insufficient. Erasmus remarks: "I do not think that even in the light of glory it will be clear that God casts someone who does not deserve it into eternal fire."[132] Erasmus's generally positive view of both man and God thus leads him to detest Luther's notion that God would punish the innocent. For Luther it was blasphemy to think of God in such human terms. For Erasmus, it was blasphemy to think of God in such devilish terms: "Who will be able to bring himself to love wholeheartedly the God who has created a hell seething with everlasting torture where he can punish his own evil deeds in wretched human beings, as though he delighted in their suffering?"[133] For Erasmus, God permits rather than wills evil deeds.[134] "God is to the highest degree just and good. If he is just, then he does not punish eternally. But in his goodness he does not give up on anyone who does not give himself up." Erasmus thus believes that we are slaves of neither Satan nor God, but occupy a middle ground between these two kingdoms.[135]

Insofar as humans occupy a middle ground, their moral choices play some role in determining their spiritual fate. Both nature and reason in Erasmus's view give us a certain inclination toward morality.[136] They sometimes even lead one who has been debased by his habits to be horrified by his sin.[137] Reason is thus not the whore of Babylon as Luther claims. In opposition to Luther's claim that Socrates, Epictetus, Aristides, Cato of Utica, and others philosophers were simply filled with vainglory, Erasmus points to Paul's admission that there is actual good in some philosophers.[138] Indeed, pagan virtue rightly puts many Christians to shame and books of philosophy contain precepts similar to those of the prophets.[139] Thus Luther is mad to believe that supremely moral men such as Socrates are evil: "Even though we grant that moral virtues are not sufficient to gain evangelical justification without faith, people still were not doing wicked deeds when they honored their parents, loved their children and wives, supported the poor, sick, and afflicted."[140]

The position that Erasmus defends here clearly moves in a Pelagian direction, although in comparison to some of his other remarks during the same period it is relatively restrained. In 1522, he has one of his characters in *The Holy Treat* declaim "Saint Socrates, pray for us," and in 1523 he uses the same phrase in his own name.[141] He also virtually proclaimed the salvation of Cicero in his introduction to the Froben edition of Cicero's *Tusculan Disputations*.[142] While this certainly diminishes the importance of Christ and his sacrifice, these claims for Socrates and Cicero do not necessarily demonstrate that Erasmus was heterodox. In fact, Luther himself comes close to Erasmus in his admiration for Cicero. He asserted, for example, that Cicero would sit higher than Duke George of Saxony in the world to come, and if he [Luther] sat where Cicero did he would be saved.[143] He also says that the pagans who obeyed the law will be punished less severely by God than those who knowingly violate it.[144] But in contrast to Erasmus, this does not mean that grace plays any less a role. As McSorley concisely puts it, Luther does not so much deny natural goodness as show a complete disinterest in it because in his view ethical goodness is totally irrelevant for salvation.[145]

Erasmus in contrast to Luther cannot believe that charitable works are irrelevant to salvation: "Although we grant that works do not confer justification, certainly they do not make a person wicked unless they spring from a perverse motive."[146] In fact, he agrees with Paul that "if our contributions were not there we would not be saved."[147] Even for pagans, works made a difference. He asks Luther to "imagine for me some pagan who never heard of the mysteries of faith (and it was through no fault of his own that he did not) but has his mind set on learning what is best and living blamelessly in so far as he can through the guidance of nature; I do not think that everything he does is sinful, whether it be loving his wife and bringing up his children in a wholesome way or contributing as much as he can to the common good."[148] While deeds do not produce justification, they do invite the kindness of God.[149]

For Luther there is literally nothing that man can do to attain salvation, since everything depends on God alone. There is thus no path to salvation for Luther. In Erasmus's view this univocal focus on divine will utterly undermines morality. Almost as if reflecting on Luther's famous advice to Melanchthon to "Sin boldly!" Erasmus remarks: "If it is predetermined that I am damned, any effort I make is useless. If I am destined to be saved, there is no reason not to follow my every whim." [150] Humans can be improved by a proper upbringing and by education. They can also improve themselves by combining *humanitas* and *pietas* within the *philosophia Christi*. Erasmus was convinced that "a large part of goodness is the will to be good. The further that will leaves imperfection behind, the closer a person is to grace." [151] To abandon morality and moral education, to see the formation of character as irrelevant to human well-being, can end only in a world in which force alone rules, a world in which the murderer, the rapist, and the tyrant rule, or worse a world in which the faithful rape, murder, and tyrannize over others in the name of God and as agents of his omnipotent and indifferent will.

ALPHA AND OMEGA

In 1516 Erasmus had written his *Education of a Christian Prince* to train the prince destined to be the greatest emperor in Europe since Charlemagne. This moment was in a sense the culmination of his project for the transformation of Europe from above. A ruling class of Christian humanists gradually spreading the fruits of an education in the philosophy of Christ would, he believed, create a new European order. However, with the appearance of Luther, the schism in the church, and the outbreak of the Peasants' Rebellion, he saw his hopes for a peaceful reformation of the Christianity and Christendom dissolve before his eyes. As a result of his quarrel with Luther, Erasmus fell into a pessimism from which he never entirely recovered. [152] His pessimism was justified. Humanism would continue to exercise an important influence on intellectuals and on some members of the upper classes, but as an agent of social change it had been surpassed by the religious passions unleashed first by the Reformation and then a few years later by the Counter-reformation. These passions reached a much broader population than humanism and moved them in more immediate and more violent ways. The humanist project in which Erasmus had placed such great hopes would be revived, but only in a world that had been radically transformed by the Wars of Religion, the exploration and colonization of the New World, the Copernican Revolution, and the development of a new mathematical natural science. The intervening period was a time of unparallel violence and religious fanaticism. Humanism would survive in a variety of forms and places, but it was generally driven from the public square into private towers and Epicurean gardens, out of ducal courts into secret societies and the privacy of individual households.

From the outset of the conflict between Luther and the church, Erasmus had feared the general breakdown of society and had done his best to prevent it. Luther, too, had recognized this possibility, but in contrast to Erasmus, he longed for it, for he believed it heralded the Apocalypse. Erasmus had believed the church and the state could be reformed by a humanistic system of education. Luther denied that any such improvement was possible, since man was powerless to change what God had already established. What were crucial for him were not moral reform and improvement but grace, faith, and the preaching of Scripture. In rejecting humanism, Luther thus also rejected the notion of a moral foundation of the social and political order.

Perhaps the greatest monument to the period in which Erasmus and Luther lived was Michelangelo's work in the Sistine Chapel. His great ceiling was painted for Julius II during the years from 1503 to 1513, when the humanist project was at its height and humanists looked toward the future with such extraordinary expectations.[153] The ceiling portrays this humanist dream in all of its magnificence. It tells the story of the genesis and destruction of the world from the separation of light and darkness to the drunkenness of Noah. It is a scriptural and at times almost liturgical story, but this story unfolds within a classical framework in which God and the figures of Genesis have been transformed into pagan gods and heroes. It is a world in which love and beauty in Neoplatonic fashion hold sway, a world in which Christian prophets and pagan Sibyls mingle with one another and teach the same lessons, and a world in which the heroic and naked human form is the measure of all things. The ceiling is thus the epitome of the humanist project that Erasmus defended to the end. Michelangelo remarked with calculated understatement that Julius II was "well pleased" with the result. The story, however, does not end there, for Michelangelo returned to paint the great altar wall of the chapel for Paul III in the years from 1534 to 1541.[154] The story reflected on this wall is not the story of the world's beginning, of a paradise lost and yet a paradise artistically continually regained. It is rather the story of the Last Judgment, and in its subject and style reflects the darkening prospects that overhung the European world. Here too heroic figures confront the viewer, but in a shaded landscape with clouds and a terrified humanity swirling eternally around the threatening figure of Christ, his hand upraised, rendering judgment, a judgment just completed but whose consequences are not quite carried out, eternally and achingly imminent. This painting is, of course, a painting of the end, the coming end, and seems to herald the decline of a human-centered world and to presage the looming age of destruction that was soon to follow. Its reception also echoed the changing mood of the times. Almost as soon as the painting was completed, it was criticized by the pious as immodest and un-Christian, and lesser men were called in to paint over the genitalia, to conceal the organs of generation that had been such an essential part of the Neoplatonic vision of love that stretched from Petrarch to Ficino. In a similar way for the next century and a half the humanists were forced to cover and conceal themselves, hiding their true intentions and enterprises away from the Inquisition and the intrusive public gaze of their fellow citizens and communicants.

The world of humanism as it is reflected in the Sistine ceiling begins with the separation of light and darkness. The world of the Reformation reflected on the altar wall mixes these two together once again. In this twilit world on the precipice of the Apocalypse, the armies of light can scarcely be distinguished from the armies of darkness. The same was true of the actual world, where each side in the conflict was convinced that God rode with them or that they were his emissaries. The creation of the modern world, as we understand it both in a scientific and a moral sense, was made possible only by finding a way once again to separate the light from the darkness. The center of Michelangelo's ceiling is the creation of the human Eve out of Adam. The center of the altar wall is the dark God-man. The center of the "ceiling" for those who opened up the modern world was neither human nor divine. In the midst of the Wars of Religion that called into question both God and man, the gaze of those who created the modern age seems to have turned to an earlier panel in Michelangelo's ceiling, to the creation of the cosmos, and thus to the material world in all its multipicitous motion. This modern "ceiling" in all of its magnificence and power is, however, painted not in the vibrant living colors of the world of ordinary experience but in the pure and brilliant, though colorless light of mathematics.

6 | *Descartes' Path to Truth*

At the very beginning of his earliest philosophical reflections, René Descartes placed the surprising proverb: "The fear of the Lord is the beginning of wisdom."[1] This work, which was never completed and which we know only from Baillet's biography and Leibniz's notes, was Descartes' earliest attempt to develop the science he had described to Isaac Beeckman a few months before in early 1619:

> What I want to produce is not something like Lull's *Ars Brevis,* but rather a completely new science, which would provide a general solution to all possible equations involving any sort of quantity, whether continuous or discrete, each according to its nature. . . . There is, I think, no imaginable problem which cannot be solved at any rate by such lines as these. . . . Almost nothing in geometry will remain to be discovered. This is of course a gigantic task, and one hardly suitable for one person; indeed it is an incredibly ambitious project. But through the confusing darkness of this science I have caught a glimpse of some sort of light, and with the aid of this I think I shall be able to dispel even the thickest obscurities.[2]

The ultimate result of these efforts, renewed and sustained over a period of many years, was a new science based on the natural light of reason that revolutionized European thought and helped to bring the modern age into being. But how are we to understand the claim that stands at its beginning? We are prone to think of modernity as a secular age, and to think of Descartes in particular as one of those most responsible for the rejection of religion. How in this light can we make sense of his claim that the fear of the Lord is the beginning of this new wisdom?

The provenance of the proverb is probably coterminous with religion as such. In the Old Testament it points to "a wrathful God" who demands strict adherence to his law. The wisdom referred to in the proverb is thus not questioning and thinking, that is, not philosophy or science, but piety and obedience. Is this, however, what Descartes means when he puts the proverb at the head of his text? And which Lord is he referring to that generates this fear? It is hard to believe that the God that Descartes has in mind is the rational God of scholasticism or the Neoplatonic God of humanism. I want to suggest that the God the young Descartes has in mind is rather the arbitrary and unpredictable God who first appeared in the thought of Ockham and who found his preeminent form in the hidden God of Luther. It was this God who appeared in such a horrifying fashion to Descartes in the Wars of Religion and who also opened up the possibility of a new wisdom. How is it possible, though, that the experience of this dark God can engender the natural light that Descartes so excitedly described to Beeckman in the letter cited above, a light that would cut through the darkness and deception engendered by this hidden God and provide the illumination needed to construct the citadel of reason that became the modern world? How is it that the light shines out of this darkness?

In this chapter I will argue that Descartes sought to construct a bastion of reason against this terrifying God of nominalism, a bastion that could provide not only individual certainty and security, and not only mitigate or eliminate the incommodities of nature, but also bring an end to the religious and political strife that were tearing Europe to pieces. Descartes aimed to achieve this and make man master and possessor of nature by developing a mathematical science that could provide a picture of the true world underlying the phenomena. Moreover, while Descartes drew upon many of the prevailing resources in the humanist tradition and particularly on Hermeticism in seeking to construct his bastion, he ultimately establishes his foundation on a very different ground than that of humanism. Like most of the humanists Descartes asserts the independence of the human will and the capacity of man to make himself master and possessor of nature by coming to understand and manipulate her hidden powers. In contrast to the humanists, however, he grounds human freedom not in the power of the individual will but in the fact that our will, like the will of God, is infinite. Indeed, it is this understanding of infinity that is essential as the foundation of his science. In this respect, Descartes' science rests in an almost paradoxical way on the God he both fears and worships. The natural light that he believes is essential to the creation of the modern world is thus the light that shines out of the darkness of this divinity.

THE HISTORICAL AND BIOGRAPHICAL BACKGROUND OF DESCARTES' THOUGHT

The development of the Reformation in Europe was rapid and widespread. Inspired by Luther and reacting to church abuses in their own areas, reformers appeared throughout Europe. Already in 1520 Zwingli had brought the Reformation to Switzerland, and many of his radical followers soon formed the Anabaptist movement that spread across Europe, especially among the lower classes. The transformation of the English church began in 1529 with Henry VIII's break with the pope and was finalized in 1536 with the Act of Dissolution. In the same year Calvin published the first edition of his *Institutes of the Christian Religion* that shaped the further development of the Reformation in Holland, Scotland, France, Hungary, and parts of Germany as well. The rapid spread of the Reformation was facilitated by the increased use of the printing press, but also by the support of many princes who found it in their interest to oppose Rome. The beginning of the Catholic Counter-reformation is usually dated from the Council of Trent (1545–63), which standardized church doctrine (thus eliminating the pluralism of Renaissance Christianity), consolidated papal power, and empowered the Inquisition, but equally important was the formation of the Jesuit order with its vow of absolute obedience to the pope. The first of the Religious Wars broke out in Germany in 1546 and was only brought to an end in 1555 by the Peace of Augsburg, which allowed princes to determine religious belief in their domains. Shortly thereafter, however, war broke out in France, which was particularly hard hit in the latter half of the sixteenth century, suffering through nine Wars of Religion lasting from 1562 to 1598 that included the horrifying massacre of St. Bartholomew's Day. This period of warfare culminated in the so-called War of the Three Henries (1584–89) and the War of the League (1589–98), which ended only when the Protestant Henry of Navarre converted to Catholicism and accepted the French throne as Henry IV. He issued the Edict of Nantes in 1598, granting freedom of conscience and a limited freedom of worship to the Huguenots, allowing them fortified cities and royal support for their pastors. This Edict remained in place until 1685, but after the assassination of Henry IV in 1610, warfare broke out again and the Edict was gradually rescinded. This accelerated after Richelieu came to power in 1624 vowing to break the Huguenots. He was as good as his word, capturing La Rochelle in 1627 and revoking the corporate independence of Huguenots with the Edict of Alais in 1629.

France was not the only country torn by religious wars. Almost all of Europe was engulfed by the conflict. The Thirty Years War (1618–48) was centered in Germany but convulsed most of central and northern Europe. This war began when Ferdinand II became Holy Roman Emperor and sought to suppress Protestantism in all of his territories. Bohemia, which was then a predominantly Protestant region, revolted and offered its throne to Frederick, the Elector of the Palatinate, champion of the Reformed Protestant cause. Frederick became king in October 1619 but ruled only until November 8, 1620, when his forces were defeated at the Battle of White Mountain. This loss tilted the balance of power and drew nearly all of the European states into the conflict.[3] The civil war within the German territories was brought to an end by the Peace of Prague in May 1635, but the fighting continued, due to the intervention of large foreign forces from France, England, and Sweden. The war ended only with the Peace of Westphalia in 1648. The last years of this war were also contemporaneous with the English Civil War that raged with similar ferocity although with somewhat less devastation from 1642 to 1651.

It would be a mistake to believe that the question of religious orthodoxy was the sole factor in the Wars of Religion. Charles Tilly has argued, for example, that these wars were in fact more the consequence of efforts to consolidate the new national states than wars of religion.[4] While there is much to be said for this argument and while it is certainly true that the consolidation of state power was part and parcel of the process, there is also little doubt that most of the leading participants in these wars and many of the most violent among them thought that they were doing God's work and not that of their sovereign. Thus, while we cannot attribute the wars simply to religious differences, there can be no doubt that religion in many different forms and ways contributed to the fanaticism and slaughter that distinguish those wars from so many others.

Descartes (1596–1650) was intimately acquainted with the struggles of the time.[5] His family was Catholic but had connections to Protestant France. They lived in Poitou, which was a Huguenot stronghold, but also had close ties to Châtellerault, a secure city under the Edict of Nantes. His mother died when Descartes was one and his father remarried, leaving him principally in the care of his maternal grandmother and perhaps his great-uncle Michel Ferrand, who was a judge in Châtellerault. Descartes' father and many of his other relations were lawyers or judges, and they clearly expected that Descartes would pursue a similar career in governmental service.[6]

Descartes was sent along with his older brother in 1606 to the Jesuit school La Flèche that had been founded two years before by Henry IV.[7] The school was intended to prepare gentlemen for state service, and it had a classical curriculum that drew both on the scholastic and the humanist tradition. The school was run in an egalitarian manner with a general although not total disregard for rank. The students' lives were carefully regulated but in a manner that excluded corporal punishment and promoted friendly interchange with their teachers. This was reflected in Descartes' experience. His distant relative, Father Etienne Charlet, S.J., paid such close attention to Descartes that the philosopher later proclaimed him his true father.[8] Even in this closed environment, however, Descartes was not completely sheltered from the events of the times. The assassination of Henry IV was particularly felt at the school, and Descartes' himself witnessed the ceremony in which Henry IV's heart was buried in the chapel at La Flèche.[9]

[Descartes' education acquainted him with the religious controversies and theological debates of the time. He studied Aristotle and Aquinas in his course on metaphysics and Suarez and Lessius in moral philosophy.[10] Through Suarez he became acquainted with Augustine, the scholastics John Scotus Erigena, Anselm, Bonaventure, and the nominalists Ockham, Robert Holcot, Marsilius of Inghen, Gabriel Biel, Gerson, Peter d'Ailly, and Andreas of Newcastle.[11] He also knew the mathematical work of the nominalist Nicholas of Oresme, the scientific works of Nicholas of Cusa, and at least the medical works of Francisco Sanchez.[12] While at La Flèche, he may have studied with François Veron, who later defended Catholicism with great zeal and ability in debates with Protestants.[13] One of his teachers was probably a nominalist, and another may have taught divine indifference, although Descartes was already well acquainted with these doctrines from his studies of the scholastic debates.[14] Descartes' education, however, was not confined to the traditional curriculum. He certainly read Montaigne, Charron, and Amades de Gaul, and either read or heard of Galileo.[15] He was apparently granted access to all of the holdings of the school library and used this opportunity to read occult texts concerned with alchemy, Hermeticism, and magic. These works had an important impact on him. Descartes tells us little about his own religious beliefs beyond the fact that his religion was the religion of his king and country. This may seem to indicate unequivocally that Descartes was French Catholic, but this is far from clear since his king at the time was Henry IV, an opportunistically converted Calvinist, and later in life his chosen country was at least as often the Protestant Netherlands, Bohemia, or Sweden as France.[16]

[Descartes studied law from 1614 to 1616 in Poitou, then in revolt against Louis XIII. However, perhaps because he was a second son, he entered the peacetime army of Maurice, Prince of Orange in 1618.[17] Descartes, however, saw no fighting and spent most of his time in Holland studying military architecture and mathematics.[18] It was during this period that he met the young physician and thinker Isaac Beeckman, who became his spiritual mentor and from whom he received the decisive intellectual impulse that redirected his life.

Beeckman, who was a philosophical talent in his own right, recognized Descartes' genius and strongly encouraged him to give up all other aspirations and become a searcher for truth.[19] They worked on mathematics and read several Hermetic texts together. Beeckman's influence was profound.[20] Descartes did not, however, immediately follow the path that Beeckman urged upon him. Instead, he headed for Germany (via Copenhagen), supposedly to join in the wars of religion that were under way at the time. It is generally assumed that he was a member of the army of Maximilian I, the Catholic Prince of Bavaria, who later allied himself with the new Emperor Ferdinand II and defeated the Protestant forces of Frederick, Elector of the Palatinate and King of Bohemia, at the Battle of White Mountain. Watson, however, points out that there is little evidence of this fact and that it is much more likely that he would have served on the Protestant side since they were allied with France. In any case, there is no documentary evidence that Descartes saw any action, and Baillet's account of his participation in the rape of Bohemia is good Catholic propaganda but highly unlikely.[21]

Descartes' stay in Germany was a time of intense intellectual activity in part certainly because of the intellectual ferment he found there. In 1613, the elector had married Elizabeth Stuart, the daughter of James I/VI of England and Scotland, and his lands had as a result been inundated with intellectual figures of the English Renaissance, and especially those Protestant thinkers who drawing on Hermetic strains of humanist thought had formed themselves into a secret scientific society modeled on but also meant to oppose the Jesuits. They were called the Rosicrucians.[22] These men drew upon the work of Italian humanists such as Giordano Bruno and Ficino but also Hermetic magi including Cornelius Agrippa and Robert Fludd. While in Germany, Descartes met some men who were attracted to this order and was very much taken with them, their goals, and their retired manner of life.[23] He also seems to have shared some of the excitement generated by their apocalyptic fantasies arising out of the same political and theological tensions that led to the Thirty Years War.[24]

Descartes was probably already acquainted with some of the alchemical and Hermetic writings they drew on from his time at La Flèche and his acquaintance with Beeckman.[25] Charles Adam believes he may have also have already read the most important Hermetic work of the time, Cornelius Agrippa's *De occulta philosophia*.[26] This sympathy for Hermeticism was further strengthened by his contact with the Rosicrucian mathematician Johannes Faulhaber during his time in Germany. Rosicrucianism clearly had an impact on Descartes, and it helped to shape his early philosophical project.[27] A brief examination of Rosicrucianism makes clear why.

The Rosicrucian project was laid out in two manifestos, *The Fame of the Order of the Rosy Cross,* written in German and published in 1614, and *The Confession of the Order of the Rosy Cross,* written in Latin and published in 1615. The third work of Rosicrucianism was *The Chemical Wedding of Christian Rosencreutz,* published in 1616. It was a thinly veiled account of the marriage of Frederick V of the Palatinate and Elizabeth Stuart.[28] The Rosicrucians were essentially Hermetic thinkers who sought to understand the hidden order of nature in order to gain power over it. Agrippa, for example, wrote in 1655 that "a magician is defined . . . as one to whom by the grace of God the spirits have given knowledge of the secrets of nature."[29] Hermetic thinkers thus divided the world into thinking substance and extension and sought to prepare themselves for the revelation of the hidden truth that lies in incorporeal substance by banishing the deceptions of the world from their minds.[30] They believed themselves to be aided in the pursuit of these truths by Olympian spirits who cleared away the shadows of the world that surround all things.[31] Nature, however, did not in their view deliver up its secrets without a struggle but had to be tortured and even torn to pieces to discover the truth.[32] Hence they recognized the need for scientific instruments. Moreover, nature in their view could be understood not in ordinary language but only by the application of mathematics.[33] The goal of such knowledge for them was not personal gain but the fundamental improvement of humanity by the prolongation of human life and the elimination of want and disease.[34] They had six explicit rules: (1) to deliver medical care without charging a fee, (2) to wear no distinctive clothing, (3) to meet one another once a year, (4) to look for a worthy successor, (5) to use the letters C.R. or R.C. as their seal and mark, and (6) to keep the fraternity secret for one hundred years.[35]

Beeckman had encouraged Descartes to follow such a path, and in Germany Descartes discovered others leading just such lives. This experience seemed to intensify his desire to continue work on the new science he had described earlier to Beeckman. Waylaid by an early winter in a small German village near Ulm with no friends or acquaintances, Descartes was convinced that the time was ripe to try to establish a foundation for the science he wanted to develop. This was the task he set himself in his small, stove-warmed room *(poêle).* Descartes describes this beginning in two places, in the *Olympica* section of his *Little Notebook,* and, more fully, in part 2 of the *Discourse on Method.* As we shall see, these two sources suggest that on November 10, 1619 Descartes spent the day in a series of reflections that began not with abstract metaphysical thoughts but with the criteria for distinguishing good technicians, lawgivers, and scientists set against the backdrop of a world that had failed to find a principle of order that could restrain the religious passions and establish political peace. The path that Descartes follows in his speculations is a path that leads away from the political and into the self, but it is not a path of retreat and withdrawal, not merely an effort to save himself or maintain his own independence on the model of Petrarch or Montaigne. The retreat into the self is part and parcel of his effort to discover the ground for a radical transformation of European society based on a certain method for determining the truth. His "retreat" in this respect follows a Rosicrucian path. Indeed, in Hermetic fashion, he tries to separate his mind from his body in order to free himself from the illusions of the world and in so doing to open himself up to a visionary revelation.[36] His goal, however, is not personal but public and in a certain sense political.

The date of his momentous day was charged with great and perhaps even mystical significance for Descartes. November 10, 1619 was St. Martin's Eve. This was the day on which Ignatius Loyola founded the Jesuit order.[37] This day was also traditionally regarded as the end of warm weather in Descartes' native Touraine, and folk wisdom saw it as beginning of winter. Rents were due on leases at this time. It was also the opening day for *parlements* (courts) in France. Descartes received his B.A. on November 9, 1614 and licentiate in canon and civil law on November 10, 1616. He first met Beeckman on November 10, 1618, and his dream occurred on November 10, 1619. He also apparently continued to regard this date as significant. On November 11, 1620, he claims he had just begun (presumably on November 10, 1620) to understand the foundation of his wonderful discovery. On November 10, 1640, he wrote to Mersenne that he had sent the *Meditations* to Huygens the day before and on the same day announced his intention to publish the *Principles*.[38]

According to his own account, Descartes spent that entire November 10, 1619 in thought, laying out the foundations for what he described as a miraculous science. After this day of feverish thinking, filled with enthusiasm, Descartes went to bed, expecting a dream that would confirm his great discovery. He was not disappointed. Indeed, he had a series of dreams (either two or three depending on the commentator) that left him convinced that he had chosen the right path in life and had discovered a method that would lead infallibly to the truth.[39]

The meaning and importance of Descartes' dream(s) have been the subject of a controversy that at one time or another has occupied nearly every prominent Descartes scholar and even, if only briefly, the greatest "dream scholar" of them all, Sigmund Freud. There are two quite different interpretations of his dream(s). The first school believes that he faithfully (and almost immediately) described what transpired that night. Even among this group there are those like Freud who believe that there is little to be learned from this account because no one can interpret the dream except the dreamer. What we can know thus comes only from Descartes' own interpretation of the dream. Other, more daring interpreters believe that they can decipher the meaning of the dream symbols even if Descartes does not explain them. For them the dreams reveal the deep intentionality behind Cartesian science, not always clear even to Descartes himself.

A second school believes that the account of the dreams is invented whole cloth or is such a complete reworking of the dream experience that it needs to be treated as a literary creation. Watson has persuasively argued that the specific details of the dream(s) were invented by Baillet and that succeeding generations of Descartes scholars have accepted them as genuine out of a burning desire to have some insight into Descartes' real motives.[40] Others accept the details as Cartesian but believe that the dream story is merely a method for Descartes to present opinions that are either politically or theologically suspect. Scholars who support this reading point to the fact that there was an existing tradition of using dream accounts in this manner in both Latin literature and the Hermetic tradition.[41] Cicero's famous "Dream of Scipio" is only the best known of these examples and one with which Descartes was undoubtedly familiar as a result of his Jesuit education.

In order to come to terms with the importance of the dream story told in the *Olympica,* it is necessary to understand more fully the structure of the *Little Notebook* of which it is a part. Descartes began the *Little Notebook* after leaving Holland (imitating Beeckman who kept a similar notebook). Its first page is dated January 1, 1619, and it was written over a number of months and contained many incomplete sections, but it was clearly important to Descartes since he retained it for over thirty years, and it was found among his papers when he died in 1650. The manuscript, as Chanut describes it, is very complicated with different texts on different sides of the page, some written upside down. As a result of the thoughtful reconstruction by Cole (drawing on Gouhier), we now know that what Descartes almost certainly did was write on one side of the paper until it was full then turn the book over and write on the other side. The manuscript thus contained seven parts. On one side there were four sections, *Parnassus* (18 sheets of mathematical considerations), untitled considerations on the sciences (2 pages), untitled algebra (1/2 page), and *Democritica* (a few lines of text), and on the other side three sections, *Praeambula*

(4 pages), *Experimenta* (5 pages), and *Olympica* (6 pages, dated November 11, 1620).[42] The first series, which does not seem to follow any particular order, corresponds to Descartes' interests in mathematics and science in the first part of the year after leaving Beeckman. The second series looks more like an early sketch of a text being prepared for publication. This notion is further supported by one of Leibniz's notes that he copied from the notebook in which Descartes promises to finish his treatise by February 23.[43]

Descartes makes clear his trepidations in the *Praeambula:* "As actors put on masks in order not to show their blush when cued in the theater, so, as I am about to ascend onto the great stage of this world, having been only a spectator until now, I advance masked."[44] Descartes repeats this claim in somewhat different language in the *Rules.*[45] Why does he believe that concealment is necessary? In part his concern probably is related to his Rosicrucian connections. He knew already from his time at La Flèche how suspicious orthodox Catholicism was of Hermeticism. The Counter-reformation had sought for many years to limit the religious pluralism that had flourished during the Renaissance and had taken aim at Hermeticism in particular, most famously burning Giordano Bruno at the stake in Rome in 1600. Descartes, however, seems to have hoped that this approach would give him the kind of knowledge he desired. While he followed this path, he also knew that he could only do so very discretely.

For all his hopes, Descartes was not uncritical of the Rosicrucians. He thought that their efforts were laudable but that they were often lost in confusion, principally because they lacked a method for analyzing nature and coming to terms with the hidden truths they sought. It was such a method that Descartes believed he could supply. This new method shone dimly through the account of his dream given in the *Olympica,* and was spelled out in the weeks and months following the event in a fuller form that first appeared in the *Rules* and then in the *Discourse.*

While we cannot investigate the dreams thoroughly to show how his turn away from religion and toward his new science was reflected in them, a short summary should give us some idea of the decisive change in his thinking that led him away from the life he had led up to then and toward a philosophic life dedicated to the establishment of a new and universal science based upon the analysis of nature.

The account of the dreams occurs in the *Olympica* section of the *Little Notebook.* The title refers to the things of Olympus, the home of the Greek gods. The probable reference is to pagan, Hermetic spirits that point us in the direction of the truth. We see this in the action of the dreams themselves. The dreams as a whole are about a turn away from religion toward natural philosophy. The predominant experience of the first two dreams is terror, while the third is characterized by a great calmness and hopefulness. Descartes himself says the first dream relates to the past, the second to the present, and the third to the future. The first dream is dominated by Descartes' fear of divine punishment for what he calls his secret sins. This notion is reminiscent of the problem of conscience posed for Luther by the omnipotent God, and given what Descartes says in the *Praeambula,* it is possible that he suffers from a similar fear as well. In the first dream his sins are personified by an evil spirit or wind that weakens him and causes him pain. He seeks to go to a church to pray and is surprised when he tries to turn aside to speak to a friend that the wind presses him toward the church. [46] He recognizes that while it might have been God who initially directed him, it is now an evil spirit at work. Descartes, however, is saved by friendship and conversation, which together lessen the force of this spirit. In the second dream Descartes hears a stroke of thunder and awakens in terror to find the air filled with sparks. In order to determine whether this is a supernatural vision or a natural phenomenon, he blinks his eyes and they pass away. His terrors are thus resolved by an experiment.[47] He tells us in his later interpretation that he felt this was the spirit of truth taking possession of him. Some commentators have identified the spirit of truth here with God, but Kennington rightly points out that such a reading is untenable.[48] In the third dream he faces the question of what path to follow in life and sees two alternatives. In his sleep, the pursuit of poetry (on the model of the humanistic volume of Ausonius, *Corpus Poetarum*) seems preferable, but when he wakes up a universal mathematics (on the model of Pythagoras) seems best.

The dreams in a veiled manner thus show how wisdom arises out of the fear of God, who threatens to punish our sins and seeks to drive us into the church to find redemption. The crucial steps that underlie Descartes' escape from this God and the terrors he engenders are a society of friends, experimentation, and a mathematical science.[49] It is important to note that in this escape Descartes does not follow the path of humanism. It is attractive to him, but only when he is asleep. The real world can be mastered only by following a different path that focuses not on man or God but on the natural world.

Many who see this account as more or less a literary fabrication point toward similar Rosicrucian stories. The account given in the dream may be modeled on such stories, but it also rejects the Hermetic notion that imagination can reveal the hidden sympathies and antipathies in the natural world in favor of an analytic mathematics that can map out and reveal the true relations among all things. While Descartes' original conception of science may thus be indebted in some respects to Rosicrucianism (and by extension to the Hermeticism of Italian humanism), it is not Rosicrucian or Hermetic in its methodology or conceptualization. It builds rather on the work of Bacon and Galileo, but uses a method that is Descartes' own.

Whatever the meaning of the dream for Descartes, he clearly felt that he had understood the foundations of his science, or at least the method for attaining the truth. Indeed, when he recounts the story in the *Discourse,* he suggests that he had thought out all four steps of the method, although this seems doubtful given that it is still inchoate in the *Rules.* He claims to have been equally certain that the development of this science would require a much fuller knowledge of the world. Thus, while he continued to work on individual problems and to conduct experiments, he did not attempt to develop this science in its entirety at the time.

Descartes returned to Paris in 1622. The political and intellectual situation was quite different there from that in Holland and Germany. Catholics had the upper hand but felt threatened by three different groups: Christian Hermetics such as the Rosicrucians who sought the secret knowledge of natural causes; deists and libertines whose rejection of the intense religiosity of Calvinism had become a rejection of Christianity; and Pyrrhonist skeptics who believed that the only justification for Catholic doctrine was fideism.[50] Marin Mersenne, who was one of the broadest thinking Catholics and the person perhaps most responsible for the propagation of Descartes' thought had, for example, attacked Ficino, Pico, Giordano Bruno, Cornelius Agrippa, and Robert Fludd, but he had also sharply criticized skeptics such as Charron.[51]

Upon his return Descartes found himself accused of being a Rosicrucian. This charge may have been leveled because of his actual opinions, but it may also have been the result of the fact that he was so reclusive. Whatever the truth of the matter, he was clearly concerned not merely for his reputation but also for his freedom and security, and he began to appear more regularly in public to alleviate suspicion and soon left Paris for Italy, where he remained for two years.

In 1625 Descartes returned to Paris and stayed for three years. The intellectual life of Paris at the time had been shaped by the long years of war and religious dispute. The Sorbonne was a bastion of scholasticism that had been revived as part of the Counter-reformation, but outside its walls a less traditional and more ardent Catholicism was also springing up. In other quarters and under the influence of Montaigne and Charron, many members of the educated classes who had received a humanist education were increasingly drawn to skepticism and fideism, while others went further into libertinism.[52] The libertines despised scholasticism, were scientifically curious, and argued for the devaluation of religion in social life. Many of them were interested in Hermetic and Rosicrucian matters. Their number included Naudé, Gassendi, Vanini, Le Vayer, Elie Diodati, Jean-Louis Guez de Balzac, Théophile de Viau, and Father Claude Picot, known as the atheist priest (who also handled Descartes' financial affairs). They were all freethinkers. Some were debauched and practiced deism and Machiavellianism, while other were more erudite and studied politics, theology, science, and philosophy.[53] While the state generally tolerated their activities when kept private, any attempt to present their ideas publicly was harshly punished.[54]

While Descartes may at some level have been a Rosicrucian and was on friendly terms with a number of the libertines, he was probably not a libertine himself and was certainly opposed to the humanistic skepticism that was at the heart of the libertine position. Skepticism in Descartes' view could not solve the problems of the time because it led only to probability and not certainty. The famous incident by which Descartes came to public attention makes this clear. The chemist/alchemist Chandoux purportedly gave a speech at the home of the papal nuncio Bagni attacking Aristotle and laying out his own mechanistic philosophy. He was praised by everyone present except Descartes. When asked why he demurred, Descartes lauded Chandoux's anti-Aristotelianism but criticized his reliance on merely probable arguments. The others present challenged him to produce something better and to their astonishment he did, apparently laying out his notion of clear and distinct ideas.[55]

It was at this meeting that Descartes first encountered Bérulle. Bérulle was an Augustinian and had founded the French Oratorians in 1611 to rival the Jesuits. He was at the time forming the Compagnie du Saint-Sacrement, a secret society of Catholic laymen to fight Protestantism that played a horrific role in the following years. Bérulle apparently took a deep interest in Descartes. Those who believe Descartes to have been an ardent Catholic assume that Bérulle became his spiritual mentor, recruiting him to write a defense of orthodox theology and metaphysics. However, it seems just as likely that Descartes was frightened by Bérulle and anxious not to be drawn into this man's schemes.[56] In the aftermath of this meeting, Descartes fled Paris for the Protestant Netherlands, concealing his whereabouts and not returning to France for sixteen years. He certainly kept in touch with some of the Oratorians, especially Guillaume Gibieuf, and may have been influenced by Gibieuf's notion of divine omnipotence, but there is little evidence that he saw himself carrying out or participating in Bérulle's project. While he was critical of humanistic science because it sought only the probable truth, he was no friend of religious fanaticism.

⟨Why did Descartes leave Paris and hide himself away from the public eye? He himself gives us a preliminary answer to this question with his famous assertion that "he lives well who lives unseen."[57] This humanist claim, however, does not capture the truth of the matter, for Descartes did not really retreat from society. In fact, he moved around a great deal, spending considerable time in Amsterdam, which he called his "urban solitude," and in a number of smaller towns. It was not therefore a bucolic, Petrarchian solitude that Descartes was seeking. It is more likely that he wanted to find a place he could work and publish more freely and without fear of retaliation. On May 5, 1632, he wrote a paean on Holland to his friend, the poet Jean-Louis Guez de Balzac: "What other land [is there] where one can enjoy a liberty so entire, where one can sleep with less inquietude, where there are always armies afoot expressly to guard you, where poisonings, treason, calumnies are less known, and where the innocence of former times remains?"[58] It is important to remember that he had already been accused of Rosicrucianism. His fears on this score were not misplaced, as the actions taken against a number of the libertines indicate. Already in the *Little Notebook,* he had recognized the need to conceal his true features and during his years in Holland he went to great lengths to develop and perfect this mask. In fact, Descartes assiduously cultivated the appearance of orthodoxy, although it is clear that at least theologically he had adopted heterodox positions from very early on.[59]

⟨During the early years of his stay in Holland, Descartes tried to lay out in print his method and the doctrine of clear and distinct ideas that he had been thinking about for the previous decade. This effort was a continuation of the work he had apparently begun the year before (1628) but left incomplete, his *Rules for the Regulation of the Mind.* This work seems on the surface to be the realization of the plan for the science that he had described as early as 1619 to Beeckman and in the interim to Mersenne and others. Descartes, however, did not complete the work, apparently because he began to reflect on the metaphysical and theological assumptions of his science and saw problems posed for it by the idea of divine omnipotence as it appeared in nominalism and in the theology of Luther and Calvin. Descartes' original idea of an apodictic science rested upon the eternal truth of mathematics. If God was omnipotent, however, such truths could not bind him. Indeed, he must have created them and in principle he thus could uncreate them. No necessity impelled God to create eternal truths, and they could have been created other than they are.[60] This realization led to a skeptical crisis and to his formulation of the astonishing theory of the creation of eternal truths, which undermined his original idea of a universal science.

A second event also apparently convinced Descartes that his project needed to be reformulated. From 1628 to 1633, Descartes sought to develop a Copernican science that ended in a manuscript entitled *The World*. He described this project to Mersenne in a letter of November 13, 1629 in much the same language he had used in writing to Beeckman more than ten years before: "Rather than explaining just one phenomenon I have decided to explain all the phenomena of nature, that is to say, the whole of physics."[61] He clearly hoped that this work would replace Aristotle.[62] Descartes was about to publish the manuscript when he learned of the condemnation of Galileo, which led him to withdraw it. He remarked in the *Discourse* that he had not seen anything objectionable in Galileo's work and therefore became uncertain of his own judgment, but it is reasonably clear that this explanation is a mere smokescreen for the truth that he believed Galileo to have been unjustly condemned.[63] He consequently became convinced that while he might be able to write and even publish his work in the relatively free circumstances then existing in Holland, it would never be accepted by orthodox Catholics and he might be declared heterodox himself. He thus concluded that he could not provide an adequate foundation for his science nor could he make it acceptable without dealing with fundamental metaphysical and theological questions.[64]

Descartes first put his science before the world with the publication in 1637 of his *Discourse on the Method of Rightly Conducting One's Reason and Seeking the Truth in the Sciences*. The work was published in French rather than Latin and was intended for a popular audience. It consisted of a discourse or introduction to his science in which he talked about his method, and scientific treatises on optics, meteorology, and geometry in which the method was presented and demonstrated. Descartes begins the work with the assertion that there is a kind of equality of mind that characterizes all human beings, in that nearly every person presumes he has all of the intelligence he needs. This ironic assertion is almost certainly drawn from Montaigne's essay "On Presumption," but it also echoes a similar claim made by Bacon. The connection to Montaigne is illuminating: it is an almost universal characteristic of human nature that human beings think they know when in fact their thinking is mostly muddled and misguided. Their presumption leaves them prey to rhetoric (including poetry) and enthusiasm that in turn produce misery and destruction. What is necessary, according to Descartes, is not more intelligence and learning, as humanism suggested, but a method to conduct intelligence to the truth. It is exactly such a method that he believes he can supply.

The *Discourse* itself is written in autobiographical fashion, and it situates Descartes' project in his own time.[65] The story is told in narrative rather than dramatic fashion, and it thus has a historical voice that distances the reader from the immediacy of the thinker but also gives historical perspective on the thought itself. In part 1, Descartes discusses his early life and education. Part 2 begins with a discussion of that wonderful day in 1619 when Descartes first conceived the foundations of his science. His account here fills in the story that is lacking in the *Little Notebook*, but it also leaves out much that was central there. In the *Discourse* the Rosicrucian elements and the account of his fabulous dream are excluded. Instead the story of his discovery is put in the context of the Wars of Religion, and his reflections begin not with mathematical or scientific matters but with practical and political concerns.

Descartes in this way ascends onto the stage of the world masked, as he originally prophesized in the *Little Notebook*. In contrast to the account in the *Little Notebook*, there is no reference to his great enthusiasm nor to his sense of being possessed by the spirit of truth. Such Hermetic elements would have endangered the acceptance of the work in orthodox Catholic circles. Rather, he constructs a Descartes who will be acceptable to his audience, a Descartes ardent to discover the truth, but a Descartes who eschews anything theologically or politically suspect. This Descartes is not a Rosicrucian but an orthodox Catholic and loyal subject. The *Discourse* is the first chapter in a fabulous history of self-creation in and through which Descartes presents himself as an exemplum to replace the exempla of antiquity that humanism presented as models of virtue.[66] He thus employs a humanistic method that goes back at least to Petrarch in order to promote a project that at its core is centered not on man but on nature and that seeks to bypass the theological issues of his time.

The account is framed by events of the Thirty Years War. The work appeared two years after the Peace of Prague had put an end to the civil war within Germany, but just at a time the European war was breaking out in Germany. The work points back to the beginning of this war almost two decades before as the starting point of Descartes' reflections. To dispel any suspicions, Descartes mentions that he had attended the coronation of Ferdinand II, thus giving the impression that he served on the Catholic side, but he does not actually say this. Descartes tells us how he was delayed by winter and forced to put up in a small German village where he began to meditate.

It is important to understand the scene Descartes unfolds. He is a young soldier idled by winter just before the beginning of the most cataclysmic event of his age. He is alone, sitting in a stove-warmed room looking out his window. Outside is a medieval German village, a collection of houses that have been built and added onto over the years, set together in haphazard fashion without any guiding principle of organization. The same is true of the political world around him. It too is the product of innumerable individual and uncoordinated decisions, driven not by reason or by any methodological use of intelligence. There is an emperor who rules this world, but at the very moment Descartes is meditating he has been (presumptuously) rejected by many of his subjects because he (presumptuously) attempted to suppress their religion. Like politics, religion too is governed by multiple conflicting and confusing rules written by those who, as he tells us at the beginning of the *Discourse,* are convinced that they have all of the good sense they need. Is it any wonder that his first thought is that "there is not usually so much perfection in works composed of several parts and produced by various different craftsmen as in the works of one man." [67] It hardly needs to be added that he means a man who has good sense. The chaos of the world around him is evidence of a long history of men acting presumptuously without good sense or at least without a uniform method for employing the good sense they have to arrive at the truth.

Descartes gives a series of examples to illustrate his point, comparing buildings patched together by several people with those designed by a single architect, cities that have developed hodgepodge from mere villages with planned towns, peoples grown together from a savage state living only according to a haphazard law of precedents with peoples such as the Spartans who have a wise lawgiver at the very beginning, religions whose articles are made by men with those laid down by God himself, and finally a science that is a mere accumulation of the opinions of various persons with one devised by a single man of good sense employing simple reasoning. All, he argues, demonstrate the superiority of the governance of a single mind when it is guided by good sense.

The choice of these examples is hardly accidental. In fact, they are part and parcel of Descartes' rejection of Aristotelianism. The series of examples he employs mimics the account of knowing Aristotle develops in the sixth book of the *Nicomachean Ethics.* Aristotle argues there that there is an unbridgeable divide between practical knowledge, which is concerned with things that change, and theoretical knowledge, which considers those things that do not change. Practical knowledge is of two sorts, the knowledge of things made *(technē)*, and the knowledge of things done *(phronēsis)*. Theoretical knowledge involves the knowledge of first principles *(nous)* and deduction from these first principles *(epistēmē)*, which together constitute wisdom *(sophia)*.

Descartes considers each of these in turn. His first two examples are the two highest forms of *technē*, that of the architect and city planner; the second two are the highest forms of *phronēsis*, human and divine lawgivers, and the last is the highest form of theoretical knowledge, the scientist who attains wisdom. While Descartes follows the general structure of knowing that Aristotle delineates, he does so in order to distinguish himself from Aristotle. First and foremost, he argues that there is not a sharp division between practical and theoretical knowledge. Good sense, as he calls it in the *Discourse,* transcends the divide between the two and thus allows us to employ theory in the service of practice. The scientist therefore will be the master not of single area of knowledge but of all knowledge. His knowledge will thus be a *mathêsis universalis,* a universal science or universal mathematics. He will thus be not merely the wisest human being but also the best technician and the best lawgiver in both political the theological matters.[68]

The conclusion that follows from this new understanding of human knowing and the relationship of knowing and practice is that all things including the state and religion should be transformed from the foundation up. Descartes recognizes that people will inevitably draw this conclusion and see him and his science as revolutionary. He thus immediately denies that he seeks such revolutionary change. Indeed, he asserts that he is absolutely opposed to those meddlesome people who try to upset states. His only goal he tells us is to rebuild his own house, that is, to reform his own thoughts and construct them upon a foundation which is all his own.

The question of course is whether Descartes is sincere or disingenuous here. Viewed against the background of the humanist tradition, Descartes' project seems to be a retreat from the polis to the *poêle,* from a desire to reform public life to a private search for self-perfection.[69] Petrarch and Montaigne had famously carried out such retreats. If Descartes is telling the truth here and this was in fact his initial reaction in the face of the chaos of his time, it dissipated fairly quickly, for in November 1629 he wrote to Mersenne that the method at the heart of his science itself presupposed "great changes in the order of things. The whole world would have to be a terrestrial paradise—and that is too much to suggest outside of fairyland."⁷⁰ Can this insight have eluded him in 1619 and 1620, as he watched (from near or far) the plundering of Bohemia? Or in the 1630s, when he looked backward over two decades of war? He tells us that it was at this time that he formulated his method but decided not to develop his science further until he had a greater knowledge of the world. But would such worldly knowledge (as opposed to experimental knowledge) change the basic character of the science itself or alter it in any of its particulars? It is hard to see how it could. We are thus left with the conclusion that the greater knowledge of the world was needed to better judge the possible reception of such a science in the theologically heated atmosphere of the time. The question was not the nature of science itself, although he still had much to work out, but the mode of presentation that would make it most acceptable. His concerns were clearly warranted, as the condemnation of Galileo demonstrated.

The *Discourse* is a more circumspect effort. In this work he does not directly or explicitly attack the Aristotelianism that had come to be re-garded as the foundation of Counter-reformation Catholicism, but rather lays out a science that calls into question the fundamental ontological and epistemological presuppositions of Aristotelian science. The goal of the work is also concealed. For example, Descartes claims he has no interest in reordering politics or education, but we know that he repeatedly tried to convince the Jesuits and others to adopt his work as their school text in place of Aristotle. If he was this concerned with education, can he have been any less concerned with politics? His late letter to Princess Elizabeth on Machiavelli, in which he shows a keen concern with and knowledge of political life, suggests otherwise.⁷¹ His explanation for his lack of inter-est in transforming the political realm is also disingenuous. He claims in the *Discourse* that custom has gone a long way toward making contem-porary political institutions palatable, but the entirety of the argument in the *Discourse* aims at showing how insufficient custom is to achieve this goal. Indeed, his argument suggests that custom can never play the role that he attributes to it here since it remains merely an accumulation of the opinions of those who act presumptuously without good sense. Indeed, almost immediately after making this claim, at the beginning of part 3, he refers to events in his own time as an example of the "declining standards of behavior" in a world in which nothing remains the same.⁷²

Descartes did not expect an immediate revolutionary change in the or-der of things, but he certainly thought that the European world would be transformed in the long run by the adoption and gradual application of his science. In the *Discourse*, he claims that he only seeks to reform himself. If this were the case, however, he would have no need to publish his work. In fact he expects others to imitate his model and undertake a thorough self-examination. The crucial question, of course, is what he imagines the consequence of such self-examination will be. Montaigne had made a similar appeal with his *Essays,* and he seems to have believed that the result would be a flowering of human multiplicity, because he did not believe that any two humans would ever reason alike. This was the inevitable conclusion of a humanism that began with a notion of human individuality in Petrarch and developed this notion to its conclusion in the Promethean individualism of Pico and others. Descartes, by contrast, was convinced that anyone who is freed from the prejudices of the world and uses his good sense will arrive at exactly the same conclusions he did. Both the method and the path of doubt lead to the same goal. Descartes thus hopes to transform European society not as a whole all at once and from above, but from within one person at a time. Moreover, as we will see, it is crucial that each individual follow Descartes' path on his own, for the truth of Cartesian science can only be known through personal experience.

[The fundamental principle and foundation of Descartes' science is *cogito ergo sum.* This is the thought that he believed everyone or nearly everyone could experience if only they followed the path he laid out. This is the basis of all Cartesian wisdom, and the Archimedean point on which he believes humanity can stand to move the world. This principle, however, can only be understood if we understand Descartes' transformation of metaphysics.

DESCARTES' REFORMULATION OF METAPHYSICS

There has been considerable debate over the last hundred years about Descartes' originality, almost all of it bound up with a debate about the origin and nature of modernity. The traditional view of Descartes growing out of the Enlightenment was perhaps best summarized by Hegel, who claimed in his *History of Philosophy* that when we come to Descartes we come home to ourselves, out of otherness, home to subjectivity.[73] Modernity is thus understood as the consequence of the Reformation and the development of human inwardness. Beginning at the end of the nineteenth century, a number of scholars, often neo-Thomist in inclination and antipathetic to modernity and Descartes, tried to show that Descartes' thought was not as original as he had contended by showing the many ways in which he drew upon scholasticism. Descartes in their view concealed the medieval foundations of his new structure, building a "mechanic's workshop" on a "cathedral's foundation." Martin Heidegger and a number of later post-modernist thinkers argued, by contrast, that while there were certainly medieval echoes in Descartes' thought, it was essentially modern because it had the doctrine of subjectivity at its foundation. However, in contrast to the earlier tradition that culminated in Hegel, they insisted that this Cartesian turn to subjectivity was not the moment of humanity's home-coming but the moment of its most profound alienation, the beginning of its "world-midnight." Since the 1980s a new view of Descartes has begun to emerge.

Descartes is often described as one of the first to attack Aristotelianism. This view, however, is simply mistaken. As we have seen, the attack on Aristotelianism had already begun in the thirteenth century. The Aristo-telianism of Descartes' time was in fact a neo-Aristotelianism (actually a neo-Thomism) that was developed in the Counter-reformation, particu-larly by Suarez. Ontologically, it was closer to nominalism than it was to Thomism itself. It is true that Descartes rejected the scholastic or Aristo-telian idea of substantial forms, but so had many of his predecessors. He also clearly accepted the basic nominalistic premise that God created the world because he wanted to and not because he was determined to do so by some antecedent reason or necessity. Thus, in contrast to scholasticism, he did not believe that the eternal truths of reason guided God in the cre-ation of the world.[74] While Descartes accepted this basic nominalistic idea, he did not build his new science on a nominalist foundation. Instead he formulated a basic principle of his own that was fundamentally at odds with nominalism.

The goal of Descartes' scientific project was to make man master and possessor of nature and in this way to prolong human life (perhaps infi-nitely), to eliminate want, and to provide security. He thus had a decidedly this-worldly goal.[75] His science seeks to employ theory in the service of practice and to ground all thinking and action in certainty. The aim of this thinking is thus not contemplation but action and production, turning the world to human use.[76]

The key to such a science for Descartes is certainty. By certainty, how-ever, Descartes does not mean the certainty of perception but the certainty of judgment. He explains this in the *Rules:*

> All knowledge is certain and evident cognition. Someone who has doubts about many things is no wiser than one who has never given them a thought; indeed, he appears less wise if he has formed a false opinion about any of them. Hence it is better never to study at all than to occupy ourselves with objects which are so difficult that we are unable to distinguish what is true

from what is false, and are forced to take the doubtful as certain; for in such matters the risk of diminishing our knowledge is greater than our hope of increasing it. So, in accordance with this Rule [#2], we reject all such merely probable cognition and resolve to believe only what is perfectly known and incapable of being doubted.[77]

Descartes thus concludes that "the aim of our studies should be to direct the mind with a view to forming true and sound judgments about whatever comes before it."[78] Such judgments are the antidote to presumption and the foundation of science.

Judging for Descartes is affirming or denying that something is the case, that is, that two things belong or do not belong together. We err when we are deceived by our senses, or our imagination, or when we become entangled in mere words. The basis of true judgment and thus true knowledge is the certainty of intuition, which is "the indubitable conception of a clear and attentive mind which proceeds solely from the light of reason."[79] This does not mean that Descartes eschews deduction.[80] Indeed, because intuition depends on the immediacy of mental vision, the number of axioms it can produce is relatively small. To comprehend more complicated and extended matters requires connecting judgments together. Therefore deduction is a necessary supplement to intuition.[81] Even with deduction, however, it is difficult to attain certainty in long chains of reasoning. In this case it is necessary to employ enumeration to minimize errors. The goal of any chain of reasoning, however, is to grasp the entirety of the chain through constant repetition in a single vision.

Descartes thus maintains that we only truly know the naturally simple things and their intermixture.[82] He does not mean merely visible or tangible things that we can imagine. Imagination can easily be mistaken. Fortunately, we can know unimaginable things like doubt and ignorance, but only when the mind dispenses with images and examines itself.[83] It thereby discovers the innate ideas, and especially mathematical ideas. The problem for Cartesian science is how to bring these purely intellectual things—particularly the mathematical objects—and bodies known to the senses and imagination together. Given Descartes' dualism, it is hard to see how these two can ever meet and thus how science can be possible. The bridge in Descartes' early thought is the imagination.[84] This is the link between the intellect and the senses that makes science possible.[85] What we sense is given figural representation in the imagination and compared there to ideas made available by the intuition and given determinate form by the imagination. On this basis, the intellect is able to affirm the representation as possible or necessary or to deny it as impossible.[86] Judgment goes astray, by contrast, when it compounds elements in the imagination without reference to intuition.

Science, as Descartes developed it in his early thought, thus depended crucially on the certainty of intuition. Descartes, however, came to doubt that intuition could provide the foundation for his science, because he saw that the idea of divine omnipotence as it appears in both Protestant and radical Catholic thought called into question the infallibility of intuition. If intuition is not certain, then the mathematical science that Descartes seeks to establish can be no better than the probabilistic science he wants to replace. [87] If there is no certain ground, no *fundamentum absolutum inconcussum veritatis,* then we cannot truly know anything and are thrown again into the arms of the skeptics. The humanist reliance on the imagination and upon poetry (that presented itself as a possibility in his dream) had been unable to provide the apodictic grounds that Descartes believed were necessary for human knowing. It thus ended in a probabilistic skepticism. In order to ground his science, Descartes consequently had to confront skepticism, and confront it not merely in its ancient Pyrrhonist form derived from Sextus Empiricus but in the form derived from nominalism that calls into question our capacity to know even the most certain things.

Descartes' pursuit of a secure foundation for his science leads to his great struggle with skepticism. He tells us in the *Discourse* that this was the task he undertook in 1629 when he had retired into the urban solitude of Amsterdam. Once again he was alone, although now in a different sense and in a different place, not in a small village but in the best planned city of his age, not in the midst of political and religious struggle but in the most liberal and tolerant society of his time. [88] It was under these circumstances that he felt himself able to confront the fundamental questions that threatened his science and his own sense of self. As we shall see, these questions at their core were bound up with the same theological problem he had faced in 1619.

Descartes describes his first meditations on this topic in part 4 of the *Discourse.* He tells us there that in pursuit of a certain foundation for his science he determined to accept only what was indubitable and to reject everything else as false. In reflecting on this topic he recognized that he would have to reject everything that came from the senses because some are illusions, the results of all reasoning because he knew that he sometimes made mistakes in reasoning, and every thought that came into his head because they might be dreams. This account in the *Discourse,* however, does not tell the whole story. Descartes is not fully forthcoming about his deepest reflections because he is concerned, as he himself admits, that they would be "too metaphysical" for a popular audience. He spells these out more fully in the *Meditations*.

The *Meditations* was originally written in Latin, but it was soon translated into French (perhaps by Descartes himself and certainly with his assistance), which made it available to a broader audience. Moreover, it was published not just on its own but with a series of objections appended to it by noted thinkers of the time, followed by Descartes' replies. It was almost certainly written to answer questions that had arisen about the *Discourse* and should be seen as a continuation or deepening of the argument presented there.[89] This connection is also made apparent in the text, for the first few paragraphs of the *Meditations* summarize the material in parts 1–3 of the *Discourse*. The *Meditations* is also written in an autobiographical fashion, but in contrast to the *Discourse,* it is in a dramatic and not a narrative form. The work thus has a greater immediacy for the reader. The *Discourse* presented readers with a life of good sense that they might imitate; the *Meditations* leads them step by step through the process, forcing them (at least vicariously) to follow the path of doubt to what Descartes believes is its inevitable conclusion.

The First Meditation retraces the path of doubt delineated in part 4 of the *Discourse*. Descartes lists the traditional sources of doubt drawn from ancient skepticism, illusions of sense, madness, and dreams, and concludes that while these might call into question the truths of physics they do not call into question the truths of mathematics. The ultimate source of doubt in the *Meditations,* however, is not simply the possibility of human error (which can be minimized or perhaps even eliminated by the consistent application of the method) but the possibility that we are deceived in an irremediable way by an omnipotent God. Such a God may have created us so that we necessarily misperceive the world, or he may have created the world such that we are continually misled, or he may even interfere with our minds or intervene in the order of nature to deceive us in an ad hoc manner.[90] The mere possibility that such a God exists is sufficient to call into question the apparently most certain truths, that is, mathematical intuitions.[91] In this light, the whole of Cartesian science might rest on a faulty foundation.

This possibility leads Descartes to the methodological hypothesis of an evil genius who continually deceives us. This assumption, he argues, will prevent him from falling into error by treating as false anything that is dubitable. On the basis of this assumption, he is then able to determine that the external world and all the abstract entities (and truths) of mathematics are dubitable. Science is thus impossible, and Descartes is forced to wonder whether he himself is anything at all. As he puts it at the beginning of the Second Meditation, "I have convinced myself that there is absolutely nothing in the world, no sky, no earth, no minds, no bodies. Does it now follow that I too do not exist?"

As rigorous and radical as this skepticism seems to be, many have doubted its sincerity. This question is bound up with the larger question of the sincerity of the *Meditations* and Descartes' metaphysics as a whole. One group of interpreters, including Louis Laird, Charles Adam, Etienne Gilson, Lucien Laberthonnière, Jean Laport, Hiram Caton, Richard Kennington, and Stanley Rosen, believes that Descartes was above all else a scientist and that he turned to metaphysics only in order to make his science palatable to believers. From their point of view, his hyperbolic doubt is thoroughly insincere.[92] For them, Descartes never truly doubts the veracity of mathematics. A second group, which includes Alfred Espinas, Alexander Koyré, Henri Gouhier, and Jean-Luc Marion, sees Descartes sincerely troubled by skepticism but rejecting it in favor of a genuine religious life. For them the metaphysics of the *Meditations* is not merely a sop for believers but the pinnacle of Cartesian thought. There is solid support for both views. Descartes, for example, clearly tries to shore up the metaphysical foundations of his science, something he believed Galileo, to his great detriment, had failed to do.[93]

While it is certainly true that this was one motive behind Descartes' hyperbolic skepticism, it is hard to believe that it is the only one, or that he was only attempting to defend himself against potential enemies among believers. In the first instance we know that at least one of the reasons for writing the *Meditations* was to answer questions that had been posed to him by a variety of thinkers, at least some of whom (for example, Thomas Hobbes) could hardly be accused of excessive piety. Descartes' concern with metaphysical and theological questions also clearly antedates the *Meditations*. For example, there are already metaphysical questions at play in the *Little Notebook*. Moreover, the challenge to the certainty of his science that so concerns him, as we noted above, does not require the actual existence of an omnipotent God but only his mere possibility. Descartes thus does not have to believe in such a God or even in any God at all to entertain such doubts. He only has to be unable to prove such a God's nonexistence. In a certain sense then even if his metaphysics is constructed only to answer wild and hyperbolic doubts, those doubts are quite real and resolving them therefore quite important for Descartes' enterprise. Unless Descartes can eliminate them, his science can never be apodictic. Thus, Descartes is not insincere when he writes to Mersenne on April 15, 1630: "I

believe that all those to whom God has given the use of reason are obliged
to use it mainly to know Him and to know themselves. That is how I tried
to begin my studies, and I would not have been able to find the basis for
my physics if I had not looked for it along these lines."[94] The fear of God,
of this omnipotent God and the skepticism that his very possibility engenders, thus reappears in the *Meditations* as the beginning of wisdom.

Some scholars have argued that Descartes cannot seriously have believed that divine omnipotence gives rise to radical doubt, because he
believes that God is constrained by the law of noncontradiction. The evidence, however, indicates that this interpretation is incorrect. Descartes,
for example, argues in a letter to Mersenne of May 27, 1630 that while God's
will is eternal there was no necessity that impelled him to create eternal
truths and, therefore, they could be different.[95] The possibility of God acting in alternative ways is thus not excluded by the law of noncontradiction. He explains this to Mésland in his letter of May 2, 1644: "The power
of God can have no limits. . . . God cannot have been determined to make
it true that contradictions cannot be together, and consequently He could
have done the contrary."[96] Therefore, he concludes in a famous letter to Arnauld of July 29, 1648 that it is not impossible for God to make a mountain
without a valley or to make one plus two not equal three.[97] This said, Descartes does not believe that God changes his laws. He writes to Mersenne
on April 15, 1630:

> Do not be afraid to proclaim everywhere that God established these laws in
> nature just as a sovereign establishes laws in his kingdom. . . . One will tell
> you that if God established these truths, He would also be able to change
> them just as a king changes his laws; to which one should reply that it is
> possible if His will can change. But I understand these truths as eternal and
> unvarying in the same way that I judge God. His power is beyond compre-
> hension, and generally we assume ourselves that God can do everything
> we are capable of understanding but not that He cannot do what we are
> incapable of understanding, for it would be presumptuous to think that our
> imagination has as much magnitude as His power.[98]

Descartes thus claims that God can contravene the laws he has established
(including the law of noncontradiction), but that he will not do so. Descartes, however, does not explain why he believes God's will to be unvarying and calls this claim into question with his assertion of the incomprehensibility of God.[99] If God is truly omnipotent, then the light of reason
might be false and apodictic science therefore impossible.

There are two traditional answers to the skepticism that Descartes
considers and rejects at the end of the path of doubt. The first, which was

originally articulated by Augustine in *Contra academicos,* sees faith as the answer to skepticism. This is the path of piety. As we have seen, this solution was also employed by Luther who proclaimed in his debate with Erasmus that "the Holy Ghost is not a skeptic." [100] While Descartes does not deny that faith may in some sense be an answer to skepticism, he argues that faith of this sort cannot provide an answer to the skeptical doubts he raises. He notes that it is not contrary to God's goodness to allow him to sometimes be deceived, so it cannot be contrary to his goodness that he always be deceived.[101] Luther's answer in this instance is no more compelling than that of Augustine. Sheer faith in God cannot alleviate these doubts because it is God himself who is the source of these doubts, and the more powerful one imagines God to be, the easier it is to imagine the possibility that he can deceive us.

The second potential answer to this form of doubt is atheism. If there is no God and everything occurs simply by an endless antecedent necessity, it would seem that such radical doubt would be impossible. Descartes suggests that such a materialist notion cannot resolve the problem because the possibility that we are accidentally constituted in such a way as to be continually deceived about the nature of the world is even greater than the possibility that God deceives us.[102] For Descartes whether we follow the path of faith that relies on God or the path of experience that depends on man, we cannot provide the foundation for science.

The skepticism that bedevils Descartes both in part 4 of the *Discourse* and at the end of the First Meditation is resolved by his fundamental principle. He concludes in the *Discourse* that in attempting to think everything false, he recognized that in so doing he who was thinking this had to be something, and thus articulated his famous principle, "I think, therefore I am." [103] This conclusion takes a slightly different form in the *Meditations,* where he writes that "this proposition, I am, I exist, is necessarily true whenever it is put forward by me or conceived in my mind." [104]

How are we to understand this principle? On the surface it looks as if it is the conclusion of a syllogism, but Descartes rejects this notion in the *Replies.*[105] If it were the conclusion of a syllogism, it could not be fundamental since it would depend on more fundamental premises and on the principle of noncontradiction. Descartes asserts in the *Discourse* and later in the *Principles* that it is a judgment.[106] In the *Meditations* he calls it a necessary conclusion, by which he means that it is the conclusion of a judgment, the affirmation of a necessary connection.[107] It is, however, a peculiar kind of judgment, for its truth lies not in its logical form but in its performance.[108] It is not a statement that is true in the abstract; it is only true and can only be recognized as true when it is performed or experienced. Or to put the matter in Kantian terms, it is a synthetic a priori truth. That said, it is not just any synthetic a priori truth; it is rather the I's self-grounding act, its self-creation. Descartes explains the nature of such self-grounding judgments in the *Replies:* "We cannot doubt them unless we think of them, but we cannot think of them without at the same time believing that they are true. . . . Hence we cannot doubt them without at the same time believing they are true, that is, we can never doubt them."[109] In order to understand the nature of this conclusion, however, we need to examine more fully what Descartes means by thinking and judging.

Descartes defines thinking in a variety of ways. In the *Rules* he lists four cognitive capacities: understanding, imagination, sensation, and memory.[110] In his later thought he expands his notion. In the Second Meditation he asserts that a thing that thinks is a thing that doubts, understands, affirms, denies, wills, refuses, imagines, and senses.[111] In the Third Meditation he characterizes himself as a thinking thing *(res cogitans)* who doubts, affirms, denies, knows a few things, is ignorant of many, loves, hates, wills, desires, and also imagines and senses.[112] In the *Replies* he asserts that thought includes everything we are immediately conscious of and falls into four general categories, will (which includes doubt, affirmation, denial, rejection, love, and hate), understanding, imagination, and sensation.[113] In the *Principles,* he argues that thinking is divided into two modes: (1) perception or the operation of the intellect which includes sensation, imagination, and the conception of things purely intellectual, and (2) action of the will that includes desiring, holding in aversion, affirming, denying, and doubting.[114] Finally, in the *Passions* he argues similarly that there are two basic functions of the soul, its actions and its passions.[115] Only those passions that originate in the body are in his view passions properly speaking; those that arise in the soul are both actions and passions and take their name from the nobler former capacity.

We saw earlier that judgment for the early Descartes was made possible by the power of the imagination that brought together the schematized images derived from sensation with formalized ideas. In his later thought, the imagination becomes more a screen on which the images are projected, the backside of the brain or pineal gland.[116] In this sense it is no longer the active power in judgment. For the mature Descartes, judgment is the combination of two different mental capacities, will and understanding. The latter is more passive than before, and the role of will much greater. Through will, for example, the understanding becomes active as perception (from *percipere,* literally "by grasping"). Will stimulates the brain to form images as an aid to understanding, usurping the previous role of imagination. It also displaces intuition as the capacity that summons up the innate ideas.[117] Judgment in this way becomes a determination of the will.[118] Thinking for the mature Descartes is thus a form of willing.[119] This becomes particularly apparent when we examine the character of the thinking that establishes itself as the fundamental principle.

Descartes fundamental principle is often understood as self-consciousness or subjectivity. What Descartes means by self-thinking, however, is quite different from the ordinary notion of self-consciousness. Thinking for Descartes is clearly reflexive. He writes to Mersenne in July 1641: "I have demonstrated that the soul is nothing other than a thing that thinks; it is therefore impossible that we can ever think of anything without having at the same time the idea of our soul, as of a thing capable of thinking all that we think about."[120] Descartes, of course, was not the first to recognize that we can think ourselves. This issue was raised by Plato in his *Charmides*, and in later Neoplatonic thought as well as in the thought of Augustine. These earlier notions of self-consciousness, however, all imagined that the self that consciousness was conscious of was somehow an object like the other objects in the world, that is, that I am conscious of myself in the same way that I am conscious of, say, a chair, or that whenever I have an idea of a chair I also have alongside it an idea of myself as conscious of the chair. Descartes' notion of the thinking of thinking, however, has little to do with such an idea.

Descartes does not think that we are self-conscious because we have ourselves as our own object. For Descartes, everything that we know is known only when it is perceived, transmitted to the brain, and represented upon the screen of the imagination by the will. The sensed object in this way is transformed into a mathematical line or form on a coordinate system, which Descartes refers to as extension. Thus the world only truly is when it is represented rather than sensed or imagined, that is, only when it is factual in a literal sense as something made or constructed (from the Latin *facere,* "to make"). This construction of the world is its representation or objectification. This representation, however, is always a representation for a subject, always only in thinking. Thinking as representing is thus always a representing for a subject. The subject is that which is established or thrown under *(sub-iectum)* the object, that is, that which is thrown off or before us *(ob-iectum).* Consequently, the subject is necessarily posited or willed in every act of thinking. Every act of thinking is thus also a self-thinking, or to put the matter in a later vocabulary, all consciousness is self-consciousness. Descartes' solution to the problem posed by the omnipotent God thus leads to a radically new vision of what it is to be a human being.[121]

A human being for Descartes is a thinking thing *(res cogitans)*. A thinking thing, however, is a representing, constructing thing, and is especially always a self-representing or self-positing thing. The Cartesian human being is thus at its core a self-positing, self-grounding being. Man in this way ceases to be considered the rational animal and instead is conceived as the willing being. Both humanism and the Reformation, as we have seen, similarly located man's humanity in the will rather than the reason. Descartes is indebted to both but also moves beyond them. In contrast to humanism, his subject is abstracted from the historical world, and has no personality, no virtues or vices, no concern with immortal fame. The willing subject, however, is thus not constrained by the finitude of this world and consequently can imagine becoming its absolute master. Similarly, the subject's will is not subordinate to or in conflict with the will of God. The problem that we saw at the heart of Luther's thought and in the debate between Erasmus and Luther thus seems at least on the surface to be resolved.

This subject's rethinking of thinking as willing is the ground of Descartes' attempt to construct a citadel of reason for human beings against the potentially malevolent omnipotence of God. This is particularly apparent in his formulation of his fundamental principle. The fundamental principle arises at the end of the path of doubt. In Descartes' later accounts of thinking, doubt is classified as a form of the will, but it occupies an unusual place, since all other forms of the will are paired opposites (affirming and denying, desiring and holding in aversion). Doubting in one sense seems to stand between affirming and denying, but in another sense it looks as if it should be paired with faith or belief, which is perhaps suppressed in Descartes' account because of its controversial place in Reformation debates. In fact, for Descartes the concealed opposite of doubt is not belief or faith but certainty. Certainty and natural science thereby replace faith and theology for Descartes.

The attainment of certainty is not an act of the intellect or understanding but an act of the will. Certainty for Descartes arises when we can no longer doubt, that means at the end of the path of doubt. Doubting as a form of willing is thus the means of reaching certainty, the foundation of Descartes' universal science. The heart of Descartes' fundamental principle is the recognition that doubt, as a form of negation, cannot negate itself, that such a negation is in fact a negation of negation and thus a self-affirmation.[122] In this manner the will constitutes itself as a self and thus as the foundation or *subiectum* upon which everything can be established.[123]

To become master of nature, Descartes tells us, one must first become master of oneself, by freeing oneself from the illusions of the imagination. We assert our freedom by exercising our will in the form of doubt to avoid being taken in by any of these illusions. Will thereby asserts its superiority and its freedom from both God and his creation.[124] However, as we have seen, such freedom is the freedom of the void. The will as doubt or negation shatters the world into a million pieces, leading Descartes to suppose that he and the world are nothing.[125] Doubt, however, discovers that it cannot doubt itself.[126] In freeing itself from illusion, the will discovers that it cannot will itself away, and in this discovery lays the foundation for its conquest of the natural world.

For Descartes doubt thus ends not in skepticism or in the aporetic wisdom of Socrates and Montaigne but in a practically useful science that makes possible the mastery of nature and the alleviation of the human estate. The principle of this new science is thus individual autonomy that arises out of the self-assertion and self-positing of the human will.[127] The self is therefore not just another object but the foundation of the representational reconstruction of the world; and the citadel of reason, the great city described at beginning of *Discourse,* is build upon this foundation.

Thinking for humanism was also a form of willing, a poetic making and self-making that painted an image of the world. Descartes accepts this humanist notion, but he believes that we cannot rely upon the imagination to bring about such a reconstruction. The "truth" of the imagination, the artwork and technology rooted in the imagination, present at best merely probable solutions to a *fortuna* that remains outside of and apart from the self. Descartes' representational reconstruction of the self and the world rests not upon the imagination but upon an analytic algebra underpinned by a self-certifying self. Descartes' "poetic" remaking of the world thus produces a world that is no longer a cosmos or a creation independent of man but a human artifact that comes to be through me and that can therefore be totally mine. It is as it is only with respect to me; it is proper to me; and it can therefore become my property. To understand how this change is brought about, however, we need to examine more carefully the manner in which Descartes expropriates this world from its previous owner, that is, from God himself.

Descartes' fundamental principle, *ego cogito ergo sum,* seems on the surface to guarantee only the existence of a self that thinks. Descartes claims, however, that it is the key to establishing the certainty of his universal science, the Archimedean point from which he will be able to move the world. How does the fundamental principle, the self-creating I, guarantee

the certainty of science and thus make possible the mastery and appropriation of nature?

(According to Descartes, the fundamental principle is not only true; it is
the standard of all other truth. That is to say, for any other judgment to be
true, it must be as clear and evident as the fundamental principle. On the
surface, it is difficult to see how other judgments could attain such clarity
and evidence. If we look a bit deeper, however, it becomes clear that other
judgments can be true only if they are derived from or rest on this principle. The truth of Cartesian science depends on the truth of mathematics
and the truth of mathematics is called into question only by the possibility
of an omnipotent deceiver. Therefore, if it is possible to show on the basis
of Descartes' fundamental principle that there cannot be such a deceiver,
the truths of mathematics will be irrefutable and the apodictic character
of Cartesian science will be guaranteed. To be sure, physics will depend
upon the actual (as opposed to the possible) existence of objects, but this
existence can be methodologically verified. Thus, the only other truth that
has to be as clear and distinct as the fundamental principle is that God
is not a deceiver. But how is it possible to demonstrate on the basis of the
fundamental principle that God is not a deceiver? Or to put the matter in
somewhat different terms, how is it possible to tame the irrational God of
nominalism and the Reformation, and demonstrate that he neither is nor
can be a deceiver?[128]

(The demonstration of this point, Descartes' so-called ontological argument, is perhaps the most controversial element of Cartesian philosophy.
The customary interpretation of this argument reads it against the background of scholasticism. The ontological argument in its classical form was
first presented by Anselm in his *Monologium* and later repeated by Aquinas at the beginning of the *Summa* in his discussion of the various proofs
of God's existence. It is probably from this source that Descartes knew
it.[129] The argument depends on the scholastic distinction between levels of
being or reality. Substance or being, according to this account, has more
reality than accidents, and infinite being has more reality than finite being. God thus is more real than things and things more real than accidents
such as colors. Descartes employs this argument but gives it a peculiar
twist. When I look into myself, I find an idea of perfection, but because
I have come to understand myself as a finite being who can be deceived,
I recognize that I am not perfect and that the idea of perfection cannot
come from me. This idea, however, must come from somewhere and that
somewhere is God. God must be the cause of this idea. God therefore exists
and is perfect. The idea of God, according to Descartes, is thus innate in us

and follows from the fundamental principle.[130] If, however, God is perfect, then he never deceives us, because all deception is the result of some lack. Consequently, God is not a deceiver, and if God is not a deceiver, the truths of mathematics are certain. Moreover, God has also led me to believe in the existence of external objects and because he is not a deceiver there must be a correspondence between the objects and what is real, or at least it must be possible for me to come to understand the relationship between them through the proper use of my faculties. As a result, not merely mathematics but physics must be possible. God thus guarantees the truth of clear and distinct ideas and belief in God is thus necessary for science, but God himself is guaranteed by the certainty of the fundamental principle.[131]

(As convincing as this traditional interpretation of Descartes' ontological argument is, Jean-Luc Marion has given us reasons to doubt that the story can be as straightforward as this account suggests. In particular he has pointed out the apparent inconsistency of Descartes' definition of God: in the Third Meditation he is called infinite; in the Fifth Meditation he is a perfect being; and in the First and Fourth Replies he is characterized as a *causi sui*.[132] If he is infinite, God must be beyond reason and therefore a potential deceiver; if he is perfect, though, he cannot be; and if he is a *causa sui,* he is subordinate to the laws of reason. This suggests that the traditional reading of the ontological argument cannot capture the richness of Descartes' account. The traditional view of the argument, at least in this case, seems to be a description of the mask that Descartes puts on to make his science more palatable to the orthodox. The fact that Descartes disguises his true opinions, however, does not mean that he is really an atheist, as a number of scholars have asserted. Rather it suggests that his understanding of God is more complicated and unorthodox than has traditionally been believed.

(In fact Descartes' understanding of God and thus the ontological argument that he uses to demonstrate God's existence depends on a new understanding of infinity that is radically different than anything that preceded it and that is essential to the formation of the mathematics that is at the foundation of modern science and the modern world. Moreover, this new notion of the infinite makes it possible to reconcile the three different definitions of God that Marion describes. To understand this we must return again to Anselm's classical formulation of the ontological argument. When Anselm says that God is infinite, he is asserting that God is fundamentally mysterious, for following Aristotle, he believes that the infinite is incomprehensible.[133] When Descartes describes God as infinite, however, he is asserting that he can be understood. This is a remarkable claim. Even

Bonaventure, who understood the difference between the finite and the infinite with great clarity, does not believe that God can be understood in this way.[134] Descartes can understand God in this way because he has already defined him as a substance different only in quantity from other beings.[135]

The infinite for the ancients and for scholasticism was regarded as the negation of the finite and therefore as something that does not exist or is not comprehensible in its own right. In ascribing the term to God, Christianity was simply asserting that he was incalculably greater and radically different than all other beings. Drawing upon his work in geometry, Descartes believed it was possible to formulate a positive idea of the infinite that was not merely a negative but a positive path to understanding God. In fact, Descartes suggested that the tradition had it exactly wrong. The infinite is not the negation of the finite; rather the finite is a negation of the infinite.[136] He adopts as his model here not an infinite sequence but an unbounded figure.[137] If we think of God's infinity as an unbounded plane extending in every direction, then all finite beings are only negations of this infinity, bounded figures inscribed upon this plane. In his view we can thus understand God in the same way we understand an infinite figure. Consequently, we do not merely have an idea of God by negation or by summation, but as a whole at one time.[138]

Now it might be objected that what Descartes is actually doing here is simply identifying God with the infinite. He tries to defend himself against this charge, claiming that the idea of the infinite is an imperfect model for God since God is infinite in every respect, infinitely infinite. Descartes thus wants to reserve the term 'infinite' for God and to call other infinite things indefinite.[139] This, however, is not a real distinction, for Descartes concludes that while we therefore cannot understand God perfectly on the model of an infinite figure, we can understand him as clearly and distinctly as a limitless figure can be understood.[140]

Since God is infinite, he cannot be imagined, but he can be conceived, which is to say that we do have an idea of God. Indeed, Descartes claims that the knowledge of our own existence includes the idea of God.[141] What he seems to mean by this is that the recognition of the self in the fundamental principle is a recognition of its own limitation, that is, the recognition that I am a finite being. This recognition is, however, at the same time the recognition of the unlimited, that is, of the will itself, and this unlimited will is God. We are only a limitation of the unlimited, finite figures inscribed upon an infinite plane, negations of this infinite whole that is God.

But in what sense is this notion of God included in the fundamental principle? The answer to this follows from our earlier examination of thinking. There we saw that thinking at its core was will and the self wills itself in the act of thinking the fundamental principle. It thus follows that in the same act that I will myself to be I, I will God to be God. This God that I will, however, is not the omnipotent and potentially malevolent God of nominalism that produced such fear and uncertainty. Nor is he Luther's hidden (or revealed) God. In fact, this God cannot be a deceiver because he is not aware of himself and therefore not aware of the difference between him and I. This is an important implication of Descartes' argument, but it is not immediately clear without some additional explanation.

For Descartes, I come to recognize myself as limited and distinct at the end of the path of doubt. In becoming self-conscious, in positing myself as a finite being, I recognized myself as distinct from other beings, as needy, as imperfect. God, however, comes to no such realization. He is not finite and thus cannot be self-conscious of himself because his will is never impeded, never limited by what it is not. God thus cannot distinguish himself from all that is. As a result, he cannot be a deceiver. And if God is not a deceiver, then Descartes' universal science is secure.

Descartes in this way tames the nominalist God by reducing him to pure intellectual substance. This was already clear in the *Little Notebook* where he asserts that God is pure intelligence. God's intelligence, however, in Descartes' mature thought is equivalent to his will. As pure intelligence, God is pure will. As infinite, God's will is not directed to anything specific; it is causality as such. God is the *causa sui* because he is pure causality, the mechanism at the heart of mechanical nature, a how and not a what.[142] Looking backward we could say that he is *fortuna,* or forward, the source of the motion of all matter.[143]

The goal of Cartesian science is to master nature, or more correctly to master this motion and this causality at the heart of nature. Put in somewhat different terms the goal of his science is to comprehend and master God. Descartes' science achieves this end by reconstructing the chaos of the world in representation, by transforming the flux of experience into the motion of objects in a mathematically analyzable space. The omnipotent God of nominalism and the Reformation is thus unable to enter into Descartes' rationalized universe unless he gives up his absolute will and lives according to the powers that Descartes ordains. He is dispossessed of his absolute power and his world, which falls increasingly under the hegemony of the scientific ego. In this reading, Descartes' proof of God's existence is a proof of God's impotence or at least of his irrelevance for human affairs.[144] As Descartes puts it, whether or not God exists, nature operates in much the same way and in either case we must use the same mathematical means to understand it.[145]

(But how can man compete with God, for the mastery of appearances and the possession of the world?[146] The answer to this is fairly clear: man can only compete with God if man himself in some sense is omnipotent, that is, if man in some sense is already God.[147] The key to understanding this titanic claim that lies at the heart of Descartes' thought is understanding that for Descartes both God and man are essentially willing beings. Descartes tells us that the human will is the same as the will of God.[148] In his view it is infinite, indifferent, and perfectly free, not subordinate to reason or any other law or rule.[149] It is consequently the sole basis of human perfection.[150]

The difference between God and man, Descartes suggests, lies not in their wills, which are identical, but in their knowledge. Man's will is infinite, he wants everything and his desires are insatiable, but his knowledge is finite. His power is thus limited by his knowledge.[151] In contrast to Kant, who would face a similar disjunction, Descartes does not counsel the restraint and accommodation of the will to the limits of the understanding, in large part because he believes that the limits of the understanding are not given but are rather the consequence of the past misapplication of the will.[152]

What is crucial for Descartes is the rational application of the will to the mastery of nature. Descartes believes that his method and *mathesis universalis* will make this possible. Humans are therefore godlike but they are not yet god. To become god, to master nature utterly and dispossess God entirely, one needs Cartesian science. This finally is the answer to the problem with which Descartes began his philosophizing: if the fear of the Lord is the beginning of wisdom, then wisdom is the means by which the Lord is captured, disarmed, dispossessed, and subsumed within the citadel of reason.

(If God is understood in this manner, Descartes believes that religious conflict will disappear. The reason for this becomes clear when we reflect on Descartes' account of his dream in *Olympica*. God and religion derive their power over human beings from the natural human fear that they will be punished for their sins, not just their public sins but their secret sins, the sins hidden in the depths of their souls, perhaps even from themselves. The fear of punishment for these sins is like a great wind or an evil spirit that whirls us about and drives us toward the church and away from our secular communities of friends. Luther is an obvious example of the

power of such fears, and the Wars of Religion were the most grievous consequence of giving in to them. The spirit of truth manifested in Cartesian
science clears our mind of the terrifying illusions of the imagination that
give force to these fears. Freed from these illusions, we can then understand the path we should follow in life, a path that is humanistic in its
development but that is finally rooted in a mathematical representation
and appropriation of nature. At the end of this process we will no longer be
governed by the fear of God but by good sense, especially when it is used,
as he tells Princess Elizabeth in a letter of 1646, by a prince guided by a
nearly divine will guaranteeing the rights of thinking subjects.[153] Indeed,
Descartes seems to suggest that with the spread of his method, good sense
will come to predominate in human beings and as a result they will all
agree to form such a regime.[154]

The generally liberal consequences of his science were not something
that Descartes could bruit about with impunity. Indeed, he only began to
reveal these consequences later in life, when he had more powerful friends
and protectors. Sadly, however, even his fame and friends were unable to
keep him safe from harm. The outbreak of the Fronde in France and the
attacks leveled against him by Voetius and others in Holland were the
principal reasons Descartes decided reluctantly to move to Sweden and
accept the protection of Queen Christiana.[155] The Queen demanded that
Descartes tutor her every winter morning before dawn, and with the repeated exposure to the frigid weather in an unheated coach, his health
deteriorated rapidly and he died.

Descartes was able in the end to resolve the fear of the Lord with his
completed wisdom. The price he had to pay for this, however, was high. In
part, like Marlowe's Dr. Faustus, he could only achieve this goal by abandoning traditional religious beliefs and following what began at least as a
Hermetic path. But this was not the greatest danger. The God that Descartes first imagined and feared was a titanic God, beyond reason and nature, beyond good and evil. Descartes won his struggle with this fearsome
God only by taking this God's power upon himself.[156] He thereby opened
up the hope and aspiration for human omnipotence, a hope that has manifested itself repeatedly since in monstrous form.

7 | *Hobbes' Fearful Wisdom*

In 1588 a young woman lay in childbirth in a small vicarage in southwestern England. The baby was coming earlier than she'd expected. But then, she'd not expected those Catholics to come with all their ships either. It had terrified her. A foreign invasion here in England! An invasion of Papists! She knew that was why she was before her time. But what a time to bring a child into the world! Fear was in the air, and everyone expected the worst. Could Queen Bess's navy stop those Spanish devils, and their Popery? She and her family would have it bad if they could not. They were Calvinists and her husband a vicar. "Will they butcher us like they did those poor Huguenots?" she wondered. "Why would they treat us any differently? We're Calvinists, too. And even if they spare us, how will we survive if my Thomas loses his living? If they bring back their cardinals and priests?"

In retrospect, it may seem as if the fears of this young woman were exaggerated, but such concerns were only too well grounded. It was a fearsome time. The son who was born that day, her Thomas, would understand this fear and give it a voice it had never had before. Indeed, recounting his birth in his *Verse Life* more than eighty years later, he remarked that "Mother Dear/ Did bring forth Twins at once, both Me, and Fear."[1] The man in question was, of course, Thomas Hobbes, and he was referring to the coincidence of his birth and the terrifying threat of the Spanish Armada. Hobbes suggests in the witty passage that his very birth was linked to fear, the passion that he famously proclaimed the wellspring of human behavior. Appearances notwithstanding, his quip was anything but lighthearted. Indeed, it points to a dark reality at the heart of Hobbes' thought, rooted in the violence of his time but reflecting what he took to be a universal fact of the human condition and a continual burden on the human psyche: the world, God's creation, seems not to be ordered for our happiness and well-being, but to be inimical to us and willing to kill us if it can.

In light of this threat, Hobbes knew that the most natural human passion is fear. It is intrinsic to the way in which we are in the world, and in order to improve our lot, we need to acknowledge this fact. Hobbes believed that his contemporaries were unwilling to do so because they were misled by three false doctrines. The first was the scholastic vision of a harmonious world that was a manifestation of divine reason and justice. The second was the humanist idea that we can attain immortality through glorious deeds. The third was the teaching of the Reformation and Counterreformation that portrayed death in the service of God as a form of martyrdom that guaranteed salvation. For Hobbes all three of these were forms of deception propagated by human beings seeking their own advantage. Such deceptions, however, could be exposed and overcome, thereby legitimizing our fear of violent death and promoting the use of reason to minimize or eliminate it. The goal of Hobbes' thought is thus to eliminate violence, secure our preservation, and promote our prosperity.

To admit that one is afraid of death is at least on the surface to admit that one is a coward. This is exactly how Hobbes described himself. Indeed, perhaps no thinker before or since has gone to such lengths to emphasize his cowardice, repeatedly reminding his contemporaries that he was among the first to flee the country at the beginning of the Civil War. Why tell such a story? It was certainly advantageous for a Calvinist in the royalist camp to emphasize his opposition to the Puritans, but it is hard to believe that this could offset the opprobrium of the cavaliers among whom he moved who were trained in the humanist tradition and who accorded courage pride of place among the virtues. Hobbes' claim, however, was not intended to curry favor with those in power. Rather, it had a deeper philosophic purpose, and it points to a fundamental revaluation of fear and courage that is intrinsic to Hobbes' thought and to modernity generally. For Hobbes cowardice is not a vice; it is the source of the greatest of all virtues, for it is rooted in a passion that promotes the wisdom and science necessary to secure and sustain peace and prosperity.

As we have seen, Hobbes and his contemporaries had good reasons for such fear. England was spared invasion in 1588 by the courage and ingenuity of its navy and by a great deal of good luck. The fears of Hobbes' mother were neither frivolous nor hyperbolic. Had the Spaniards succeeded in landing in England, the results would almost certainly have been horrifying. However, the fear of violent death in Hobbes' view does not only arise in dangerous times and situations; it continually besets us even if we do not ordinarily perceive or understand this fact.

Hobbes believes that our goal should not be to overcome the fear of violent death but to eliminate the violence that is its source. Death in his view is the result of an interruption of our vital life processes brought about by a collision with other human and nonhuman things that interrupt our vital motions. The fear of violent death is thus really the fear of such collisions. In order to preserve ourselves, we thus must understand and eliminate the causes of such collisions. The search for the ultimate causes of such collisions, however, leads us back to the beginning of all motion and that for Hobbes is God. Insofar as fear inspires us to reason, it is thus the fear of the Lord that for Hobbes (as for Descartes) is the beginning of wisdom. Hobbes' science in general and his political science in particular thus involve an investigation of God.

(The fear of gods was well known in the classical world, but this fear was generally considered a distraction and not the source of wisdom. Thinking for Aristotle begins in the experience of wonder, and it is a love of things that are higher and more beautiful than we are. For Hobbes thinking begins not with a sense of the overwhelming and inexplicable bounty of being but with a recognition that misery and death are close at hand and that we need to preserve ourselves. Fear leads us to search for to the invisible causes behind all things.

(Our initial response to the fear of such invisible powers is to propitiate them. According to Hobbes, this is the source of the natural piety that is the foundation of all religions.[2] The world for natural man is a dark place ruled by a mysterious and indefinable force that ultimately produces our death.[3] While our fear of this dark power typically ends in superstition, Hobbes suggests that under the right conditions it can also induce us to the kind of reflections that improve our earthly lot. The first step toward this end is the recognition that the gods or God do not intervene directly in earthly affairs. Once this becomes clear, fear pushes human beings in a new direction, away from a concern with a malign divine will that has singled us out and toward an encounter with the reality of the natural world. This in turn gives rise to the joy in discovering the causes of things that Hobbes calls curiosity. The final step is the recognition that by understanding causes we can develop a science that will make us masters and possessors of nature and enable us to eliminate the danger of violent death.

(This brief summary of Hobbes' argument is sufficient to allow us to see the deep connection between theology, politics, and science in his thought. In what follows, I will argue that his dark view of the world is the result of his acceptance of the basic tenets of nominalism, especially as it is received and transmuted by the Reformation. I will argue further that Hobbes transforms this thought in essential ways. Luther and Calvin sought to show that nothing we do on earth can affect our chances of salvation, which depend solely on divine election. Hobbes accepts this doctrine of unconditional election, but he turns it on its head. If nothing we do on earth affects our salvation, then there is no soteriological reason to perform any earthly action. Properly understood, the nominalist doctrine of divine omnipotence and the Calvinist notion of election that follows from it thus undermine the authority of religion in secular affairs. Therefore, it is not the rejection of religion that produces modern natural and political science but the theological demonstration of religion's irrelevance for life in this world. Before we discuss this more fully, we need to examine the background of Hobbes' thought.

THE HISTORICAL BACKGROUND OF HOBBES' THOUGHT

In the three hundred years between Ockham and Hobbes England underwent a remarkable transformation. The first two centuries were torn by a series of wars that ended with the establishment of the Tudor dynasty (1486–1603) under Henry VII. While the Tudor period was relatively peaceful, it was a time of immense change. Politically, the Tudors transformed England from a feudal society to a centralized state. Intellectually, the almost simultaneous arrival of humanism and the Reformation swept away traditional forms and practices. Humanism arrived in the time of Henry VII and reached its zenith in the mid-sixteenth century with the ascendancy of More, Colet, Spenser, Sidney, and (somewhat later) Shakespeare. English humanists on the whole were less given to Prometheanism than the Italians and more rooted in the Christian humanist tradition.[4] However, they were deeply interested in Hermeticism and the magical knowledge of unseen causes. Marlowe's Doctor Faustus, Shakespeare's Prospero, and the scientists of Bacon's *New Atlantis* are literary reflections of such famous magi as John Dee and Robert Fludd, who had an impact not merely in England but also in Bohemia and the rest of Europe.

The English Renaissance was foreshortened by the advent of the Reformation. The English Reformation began as a movement from above with Henry VIII's nationalization of the church, but it soon became more radical as the pressure for changes like those on the continent percolated up from below. This is hardly surprising. The English had long been more radical theologically than the rest of Europe. Scotus and Ockham were two obvious early examples, but John Wycliff (1324–84) was more important, raising the challenge to the church that culminated in Hus and Luther.

Despite his rejection of papal authority, Henry VIII did not attempt to transform religious doctrine or practice in fundamental ways, and he sided with the church, for example, against Luther. After his death and the ascension of his young son Edward VI (1547), Protestants gained the upper hand. When Edward's early death (1553) brought his half-sister "Bloody" Mary to the throne, she sought to reestablish Catholicism through force. Her marriage to the (Catholic) King of Spain produced no offspring and she died in 1558. Her successor Elizabeth I reached a settlement with the various religious groups in 1559 (embodied in the Thirty-Nine Articles of 1563) that guaranteed the independence of the English church with a centralized, episcopal structure. However, radical Protestantism continued to grow with the return of refugees who had gone to Geneva and Germany during Mary's reign. They brought with them religious views that led to the emergence of Presbyterianism in Scotland and Independency in England. These Calvinist Dissenters from the Elizabethan settlement were characterized by their opponents as Puritans.

The opposing parties continued to agitate for change, and concerns were heightened by religious warfare in France and the Netherlands. For many Calvinists the slaughter of St. Bartholomew's Day and the threat of the Spanish Armada in 1588 were ominous signs. Their Protestant queen could not live forever, and they knew that her successor would likely be less friendly to their cause. Still, their strength was growing, and in 1590 the Archbishops of Canterbury and York both endorsed the Calvinist notion of absolute predestination.

At the same time, a new religious movement, Arminianism, had sprung up. Arminianism was named after its Dutch founder Jacobus Arminius (1560–1609), who had been a student of Calvin's successor Theodore Beza but rejected Calvinism because he believed it made God the author of sin. Drawing on Erasmus, he argued that free will was important in determining salvation and damnation. Such a theology appealed to many in England, and Arminianism grew rapidly. This new theology, however, was viewed with suspicion by Calvinists who saw it as crypto-Catholicism, a disguised form of "Popery."

The struggle between the Calvinists and the Arminians, which mirrored the earlier debate between Luther and Erasmus, became more pronounced after the death of Elizabeth and the coronation of James VI of Scotland as James I. He was the son of Mary Stuart, Queen of Scots, who had tried to revive Catholicism in Scotland. Although raised as a Protestant, he had to navigate between Catholics and Protestants in Scotland. He preferred Episcopalianism in part because it steered a middle course but also because it provided the strongest theological support for his belief in divine right. The king in his view was God's anointed and was thus subject to no man, including the pope.

The Calvinists demanded the suppression of Catholicism, but James continued Elizabeth's policy of toleration, although with greater difficulty after 1605, when the Gunpowder Plot rekindled Protestant fears.[5] Calvinists, however, were not alone in seeking reform. The Arminians too were gaining ground, especially in the universities. One of the king's closest advisors, the Arminian William Laud, attacked Calvinism in 1615.[6] The struggle between the two groups continued for the next decade and mirrored the similar struggle in Holland.[7] Laud's influence gave the Arminians the upper hand, and Calvinism was outlawed at Oxford in 1626 and at Cambridge in 1632. In the interim the dispute became so disruptive that in 1628 the king banned all debates between the two groups.[8]

The outcome in England was the reverse of that in Holland, where Arminianism was condemned at the Synod of Dort in 1619. As a result many Calvinists left England for Holland (or the New World) or joined one of the new nonconforming sects.[9] Many nonconformists were convinced that the institutionalization of Arminianism was only a preparation for "Popery." Even moderate Calvinists saw Arminianism as a form of philosophical skepticism and thus as an extension of the humanism of More and Erasmus that had characterized English Catholicism in the preceding century. Calvinists were somewhat mollified by the marriage of the king's daughter Elizabeth to the Protestant Elector of the Palatinate (1613), but they were furious with his attempt to marry his son Charles to a Catholic Spanish princess and only somewhat less angry when he instead married him to the Catholic sister of the king of France.

When Charles became king in 1625, he pursued a complicated and duplicitous strategy in dealing with the Calvinists. He was a high Anglican and opposed to all forms of Calvinism, but he desperately needed parliament's support because of the dire financial condition of the monarchy. He sought to win Calvinist support by promising not to tolerate Catholicism, while he secretly promised the French king to do just that. He sought to gain funding for his foreign policy and to circumvent the religious struggle by appealing to the Republicans but was forced to grant the Petition of Right in 1628 as the condition of their support. In fact Charles I was never really willing to work with parliament and invariably viewed it as a barrier to his power. To consolidate his power, he needed the church firmly under his control, and therefore appointed Laud Archbishop of Canterbury in 1633.

The dominance of the Arminian faction exacerbated relations with the Calvinists, who believed that Laud intended to reintroduce Catholicism, and with the Republicans, who thought he wanted to repeal the Petition of Right. Before the Civil War parties formed around these religious and political differences. The Arminians, Episcopalians, and supporters of divine right stood on one side and the Presbyterians, Independents, and Republicans on the other.

(The war began when Charles attempted to impose episcopal church government on Scottish Presbyterians.[10] The Scottish Civil War spilled over to England and Ireland almost immediately, with shifting alliances among the various parties. Before 1643, the Puritan side included moderate Presbyterians, Scottish Presbyterians, Erastians, and Independents, but when they gained power in the Long Parliament, they split into competing groups. The Westminster Assembly of 1643 attempted to hold the alliance together but failed to find common ecumenical ground. The broader conflict lasted for many years with horrific casualties on both sides and among the civilian population. After much bitter warfare and with factions shifting from one side to the other, the Independents eventually gained the upper hand. They executed the king in 1649 and drove his son, Charles II, into exile in 1651. Their triumph, however, did not bring peace, for the victors found that their own theological differences made it impossible for them to work with one another or even to live peaceably together. The Protestant sects that had proliferated were not merely idiosyncratic in their beliefs and practices but also often intolerant of each other. Order was sustained only by the army under Oliver Cromwell, who became Lord Protector in 1653. With Cromwell's death and the failure of his son to win the army's confidence, parliament recognized the necessity of an accommodation with the Stuarts and agreed to a restoration of the monarchy in 1660.

Although Charles II was a high church Anglican, religion was less important to him than to his predecessors, and England settled into a period of peace. However, the peace was overhung by the recognition that the king had no legitimate son and would thus be succeeded by his brother James, a crypto-Catholic until 1673 and a professed Catholic thereafter. This produced the Exclusion Controversy (1679–81) based on a plan to exclude James from the throne, and to the Glorious Revolution (1688) that deposed him three years after he had become king.

HOBBES' LIFE

Born in 1588, Hobbes grew up in the small town of Malmesbury. He came from the middle-class, though his father was an ill-educated and often drunk Calvinist cleric.[11] As a child he studied with Robert Latimer, "a good Grecian," at Westport church, and remarkably translated *Medea* from Greek into Latin at the age of 14. This play with its terrifying vision of the dissolution of society perhaps appealed to him because of what his earliest biographer Aubrey called his melancholic disposition.[12] His studies followed a generally humanist path with a focus on languages and ancient authors, but with a Greek rather than a Latin focus.

In 1603 Hobbes went to Magdalen Hall, earlier a center of Puritanism, whose rector was John Wilkinson, a staunch Calvinist who emphasized the sinfulness of human nature.[13] Hobbes studied logic and Aristotelian physics, although he was not interested in either, and actually spent most of his time reading about astronomy and the New World. While the curriculum was probably scholastic, it is not clear whether it was realist or nominalist.[14] Some believe that the humanistic reforms of the mid-sixteenth century had brought a rhetorical element to the curriculum that remained strong even with the revival of Aristotelianism, and that Hobbes' education was more humanistic than most scholars assume.[15]

Completing his degree in 1608, Hobbes became the tutor for William Cavendish on the recommendation of Wilkinson. The Cavendishes were one of the great royalist families of Stuart England, and through them Hobbes entered the highest echelons of society and participated in discussions of the great political, theological, and intellectual issues of the day.[16] With only a few interruptions he stayed with them for the rest of his life.

Hobbes benefited from the family's extensive library, reading broadly in the humanist and Christian traditions, focusing more on Greek history and poetry than philosophy, and less on Roman moral and political thought than had earlier humanists.[17] He apparently had no interest in Platonism or Neoplatonism, and little sympathy for civic republicanism, but showed a keen interest in the Hermetic tradition.[18]

While many scholars treat the young Hobbes as a humanist, his concerns were distant from those of earlier humanists, who sought to reconcile Christian doctrine and Roman moral thought within a Platonic horizon. Hobbes insisted that Roman moral and political philosophy was pernicious and that Platonism was demonic and anti-Christian. In this respect, he was closer to Luther than to Petrarch and Ficino, or even to Erasmus and More.

William Cavendish was only slightly younger than Hobbes, and, as a result, Hobbes was more companion than tutor. They toured the continent from 1614 to 1615. During this trip, Hobbes saw Catholicism at first hand, and he became convinced that it had been corrupted by paganism. In one of his earliest essays, he argued that the ambition of the bishops of Rome had subverted the empire and that their sumptuousness and pride continued to corrupt Catholic doctrine and practice.[19] During this time in

Italy, he may have heard or met Paolo Sarpi, the nominalist and materialist whom David Wootton has called the only admitted atheist of his age.[20]

During this trip, Hobbes became more interested in Roman historical writing. According to Aubrey, he bought Julius Caesar's *Gallic Wars,* and he read Tacitus's account of the Cataline conspiracy, which was the topic of another early essay. He showed some admiration for Brutus and Cassius, but he had little sympathy for democracy and republicanism and continued to stress the importance of the sovereign's monopoly of force and the dangers of anarchy and civil war.

During this period he also became acquainted with the work of Bacon and came into contact with the Lord Chancellor, perhaps as early as 1615 but no later than 1620, when he served briefly as Bacon's amanuensis and translated some of his essays into Latin.[21] The extent of Bacon's influence on Hobbes is much debated. Most believe it was minimal since Hobbes did not like Bacon personally and rejected his empiricism and inductive method.[22] However, there are reasons to doubt this conclusion. First, Aubrey tells us that Bacon liked Hobbes best of all his secretaries because he understood what Bacon was talking about. Hobbes must have entered deeply into Bacon's thought to have so impressed the astute Lord Chancellor. Also, like Bacon he was a nominalist, and he adopted Bacon's notion that science must be practical rather than theoretical. He also shared Bacon's core notion that knowledge is power. All this suggests that Bacon was more important for Hobbes than is generally assumed. Moreover, a recent discovery further supports this view. In their investigation of the authorship of Bacon's works, Noel Reynolds and John Hilton found that in all likelihood a major portion of the *New Atlantis* was identifiably Hobbesian.[23] They do not suggest that Hobbes was the author of this work, which was found among Bacon's papers, but they do believe he played some substantial role in its composition. Bacon often had his secretaries write up his ideas. How great a role they played probably depended a great deal on their ability. It is at least fair to say that this stylistic analysis demonstrates that Hobbes was thoroughly familiar with this work and thus with Bacon's idea of the scientific transformation of society. Can we doubt that he was influenced by this notion?

Bacon's impact is often discounted because it does not seem to have deflected Hobbes from his humanistic concern with history and poetry. Indeed, the first work published in his own name, an edition of Thucydides, was a model of humanistic scholarship. However, Hobbes' interest in Thucydides was unusual for a humanist. Thucydides was perceived by the humanists to be a critic of republicanism. The similarity of Hobbes' edition to Machiavelli's *Discourses,* that some scholars see, is thus mistaken. Machiavelli uses Livy to promote Roman republicanism in a fashion that goes back to Petrarch. Hobbes, by contrast, uses Thucydides to demonstrate the inevitable *instability* of republicanism.[24] At the very least his interest in Thucydides reflects a more scientific approach to history, less concerned with history as moral rhetoric (as Cicero imagined it) than with history as an ineluctable chain of causes. Such a view of history puts Hobbes not in the humanist camp but in the company of Luther, Calvin, and Bacon.

Hobbes' companion William suddenly died in 1628. Hobbes accepted a position as a tutor for Gervase Clifton and accompanied him on a trip to the continent in 1629–30. During this trip Hobbes glanced at a copy of Euclid's *Elements* in a gentleman's library in Geneva, and, as Aubrey tells us, was transfixed by reading the 47th Proposition of book 1: "By God, sayd he . . . this is impossible! So he reads the Demonstration of it, which referred him back to such a Proposition; which proposition he read. That referred him back to another, which he also read. *Et sic deinceps* that at last he was demonstratively convinced of that truth. This made him in love with Geometry."[25]

This event is often taken to be the decisive moment in Hobbes' turn away from humanism to science. The development of Hobbes' science, however, depended not on a single event but on a series of factors. At its foundation, was Hobbes' belief in the Calvinist notion of predestination, which was the basis of his mechanistic notion of causality. Of similar importance was the impact of Bacon's notion that science was practical rather than theoretical. His "discovery" of Euclid provided Hobbes with the method he needed to realize his science, but even with this method, his science would have remained stillborn without two further insights that we will discuss below. In part the notion that Hobbes abandoned humanism is an illusion fostered by a misunderstanding of the nature of Hobbes' humanism. In contrast to earlier humanists he was more concerned with the Greeks than the Romans and with history than with philosophy. He was also more prone to see humans in a Calvinistic light as natural creatures subject to God's all-powerful will and less apt to see them humanistically as quasi-divine beings freely choosing their own natures or even as artists shaping their own characters. Hobbes' humanism was thus much closer to Calvinism and to modern natural science than the humanism from which Descartes began.

Hobbes' discovery of Euclid did change his approach, but it did not lead him to reject humanism in favor of science. He seems rather to have pursued both simultaneously. Returning to England, he became tutor to Cavendish's thirteen-year-old son. They translated and summarized Aristotle's *Rhetoric,* certainly an archetypal activity by humanist standards.[26] Hobbes also expanded his scientific studies and had greater contact with the Walbeck Cavendishes (including the earl of Newcastle, his brother Sir Charles Cavendish, and their chaplain Robert Payne), who were deeply interested in Galileo and the new science.[27] He was part of their circle in 1630, when the *Short Tract* was written. This work, which uses the geometric method to sketch the idea of a philosophic system, has often been attributed to Hobbes, but we now know it was written by Payne.[28] Nonetheless, we know that Hobbes was on intimate terms with Payne and that this manuscript reflects the developing scientific views of both men.

Through his connection with Newcastle he also became acquainted with members of the Great Tew Circle of Viscount Falkland, including Chillingsworth, Sheldon, Hyde, and others. While these men had some interest in science, their real concern was religion and politics. Most were Arminians, and their moral and political ideas were derived from Erasmus, Hooker, and Grotius.[29] They were sympathetic to Scripture but were convinced, as Chillingsworth put it, that nothing in Scripture contradicted right reason and sense, a position to which Hobbes also subscribed.[30]

Hobbes returned to the continent in 1634 and came in contact with Mydorge, Mersenne, and Gassendi. Tuck has argued that his interactions with the Mersenne Circle (and through them Descartes) were essential for the development of his science. As we saw in chapter 3, late sixteenth-century humanism particularly as exemplified by Montaigne and Charron called into question the veracity of sensation. Galileo was the first to explain why this was the case, pointing out that heat was not something in nature but only a perception caused by something we do not experience directly.[31] Gassendi, Descartes, and Hobbes independently came to the conclusion that we only have veridical knowledge of our sense-perception and "know" the external world only because of the impact of objects on our sense organs that transmit signals to the brain that we interpret as external objects. This notion played a crucial role in the development of Hobbes' science.

The final element necessary to Hobbes' science was the insight that everything is a form of local motion. The source of this idea is disputed, but we know that he first articulated it to Newcastle during the month he visited Galileo. Donald Hanson and others have claimed that the impact of Galileo and Paduan science on Hobbes has been overrated, but the outlooks of both men are clearly similar.[32] We do know that this visit had a catalytic effect on Hobbes, who returned to England and devoted himself to philosophical work, striving to articulate a scientific system.[33]

During this period, Hobbes also carefully examined Descartes' work. When he received a copy of Descartes' *Discourse* and *Dioptrics* in 1637, he was immediately cognizant of the similarities to his own thought but also of the differences. His *Tractatus opticus* (written at the time but published only in 1644) is almost a running critique of Descartes.[34] In 1640 he sent Mersenne a fifty-six-page commentary on the *Discourse* and *Dioptrics* that he assumed would be forwarded to Descartes. In this critique (since lost) he apparently attacked Cartesian dualism, challenging the idea that the mind could be affected by the motion of bodies without itself being corporeal.

Hobbes' investigation of such questions was cut short by the political and religious crisis in England in which he and his royalist patrons were deeply involved. At the urging of Devonshire, Hobbes unsuccessfully ran for parliament in 1640. During the same period, Hobbes wrote *Human Nature* and *De corpore politico,* which circulated in royalist circles although they were only published ten years later as the first two parts of the *Elements of Law.* The work was dedicated to Newcastle and intended to provide arguments to bolster the king's claims to sovereignty. Miller and Strong have argued that Newcastle hoped to convince the king to use Hobbes as a weapon in the debate with parliament and that these works were a demonstration of what he could do.[35] Events, however, soon made such words superfluous. Parliament was so obstinate the king dissolved it, and when he was forced by financial exigency to call a new one, the Republican and Presbyterian members attacked his ministers. Mainwaring was sent to the Tower for supporting the doctrine Hobbes had laid out in his manuscript. Fearing he would be next, Hobbes fled to France.

He remained in France for more than a decade, working initially on sections of his system dealing with first philosophy. He also began studying chemistry and anatomy. He spent considerable time with the Mersenne and his circle. Hobbes' brilliance was quickly apparent to Mersenne, who asked him to write a critique of Descartes' *Meditations.* His objections (and Descartes' replies) were added to those included with the work when it was published in 1641. As we will see in the next chapter, the debate between the two concerned the nature and relation of man and God, and consequently the meaning of freedom and necessity in the new science.

In 1642 Hobbes published *De cive,* which was the third section of the *Elements of Law.* The work was motivated by English politics but had a universal success, establishing Hobbes' European reputation. He saw it as an integral part of his system that would only be fully comprehensible when he completed the antecedent sections, but even as it stood, it was in his opinion the first truly scientific work on politics.

With the publication of *De cive*, Hobbes began working at a feverish pitch. In 1642 he began an optics, worked on *De corpore*, and wrote an extensive critique of Thomas White's *De mundo*.[36] White had sought to reconcile Aristotle and atomism. In his critique Hobbes tried to reconcile modern science and Christianity. In 1644 he completed the *Tractatus opticus* and Mersenne published his *Ballistica* with a summary of Hobbes' thought, probably written by Hobbes himself. Mersenne was attracted to Hobbes because he seemed to offer an answer to skepticism. This was less important to Hobbes, who was never troubled by skeptical doubts.

In 1645 Charles Cavendish and his brother arrived in Paris, bringing Hobbes into closer contact with the court.[37] As a result, he was asked in 1646 to tutor the future Charles II in mathematics.[38] Fortunately, this work was not demanding, and he was able to complete a revised edition of *De cive* as well as his *Optical Treatise* during this period.

The death of Mersenne and the departure of Gassendi in 1648 deprived Hobbes of his closest intellectual companions. Moreover, when Charles I was executed in 1649, the court became a more treacherous environment because of the increased influence of the Catholics around the Queen Mother. During this time, Hobbes began working on *Leviathan* (published in London in 1651).

Leviathan was an attempt to lay out the grounds for a just and lasting political order on the basis of the new science. Hobbes believed that it could serve as the basis for a solution to the political and theological problems at the heart of the Civil War by demonstrating that reason and revelation mandated the rule of the sovereign over both church and state as the basis for a lasting peace. This was a distant but not impossible goal. In the short term, however, the work did not bring peace but a firestorm. The work contained something for almost every one of the competing parties to dislike. Also, while it was written in 1649–50, it only appeared after Charles II had been defeated by Cromwell and driven from England. It was thus portrayed by some of Hobbes' royalist enemies as an effort to win favor with Cromwell, since it justified the rule of whomever was in power at the moment.

This reaction was perhaps inevitable. Theologically, Hobbes had tried to walk a narrow path between the conservative Arminians who defended clerical power on the basis of divine law and the radical Protestants who believed themselves bound only by the will of an omnipotent and unpredictable God. The theological position that Hobbes worked out was surprisingly reminiscent of the Calvinism of his youth, although transformed in important ways by his materialism.[39] The Queen Mother was already angry about the publication of *De cive,* and, after the *Leviathan* appeared, banned him from court. He seems to have thought the Anglicans would see the work as a powerful argument for episcopal government, but even royalist Anglicans such as Payne, who had admired *De cive,* thought *Leviathan* was dangerous because it was fideistic.[40] Hammond called it "a farrago of Christian atheism."[41] The first two parts of the book were not so disturbing, although they pushed claims for reason further than many Christians were willing to go. The last two sections, however, were especially threatening, not because they were anti-Christian but because their scriptural theology was both heterodox *and* persuasive.[42]

∠Hobbes may already have planned his return to England, and he fled there in 1651, when French Catholics moved to have him arrested. Settling in London, he again came into contact with Charles Cavendish and was soon back in the employment of Devonshire.[43] He renewed friendships with John Seldon, Ben Jonson, Samuel Cowper, John Vaughan, and William Harvey and was drawn into to freethinking circles that included men such as Thomas White.

∠The uproar over *Leviathan,* however, would not go away. In 1654 Hobbes was drawn into a debate with the Bishop Bramhall over liberty and necessity of the will. Bramhall was an Arminian and an ally of Stafford and Laud.[44] The debate began as a private discussion but became a vitriolic public debate when the initial discussions were published without permission by one of Hobbes' supporters. This debate recapitulates in many ways the debate between Luther and Erasmus, as well as Hobbes' earlier debate with Descartes in the Objections and Replies to the *Meditations.* Bramhall argued that human beings have a free will that they must use to respond to divine grace. Hobbes maintained that everything happens as the result of God's predestining will, the same position that Luther and Calvin defended, but he supplemented this theological assertion with the claim that this divine will operates in the world according to sheer mechanical causality. Bramhall was deeply disturbed, but more because of Hobbes' Calvinism than his materialism.[45] He also rejected the view of divine omnipotence that underlay Hobbes' notion of predestination, asserting he would rather be a heretic than admit the absoluteness of God's creative power.[46] Hobbes too worried that the doctrine of predestination might lead to atheism or despair.[47] However, he tried to show that the absence of free will did not mean that humans had no responsibility for their actions. In his view human beings are not blamed for choosing to do what they wrongly desire but for wrongly desiring it.[48] They are thus blamed not for their choices but for their character.

In 1655 Hobbes published the first part of his philosophical system, *De corpore*. It was his attempt to show definitively that the only substances that exist are bodies. The demonstration of this position was crucial as a ground for the arguments in his earlier works and for the position that he maintained in his debates with Descartes and Bramhall. In that same year Hobbes became involved in what proved to be a long debate with the mathematician John Wallis about the nature of mathematics. Wallis was not merely a mathematician; he was also a clergyman and a leading Presbyterian, indeed someone Hobbes held responsible for fomenting the Civil War.[49] Hobbes believed that the success of his political work was at stake since he saw it as rooted in the mathematical and physical arguments of *De corpore*, an opinion shared by his opponent.[50] The length and bitterness of this debate was less a result of the importance of the mathematical questions than their perceived political and theological significance.

Hobbes' notoriety also played a role in his exclusion from the Royal Society. A few members (Wallis in particular) detested Hobbes, and others found it difficult to forgive his attacks on their religious views.[51] Hobbes also had no sympathy for the Society's Baconian emphasis on experimentation. Still, he was an important scientist and had many friends among the members. In all likelihood the real barrier to admission was the similarity of his proclaimed views on religious and political matters to the less loudly expressed views of many members, who were reluctant to share his opprobrium.[52] In any case, their unwillingness to admit him had little to do with his science, which was seldom questioned by any of them.[53]

The critique of his work aroused ire against Hobbes in England, but it did little to dim his continental reputation. Moreover, after the Restoration Hobbes returned to court and was considered one of its finest wits. As a result, "Hobbism" became popular at court and among the young.[54] Royal favor and popular success, however, only intensified attacks on him. In part, this was because the libertinism of Charles II and his court was often wrongly attributed to his influence.[55] The anger of his enemies was so pronounced that, after the London Fire in 1666, a number of radical parliamentarians argued the disaster was divine punishment for sin and suggested that Hobbes was its cause. They appointed a committee to investigate him and consider charging him with atheism.[56] Hobbes was frightened and, according to Aubrey, burned some of his papers, but the king came to his defense, although he required Hobbes to cease publishing polemical works. Hobbes continued to write, producing *Behemoth*, his account of the Civil War (1672, published posthumously in 1682). In 1672 he also wrote both his prose and verse autobiographies. Unable to publish polemical work, Hobbes returned to translation, producing an English *Iliad* and *Odyssey* in 1675 at the age of eighty-seven. He died peacefully at Hardwick in 1679, probably from the Parkinson's disease that had long afflicted him.

HOBBES' PROJECT

Given the character of his age, it is perhaps not surprising that from his translation of *Medea* at age 14 to his translation of the *Iliad* and *Odyssey* at the age of 87, Hobbes demonstrated a concern with the impact of violence on political institutions and practices. The preeminent example of such violence in his mind was civil war, which was the subject of his early translation of Thucydides as well as his late *Behemoth*. In between, he developed a science that he believed could eliminate violence, establish peace, and promote prosperity. This science consisted in a physics that described the nature of bodies and the laws governing their motions, an anthropology that described human bodies and their motions, and a political science that established a mechanism to minimize the violent collisions of human bodies.[57]

This science is similar to Descartes' *mathesis universalis* but is both broader and more ambitious. As we saw in the last chapter, Descartes sought to develop an apodictic science that would enable us to understand and control the motions of all bodies. Since humans are only partly bodily, this science could only understand corporeal human processes and had nothing to say about actions deriving from the free will. Descartes' system of science thus included only an abbreviated anthropology (*The Passions of the Soul*) and did not include social or political science. As a result, his science did not directly address the crisis of his time. As we saw in the last chapter, he hoped to have a powerful indirect effect, but he knew this could occur only in the long term.

Hobbes too seeks to make man master and possessor of nature, but in contrast to Descartes, he denies that human beings have any special status. They are no different than all other beings. A science that seeks to make humans masters and possessors of nature by revealing the causes of motion thus must necessarily consider the mastery and possession of other human beings. Hobbes therefore had to consider the motives of human action and the means to regulate and control such actions. Anthropology and political science are thus a necessary part of Hobbes' system. While

Descartes hoped that his new science might indefinitely extend human life, he had little to say about how such long-lived beings could live peacefully with one another. The idea of generosity he developed in the *Passions* points to something like a humanist notion of friendliness, but it does not deal with the desire for property, the longing for preeminence, or the preference for one's own that have been enduring sources of human conflict. It is thus hard to see why Descartes' scientifically empowered, freely acting human beings would peacefully co-exist, sharing the mastery and possession of nature rather than using their vast powers to kill, dominate, and exploit one another. Hobbes, by contrast, confronts these questions directly, leaving no doubt about the importance of his science for the political and theological struggles of his age.

Hobbes' attempt to develop a comprehensive science has led to questions about the coherence of its parts.[58] He had a general idea of the variety of the sciences and a vision of the hierarchy of knowledge, but he was never as certain as Descartes about how all the separate branches of science fit into his larger tree of knowledge. On this matter, Hobbes is actually closer to Bacon, who saw himself initiating a new science, mobilizing humanity to engage in a scientific investigation of a whole variety of areas without a final idea of the exact relation of these areas to one another. Hobbes remained similarly unclear about how these fields would fit together, but that is more an indication of his honesty than any attempt to camouflage basic incompatibilities. Indeed, in comparison to Descartes, who was convinced from his initial letter to Beeckman until near the end of his life that he could complete his science without external assistance and provide humanity with an explanation for everything, Hobbes recognized the vast scope of his endeavor and the insuperable difficulties facing anyone who wanted a thorough knowledge of the whole.

This question of the coherence of Hobbes' science is a central issue for Hobbes scholarship. While everyone admits Hobbes sought to develop a mechanistic science that could explain the motions of all natural and human bodies, there is considerable disagreement whether he succeeded in doing so. At the heart of this debate is the question of the relationship of his natural science to his anthropology and political science, a question which Hobbes addressed on several occasions and to which he gave varying answers. Many scholars accept Hobbes' claim that his political science follows from his natural science. Others such as Leo Strauss and Quentin Skinner see a disjunction between the two.

For Strauss the early Hobbes was a humanist, not so much in the school of Petrarch or Ficino as in that of Machiavelli. Strauss believes that, after his discovery of Euclid, Hobbes developed a mechanistic science on a radically new foundation but that he was unable to explain human beings and political life mechanistically and fell back on a vitalistic account more characteristic of humanism.[59] Strauss thus sees Machiavelli lurking behind Hobbes' political science, but he sees this disguised by the scientific veneer he derives from Euclid and Galileo. He consequently argues that while Hobbes does develop a new mechanistic science, this science cannot really explain human action especially in the context of political communities. Hobbes' supposed political science is thus in the end only a kind of political prudence. Moreover, in reducing human action to the pursuit of self-interest, Hobbes in Strauss's view diminishes the importance of higher motives such as nobility or piety and like Machiavelli lowers the sights of the modern age.

Skinner, too, believes that Hobbes was unable to construct his political science on a simply mechanistic foundation. He argues that after Hobbes returned to England in 1615 he devoted himself to the *studia humanitatis*.[60] In contrast to Strauss, Skinner sees this as the study not of philosophy but of rhetoric. The Thucydides edition and his synopsis of Aristotle's *Rhetoric* were the product of this dedication. Skinner suggests, however, that after Hobbes discovered Euclid and published *De cive* he was in revolt against humanism.[61] However, this too was unsatisfying, as Hobbes realized during the Civil War that he could only have a broader impact if he employed rhetoric. Consequently he combined rhetoric and science in the *Leviathan* to construct his political science.

While these views have had a powerful impact, they are not universally shared. Noel Malcolm, for example, is representative of a competing view that sees Hobbes' natural and political science as independent of one another but parallel, differing not in principle but in type, the first based on Hobbes' resolutive method (analysis) and the second on his compositive method (construction).[62] Both, however, are scientific. Other scholars are more dismissive of the idea of a disjunction, which they believe rests on a misunderstanding of Renaissance science. As Reik points out, Hobbes himself simply does not recognize a difference between his humanistic and scientific work.[63]

Many of those who see a disjunction in Hobbes' thought put great weight on Hobbes' discovery of Euclid (or the influence of Galileo) in explaining the origins and nature of his science. Such an explanation is not convincing. On closer examination, Aubrey's account of the supposed discovery of Euclid is hard to swallow. The 47th Proposition is a stunning proof, but Hobbes was almost certainly acquainted with it long before coming to Geneva. It is in fact the most famous proof in mathematics, the Pythagorean Theorem, which Hobbes must have known from his schooldays.

[Euclid certainly played an important role in the formation of Hobbes' science, but Hobbes himself suggests in his prose autobiography that this was because of what it taught him about method. Method, however, can only make a difference after a number of other factors are already in place. As Funkenstein and others have shown, Hobbes' "geometric" science is crucially dependent on the acceptance of a number of other presuppositions derived from earlier theological accounts. To take just the most important example, the universal and necessary concatenation of events that lies at the heart of his notion of mechanical causality is clearly related to and in many ways derived from the Calvinist notion of predestination. The tendency to see Hobbes' science as essentially Euclidean (or Paduan) is in fact bound up with a devaluation of the importance of these theological elements of his science, and particularly the identification of divine will or providence with a universal and unbreakable material causality.[64] This notion decisively distinguishes the Hobbesian universe from the humanist cosmos governed by the capricious goddess *fortuna*.

[This attempt to devalue the importance of the theological origins of Hobbes thought is also evident in the attempt to assimilate him to Machiavelli or the civic republicans. Such efforts are misplaced. From his youth he focused on the Greeks rather than the Romans and was more interested in works that emphasized fate and necessity than freedom and chance. His reading of the ancients also convinced him that ordinary human beings could not govern themselves and that civic republicanism inevitably produced anarchy and war. Hobbes' supposed humanism was thus quite distant from the humanism we examined in the earlier chapters of this book.

[The tendency to see a discontinuity between Hobbes' science of nature and his science of man is also a reflection of the difficulty of understanding how a science that explains mindless matter could also explain the motions of bodies controlled by minds. Such a distinction, however, is foreign to Hobbes. Not only are there no minds apart from matter, but matter itself is always "minded," or at least "willed." Natural bodies are imagined to move as they do not simply because they are impacted by other mindless bodies but because they are willed to do so by God. Hobbes' physics is thus not an investigation of "mindless" matter and his account of the motions of matter is not an account of sheer mechanism. In his physics he seeks to analyze and comprehend what God has willed. The cosmos in this sense is no less "minded" than the commonwealth. To understand what this means, however, we need to investigate Hobbes' science more carefully and systematically.

HOBBES' PHYSICS

Joshua Mitchell has suggested that there are four different scholarly views of the relation of Christianity and early liberalism. Scholars such as Strauss, MacPherson, and Oakeshott have argued that there is a sharp break between Christianity and liberalism, which is certainly un-Christian and in many respects anti-Christian. A second view, evident in Weber, Löwith, and Blumenberg, sees liberalism arising as a result of Protestantism's disenchantment of the political world, that is, as a result of the elimination of the sense of divine presence in the world, whether it is in the sacred character of the king's body, the real existence of God in the host, the importance of religious images and the doctrine of the saints, etc. A third view, defended by Tawney and Wolin, sees Christianity itself implicated in the development of the modern world. By separating religion and politics, it makes possible a reenchantment of the political realm that has been unavailable since antiquity. According to Mitchell, the first of these views discounts Christianity, the second acknowledges its importance but leaves the present epoch disenchanted, and the third acknowledges the importance of Christianity but not its continuing relevance. A fourth view, favored by Eisenach, Reventlow, MacIntyre, and Mitchell himself, sees modern liberalism as a form of Christianity and of Protestantism in particular.[65] What I have tried to show in the preceding chapters and what is especially clear in the case of Hobbes is that all four of these ways of reading the relation between Christianity and modernity make some sense but that a great deal depends upon how one understands Christianity. If one identifies Christianity with scholasticism, there can be no doubt that liberal modernity is something radically new. As we have seen, however, the critique of scholasticism that Descartes and Hobbes undertake is in its origins and in most of its incarnations itself Christian. There also can be no doubt that Protestantism disenchants the world. However, again as we have seen, this disenchantment is not a form of secularization but a theological transformation within Christianity that imagines God as a *deus absconditus*. There is also no doubt that the separation of religion and politics that characterized the early modern period facilitated the humanists' recovery of ancient republicanism, but, as we have seen, humanism was itself not unreligious or antireligious but an effort to recover a more authentic (if at times also a more Pelagian) Christianity. It also could not have been successful without the concomitant struggle within Christianity to purge the church of corruption that inevitably accompanied its involvement in temporal affairs. Does all of this then mean that the modern liberal world is a form of Protestant Christianity as Mitchell suggests? The modern world certainly arises out of the Reformation and has a strongly Protestant character even when it seems most secular. Insofar as Protestantism always defined itself in terms of the *deus absconditus,* secularism can be understood as merely one of its extreme forms. Indeed, even if our age is defined by the death of God, as Nietzsche proclaimed, it is still defined by its relationship to God and therefore still defined theologically, even if only by a thoroughly negative theology. Nonetheless, it is also undeniable that theology in the modern age was itself transformed by its encounter with the ancient world and the development of a secular and a civic humanism. The humanist recovery of ancient ideas and practices has thus had an impact directly or indirectly (through Christianity) on the formation of modernity. Here it is principally a question of how much weight should be assigned to each element, and it is not surprising that different scholars come to different conclusions about this point.

The most powerful argument for the revolutionary character of modernity, however, lies in the role it assigns to natural science. It is science that defines the modern world and science (or philosophy) that is widely considered to be incompatible with religion. However, over the last twenty years scholarship has demonstrated the deep debt that seventeenth-century science owes to Christianity and to the nominalist revolution in particular. Determining the importance of Christianity for modernity and for modern science is made more difficult in the Reformation period by two factors, first, the increasing importance of belief or faith and decreasing importance of practice as a measure of one's religiosity and, second, the proliferation of Christian sects. Christianity had long sought to define and enforce orthodoxy, but from the fourteenth century on the church found it increasingly difficult to sustain dogmatic unity. Even before Luther there was a growing multiplicity of ideas and practices within Christianity, and the Reformation saw an explosion of sectarian diversity. It is difficult to judge whether these sects are Christian in a narrow sense, but there is no question that most of their members were deeply religious. In trying to determine the impact of religion on modernity it is crucial to recognize this diversity and not simply assume that those who dissent from a particular doctrine are irreligious or atheistic.

Hobbes has often been characterized as an atheist, for the most part in his own time by sectarians who believed that anyone who did not share their dogmatic opinions must be irreligious. While we cannot know what Hobbes actually believed, we can know what he says and what sources he relies on. What is immediately clear is that Hobbes' thought is deeply indebted to nominalism. He accepted nominalism's basic tenets: that God is omnipotent, that only individuals exist, and that the meanings of words are purely conventional. However, he tried to show that these principles were compatible with a physics, anthropology, and theology that were different from the ones nominalism had developed.

Hobbes was first instructed in the nominalist notion that God was supremely powerful and arbitrary in his election of human beings for salvation at his father's table. It was further explained by his Calvinist teachers, and cemented by his university education. It was an article of faith on which he never wavered, and one that he explicitly affirmed not only in his debate with Descartes and in *Leviathan* but also in his critique of White and in his later debate with Bramhall.[66]

Hobbes also accepted and often repeated the nominalist critique of scholastic realism and syllogistic reasoning as well as the related doctrine of ontological individualism. Moreover, he was convinced of the individuality of all things not as the result of any direct knowledge of such entities but as an inference from a belief in divine omnipotence.

This nominalist ontology served as the foundation for Hobbes' physics. According to Hobbes, the bodies that make up the universe are constantly changing.[67] On the surface, this claim does not seem particularly novel or revolutionary. Aristotle made a similar claim, and it was repeated by many others including the scholastics Hobbes criticized. They claim that things change in multiple ways and for multiple reasons. For Hobbes, however, while everything is changing, there is only one kind of change and it is the result of local motion caused by the impact of one body on another.[68] Bodies themselves are not created or destroyed but moved about and rearranged.[69] Every act thus may be understood as generated and passing away in a mechanical fashion, that is, as a result of the impact of another body and without any further input from God. In addition, there is no kind of motion that is unique to a particular body. Every body is capable of every possible motion. All bodies as bodies are thus homogeneous and subject to the same effects from the impact of other bodies. Moreover, no body can produce any act within itself, and everything thus occurs as the result of bodies striking one another.[70] Motion has no other cause than motion.

The question this claim leaves unanswered is the nature and origin of motion itself. This question is not new. It was addressed by ancient atomists who posited an initial, uncaused "swerve" that brought atoms into contact with one another and began the interactions that formed the cosmos. Christian thinkers attributed this beginning to a mysterious divine will. It has often been suggested that Hobbes' thought on this issue is indebted to atomism, but in fact this idea owes a great deal more to nominalism, as the arguments he develops in his critique of White make clear. For Hobbes, all motion begins with God. Surprisingly little, however, follows from this fact in Hobbes' case. Indeed, from reflecting on motion, he believes that we can only know that God is the source of motion. Everything that we otherwise believe we know, we know only from revelation.[71]

Hobbes does not even make the traditional claim that God is a first, unmoved mover.[72] God is not a *demiurgos* that sets the mechanism of nature in motion and then looks on but is instead present in some sense in the continual and sustaining motion of the universe.[73] We can infer a first mover, according to Hobbes, but we cannot infer that he was eternally unmoved. Indeed, what logically follows is that he was (and consequently is) eternally moving. Hobbes thus rejects the Platonic claim essential to medieval Christianity that God and thus true being are unchanging. Rest in Hobbes' view cannot be attributed to God and the idea of the eternity of God, of a *nunc stans,* is an absurdity.[74] Motion is the action of God, and this action in nominalistic fashion is not governed by any reason or purpose other than God's omnipotent and indifferent will. The cosmological consequence of this position is that there is no rational or natural goal of bodily motion. Effectively then for Hobbes, God is the same as the causal process or, in the words of *Leviathan,* nature is God's artifice, his continuing activity.[75]

Although motion for Hobbes does not have a natural end, it is not random or unintelligible. In order to understand how this can be the case, we need to understand what Hobbes means by causality. Like Bacon, Hobbes develops a notion of causality using the Aristotelian language of substance and accidents. Aristotle argued that everything is predicated of substance. Accidents, such as greenness, are predicated of substances such as trees. While Aristotle or at least his scholastic followers recognized that accidents could not be in the same sense as substance, they were convinced that they had a real existence apart from substance. Thus colors, for example, exist apart from the bodies that are colored, even if in some sense they have less being than the substances themselves. Hobbes denies this. In his view accidents are not separable from body. Accidents are rather characteristics of bodies, the particular kinds of internal and external motions that characterize them. The cause of an effect thus is not in the body itself but in its motions, or, to use the Aristotelian term, in its accidents.

Aristotle famously defined four causes, a material, formal, efficient, and final cause of every effect. The material cause of a golden chalice, for example, is the gold out of which it is made. While a chalice could be made from many elements, it could not be made from air or water to take only two examples. The gold is a cause in that it contributes to the chalice. The formal cause is the shape of the chalice. Again, while a number of shapes are possible, not all of them are since the chalice must hold liquids. The efficient cause is the means by which the chalice comes to be, in this case the craftsman who chooses the material and form of the chalice to meet the purpose or final cause for which it is made. In making the chalice, the craftsman thus does not create it or its idea out of nothing. The act of creation is a form of *mimēsis* or imitation. Aristotle asserts that this notion of the causes of things applies not merely to manmade things but to natural things as well, many of which (e.g., all living things) have their efficient cause within themselves (e.g., the acorn has the capacity to form itself into an oak).

Hobbes reworks this Aristotelian notion of causality. He recognizes only a material and an efficient cause. He sees the efficient cause as the sum total of all the motions that lead something to push on and move something else and the material cause as the sum total of all the motions in the thing that is pushed or moved. Together they constitute a necessary cause in the presence of which the effect necessarily occurs.[76] In keeping with his rejection of universals, he believes that formal and final causes do not really exist for natural objects but are really efficient or material causes. Final causes exist only for beings with reason and will.[77] Causality for Hobbes thus becomes the aggregate interaction of all motions, or, to put the matter in more theological terms, it is the purely indifferent will of God that has no rational form and no rational or natural end but consists in the interacting motions of all things acting corporeally upon one another.[78] While Hobbes employs Aristotelian terminology to describe causality, he thus rejects the *via antiqua* reading of Aristotle in favor of a *via moderna* reading favored by Ockham and his followers.

The practical conclusion that follows from this account is that the world of matter in motion is governed by an omnipotent God who is indifferent to our preservation and well-being. Hobbes was not the first thinker to reach this sobering conclusion. As we saw in chapters 2–4, both the humanists and Reformers had recognized this fact. Hobbes holds a similar view of God's apparent indifference to human suffering or thriving. In contrast to both the humanists and Reformers, however, Hobbes does not accept this view as final but seeks to show, as we will see, that through the natural law

God provides a impulse toward self-preservation that is the foundation for a human science that will make us masters and possessors of nature.[79]

The goal of Hobbes' science is thus not merely to understand the world but to change it, to give human beings the power to preserve themselves and improve their earthly lot. He asserts in *De corpore:*

> The end or scope of philosophy is, that we may make use to our benefit of effects formerly seen; or that by application of bodies to another, we may produce the like effects of those we conceive in our mind, as far forth as matter, strength, and industry, will permit, for the commodity of human life. For the inward glory and triumph of the mind that a man may have for the mastering of some difficult and doubtful matter, or for the discovery of some hidden truth, is not worth so much pains as the study of Philosophy requires; nor need any man care much to teach another what he knows himself, if he thinks that will be the only benefit of his labour. The end of knowledge is power . . . and lastly, the scope of all speculation is the performing of some action, or thing to be done.[80]

The goal of philosophy or science is thus not theoretical, nor is it pursued because it brings its possessors fame.[81] Rather it is eminently practical, pursued because it gives one power, security, and prosperity, and pursued not out of idle curiosity or piety but in response to the pervasive fear that unsettles human life. Science, as Hobbes understands it, will thus make it possible for human beings to survive and thrive in the chaotic and dangerous world of the nominalist God.

The knowledge that this science seeks is not the knowledge of *what* is but of *how* things work, that is, *how* they are or can be brought into being or prevented from coming into being. Such knowledge is artifice, that is, the technical or mechanical knowledge of what scholasticism called the secondary causes by which divine will moves matter. Attaining such knowledge, however, is much more difficult than one might first suppose because we do not have immediate knowledge of the real world. We know only the effect that this world has upon us.[82] Our perceptions are thus not real representations of the actual world but obscure signs of hidden natural events that must be deciphered.[83]

On the surface, the merely inferential knowledge of the real world would seem to make science difficult if not impossible. As we saw in the last chapter, Descartes held a similar view of perception and yet thought he could construct an apodictic science by demonstrating that God guaranteed the correspondence of ideas and objects. Hobbes doubted this proof and thought that we could never know what actual causes were responsible for any particular effect because of our lack of access to the things themselves. He like Bacon recognized that the same effect could be produced by a variety of causes, and he contented himself in the belief that while much God did might be above or beyond reason, he would never contradict it.

Such a probabilistic position cannot serve as the basis for an apodictic science, because there can be no guarantee that the picture science paints of the world corresponds to reality.[84] The brilliance of Hobbes' position is that this does not matter. It is not crucial that we know the actual causal chains that govern the motions of matter. For science to achieve its goal we need only hypothetical truth. The hypothetical picture that we construct need not correspond to the actual causal pathways by which events occur; it need only explain how to produce or prevent effects. The account that science gives of the world is thus only a construction, that is, a hypothesis. In a certain sense, however, hypothetical knowledge is superior to apodictic knowledge—apodictic knowledge is merely a description of what God did do, according to his *potentia ordinata,* while hypothetical knowledge describes what God could have done by his *potentia absoluta.*[85] Hypothetical reasoning in this case is an exercise not in mere analysis and description but in artifice itself. The hypothetical construction undertaken by science is thus akin to the actual construction by which God creates the natural world, and it can serve as the basis for the construction of one that is more conducive to human thriving.[86]

This new science that Hobbes develops rests upon an essentially nominalist theory of knowing that understands words as signs. Everything we know in his view we know through sensation. We are struck by external objects that impart a motion to our organs of sense, thus producing a motion in us, a phantasm.[87] The motions that continue in us Hobbes calls imagination. All knowledge, he argues, is either sensation or imagination. Our ability to think using these images, however, is limited because of our inability to hold them all together in our mind. This is due to the fact that each phantasm is unique. The solution to this problem and the foundation for science is the use of signs.

Signs, Hobbes argues, are marks that serve to bring a particular thing before the mind. They do not have to be words, as in the case of rocks that mark the end of a path, but the signs we most employ are words. Words name and link things. Words are either proper names, which point to specific things, or they are the names of names that link things together. Insofar as words bring different things together under a single term, they both assist and mislead the understanding.[88] The danger is that we forget the uniqueness of the similar things and imagine some one universal thing of which they are all exemplars. Words are essential to reasoning but often lead to reification. As we saw in chapter 1, Ockham's razor was designed to minimize such reification. Hobbes is equally aware of this danger. Every error in philosophy, he asserts, is the result of too much freedom in the use of tropes. This is especially true in philosophy that abuses abstract names in its confusion about the difference between the universality of names and things.

Like Descartes, Hobbes believes philosophy must begin with epistemological destruction. In Descartes this is his famous path of doubt by which he thinks away the material world, leaving only the bare *cogito ergo sum*. Hobbes too begins by imagining the world to be annihilated.[89] Both thinkers in this respect build on the nominalist method for eliminating reified universals by asking what would still exist if the rest of the world were destroyed.[90] Such a method reveals the truly individual things. Instead of accepting the world as it appears to us, we construct it anew in the imagination on this foundation. We thereby come to know things not by nature or sense but by ratiocination.

Knowing for Hobbes is the connecting of names into propositions that are essentially forms of computation (either addition or subtraction) by means of which we recognize the similarities and differences among things. These propositions are connected into syllogisms, and syllogisms are linked together to form demonstrations. Such a capacity for reasoning is naturally available to all men, but where a long series is necessary most fall into error. The reason for this, according to Hobbes, is the want of method.[91] Using the correct method is the most efficacious means of discovering effects by their known causes or causes by their known effects. Method is thus essential.[92] Previous philosophy lacked a method and constantly found itself entwined in contradiction. Hobbes thought he had found such a method in Euclidean geometry.

Hobbes' geometric method is often compared with Descartes' but they are quite different. For Descartes, thinking is not limited to what we can imagine. Indeed, the ideas are altogether nonrepresentational. The example that he employs to make this point is a chiliagon (a thousand-sided polygon), which can be known but not imagined. Hobbes rejects this way of thinking. There is no knowledge except through the imagination.[93] We may not be able to imagine a chiliagon but we can construct one, and it is only because we can thereby imagine it piece by piece that it is knowable. The infinite in his view (and contrary to Descartes) is thus completely unknowable. Moreover, speaking about infinite numbers is misguided. However large a number is, it is still finite. What is infinite (including God) is inaccessible and incomprehensible.

Hobbes' reconstruction of the world is thus different from Descartes' *mathesis universalis,* which is always a literal *mathesis* or mathematics that captures the reality of things. For Hobbes, the geometric method is metaphorical. It is not the actual numbers or figures that capture the world but the precise definitions and the process of construction based upon these definitions. Geometry is one form of such a construction, but it is not the only or even the primary one. Hobbes' representation of the world thus depends upon signs that provide a useful reconstruction of reality that specifies the necessary connections among things and thus allows for certain deduction on the basis of the assumed truth of hypothetical premises rather than upon numbers that portray the actual essence of things.

This does not mean that science is merely a story. It is different from both experience and history. It is not description but indubitable reasoning on the basis of self-evident truths.[94] Hobbes' science is thus quite distant from the historical and prudential thought of Renaissance humanism and even from the empirical or experimental thought of Bacon. Indeed, its goal is not to understand the causal relations that govern the world God ordained and created but to understand the causal power of God himself and use this power to reconstruct the world in ways that will facilitate human thriving. Hobbes nominalism in this case places him close to the Reformers, but he is less concerned with salvation and eternal life than with preserving and improving life in this world. We see this most clearly in his account of man and the state.

HOBBES' ANTHROPOLOGY

In almost any metaphysical system the transition from physics to anthropology presents real difficulties. Almost everyone agrees that humans are natural beings, but few are willing to assert that they are only natural beings. Descartes saw man as *res extensa* but also as *res cogitans.* He did not thereby mean to suggest that human bodies were not subject to natural causes but only that they were also moved by a free human will. Hobbes, by contrast, argues that humans are governed by the same mechanical causality that governs all beings. He rejects the idea that humans have a supernatural component as a ploy of priests to gain power over others.

This does not mean that there is nothing unusual or distinctive about humans for Hobbes. Indeed, in his view we are complex *automata,* mechanisms like clocks that are, as it were, spring-loaded, and when the energy stored in these "springs" is released we move. We seem to ourselves to be freely self-moving, but this is an illusion. Our so-called actions are always only reactions, determined by our passions, which are aroused by the impacts of external objects on our bodies. These impacts trigger a mechanism that releases a "spring" and catapults us into action. The direction we move and the speed with which we move are determined by the character of the initial impact and by the energy stored up in the "spring." Thus I may be moved to eat if I am offered food when I am hungry, but less likely to do so when I am full. I would also be less likely to eat, whatever my hunger, if I were in the throes of grief or entranced by a Beethoven symphony. I may believe that I choose one thing rather than another, but that choice is determined by the nature and intensity of my passions at that moment. I may seem subjectively to choose to do what I want, according to Hobbes, but even if this is the case I can never choose to want what I want. That is the result of a series of causes that are independent of me.

For the most part our dependence on such external causes is hidden from us. We believe that we act freely, but if we read ourselves, as Hobbes recommends at the beginning of *Leviathan,* we recognize that we and all other human beings are moved by our passions. In one sense this recognition is humbling because it diminishes our autonomy, but in Baconian fashion Hobbes turns this humiliation into our salvation. In reading ourselves in this way, we can discover what we need to be happy. In giving up belief in our freedom, we recognize that happiness consists not in a striving for moral perfection, immortal fame, or perfect piety but in satisfying our bodily desires. In the course of this examination we also recognize that while we want different things at different times, the one thing we want everywhere and always is to be alive. We thus come to understand that the most powerful "spring" within us moves us to seek our own preservation, overriding all of other passions. Hunger, lust, thirst, and wonder all disappear in the moment we are confronted with a threat to our lives. This is the meaning of Hobbes' claim that the wellspring of human action is the fear of violent death.[95]

While we can understand that violent death is the one thing we all want to avoid, it is not possible to define more fully or explicitly the other goods necessary to our happiness. In a humanistic fashion, Hobbes asserts that we are all radically individual beings with idiosyncratic passions. Thus, while we all desire to exist, what any one of us wants to exist for or wants out of existence can only be specified by that individual. The happiness of each individual thus depends upon his getting what he wants, and this is related to his power. Power, however, arises out of our ability to master and manipulate the world in motion around us, minimizing or avoiding collisions with objects that could injure or destroy us and maximizing collisions with objects we desire. Such power is the basis for what Hobbes believes is rightly called freedom.

As we discussed above, Hobbes denies that we have a free will. However, he does not therefore subscribe to the Lutheran doctrine that man is nothing other than an ass ridden by God or the devil. There is no freedom God bestows on us with an infusion of his will. Hobbes believes such pious hopes merely subordinate us to the passions of priests and religious fanatics. Humans are bodies driven by passions, and to be free for Hobbes is to pursue the objects of our passions without external constraints. This is practical but not metaphysical freedom. Human beings are the motions that are imparted to them. Like all other beings they are manifestations of divine will that foreknows and forewills every event. While we are thus predestined to be the kinds of beings we are and to have the passions that we have, this does not affect our freedom because it is precisely these passions that define our identity.[96] For us to be the individuals we are, it is thus only necessary to be able to will without hindrance from other created beings.

The degree of our freedom depends on our power. The greater our power, the more freely and safely we move amidst other beings. Our power depends on the strength of our bodies, the number of our supporters, the extent of our external resources, and above all on our capacity to reason. For Hobbes reason means something different than what it did for his predecessors. It is not a separate power that can discern the appropriate ends of life and guide us in the proper direction. It is thus not teleological but instrumental, the spy and scout of the passions.[97] It thus helps us to maximize the satisfaction of our desires but not to train, direct, or control them. To live by right reason, for Hobbes, is thus not an end but a means. Indeed, the purpose of deliberation is not to moderate the passions, as Petrarch believed, but to increase our power in order to get what we want.

Living and acting according to the impulses that are imparted to us and that guide us in life is happiness, according to Hobbes. Put in these terms, it is immediately apparent how distant Hobbes is from both humanism and the Reformation.[98] There is no notion of a Neoplatonic ladder of love that leads to perfection, nor is there any suggestion that our actions are guided by Satan. We are neither superhuman nor are we depraved. We are all only individual beings, determined by our idiosyncratic passions. Good and evil for each of us is thus measured not by our progress toward a rational, natural, or supernatural end but by the vector of our desire. No direction is naturally better than any other. Good is what pleases us, evil what displeases us, good what reinforces our motion, evil what hinders it.

Or to put the matter in different terms, good is an increase in our power and evil its decrease. The greatest good is thus progressing towards satisfaction with the least hindrance, and the greatest evil the cessation of all movement in death. Each person in Hobbes' view is thus a self-interested individual who seeks to maximize his own power and satisfaction. The problem is that we are also in competition with other human beings. In our efforts to become masters and possessors of nature we are driven to seek mastery not only over natural beings but over human beings as well. In the state of nature, we are thus constantly at war with one another.

(Indeed, the principal threat to our preservation and power, according to Hobbes, comes from other humans. The reasons for this are not obvious, given Hobbes' physics. Disease, drought, predatory animals, earthquakes, storms, and the like threaten us in real and unmistakable ways. Why then are humans more dangerous than more massive, speedy, and numerous nonhuman beings? The simple answer is that for Hobbes humans are more powerful because they use language. Language enables humans to extend their sway over the world and thus to become extraordinarily dangerous to other human beings. For Hobbes, the use of signs gives humans an extended memory that opens up both a past and future and thus makes self-awareness possible.[99] In contrast to all other beings, we have a capacity to recognize the ends towards which our passions direct us, the means for attaining these ends, the obstacles that stand in the way, and the dangers that threaten our existence. The world for humans is thus both more promising and more threatening than it is for animals. Insofar as we recognize this danger and are driven by fear to seek a remedy, we find ourselves in a life and death struggle with other humans for dominance. Unlike ants or bees, we have no natural hierarchy and are more or less equal individuals driven by a desire for preservation and well-being.[100] We recognize that this can only be achieved by obtaining the means necessary to meet our needs. Since these needs extend into the future, our needs are limitless. Therefore only the mastery of all human and natural motion can provide security and put an end to fear. The desire that all humans have for such means leads them into the war of all against all.

/Fortunately, the use of language that makes humans so dangerous also makes it possible to eliminate this danger. The war of all against all that characterizes life in the state of nature can be overcome by reason through the construction of an artificial world, the commonwealth, to supplement the world that God created. Human artifice thus can repair the work of divine artifice, so that humans can live peacefully with one another. In contrast to Descartes, who sought only to control the motions of natural bodies, Hobbes recognized the need to control the *interactions* of human bodies, ordering their motions to minimize violent collisions. He thus saw that physics and anthropology must be completed by political science.

HOBBES' POLITICAL SCIENCE

The three great works that constitute Hobbes' political science, *The Elements of Law, De cive,* and *Leviathan,* were written against the backdrop of the English Civil War. *The Elements* was written and circulated during the bitter struggle between the king and parliament that precipitated the war. *De cive* and *Leviathan* were written after Hobbes fled to France. The carnage in his own country turned his attention to his political science, which he had intended as the final section of his system.

Hobbes knew that this science could not be fully convincing without his physics and anthropology.[101] He believed, however, that it could stand in part on its own since its starting points were accessible through introspection.[102] In his view political science, like geometry, is a constructive science that starts with definitions. On the basis of these definitions, it is possible to come to true conclusions.[103] We can know these definitions by reading ourselves, although we cannot know whether they are universally valid without an account of nature as a whole.[104] Hobbes attempted to demonstrate the validity of his initial definitions through his account of the nature of man in *Leviathan,* but this account was sketchy at best.[105] While his political science could be useful on its own, it could only be completely convincing if it was grounded in a comprehensive anthropology and physics. Both are resolutive sciences that disassemble the world and examine its parts before putting them back together. They are thus the foundation for political science, which is purely constructive, more a form of engineering or what Hobbes calls artifice than science. Indeed, political science is akin to the supreme artifice with which God created the world. Since the commonwealth, however, is not constructed ex nihilo, it must make sense within the existing natural world. Without a physics and anthropology, it remains merely an imaginary construction like Plato's Kallipolis or More's Utopia.[106]

Hobbes believed that his physics and anthropology did confirm the validity of the premises of his political science, that human beings are driven by their passions, that their overriding passion is a fear of violent death, and that they seek to accumulate power in order to preserve themselves and maximize the satisfaction of their desires. On the basis of these premises, Hobbes thought that he could show that human beings living in proximity to one another inevitably live in a state of war and that this war can only be brought to an end in a commonwealth ruled by an absolute sovereign.[107]

The war of all against all is a consequence of the radical individuality of human beings. Each individual strives for power but can never have enough because the amount he needs depends on the power of those in his vicinity. The more each has the more all others need. War may begin because some are greedy or vainglorious, but even if everyone were moderate and virtuous our inability to know others' intentions would lead us to fear for our lives, prepare for self-defense, and thus become threats to others. As Hobbes sees it, the fear of violent death and the desire for preservation thus lead to the pursuit of "power after power that ceaseth only in death."[108] Under such circumstances, life becomes solitary, poor, nasty, brutish, and short.

⟨It is in this abyss of despair where no one is secure and the fear of violent death possesses everyone that the path to earthly salvation begins.[109] It is in this moment when flight is no longer possible because death waits everywhere that one has to choose between peace and war. Hobbes argues that in these circumstances reason dictates that one first seek peace and only if that fails that one pursue war. Indeed, for him this is the first and fundamental law of nature. But how does reason reach this decision and in what sense is it a law? Reason for Hobbes certainly does not supply us with this precept out of itself. In fact, in this case it seems to be merely the spokesman for the body and its overwhelming desire for preservation.

⟨To understand how this can be a law rather than a merely prudential maxim, we need to return to Hobbes' anthropology. According to Hobbes, human bodies are characterized by both vital and voluntary motion. The former consists in autonomic processes such as respiration and digestion. These matters are not under our conscious control, since they are essential to our existence from the moment we are born. Voluntary motion, by contrast, involves choices about those things that are pleasurable or advantageous to us but that are not immediately essential to our preservation. The crucial question for Hobbes is which of these forms of motion best describes our reaction to the fear of violent death. Hobbes believed that the motion this fear engendered was like respiration. We can hold our breath, but not indefinitely. Similarly, we can stand and fight or at least some of us can some of the time. We all do this naturally when we must in order to preserve ourselves. Some of us do so for short periods of time when we believe it to be to our advantage, just as we hold our breath when we dive beneath the water, but Hobbes seems to have been convinced that even those who face death in this way are always afraid and feel (although they resist) the impulse to run.[110] He thus concludes that the fear of violent death is universal. It is a command that we all receive directly from nature, and it directs us even without the intervention of language. It is a universal natural impulse, a part of nature's artifice that directs us for our own good. The source of the law of nature is thus nature's artificer. The natural law is thus the law of God written into the natural world, analogous to the law of gravity or the law of inertia. What Hobbes thus seems to suggest is that while the world that the omnipotent God of nominalism and Calvinism opens up is dangerous and terrifying, there is also a natural impulse that directs us to our own earthly salvation.

Hobbes' recognition that we are driven to preserve ourselves was not novel, but the means he develops to achieve this goal were. He begins by asserting that we must seek peace rather than war. With this assertion he rejects the courage of the warrior and the martyr as means to peace and security. Both, he suggests, are rational at times for some, but they are ultimately irrational because they are not conducive to the natural human end of preservation. Hobbes believes that he can demonstrate this fact by showing us the consequences of following the chain of causes to their bitter end. The demonstration that courage cannot give us what our being demands is the basis for the decisive second law of nature that specifies the true means to peace and preservation: one must be willing to covenant with others, giving up one's right to all things and being content with as much liberty against other men as one would allow others against oneself. This law follows from the first law of nature but is not derived or deducible from it. It is thus the principal act of human artifice. According to Hobbes, all the other laws of nature derive from these two. The first describes the end and the second the means of all political striving. The rest of political science follows from this beginning.

The first law is a law rather than a prudential maxim because it rests on our involuntary will to live. Our desire to preserve ourselves is different in kind from our desire for food or drink. It is not something about which we have any choice, just as we have no choice about respiration or digestion. In order to maintain our vital motion, Hobbes believes we will always give up our voluntary motions. It is an autonomic response. This fact for the most part is concealed from us by the protection afforded by the state, but it becomes apparent to us when we are plunged into the war of all against all. Under these circumstances we thus come to see the truth.

The second law, by contrast, is not the result of an autonomic response. Our initial natural impulse is to fight or flee, not to negotiate a covenant.

In fact, such an alternative only becomes evident in an extreme situation as a result of a chain of reasoning, that is, it only becomes apparent when we cannot fly because death is everywhere and when we cannot hope to successfully fight because we can never be strong enough to overpower everyone else. Only under such circumstances do we realize that nature pushes us to establish covenants and that this decision is therefore not entirely voluntary.

Of course, we may lie for strategic reasons, intending to break our covenant when it is to our advantage to do so. Here the voluntary component of the act becomes obvious. The law of nature thus is not self-enforcing. We do not automatically die when we break our promises; indeed, we sometimes thrive. In Hobbes' view sanctions are thus necessary to sustain the agreements that make it possible for us all to escape from the war of all against all. We break our oaths to increase our power in order to gain something we desire, and this can only be counteracted by institutionalizing the threat of violent death that the covenant eliminates, by reminding us of the priority of preservation to the other passions. In Hobbes' view this fear is originally institutionalized by swearing an oath that invokes God's wrath as punishment for violation.[111] The fear of the lord here plays a crucial role in leading us to wisdom. Indeed, in Hobbes' view it is only through the terrifying fear of divine sanction that a covenant among human beings can originally be sustained, and even after human authority is in place, fear of divine sanction is a necessary support for the sovereign who cannot be everywhere at once.[112]

In the long term, this solution can only succeed in Hobbes' view if some actual power is put in place of God to enforce the covenant. This is Hobbes' Leviathan, who like Moses "personates" God. He is a "mortal God" who instills obedience to covenants by means of the same overwhelming and overawing force that one finds in God. Peace, Hobbes believes, is only possible if humans are convinced they will suffer a violent and painful death if they break their covenant.

The Leviathan is necessary to assure everyone that no one will break the fundamental covenant that guarantees the peace. Most men in Hobbes' view are unlikely to do so in any case, and for them the Leviathan is not a threat but a bulwark of their security. The real danger in Hobbes' view comes from those proud or vainglorious men who think that they are superior to others and deserve to lord it over them. These are the men the Leviathan must restrain, and it is for this reason that he is called the king of the proud.[113] As the biblical passage makes clear, "There is nothing on earth to be compared with him. He is made so as not to be afraid. He

seeth every high thing below him; and is king of all the children of pride"
(Job 41:33–34). Human beings in Hobbes' view are basically equal because
they are equally mortal. No one is so strong that he cannot be killed. The
Leviathan, like Machiavelli's prince, is needed to control those who believe they are more than human and thus deserve to rule over others. They
need to have their pride affirmed by the obedience and adoration of their
subjects. There is a strong temptation to see these men as the warriors or
conquerors.[114] Hobbes, however, suggests that physical strength and prowess is only one source of pride. Human beings also pride themselves because
of what they consider their superior intelligence or closeness to God. All of
these forms of superiority can have pernicious political consequences.

Hobbes' notion of such a ruler as a prerequisite for peace was not surprising. Indeed, the principal goal of the treaties of Prague (1635) and
Westphalia (1648) was to create and legitimate such sovereigns. It was less
apparent at the time, however, that such a sovereign needed be an absolute
monarch. While Hobbes believes there are strong prudential arguments
for a monarch, he admits in *De cive* that this cannot be demonstrated.

At the root of Hobbes' preference for an absolute monarch is a nominalist
understanding of human relations. He believes that humans cooperate and
keep their covenants only because it is in their interest to do so and that they
will break them when they can achieve some benefit by doing so. Thus they
must be forced to keep their promises. This argument rests on Hobbes' assumption that human beings are absolute individuals. It is important to see
that this idea is not rooted in experience. As Aristotle and others pointed
out, we all begin as members of families, tribes, villages, or cities and most
remain a part of such communities. We have children, parents, friends, and
loved ones whom we trust not merely with our wealth but with our lives.
Moreover, there are many for whom we would sacrifice our fortunes and
even our lives to save or to assist them in significant ways. Hobbes' emphasis
on human individuality is thus rooted not so much in his observation of everyday social life but in the experience of the breakdown of social life in civil
war. He clearly has in mind events like the revolution in Corcyra, described
by Thucydides, and the slaughter in Bohemia or Magdeburg. These extreme
situations confirm the truths he obtained from reading himself, that we put
preservation above all other things. He thus believes that in this worst case
scenario no human institution other than the sovereign can maintain order
and guarantee peace. In fact, all other institutions, families, churches, parties, etc. become merely means to sustain the conflict that endangers everyone. The sovereign alone rises above the fray.

In "personating" God, the sovereign stands in the state just as the nominalist God stands in the universe, the source and union of all things. He is similarly separate from them. While the medieval king, like the God of Dante and Aquinas, was part of a hierarchy that included all of creation, Hobbes' Leviathan is of a different order of being than his subjects, a figurative monster who owes them nothing and enters into no covenants with them. His sole purpose is to overawe those who would break their covenants, threatening them with violent death. Like the nominalist God he is no man's debtor. His superiority has a number of practical advantages that Hobbes lays out in detail. The foremost is that it makes it impossible for the proud to dream of someday becoming preeminent. They cannot compare themselves with him. Similarly, it makes it unnecessary for him to constantly reassert his superiority by using his power to humiliate or destroy his subjects. The existence of the Leviathan thus eliminates or at least minimizes all status competition and creates conditions of general equality, which Hobbes asserts are the sine qua non of peaceful coexistence. While he is God's agent on earth, he is not completely self-sufficient. He has bodily needs and is mortal. The former might make him dangerous to his subjects, but Hobbes seems to share Shakespeare's conviction that a single man's passions cannot be that great a danger to the state.[115] The Leviathan's mortality also restrains him, for he does have to fear divine punishment for not doing his duty. However, this very fact also opens him up to the manipulations of priests and religious fanatics who claim to have special knowledge of God's will. As we will see, this is one of the reasons that the Leviathan must rule the church as well as the state.

The crucial question that Hobbes sought to answer in the midst of the Civil War was why the existing English sovereign had been unable to use his power to sustain order and maintain peace, and how such a failure could be avoided. While all conflicts in Hobbes' view originate in disagreements about *meum* and *tuum,* about mine and thine, such conflicts for the most part are settled by the institution of the commonwealth and the establishment of law that guarantees property rights, which determine where my property ends and where yours begins. While most conflicts over property are thus minimized or eliminated by the institution of law, this only displaces the conflict to a higher level. If law or right determines my property rights under the general covenant, then I can increase my power by writing the laws in my favor, or even more profoundly by articulating general notions of good and evil that tilt all the laws in my favor. Here the power of rhetoric and particularly religious rhetoric is decisive. The Civil War in Hobbes' view was the result of the sovereign's failure to limit debate on the nature of good and evil. This opened the door for the will to power of those who thought they were superior to others and wanted to use the power of the state to institutionalize their superiority.

The Civil War in other words was the consequence of a failure to recognize that the sovereign must decide and enforce religious doctrine, laying out the public standards of good and evil that shape law and policy. The sovereign thus must determine what can be preached because, as we will examine below, there is no other way to decide the issue.[116] In the absence of a sovereign determination of what counts as good and evil, the competition that arises naturally in the state of nature is recapitulated in conflicting religious views that articulate sweeping doctrines of good and evil. Such articulations vastly increase the stakes in any conflict. Consequently, the conflict does not remain merely a conflict over the ownership of particular things but becomes a conflict over ideas about ownership, justice, morality, and the differences between a pious and impious life. Since there is no way to know which of these is correct, the only way that such conflict can be brought to an end is by imposition. The sovereign in Hobbes' view thus must bring these calamitous disputes to an end by establishing and enforcing a uniform standard of good and evil.

Only the sovereign can bring these moral and religious disputes to an end because each person's view of good and evil is a reflection of his or her idiosyncratic passions. Self-restraint is thus impossible. Hobbes claims that this is the lesson of the Old Testament. The story begins in Eden, a peaceful garden in which humans do not need to fear death.[117] The sole requirement is that they obey God's one commandment not to eat of the tree of good and evil, that is, that they not make individual judgments about good and evil. This prelapsarian state is brought to an end by human desire that leads to disobedience and the advent of private judgment.[118] Humans cannot resist making such judgments. The world in which they find themselves after the Fall is for Hobbes the original state of nature, the state in which God is absent and in which men live according to their conflicting notions of good and evil, each emulating God and elevating himself and his moral judgment above all other men.[119] This is the calamitous age of pride.[120] The lesson to be learned from this event for Hobbes is that unarmed gods fail to provide the order necessary to sustain a peaceful, communal life.

Human beings (or at least the Jewish people) in Hobbes view were given a second chance to live directly under God without coercive authority through the covenant with Abraham and Moses. They consented to live in obedience to divine law as interpreted for them by their judges and prophets. This regime, however, already exhibited its flaws in the time of

Moses and was later rejected by the Jews themselves in their desire to have a king, a decision to which God consented, according to Hobbes.[121] This is a second and more clearly historical indication of the inability of human beings to live peacefully without a monarch to enforce obedience to law. Divine commandments, even reinforced by the harangues of the prophets and the moral authority of the judges, cannot solve the problem of private judgment. Only the armed monarch can solve this problem, serving as God's agent on earth to enforce a prohibition on conflicting moral judgment. Sovereigns are thus essential to peace and will remain so until that (distant) time when Christ returns to earth to rule. However, even then Christ's rule will be based on real temporal power and will not depend on moral persuasion or faith. There is thus, for Hobbes, no simply religious (or moral) solution to the war of all against all.

Such a Leviathan, of course, will not be acceptable to all. Religious leaders in particular are driven by their own beliefs about what is right and wrong and jealous of their own power. They are thus unwilling to allow the sovereign to impose his standards of good and evil on them and their followers. They will fight long and hard to prevent this from happening, seeking either to establish an alternative base of power or to usurp the power of the state and use it to achieve their own moral or religious ends. The former, of course, was the strategy of the Catholic church, and the latter the path followed by the Puritans in the English Civil War. Religion in this way poses a perpetual danger to peace and prosperity.

While religious disputes do continually endanger public peace, Hobbes does not favor a secular state that takes no stance on religious issues. The failure of the sovereign to establish and maintain standards of good and evil would leave the determination of these questions to the same private judgments that produced the problem in the first place. Hobbes thus believes that all successful states must have an established form of religious practice, but with the great caveat that political and religious authority must be in the hands of one sovereign who enforces standards of public judgment in religious matters and disallows the public expression of private religious judgment, although perhaps allowing privately held dissenting views. This religious state brings the war of all against all to an end by establishing and enforcing uniform moral and legal standards.

Here Hobbes builds on Luther's *Appeal to the German Nobility* but moves beyond it by rooting the argument for the princely rule of religion in an argument that is itself not expressly religious, that is, by grounding the establishment of religion and state control in an argument based on natural law. While this state in Hobbes' view must be rooted in and support a particular religious view of good and evil, its justification lies not in religion in the narrow sense but in the laws of nature which are not just for a particular people but for all human beings, based upon the universal human desire for self-preservation and aimed at eliminating the "great enemy of nature," that is, violent death.[122] These laws spell out a justification for obedience to the sovereign rooted in nature. They explain why any sovereign who does rule should be obeyed, and not how a sovereign comes to rule.

The law of nature, which is the foundation of this science, follows from these premises. If this law were simply the result of introspection, it would at best be a prudent suggestion. Its obligatory character, however, follows from the fact that it is not merely rooted in nature but is the embedded command of nature's God.[123] We may find this idea strange because we imagine obligation to arise only from situations in which we have freely given our consent. For Hobbes, however, there is nothing that is freely given in an absolute sense. Everything we do, we do because we are in a real sense pushed to do it. Obligation thus is not something chosen but something imposed as a result of an unequal power relationship. We are thus obliged only because we are commanded.[124]

HOBBES' THEOLOGY

While Hobbes was convinced that human beings could eliminate violent death in a commonwealth ruled by an absolute sovereign, he also knew that death itself was inevitable. Descartes had suggested in the *Discourse* that science might eventually overcome death and indefinitely extend human life, but Hobbes was under no such illusions. Moreover, he knew that the fear of death inevitably led to questions about the afterlife, and that such questions posed tremendous problems for political stability since the possibility of gaining eternal life in some cases could outweigh the desire to preserve this life. The proclamations of priests and the delusions of religious fanatics about the nature of good and evil thus could become more compelling than the commands of the sovereign and throw the state into chaos. The Wars of Religion in his view were the result of such a state of affairs, and the only way to avoid this problem was for the sovereign to rule both the church and the state.[125]

While both offices must be united, Hobbes did not favor a theocracy. In fact, the rule of priests with exclusive intercessionary powers or of inspired saints was exactly what he feared. Such theocratic impulses in his view can only be quelled by granting the civil sovereign both temporal and ecclesiastical dominion. However, this solution, which is known as Erastianism, requires theological doctrines that are commensurate with his political imperatives. Therefore, political science cannot leave the question of the content of religious doctrine and practice to the private determination of the citizens. His goal in the last chapters of *De cive,* in the second half of the *Leviathan,* in his critique of White, in his debate with Bramhall, and in his other works on religion is thus to spell out a theology for a Christian commonwealth in which the commandments of church and state are one and the same. As we will see, this theology is essentially Protestant, largely Calvinist, and with a few exceptions compatible with Anglicanism as spelled out in the Thirty-Nine Articles of 1563.[126]

This subordination of theology to politics has led to the widespread belief that Hobbes was irreligious. His belief that the civil sovereign should also have ecclesiastical dominion, however, provides no grounds for doubting his religiosity. The fact that he defends unpopular doctrines at some danger to himself suggests that he did not do so insincerely or in order to conceal his real views. Had he said nothing about religion, he would certainly have put himself in less danger, and if he merely wanted to camouflage his atheism, there were many other more orthodox versions of Christianity he could have used.[127] To believe that Hobbes was irreligious is thus historically anachronistic and contradicted by his own actions.[128]

One might more reasonably question his orthodoxy. By the standards of his time, however, most of the doctrines and practices he espoused were orthodox, and even those that were contestable were often better grounded in Scripture than those he opposed. Hobbes' version of Christianity is very simple, requiring only that one to believe Jesus was the Christ.[129] This is not quite as simple as it sounds, but it requires little beyond belief in the Nicean Creed and thus in Hobbes' view should be acceptable to most Christians.[130] Disagreements within Christianity, as he saw it, did not arise over basic tenets of faith but about practices derived from the pagans concerning the power, profit, or the honor of clerics.[131] Like many Reformers Hobbes sought to purge Christianity of these accretions. He was particularly concerned by the revival of paganism in the Catholic Church under the influence of humanism.[132] This was one of the factors that produced what he called the Kingdom of Darkness. Hobbes was also convinced that the radical Reformation's emphasis on private revelation and prophecy was wrong-headed and dangerous to public peace. Both these forms of Christianity were thus incompatible with good government. The former produced endemic corruption and the latter civil war.[133] Hobbes rejected both as false theology.

Since theology is concerned with matters that transcend our experience and are indemonstrable, it cannot be a part of science, but it is not therefore meaningless.[134] In fact, Hobbes puts theology in the same category as civil and natural history.[135] Moreover, while Hobbes believed theology is not scientific, he was convinced that none of its conclusions could ever contradict the teachings of science.[136] His theology was thus developed within the framework of a metaphysics that granted priority to nature rather than to man or God. In contrast to the Reformers who fit their notion of nature to their theology, Hobbes sought to fit his theology to his understanding of nature. As a result, his theology at times appears to be "deformed" by his materialism.[137] This fact, however, is less significant than it might at first seem and does not ultimately call into question either his science or his theology.

Hobbes like the nominalists and their followers in the Reformation denied that there is a natural or rational theology. Indeed, by nature we can know only that God is the origin of motion. What we otherwise believe about him we learn only from faith. Faith in Hobbes' view arose originally from true prophecy confirmed by miracles, but since apostolic times miracles had ceased and faith was thus always faith in the account of miracles and prophecy embodied in Scripture.[138] Since Scripture is a human product, faith is belief in those who wrote Scripture. This fact for Hobbes poses two questions: how do we know what real Scripture is and how do we decide on the true interpretation of Scripture?[139] Since neither of these questions can be answered by reason, they depend on authority. If such authority rests in individuals, congregations, or even synods, disagreement and religious war in Hobbes' view are inevitable. If such authority is given to a priestly caste, they will use it to consolidate their own power against the power of the sovereign. Thus for Hobbes it is crucial that the sovereign determine what constitutes Scripture, how it is interpreted, and what practices follow from it.[140] Hobbes thus converts all questions of faith into questions of obedience, excludes privileged sources of religious knowledge, and invokes reason to authorize the sovereign as the ultimate biblical interpreter.[141] He is specifically concerned about the account of God's nature, providence, salvation, and the afterlife.

Hobbes' view that God is infinite and unimaginable is remarkably similar to that of Ockham.[142] While both believe our knowledge of God comes from Scripture, Hobbes only asserts that God exists because that is how God describes himself.[143] Hobbes' God is thus remarkably remote from man, a *deus absconditus* akin to Luther's hidden God. In contrast to Luther, however, Hobbes does not believe that God bridges this divide by infusing himself in human hearts. There is thus no possibility of a direct and loving relation between them. For Hobbes inner faith is nearly irrelevant, prayers do not move God but honor him, and there are no possible covenants with him.[144] While Hobbes never questions God's existence, causality, infinity, or omnipotence, he thus does call into question his goodness, justice, wisdom, and mercy since all these scriptural terms are not descriptive but merely forms of praise.[145] In this respect he only echoes earlier nominalists.

The distance of Hobbes' God from both man and nature opens up a vast space for the development of a natural and political science that is independent of theology. This distance does, however, pose real problems for explaining the relationship between God and his creation. Hobbes dismisses the Cartesian dualism of corporeal and incorporeal substance as a mystification, but in seeking to overcome it he is driven to the conclusion that God is corporeal. At least on the surface this was a heterodox position, seriously defended in the Christian tradition only by Tertullian and explicitly contradicted by the first of the Thirty-Nine Articles.[146] This would seem to be a case in which Hobbes' dedication to the ontic priority of nature distorted his theology.[147]

Appearances notwithstanding, this doctrine of the materiality of God may not have been as radical as it at first appeared or as it has often been portrayed. As we discussed above, Hobbes had a different notion of matter than his predecessors. In his view we have no direct experience of matter and know it only by inference. His belief in God's materiality is thus analogous to his belief in bodies since both transcend the senses. This is, however, very much like the traditional belief in an incorporeal God.

While such an interpretation may save Hobbes from the imputation that his theology is merely an appendage of his science, it is still hard to see how it can make the interaction of an infinite God and a finite world comprehensible without moving either in the direction of Meister Eckhart's mysticism or Spinoza's pantheism, both of which Hobbes wanted to avoid. To say that God is some small and subtle matter interspersed in everything, as Hobbes at times does, seems to deny the divine infinity that Hobbes repeatedly insists upon. In fact, Hobbes really only needed to focus on the priority of motion and treat body as an assumption we make in order to understand and explain motion. The term 'body' then would be the sign we use as a means of explanation. Hobbes could then have defined God consistently as the motion or causality in all things.[148]

A second and related difficulty that Hobbes faces in attempting to reconcile his theology with his science is in explaining the Trinity. Here the problem arises less from materialism than from his individualism. This was a problem not merely for Hobbes but for all nominalists, since ontological individualism made the notion of a common essence of the three persons inconceivable. Most nominalists became either Tritheists or Arians (or some variation thereof, for example, Socinians or Unitarians).[149] Hobbes sought a different solution. He argues in the English version of *Leviathan* that the God is "personated" or represented by Moses (the Father), Christ (the Son), and the Apostles and doctors of the church (the Holy Spirit). While this view contradicted the second of the Thirty-Nine Articles and pushed Hobbes toward Arianism, he believed it was better founded in Scripture than the traditional Trinitarian view that in his opinion was the result of the corrupting influence of Platonism on patristic Christianity.[150]

The question of the relation of the persons within the Godhead was a vital and contentious question in the early church, and was revived during the Reformation. While Hobbes' interpretation of the Trinity was heterodox, it was shared by a number of the dissenting Protestant sects. Still, in response to the furor evoked by the *Leviathan,* Hobbes modified his account in the Latin translation to bring his interpretation more into line with the Thirty-Nine Articles.[151]

While Hobbes struggled to make sense of the ontological divide between man and God, he was resolute and unvarying in his rejection of the existence of all beings who were supposed to inhabit the ontological space between them. He goes to great lengths to show that angels and devils are not real beings. He also denies that the saints dwell with God and can intercede with him on our behalf. The worship of the saints in his view is idolatry. Although Hobbes' rejection of such beings has been taken as an indication of his hostility to religion, he is no different in this respect than most of the Reformers.

Although Hobbes (like many nominalists) had difficulty explaining a Trinitarian God, he found it easier to explain the connection between divine providence and mechanical causality. Both the scholastics and nominalists argued that God could act directly or by means of secondary causes. His initial creation of the world ex nihilo and miracles are examples of the former. Everything that follows by the action of one created object on another is produced by the latter. In such cases, while God may still have planned, willed, or foreseen the result he did not produce it directly. To construct a causal science of motion would be impossible if God constantly intervened in the order of events. Under such circumstances an analysis of secondary causes would not be useful. Hobbes argues that God acts after the creation only by means of secondary causes, according to a strict mechanical necessity. Even miracles in his account do not violate this law. God foresaw the need for them at the creation and organized the

world to produce what appeared to be miracles at certain moments to affirm his messengers. Appearances notwithstanding, they thus do not violate the laws of nature. This view would seem to make Hobbes a probablist,
but this is not the case. In his view God does not overturn his ordained order not because he cannot but because he would have already always have
done so. The will of God therefore can be understood as the concatenation
of secondary or mechanical causes that move and connect all things.

If God is the source of all motion, the question necessarily arises
whether this motion is merely a regular but aimless unfolding of things
or the purposeful development of events. The latter would not necessitate
a return to teleology but might point to the realization of God's purposes
historically. There are two possible answers to this question, each of which
has some warrant in Hobbes' thought. The first possibility is that God wills
merely capriciously and thus has no ends. This seems to be the conclusion
one would draw if one were only looking at the God of nature. Providence
would then be effectively the same as *fortuna*. To read Hobbes in this way
is to read him against the background of Lucretius and Machiavelli. Such
a view renders God irrelevant for human beings because he has no ends in
this world that we can either advance or impede.[152] A second view is that
Hobbes like the nominalists and Reformers believed that God's will was
utterly decisive in the unfolding of creation. If this is the case, then the goal
of all creation would be revealed to us only by Scripture.[153]

Hobbes seems on the whole to adopt the latter view. For him the world
as we know it will thus not go on forever but will end in an apocalyptic
transformation. God will come to rule on a renewed earth, everyone will
be resurrected, and the elect will live on this new earth in renewed bodies in God's presence and governed by his will alone. The rest of humanity will be consigned to a second death but not to the eternal tortures of
hell, which Hobbes believes is incompatible with divine mercy. Until this
event occurs, that is, between the first and second coming, God in Hobbes'
view has put us in charge of the government of the world.[154] Ruling under
such circumstances, as we saw above, requires a Leviathan. In contrast to
Luther, it is thus irrelevant to Hobbes whether the last days are near or far
since we must rule until God returns. The possibility that the world will
end thus makes no difference to politics and is no justification for resistance to the sovereign. There is no need to prepare for God's imminent
arrival, and all such efforts are irrelevant to our spiritual fate. Hobbes' account of the end of the world thus consciously (and ironically) undermines
millenarian arguments for political change.[155]

In keeping with his Calvinism and in contradistinction to the Arminianism regnant among the royalists, Hobbes believed that all human action in every detail is foreknown and forewilled by God. This is the famous doctrine of double predestination. According to this doctrine, human beings have no free will and are merely manipulated by God. The consequence of this position is that God is the origin not merely of good but also of evil. Like Luther, Hobbes admits this fact, arguing, however, that while God is the origin of evil he is not its author.[156] The most important consequence of this doctrine of predestination for Hobbes is that it demonstrates that what man does in this world is largely irrelevant to his fate in the next. The highest form of worship is obedience to the law of nature, but this does not have any impact on our spiritual fate.[157] It is true God chooses some rather than others for salvation, but it is also true that he does so for no reason other than his will to do so. Thus there is nothing that human beings can do to appease or win the favor of this God. He is as indifferent to their well-being as he was to Job's. The consequence of the acceptance of this Calvinist doctrine in Hobbes' view is thus the recognition that God neither can nor will do anything other than he has already done in creating the law of nature to aid us in the face of death and thus that religion can do nothing to quell the terrors of this life. Calvinism in this roundabout way prepares the ground for Hobbes' natural and political science.

Hobbes asserts that the biblical notion of the afterlife has been grossly distorted by Catholic priests to gain power over ordinary Christians and turn them away from their rightful obedience to their sovereigns. In place of these false views Hobbes articulates a scripturally based alternative that is compatible with his Erastianism and materialism. The great source of the wealth and power of the Catholic Church in Hobbes' view was belief in its monopoly of the power to intercede with God and influence one's fate in the afterlife. As we have seen, this became especially important in the aftermath of the nominalist revolution, with the advent of the idea of an unpredictable and terrifying God. The church had always administered the sacraments, but after Ockham extraordinary means of exercising theological influence became increasingly popular. Special masses, indulgences, etc. were the rule of the day. All of these in Hobbes' view were based on the pagan notion of the immortality of the soul, the idea that some essential but immaterial part of our being survives the death of our body. This false notion in Hobbes view was the basis for the greatest of all frauds, the idea of purgatory. The idea of purgatory was extraordinarily useful to the church because of its supposed ability to gain reductions in the sentences of sinners in purgatory, both before and after death. This was the source of the indulgences that so infuriated Luther. In denouncing these beliefs Hobbes was thus in the mainstream of the Reformation.

Hobbes seeks to further reduce the influence that clerics derive from the fear of judgment by clarifying what is to occur on the basis of Scripture. Christ at his return will establish an actual kingdom and rule directly over humans. Hobbes ties this interpretation of the coming kingdom to the resurrection and immortality of the body promised in Scripture and articulated in the Creed. Everyone in his view will be resurrected in the body, some few will be chosen to live forever in the Kingdom of God, and the rest will be condemned to a second death though not to the eternal tortures of hell. There are no unending tortures awaiting the damned. Hobbes thus seeks to eliminate the terrors of eternal damnation.[158] The fear of the fires of hell in his view is used by many radical sects to turn men against the state, and in eliminating it he hopes to strengthen the authority of the sovereign. This argument is unusual but is not without scriptural support.

CONCLUSION

In a time of relative peace in his native France, Descartes laid out the foundations for a new science in his *Discourse*. In confronting the theological-political problem, he simply asserted that he held it wrong to do anything to upset the existing order. However, as he well knew, his science would certainly bring about a transformation in the order of things. His contemporaries, as we saw, were not deceived. His philosophical and theological views were similar in many ways to those of the Arminians, and as a result he was attacked by the dominant Calvinists in Holland and the dominant Catholics in France. Hobbes too had to deal with the theological-political problem, not however in a time of peace but in a time of brutal civil war. In his case there was no regnant church and state to support. Hobbes too had a vision of a science of motion, but he realized that this vision could only be realized if political conditions were more stable. He thus had to provide grounds for a political and religious order that would make science possible. He sought to do so by spelling out an order justified by both natural law and Scripture, as revealed by both his science and his theology. The picture of the commonwealth governed by a mighty Leviathan resembled in many ways the institutions of Elizabethan England, but it was rooted not in mere traditionalism but in reason and a limited form of consent. Theologically, Hobbes found it necessary to depart in two respects from Anglican orthodoxy, but he was careful that even his deviations were scripturally justifiable. Moreover, his ultimate goal was not to push Anglicanism to the left or the right but to bolster it against opponents on both extremes. His interpretation of Anglicanism, however, was more Calvinist than that of his contemporaries, especially on the doctrine of predestination, again in a manner similar to Anglicans of the previous century. This brought him into conflict with both the dominant Arminians and the dissident Presbyterians. His fate was thus much like that of Descartes. However, while his theology was attacked in his own lifetime and in the period immediately after his death, it was also silently adopted by people such as Locke and the Latitudinarians.

Hobbes' God is a being less to be loved than feared. This is apparent in Hobbes' argument that the love of God is best displayed in the obedience to his laws. This God sets standards of good and evil, but they are arbitrary. He governs nature, but he gives it no determinate form or end. He is distant from human life, and human happiness thus depends not on God but on human wisdom. This is a wisdom that arises out of our intrinsic humanity, out of our finitude and corresponding fear of death. The solution to the human dilemma for Hobbes is a science that accepts this distant God as the origin of all things and seeks to emulate his power and artifice through the mastery of the causal order of the world. In the end, while God may reign for Hobbes, it is the space he leaves free that is the site for the triumph of the fearful wisdom that he bequeaths to humanity.

Hobbes in this way provides the foundation for the acceptance of the radically omnipotent God that nominalism proclaimed by showing how this God was compatible with the human mastery of both the natural and the political world. In doing so, he articulates a doctrine that in contrast to both Descartes and the humanists diminishes the divinity of man and that also in contrast to Luther diminishes the role that God and religion play in human life. While some may see this as just another step in the path of secularization that began with Ockham and ended in Nietzsche, it was a stunning achievement, and it was an achievement that was rooted as much in a new theological vision as in science.[159] And unless and until we understand this theological vision we will be unable to understand either modern science or modernity itself.

The Contradictions of Enlightenment and the Crisis of Modernity

On a cold and rainy January day in 1793, a corpulent gentleman, just thirty-eight years old, stepped out of his carriage in the midst of a hostile Parisian crowd. He loosened his scarf, turned down his collar, and with some assistance ascended the steep steps of the scaffold. Speaking in a surprisingly loud voice, he declared himself innocent, pardoned those who were about to kill him, and prayed that his blood would not be visited upon his country before placing his neck on the block of the guillotine. As the blade was released and began its swift downward course, few of those present realized that it was bringing to an end not merely the life of the King of France but also the purest hopes of the modern age. The cut was not clean, but it was mortal and final. One of the revolutionaries grasped the head by the hair and displayed it to the crowd. After a brief silence, cries of "Vive la Révolution!" began slowly and then swelled to a roar, as if the mob needed to reassure itself that what it had seen, and in a sense achieved, was something positive. And with good reason. While it is almost certain that Louis XVI was guilty of treason and by the standards of his times deserved to be put to death, his execution carried the Revolution across a line that could not be crossed with impunity. Having transgressed this boundary, there was nothing left to constrain revolutionary passions, and within a few months executions had become a daily ritual, producing a Reign of Terror that lasted until July 1794, leaving more than thirty thousand dead across France. Despite the king's pardon and his prayer, his blood was visited upon his native land and particularly upon those who had put his neck on the block. The Terror swallowed not just the members of the *ancien régime* but also many of the leaders of the Revolution as well. While the number killed was not great by comparison to the earlier butchery of the Wars of Religion or to the later slaughter of the twentieth century, the Reign of Terror had an extraordinary impact on the intellectual elite of its time, shattering their faith that reason could rule the world, that progress was inevitable, and that the spread of enlightenment would usher in an age of peace, prosperity, and human freedom. The Terror convinced them that when universal reason came to power it wore a devil's mask and opened up the gates not of heaven but of hell.

The hopeful dreams of the "century of lights" were swept away, and reaction set in on all sides. The blade that separated the muddled head of an ineffectual king from his body thus also severed the unblemished ideal of modernity from the reality of modern practices and institutions that were taking hold all over Europe. Since then modernity has swept in everywhere and changed the face of Europe and the world, but despite this triumph no one has ever been quite able to forget that modernity has an edge that cuts for good *and* ill.

As we have seen, questions about the modern project had been raised before. Indeed, while modernity had increasingly engaged the imagination of European intellectuals since the latter half of the seventeenth century, there had always been those who had doubts that it was an unqualified good. In the late seventeenth and early eighteenth centuries, the broadest claims of the modern project had been called into question in the famous Quarrel of the Ancients and the Moderns, but this for the most part was merely a rear-guard effort by humanists defending the authority of classical thought against Cartesian modernists. Rousseau launched a similar but broader attack in his *Discourse on the Arts and Sciences,* arguing that modernity not only failed to improve human beings but actually made them worse, producing not virtue, strength, or truthfulness, but vice, weakness, and hypocrisy. And finally, Hume mounted a skeptical attack that called into question the idea of a necessary connection between cause and effect that was essential to the modern idea of an apodictic science. While such criticism did not go unheard, European intellectuals were still overwhelmingly committed to modern thought in the broadest sense in 1789, in large part certainly because the power of modern rationality seemed to have been borne out by the success of the Americans in peaceably establishing their own laws and choosing their own leaders in the aftermath of the American Revolution.[1] This example led most European intellectuals to conclude that human reason could give order to human life if only given a chance. As a result, the critique of modernity often fell on deaf ears.

Even those who recognized the profundity of Rousseau's and Hume's critiques more often than not came to the defense of modern reason. Kant was a case in point. While he was deeply impressed by the arguments of Rousseau and Hume, he remained convinced that modern science and morality were both possible and eminently desirable. Indeed, he believed that he could defend modern science while leaving space for morality and religion. Such a defense of modern rationality was crucial because in his view this notion of rationality opened up the path to the universal enlightenment of the human race.

The crucial word here is enlightenment. In our discussions in the earlier chapters of this book, we have scarcely mentioned the Enlightenment, although for many today the Enlightenment *is* modernity, and modernity is or at least begins with the Enlightenment. Indeed, one of the purposes of the preceding argument has been to demonstrate that modernity is broader, deeper, and older than the Enlightenment. That said, at the core of the project initiated by Descartes and Hobbes is a faith or self-confidence that an enlightened humanity can discover a ground for an apodictic or at least an effectual truth, and that this truth will provide the foundation for an unprecedented human flourishing. It was the recognition of this widespread and deeply held belief in the enlightening force of reason that led nineteenth-century scholars to characterize this earlier period as the age of Enlightenment.[2] While the concept of the Enlightenment as a historical period only arose in the nineteenth century, the idea that reason could enlighten humanity had certainly been present in modern thought since at least the mid-seventeenth century, as we saw in our discussion of Descartes and Hobbes. The term 'enlighten' was actually first used in print in English in 1667 by Milton, whose God in *Paradise Lost* commands the archangel Michael to "reveal to Adam what shall come. . . . As I shall thee enlighten."[3] Addison used the term obliquely in 1712 in referring to the time before "the World was enlightened by Learning and Philosophy."[4] On this basis, Kant used the equivalent German term, 'Aufklärung,' in "What is Enlightenment" in 1784. This usage almost certainly derives from the earlier theological and philosophical usage of the term 'light.' In the dedicatory epistle to *The Great Instauration,* for example, Francis Bacon expressed his hope that "the kindling of this new light in the darkness of philosophy, be the means of making this age famous to posterity [for] the regeneration and restoration of the sciences."[5] Bacon's two great successors, Descartes and Hobbes, used the term 'light' in a similar sense. Descartes repeatedly spoke of the "great light in our intellect" and of our "natural light," while Hobbes famously pointed to "perspicuous words" as "the light of human minds."[6] This usage itself clearly derived from the earlier distinction of the divine and natural light in scholastic thought, which in turn was indebted in different ways to the Augustinian notion of divine illumination and the Platonic analogy of the idea of the good to the sun. *"Light" in Bible?*

While the light at the core of the Enlightenment thus had an origin in the theological and philosophical thought of the High Middle Ages, it would be a mistake to believe that this concept was parasitic upon scholastic metaphysics. The terminology had a genealogical debt to scholasticism, but, as we have seen in our preceding discussion, it was employed within a new metaphysics that had broken with scholasticism in almost every respect. Descartes' notion of the natural light was different in its nature and function from the natural light that Aquinas, for example, attributes to human reason. It was the increase and spread of this new notion of natural light or what came to be called *reason* that was the source of enlightenment. As Hegel put it, consciousness at this time discovered in the world the same reason that it found in itself.[7] The increase in this light makes possible the progressive mastery of nature that eighteenth-century thinkers believed would produce universal freedom, general prosperity, and perpetual peace.

The Enlightenment as a historical period is generally reckoned by later historians to have begun with Locke and then spread to the rest of Europe. While the transmission and reception of his thought in the different social and intellectual contexts produced different strains or schools of thought, many thinkers throughout Europe were in general agreement that a new age was dawning, an age of reason. In 1759, Jean d'Alembert, the French mathematician and Encyclopedist, spoke for the intellectual class of his age when he declared that "our century is the century of philosophy par excellence. If one considers without bias the present state of our knowledge, one cannot deny that philosophy among us has shown progress."[8] The idea of the progress in enlightenment had taken such hold of European thought that Voltaire could claim that the young graduate of a French Lycée knew more than the philosophers of antiquity. Kant summarized the goals and aspirations of this "century of lights:" "Enlightenment," he argued, "is man's emergence from his self-imposed immaturity. Immaturity is the inability to use one's understanding without guidance from another. This immaturity is self-imposed when its cause lies not in lack of understanding, but in lack of resolve and courage to use it without guidance from another. *Sapere Aude*! 'Have courage to use your own understanding!'—that is the motto of enlightenment."[9] Laziness and cowardice enslave human beings to others, and they cannot be freed by revolution but only by the growth of reason. Thus, for Kant "nothing is required for this enlightenment . . . except freedom; and the freedom in question is the least harmful of all, namely, the freedom to use reason publicly in all matters."[10] This is not a vain or utopian hope in his view, for "we do have clear indications that the way is now being opened for men to proceed freely in this direction. . . . The inclination to and vocation for free thinking . . . finally even influences the principles of government, which finds that it can profit by treating men, who are now more than machines, in accord with their dignity." [11]

While Kant perhaps never doubted that universal enlightenment and the rule of reason could be attained, he recognized, especially from his reading of Hume, that there were powerful reasons to doubt that the notion of reason that modern thinkers employed could provide the foundation for the two great goals of modern thought, the mastery of nature through modern science and the realization of human freedom. These doubts arose from the fact that reason itself seemed inevitably and ineluctably to become entangled in aporiae and contradiction. These aporiae or, as Kant called them, antinomies, threatened to undermine the modern project of *mathesis universalis* and leave humanity lost in the abyss of Humean skepticism.

Kant first considered the problem of the antinomies in his dissertation (1770), he but did not appreciate their full significance until after reading Hume. In the period before he began writing the *Critique of Pure Reason* (published in 1781), he came to understand their deeper significance. He explained this in a letter to Garve on September 26, 1798, asserting that it was "not the investigation of the existence of God, of immorality, etc. but the antinomy of pure reason . . . from which I began. : 'The world has a beginning—:it has no beginning, etc., to the fourth [?] There is freedom in human being,—against there is no freedom and everything is natural necessity'; it was this that first woke me from my dogmatic slumber and drove me to the critique of reason itself to dissolve the scandal of the contradiction of reason with itself." [12] The central reference here is to the Third Antinomy (the seventy-four year old Kant misspeaks himself in his reference to the Fourth Antinomy). This antinomy purports to show that it is impossible to give a meaningful causal explanation of the whole without the assumption of a first cause through freedom, and yet that the very possibility of such freedom undermines the necessity of any causal explanation. [13] In other words, modern natural science, which analyzes all motion in terms of efficient causes, is unintelligible without a freely acting first cause such as God or man, but such causality through freedom, which is essential to morality, is incompatible with natural necessity. Freedom is thus both necessary to causality and incompatible with it. Kant recognized that if this conclusion were correct, the modern project was self-contradictory and that modern reason could give man neither the mastery of nature nor the freedom that he so desired.

Kant's philosophical enterprise aimed at resolving the problem posed by the antinomies.[14] The antinomies, as Kant sees them, are only apparent and not real contradictions. They arise as the consequence of an attempt by the understanding (which deals only with finite things) to grasp the infinite. In struggling to understand what it cannot understand, it inevitably falls into perplexity. Kant believes we can solve the problem of the antinomies by recognizing and accepting the limits of our rational capacities. We must, in other words, confine the understanding to its native realm, to what Kant calls "the island of truth," and resist the lure of a fatal voyage in search of the infinite on the foggy, iceberg-infested seas that surround this island. The critique of reason that establishes these limits is thus an effort to know oneself and hence an integral moment of enlightenment. What Kant believes he can show through such a critique is that reason "knows" in two different ways: first, through the understanding (pure reason), which gives us a scientific (and causal) account of existence, and second, through a moral sense (practical reason) rooted in our transcendental freedom, which tells us what is right and wrong. The apparent contradiction of reason with itself is thus the consequence not of the contradictory character of existence or the inadequacy of reason but of the misuse of reason. The correct use of reason, Kant believes, will make possible the mastery of nature and attainment of human freedom, which will produce prosperity and morality and consequently political liberty and perpetual peace. Kant thus believed that transcendental idealism could save the modern project by providing the philosophical ground for the reconciliation of freedom and science, and that it would thus make possible the continued growth in enlightenment and human progress.

This "solution," however, was not universally accepted, largely because Kant did not, and perhaps could not, explain how the two faculties of knowing, pure and practical reason, could be conjoined in consciousness.[15] Kant recognized that this was a problem and argued that these two capacities were unified in the transcendental unity of apperception (or self-consciousness), but he did not explain how such a unity was possible. Rather he simply asserted that without such a unity experience would be impossible. Since we do have experience, he concluded that such a unity must exist. However, to many of his immediate successors it seemed as if Kant had not solved the problem of the antinomies but displaced it, saving science and morality only by making self-consciousness itself unintelligible. Nineteenth- and twentieth-century continental thought is in large measure a series of attempts to come to terms with the question that Kant posed in the antinomies, that he himself failed to adequately answer, and that was driven home by the French Revolution.

If the antinomy cannot be resolved, then it is difficult to see how the modern scientific and technological project that seeks to make man the master and possessor of nature can be compatible with a moral and political project that aims to realize and secure human freedom. As Kant and his successors realized, this is thus the question on which the fate of modernity turns. The antinomy, however, did not spring full-grown from the head of Kant. The antinomy is decisive for modernity precisely because it brings into the open the contradictions that were hidden in the modern project from the very beginning, and from before the beginning. The antinomies, and the decisive third antinomy in particular, are deeply rooted in early modern and premodern thought. Indeed, as we will see, the problem that appears in the third antinomy and that has had such an important impact on later thought appeared first in the debate between Erasmus and Luther, and then more explicitly in the debate between Descartes and Hobbes in the "Objections and Replies" to the *Meditations*. We have already examined the earlier debate in detail. In this chapter we will examine the latter.

As we have seen, modernity in the broadest sense was a series of attempts to answer the fundamental questions that arose out of the nominalist revolution. These questions were both profound and comprehensive, putting into doubt not merely the knowledge of God, man, and nature, but reason and being as well. The humanist movement and the Reformation were comprehensive attempts to answer these questions. They both accepted the nominalist ontology of radical individualism, but they disagreed ontically about which of the traditional realms of being was foundational. The humanists began their account with man and interpreted the other realms of being anthropomorphically. The Reformers, by contrast, believed that God was primary and interpreted man and nature theologically. As we have seen, however, neither the humanists nor the Reformers were willing to eliminate either God or man. The humanists did not suggest that God did not exist, and the Reformers did not deny the independence of human beings. However, such qualifications, especially in times of persecution, are often merely camouflage for deeper claims. To the extent that their differences were foundational, each position denied the ground of the other, as we saw in our examination of the debate between Erasmus and Luther. If one begins as Erasmus does with man and asserts even a minimal efficacy for human freedom, divine omnipotence is compromised and the reality of the Christian God is called into question. Morality in this way renders piety superfluous. If one begins with a doctrine of divine freedom and omnipotence manifested as divine grace, no human freedom is possible. Religion crushes morality and transforms human beings into mere marionettes. The Luther/Erasmus debate thus actually ends in the same unsatisfying juxtaposition of arguments as the later Kantian antinomy. If we were to schematize that debate in a logical form corresponding to the antinomy, the thesis position (represented by Erasmus) would be that there is causality through human freedom in addition to the causality through divine will, and the antithesis position (represented by Luther) that there is no causality through human freedom but only through divine will. There is no solution to this problem on either a humanistic or a theological basis that can sustain both human freedom and divine sovereignty. As we saw above, the gulf that is opened up by this contradiction was unbridgeable. It was also unavoidable since each claim is parasitic on the other. This antinomy, which played an important role in propelling Europe into the Wars of Religion, was thus in a certain sense inevitable.

As we saw in the last two chapters, modernity proper was born out of and in reaction to this conflict, as an effort to find a new approach to the world that was not entangled in the contradictions of humanism and the Reformation. To this end, thinkers such as Bacon, Descartes, and Hobbes sought a new beginning that gave priority not to man or to God but to nature, that sought to understand the world not as a product of a Promethean human freedom or of a radically omnipotent divine will but of the mechanical motion of matter. Modernity in this sense was the result of an ontic revolution within metaphysics that accepted the ontological ground that nominalism established but that saw the other realms of being through this new naturalistic lens. While this revolutionary approach seemed at first to eliminate the conflict within metaphysics which we examined in chapters 2 through 5, as we will see, it was finally unable to erase it and in the end actually reinscribed it within modern metaphysics as the contradiction between natural necessity and human freedom. Thus, while modern metaphysics began by turning away from both the human and the divine toward the natural, it was able to do so only by reinterpreting the human and the divine naturalistically. However, both were thereby incorporated within the naturalistic perspective. In incorporating them in this manner, however, the earlier conflict between the human and the divine was not resolved but concealed within the new metaphysical outlook. In order to explain how this occurs, we must examine this process more carefully.

As prototypical modern thinkers, both Descartes and Hobbes agree that in our analysis of the world we must grant ontic priority to nature.[16] Insofar as they represent opposing poles within modernity, they disagree about the way in which we should interpret the human and the divine within this naturalistic horizon. As we have seen, Descartes sees human beings as corporeal *(res extensa)* and thus as comparable to all other natural beings, but he also sees humans as incorporeal *(res cogitans)* and thus as comparable to God. Hobbes, by contrast, argues that human beings are no different than the rest of nature, mere bodies in motion that can no more act like God than create something out of nothing. Descartes is thus able to retain a space for human freedom, while Hobbes concludes that everything happens as the result of necessity. In this way, the disagreement that tore the premodern world to pieces reappears as the disagreement about the nature of human freedom and natural necessity. And as we shall see, it is this deep disagreement at the beginning of modern thought that reemerges in the end in and as Kant's antinomy. Therefore, the antinomy that is taken to mark the end of the Enlightenment and thus the end of modernity is only the recognition of the fundamental contradictions that were always hidden in the heart of the modern project.

While they disagreed about the nature and relation of man and God, Descartes and Hobbes otherwise followed remarkably similar paths. Both were acutely aware of the dangers of religious fanaticism. They were also both opponents of dogmatism, particularly in its scholastic form, and similarly believed that that the idea of individual revelation was extraordinarily dangerous.[17] They also shared similar epistemological views. Both agreed that the senses do not give us immediate knowledge of the external world but only stimulate our sensory apparatus to form images in us. Knowledge of the truth then cannot be attained by relying on the senses and observation. Instead it is necessary to free reason from the snares of the senses and open up a space for the reconstruction or representation of the world hidden behind the veil of perception. In this way, epistemology for both became the prelude to any metaphysics. In seeking this new path to truth both drew on Bacon's notion of science, but they recognized that his method was inadequate to establish such a science. In their opinion, his inductive empiricism would never produce the science he imagined and desired. Science required a better method, and this they hoped to establish by applying Galileo's mathematical analysis of motion to broader problems.

Descartes and Hobbes thus agreed about the dangers of religion, the difficulties that confronted understanding, the priority of epistemology, the need for science, and the importance of a mathematical method at the basis of such a science. However, as we have seen, they disagreed about the nature of the world hidden behind the veil of perception, about the capacity of science to comprehend it, and most importantly about the nature and relationship of man and God within this naturalistic worldview. Their ontic agreement about the priority of nature and the logic of the science needed to master it thus concealed their disagreement about the nature and relation of the human and the divine. This disagreement became particularly evident in their debate in the Objections and Replies to the *Meditations.*

There is a certain disproportion in the exchange between Hobbes and Descartes in the Objections and Replies. At the time this debate occurred, Descartes was already a well-known and highly regarded intellectual figure. Although Descartes' senior by eight years, Hobbes was by contrast a political exile who had published almost nothing. Within the Mersenne circle, however, Hobbes was highly regarded, and it was no accident that Mersenne asked Hobbes to comment on Descartes' new work. Hobbes had already written a lengthy and apparently penetrating critique of the *Discourse* and *Dioptrics.* There can be no doubt that Hobbes took the task Mersenne assigned him seriously, even if his objections at times seem petty or malicious. As Richard Tuck and others have shown, there was already some animosity between the two men, especially on Descartes' side, due in part to Hobbes' earlier critique of the *Discourse* but also because that critique had raised Descartes' suspicion that Hobbes was out to steal his ideas and his fame.[18] Hobbes, by contrast, was continually irritated by what he took to be Descartes' failure to read and carefully consider his criticisms. This said, a careful reading suggests that neither Hobbes' objections nor Descartes' replies were significantly shaped by this animus. Tuck has shown how important this exchange was for the development of Hobbes' thought, and a careful examination of the text shows that Descartes actually paid a great deal more attention to Hobbes than Hobbes imagined, often where he seems most dismissive. For example, he goes to great lengths—greater than in any of the other Objections and Replies—to make the exchange look like an actual debate. It is the only section in the Objections and Replies that Descartes actually organized as a debate, with each objection followed by an immediate reply, rather than globally replying to all of his critic's objections. Moreover, in response to Hobbes, Descartes often writes proleptically, inserting in his reply to a specific objection examples or arguments that Hobbes turns to in his succeeding objection, thus giving the exchange a greater coherence than it might otherwise have had. The literary composition of the exchange thus argues strongly for Descartes' recognition of its importance.

While Descartes almost certainly did take Hobbes' objections seriously, he apparently also recognized that the differences between them were so profound that there was really little basis for an exchange of views that could bring either of them to meaningfully alter his position. Their dialogue thus is really more two monologues that present statements of their opposing views. These statements, however, are quite valuable because they reveal the necessary and irremediable character of their disagreement and thus the necessary and irremediable brokenness at the heart of modernity.

Hobbes begins his critique of the *Meditations* by affirming the truth of Descartes' demonstration in the first meditation that sense-deception calls into question the reality of external objects. On this point he and Descartes agree. Indeed, as we saw above, it is this crucial point that is behind the modern effort to discover an underlying rational order that is not accessible to the senses. Hobbes, however, points out that Descartes' argument is not original but merely repeats the arguments of Plato, that is to say, of the Academic skeptics, a point which Descartes admits in his reply.

What is surprising about this assertion and Descartes' agreement with it is that it is manifestly false. The crucial difference between the argument in the *Discourse* and in the *Meditations* is the claim that the ultimate source of skepticism is the possibility of deception by an omnipotent God. This argument, however, appears nowhere in Plato or the Academic or Pyrrhonian skeptics. One could plausibly suspect that Hobbes merely builds here on his earlier critique of the *Discourse* (where Descartes does not refer to divine omnipotence) and simply overlooks the importance of the role of God in this context, but he asserts later that Descartes' whole argument depends upon a demonstration that God is not a deceiver. It thus seems unlikely he overlooks the importance of this point here.

What is more important to Hobbes seems to be the assertion at the very beginning that Descartes' claims are not new, and that he is thus not modern. By tying Descartes to Plato in this way, Hobbes attempts to connect him to a dualistic (Catholic) metaphysics of body and soul that Hobbes believes is outmoded and deeply complicit in the religious conflicts of the time. As we have seen, Descartes does draw on Plato (and Plato's Christian follower Augustine), but he certainly is less Platonic than Hobbes suggests. Why then does he agree with Hobbes on this point? The most likely explanation for his willingness to allow this mischaracterization or exaggeration of his position is that he is anxious to appear less revolutionary to his Catholic audience (and especially the doctors of the Sorbonne) than he actually is.[19] What is certainly clear is that both thinkers are aware of how crucial the question of the nature and relation of God and man is in this context.

Whatever the reason that Hobbes and Descartes are silent on this matter here, it comes to occupy the center of their debate.[20] This is already apparent in Hobbes' second objection that calls into question Descartes' characterization of man as *res cogitans*. While both thinkers agree that nature is a mechanical process, they disagree fundamentally about whether man is a part of this process and subject to its laws. For Descartes, the human body is a mechanical thing, but the human self or soul is independent of this realm and its laws, a *res cogitans,* a thinking thing. For Hobbes, man like all other created beings is matter in motion and nothing besides. Hobbes points out that Descartes' proof of his own existence rests on thinking but argues that Descartes' further conclusion that it follows from this that man is a thinking thing is faulty. He should rather have concluded that man is an extended or corporeal thing. A thinking thing in Hobbes' view is necessarily corporeal because we cannot conceive of thinking except as matter that thinks. Therefore, in his view man is not a thinking thing but a thing that thinks. My being is not thought; thought is a motion of my corporeal being.

Descartes agrees with Hobbes that the *res cogitans* is first a *res* and then a *cogitans,* but he argues that this does not make it corporeal, since there are both corporeal and incorporeal substances. Descartes thus does not deny the basic fact that there is a substance underlying thinking but argues that this substance is ontologically distinct from corporeal substance or body. In effect, Descartes thereby reinscribes his dualism in substance itself and sets it off against Hobbes' monistic materialism. Descartes frames his answer in this way to undercut Hobbes' third objection in which he declares that the Cartesian definition of man as *res cogitans* is merely the reification of the activity of thinking. Descartes denies this, asserting that the thinker is distinct from his thought, but he does not explain what this means other than to reassert the character of the thinker as an incorporeal substance.

If we are essentially incorporeal, then true knowing cannot be derived from the images formed as a result of our interactions with bodies. For Descartes, the realm of pure thought is thus independent of body and of the corporeal imagination. In the fourth objection, Hobbes denies the possibility of such non-imagistic thinking. Reasoning, he argues, is a connecting of names, and names are merely the signs of images. We have no immediate or even mediate knowledge of what is. Words are merely tools that we use to obtain power over and manipulate things. Therefore, as Hobbes tells us elsewhere, all thinking is hypothetical and is measured not by its truth or correspondence to what ultimately is, but by its effectiveness. For

Descartes by contrast, we reason not about words but about the objects that they signify, and *mathesis universalis* aims not merely at probable knowledge that gives us an effective mastery of nature at this time and place but at apodictic knowledge that can guarantee our mastery everywhere and always.

If Hobbes is correct about the nature of reasoning, then as Descartes well knows, we can never be certain that our ideas correspond to the things themselves. For Descartes, the guarantee of such a correspondence is provided by God, but only if God is not a deceiver. *Mathesis universalis* thus depends on the demonstration of this fact, but such a demonstration itself depends on our being able to know God, on having an idea of God in us. Hobbes considers this impossible because God is infinite, and all of our ideas are drawn from the imagination of finite bodies. We can thus know of God's existence only inferentially by the logical necessity of a first cause.

Here we see a great divide. For Descartes there is a pure thinking separate from the imagination. Our capacity for such pure thinking is in fact something that we share with God. Descartes explains in the fifth Reply that our true "ideas" are the same as those in the divine mind that has no corporeal imagination. Implicitly, Descartes thus argues here that man as *res cogitans* is divine or at least participates in some aspects of the divine. As we have seen, this is a point he makes explicitly in the body of the *Meditations* where he identifies man's infinite will with the will of God.[21] For Hobbes, by contrast, we can have no idea of an incorporeal thing. Even things like emotions, which Descartes educes to support his point, are in Hobbes' view nothing other than the thing that evokes the emotion plus its effect on our body. Hobbes thus concludes that since we have no idea of our self or of God except as body, Descartes' whole argument collapses. Descartes argues, on the contrary, since we *do* have an idea of God, Hobbes' objection collapses. Argument at this point can go no further, since the parties fundamentally disagree about the nature of man, his capacities, and his relation to God.

Hobbes bolsters his argument in the next four objections. He first argues that there is no distinction between the imagination of things and the astronomical or mathematical idea of them. Both images or words and mathematical symbols are tools that we use to grasp and manipulate bodies. Mathematics thus does not give us access to a trans-corporeal reality as Descartes suggests. In a similar vein, Hobbes denies that there are different levels of being of the sort that Descartes employs to identify divine infinity with perfection. There is no sense in which some being has more "reality" than another being. God's infinite being thus does not have more reality and perfection than our finite being. Indeed, the idea of the infinite is always only the idea of the in-finite, and is thus formed only by reflecting on our own limitations. We simply cannot understand God, and it is in fact contrary to Christian doctrine to try to do so.

This argument is, of course, aimed at Descartes' demonstration that God cannot be a deceiver because it would be incompatible with his perfection as an infinite being. Hobbes suggests that the infinite is no more perfect than the finite, and that we can have no positive knowledge of the infinite in any case and thus no knowledge of God. If Hobbes is correct on this point, then Descartes' crucial demonstration that God cannot be a deceiver is defective. Descartes recognizes this and argues that we can in fact understand God positively by indefinitely extending the idea of the understanding that we already have. What Descartes is arguing here and spells out more fully in the exchange with (Hobbes' friend) Gassendi in the fifth set of Objections and Replies is that we have the capacity to grasp the infinite on the model of an unbounded figure.[22] Seen in this way, finite things are figures inscribed on an infinite plane. The finite is thus the negation of the infinite and not the reverse. Such an argument, however, cannot convince Hobbes, who denies that we could ever have an idea of an infinite plane in the first place.

Believing that he has disposed of the central pillar of Descartes' argument that rests on our knowledge of God, Hobbes moves on in the twelfth objection to attack his notion of man as a freely willing being. Descartes, he claims, believes we err because our will is not confined by our understanding and ranges freely to the infinite, but Descartes never demonstrates the freedom of the will and such freedom is called into question by predestination. He refers here to predestination, but as we have seen he interprets this mechanistically.

This conclusion follows from everything Hobbes has argued in the earlier objections. Man for him is not a thinking thing but a body and does not rise above the natural world that is governed by a universal and inexorable mechanical causality. However free we may seem to be when we examine ourselves, we thus cannot really be free, that is, we cannot be an uncaused cause. This crucial point is bound up with Descartes' and Hobbes' basic disagreement about the relationship of the human and the divine. For Hobbes, man is radically separate from God. God is no man's debtor, and everything that occurs is the result of God's preordination. Human freedom is thus an illusion that arises as a result of our ignorance of the manner in which God has organized all motion. Descartes admits that it is very difficult to grasp how God's preordination is compatible with freedom but claims that we all experience freedom within ourselves and know it by our natural light.

Hobbes tries to show that this argument is unconvincing because there is no light in the intellect such as Descartes describes. This term is merely metaphorical, and the assertion that it is anything more is not only wrong but also dangerous. Indeed, in his view there have been many fanatics who have claimed to know the truth by an inner light. Hobbes here is certainly thinking of the religious fanatics on all sides who had produced the bloodbath of the Wars of Religion. He is thus arguing that Descartes' demand for apodictic truth based upon the certainty of the inner light is not only over-drawn, it is also dangerous, indeed that it repeats the error that produced the Wars of Religion. Knowing and willing for Hobbes are two different things. If we know the truth, we are convinced by it even in opposition to our will. Thus the inner assent that Descartes suggests follows from our inner light is not necessary to knowledge. Moreover, the source of error thus does not lie in the improper use of the free will as Descartes suggests. We come to know things from an examination of the nature of things that actually exist. There are no objects of knowledge that transcend these things, no essences that we can know by pure thinking. Thinking is a linking of names by the word 'is.' Essences are consequently only mental fictions. We therefore cannot know anything that does not exist since there are no natures, even of such things as triangles, apart from existing things.

Descartes' science, Hobbes claims, depends on the demonstration that God is not a deceiver. However, we know that doctors and fathers, for example, often deceive others for their own good. Since deception is sometimes a good thing, we cannot assume that even a good God is not a deceiver. As a result, we cannot know that external objects exist on the basis of the propensity that God puts in us to believe in them. The consequences of this for Descartes' argument are profound, for by his own logic, Hobbes asserts, we cannot know with certainty that we are awake rather than dreaming. The unstated conclusion to Hobbes' argument is, of course, that Descartes' *mathesis universalis* as he conceives it is impossible. This conclusion does not mean that science as such is impossible but it does mean that science can only be hypothetical and not apodictic. Such a hypothetical science that aims not at absolute truth but at effective truth remains a possibility. As we saw in chapter 7, it was this possibility that Hobbes explored and spelled out in his work.

What is clear from this examination of the exchange between Descartes and Hobbes is that the issues that divide them and that remain at the heart of modernity reprise in a surprising way the earlier issues in the debate between Erasmus and Luther. This is not accidental. Both debates in fact are a reflection of contradictions that are intrinsic to the metaphysical inheritance within which modernity unfolds. Granting ontic priority to nature directs attention away from the question of the superiority of the human or the divine but it does not eliminate it. In fact, it merely conceals the question within the naturalistic worldview that science articulates. However, this is not a question that can be long concealed, if only because it is the question of the nature of the being who poses questions. In fact, it is this question that in the late eighteenth century reemerges in all of its power and brings the Enlightenment to an end.

SECULARIZATION OR CONCEALMENT?

The persistence of the question of the nature and relationship of the human and the divine from Luther and Erasmus through Hobbes and Descartes to Kant points to the deeper question of the enduring importance of theology for modernity. In the preceding chapters, we have seen that the series of transformations that brought the modern world into being over a three hundred year period were the result of repeated (though ultimately unsuccessful) efforts to develop a consistent *metaphysica specialis* that could account for the relationship between man, God, and nature within a nominalist ontology. While the importance of theology in this development is relatively clear, its continuing relevance to the further development of modernity is less obvious. Indeed, many would argue that religion in general and theology in particular have become increasingly less important for the modern world. From this point of view, the problem of explaining the relationship between the three traditional realms of being within a consistent *metaphysica specialis* is "solved" in modernity by excluding the divine from the equation. As a result, knowing ceases to be conceived as metaphysics and is reconceptualized as a universal science that consists of only physics and anthropology. Theology is no longer regarded as a form of knowledge and becomes an expression or interpretation of faith, more akin to rhetoric or poetry than science.[23]

This decline in the importance of religion and theology in modern times has been characterized as the process of secularization. Secularization refers in the first instance to the development of a secular or nonreligious realm alongside the world informed by religion, but during the course of modernity it has come to mean the expansion and dominance of the secular realm and the concomitant diminution or disappearance of the sphere of religion.[24] The idea that modernization produces secularization was a product of the later nineteenth- and early twentieth-century thinkers such as Marx, Freud, Dilthey, Weber, Durkheim, and Troeltsch. They argued that the development of modernity, especially in the aftermath of the Enlightenment, inevitably brought about what Weber referred to as the disenchantment of the world, a decline in religious belief and authority, first in the political realm but then increasingly in other realms of human life as well. To take just one example, the cosmos as the embodiment of divine reason first was reconceptualized as the contingent creation of an arbitrary divine will, then as pagan *fortuna,* and finally as matter in motion.[25] A similar process in their view was evident in other realms as well. This transformation diminished the role of God and the authority of religion in human life. Practically, it led to the increasing limitation of religious authority first in the political and economic realms and then gradually in the social and cultural realms as well, transforming religion into a private belief or practice and religious institutions into voluntary associations similar to clubs and lodges. This transformation was accelerated by the Enlightenment, which sought (at least in its most radical form) not merely to privatize religion but to eliminate it, imagining it to be a crutch for an immature humanity or a pernicious fraud perpetrated and sustained by corrupt clerics. In the aftermath of the Enlightenment, Weber could thus proclaim that secularization ended with the replacement of both traditional authority (of the Catholic Church and the state institutions it underpinned) and charismatic authority (of Protestant preachers and their like) by rational bureaucratic authority. Secularization theorists understood that some vestiges of religion might persist, but they imagined these would all essentially be forms of deism or Unitarianism.[26]

As we have seen, there is evidence in the thought of Descartes and Hobbes of an attempt to delimit the sphere of divine will and religious authority. But was this an example of secularization? There are good reasons to think that it was not. Their efforts, as we argued above, were not driven by an antipathy to or disbelief in religion per se but by the attempt to develop a new science that granted priority to nature. They believed that giving priority to such a science and to nature generally would not merely help to defuse the internecine conflict about the relation of God and man but would also give human beings the capacity to master nature, improve security, expand freedom, and promote prosperity. Their goal was not to eliminate religion but to limit its role within a more naturalistic *metaphysica specialis.* It is thus difficult to believe that Descartes and Hobbes were consciously in favor of a wholly secular life. Indeed, Hobbes, as we saw in the last chapter, was convinced that religion would always be necessary because human mortality inevitably provoked questions about the afterlife that in one way or another had to be answered.

Even if one accepts the view that Descartes and Hobbes were believers and supporters of religion of one kind or another, one might well imagine that their attempts to reduce the importance of religion were in fact important steps in the process of secularization.[27] Despite their own faith and against their own intentions, their actions may have promoted a more secular outlook. In providing the grounds for the independence of man as the *res cogitans*, Descartes opened up a space for the human self that was not subject to the manipulation or control of even the most radically omnipotent God. Similarly, with his interpretation of predestination and his account of natural law, Hobbes facilitated a turn away from a morality and politics based in Scripture to one rooted in a more naturalistic understanding. Both of these changes appear to have been steps in the process of secularization. But is this an adequate explanation for what actually occurred?

The underlying assumption of the secularization thesis is that God does not exist and that religion is merely a human construction. The idea that modernization produces secularization rests on the notion that modernization produces enlightenment, that enlightenment reveals the truth, and that the truth is that there is no God (or at least that there is no God that matters for the conduct of human life). A philosophically astute believer might see the process in a radically different way. Heidegger, for example, argued in opposition to this point of view that what appears to be a process of secularization that ends in the death of God is in fact only God's withdrawal and concealment. Christians of various persuasions have developed similar explanations to account for this phenomenon. It is clear that there is no possible way of deciding which of these explanations is correct. The secularization thesis depends on the belief that God is a human construct, the notion of God's withdrawal on the view that the world and everything in it are divine creations. Whether one or the other is correct cannot be empirically determined and thus rests on the faith that God does or does not exist.

Rather than enter into this fruitless debate, I want to explore a different possibility. The argument presented in the first half of this chapter suggests that the apparent rejection or disappearance of religion and theology in fact conceals the continuing relevance of theological issues and commitments for the modern age. Viewed from this perspective, the process of secularization or disenchantment that has come to be seen as identical with modernity was in fact something different than it seemed, not the crushing victory of reason over infamy, to use Voltaire's famous term, not the long drawn out death of God that Nietzsche proclaimed, and not the evermore distant withdrawal of the *deus absconditus* Heidegger points to, but the gradual transference of divine attributes to human beings (an infinite human will), the natural world (universal mechanical causality), social forces (the general will, the hidden hand), and history (the idea of progress, dialectical development, the cunning of reason).

(We see this already in Descartes and Hobbes. God for Descartes is no longer the wild and unpredictable God of nominalism. In fact, it is precisely this God that Descartes suppresses in favor of a more rational God, or at least a God that can be comprehended by human reason. At the same time he brings God downward towards man, Descartes elevates man towards God with his claim that man has the same infinite will as God. Hobbes, by contrast, accepts a more orthodox Calvinist position that asserts the absolute power of God and the insignificance of man. According to the doctrine of predestination, each individual either is or is not saved by God's will alone. Since God is no man's debtor, man can do nothing to influence God. In an ironic fashion, God thereby becomes irrelevant for human conduct and human life, that is, he becomes nothing other than the enduring first cause, or the motion of matter determined by a series of mechanical causes. While God in a narrow sense may be disposed of in this way, it would be a mistake to believe that any explanation of the whole can do without those powers and capacities that were attributed to him. Indeed, it is no accident that as the Calvinist God becomes less important for human life in Hobbes' account, the "mortal God," that is, the sovereign becomes more important. Moreover, while this transference does serve to moderate and ultimately eliminate the expressly theological debate that had been so contentious and violent, it also conceals the theological nature of the claims made by the contending parties. They thus cease to be disputable theological assertions and become unquestionable scientific or moral givens.

That the deemphasis, disappearance, and death of God should bring about a change in our understanding of man and nature is hardly surprising. Modernity, as we have seen, originates out of a series of attempts to construct a coherent *metaphysica specialis* on a nominalist foundation, to reconstitute something like the comprehensive summalogical account of scholastic realism. The successful completion of this project was rendered problematic by the real ontological differences between an infinite (and radically omnipotent) God and his finite creation (including both man and nature). As we have seen in the preceding chapters, these different attempts to find a solution to this problem rested on opposing notions of the ontic status and hierarchy of the different realms of beings. These ontic differences led to differing views about the relative weight that ought to be assigned to particular beings in the metaphysical account of the whole. Ockham and Luther, to take just one example, gave more weight to divine power than did Petrarch or Descartes.

Central to the whole period, as we have seen, was the question of the relation of divine and human will, which played an important role in the Wars of Religion. The purpose of the turn to a naturalistic science was to eliminate or at least moderate this conflict. This scientific turn, however, could not simply reject or abandon everything that had been hitherto included under theology. Purely supernatural matters could be set aside or relegated to the province of a wholly scriptural theology separate from science, but previous theology had not been merely concerned with man's spiritual fate in another world but also with explaining what happened in this world. Nominalists, for example, understood God as the freely acting, infinite, and radically omnipotent creator of heaven and earth, the first cause and source of all motion, the unity of all things, and the source of all standards of good and evil, to name only his most prominent attributes. All or at least most of these characteristics must be included in any coherent and comprehensive explanation of actuality. To simply erase God and all of his attributes from the mix would have left gaping holes in any purportedly comprehensive account of the whole.

What actually occurs in the course of modernity is thus not simply the erasure or disappearance of God but the transference of his attributes, essential powers, and capacities to other entities or realms of being. The so-called process of disenchantment is thus also a process of reenchantment in and through which both man and nature are infused with a number of attributes or powers previously ascribed to God.[28] To put the matter more starkly, in the face of the long drawn out death of God, science can provide a coherent account of the whole only by making man or nature or both in some sense divine.[29]

While on the surface the Enlightenment in general is positively hostile to religion, this hostility did not prevent (and in many instances facilitated) this transference. Indeed, Enlightenment thinkers repeatedly "discovered" powers and capacities in man and nature that had previously been ascribed to God. Pope spoke for the Enlightenment as a whole when he proclaimed: "The proper study of mankind is man."[30] The "man" that the Enlightenment discovered, however, was a vastly more exalted being than the sinful *viator* of Christianity or the rational animal of antiquity. Building on the earlier work of Descartes (who himself drew on the humanist tradition), Malebranche argued that in contemplating ideas and eternal truths the human mind participates in God. Leibniz made a similar claim in his monadology, imagining in Neoplatonic fashion that human being participated in or was an emanation of divine being. Many Enlightenment thinkers, however, were convinced that such views did not go far enough. They believed that one could only truly understand human being if it was completely freed from the tyranny of God and the church. Religion filled the world with so many imaginary entities and powers that under its sway human beings could not comprehend what was distinctive and valuable about their own being. Lamettrie argued that humans could not come to terms with themselves or be happy as long as they believed in God. In his view man is a natural being and must understand himself as such. What this meant for those who took their inspiration from Descartes was that man thereby replaced God. Trying to determine what was distinctive about the human will, Rousseau looked beneath the finite will to self-aggrandizement and found a general will that could never err, a will that Patrick Riley has shown is a direct descendent of God's will that all men be saved.[31] Others saw this divine element not so much in man and his will but in the rationality of the natural world. Following Hobbes' identification of mechanical causality and divine will, Spinoza developed a pantheistic account that identified God and substance. Locke believed that one could find moral imperatives sufficient to guide human life within the divinely created natural world.[32] Newton saw time and space as the forms of divine being. After these divine capacities had been transferred to man or nature, it was easy for the Encyclopedists Diderot, D'Alembert, and Holbach to demonstrate that revealed religion was not only false but also superfluous.[33] By the end of the Enlightenment, many thinkers treated human beings as quasi-divine. This is especially clear in someone like Kant who asserts that human beings are infinitely valuable ends in themselves.[34] Such a view is only possible because of the transference of what hitherto were considered divine attributes to human beings. The Enlightenment (and post-Enlightenment) exaltation of human individuality is thus in fact a form of radical (although concealed) Pelagianism. Divine or at least quasi-divine powers reemerge although always in disguise. Nature is an embodied rational will; the social world is governed by an "invisible hand" that almost miraculously produces a rational distribution of goods and services; and history is the progressive development of humanity toward perfection.

This transference of divine attributes to other realms of being was not without its dangers. At one extreme it led to the view that man was super-human, a godlike being who by the mere application of his will could bring into being the ideal world. Viewing the world from such a Promethean perspective, Enlightenment thinkers saw any resistance to their titanic projects as either irrational or malicious. In the face of such resistance, they were, as it turned out, all too willing to use increasingly greater amounts of force to achieve what they saw as rational ends.[35] At the other extreme, the understanding of nature as a quasi-omnipotent force often ended in a fatalistic view that saw man as nothing other than a marionette (Holbach) or a machine (Lamettrie).[36] While one strain of Enlightenment thought thus came to believe that humans were gods, the other strain saw them as beasts or even mere matter in motion, driven by desire and sheer self-interest. While both of these alternatives had problems of their own, what was perhaps most distressing was the fact that the two greatest thinkers of the Enlightenment, Diderot and Kant, realized that it was not possible to affirm either of these positions without also affirming the other and that they were mutually contradictory. The hopes of the Enlightenment were deeply shaken by the realization of the contradiction of its essential goals.

That the Enlightenment ended in such an impasse is not surprising. From the beginning, it sought to sidestep the decisive and contentious question of the freedom or bondage of the human will in a world determined by the predestining will of an omnipotent God. The end result, however, was simply the displacement of the question and its reemergence as the question of the relation of the freedom of the human will in a world determined by the unbreakable necessity of an infinite chain of natural causes. Thus, as we have seen, the contradiction that appeared in such starkly rational form in Kant's third antinomy was essentially a repetition of the contradictions that we saw in the debates between Erasmus and Luther, and Descartes and Hobbes. However, there was one crucial difference. In the earlier two debates the central question was the extent of divine power, which was always understood to be a matter of faith. In the Kantian antinomy, the disputable predestining will of God is transformed into the indisputable necessity of nature. The truth of natural causality, in this context, is not taken as a matter of faith to be believed or not but as a self-evident truth of reason. In this way, the theological foundations of the two sides in the debate are concealed and thus cease to be open to debate. The contradiction at the heart of the antinomy is thus solidified and made insoluble by the forgetfulness of its theological origin.

As we have seen, Kant was impelled to his critique of reason by his recognition that the antinomies posed an earthshaking problem for the Enlightenment. He believed, however, that his transcendental idealism offered a solution to the problem that would make it possible to achieve the goals of the Enlightenment by differentiating the phenomenal realm of nature and necessity from the noumenal realm of freedom and morality. However, if this differentiation was not tenable, as most of his successors maintained, then humanity was caught in a nest of contradictions. Freedom, for example, could only be attained by the use of a science that at its core denied the very possibility of freedom. Similarly, if humans were natural beings, they could not be free because they would be subject to the laws governing the motion of all matter, and if they were free they could not be natural beings. Humans were thus either mere matter in motion or they were gods, or to put the matter more clearly they constantly lived the contradiction of being both mere matter in motion and gods.

These contradictions revealed themselves in all of their power in the Reign of Terror. From the very beginning of the Revolution, the French Revolutionaries were deeply concerned that the new regime would be overthrown by conspiracy.[37] The historical example that engendered their fear (and dominated almost everything they wrote about the matter) was the Cataline conspiracy in republican Rome. As described by Sallust, Tacitus, and Cicero this conspiracy was the result of moral corruption. The French Revolutionaries shared this Roman fear of corruption, but understood it not in a Ciceronian but in a Rousseauan manner. Rousseau had argued that all action that was moral was in harmony with the general will. For the Revolutionaries, action thus could only be moral if it conformed to the universality of reason and if it realized human freedom. To put the matter in Kantian terms, freedom and reason could only be compatible if each individual always willed only categorically, that is, in accordance with the general will. However, such a categorical will is only possible in the abstract. As soon as the will settles on a finite object it ceases to be general and becomes particular and self-interested. While the Terror undoubtedly drew much of its energy and vehemence from class resentment, political infighting, and opportunism, it found its continuing justification in the repeated need to eliminate corruption, that is, to eliminate the particular will.[38] Such a task, however, can never be completed, for as finite beings humans are necessarily rooted in particularity. Thus, even the most virtuous citizen, the "incorruptible" Robespierre, could not meet these impossible standards and had to be eliminated. The Terror was in this way the first modern example of the danger in ascribing divine attributes to human beings.[39] A transcendent God could perhaps always will in a truly general or universal manner, as

Arnauld and later Malebranche maintained, but finite human beings could not, and the demand that they to do so inevitably ended in tragedy.

AFTER ENLIGHTENMENT: THE CONCEALED
THEOLOGY OF LATE MODERNITY

Post-Enlightenment thought has continued to struggle with these same questions in ways that I have examined in great detail elsewhere.[40] What later modern thinkers have not done is come to terms with the concealed theological/metaphysical essence of these questions. Indeed, such questions have seldom been perceived let alone posed.

Much of nineteenth- and twentieth-century philosophy was shaped and directed by the perceived need to escape from the contradictions of the Enlightenment that appeared in Kant's antinomies and that manifested themselves in the French Revolution and Terror. The Enlightenment expulsion of God from the metaphysical constellation of beings left man locked in juxtaposition to nature. Post-Enlightenment thinkers were forced to recognize that a coherent and comprehensive account of actuality could not be constructed on the basis of such a dualism. A number of possible solutions presented themselves, from the notion that everything might be explained as the product of a freely acting will, to the idea of an infinite series of material causes, or finally to some interaction of the two. The first was explored by the German Romantics and post-Kantian idealists as well as by a variety of fellow travelers in other countries. The second possibility was investigated by a variety of natural scientists who focused not merely on the motion of matter but upon the interplay of natural forces that governed motion. The third possible solution was developed by a variety of thinkers who fall generally under the rubric of historicism.

The German Romantics, early German idealists, and their nineteenth-century followers were convinced that the Enlightenment had misconstrued nature as a mechanical rather than as an organic or spiritual process. They believed that if nature were grasped in a pantheistic fashion as the product of a world-spirit (Goethe), a world-soul (Emerson), an absolute I (Fichte), or a primordial will (Schelling, Schopenhauer), it would be compatible with human freedom, since both natural motion and human action would spring from a common source. The real barrier to human freedom in their view lay not in nature but in the institutions and practices that had been created and propagated by the Enlightenment with its dedication to a mechanistic understanding of nature, universal rights, bureaucratic politics, the development of commerce, and bourgeois morality. True human freedom for these thinkers thus could only be attained by expressing one's will (including one's natural passions and desires) regardless of the consequences for social, political, or moral order. The truly free "natural" man thus asserts his will against all bounds and consequently appears to enlightened society to be a moral monster (Tieck's William Lovell, Byron's Manfred, Goethe's Faust) or a criminal (Stendhal's Julian Sorel, Balzac's Vautrin, Shelley's Prometheus). A life led in harmony with nature is a life in contradiction to convention. To live in this way it is thus necessary to liberate oneself from Enlightenment rationalism and to reconceptualize nature as the motion of spirit rather than the motion of matter. Hence in place of reason these thinkers put passion or will; in place of mathematics, art; in place of universal rights, national mores; and in place of the bureaucratic state, the charismatic leader. Romantic nationalism and later Fascism and Nazism were among the consequences of this development.

In contrast to these thinkers, natural scientists such as Michael Faraday and James Clerk Maxwell sought to give a comprehensive account that saw the motion of matter as the result of the interplay of natural forces. This led to the development of the chemical and physical sciences, but also, and more importantly, to a new biological science that tied the development of man to the chemical and physical development of the universe as a whole. In the first instance this took the form of an evolutionary theory that saw man as a moment in the development of life as such, but this was followed in the twentieth century by a molecular biology that saw life itself as merely a subset of material motion. In this way the distinctiveness of humans and of life itself was effaced, as the difference between the animate and inanimate was eliminated.[41] A similar reductionism was apparent in the consideration of human action. All (free) human action from a scientific point of view became mere behavior, that is, mere reaction to stimuli. The most obvious early example of this development was utilitarianism, which sought to explain all human behavior in terms of a calculus of pleasure and pain. The development of behavioralism in the twentieth century was another example of this way of thinking. More recently we have witnessed a new account of motion that focuses on our selfish genes. Just as Romanticism attempted to show that there was no contradiction between natural necessity and human freedom because nature was itself a vital spirit or world-will akin to the human will, natural science has attempted to show that there is no contradiction because there is no human freedom since there is nothing that distinguishes human beings from the rest of the natural world. Thus, everything can be explained by natural causes.

From a metaphysical point of view, these two strains of post-

Enlightenment thought sought to solve the problem of the contradiction of nature and freedom by erasing the ontic distinction between the natural and the human. Before the Enlightenment, *metaphysica specialis* consisted of theology, anthropology, and cosmology, with man floating somewhere between God and his other creatures. The Enlightenment eliminated theology from the mix. Post-Enlightenment thought sought to show in different ways that there was no distinction between the two remaining ontic realms, that is, that there were no distinct realms of being as philosophy had hitherto imagined.

While these strains of post-Enlightenment thought thus offer different answers to the problem of the antinomy, neither offers (nor can offer) an account of the whole that is both consistent and complete. Each thus produces a partial explanation that achieves coherence by sacrificing completeness or achieves completeness by sacrificing consistency.[42] While both are generally considered to be atheistic from a traditional Christian point of view, each is in fact parasitic on the Christian worldview. This is obvious in the case of the idea of a world-spirit, but it is equally true of the notion of natural causality that derives the certainty of the necessary concatenation of events from the notion of divine predetermination.[43]

While the Romantics and materialists sought to explain the whole on the basis of freedom or nature alone, other thinkers tried to explain their interaction. The idea that nature acted upon human beings was not new. Indeed, almost all ancient philosophy and much medieval thought as well assumed that human action unfolded within an unchangeable natural order that shaped and set limits on all human striving. As we saw in the preceding chapters of this book, the nominalist revolution gave birth to a new vision of metaphysics that opened up the possibility that human beings need not merely accommodate themselves to the natural world. Instead they could become masters of nature and reshape it to meet their needs through the methodological application of will and intelligence. This new understanding of the relation of man and nature had profound implications for man's own understanding of his place in the time. In antiquity, time had been identified with the coming into being and passing away of all things according to the (circular) order of nature. From a human point of view, time was thus always identified with birth and degeneration, with ascent and fall, which meant that all human projects inevitably succumbed to what Plato called the "laws of time."[44] The apocalyptic vision of time within which Christianity operated was even more obviously immune to the impact of human action. Not only were human beings disabled by sin, but they were also subordinate from the beginning to divine power. With the development of a new notion of human will and freedom, however, the time in which humans lived, that is, history, appeared in a new light. The relevant story of humanity from this perspective was not the cyclical pattern the ancients imagined, nor the biblical story of a past fall and a future (divine) redemption, nor even the humanistic account of man's Sisyphean efforts to master *fortuna,* but the story of humanity's ever increasing conquest and transformation of the natural world. History in this way came to be seen as the story of human progress that had a direction and an end. To be human meant to be progressive, to move toward that end. Humanity may once have been subject to nature, but since the advent of civilization humans had made intermittent progress in achieving mastery, and, now that the true method had been found, could rapidly complete the conquest of the natural world, establishing a peaceful world in which they could freely pursue whatever they desired and in which they could live a commodious life. At the core of this modern notion of progress was the (Pelagian and at times Promethean) notion that, while humans are in some sense natural, they are also in some sense transcendent beings who can master and transform the natural world.

As we saw in chapter 1, this notion of history as progress is intrinsic to the modern age and an essential moment of modernity's self-understanding. The modern conception of history was developed in the late eighteenth century by thinkers such as Vico, Motesquieu, Voltaire, Gibbon, Herder, Turgot, and Condorcet, who imagined history as the process by which human beings employed their reason to create a free world in which human being could live prosperously and at peace with one another.[45] The implicit goal of history that underlay all of their work was the realization of a perfectly rational and secularized world, an earthly paradise. For them history was thus also the source of a moral imperative that compelled all those who understood it to do everything in their power to accelerate the historical process and bring this new world into being. This imperative played an important role in motivating and justifying many of the French Revolutionaries. Their principal goal, as we discussed above, was to establish the rule of reason, which they understood in Rousseauian fashion to be identical with absolute freedom. When the realization of such freedom proved difficult, they were able to justify the use of terror to attain this exalted end. The problem with this Revolutionary project was that no amount of violence could bring about the world they desired since it depended on an impossible transformation of human nature.

In the aftermath of the Revolution, thinkers such as Hegel began to rethink the grounds of history. Hegel, too, believed that history was progressive. He also believed that it would end with the rule of reason. The rational order he had in mind, however, differed considerably from that of the French Revolutionaries. In his view the pursuit of absolute freedom could only lead to disaster. Rational freedom required an accommodation with nature in general and with the natural, self-interested desires of individual human beings in particular. He thus argued that while freedom was the necessary and inevitable goal of history, this freedom was an embodied freedom rooted in individual property rights, Kantian morality, the nuclear family, a market economy, a bureaucratic state, and cultural productions of art, religion, and philosophy. Moreover, this was not a regime that lay in the distant future or that could only be attained by an apocalyptic transformation but that was coming into being in the European world of his time.

The historical process he described culminated in the recognition that the three traditional realms of *metaphysica specialis*, God, man, and nature, were ontologically the same, although they remained ontically separate from one another. History then is the process in and through which humans come to recognize that as rational self-conscious beings they are God, that God is only in and through them, and that the same rationality that they find in themselves is present in the natural world. Hegel's thought thus is a comprehensive effort to resolve the contradictions that had troubled modern thought from the very beginning. However, in his view the achievement of such a reconciliation is not the result of his or any other individual's planning or will but is the consequence of the "cunning of reason." The path and goal of historical development is thus preordained, rooted in the nature of self-consciousness and spirit itself. On these grounds, he thought that he could show that history was coming to an end, and that no further revolutionary efforts were necessary to bring the best of all possible human orders into being.

Hegel's titanic vision of reconciliation dominated much of European life in the period between 1820 and 1848, but it went into rapid decline and quickly lost its hold on the European imagination in the years thereafter. There were several reasons for this. First, the speculative foundations for Hegel's reconciliation of man, God, and nature were never very clear and were thus increasingly regarded as an *unio mystico*. Second, his teleological conception of nature was repeatedly called into question by the discoveries of natural science.[46] And finally and perhaps most importantly, his prediction that current European states would inevitably develop into more liberal constitutional monarchies seemed to have been contradicted by the failure of the Revolutions of 1848.

After 1848, Hegel's more conservative followers increasingly turned away from the liberal cause to Romantic nationalism (and in the twentieth century to Fascism and Nazism). His more radical followers, by contrast, were pulled toward populism or nihilism (Cherneshevsky, Pisarev), anarchism (Bakunin), and revolutionary socialism or communism (Marx, Engels). Almost all of these more radical Hegelians rejected Hegel's notion that rational freedom required a reconciliation with nature and an acceptance of existing social, economic, and political institutions, arguing that history was a teleological process that could end only with the realization of absolute freedom for all of humanity. Indeed, they believed that they could scientifically demonstrate that such a goal was inevitable. As a result, they were convinced that the pursuit of such a liberation was a moral imperative and that those like Hegel who argued for a more limited notion of freedom were merely quietists or bourgeois ideologists seeking to maintain the status quo. They thus turned to a more a more radical view of freedom that envisaged the ultimate liberation of all human beings. In place of the existing order they imagined a world in which everyone would be able to do whatever they wished, to "hunt in the morning, fish in the afternoon, and be a critical critic in the evening." However, such universal freedom and prosperity could only be achieved if nature were completely mastered. To achieve this goal, they believed it would thus be necessary to free human productive forces by means of a revolutionary overthrow of the existing social and political order. In this way the artificial constraints on the productive power of technology would be removed, a superabundance created, and all want eliminated. Radical Hegelians thus abandoned Hegel's notion that humanity had already attained its historical goal, which in their minds was near but which could only be attained through one last apocalyptic act of violence. In this way, these radicals returned to the millennarian politics that Hegel had sought to constrain. In doing so, however, they also returned to the same Enlightenment optimism about human progress that had characterized earlier historical thinking and that had played such an important role in the extremism of the Revolution.

The view of history as progress was severely shaken by the cataclysmic events of the first half of the twentieth century, the World Wars, the Great Depression, the rise of totalitarianism, and the Holocaust. What had gone wrong? Modernity, which had seemed on the verge of providing universal security, liberating human beings from all forms of oppression, and producing an unprecedented human thriving, had in fact ended in a barbarism almost unknown in previous human experience. The tools that had been universally regarded as the source of human flourishing had been the source of unparalleled human destruction. And finally, the politics of human liberation had proved to be the means to human enslavement and degradation. The horror evoked by these cataclysmic events was so overwhelming that it called into question not merely the idea of progress and enlightenment but also the idea of modernity and the conception of Western civilization itself.

[At the heart of the matter were the unresolved contradictions that had bedeviled modern thought from the beginning. The modern idea of history was an attempt to reconcile freedom and necessity, but as Kant had shown such a reconciliation was impossible. Freedom is understood to be the goal of history, but history itself is imagined to be a necessary process. To put matters in the terms of our earlier argument, history is imagined in a Pelagian fashion to be the product of free human willing but at the same time the unfolding of history is imagined to be guided by an "invisible hand," or by "the cunning of reason," or by "dialectical necessity." The fact that this motion is imagined to be necessary or preordained is an indication of the concealed theological assumptions that underlie such a view of change. This view, as we have seen, contradicts the notion that humans act freely. This contradiction, however, is not obvious and in practice is not troubling when things seem to be moving in a positive direction. Thus as long as history was identified as "manifest destiny," or the "spread of civilization," or "procession of God through the world" (as Hegel put it), it was not particularly troubling.

The series of catastrophes that befell humanity in the twentieth century called this positive or progressive notion of history into question. From this perspective, the hidden hand looked more like the hand of Satan than of God, the cunning of reason more like the diabolic shrewdness of an evil deceiver than the will of a beneficent deity, and dialectical necessity more like the iron chains of tyranny than a path to freedom. In short, the dominant Pelagian view of history as the product of free human willing gave way in the midst of these troubling times to a more Manichean vision of historical change that saw individuals as mere cogs in a machine or moments of an inhuman causal process.

Such a view of history was not new. Counter-Enlightenment thinkers such as Rousseau had already argued in the eighteenth century that the development of the arts and sciences had not only not improved humans but had actually made them worse, depriving them of a happy natural existence and replacing it with a miserably alienated and conflict-ridden life in modern society. Elements of this counter-Enlightenment vision of history persisted in the thought of thinkers such as Tocqueville, who saw the dark underside of what they recognized as human progress. More decisively, late-nineteenth-century thinkers such as Nietzsche viewed history more pessimistically. In this view, European history since Plato had been a process of decline, and while he hoped that this process could be reversed by a titanic act of will, he knew that decadence and degeneration might well continue to increase and spread. Building on this view in the aftermath of the First World War, thinkers like Spengler *(The Decline of the West)*, Husserl *(The Crisis of the European Sciences)*, and Heidegger presented a much darker image of the historical destiny of European humanity. Heidegger argued that European humanity had been in continual decline since the time of the Presocratic Greeks. In fact, Europeans had sunk to such depths that they were no longer even capable of recognizing their own degradation. In his view modern human beings believed that they were becoming masters and possessors of nature when in fact they were being enslaved by the very technology that they imagined to be the means of their liberation. This technology in fact converted humans into mere raw material for a productive process that was itself an aimless and pointless pursuit of nothing other than more production. In this way the Manichean vision of a demonic force at the heart of things that so concerned Luther and that resurfaced on a number of occasions in the development of modernity comes to light as the dominant force behind history.

The idea of history had its origin in the attempt to make sense of the modern project in light of the contradictions that became increasingly evident in the Enlightenment. The idea of history itself, however, is rent by these same contradictions. It too vacillates between a Pelagian notion of individual freedom and a Manichean notion of radical determinism. We see this in the development of history as an explanation that replaces philosophy and metaphysics in the nineteenth and early twentieth centuries but also in our continuing efforts to make sense out of modernity. This is particularly evident in the prevailing debates about globalization with which we began our discussion.

The initial image of globalization that came to predominate in the period after the fall of the Berlin Wall rested on a liberal view of history and society that saw human development as the result of the increasingly intertwined interactions of human beings connected by free trade and almost instantaneous communications. This was a liberal vision of a process that many believed would produce global peace, freedom, and prosperity. This extraordinarily positive view of globalization rested on a faith in the hidden hand of the free market and a sense that the dialectic of history had finally reached the end that Hegel had predicted. Those who held this view imagined worldwide economic development, a growing tolerance for all kinds of differences, an end to oppression and the realization of human rights, the spread of democratic government, and peaceful and fruitful cultural interchange. Opponents of globalization, by contrast, saw this process as motivated not by free choices of individual human beings but by the logic of global capitalism, or the demands of world technology, or the needs of American imperialism.[47] In this Manichean vision, globalization—typically understood as the triumph of global capital—leads not to peace, freedom, and prosperity but to war, enslavement, and immiseration. Globalization institutionalizes inequality, promotes wage slavery, props up authoritarian regimes, undermines traditional social structures, crushes indigenous cultures, and despoils the environment. While these two views of globalization are deeply at odds with one another, they share a set of common values. Their disagreement reflects the opposing views that we have noted throughout our discussion, and it betrays in this way the concealed metaphysical/theological commitments within which we think and act.

As deeply at odds as these proponents and opponents of globalization are, they generally remain within the horizon of Western civilization. For example, they generally share a belief in the value of tolerance, peace, freedom, equality, rights, self-government, and prosperity. They disagree only about whether globalization will bring these goods about and if so whether they will be equitably divided.

The attacks of 9/11 drew varying responses from supporters and opponents of globalization. For those who took a more liberal view of globalization, these attacks were the acts of a few benighted religious fanatics who were anxious to derail modernization and the spread of liberalism in their traditional societies. The solution seemed equally clear to them—eliminate or neutralize these fanatics so that the great mass of people in the Islamic world could pursue their desire for a better life by participating in the global economy and joining the march to modernity. Those who opposed globalization, on the contrary, saw 9/11 as a legitimate or at least understandable form of resistance to global injustice, the response of those who had been exploited by the system of global capitalism and American hegemony. From this perspective the solution to the problem of terrorism was to end American imperialism and American support for authoritarian governments in the developing world. Both sides in this debate, however, found it difficult to sustain their explanations in the face of succeeding developments. It has become clear that the preference for Islamic beliefs and practices is much deeper and more broadly shared than the liberal defenders of globalization initially believed. It has also become obvious that the values of many of the Islamic fundamentalists—intolerance of different religious sects and lifestyles, the denial of the rights of women, and a marked preference for theocracy—are deeply at odds with core beliefs of the opponents of globalization. The failure of both explanations suggests that we need to examine the question of Islam and the West more carefully.

(The argument presented in this book presents a first effort to come to terms with the implicit metaphysical/theological commitments that characterize our often concealed tradition. We can only begin to take Islam seriously if we recognize the ways in which Muslims' views parallel, intersect, and veer away from our own. Thus, only by coming to terms with our own tradition can we hope to transform the current clash of our two cultures into a more productive, although undoubtedly at times still painful, encounter of beliefs and ideas. It is imperative that we make the effort, for if we do not we are almost certainly doomed to a clash of a different kind, not in the realm of ideas but on some "darkling plain / Swept with confused alarms of struggle and flight / Where ignorant armies clash by night." [48]

He remembered it as if it were yesterday. He had been a young student in the Nizamiya Madrasa in Baghdad, the greatest city in the world. He had risen early, walked to the school down broad streets and dark alleyways, past palaces with towering iron gates guarded day and night by large men with great scimitars, by marbled mosques with golden spires blazing in the sun, and through shaded bazaars filled with goods from Samarkand, Cordoba, Lahore, and Marrakesh, jostled by the endless multitude of the faithful and the unfaithful who called the city home. He had been on his way to hear his teacher, the one they called The Guide to the True Faith. He'd hoped to arrive early to find a place amidst the throngs of students and scholars who came to hear the teacher speak. But that day there had been no soft voice explaining the words of the Prophet and the wisdom of the philosophers. His teacher was not there. No one knew why. Later, they'd learned that he had been overcome by some kind of ailment, unable to eat or drink or speak. What could have caused such a thing? They'd prayed that God the beneficent would cure him, but as the days passed he did not return to the school. Years later they learned he had been overcome by doubt and despair. Who could blame him? There was reason to despair. Their world was falling to pieces. Vizier Nizam al-Mulk, the great patron of learning, had been murdered by an Isma'ili assassin, and the Seljuk Sultan Malikshah, who had brought victory to the faithful, and with it peace and prosperity, had died suspiciously of food poisoning less than a month later. Both were replaced by incompetents.

Their teacher had left Baghdad, abandoning all of his worldly goods and his glittering career, wandering for ten years in the west from Damascus and Jerusalem to Alexandria, Medina, and Mecca, before settling in his ancestral Tus far in the east. What years those had been! The empire shaken by internal strife, coarse Turkomen appearing everywhere, menacing the faithful, and Christian barbarians marauding throughout the Caliphate. He too had despaired. But during his wanderings, the Teacher had found a new way, derived from the Sufis, but now open to all the faithful who chose to follow it. He taught them to lose themselves in God, to dwell in what lies beyond words, in ecstasy, like the Prophet, beloved of God. Now, even if their rulers failed them and they were beset by the ruffians and crusaders, he knew that, God willing, the faithful would prosper and triumph. For God is Great!

The teacher in this vignette was Abu Hamid al-Ghazali (1058-1111), after the Prophet perhaps the most influential figure in all Islam. Orphaned as a young boy, he studied Islamic law and theology under an Ash'arite teacher and Sufism with a master in his native Tus. He later joined the circle of scholars in Baghdad around the Seljuk Vizier Nizam-al Mulk that included such luminaries as Omar Khayyam. He became the most famous intellectual of his time, surrounded by scholars and students who came from the ends of the earth to hear him speak. After the death of the vizier and the ensuing chaos described above, Ghazali, was plagued by skeptical doubts that his philosophy could not answer. As he tells us in his autobiography, *Deliverance from Error,* he vacillated for a time, unable to decide between continuing his academic career and following a religious and mystical path, but was finally overcome by a crisis that he took as a sign to leave the academic world, adopt an ascetic way of life, and follow a new path. It was this path that helped reshape Islam.

Islam developed in the period after Christianity had already become the official religion of the Roman world, and while it shared an Abrahamic origin with Christianity, it differed in several crucial respects. First, there was no notion of a human fall and thus no need of a redemption. As a result, there was no doctrine of incarnation. In contrast to Christianity, Islam rested not on the ontological connection of God and man but on their absolute difference and thus on the necessity of the submission of finite men to an infinite God. Indeed, the term 'Islam' means submission. The dominant school of Islamic theology (*kalam*) was founded by Ash'ari (ca. 873-935) at the end of the ninth century and portrayed God as radically omnipotent. Indeed, Ash'ari defended an occasionalist doctrine that denied the efficacy of all secondary causes and attributed everything to the immediate causal power of God. From this Ash'arite point of view there was thus no natural or mechanical causality, indeed no orderly flow of events since everything, including all human volitions, acts, and cognitions, are the direct creation of God. This belief put the Ash'arites firmly in opposition to the Aristotelianism and Neoplatonism of the Mu'tazilites, the other philosophical/theological school that had developed within Islam. Members of this school such as Alfarabi (al-Farabi, 870-950) and Avicenna (Ibn Sina, 980-1037) defended a more rationalist view of God. These thinkers believed in divine unity and divine justice, and tried to combine them with divine omnipotence. As we have seen in our earlier discussion, this is not easy task, and the effort to achieve some kind of harmony or reconciliation led the Mu'tazilites to deny divine freedom. To save divine justice and unity, they had to argue that God's will was eternal and for similar reasons that it was always just. God thus could not save whomever he would, but had to save all who acted justly.

The Ash'arites found these views blasphemous. They denied that God's will was one with his essence and saw it rather as one of his attributes. While God was eternal, his will thus was not necessarily invariable. As a result he could act freely without contradicting himself. He could thus also will both just and unjust acts, since all acts in themselves are morally neutral and receive their value only by being willed by God. In their rejection of realism (or necessitarianism) these Ash'arite theologians thus blazed a path remarkably similar to the one later traversed by Christian voluntarists and nominalists.

The great opponent of this Islamic rationalism was Ghazali.[1] He was at first attracted to this path and described it in great detail in his *The Intentions of the Philosophers* (1094), summarizing the work of Avicenna. Shortly after completing this text, however, he was thrown into the skeptical crisis alluded to above. At about this time, either before or shortly after he left Baghdad, he wrote his seminal work *The Incoherence of the Philosophers,* that vigorously and relentlessly attacked all Mu'tazilite thought.[2] Thereafter, he increasingly turned in a more conservative theological direction that was deeply influenced by earlier Ash'arite thought but that also (importantly) drew on the mystical Sufi tradition. He articulated a doctrine of a supremely powerful God. In this respect his position was not unlike that of the voluntarist and nominalist tradition from Ockham and Luther. However, where Luther believed that one could become one with God through the experience of Scripture, Ghazali believed that one could experience God directly through mystical or ecstatic experience. In this respect, his path was more akin to that of Meister Eckhart than either Luther or Ockham. Man, for Ghazali, was a slave to God, but he could also be his regent on earth. This extreme voluntarist position rejected all natural theology and all independence of human beings from divine will.[3]

As we remarked above, one of the chief factors that distinguishes Christianity from Islam is the notion of incarnation.[4] While this notion is a continuing source of tension and conflict within the Christian tradition, it does open up the possibility for a form of humanism that grants quasi-divine status to human beings. As we have seen, such a view is manifest in thinkers such as Pico and Erasmus, but it also plays an important (although often concealed) role in making concepts such as Locke's notion of natural right or Kant's notion of human beings as infinitely valuable ends in themselves believable. Moreover, the idea of the Incarnation provides the justification for a Christian humanism. For the strain of Islam that derives from Ghazali, by contrast, humanism is generally regarded as a rebellion against God. The intrinsic value of the individual, as modernity has understood it since Petrarch, is thus theologically problematic for orthodox Islam.[5]

In contrast to Christianity, which turned in a humanistic and later naturalistic direction in response to the problems posed by divine omnipotence, mainstream Islam followed the path blazed by Ghazali. As a result of his devaluation of the individual and a mystical focus on an omnipotent God, this strain of Islam was generally unreceptive to the ideas that came to characterize modernity in the European world. From this Ash'arite perspective, western modernity seemed to be either a secular or a Christian phenomenon, in any case hard to reconcile with faithfulness and obedience to God. Moreover, when modernity came to the Islamic world, it was often due to the impact of western imperialism. As a result, it was not only at odds with Islam's ontological and theological commitments but was also at odds with many of the traditional social conventions and mores of Islamic society. The impact of modernity in the Islamic world was thus muted and contradictory. While many accepted certain aspects of modernity, often wholly and unquestioningly, many also found other aspects of modernity alien and impious. As a result, Western modernity was often greeted with skepticism and occasionally was met with open opposition.

This was especially true of several schools that arose in opposition to modernism. Islamic traditionalism found an early defender in the eighteenth-century thinker Muhammad ibn Abd-al-Wahhab (1703-92), who built on the Ash'arite notion of radical omnipotence. Wahhab inspired a movement called Salafism that insisted on the need to return to Islam as practiced during the first three generations after the Prophet, the time of the "pious ancestors" or Salafis. Such a return entailed the abandonment of systematic theology as a Hellenistic import, the rejection of anything that verged on polytheism, including the veneration of saints or idols, a rejection of mysticism, and an insistence on the foundation of Islamic life in Scripture. In this respect Wahhab played a role in Islam that was similar to that of Luther within Christianity.

In the twentieth century, a number of Islamic thinkers sought to articulate a theological foundation for opposition to Western modernism, which came to the Islamic world with great force from many different directions. Perhaps the foremost among these radicals were Sayyid Qutb (1906-66), the founder of the Muslim Brotherhood, who argued that Muslims must live under Sharia law in a state governed by truly believing Muslims, separate from Christians and Jews, who he argued were infidels and not people of the book, and Mawlana Mawdudi (1903-73) an Indian/Pakistani Muslim who preached the imminence of the coming apocalyptic battle of Muslims against Christians and Jews.[6] They both in different ways inspired the work of later radicals such as Osama Bin Laden. Their versions of Islam did not exclude all modernist elements. Indeed, beginning with Ghazali and including even contemporary Islamic radicals, Islam has been remarkably hospitable to science. Radical Islam, however, has been generally disinclined to accept modern humanism and individualism, which they believe (with some justification within Islam) is or at least verges on idolatry. As we saw in our discussion of Luther and the Reformation, this is not a position that is entirely foreign to the Christian tradition. Indeed, recent attacks by Christian fundamentalists on "secular humanism" reemphasize this point, although they are typically less troubled by individualism and more troubled by modern science than their Islamic counterparts.

The ways in which we in the Western world misunderstand Islam are complicated by the ways in which we misunderstand ourselves. This is especially true of our ignorance of the theological provenance of our own liberalism. Since we do not understand the way in which our Christian past has shaped the individualism and humanism at the heart of liberalism, we do not understand why radical Islam sees our liberal world as impious and immoral. We similarly do not understand the ways in which our liberal institutions are ill-suited to the Islamic view of the proper order of the world.

But perhaps such a misunderstanding is inevitable. After all, modernity is above all things convinced that it owes nothing to the past, that it has made itself, that what matters is what is happening right now. Indeed, this is the meaning of the freedom, power, and progress that we all prize. This belief, however, leaves us in a precarious situation, for reasons that Sophocles made clear long ago. His great hero Oedipus had risen to power in Thebes by means of his own abilities. He was an immigrant who had tamed a new world and established himself as its master. What he did not remember was his origin, proclaiming himself "fortune's child," the world's first self-made man. Was there ever a clearer expression of the dangers inherent in modernity? For none of us is fortune's child. We all come from somewhere, and our genealogy is more than just a list of names on a page. Unless and until we become aware of this fact, we may storm through the world like Oedipus, brilliant in our ability to answer questions and astonishing in our drive to mastery, but blind to the truth of who we are and what we are doing. We too like him may become the one "all men call great," but like him we may also have to confront the abysmal questions that spring forth from our finitude.

1. Thomas L. Friedman's experience is exemplary. In a chapter entitled "While I was Sleeping," he writes: "Before 9/11, I was focused on tracking globalization and exploring the tension between the 'Lexus' forces of economic integration and the 'Olive Tree' forces of identity and nationalism. . . . But after 9/11, the olive tree wars became all-consuming for me. . . . During those years I lost the trail of globalization." *The World is Flat: A Brief History of the Twenty-First Century* (New York: Farrar, Strauss and Giroux, 2005), 8–9. What he fails to see is that he was not sleeping but being driven by (and as a journalist also intensifying) the underlying anxiety that is the necessary complement of the progress that he finds so exhilarating. For a thoughtful discussion of the pre-9/11 debate on globalization, see David Held, Anthony McGrew, David Goldblatt, and Jonathan Perraton, *Global Transformations: Politics, Economics, Culture* (Stanford, Calif.: Stanford University Press, 1999).

2. One has to wonder whether in the midst of our prosperity and enlightenment, we are not like that earlier lost generation, a people who "Cling to their average day . . . / Lest we should see where we are, / Lost in a haunted wood, / Children afraid of the night / Who have never been happy or good." W. H. Auden, "September 1, 1939," lines 46, 52–55.

3. I am aware of the fact that many today use the term 'modernity' to refer to a period of time that begins in the latter half of the nineteenth century. This usage seems to be largely derived from the identification of modernity with modernism. This usage is relatively recent. I use the term in the more traditional sense that sees modernity extending back at least to the seventeenth century.

4. Others have pointed back to a hidden wellspring of modernity in the thought of Machiavelli or recently even Leonardo da Vinci. Indeed, a noted scholar seriously maintained modernity began on the night that Machiavelli met Leonardo da Vinci. Roger Masters, *Fortune is a River: Leonardo da Vinci and Niccolò Machiavelli's Magnificent Dream to Change the Course of Florentine History* (New York: Free Press, 1998).

5. This is true even of most postmodern critics who turn this modern story back against itself.

6. Hans Blumenberg, *The Legitimacy of the Modern Age* (Cambridge, Mass.: MIT Press, 1989); Amos Funkenstein, *Theology and the Scientific Imagination from the Middle Ages to the Seventeenth Century* (Princeton, N.J.: Princeton University Press, 1986).

INTRODUCTION

1. Sugurus Abbas S. Dionysii, *Vita Ludovici,* ed. Henri Waquet (Paris: Belle Lettres, 1929), 230.

2. Aristophanes, for example, distinguishes the "old" style of Aeschylus from the "new" style of Euripides and the sophists in his *Frogs.* This topos was adopted by Callimachus in the third century and then by many different Roman authors in their discussions of art and aesthetics. Tacitus and Marcus Aurelius distinguished old and new kinds of historical writing, but they never used these distinctions to name historical periods. See G. Gordon, "Medium aevum and the Middle Ages," *Society for Pure English Tracts* 19 (1925): 3–28; and Mircea Eliade, *Cosmos and History: The Myth of the Eternal Return,* trans. W. R. Trask (New York: Harper, 1959).

3. Daniel 2:17–45. This idea goes back at least to Hesiod and seems to be associated with the cycle of the seasons and the idea of the rebirth of a golden age. This connection, however, should not be overemphasized.

4. From our perspective, it is difficult to see how this notion could have survived the fall of Rome, but from the medieval point of view, the Eastern Empire had never fallen and the Western Empire had been reestablished by Charlemagne. Moreover, while some early Christian thinkers drew a clear distinction between their own time and that of pagan Rome, medieval Christianity generally did not recognize this break. As Reinhart Koselleck has shown, as late as 1529 Christians still treated Alexander the Great's victory at Issus as a current event. Koselleck, "Modernity and the Planes of Historicity," *Economy and Society* 10, no. 2 (May 1981): 166–67. While there were vast differences between the medieval and ancient worlds, medieval Christians did not recognize them. They lacked concrete knowledge of the ancient world, and Roman Christianity itself had gone to great lengths to conceal the profound transformation it was bringing about. Still, the most important reason that medieval Christianity did not recognize these differences was that in comparison with the purified world to come both their world and the world of the pagans were all-too-similar worlds of sin.

5. For a brief discussion of Joachim of Fiore, see Norman Cohn, *The Pursuit of the Millennium* (New York: Oxford University Press, 1972), 108–26. For a fuller discussion see Matthais Riedl, *Joachim von Fiore: Denker der vollendeten Menschheit* (Würzburg: Königshausen & Neumann, 2004).

6. On this point see Theodore E. Mommsen, "Petrarch's Conception of the 'Dark Ages,'" *Speculum* 17, no. 2 (April 1942): 226–42.

7. Rudolf Pfeiffer, *History of Classical Scholarship from 1300 to 1850* (Oxford: Clarendon, 1976): 35–41.

8. This was reflected in terminology employed in the discussion of architecture that distinguished *antico* and *moderno* but identified *moderno* with the "Gothic," the pejorative term used by Raphael in the early sixteenth century to describe the decadent art that had characterized the period between antiquity and his time. Erwin Panofsky, *Die Renaissance der europaischen Kunst* (Frankfurt a.M: Suhrkamp, 1979), 47–54.

9. Vasari described the Renaissance style as "buona maniera moderna." Quoted in Panofsky, 23. On the similar aesthetic usage of the French term *antique,* see J. Huizinga, *The Waning of the Middle Ages* (New York: Doubleday, 1954), 327.

10. Christophus Cellarius, *Historia universalis breviter ac perspicue exposita, in antiquam, et medii aevi ac novam divisa, cum notis perpetuis* (1708), 233. A similar three-part scheme was developed by Leonardo Bruni (1370–1444) and fleshed out by Flavio Biondo (1392–1463), although they did not think of the period beginning after the end of the Middle Ages as modern in our current sense but as the beginning of a return to antiquity.

11. On this point see Hans Baron, "The Querelle of the Ancients and Moderns as a Problem for Renaissance Scholarship," in *Renaissance Essays,* ed. Paul Oskar Kristeller and P. P. Wiener (Rochester: University of Rochester Press, 1992), 95–114. Baron argues that George Hakewill's 1627 work *Apology . . . of the Power and Providence of God, . . . and Censure of the Common Errour Touching Nature's Perpetuall and Universal Decay* was decisive for the development of this notion of progress.

12. In 1575 Loys le Roy had already argued that the invention of printing, the marine compass, and the bombard had elevated present times above anything known in previous ages. Loys le Roy, *De la vicissitude ou variété des choses en l'univers,* ed. B. W. Bates (Princeton: Princeton University Press, 1944), 35–44.

13. Francis Bacon, *The New Organon,* ed. F. Anderson (New York: Macmillan, 1960), 7–8.

14. The concept of the Renaissance itself was the creation of nineteenth-century historians and was given its classic portrayal in Jacob Burckhardt's *The Civilization of the Renaissance in Italy* (1860). The term first appears in English in 1845. It is associated with 'humanism,' a term which itself was first used in English only in 1838.

15. Even Pope tacitly admitted this in his famous couplet inscribed on Newton's tomb: "Nature and nature's laws lay hid in night. / God said: Let Newton be. And all was light."

16. Judith Shklar, "Hegel's *Phenomenology:* An Elegy for Hellas," in *Hegel's Political Philosophy: Problems and Perspectives,* ed. Pelczynski (London: Cambridge University Press, 1971), 73–89. Such nostalgia for antiquity at times broke out even among those Romantics typically more focused on Gothic themes. Edgar Allen Poe's well known line, "the glory that was Greece and the grandeur that was Rome," is typical. "To Helen" (1831).

17. Robert Pippin, *Modernism as a Philosophical Problem: On the Dissatisfactions of European High Culture* (Cambridge: Blackwell, 1991), 120.

18. The repeated emphasis of the superiority of the new contains at its core the demand for constant change and the concomitant anxiety that one will fall behind the curve and become outmoded. Fixed and lasting tastes or opinions thus are unacceptable in the face of the onrushing future. Modern man in this sense has to be thoroughly protean in order to retain his status as a member of the avant-garde.

19. Pippin, *Modernism as a Philosophical Problem*, 7. See also Marshall Berman, *All That is Solid Melts in Air: The Experience of Modernity* (New York: Penguin, 1988). Marx and Engels were devoted to the idea of science. They did not believe that freedom had any historical efficacy and that it could only be attained when the political constraints on science and technology were removed. The elimination of such fetters would in their view unleash the productive powers of technology and usher in an age in which human beings were no longer driven by the natural need to produce their own subsistence and thus could exist at their leisure.

20. Ostwald Spengler, *The Decline of the West*, trans. Charles Atkinson, 2 vols. (New York: Knopf, 1976), 1:13–23. Spengler developed the concept of the West to replace what he saw as the defective ancient/modern distinction. On this point see my "Liberal Education and the Idea of the West," in *America, The West and the Liberal Education*, ed. Ralph Hancock (Lanham, Md.: Rowman & Littlefield, 1999), 7–11.

21. Francis Fukuyama, *The End of History and the Last Man* (New York: Free Press, 1992). For Fukuyama as for Hegel, history ended in 1806 with the advent of parliamentary democracy. While some see his thesis as merely a continuation of the Whig interpretation of history, it should be noted that Fukuyama sees the triumph of liberalism not as an unadulterated good but more pessimistically as the triumph of something like Nietzsche's last man. It should also be noted that Fukuyama himself later concluded that genetic engineering might well change human nature and establish a new transhuman future. See his *Our Posthuman Future: Consequences of the Biotechnology Revolution* (New York: Farrar, Strauss and Giroux, 2002).

22. See, for example, Etienne Gilson, *Études sur le rôle de la pensée médiévale dans la formation du système cartésien* (Paris: Vrin, 1930) as well as Alexander Koyré, *Descartes und die Scholastik* (Bonn: Cohen, 1923).

23. Funkenstein describes these similarities and connections in great detail and breadth in his *Theology and the Scientific Imagination*.

24. Karl Löwith, *Meaning in History: The Theological Implications of the Philosophy of History* (Chicago: University of Chicago Press, 1949).

25. Blumenberg has developed this argument in many of his works, but it is the central topic of his *Legitimacy of the Modern Age*.

26. Friedrich Nietzsche, *Kritische Gesamtausgabe*, ed. Giorgio Colli und Mazzino Montinari (Berlin: de Gruyter, 1967–), V 2:256.

27. Ibid., VI 1:136; VI 2:417.

28. Or, to put the matter in other terms, the Christian theological enterprise from the second century on was an attempt to unite Athens and Jerusalem. This new combined city was in their view the coming city of God and was opposed to the city of the pagans whether it was called Rome or Babylon.

CHAPTER ONE

1. Umberto Eco brilliantly portrayed this conflict and collapse in his novel, *The Name of the Rose* (New York: Harcourt Brace Jovanovich, 1983).

2. On this point see Joseph Michael Incandela, "Aquinas's Lost Legacy: God's Practical Knowledge and Situated Freedom" (Ph.D. diss., Princeton University, 1986), 82–83.

3. As we find ourselves entangled in a struggle against antimodern forces that draw much of their inspiration from Islam, it is important to recognize that the decisive turn away from the medieval world in the direction of modernity was rooted in a fear and rejection of Islamic influences on Christian thought. It is probably not accidental that this fear arose in tandem with the actual military threat of Islam to Europe itself. Ironically, as we will see below, the nominalist alternative that arose in reaction to scholasticism was probably also indebted to Islamic thought, although to a less philosophical and more "fundamentalist" strain of Islam.

4. On this point see Edward Grant, "The Effect of the Condemnation of 1277," in *The Cambridge History of Later Medieval Philosophy*, ed. Norman Kretzmann et al. (London: Cambridge University Press, 1982), 537–39. It would probably be more accurate to say that the condemnation focused primarily on those elements of Aristotelianism that were most deeply influenced by Averroism.

5. One should not be misled by the fact that Ockham presents himself in the guise of a traditional scholastic, in fact as a follower of the *via antiqua*. It is important to remember the context within which he wrote and particularly his Thomistic adversaries at Oxford. They had no doubts about the revolutionary character of his thought in spite of his efforts to portray himself as a traditionalist. Indeed, they denounced his thought as heretical. Contemporary scholars who are anxious to demonstrate his orthodoxy are in part interested in defending his Catholicism against the longstanding charge that he was the father or at least forefather of the Protestant Reformation. Whether or not he was in part responsible for the Reformation, there can be no doubt that his thought represents a metaphysical and theological break with scholasticism. Perhaps the best secondary work on Ockham is Jürgen Miethke, *Ockhams Weg zur Sozialphilosophie* (Berlin: de Gruyter, 1969). For an excellent introduction to nominalism in English, see William Courtenay, "Nominalism and Later Medieval Religion," in *The Pursuit of Holiness in Later Medieval and Renaissance Religion*, ed. Charles Trinkaus and Heiko Oberman (Leiden: Brill, 1974), 26–58. For an encyclopedic account of Ockham's thought, see Marilyn McCord Adams, *William Ockham*, 2 vols. (Notre Dame, Ind.: University of Notre Dame Press, 1987). See also my *Nihilism Before Nietzsche* (Chicago: University of Chicago Press, 1995), 14–28.

6. Ockham I *Sent.* d. 43 q. 2, *Opera philosophica et theologica*, ed. Stephen Brown (New York: Bonaventure Press, 1967). On this point, see A. B. Wolter, "Ockham and the Textbooks: On the Origin of Possibility," *Franziskanische Studien* 32 (1950): 70–92; Miethke, *Ockhams Weg*, 139–40, and Blumenberg, *Legitimacy*, 161–62.

7. William of Ockham, *Predestination, God's Foreknowledge, and Future Contingents*, ed. and trans. Marilyn McCord Adams and Norman Kretzmann, 2d ed. (Indianapolis: Hackett, 1983), 13.

8. The divine creation of a universal would thus entail a performative contradiction. Ockham I *Sent.* d. 2. q. 6.

9. God can sustain any one thing in existence without the necessity of the existence of anything else in the universe. Funkenstein, *Theology*, 135. See also André Goddu, *The Physics of William of Ockham* (Leiden and Cologne: Brill, 1984).

10. On the ontological uniqueness of God as the nominalists understood him, see Martin Tweedale, "Scotus and Ockham on the Infinity of the Most Eminent Being," *Franciscan Studies* 23 (1963): 257–67.

11. On this point, see Jean Largeault, *Enquête sur le nominalisme* (Paris and Louvain: Beatrice-Nauwelaerts, 1971), 154. God does not need universals since he can understand everything individually by means of his *cognitio intuitiva*. Adams, *Ockham*, 2:1036–56.

12. II *Sent.* q. 14–15; q. 17; q. 18; q. 22; q. 24; IV *Sent.* q. 3; q. 8–9. The principle has several other forms. "No plurality should be assumed unless it can be proved by reason, or by experience, or by some infallible authority." *Ord.* I, d. 30, qu. 1. Also: "One should affirm no statement as true or maintain that something exists unless forced to do so by self-evidence, that is, by revelation, experience, or logical deduction from a revealed truth or a proposition verified by observation." I *Sent.* d. 30 q. 1; III *Sent.* q. 8.

13. On the contingency of created things for Ockham, see I *Sent.* d. 35 q. 2; and II *Sent.* q. 4–5.

14. *Centiloquium theologicum* conc. 6, 7a, ed. Philotheus Boehner (St. Bonaventure, N.Y.: St Bonaventure University Press, 1988), 44.

15. Miethke, *Ockhams Weg*, 227, 275, 284; Blumenberg, *Legitimacy*, 164; Tweedale, "Scotus and Ockham," 265.

16. As severe as this position might seem, in one sense it ameliorates the Thomistic doctrine of original sin since Ockham believes that no man intrinsically deserves damnation. On this point, see Adams, *Ockham*, 2:1257–1337.

17. Ockham even asserts that God's love of man is only a passage back to himself and thus an act of self-love. Blumenberg, *Legitimacy*, 174–77.

18. On this point see David Clark, "Ockham on Human and Divine Freedom," *Franciscan Studies* 38 (1978): 160.

19. John Calvin, *Institutes of the Christian Religion*, ed., John McNeill, trans. Lewis Battles, 2 vols. (Philadelphia: Westminster, 1960), 1:162. On similar grounds, Hans Blumenberg has argued that we should understand nominalism as the second coming of Gnosticism. *Legitimacy of the Modern Age*, 127–36.

20. Henning Graf Reventlow, *The Authority of the Bible and the Rise of the Modern World* (Philadelphia: Fortress, 1985), 35.

21. They wanted the pope, for example, to allow communal ownership of property.

22. They believed that God was not bound by his past acts and could predestine individuals as he wished. Adams, *Ockham*, 2:1201, 1257.

23. On this point see Louis Dupré, *Passage to Modernity: An Essay in the Hermeneutics of Nature and Culture* (New Haven: Yale University Press, 1993), 7.

24. Antony Levi, *Renaissance and Reformation: The Intellectual Genesis* (New Haven: Yale University Press, 2002), 29. In my discussion of the variations in the nominalist school I draw on the argument he develops in his excellent book (30–65).

25. Pelagianism was the doctrine named after Pelagius (354–ca. 420/440), who argued that original sin did not affect human nature and that moral will was capable of choosing between good and evil without divine assistance. Human beings in this view are thus responsible for their own salvation and do not require grace to be saved. Thus Jesus' sacrifice was not the source of redemption, and his life is merely a moral example. Humans thus can win salvation by a rigorous moral life whether God wills that they be saved or not.

26. As Levi has pointed, out Ockham's follower Gregory of Rimini went even further, arguing that God can even reject acts inspired by grace and refuse salvation to the justified. Like Holcot, he too was skeptical of all rational or natural theology. Ibid., 60–63.

27. Ibid., 64–65.

28. The great European famine of 1315–17 was the best-known consequence of this climatic change, but there was also famine in France in 1304, 1305, 1310, 1330–34, 1349–51, 1358–60, 1371, 1374–75, and 1390 as well. In England, the most prosperous medieval realm, there was famine in 1321, 1351, 1369 and the following years. As a result of decreased food production, the average lifespan was reduced in England from 35 to 30 in the period before the Black Death. Immediately after the Plague it fell to 17. Over the hundred year period ending in 1420, the German population declined by 40 percent, and the populations of Provence and Tuscany by 50 percent.

29. In this light we should perhaps ask how anyone could continue to believe in a predictably beneficent God. Levi has convincingly argued that the uncertainty about ultimate destination of the *viator* helps explain the origin of indulgences, chantry bequests, prayers for the dead, and posthumous conversion. Ibid., 56. The terrors of the time are depicted in the four *Dialogues* of Gregory the Great. Ibid., 59.

30. Or as one of his successors, Francesco Guicciardini, would put it two hundred years later, God's "ways are so past finding out, that they are rightly called *abyssus multa*." *Maxims and Reflections (Ricordi)* (Philadelphia: University of Pennsylvania Press, 1965), 64. He like Petrarch was convinced that scholasticism was not a body of collected wisdom but rather thousands of insane ideas (72–73).

31. For an uncompromising portrayal of the corruption of the contemporary church and its saints, see the first two tales in Giovanni Boccaccio's *Decameron,* trans. M. Musa and P. Bondanella (New York: Norton, 1977), 18–31. Boccaccio was Petrarch's friend and admirer.

32. On this point, see Charles Trinkaus, "The Problem of Free Will in the Renaissance and the Reformation," in *Renaissance Essays,* ed. Kristeller and Wiener (Rochester, N.Y.: University of Rochester Press, 1992), 187–98.

33. For a discussion of the Renaissance vision of the state as an artwork, see Funkenstein, *Theology and the Scientific Imagination*, 342.

34. It was already apparent to Heinz Heimsoeth in 1922 that there was a clear connection of the early Renaissance to Ockham. Heimsoeth, *The Six Great Themes of Western Metaphysics and the End of the Middle Ages,* trans. R. Betanzos (Detroit: Wayne State University Press, 1994), 31. This connection has become increasingly clear, especially in the history of science. See, for example, Alexander Koyré, *From Closed World to Infinite Universe* (Baltimore: Johns Hopkins University Press, 1957); A. C. Crombie, *Robert Grossete and the Origins of Experimental Science* (Oxford: Oxford University Press, 1953); and of course Blumenberg's *Legitimacy of the Modern Age* and Funkenstein's *Theology and the Scientific Imagination.*

35. Martin Luther, *The Freedom of a Christian,* in D. *Martin Luthers Werke: Kritische Gesamtausgabe,* 67 vols. (Weimar: Hermann Böhlaus Nachfologer, 1883–1997), 7:61 (hereafter cited as *WA*); *Luther's Works,* 55 vols. (St. Louis and Philadelphia, 1955–75), 31:361 (hereafter cited as *LW*). When citing the *Weimar Ausgabe,* I have followed the standard scholarly convention by giving first the volume:page.line. Roman numerals indicate the first or second part of a volume.

36. *WA* 7:49.7–19; *LW* 31:343.

37. Luther insists on the necessity of Scripture and rejects the extreme subjectivism of the evangelicals who followed not the word of God but the illumination they received in direct communion with God, their so-called inner light.

38. Heimsoeth argued that Eckhart represents the first step toward an affirmation of creation. *Six Great Themes,* 47.

39. I do not mean to assert in this way that all early modern materialists are atheists. Indeed, the reverse is the case. It is their particular notion of God that provides the assurance that he is irrelevant for their interpretation of nature. Charles Larmore captures this view with his assertion that in modernity, "God is so great he does not have to exist." Larmore, *The Morals of Modernity* (Cambridge: Cambridge University Press, 1996), 41.

40. Francis Bacon, *The New Organon and Related Writings,* ed. F. H. Anderson (New York: Macmillan, 1960), 122.

41. Ibid., 12.

42. Ibid., 3.

43. Ibid., 47–66.

44. Ibid., 23, 29.

45. Ibid., 80, 90.

46. Ibid., 4.

47. Ibid., 23, 78, 118, 267.

48. Ibid., 5, 132. Funkenstein argues that this is the beginning of a new ideal of knowing as construction. *Theology and the Scientific Imagination,* 297.

49. Bacon, *The New Organon,* 29; see also 39.

50. Ibid., 13, 66, 119.

51. Ibid., 6, 112.

52. Ibid., 20, 22, 25, 95, 113.

53. Ibid., 23.

54. Ibid., 109.

55. On this point see Thomas Spragens, *The Politics of Motion: The World of Thomas Hobbes* (Lexington: The University of Kentucky Press, 1973), 60–74.

56. Bacon, *The New Organon*, 39.

57. This project finds its preeminent form and definitive methodology in the calculus developed by Leibniz and Newton.

58. Descartes, *Oeuvres de Descartes,* ed. Charles Adam and Paul Tannery, 13 vols. (Paris: Vrin, 1957–68), 7:57–58 (hereafter cited as AT); *The Philosophical Writings of Descartes,* trans. John Cottingham, Robert Stootfhoff, and Dugald Murdoch, 3 vols. (Cambridge: Cambridge University Press, 1985), 2:40 (hereafter cited as CSM). See also Descartes to Mersenne, December 25, 1639, AT 2:628; Descartes to Elizabeth, 3 November 1645, AT 4:332. See also Margaret Wilson, "Can I Be the Cause of My Idea of the World? (Descartes on the Infinite and the Indefinite)," in *Essays on Descartes' Meditations,* ed. Amélie Oksenberg Rorty (Berkeley and Los Angeles: University of California Press, 1986), 350.

59. Thomas Hobbes, *Leviathan,* ed. Edwin Curley (Indianapolis: Hackett, 1994), 33.

CHAPTER TWO

1. Francesco Petrarca, *Rerum familiarum libri,* trans. Aldo S. Bernardo, 3 vols. (Albany: State University of New York Press, 1975–85), I, 1 (1:7).

2. Ibid., 1:12.

3. Ibid., 1:3.

4. Ibid., 1:14.

5. Ernest Hatch Wilkins, *Life of Petrarch* (Chicago: University of Chicago Press, 1961), 3–4.

6. Ibid., 6; Kenelm Foster, *Petrarch: Poet and Humanist* (Edinburgh: Edinburgh University Press, 1984), 2.

7. Petrarch "On his Own Ignorance and that of Many Others," in *The Renaissance Philosophy of Man,* ed. Ernst Cassirer et al. (Chicago: University of Chicago Press, 1948), 69.

8. Questions have been raised about the identity and even the reality of Laura since Petrarch's own time. Some have noted the striking parallel between Dante's account of his falling in love with Beatrice and Petrarch's attachment to Laura and have speculated that she was more likely a literary trope than a real person. The close connection of the name Laura to laurel and the laurel crown with which Petrarch by his own account was crowned have led others to believe that it was not a real person but fame that Petrarch fell in love with. Others have seen a hidden Christian symbolism in the name Laura since the cross was supposedly constructed out of laurel. On this point, see Marjorie O'Rourke Boyle, *Petrarch's Genius: Pentimento and Prophecy* (Berkeley and Los Angeles: University of California Press, 1991). There can be no definitive answer to this question, since almost all of our knowledge of Petrarch's life is derived from the various collections of his letters he put together late in life. From his own testimony we know that he reworked many of these, and from scholarly detective work we know some

were simply invented. In my view the status of the letters should not disqualify them. They should be treated in the way all autobiographical material is treated, with skepticism on details but with a general trust that the author is not inventing himself out of whole cloth. Many of these letters appeared while the persons involved were still alive, and there is little conflicting testimony about their veracity.

9. Petrarch served mostly in a secretarial capacity and never accepted a position that involved pastoral duties. Petrarch's brother, by contrast, continued to lead a secular and rather dissipated life until 1343 when, much to Petrarch's surprise, he entered a Carthusian monastery.

10. After his discovery in 1345 of Cicero's Letter to Atticus, "the personal (not private) letter was henceforth to serve as the chief medium through which he sought to act on the world of his time." Foster, *Petrarch,* 159.

11. Wilkins, *Life,* 183. Other works were of course later discovered and added to this corpus, especially the works of Greek poets and philosophers who were only poorly known by Petrarch, but many of the classical works that we today still consider most important were first resurrected by Petrarch.

12. Petrarch, *Remedies for Fortune Fair and Foul,* trans. with commentary by Conrad H. Rawski, 5 vols. (Bloomington: Indiana University Press, 1991), 3:4. See also Giuseppe Mazzotta, *The Worlds of Petrarch* (Durham: Duke University Press, 1993), 89.

13. *Remedies,* 3:8.

14. Ibid., 3:10.

15. Ibid., 3:10–12.

16. Ibid., 3:10.

17. Envy is a persistent poison. Petrarch, "Ignorance," 49.

18. *Remedies,* 1:238. The wheel here is the wheel of fortune, a widely used medieval and Renaissance image.

19. Ibid., 1:234, 284. In a 1352 letter to Stefano Colonna, he surveys the world and finds some promise of peace and freedom only in Venice and Paris. *Familiarum* XV, 7 (2:267, 269).

20. *Remedies,* 1:38. He wrote to his brother Gherardo: "Divide the day into hours, and the hours into minutes, and you will find the desires of a single man more numerous than the number of minutes." *Familiarum* X, 5 (2:70).

21. *Remedies,* 1:286.

22. Ibid., 1:294.

23. Petrarch, *Book without a Name: A Translation of Liber sine nomine,* trans. Norman P. Zacour (Toronto: Pontifical Institute of Medieval Studies, 1973), nos. 2–5, 9, 14. See also Petrarch, *Bucolicum Carmen,* trans. Thomas Bergin (New Haven: Yale University Press, 1974), 74–113; and Ernst Hatch Wilkins, *Studies in the Life and Works of Petrarch* (Cambridge: Medieval Academy of America, 1955), 48. This corruption is graphically portrayed by Petrarch's friend and follower Boccaccio in his *Decameron.*

24. *Familiarum* IV, 1 (1:288).

25. Foster, *Petrarch,* 154–55.

26. *Rerum senilium libri,* 2 vols., trans. Aldo S. Bernardo (Baltimore: St. Johns University Press, 1992), V, 2 (1:162–66)(henceforth *Seniles*). See also Foster, *Petrarch,* 154–55.
27. Cassirer, *Individual and Cosmos in Renaissance Philosophy,* trans. M. Domandi (Philadelphia: University of Pennsylvania Press, 1963), 127–28.
28. *Seniles,* V, 2 (1:162–66); XV, 6 (2:580).
29. Charles Trinkaus, *The Poet as Philosopher: Petrarch and the Formation of Renaissance Consciousness* (New Haven: Yale University Press, 1979), 55.
30. Paul Oskar Kristeller, *Eight Philosophers of the Italian Renaissance* (Stanford: Stanford University Press, 1964), 6; *Familiarum* I, 7 (1:37–40).
31. Foster, *Petrarch,* 153. See also Charles Trinkaus, *The Scope of Renaissance Humanism* (Ann Arbor: University of Michigan Press, 1983), 260.
32. For example, while in Naples, Petrarch lived in the Franciscan monastery of San Lorenzo and was shocked by the political authority exercised in the city by the Franciscan spiritual Roberto da Mileto, a member of the Brethren of the Life of Poverty, who was at odds with the other Franciscans and the pope. Petrarch thought he was a hypocrite. Wilkins, *Life, 40.*
33. Petrarch, *The Life of Solitude,* trans. and intro. Jacob Zeitlin (Champaign: University of Illinois Press, 1924), 64.
34. *Remedies,* 1:1.
35. Fortune is not an independent force for Petrarch, but a manner of speaking about the basic human condition in a world of strife and change. Trinkaus, *Poet as Philosopher,* 120.
36. Mazzotta, *Worlds,* 127.
37. Ibid., 7.
38. J. H. Whitfield, *Petrarch and the Renasence* (Oxford: Blackwell, 1943), 90.
39. Ibid., 40.
40. Wilkins, *Life,* 29.
41. This new idea of community eventually became the republic of letters.
42. Petrarch, "Ignorance," 104; *Remedies,* 3:252. Aristotle, in Petrarch's view, never fulfills his initial promise in the *Nichomachean Ethics* of making man better: "It is one thing to know, another to love, one thing to understand, another to will. He teaches what virtue is. I do not deny that; but his lesson lacks the words that sting and set afire and urge toward love of virtue and hatred of vice or, at any rate, does not have enough such power." Petrarch, "Ignorance," 103. He is comparing Aristotle to Cicero and Seneca, and he almost certainly did not realize that he was dealing with Aristotle's lecture notes rather than his published works.
43. Foster, *Petrarch,* 155.
44. Petrarch, *The Canzoniere (Rerum Vulgarium Fragmenta),* 2 vols., trans. Frederic Jones (Market Harborough: Troubador: 2001), 2:3.
45. Trinkaus characterizes him as the first to write subjective poetry. *Poet as Philosopher,* 2.
46. Mazzotta, *Worlds,* 44.
47. Mazzotta argues that Petrarch operates with a peculiarly modern notion of the self as an isolated subject who reflects on his memories, impulses, and desires in

the attempt to create a self-enclosed fictional universe that rejects time and history and makes the self the idolatrous counterpart of God. *Worlds*, 3. Such a view, however, wrongly assimilates Petrarch's notion of the individual to the Cartesian notion of subjectivity. For Petrarch the self is always in and of the world. It is not a *res cogitans* over and against a *res extensa*. It constantly struggles with the world but the world is not an alien other.

48. The disordered mind of the impetuous lover, in Petrarch's view, knows no peace. See his *Africa*, trans. T. G. Bergin and A. S. Wilson (New Haven: Yale University Press, 1977), 88.

49. Drawing on Cicero, Petrarch asserts in his Coronation oration that passion and the desire for glory are essential to any great work of spirit. Hans Baron, "Petrarch: His Inner Struggles and the Humanistic Discovery of Man's Nature," in *Florilegium historiale* (Toronto: University of Toronto Press, 1971), 30.

50. In this respect, Petrarch found the Romans superior to Greeks because they avoided excessively intellectualizing the question of virtue. Foster, *Petrarch*, 151. On the question of moral virtue, Petrarch firmly believed that Romans had improved what they received from Greeks. Whitfield, *Petrarch and the Renascence*, 103 and 107.

51. Jerrold Seigel, *Rhetoric and Philosophy in Renaissance Humanism: The Union of Eloquence and Wisdom, Petrarch to Valla* (Princeton: Princeton University Press, 1968), 58.

52. Mazzotta, *Worlds*, 117.

53. Ibid., 118.

54. Trinkaus, *Scope*, 353.

55. Later in life, Petrarch became increasingly interested in Caesar and wrote an extensive life of him as well, entitled *De gestis Caesaris*. He apparently never believed that he was as virtuous as Scipio, but was attracted to him against his sympathies by his greatness. Foster, *Petrarch*, 156.

56. Petrarch, *Africa*, x. This is reflected as well in Petrarch's critique of Pompey for not destroying Caesar earlier when he had the chance. This view has no parallel in medieval thought. Baron, "Petrarch," 27.

57. *Africa*, 70–77.

58. Foster, *Petrarch*, 148.

59. *Africa*, 166.

60. Ibid., 37, 227. Scipio, however, in a certain sense is merely emblematic for the Roman people themselves. Ibid., 74.

61. "For well schooled, the leader of the victorious hosts had marked Fate's oscillations and 'gainst every chance prepared himself." Ibid., 126.

62. This picture of Scipio is quite similar to Petrarch's later vision of the characteristics of a good prince. According to Petrarch, the prince should be lovable, just, promote public works, be careful in the use of public funds, contribute to new taxes, avoid cruelty and excessive delegation of power, cherish friendship, and be free from vanity and overweening pride. Wilkins, *Life*, 242–43. The power of this idea is evident in its continuing impact many years later on Erasmus. See

Erasmus, *The Education of a Christian Prince,* trans. Neil Cheshire and Michael Heath (Cambridge: Cambridge University Press, 1997). This work was contemporaneous with Machiavelli's *The Prince.*

63. *Africa,* xv.

64. Ibid., 26.

65. Ibid., 34. This is a prominent theme in his work: "Nothing man does lasts forever, nothing that pertains to man, save his immortal soul. Works shall fail, lands shall decay, buildings shall fall down." *Remedies,* 3:330.

66. *Africa,* 37.

67. Foster, *Petrarch,* 157. *Africa* was left unfinished in 1345 and never published in Petrarch's lifetime. Mazzotta argues that Petrarch attempted to write political poems, but, as their rhetoric failed, the failures gave him an alibi to retreat from a ghostly, unrealizable world of history to the obsessive absorption with his own private self, which was simultaneously empowered by love and powerless in love. Mazzotta, *Worlds,* 139. This view of Petrarch, however, fails to see the multiple ways in which the self he imagines remains in and part of this world, especially in and with his friends.

68. Petrarch lays out this argument in his *Trionfi* or *Triumphs,* which were written between 1340 and 1374. The first details the triumph of carnal love (*cupido*) over the human heart; the second the triumph of a chaste love (represented by Laura) over *cupido;* the third the victory of death over chaste love; the fourth the triumph of fame over death; the fifth the victory of time over fame; and the sixth the triumph of eternity over time (with Laura reappearing in heaven). Foster, *Petrarch,* 19. The *Triumphs* sum up Petrarch's entire philosophical position. They restore the coherent order of the world as a hierarchical arrangement of values from love of self to love of God in a linear and progressive movement. Mazzotta, *Worlds,* 99.

69. Wilkins, *Life,* 170.

70. Foster, *Petrarch,* 160.

71. Georg Voigt, *Pétrarque, Boccace et les débuts de l'humanisme en Italie d'après la Wiederbelebung des classischen Altertums,* trans. Le Monnier (Paris: H. Welter, 1894).

72. Whitfield, *Petrarch and the Renascence,* 39.

73. Ibid., 85.

74. Foster, *Petrarch,* 169.

75. Petrarch, *Petrarch's Secret or the Soul's Conflict with Passion: Three Dialogues Between Himself and S. Augustine,* trans. William Draper (London: Chatto and Windus, 1911), 112.

76. Trinkaus, *Scope,* 244.

77. Foster, *Petrarch,* 161. Cassirer remarks that the lyrical genius of individuality (Petrarch) takes fire at the religious genius of the individual (Augustine). *Individual and Cosmos,* 129.

78. William J. Bouwsma, "The Two Faces of Humanism: Stoicism and Augustinianism in Renaissance Thought," in *Itinerarium Italicum* (Leiden: Bill, 1975), 13.

79. Bouwsma suggests that Augustinianism seemed to provide an answer to the problems of modern society that scholasticism did not, because it treated men not just as disembodied minds but as bodies and passions as well. Ibid., 33.

80. *Familiarum* XVII, 1 (3:2–4); Foster, *Petrarch*, 175.

81. *Familiarum* X, 5 (2:77). See also Foster, *Petrarch*, 15. Petrarch elaborates this point in the *Remedies:* "Philosophy offers not wisdom but the love of wisdom. Therefore, whoever wants her must win her through love. . . . True wisdom can be grasped and loved only by pure and pious minds. Regarding this it is written: *pietas est sapientia*—piety is wisdom. . . . The philosophers, likewise, discuss the mysteries of nature as if they came straight from heaven and had attended the privy council of Almighty God—forgetting that it is written: *For who hath known the mind of the Lord?*" *Remedies*, 1:147. See also, Foster, *Petrarch*, 16–17.

82. Almost all scholars now believe that this ascent never took place or at least that it did not take place as Petrarch describes it. It is rather a spiritual allegory.

83. *Familiarum* IV, 1 (1:178).

84. Ibid.

85. In this admission we see a movement from Petrarch's earlier Stoic humanism to Augustinian humanism. On this point see Bouwsma, "Two Faces," 36.

86. *Secret,* xii. Augustine wanted to convert others, while Petrarch's self-examination (which remained unpublished) was only undertaken on his own behalf. Erich Loos, "Selbstanalyse und Selbstbewusstsein bei Petrarca und Montaigne," *Abhandlungen der geistes- und sozial-wissenschaftlichen Klasse*, 1988, no. 13 (Wiesbaden: Steiner, 1988), 11. Foster reminds us that while Petrarch cultivated self-disclosure more than any previous human being of whom we have a record, there is some deliberate impersonation in his account. *Petrarch*, 2–3.

87. *Secret,* 7; cf. also 14.

88. Ibid., 13. Augustine begins with the demonstration that no one is happy against his will and therefore that the first step to reform is to desire it, which in the last resort depends on the will and not reason, which only clarifies the issues. Foster, *Petrarch*, 165.

89. Ibid., 170.

90. *Secret,* 41. Petrarch recognized that the will had been crucial in Augustine's own conversion. On this point see Bouwsma, "Two Faces," 37.

91. *Secret,* 25, 32. Foster argues that while Petrarch seeks to purge himself of many of his passions, he never renounces the classics, which remain for him the incomparable patrimony of human wisdom. Indeed, in Foster's view, the whole work is classicist propaganda that finds common ground between ancient paganism and Christianity in opposition to the real Augustine who rejected Platonic dualism and the Stoic idea of passionless virtue. Foster, *Petrarch*, 170–71.

92. Ibid., 172. There is considerable disagreement about the meaning of *accidia* in Petrarch's thought. In the Christian context it generally means sloth, but in Petrarch's case it seems to be much closer to melancholy. Indeed, some scholars trace the modern notion of melancholia to this discussion of *accidia* in *My Secret*.

93. Foster, *Petrarch*, 173; Seigel, *Rhetoric and Philosophy,* 54.

94. *Secret,* 104. This becomes the basic theme of the *Remedies.*
95. Ibid., 125, 132. Foster, *Petrarch,* 174. Later humanists, drawing on Plato's *Symposium,* were able to describe a ladder of love by which thought was led upward, but the *Symposium* had not yet been translated into Latin in Petrarch's time.
96. Foster, *Petrarch,* 175. The danger is not just Laura but all created beauty and all human culture that has the power to distract man from true self-knowledge and correlative genuine awareness of God. Foster, *Petrarch,* 141.
97. Foster, *Petrarch,* 176; Baron, "Petrarch," 33.
98. *Secret,* 182–83.
99. Petrarch's path in this respect is quite different from that of Descartes, who also comes to terms with himself through a dialogue but a dialogue that excludes all others. The exploration of the self in Petrarch is a manifestation of the phenomenon of friendship.
100. *Remedies,* 3:114. Trinkaus, *Poet as Philosopher,* 128.
101. Loos, "Selbstanalyse," 7. This said, it must be admitted that Augustine is a saint and that the saints were often conceived as mediators or intercessors for man with God. There is almost no indication in *My Secret* itself that Petrarch seeks any such intercession. Trinkaus suggests that in *My Secret* Petrarch's goal is to offer cures for his contemporaries' spiritual maladies. *Poet as Philosopher,* 94.
102. Cassirer sees this as the essential moment of humanism in that man attains his true nature when he gives himself his own nature. *Individual and Cosmos,* 97.
103. Foster, *Petrarch,* 163.
104. Trinkaus, *Poet as Philosopher,* 24. This Augustine is thus more akin to the early Augustine of *De vera religione.*
105. *Secret,* 191.
106. Petrarch in this case stands at the end of a long tradition of differing assessments of the proper relation of the *vita activa* and the *vita contemplativa* that begins with Seneca and passes through Philo of Judaea, Anthony, Basil, Jerome, Augustine, Julianus Pomerius, Gregory the Great, Isidor of Seville, Peter Damiani, Bernard of Clairvaux, Victorine, and Aquinas to Petrarch. On this point, see Zeitlin's discussion in Solitude, 33–55. Cf. also Petrarch's later *De otio religioso. On Religious Leisure,* ed. and trans. S. Schearer (Ithaca, N.Y.: Ithaca Press, 2002).
107. Petrarch's aim is leisure, but it is a leisure remote from both idleness and from active affairs. *Solitude,* 99.
108. Ibid., 122.
109. He thus writes to his brother Gherardo that one should not follow the lead of the multitude because they have proven by being the multitude that they do not know how to lead. *Familiarum X,* 3 (2:59). See also *Remedies,* 1:33.
110. *Solitude,* 109, 101.
111. Ibid., 105.
112. Ibid., 128. Petrarch found silence absolutely essential to literary production.
113. Ibid., 125–26.
114. Ibid., 105.
115. *Familiarum X,* 5 (2:77). See also Foster, *Petrarch,* 147.

116. Gustav Körting, *Geschichte der Literatur Italiens im Zeitalter der Renaissance*, 3 vols. (Leipzig: Tues's Verlag, 1874–84), 1:578.
117. Loos, "Selbstanalyse," 4. See also Mazzotta, *Worlds*, 2.
118. Petrarch remarks that "in this little mirror you will behold the entire disposition of my soul." *Solitude*, 102.
119. Ibid., 90.
120. Ibid., 131.
121. Ibid., 131.
122. Ibid., 134.
123. Ibid., 87. Importantly, this is not the case with the orator who must constantly think of what his audience wants to hear. In *Solitude*, Petrarch thus stakes out a claim for the superiority of philosophers to orators. They seek to know themselves and thereby to return the soul to itself, despising the empty glory sought by the orators. Seigel, *Rhetoric and Philosophy*, 47.
124. *Solitude*, 133, 139.
125. *Solitude*, 149. This position also seems to include granting all others a sphere of autonomy in their own actions: "What business of yours is the conduct of others, as long as you conduct yourself in a decent fashion?" *Remedies*, 2:207.
126. *Solitude*, 150. The image first is used by Lucretius in *De rerum natura*, but Petrarch may have adopted it from many other sources.
127. Trinkaus imagines that Petrarch simply adopts this notion from the Romans. *Poet as Philosopher*, 22. Such a conclusion fails to see the importance of the new notion of individuality that Petrarch deploys.
128. *Solitude*, 88.
129. "Ignorance," 115.
130. *Solitude*, 56.
131. Ibid., 182–83.
132. Ibid., 183.
133. Ibid., 288.
134. Ibid., 291.
135. Ibid., 131.
136. Ibid., 152.
137. Ibid.
138. Ibid., 205. Petrarch remarks that all other lives, as Cicero and Augustine have made clear, are really death. Kristeller plausibly suggests that Petrarch here transforms the monastic ideal of solitude into a secular and literary ideal, and in this form it has been valued and praised by poets, writers and scholars to the present day. *Eight Philosophers*, 14.
139. *Solitude*, 66.
140. Ibid., 162.
141. Ibid., 292.
142. Ibid., 164.
143. Zeitlin points out that Petrarch celebrates the life of leisure, retired from crowded haunts and importunate cares and devoted to reading, literary creation, peaceful

brooding, and the society of a few chosen friends, more like the life of Horace and Epicurus than that of the Christian mystics. *Solitude,* 55.

144. On the importance of intercourse with wise men through books, see *Remedies,* 1:2–3.

145. Trinkaus points out that Petrarch recognizes the danger of Carthusian overemphasis on solitude in *De otio religioso. Poet as Philosopher,* 53. Petrarch's implied mistrust of the *otium* of the monks precedes Machiavelli's and Bacon's reversal of the contemplative ideal. Whitfield, *Petrarch and the Renascence,* 107.

146. *Solitude,* 137.

147. Ibid., 301.

148. Ibid., 307, 310.

149. Kristeller, *Renaissance Thought,* 170.

150. On this point see, Whitfield, *Petrarch and the Renascence,* 94.

151. In this respect he is the predecessor of Montaigne, as Zeitlin points out. *Solitude,* 58.

152. Whitfield, *Petrarch and the Renascence,* 120.

153. Ibid., 117.

154. To gain some idea of the power of this idea, one has only to examine Valla's *On Pleasure,* which presents an explicit and global defense of what might be called a Christian hedonism.

155. Whitfield, *Petrarch and the Renascence,* 142–43.

156. *Remedies,* 2:226.

157. Ibid., 2:225.

158. *Solitude,* 139. See also 59.

159. "Ignorance," 10.

160. *Familiarum* XVII, 1 (3:4).

161. "Ignorance," 98.

162. Ibid., 99.

163. *Familiarum* IV, 1 (1:180).

164. "Ignorance," 63.

165. Ibid., 105–6.

166. Foster, Petrarch, 168.

167. *My Secret,* 23.

168. *Remedies,* 1:32.

169. Bouwsma, "Two Faces," 43.

170. See also "Ignorance," 115.

CHAPTER THREE

1. On this point see Joseph Trapp, *Studies of Petrarch and His Influence* (London: Pindar, 2003). One measure of his influence was his impact on his contemporaries. At the time Boccaccio met Petrarch, he was certainly the greatest living writer of Italian. He fell so quickly and so fully under Petrarch's spell that he thereafter wrote almost exclusively in Latin and began to study Greek. Petrarch had a similar effect on many during the late fourteenth and fifteenth

centuries. Petrarch's own description of the effect his work on his contemporaries is telling:

> Within our memory, it was rare enough for people to write verses. But now there is no one who does not write them; few indeed write anything else. Some think that the fault, so far as our contemporaries are concerned, is largely mine. . . . I fear that the reproaches of an aged father, who unexpectedly came to me, with a long face and almost in tears, may not be without foundation. "While I," he said, "have always honoured your name, see the return you make in compassing the ruin of my only son!" I stood for a time in embarrassed silence, for the age of the man and the expression of his face, which told of great sorrow, went to my heart. Then, recovering myself, I replied, as was quite true, that I was unacquainted either with him or his son. "What matters it," the old man answered, "whether you know him or not? He certainly knows you. I have spent a great deal in providing instruction for him in the civil law, but he declares that he wishes to follow in your footsteps. My fondest hopes have been disappointed." . . . If I . . . venture into the street. . . wild fellows rush up from every side and seize upon me, asking advice, giving me suggestions, disputing and fighting among themselves. . . . If the disease spreads I am undone. (*Familiarum* XIII, 7 [3:200–201])

We are prone to see such claims as self-serving, but in Petrarch's case the evidence of his influence is so massive that if anything his comments understate the impact he had on his age. Without Petrarch, the poetry of Aristo, Tasso, Chaucer, Shakespeare, and Donne, to mention only the most famous, would be inconceivable.

2. Paul Oskar Kristeller, *Renaissance Thought and Its Sources,* ed. Michael Morney (New York: Columbia University Press, 1979), 99.

3. Ibid., 30.

4. There was no humanist philosophy in the narrow sense before Nicholas of Cusa (1401–64). Those scholars such as Cassirer who see humanism as a metaphysical or philosophical alternative to scholasticism typically explain earlier humanist thought as proto-philosophical. Cassirer, *Individual and Cosmos in Renaissance Philosophy,* trans. M. Domandi (Philadelphia: University of Pennsylvania Press, 1963), 1–6. On the opposite extreme some scholars, and Kristeller is the principal proponent of this view, argue that it is a mistake to understand humanism in philosophical terms at all. See for example, Paul Oskar Kristeller, *Renaissance Thought and Its Sources,* ed. Michael Morney (New York: Columbia University Press, 1979), 30–31. In fact, both schools go astray because they operate with displaced notions of philosophy. The former understand philosophy from the perspective of Cartesianism and the latter from the perspective of scholasticism. By either of these standards, humanism is not a philosophy. What I want to suggest is that humanism represents a philosophical position that is neither Cartesian nor scholastic.

5. Kristeller, *Renaissance Thought*, 86.

6. Jerrold E. Seigel, *Rhetoric and Philosophy in Renaissance Humanism: The Union of Eloquence and Wisdom, Petrarch to Valla* (Princeton: Princeton University Press, 1968), 210–22.

7. Kristeller, *Renaissance Thought*, 90.

8. Ibid., 97.

9. Although both of these in Petrarch's mind are linked to a Ciceronian notion of oratory, they are not the same thing. Seigel, *Rhetoric and Philosophy*, 36–37.

10. This notion led Gilson to assert that the Renaissance was not the Middle Ages plus man, but Middle Ages without God and therefore also without man. Etienne Gilson, *Humanisme médiéval et Renaissance* (Paris, Vrin, 1986), 192.

11. Reinhold Niebuhr, *The Nature and Destiny of Man*, 2 vols. (New York: C. Scribner's Sons, 1941–42), 1:61–64; 2:157–61.

12. Hans Baron argued that Renaissance Italy was proto-modern, at least in its political ideas. His classic work is *The Crisis of the Early Italian Renaissance: Civic Humanism and Republican Liberty in an Age of Classicism and Tyranny* (Princeton: Princeton University Press, 1966). He actually comes close to espousing the Burckhardtian thesis that sees the Renaissance as the first moment of modernity. On his contributions see Heiko Oberman, "The Shape of Later Medieval Thought: The Birthpangs of the Modern Era," in *The Pursuit of Holiness in Later Medieval and Renaissance Religion*, ed. Charles Trinkaus and Heiko Oberman (Leiden: Brill, 1974), 4; and James Hankins, "The Baron Thesis after Forty Years," *The Journal of the History of Ideas* 56 (1995): 309–38.

13. The foremost representatives of this position are J. G. A. Pocock, *The Machiavellian Moment: Florentine Political Thought and the Atlantic Republican Tradition* (Princeton: Princeton University Press, 1975), and Quentin Skinner, *Machiavelli* (Oxford: Oxford University Press, 1981).

14. Charles Trinkaus, "Italian Humanism and Scholastic Theology," in *Renaissance Humanism: Foundations, Forms, and Legacy*, ed. Albert Rabil, 3 vols. (Philadelphia: University of Pennsylvania Press, 1988), 3:327–44.

15. Seigel, *Rhetoric and Philosophy*; Charles Trinkaus, *The Poet as Philosopher: Petrarch and the Formation of Renaissance Consciousness* (New Haven: Yale University Press, 1979), 28–29.

16. Kristeller, *Renaissance Thought*, 100.

17. The late arrival of scholasticism in Italy led to considerable variation in its reception. For example, as Kristeller has pointed out, Ockhamism and Averroism played an important role at Bologna in law and the arts, while Thomism and Scotism flourished among theologians. Ibid., 42.

18. Charles Trinkaus, *In Our Image and Likeness: Humanity and Divinity in Italian Humanist Thought*, 2 vols. (Chicago: University of Chicago Press, 1970).

19. Marvin Becker, "Quest for Identity," *Florilegium historiale: Essays Presented to Wallace K. Ferguson* (Toronto: University of Toronto Press, 1971), 295–96.

20. Beryl Smalley, *English Friars and Antiquity in the Early Fourteenth Century* (Oxford: Blackwell, 1960), 287–92; Trinkaus, *Poet as Philosopher*, 57.

21. Charles Trinkaus, *The Scope of Renaissance Humanism* (Ann Arbor: University of Michigan Press, 1983), 244.

22. On this point see ibid., 241–44; Trinkaus, *Poet as Philosopher,* 54; Smalley, *English Friars;* and Heiko Oberman, "Some Notes on the Theology of Nominalism with Attention to Its Relation to the Renaissance," *Harvard Theological Review* 53 (1960): 47–76.

23. Ultimately there is a conjunction of these two in later humanist thought. Beginning with Nicholas of Cusa and extending through Leonardo da Vinci, Galileo, and their successors this becomes a logic of number, which serves as the foundation for a mathematical science of motion. On this point` see Amos Funkenstein, *Theology and the Scientific Imagination from the Middle Ages to the Seventeenth Century* (Princeton, N.J.: Princeton University Press, 1986); and Alexander Koyré, *From Closed World to Infinite Universe* (Baltimore: Johns Hopkins University Press, 1957).

24. Petrarch wrote to his brother Gherardo that it is "the simplest matter for [God] to change not only a single mind but the entire human race, the entire world, in short, the entire nature of things." Petrarch, *Rerum familiarum libri,* trans. Aldo S. Bernardo, 3 vols. (Albany: State University of New York Press, 1975–85), X, 5 (3:80). See also Petrarch, "On his Own Ignorance and that of Many Others," in *The Renaissance Philosophy of Man,* ed. Ernst Cassirer et al. (Chicago: University of Chicago Press, 1948), 94, and Kenelm Foster, *Petrarch: Poet and Humanist* (Edinburgh: Edinburgh University Press, 1984), 150. Cf. also Petrarch, *De otio religioso. On Religious Leisure,* ed. and trans. S. Schearer (Ithaca, N.Y.: Ithaca Press, 2002), 37. On this point see Trinkaus, *Scope.*

25. Petrarch endorses the primacy of the will in striving to be good as developed by Scotus and Bonaventure's emphasis on charity, widely taken up by Augustinian Friars with whom Petrarch had intimate ties. Trinkaus, *Poet as Philosopher,* 111. On this point, see Ugo Mariani, *Il Petrarca e gli Agostiniani* (Rome: Storia e Letteratura, 1957). The primacy of the will is even clearer in later humanists, especially Salutati and Pico.

26. Ockham and Marsilius of Padua both developed heterodox doctrines of authority that are strikingly similar to many of the more Augustinian humanists. Giuseppe Mazzotta, *The Worlds of Petrarch* (Durham: Duke University press, 1993), 26. On this point and particularly on the different political outlooks within humanism see William J. Bouwsma, "The Two Faces of Humanism: Stoicism and Augustinianism in Renaissance Thought," in *Itinerarium Italicum* (Leiden: Bill, 1975).

27. Trinkaus, "Italian Humanism and Scholastic Theology," 330.

28. The publication of Diogenes Laertius'compendious if superficial *Lives of Eminent Philosophers* in 1431 played an important role in this revival.

29. John F. D'Amico, "Humanism and Pre-Reformation Theology," in *Renaissance Humanism,* ed. Rabil, 3:355.

30. Anthony Levi, *Renaissance and Reformation: The Intellectual Genesis* (New Haven: Yale University Press, 2002), 99.

31. Giannozzo Manetti (1396–1459) was one of the first to explicitly articulate the doctrine of the dignity of man. On this point, see D'Amico, "Humanism and Pre-Reformation Theology," 359.

32. Kristeller, *Renaissance Thought,* 73.

33. Trinkaus, "Italian Humanism and Scholastic Theology," 334–36. In his *On Pleasure* Valla creates a dialogue between a Stoic, an Epicurean, and a Christian hedonist who sees beatitude as the supreme pleasure and virtue the means to obtain it. Valla's supposed Epicureanism thus has to be understood in the context of his Neoplatonism, and hence as an effort to climb Plato's ladder of love from sensual pleasure to beatitude.

34. Funkenstein calls this ergetic knowledge. *Theology and the Scientific Imagination,* 296–99.

35. Quoted in Trinkaus, "Italian Humanism and Scholastic Theology," 343.

36. Ibid., 344.

37. Manicheanism was originally a dualistic religious philosophy taught by the Persian prophet Manes that combined elements of Zoroastrian, Christian, and Gnostic thought. Like Zoroastrianism it saw the world as the battleground of two gods or principles, one good and the other evil. In late antiquity it offered a powerful alternative to orthodox Christianity by explaining the perplexing question of the origin of evil. Augustine was intitially attracted to Manicheanism but later rejected and attacked it. It has been generally recognized by Christianity as heretical. In modern times it has come to define anyone who sees the world in black and white terms as a fundamental and irreconcilable struggle of good and evil.

38. On the importance of Plato and Platonism for the Renaissance see, James Hankins, *Plato in the Italian Renaissance,* 2 vols. (New York: Brill, 1990).

39. Since the end of the Crusades in 1291, Islam had surged onto the offensive. In the early fourteenth century, while still recovering from the devastation of the Black Death, Christendom was both divided and under assault. The Moors continued to fight against the Christians in Spain and the Turks had overrun almost all of the Eastern Roman (Byzantine) Empire, except for Constantinople, which fell in 1453. Moreover, until 1453, England and France were still locked in the Hundred Years War. Italy and Germany were also at odds throughout this period.

40. Augustine argued in *Against the Academics* that Plotinus' thought was a revival of the true Platonism that had been submerged in the skepticism of the later Academy. This interpretation, which is questionable at best, was taken as a statement of fact by almost all humanists.

41. On Ficino and the revival of Platonism, see Michael J. B. Allen, *Synoptic Art: Marsilio Ficino on the History of Platonic Interpretation* (Florence: Olschki, 1998).

42. In the popular imagination, however, the idea of a secret wisdom that antedates both the Greeks and the Jews continues to resonate widely and strongly, especially in various forms of New Age Spirituality.

43. Kristeller, *Renaissance Thought,* 152.

44. Ibid., 53, 156.

45. Later in life Ficino condemned the magical elements in Hermes and put him after Zoroaster as the source of Greek and Christian thought, but he never abandoned the theological Hermes. The importance of Hermes for the Renaissance imagination is visible on the floor of the Siennese Cathedral, which portrays an Egyptian Sibyl, with the title *Hermes theologus.*

46. It was not until 1614 that Hermetic thought was shown to have a Christian rather than Mosaic/Egyptian origin. On the importance of Hermetic thought for the origin of modern science, see Frances Yates, *Giordano Bruno and the Hermetic Tradition* (Chicago: University of Chicago Press, 1964). Yates argued in this work and elsewhere that modern science had to be understood against the background of the Hermetic, alchemical, and Rosicrucian traditions. Other works such as Walter Pagel, *Paracelsus: An Introduction to Philosophical Medicine in the Era of the Renaissance,* 2d ed. (New York: Karger, 1982); Allen Debus, *Chemical Philosophy: Paracelsian Science and Medicine in the Sixteenth and Seventeenth Centuries,* 2 vols. (New York: Science History Publications, 1977); and Paolo Rossi, *Francis Bacon: From Magic to Science* (Chicago: University of Chicago Press, 1968) paint a similar picture. Umberto Eco correctly parodies the contemporary appeal of such spiritualist views in his *Foucault's Pendulum,* trans. William Weaver (New York: Random House, 1989), but we should not therefore assume that they were not important for the intellectual development of humanism in the earlier period.

47. Neoplatonism became important for early Christian theology as part of an effort to bolster trinitarianism against the attacks of the Arians, who denied that Jesus was one with God and believed him to he only the highest of the creatures. Victorinus was seminal in this effort, and his thought informed that of all of his successors. Levi, *Renaissance and Reformation,* 28.

48. Josephus taught that Pythagoras like other Greek philosophers had garnered his wisdom from the Mosaic teaching of the Pentateuch. Levi, *Renaissance and Reformation,* 22.

49. Ficino remarks that Socrates was sent by God "in the fullness of time," a term usually reserved for the incarnate Christ. Levi, *Renaissance and Reformation,* 429.

50. Levi, *Renaissance and Reformation,* 121.

51. Ficino played an important role in convincing the church to accept the immortality of the soul as doctrinal, which was authorized by the Fifth Latern Council in 1512.

52. Paul Oskar Kristeller, *Eight Philosophers of the Italian Renaissance* (Stanford: Stanford University Press, 1964), 43, 66.

53. *The Letters of Marsilio Ficino* (London: Fellowship of the School of Economic Sciences, 1975–), 1:190. Milton's Satan is obviously modeled on such a humanist vision.

54. Kristeller points out that Ficino identifies the love described by Plato in the *Phaedrus* and *Symposium* with Christian *caritas* as taught by Paul. Kristeller, *Eight Philosophers,* 47.

55. Ficino stresses the divinity of man's soul and the personal relationship to God: "Let him revere himself as an image of the divine God. Let him hope to ascend

again to God, as soon as the divine majesty deigns in some way to descend to him. Let him love God with all his heart, so as to transform himself into him, who through singular love wonderfully transformed himself into man." *The Christian Religion, Opera omnia*, 2 vols. (Turin: Bottega d'Erasmo, 1962), 1:22–23. For Ficino, the ascent of soul to God requires two wings, the intellect and will. The knowledge and love of God are thus only two different aspects of the same thing. Kristeller, *Eight Philosophers*, 45.

56. Ficino, *The Christian Religion*, 1:4.

57. This notion is semi-Pelagian, but during the fourteenth and fifteenth centuries, it was considered orthodox by many Christians due to the almost universal ignorance of the condemnation of semi-Pelagianism at the second Council of Orange (A.D. 529).

58. Kristeller, *Eight Philosophers*, 54–56, 66.

59. Richard C. Marius, *Martin Luther: The Christian Between Life and Death* (Cambridge, Mass.: Harvard University Press, 1999), 95.

60. Kristeller, *Renaissance Thought*, 205.

61. Kristeller, *Eight Philosophers*, 67.

62. David Wootton, *Paolo Sarpi: Between Renaissance and Enlightenment* (Cambridge and New York: Cambridge University Press, 1983).

63. The deification of man is perhaps even clearer in Giordano Bruno's late sixteenth-century work *Degli eroici furori*. Cassirer, *Individual and Cosmos*, 77. For Bruno we must in godlike fashion seek to penetrate to the true essence of the infinite universe and draw it into ourselves. This, in his view, is the basis not only for our domination of nature but for the transfiguration of man into God. Ibid., 188–89. Even Nicholas of Cusa, a cardinal, uses the idea of Christ as the model for humanity, the *natura media* that embraces both the finite and infinite as an articulated ground for human self-deification. Ibid., 38.

64. D'Amico, "Humanism and Pre-Reformation Theology," 364. The skepticism of the pre-Reformation period was Academic skepticism and not the more radical Pyrrhonian skepticism that became dominant after the publication of the work of Sextus Empiricus in 1562. This late fifteenth-century skeptical crisis also led to a sixteenth- and seventeenth-century revival of interest in the thought of Aquinas, although an Aquinas who was understood in a more nominalist manner. See Levi, *Renaissance and Reformation*, 12.

65. Savonarola emphasized the irrelevance of *studia humanitatis*. Peter Godman, *From Poliziano to Machiavelli: Florentine Humanism in the High Renaissance* (Princeton: Princeton University Press, 1998), 139.

66. Ibid., 186.

67. Ibid., 163, 181.

68. Sebastian De Grazia, *Machiavelli in Hell* (Princeton: Princeton University Press, 1989), 87, 379. Machiavelli shows some curiosity about other religions but ridicules demonology and astrology. Ibid., 65.

69. Ibid., 353.

70. Ibid., 121, 217, 378.

71. Ibid., 216, 381, 382.

72. Ibid., 385. According to De Grazia, those saved in Machiavelli's view included Trajan, and David by direct confirmation; Moses, Cyrus, and Theseus as God's friends; Scipio Africanus, a divine man, and those most gratifying to God, including reformers, etc. He also added Solon, Lycurgus, Aristotle and Plato, and Lorenzo the Magnificent. By his criteria, it might also include Xenophon, Cicero, Marcus Aurelius, Plutarch, Thucydides, Tacitus, Dante, Petrarch, Boccaccio, Ficino, Pico, Numa, Augustine, Francis, Dominic, and Jerome. Ibid., 52.

73. Ibid., 356.

74. While this is Machiavelli's articulated theological position, and one that he either believed, wanted to believe, wanted others to believe, or at least to believe that he believed, it is not clear how deep his religious convictions were. It is obvious that his account of the rewards that God gives to the effective prince mirrors his account of the support such a prince gains from his people and the immortal fame he wins from future generations. All of these are clearly incentives for the prince to act for the common good and not merely in his narrow self-interest. That Machiavelli's doctrines of salvation and glorification were instrumental to the production of a well-governed state has led many scholars to believe that he was disingenuous about both Christianity and morality. While this *may* have been the case, there is no evidence that it *was* the case. Moreover, it is perfectly clear that beliefs such as these were widespread among many of Machiavelli's humanist contemporaries who certainly were Christians. Our difficulty in believing that Machiavelli was Christian has more to do with the fact that we have generally accepted the Reformation view that Christianity is principally a matter of faith and not practice. By this measure we judge Machiavelli to be an atheist.

75. See "Tercets on Ambition," in *Machiavelli: The Chief Works and Others,* trans. Allan Gilbert, 3 vols. (Durham, N.C.: Duke University Press, 1965), 2:735–36.

76. De Gazia, *Machiavelli in Hell,* 79.

77. Levi, *Renaissance and Reformation,* 368.

78. It is important not to confuse the *devotio moderna* with the *via moderna,* although there were some thinkers such as Biel who tried to combine them.

79. As Albert Rabil has pointed out, "to a man humanists believed that Reuchlin's enemies were out to undo the cause of good learning altogether." "Desiderius Erasmus," in *Renaissance Humanism: Foundations, Forms, and Legacy,* ed. Albert Rabil, 3 vols. (Philadelphia: University of Pennsylvania Press, 1988), 2:247.

80. Ibid., 220.

81. Ibid., 225.

82. Levi, *Renaissance and Reformation,* 186.

83. Rabil, "Desiderius Erasmus," 231.

84. Gordon Rupp, trans. and ed., *Luther and Erasmus: Free Will and Salvation* (Philadelphia: Westminster Press, 1969), 6.

85. Rabil, "Desiderius Erasmus," 216.

86. Levi, *Renaissance and Reformation,* 180.

87. Martin Brecht, *Martin Luther*, 3 vols. (Stuttgart: Calwer, 1983–87), 2:232. According to Trinkaus, "Erasmus was striving for an open, as well as an irenic, Christianity in which all, except the fanatical extremes, could exist together." Charles Trinkaus, "Erasmus, Augustine, and the Nominalists," *Archiv für Reformationsgeschichte* 67 (1976): 31.

88. No one had used satiric irony in such a way since antiquity. Rabil, "Desiderius Erasmus," 234–36. Socrates, for Erasmus, was a Silenus who lured men into virtue. In Erasmus's view there were a number of similar moral and religious figures, the greatest of whom was Christ. Ibid., 237.

89. In this respect, Erasmus was an unrelenting critic of *via moderna* practices. Levi, *Renaissance and Reformation*, 15.

90. *The Collected Works of Erasmus,* vol. 76: *Controversies: De libero arbitrio. Hyperaspistes 1,* ed. Charles Trinkaus (Toronto: University of Toronto Press, 1999), xxi.

91. In evaluating Erasmus's pacifism it is important to keep in mind his acknowledged lack of personal courage. He wrote to Richard Pace in July 1521: "Mine was never the spirit to risk my life for the truth. Not everyone has the strength for martyrdom. . . . When Popes and Emperors make the right decisions I follow, because it is godly; if they decide wrongly I tolerated them, which is safe." Ep. 1218, *The Correspondence of Erasmus,* trans. R. A. B. Mynors (Toronto: University of Toronto Press, 1974–), 8:259. In his view "an unjust peace is far preferable to a just war." Rabil, "Desiderius Erasmus," 243.

92. Gordon Rupp, *The Righteousness of God: Luther Studies* (London: Hodder and Stoughton, 1953), 261.

93. Rabil, "Desiderius Erasmus," 240.

94. Cited in Bernard C. Flynn, "Descartes and the Ontology of Subjectivity," *Man and World* 16 (1983): 5.

95. Trinkaus, "Erasmus, Augustine, and the Nominalists," 30.

96. Charles Trinkaus was the first to interpret Erasmus's thought in this way, but many others have elaborated it. Manfred Hoffman, *Rhetoric and Theology: The Hermeneutic of Erasmus* (Toronto: University of Toronto Press, 1994), 6.

97. Erasmus, *Collected Works,* 76:xviii.

98. Rabil, "Desiderius Erasmus," 244.

99. Manfred Hoffmann, "Erasmus im Streit mit Luther," in *Humanismus und Reformation: Martin Luther und Erasmus von Rotterdam in den Konflikten ihres Zeit,* ed. Otto Hermann Pesch (Munich: Schnell und Steiner, 1985), 94.

100. Ibid., 100.

101. Ibid., 103.

102. On this point, see Erasmus's letter to More in Spring 1527. Ep. 1804, in P. S. Allen, M. M Allen, and H. W. Garrod, eds., *Opus epistolarium Des. Erasmu Roterodami,* 12 vols. (Oxford: Clarendon, 1906–58), 7:5–14.

103. Erasmus believed that it is demoralizing to be told that there is nothing one can do that effects one's salvation, and that this could lead to indifference, wild indulgence, or despair. Erasmus, *Collected Works,* 76:xcv.

CHAPTER FOUR

1. Richard C. Marius, *Martin Luther: The Christian Between Life and Death* (Cambridge, Mass.: Harvard University Press, 1999), 1.

2. Martin Luther, *Selections from His Writings*, ed. and intro. John Dillenberger (New York: Doubleday, 1962), xi; Heiko Oberman, *Luther: Man Between God and the Devil* (New Haven: Yale University Press, 1989), 29.

3. Oberman, *Luther*, 51.

4. Ibid., 52–53.

5. Ibid., 96.

6. Ibid., 114.

7. Ibid., 116. Indeed, from a theological perspective, Erfurt was considered the stronghold of the nominalist *via moderna*. On this point, see. E. Kleineidam, *Universitas Studii Erffordensis: Überblick über die Geschichte der Universität Erfurt im Mittelalter, 1392–1521*, 2 vols. (Leipzig: Benno, 1988), 2:146.

8. Alister E. McGrath, *Iustitia Dei: A History of the Christian Doctrine of Justification, the Beginnings to the Reformation* (Cambridge, Mass.: Blackwell, 1994), 70–75; Marius, *Martin Luther*, 35.

9. They were thus opposed to More, for example, who argued that God knocks at door but the choice to open it is the sinner's own. Marius, *Martin Luther*, 197.

10. W. Urban, "Die 'via moderna' an der Universität Erfurt am Vorabend der Reformation," in *Gregor von Rimini: Werk und Wirkung bis zur Reformation*, ed. H. A. Oberman (New York: de Gruyter, 1981), 311–30.

11. Oberman, *Luther*, 118–19.

12. *D. Martin Luthers Werke*, 67 vols. (Weimar: Hermann Böhlaus Nachfologer, 1883–1997), 6:600.11, Oct. 1520 (hereafter cited as *WA*).

13. Henri Busson's *Le rationalisme dans la literature française* refutes the notion that there was no religious skepticism in the sixteenth century. Cited in Marius, *Martin Luther*, 30.

14. Ibid., 112.

15. The search for the merciful God was a crucial part of monastic life. Oberman, *Luther*, 127.

16. Ibid., 138. Biel, alone of the major theologians of his time, tried to combine the *via moderna* and the *devotio moderna*.

17. Marius, *Martin Luther*, 57.

18. Oberman, *Luther*, 180.

19. Ibid., 181.

20. Ibid., 182.

21. Ibid., 183.

22. *Preface to the Complete Edition of Luther's Latin Writings, 1545*, *WA* 54.I:179–87; *Luther's Works*, 55 vols. (St. Louis and Philadelphia, 1955–75), 34:323–38 (hereafter cited as *LW*).

23. Ibid., *WA* 54.I:186.3–13; *LW* 34:337.

24. Ibid., *WA* 54.I:186.8–9; *LW* 34:337.

25. Heiko Oberman, "'Iustitia Christi' and 'Iustitia Dei': Luther and the Scholastic Doctrines of Justification," *Harvard Theological Review* 55, no. 1 (1966): 1–26.

26. *WA* 6:195.4–5. See also Oberman, *Luther,* 120.

27. On this point see Luther's "Disputation Against Scholastic Theology, 1517" in *WA* 1:221–28; *LW* 31:3–16.

28. Leo X's "chief pre-eminence lay in his ability to squander the resources of the Holy See on carnivals, war, gambling, and the chase. . . . The resources of three papacies were dissipated by his profligacy: the goods of his predecessors, himself, and his successor." Roland H. Bainton, *A Life of Martin Luther* (New York: Mentor, 1950), 56. Indulgences in this way served as a kind of philosopher's (or better "theologer's") stone for the church, turning the straw of sin into gold.

29. *Lectures on Galatians,* 1535, *WA* 40.I:39.14–28; *LW* 26:3.

30. Luther, *The Bondage of the Will,* trans. J. I. Packer and O. R. Johnston (Grand Rapids: Baker, 1957), 24. This was one of the first events created by the existence of the printing press.

31. Oberman, *Luther,* 68–70.

32. Marius, *Martin Luther,* 249.

33. Joachim Rogge, *Luther in Worms* (Witten: Luther, 1971), 100–101.

34. *WA* 7:49.22–23.; *LW* 31:344.

35. Marius, *Martin Luther,* 365.

36. Ibid., 491.

37. Ibid., 398. Anabaptists were more prone to believe in individual revelation and inspiration or enthusiasm and were less constrained by Scripture than was Luther.

38. Ibid., 400.

39. Indeed, he typically refers to the scholastics as the sophists.

40. He apparently thought that Aristotle achieved such a univocity or oneness of being by leveling everything down to matter. Marius, *Martin Luther,* 154. In this matter, he may have followed his favorite, Bernard of Clairvaux, who had opposed Abelard's introduction of Aristotle in Christian theology. Ibid., 120.

41. Not all of the Reformers followed Luther in this decisive emphasis on the incarnation. Calvin in particular put much greater weight on the role of spirit.

42. Ibid., 99.

43. Ibid., 101.

44. On this question see the discussion in Alister McGrath, *Scientific Theology,* vol. 3, *Theory* (Grand Rapids: Eerdmans, 2001), 115–17. See also Packer and Johnston, "Introduction," in Luther, *Bondage of the Will,* 46.

45. *WA* 40.I:77.20–22; *LW* 26:29. In other words, man's finite nature cannot tolerate knowledge of an infinite God.

46. Marius, *Martin Luther,* 461.

47. Marius, *Martin Luther,* 186. Luther does hold out hope that while we do not understand this God now we will understand him later when we see him face to face. *WA* 18:784–85; *LW* 33:289–92; *Bondage,* 56.

48. *WA* 18:750.5–14; *LW* 33:237.

49. Oberman, *Luther,* 258.

50. Packer and Johnston, "Introduction," in *Bondage,* 47.

51. *WA* 18:684.26–686.13; *LW* 33:138–40. On Luther's *deus absconditus,* see David C. Steinmetz, "Luther and the Hidden God," *Luther in Context,* 2d ed. (Grand Rapids: Baker, 2002), 23–31.

52. Packer and Johnston, "Introduction," in *Bondage,* 54.

53. Marius, *Martin Luther,* 187. See also Gerhard Ebeling, *Evangelische Evangelienauslegung,* 3d ed. (Tübingen: Mohr, 1991), 258. "Luther's God comes to us in darkness except for the light of Christ." Marius, *Martin Luther,* 224.

54. Oberman, *Luther,* 156.

55. Marius, *Martin Luther,* 216.

56. This claim is repeated throughout Luther's work. For a relatively early example see his Second Christmas Sermon; Titus 3:4–8, taken from his Church Postil of 1522. "God's Grace Received Must be Bestowed, " *WA* 10.Ia:95–128 .

57. Packer and Johnston, "Introduction," in *Bondage,* 58.

58. Oberman, *Luther,* 164.

59. *D. Martin Luthers Werke: Die Deutsche Bibel,* 12 vols. (Weimar: Hermann Böhlaus Nachfolger, 1906–61), 7:9.23–29 (hereafter *WADB*); "Preface to the Epistle of St. Paul to the Romans," in *Martin Luther: Selections from his Writings,* ed. John Dillenberger (New York: Doubleday), 23 (hereafter, Dillenberger).

60. *WA* 40.I:235.15–17; *LW* 26:133. It is in this vein that we need to understand his advice to Melanchthon to sin bravely. He does not encourage him to sin but reminds him that we finite human beings are doomed to sin but that we must not forget that God forgives us our sins if we believe in him.

61. "An Introduction to Martin Luther," in Dillenberger, xxvi.

62. *WADB* 7:10.16–17; Dillenberger, 24.

63. This move has far-reaching consequences, not the least of which is the destruction of traditional Christian ethics, for this view separates reward and merit and deprives good works of their scriptural warrant. Oberman, *Luther,* 154.

64. *WA* 40.I:64.14–65.8; *LW* 26:21–22.

65. Marius, *Martin Luther,* 204.

66. Dillenberger, xxvii.

67. Marius, *Martin Luther,* 232.

68. *WA* 7:51.17; *LW* 31:346.

69. Marius, *Martin Luther,* 255. Ernst Bizer follows the texts carefully to his conclusion that the "gospel" became for Luther not only revelation but the medium through which a Christian achieved righteousness. The gospel wakened faith. Bizer, *Fides ex auditu: Eine Untersuchung über die Entdeckung der Gerechtigkeit Gottes durch Martin Luther,* 3d ed. (Neukirchen-Vluyn: Neukirchener Verlag, 1966), 166–67. On this point see Marius, *Martin Luther,* 202.

70. "For Luther, as for many others in his time, the belief that there was a God without knowing that He was a God for oneself was tantamount to atheism, that is, to acting as if His existence made no difference. . . . The transition from un-faith to faith occurs through the Word—usually the proclaimed Word—which is given and received in the miracle of faith." Dillenberger, xxvii.

71. "Sermons on the Catechism (1528)," *WA* 30.I:100–102; *LW* 51:174.

72. *WA* 40.I:54.12–16; *LW* 26:14.

73. *WA* 40.I:14.17; *LW* 26:64.

74. *WA* 40.I:345.27–30; *LW* 26:215.

75. Preface to the Psalter, 1528, *WADB* 10.I:102.30–32; Dillenberger, 40.

76. His lectures and ceaseless publication should thus be understood as an act of worship, a way of living in the word. On this point, see Marius, *Martin Luther,* 104.

77. *D. Martin Luthers Werke: Tischreden,* 6 vols. (Weimar: Hermann Böhlaus Nachfolger, 1912–21), 5:653 (hereafter, *WATr*); English translation from Oberman, *Luther,* 169–70. Luther's great insight would in fact have been impossible without the knowledge of the different meanings of *dikaiosune,* the Greek term usually translated as "justification."

78. Dillenberger, xxxi.

79. *Archiv zur Weimarer Lutherausgabe,* vol. 2: *D. Martin Luther Operationes in psalmos 1519–1521,* part III: Psalm 1–10 (Cologne, 1981), 2.389, 15f.; exegesis of Ps. 6:11 (hereafter *AWA*); On this point, see Oberman, *Luther,* 173, 248.

80. "Preface to the New Testament, 1522," *WADB* 6:10.29–35; Dillenberger, 19.

81. *WADB* 10.I:100.13–15; Dillenberger, 38.

82. *WADB* 7:20.31–21.12; Dillenberger, 31.

83. *WA* 40.I:241.12–16; *LW* 26:137–38. Marius insightfully remarks that Luther's cosmic drama is reminiscent of the cult of Dionysus, guaranteeing salvation through the mystic joining of the initiate to the god. *Martin Luther,* 271–72. It is also important to note that for Luther the primal Christian experience is a radically *individual* encounter with God.

84. *WA* 40.I:282.17–22, 283.21–23; *LW* 26:166–67.

85. *WA* 40.I:283.26–32; *LW* 26:167.

86. *WA* 40.I:287.27–29; *LW* 26:169–70. Recently, the "Finnish school" of Luther interpretation, founded by Tuomo Mannermaa, has asserted that the center of Luther's understanding of justification by faith is based on the idea of union with Christ: *in ispe fide Christus adest.* See Mannermaa's *Christ Present in Faith: Luther's View of Justification,* ed. Kirsi Stherna (Minneapolis: Fortress, 2005). For a critical evaluation of this position see Dennis Bielfeldt, "Response," in *Union with Christ: The New Finnish Interpretation of Luther,* ed. Carl E. Braaten and Robert W. Jenson, (Grand Rapids: Eerdmans, 1998), 161–66.

87. *WA* 40.I:313.19–21; *LW* 26:189.

88. *WADB* 7:23.23–25; Dillenberger, 32.

89. *WA* 40.I:45.27–46.2; *LW* 26:7.

90. *WA* 7:60.21–23; *LW* 31:359.

91. Oberman, *Luther,* 291.

92. *"Temporal Authority: To What Extent It Should Be Obeyed, 1523,"* *WA* 11:250.18–20; *LW* 45:89.

93. *WA* 11:250.26–29; *LW* 45:90.

94. *WA* 11:251.12–15; *LW* 45:91.

95. On this point see G. Ebeling, "Die Notwendigkeit der Lehre von den zwei Reichen," in *Wort und Glaube,* 3d ed. (Tübingen, 1967), 1:407–28.

96. Marius, *Martin Luther,* 366.

97. *WA* 11:251.25–28; *LW* 45:91. This argument could easily remind one of Machiavelli's prediction that unarmed prophets invariably come to grief.

98. Marius, *Martin Luther,* 230–31.

99. The true Christian, according to Luther, lives and labors on earth not for himself but for his neighbor, and therefore the whole spirit of his life impels him to do what he need not do but what is profitable and necessary for his neighbor. *WA* 11:253.17–32; *LW* 45:93–94. While it is not right to seek vengeance for oneself, it is proper to do so for others. *WA* 11:259.7–16; *LW* 45:101.

100. *WA* 40.I:51.26–31; *LW* 26:12.

101. *WA* 11:277.16–27; *LW* 45:125.

102. Marius, *Martin Luther,* 366. "The temporal government has laws which extend no further than to life and property and external affairs on earth, for God cannot and will not permit anyone but himself to rule over the soul." *WA* 11:262.7–10; *LW* 45:105.

103. *WA* 11:267.1–13; *LW* 45:111–12. In praying for one's daily bread, Luther suggests that the subject is praying for good government, that is, for peace, just weights and measures, solid currency, etc. Luther, "Ten Sermons on the Catechism, 1528," *WA* 30.I:103–104.22; *LW* 51:176–78.

104. *WA* 11:246.23–25; *LW* 45:83.

105. *WA* 11:267.31–268.1; *LW* 45:113.

106. *WA* 11:269.32–33; *LW* 45:115.

107. *WA* 11:268.17–18; *LW* 45:114.

108. *WA* 11:270.16–24; *LW* 45:116.

109. *WA* 11:273.7–24; *LW* 45:120. Marius believes that it would have taken a superhumanly sophisticated reader to believe obedience was due to such stupid wretches as Luther describes, but Luther never saw himself as the leader of a rebellion. He thus could extol a democracy of true believers and certify a tyranny for ordinary men. Marius, *Martin Luther,* 368–370.

110. *WA* 40.I:410.24–412.14; *LW* 26:262.

111. Oberman, *Luther,* 255.

112. It is important to note that in Luther's view all of Christ is present in the Eucharist and not just some part, just as all of Christ is present in us in the infusion of grace. While it is sometimes imagined that Luther favored the doctrine of consubstantiation, his own language seems to leave him closer to transubstantiation. God is not beside the host, for Luther, he is in the host. The crucial difference is the role of the priest in bringing this transformation about.

113. Oberman, *Luther,* 245.

114. Oberman, *Luther,* 310.

115. Roland Bainton, *Here I Stand: A Life of Martin Luther* (New York: Mentor, 1950), 47.

116. Ibid., 155.

117. Ibid., 243.
118. Marius, *Martin Luther*, 385.
119. "What made Luther's theology so vivid and intelligible was not the outer rhetoric, but the connection of the Word of God with corporeality." Oberman, *Luther*, 274.
120. Ibid. The apparent connection here to Ficino's conception of love is probably illusory. For Luther God is in the world as love but that love is not in me until I am infused with Christ. There is thus no general human attraction to God. Only through grace are the elect redirected to the divine.
121. Oberman, *Luther*, 327.
122. Marius, *Martin Luther*, 453. Jesus uses *charis* five times in the Gospels but never in the salvific sense Luther employs. There are also two uses of the word in Acts 15:6–11 and 18:27–28 and one use in John 1:14–17 that may in a general way support Luther's reading, but they are at best contestable.

CHAPTER FIVE

1. While Tilly was a religious zealot, he apparently did not want to destroy the city since he needed it as a bastion against the fast-approaching Gustavus Adolphus. That said, he seems to have had little concern for the fate of its inhabitants and did nothing for the women who had been carried off to the camp. The destruction of Magdeburg earned him a principal place in John Foxe's famous *Book of Martyrs* (1663) as the epitome of evil. For years afterwards, Protestants replied to Catholic pleas for mercy with assurances that they would show them "Magdeburg mercy" and "Magdeburg justice." The various contemporary accounts of the destruction of the city—Europe's first media event—are contained in Werner Lahne, *Magdeburgs Zerstörung in der Zeitgenössichen Publizistik* (Magdeburg: Magdeburgs Geschichtsvereins, 1931).
2. For an account that calls into question the religious origins of the Wars of Religion, see William Cavanaugh, "'A Fire Strong Enough to Consume the House': The Wars of Religion and the Rise of the State," *Modern Theology* 11, no. 4 (October 1995): 397–420. I do not mean to deny that the consolidation of the state was an important factor in these wars. I do want to assert, however, that without religious fanaticism they would have taken a different and much less violent form.
3. Cited in Gordon Rupp, *The Righteousness of God: Luther Studies* (London: Hodder Hodden and Stoughton, 1953), 259.
4. Rupp, *The Righteousness of God*, 263.
5. A. G. Dickens, "Luther and the Humanists," in *Politics and Culture in Early Modern Europe*, ed. Phyllis Mack and Margaret Jacob (New York: Cambridge University Press, 1987), 202. Lewis Spitz, *Luther and German Humanism* (Aldershot: Variorum, 1996), 70, 76, 78.
6. Martin Brecht, *Martin Luther*, 3 vols. (Stuttgart: Calwer, 1983–87), 2:212.
7. Harry J. McSorley, *Luther: Right or Wrong? An Ecumenical-Theological Study of Luther's Major Work, "The Bondage of the Will"* (New York: Newman Press, 1968), 63.

8. Albert Rabil, "Desiderius Erasmus," in *Renaissance Humanism: Foundations, Forms, and Legacy,* ed. Albert Rabil, 3 vols. (Philadelphia: University of Pennsylvania Press, 1988), 2:250.

9. Ep. 1113, *Correspondence,* 7:313.

10. Erasmus, *The Collected Works of Erasmus,* vol. 76: *Controversies: De libero arbitrio. Hyperaspistes 1,* ed. Charles Trinkaus (Toronto: University of Toronto Press, 1999), xlii.

11. Cited in Rupp, *Righteousness of God,* 265–66.

12. Erasmus, *Collected Works,* 76:lvii.

13. Cited in James D. Tracy, "Two Erasmuses, Two Luthers: Erasmus' Strategy in Defense of De Libero Arbitrio," *Archiv für Reformationsgeschichte* 78 (1987): 40.

14. Brecht, *Martin Luther,* 2:276.

15. Rabil, "Desiderius Erasmus," 251.

16. Rupp, *Righteousness of God,* 268.

17. Erasmus, *Collected Works,* 76:lxxi.

18. On this point, see his letter to Pirckheimer of 21 July 1524. Ep. 1466:67, *Opus Epistolarium,* 5:496.

19. He may have been influenced in his choice of topic by the English bishop John Fisher, who wrote an essay against Luther's *Assertion,* and by Cuthbert Tunstall, who said that Luther's view of freedom made God the source of sin. Rupp, *Righteousness of God* 269; Brecht, *Martin Luther,* 2:219.

20. Brecht, *Martin Luther,* 2:220.

21. Rupp, *Righteousness of God,* 268.

22. Rupp remarks that Erasmus wrote with grace and clarity but also with a poisoned barb, while Luther was heavy-handed and destructive; it was, in Erasmus's view, a conflict between a wasp and an elephant. Ibid., 270.

23. Erasmus, *Collected Works,* 76:93; Ep. 1667 in Allen, *Opus epistolarium,* 6:262–63.

24. Marjorie O'Rourke Boyle suggests that Luther may not have read *Hyperaspistes* because the *Diatribe* had evoked his latent doubts about his own position. *Rhetoric and Reform: Erasmus' Civil Dispute with Luther* (Cambridge, Mass.: Harvard University Press, 1983), 130.

25. Erasmus, *Collected Works,* 76:xl.

26. *WATr,* 1:195. Rupp, *Righteousness of God,* 267.

27. In the following discussion of the Hellenistic notion of freedom and the will, I draw on Bernard Wills, "Ancient Scepticism and the *Contra Academicos* of St. Augustine," *Animus* 4 (1999):1–17.

28. Lucretius *De rerum natura* 2.251–60.

29. Ibid., 4.877–91.

30. Cicero *Tusculan Disputations* 4.6. See Neal W. Gilbert, "The Concept of Will in Early Latin Philosophy," *Journal of the History of Philosophy* 1 (1963): 22.

31. Seneca *De ira* 2.1–2.

32. McSorley, *Luther: Right or Wrong,* 57–58.

33. Gilbert, "Concept of Will," 32.

34. McSorley, *Luther: Right or Wrong,* 204.

35. Philip Watain, *Let God be God! An Interpretation of the Theology of Martin Luther* (Philadelphia: Fortress Press, 1947), 34–35; McSorley, *Luther: Right or Wrong*, 218, 222, 224–26. McSorley sees the first evidence of a break with the Biel school in Luther's marginalia of 1515 to Biel's *Collectorium*. In the same year, he denounced the *Facientibus* principle.

36. *Lectures on Romans*, 1515–16, WA 56:382.21–383.19; LW 25:373.

37. Erasmus, *Collected Works*, 76:305.

38. Ibid., 76:306.

39. Ibid., *Collected Works*, 76:306 The German version is more circumspect. Luther concludes: "I wish that little word 'free will' had never been invented. It is not found in Scripture and should more aptly be called 'self-will.'" *WA* 7:448.25/449.24. B. A. Gerrish, "*De Libero Arbitrio* (1524): Erasmus on Piety, Theology, and Lutheran Dogma," in *Essays on the Works of Erasmus* (New Haven: Yale University Press, 1978), 187.

40. McSorley, *Luther: Right or Wrong*, 255.

41. Ibid., 254.

42. Ibid., 259.

43. Erasmus, *Collected Works*, 76:307.

44. Cicero deals with these topics in several works, including *On Fate, Stoic Paradoxes,* and *On the Nature of the Gods.* Neither Erasmus nor Luther knew anything about Pyrrhonian skepticism.

45. Boyle has made the most comprehensive argument for viewing the debate between Luther and Erasmus against the background of this ancient debate in her *Rhetoric and Reform,* and the argument that follows is indebted to her work. That said, I push the argument further than she is willing to go and use the ancient sources to read not merely the rhetorical structures in the works but the argument carried on between the lines of the text.

46. Manfred Hoffmann, "Erasmus im Streit mit Luther," in *Humanismus und Reformation: Martin Luther und Erasmus von Rotterdam in den Konflikten ihres Zeit,* ed. Otto Hermann Pesch (Munich: Schnell und Steiner, 1985), 107.

47. Boyle has argued that the *Diatribe* was an attempt to disrupt the entire judicial process against Luther, by ushering it out of the civil and ecclesiastical courts and into the senate of learned men. *Rhetoric and Reform,* 33–36.

48. Boyle claims that the real goal of the *Diatribe* is to instruct Luther and that the question of free will is only a red herring (ibid., 5). However, there is no reason the *Diatribe* could not both seek to instruct Luther and be a real consideration of free will. Boyle asserts that Erasmus was convinced free will was not that important an issue (29). Considering the fact that he sets the debate with Luther against the background of the important ancient debate on this question, this contention seems implausible.

49. While he thought Luther often acted too vehemently, Erasmus expressly states that he does not believe Luther's doctrine is heretical. *Adversus calumniosissimam epistolam Martini Lutheri (1534),* in *Desiderii Erasmi Roterodami Opera Omnia,* ed. Jean LeClerc, 10 vols. (Leiden, 1703–6), 10:1537D.

50. Erasmus, *Collected Works,* 76:199.

51. Ibid., 76:210.

52. Ibid., 76:218.

53. Ibid., 76:252.

54. Ibid., 76:245, 261.

55. Ibid., 76:190.

56. Ibid., 76:286, 77:349.

57. Ibid., 76:289.

58. Cornelis Augustijn, *Erasmus: His Life, Works, Influence,* trans. J. C. Grayson (Toronto: University of Toronto Press, 1991), 139.

59. Charles Trinkaus, "Erasmus, Augustine, and the Nominalists," *Archiv für Reformationsgeschichte* 67 (1976): 9. Erasmus was especially concerned by Luther's radical claim that man remains a sinner even after he is justified by grace (8).

60. Rabil, "Desiderius Erasmus," 254.

61. The view of freedom that Erasmus assigns to Scotus is more properly assigned to Biel. Gordon Rupp, trans. and ed., *Luther and Erasmus: Free Will and Salvation* (Philadelphia: Westminster Press, 1969), 11. In contrast to Luther, Erasmus sees nothing unacceptable in Biel's position. McSorley, *Luther: Right or Wrong,* 290–91.

62. Gerrish, "*De Libero Arbitrio* (1524)," 196.

63. Tracy, "Two Erasmuses, Two Luthers," 72.

64. Ibid., 208.

65. McSorley, *Luther: Right or Wrong,* 285.

66. Oberman, *Luther,* 216. Luther was convinced that little time was left. Köselleck notes that he became extremely angry when Melanchthon suggested that the Apocalypse might not occur for another four hundred years. Cited in Reinhardt Köselleck, "*Historia Magistra Vitae.* Über die Auflösung des Topos im horizont neuzeitlich bewegter Geschichte," in *Natur und Geschichte: Karl Löwith zu 70. Geburtstag,* ed. G. Braun and M. Riedel (Stuttgart: Kohlhammer, 1967), 212.

67. Surprisingly, Luther never seizes on Erasmus's truly Pelagian notion that nature is itself divine grace. Tracy, "Two Erasmuses, Two Luthers," 43.

68. Boyle, *Rhetoric and Reform,* 60.

69. Oberman, *Luther,* 301; Tracy, "Two Erasmuses, Two Luthers," 44.

70. *WA* 18:600–601.29; *LW* 33:15–17.

71. Boyle, *Rhetoric and Reform,* 46.

72. *WA* 18:603.22–23; *LW* 33:20.

73. Boyle, *Rhetoric and Reform,* 47–48. Bernard Wills defines this notion: "A kataleptic impression was defined as one . . . stamped and molded out of the object from which it came with a character such as it could not have if it came from an object other than the one which it did come from (Cicero, *Academica* 2.18). . . . If a certain impression had the character of a kataleptic impression, it could compel assent to the objective reality of that which was conveyed in the impression. . . . On this basis all forms of conceptual knowledge were thought to rest. Secure in his grasp of the physical *Cosmos* the Stoic was secure as well in his grasp of the divine

Logos which was identical with it and thus could transcend the limitations of his particular existence through his love of fate." "Ancient Scepticism and the *Contra Academicos,*" 4.

74. Boyle, *Rhetoric and Reform,* 53–56.

75. *WA* 18:605.32; *LW* 33:24.

76. *WA* 18:719.9–12; *LW* 33:190.

77. *WA* 18:614.12–35; *LW* 33:37.

78. *WA* 18:712.35–37; *LW* 33:181.

79. *WA* 18:634.21–635.7; *LW* 33:64–65.

80. Robert W. Jenson, "An Ontology of Freedom in the *De Servo Arbitrio* of Luther," *Modern Theology* 10, no. 3 (July 1994): 248; Rupp, *Luther and Erasmus,* 18.

81. *WA* 18:635.17–22; *LW* 33:65–66.

82. *WA* 18:743.35–744.2; *LW* 33:227.

83. McSorley, *Luther: Right or Wrong,* 339.

84. *WA* 18:653.14–24; *LW* 33:90–91.

85. On this point, see McSorley, *Luther: Right or Wrong,* 336–38.

86. *Hypognosticon* 2.11.20, in Migne, *Patrologia Latina* 45:1632. For a comprehensive discussion of the origin of this analogy, see Marjorie O'Rourke Boyle, "Luther's Rider-gods: From the Steppe to the Tower," *The Journal of Religious History* 13 (1985): 260–82.

87. Rupp, *Righteousness of God,* 277.

88. Hans Blumenberg, *The Legitimacy of the Modern Age* (Cambridge, Mass.: MIT Press, 1989), 127–43.

89. This in the end is what Luther means by Christian liberty.

90. *WA* 18:685.5–31; *LW* 33:139–40.

91. Quoted in Albrecht Peters, "Verborgener Gott—Dreieiniger Gott: Beobachtungen und Überlegungen zum Gottesverständnis Martin Luthers," in Peter Manns, *Martin Luther: Reformator und Vater im Glauben* (Stuttgart: Steiner, 1985), 74. See also Marius, *Martin Luther,* 461.

92. *WA* 18:712.32–38; *LW* 33:181.

93. *WA* 18:708.37–38; *LW* 175.

94. Rupp, *Luther and Erasmus,* 19; McSorley, *Luther: Right or Wrong,* 340.

95. Milton raises the supreme question in *Paradise Lost:* if divine power is the sole source of both good and evil, is Satan not himself then unjustly punished by God? Indeed, might it not be the case that Satan is the victim rather than the victimizer, a new Prometheus unjustly bound to his rock and tortured by a tyrannical Zeus?

96. *WA* 18:709.29–33; *LW* 33:176.

97. Rupp, *Righteousness of God,* 280.

98. *WA* 18:633.15–19; *LW* 33:62–63.

99. *WA* 18:706.22–32; *LW* 33:171–72.

100. *Evangelion am Ersten Sontage ynn der fasten.* Matthew 4. *WA* 17, ii, 192.

101. *WA* 18:615.31–33; *LW* 33:37–38.

102. *WA* 18:729.21–23; *LW* 33:206.

103. *WA* 18:750.5–10; *LW* 33:237.

104. *WA* 18:783.17–36; *LW* 33:288–89.

105. *WA* 18:626.38–40; *LW* 33:53.

106. *WA* 18:627.10–12; *LW* 33:53.

107. *WA* 18:627.22–23; *LW* 33:54.

108. *WA* 18:632.11–12; *LW* 33:53.

109. Erasmus, *Collected Works,* 76:293.

110. Ibid., 76:294.

111. Ibid., 76:11.

112. Erasmus, *Collected Works,* vol. 77: *Controversies: Hyperaspistes* 2, 729.

113. Ibid., 77:737.

114. Ibid., 77:339.

115. Ibid., 77:471.

116. Ibid., 77:554–55.

117. Ibid., 77:650.

118. Ibid., 77:711.

119. Ibid., 77:340.

120. Ibid., 77:476.

121. Ibid., 76:lxxxii. Tracy, "Two Erasmuses, Two Luthers," 57.

122. Erasmus, *Collected Works,* 77:622. These exceptional divine interventions in the order of nature are, of course, miracles.

123. Ibid., 77:723.

124. Augustine *Contra duas epistolas Pelagianorum* 2:21.

125. Erasmus, *Collected Works,* 77:420.

126. Ibid., 77:573.

127. Ibid., 77:455.

128. Ibid., 77:557.

129. Ibid., 77:690.

130. Ibid., 77:473.

131. This position is almost identical to that of Ivan Karamazov in Fyodor Dostoevsky's *The Brothers Karamazov,* trans. Constance Garnett (New York: Random House, 1950), 245–55.

132. Erasmus, *Collected Works,* 77:709.

133. Ibid., 76:13; Augustijn, *Erasmus,* 144; Gerrish, "*De Libero Arbitrio* (1524)," 199.

134. Erasmus, *Collected Works,* 77:710.

135. Ibid., 77:591.

136. Ibid., 77:593.

137. Ibid., 77:703.

138. Ibid., 77:539, 587.

139. Ibid., 77:734–35.

140. Ibid., 77:648.

141. Erasmus, *The Colloquies of Erasmus,* trans. N. Bailey, ed. E. Johnson, 2 vols. (London: Reeves and Turner, 1878), 1:186.

142. Cited in M. M. Phillips, "Erasmus and the Classics," in *Erasmus,* ed. T. A. Dorey (Albuquerque: University of New Mexico Press, 1970), 14; see also Rabil, "Desid-

erius Erasmus," 255–56; Anthony Levi, *Renaissance and Reformation: The Intellectual Genesis* (New Haven: Yale University Press, 2002), 213.

143. Cited in Spitz, *Luther and German Humanism,* 81.
144. *WA* 1:146, Cor. 3.
145. McSorley, *Luther: Right or Wrong,* 241.
146. Erasmus, *Collected Works,* 77:662.
147. Ibid., 77:676.
148. Ibid., 77:672.
149. Ibid.
150. Ibid., 77:659.
151. Ibid., 77:743.
152. Marius, *Martin Luther,* 467.
153. For a thoughtful discussion of this project, see Ross King, *Michelangelo and The Pope's Ceiling* (New York: Walker Publishing, 2003).
154. This project was begun six years after the sack of Rome by the imperial army with many Lutheran knights leading the charge. On this painting see Charles Burroughs, "The 'Last Judgment' of Michelangelo: Pictorial Space, Sacred Topography, and the Social World," *Artibus et Historiae* 16, no. 32 (1995): 55–89.

CHAPTER SIX

1. This aphorism appeared at the beginning of what was apparently a sketch for an essay contained in the *Little Notebook,* found among Descartes' papers after his death. Cited in John R. Cole, *The Olympian Dream and Youthful Rebellion of René Descartes* (Urbana and Chicago: University of Illinois Press, 1992), 23.
2. Descartes to Beeckman, March 26, 1619, AT 10:157–58; CSM 3:2–3 (for abbreviations, see chap. 1, n. 58).
3. Timothy J. Reuss, "Descartes, the Palatinate, and the Thirty Years War: Political Theory and Political Practice," *Yale French Studies* 80, *Baroque Topographies* (1991): 110.
4. Charles Tilly, "War Making and State Making as Organized Crime," in *Bringing the State Back In,* ed. Peter B. Evans, Dietrich Rueschemeyer, and Theda Skocpol (Cambridge: Cambridge University Press, 1985), 169–91.
5. The two best books in English on Descartes' life are Richard Watson, *Cogito, Ergo Sum: The Life of René Descartes* (Boston: David. R. Godine, 2002), and Stephen Gaukroger, *Descartes: An Intellectual Biography* (Oxford: Clarendon Press, 1995). Watson's biography is indispensable for coming to terms with the prejudices of previous Descartes' scholarship and particularly the early efforts to transform Descartes into a defender of Catholic orthodoxy.
6. On Descartes' family, see John R. Cole, *The Olympian Dream and Youthful Rebellion of René Descartes,* 89–113.
7. Gaukroger, *Descartes,* 42. On life at La Flêche see Camille de Rochmonteix, *Un Collège de Jesuites aux XVIIe et XVIIIe siecles,* 4 vols. (Le Mans: Leguicheux, 1839).

8. Cole, *Olympian Dream,* 93. While it is clear that Descartes was never close to his father, his assertion that Charlet was his true father must be viewed with some skepticism, since it was made while Descartes was trying to convince the Jesuits to adopt his works for their curriculum and Charlet was secretary to the head of the order.

9. Descartes almost certainly did not participate in the actual ceremony. Watson, *Cogito,* 70.

10. See Etienne Gilson, *La Liberté chez Descartes et la Théologie* (Paris: Alcan, 1912), 6; Camille de Rochmonteix, *Un Collège de Jesuites,* 4:2–3, 30; and Norman Wells, "Descartes and the Scholastics Briefly Revisited," *New Scholasticism* 35, no. 2 (1961): 172–90.

11. On this point see Georg Freiherr von Hertling, "Descartes' Beziehung zur Scholastik," Königliche Bayrisch Akademie der Wissenschaften in München, *Sitzungber. d. philos.-histor. Klasse* (1897); Alexander Koyré, *Descartes und die Scholastik* (Bonn: Cohn, 1923); and Gilson, *Études sur le rôle de la pensée médiévale dans la formation du système cartésien* (Paris: Vrin, 1930), 221; and *Index scholastico-Cartesien* (Paris: Alcan, 1913). It is also likely that Descartes at some point read Rudolph Gloclenius, *Lexicon Philosophicum. . .* (1613), which contains a concise but detailed description of the realist-nominalist debate (757–58).

12. Koyré, *Descartes und die Scholastik,* 81–82, 86, 94, and 95.

13. Richard Popkin calls this into question. See his *The History of Scepticism from Erasmus to Spinoza* (Berkeley and Los Angeles: University of California Press, 1979), 70–75, 173.

14. Hertling, "Scholastik," 18; Geneviève Rodis-Lewis, "Descartes aurait-il eu un professeur nominaliste?" *Archives de Philosophie* 34 (1971): 37–46; and Gaukroger, *Descartes,* 54.

15. Watson, *Cogito,* 73–74.

16. Ibid., 59. Watson suggests that Descartes may have harbored Protestant sympathies, although he was probably closer to the Arminians than to the Calvinists.

17. While Maurice was officially a Protestant (and certainly not very religious in any case), Descartes' entry into his service should not be taken to indicate treasonous intentions toward either his religion or his country, for Maurice was allied with the King of France against Spain. Gaukroger, *Descartes,* 65. Watson suggests that Descartes could have served in France but that he joined Maurice's army (which had a Protestant chaplain) to avoid the religious wars in France. *Cogito,* 80.

18. Watson, *Cogito,* 30.

19. Cole, *Olympian Dream,* 115; Watson, *Cogito,* 86. Beeckman was the first to recognize the modern law of inertia, and he later became the head of one of the most famous schools in Holland.

20. Descartes wrote to Beeckman on April 23, 1619: "For you, in truth, have awakened me from my idleness, and evoked in me a science I had nearly forgotten. You have brought me back again to serious occupation and have improved a mind that had been separated from them. If, therefore, I produce anything that is not contemptible, you have a right to claim it as yours." Cited in Cole, *Olympian Dream,* 121.

21. Watson, *Cogito*, 116–17.

22. For a comprehensive discussion of the Rosicrucians, see Frances A. Yates, *The Rosicrucian Enlightenment* (London: Routledge and Kegan Paul, 1972). She portrays the Rosicrucians as an extension of the Elizabethan Renaissance. See also Susanna Åkerman, *Red Cross Over the Baltic: The Spread of Rosicrucianism in Northern Europe* (Leiden: Brill, 1998), and Roger Lefèvre, *L'Humanisme de Descartes* (Paris: P.U.F., 1957), 188–93. See also Christopher McIntosh, *The Rosicrucians: The History, Mythology, and Rituals of an Esoteric Order* (York Beach, Minn.: Samuel Weiser, 1998).

23. We know from Leibniz's notes taken from the *Little Notebook* that Descartes clearly supported at least the scientific work of Rosicrucians, and that he intended to offer his first philosophical work to the savants of the world and especially the Rosicrucians of Germany. Cited in Cole, *Olympian Dream*, 25.

24. Michael H. Keefer, "The Dreamer's Path: Descartes and the Sixteenth Century," *Renaissance Quarterly* 49, no. 1 (Spring, 1996): 45.

25. He asks Beeckman in a letter of April 29, 1619 to check a reference in a text they had read together written by Cornelius Agrippa, a leading Hermetic. AT 10:165; CSM 3:5.

26. Keefer, "Dreamer's Path," 51.

27. On Faulhaber see Kurt Hawlitschek, *Johan Faulhaber, 1580–1635: Eine Blutezeit der mathematischen Wissenschaften in Ulm* (Ulm: Stadtbibliothek Ulm, 1995), and Ivo Schneider, *Johannes Faulhaber 1580–1635: Rechenmeister in einer Zeit des Umbruchs* (Basel: Birkhauser, 1993).

28. Watson, *Cogito*, 98–102.

29. Henricus Cornelius Agrippa, *Henry Cornelius Agrippa his Fourth Book of Occult Philosophy . . . Arbetel of Magick*, trans. Robert Turner (London: Printed by J. C. for John Harrison at the Lamb at the East-end of Pauls, 1655), 213.

30. Hermes Trismeistus [pseud.] *Mercurii Trismegisti Pymander, de potestate et sapientia Dei*, trans. Marsilio Ficino, ed. Jacques Lefèvre d'Étaples and Michael Isengrin (Basel: Mich. Isingrinium, 1532), sig. B4. On this issue see, Keefer, "Dreamer's Path," 57–59.

31. Keefer, "Dreamer's Path," 61.

32. As we saw in chapter 1, this path was delineated by Bacon in his *Novum Organon*. Bacon clearly should be counted among those who followed a Hermetic path. The fascination with such magi during this period is evident in both Marlowe's *Dr. Faustus* and Shakespeare's *The Tempest*.

33. Watson, *Cogito*, 99.

34. There is some evidence that Rosicrucianism played an important role in the formation of Freemasonry.

35. As Watson has pointed out, Descartes clearly practiced the first two of these and probably the fifth as well, signing most of his letters with the initials R.C. While living in Holland, he also met regularly with his friend Cornelius van Hogeland, a self-professed Rosicrucian. *Cogito*, 108.

36. Keefer, "Dreamer's Path," 55.

37. Watson, *Cogito*, 134.
38. Cole points to the significance of this date. "Olympian Dream," 63–86.
39. Baillet refers to three dreams even though by his own account there were only two. In all likelihood his emphasis on three dreams is an attempt to assimilate Descartes to Ignatius Loyola, who also had three dreams that determined the course of his life. Watson, *Cogito*, 134.
40. Ibid., 109–110.
41. Alan Gabbey and Robert Holly, "The Melon and the Dictionary: Reflections on Descartes's Dreams," *Journal of the History of Ideas* 59, no. 4 (1998): 655. Paul Arnold claimed that *Olympica* was allegorical fiction composed in the manner of the Rosicrucians. "Le songe de Descartes," *Cahiers du Sud* 35 (1952): 274–91.
42. Watson has pointed out that these subtitles are very likely Rosicrucian. Traiano Boccolini's *Advertisements from Parnassus* was published with *The Fame of the Order of the Rosy Cross* in 1614, and the prolific Rosicrucian writer Michael Maier speaks of Olympic Houses where brethren might work and dwell in his *Golden Themis. Cogito*, 108. The connection to the scientific houses described in Bacon's New Atlantis is clear, although this work was not published until 1627. It thus could not have been the source of the ideas in the *Little Notebook*. The similarities are probably the result of a mutual indebtedness to Hermeticism.
43. Cited in Cole, *Olympian Dream*, 28.
44. Ibid., 25.
45. He probably derived this notion from Bacon or Pico, as Richard Kennington points out in his "Descartes' 'Olympica,'" *Social Research* 28, no. 2 (Summer, 1961): 184.
46. The evil spirit is clearly linked to Descartes' sins, and therefore sin and not a spirit is the cause of the first dream. Ibid., 177. Descartes is perhaps reflecting here on the problems that arise for both Luther and Calvin in their attempts to explain evil. As omnipotent, God must also be the source of evil. This is the hidden God that Luther argues we must not investigate and that he fruitlessly sought to placate by entering the monastery.
47. And not reasons in the simple sense, as Kennington asserts. Ibid., 180.
48. Ibid., 200.
49. Georg Sebba, *The Dream of Descartes* (Carbondale: Southern Illinois University Press, 1987), 53.
50. Keefer, "The Dreamer's Path," 47. Pyrrhonist skepticism was more radical than Academic skepticism. It was founded by Aenesidemus in the first century B.C.E. and named after the earlier skeptic Pyrrho. It became increasingly important for early modern thought, when the *Outlines of Pyrrhonism* by Sextus Empiricus was published in 1562.
51. Ibid., 45.
52. On the challenge of skepticism for Descartes, see Popkin, *Skepticism*, 178–79. For an alternative account of Descartes' relationship to skepticism, see Gaukroger, *Descartes*, 311–15. On the libertines, see ibid., 135–39; and René Pintard, *Le Libertinage érudit dans la première moitié du XVIIe siècle* (Paris: Boivin, 1943).

53. Gaukroger, *Descartes,* 136.
54. Ibid., 136–37.
55. Descartes to Villebressieu, summer 1631, AT 1:213. This story first appears in Baillet's biography, and some modern historians have questioned its authenticity. Watson argues that Baillet's account is almost certainly based upon a letter that was probably fabricated by Clerselier. *Cogito,* 142. While this may have been the case, it is difficult to deny some of the essentials of the account, and particularly Descartes' rejection of probable reasoning.
56. Watson argues that the link to Bérulle was part of an effort to transform Descartes into an orthodox French Catholic. Bérulle was a totalitarian, "genocidal maniac," whose chief goal in life was the elimination of Protestantism through the extermination of Protestants. Descartes, by contrast, maintained friendly relations with many Protestants throughout his life. This alternative reading of Descartes also helps to explain why France's preeminent philosopher abandoned an increasingly intolerant France to spend most of the rest of his life in the Protestant and republican Netherlands. Watson, *Cogito,* 146–53.
57. Descartes to Mersenne, end of November 1633, February 1634, and April 1634. AT 1:270, 281, 285. See also Gaukroger, *Descartes,* 292. This maxim was the motto of the Rosicrucians. Watson, *Cogito,* 32.
58. AM 1:204.
59. He remarks in the "Olympica" section of the *Little Notebook,* for example, that, "Genesis says that God separated the light from the darkness, meaning that he separated the good angels from the bad. Because it is impossible to separate a positive quality from a privation, this cannot be taken literally. God is pure intelligence." Cole, "Olympian Dream," 29.
60. Descartes to Mersenne, May 27, 1630, AT 1:151.
61. AT 1:70; CSM 3:7.
62. Watson, *Cogito,* 166.
63. AT 6:60; CSM 1:142.
64. Gaukroger, *Descartes,* 304. See also Lefèvre, *L'Humanisme de Descartes,* 187.
65. Watson has suggested that the autobiographical character of the work was a response to Balzac's request for a story of his intellectual development. *Cogito,* 182.
66. David Lachterman, "Descartes and the Philosophy of History," *Independent Journal of Philosophy* 4 (1983): 37, 39. Descartes here rejects the humanist notion that we know ourselves in and through our friends, a position that he certainly knew from Montaigne, if not from Plato and Aristotle. Ibid., 41.
67. Descartes here seems to be moving toward the Baconian notion of an autocratic scientist. Kevin Dunn, "'A Great City is a Great Solitude': Descartes's Urban Pastoral," *Yale French Studies* 80, *Baroque Topographies* (1991): 97. It is useful to remember that the *Discourse* was originally entitled "The Project of a Universal Science Which Can Elevate Our Nature to its Highest Degree of Perfection." Lachterman, "Descartes and the Philosophy of History," 35.
68. The technician will of course be different than the Aristotelian craftsman because his technique will rest on science.

69. Lachterman, "Descartes and the Philosophy of History," 38.
70. AT 10:82; CSM 3:13. This is not to say that it is fictional but that it can only be proposed by means of a fiction for it would otherwise be condemned and prohibited by the authorities.
71. AT 4:486–92; CSM, 3:292–95.
72. AT 6:23–24; CSM 1:122–23.
73. G. W. F. Hegel, *Sämmtliche Werke,* ed. Eva Moldenhauer and Karl Markus Michel, 20 vols. (Frankfurt a. M.: Suhrkamp, 1970), 12:524.
74. Descartes to Mersenne, May 6, 1630, May 27, 1638. AT 1:148, 2:138.
75. For all of his discussion of theology, Descartes says almost nothing about salvation, damnation, or a life after death.
76. *Discourse,* AT 6:61–63; CSM 1:142–43.
77. AT 10:362; CSM 1:10–11.
78. AT 10:359; CSM 1:9.
79. AT 10:368; CSM 1:14.
80. Even for Aristotle, deduction depends upon the knowledge of first principles which are known by intuition (*nous*).
81. AT 10:368–70; CSM 1:15.
82. AT 10:421–27; CSM 1:46–49.
83. AT 10:419–20; CSM 1:44–45.
84. On the role of imagination in Descartes see Jacob Klein, *Greek Mathematical Thought and the Origins of Algebra,* trans. Eva Brann (Cambridge: M.I.T. Press, 1968), 197–211, 293–309; and Dennis Sepper, *Descartes' Imagination: Proportion, Image, and the Activity of Thinking* (Berkeley and Los Angeles: University of California Press, 2004).
85. Burman, AT 5:176–77. On this point see Stanley Rosen, "A Central Ambiguity in Descartes," in *Cartesian Essays: A Collection of Critical Studies,* ed. Bernd Magnus and James B. Wilbur (The Hague: Nijhoff, 1969), 24.
86. AT 10:420; CSM 1:45.
87. Descartes rejects here a science that determines only what is likely. Such a science is not concerned with probability in the modern sense. Our notion of probability as it is understood within mathematical statistics helps us determine degrees of doubtfulness or probability. This idea was unknown in Descartes' time. On the development of the modern notion of probability, see Ian Hacking, *The Emergence of Probability* (Cambridge: Cambridge University Press, 1975) and Lorraine Daston, *Classical Probability in the Enlightenment* (Princeton, N.J.: Princeton University Press, 1995).
88. Dunn, "A Great City," 100–101.
89. Although the *Meditations* presents itself as the inner dialogue of an isolated man, it is really part of a dialogical interaction with some of the most noted thinkers of the time. On the centrality of the *Objections and Replies* to Descartes' thinking, see Jean-Luc Marion, "The Place of the Objections in the Development of Cartesian Metaphysics," in *Descartes and his Contemporaries: Meditations, Objections, and Replies,* ed. Roger Ariew and Marjorie Grene (Chicago: University of Chicago Press, 1995), 7–20.

90. Some scholars believe that this Cartesian claim that everything in the world may be an illusion is meaningless, since if this is the case there is only a nominal difference between illusion and reality. See, for example, O. K. Bousma, "Descartes' Evil Genius," in *Meta-Meditations: Studies in Descartes,* ed. Alexander Sesonske and Noel Fleming (Belmont, Calif.: Wadsworth, 1965). This would only be true, however, if Descartes' God were a consistent deceiver, and there is no evidence that this is the case.

91. On this point see Karlo Oedingen, "Der 'genius malignus et summe potens et callidus' bei Descartes," *Kant-Studien* 50 (1958–59): 178–87; Popkin, *Skepticism,* 178–79.

92. It is true that in the Synopsis Descartes says that one would have to be mad to believe in such things, but this might be an effort to mask his skepticism in order to deflect potential criticism by the church.

93. Descartes to Mersenne, August 14, 1634, June 22, 1637, and October 11, 1638, AT 1:305, 392; 2:380.

94. AT 1:135.

95. AT 1:151.

96. AT 4:110.

97. AT 5:223–24. See also Descartes to Henri More, February 5, 1649 (AT 5:275), and Descartes to Clersellier, April 23, 1649 (AT 5:377, 545). Stephen Nadler argues that Descartes has a more radical notion of divine omnipotence than the nominalists. "Scientific Certainty and the Creation of Eternal Truths: A Problem in Descartes," *Southern Journal of Philosophy* 25, no. 2 (1987): 175–91.

98. AT 1:135–36.

99. Margaret Osler suggests: "In God willing and knowing are a single thing in such a way that by the very fact of willing something he knows it and it is only for this reason that such a thing is true." Thus, any change in divine understanding would entail divine imperfection. "Eternal Truths and the Laws of Nature: The Theological Foundations of Descartes' Philosophy of Nature," *Journal of the History of Ideas* 46, no. 3 (July–Sept. 1985): 352. This interpretation, however, can hardly suffice, since God could, for example, in principle will from and for all eternity that one plus two not equal three on Thursday. Hence, while his will might be unvarying, from the human point of view it could still appear to be contradictory.

100. WA 18:605.32; LW 33:24 (see chap. 4, note 13 for abbreviations).

101. This position, represented by Copernicus and Kepler, was not merely dangerous to religion in Descartes' view but also to physics. See Gérard Simon, "Les vérités éternelles de Descartes, evidences ontologiques," *Studia Cartesiana* 2 (1981): 133.

102. Hiram Caton, *The Origin of Subjectivity* (New Haven: Yale University Press, 1973); Walter Soffer, *From Science to Subjectivity: An Interpretation of Descartes' Meditations* (New York: Greenwood, 1987), 19–40. This notion does seem to confront us with a problem. If a radical materialism is even more likely to lead us into error, why is the supposition of an omnipotent God or an evil genius necessary at all? The answer to this lies in the distinction between the origin of doubt and the solution to doubt. Sheer materialism for Descartes is more likely to lead to deception, but it is in principle remediable through a strict application of the method. An

intentional omnipotence by contrast may be less likely to produce error, but it is also impossible to remedy.

103. AT 6:32; CSM 1:127.

104. AT 7:25; CSM 2:17.

105. AT 7:140-41; CSM 2:100. For the best alternative argument, see Heinrich Scholtz, "Über das Cogito, Ergo Sum," *Kant-Studien* 36, no. 1/2 (1931):126-47.

106. AT 6:33; 8A:8-9; CSM 1:127, 196.

107. AT 7:25; CSM 2:16-17.

108. On this point see Jaakko Hintikka, "Cogito, ergo sum: Inference or Performance?," in *Meta-Meditations,* 50-76.

109. AT 7:145-46; CSM 2:104; cf. *Principles,* AT 9B:9-10, CSM 1:183-84.

110. AT 10:411; CSM 1:39.

111. AT 7:28; CSM 2:19.

112. AT 7:34; CSM 2:24.

113. AT 7:160; CSM 2:133. See also Descartes to Mersenne, May 1637; and to Reneri, April-May 1638; AT 1:366; 2:36. Descartes gives a similar account plus memory in *The Description of the Human Body,* AT 11:224.

114. AT B:17; CSM 1:204.

115. AT 11:342-49; CSM 1:335-39. See also Descartes to Regius, May 1646; AT 3:372.

116. *Meditations,* AT 7:27; CSM 2:18-19.

117. *Replies,* AT 7:188-89; CSM 2:132.

118. Comments on a Certain Broadsheet, AT 8B:363; CSM 1:307.

119. On this point see Peter Schouls, *Descartes and the Enlightenment* (Edinburgh: Edinburgh University Press, 1989), esp. 35-50, and Antony Kenny, "Descartes on the Will," in *Cartesian Studies,* ed. R. J. Butler (New York: Barnes and Noble, 1972), 4. Descartes' identification of thinking as willing recalls the nominalist notion that for God knowing and creating are one and the same thing.

120. AT 3:394; cf. *Principles,* AT 8A:7; CSM 1:195.

121. On this point, see Gerhard Kruger, "Die Herrschaft des philosophischen Selbstbewusstseins," *Logos, Internationale Zeitschrift für Philosophie der Kultur* 22 (1933): 246.

122. On this point, see Simon, "Les vérités éternelles de Descartes," 126-29.

123. See Heidegger, *Nietzsche,* 2 vols. (Pfullingen: Neske, 1961), 2:148-58.

124. My interpretation thus is radically at odds with Sartre's claim that Descartes attributes absolute freedom to God but not to man. *Descartes* (Paris: Trois collines, 1946), 9-52.

125. *Meditations,* AT 7:21-22; CSM 2:14-15.

126. This conclusion is even more explicit in Descartes' unfinished dialogue, *The Search for Truth,* where Eudoxus calms the fears of Epistemon that the path of doubt leads to the skepticism of Socrates and the Pyrrhonists (AT 10:512; CSM 2:408) by demonstrating that because I doubt, that is, think, I am. AT 10:523; CSM 2:417. This is also highly reminiscent of the argument Augustine develops in the *Confessions.*

127. "To be autarchic, one's own commanding source, is both to be a principle oneself, that is, the generative or productive source of all that can be invented by sci-

ence, *and* to be the principle of oneself, that is, to have one's life and work under command. Later, in the *Passions of the Soul,* Descartes will give this autarchy the name 'génerosité'—the key and coping-stone of all the other virtues." Lachterman, "Descartes and the Philosophy of History," 43.

128. *Replies,* AT 7:144; CSM 2:103.

129. *Replies,* AT 7:165; CSM 2:116–17.

130. *Replies,* AT 7:106–7; CSM 2:77, 88. One might note that this is a proof of the existence of perfection and not of God per se.

131. Oedingen, "Der Genius Malignus," 182; Harry G. Frankfurt, *Demons, Dreamers, and Madmen: The Defense of Reason in Descartes' Meditations* (Indianapolis: Bobbs-Merrill, 1970), 172. Thus, according to Descartes, an atheist cannot attain certainty and cannot be a scientist. AT 7:139; CSM 2:99; cf. also *Replies,* AT 7:384; CSM 2:263.

132. On this point I follow Marion's argument in "The Essential Incoherence of Descartes' Conception of Divinity," in *Essays on Descartes' Meditations,* ed. Amélie Rorty (Berkeley and Los Angeles: University of California Press, 1986), 297–338.

133. That said, Anselm does not believe that God is therefore entirely incomprehensible. In fact, he argues that despite his inaccessibility God is the light that makes everything else comprehensible. The connection to the Platonic tradition is palpable.

134. Where Descartes sees God *sub specie infinitatis,* Bonaventure sees him *sub specie divinitatis. Itinerarium mentis in Deum* 3.4. See Koyré, *Descartes und die Scholastik,* 115–17.

135. Jean Marie Beyssade, "Création des vérités éternelles et doubte metaphysique," *Studia Cartesiana* 2 (1981): 93; and Marion, "Essential Incoherence," 303–7.

136. Descartes to Clersellier, 1646, AT 4:445–46; Descartes to Hyperaspistas, August 1641, AT 3:427.

137. *Replies,* AT 7:367–68; CSM 2:253.

138. *Replies,* AT 7:371; CSM 2:256.

139. *Principles,* AT 8A:15; CSM 1:202, Descartes to Chanut, June 6, 1647, AT 5:51. Margaret Wilson suggests the infinite/indefinite distinction may be a ploy since Descartes characterizes the human will as infinite. Margaret Wilson, "Can I Be the Cause of My Idea of the World? (Descartes on the Infinite and the Indefinite)," in *Essays on Descartes' Meditations,* 349–50.

140. *Replies,* AT 7:112; CSM 2:81.

141. *Replies,* AT 7:111–12, 365; CSM 2: 80, 252.

142. The Cartesian understanding of the relation of God and nature is thus the culmination of the mystical identification of the cosmos with the divine that began, as we saw in chapter 1, with Meister Eckhart.

143. Or as Soffer puts it: "Cartesian nature has become de-theologized by means of a divine inscrutability as the personification of Cartesian mechanics." *From Science to Subjectivity,* 155.

144. This reading of Descartes' ontological argument pushes Descartes in the direction of Spinoza, who sees God as unthinking substance, Fichte, who sees God as an

absolute subject, and perhaps even Hegel, who in Neoplatonic fashion sees human self-consciousness as the self-consciousness of the absolute.

145. *Discourse,* AT 6:43–44; CSM 1:132–33.

146. Amos Funkenstein, *Theology and the Scientific Imagination from the Middle Ages to the Seventeenth Century* (Princeton, N.J.: Princeton University Press, 1986), 191–297.

147. See Bernard C. Flynn, "Descartes and the Ontology of Subjectivity," *Man and World* 16 (1983): 13.

148. *Meditations,* AT 7:57; CSM 2:40; see also Descartes to Mersenne, December 25, 1639, AT 2:628. One has to note the date of the letter to begin to have some appreciation for the more than titanic character of Descartes' claim. Gilson, *Liberté chez Descartes et la Théologie,* 25.

149. Koyré, *Descartes und die Scholastik,* 44; Gilson, *Liberté,* 26; Wilson, "Can I Be the Cause," 350. The best counterargument to the interpretation presented here on this point has been developed by Antony Kenny, who claims that for Descartes we are not indifferent in the same sense God is. *Descartes and the Enlightenment,* 90. In opposition to Kenny, see Georges Moyal, "The Unity of Descartes' Conception of Freedom," *International Studies in Philosophy* 19, no. 1(1987): 46.

150. AT 11:445; CSM 1:384.

151. When freedom goes beyond the limits of understanding, it falls into error. *Meditations,* AT 7:56–57; CSM 2:39; *Replies,* AT 7:314–15; CSM 2:218–19; see also Descartes to Hyperaspistas, August 1641, AT 3:432.

152. *Burman,* AT 5:159. Koyré argues that for Descartes we have the capacity to overcome our errors and attain the absolute perfection of God. *Descartes und die Scholastik,* 47, 52.

153. Reuss, "Descartes, the Palatinate, and the Thirty Years War," 129.

154. OP, 3:628. On this point see James V. Schell, "Cartesianism and Political Theory," *The Review of Politics* 24 (1962): 263–64. See also Reuss, "Descartes, the Palatinate, and the Thirty Years War," 119.

155. Voetius attacked Descartes because he saw in Descartes' philosophy a rebirth of the Pelagianism of Arminius. The argument presented here suggests that Voetius in fact did not appreciate how radically Pelagian Descartes actually was. On Voetius and Descartes see Theo Verbeek, *Descartes and the Dutch: Early Reactions to Cartesian Philosophy, 1637–1650* (Carbondale: Southern Illinois Press, 1992); and my essay "Descartes and the Question of Toleration," in *Early Modern Skepticism and the Origins of Toleration,* ed. Alan Levine (Lanham, Md.: Lexington Books, 1999), 103–26.

156. Leibniz and Malebranche rejected the radical omnipotence of Descartes' God and thus did not need to exaggerate human capacities so tremendously. In this respect they established the grounds for the Enlightenment that exalted but did not deify humanity. It was only with the foundering of the Enlightenment on the rocks of Humean skepticism and the Kantian antinomy doctrine that the radical implications of Descartes' thought were resurrected and embodied in the thought of the German Idealists.

CHAPTER SEVEN

1. Thomas Hobbes, *Elements of Law Natural and Political* (New York: Penguin, 1994), 254.
2. *The English Works of Thomas Hobbes of Malmsbury,* ed. William Molesworth, 11 vols. (London: Bohn, 1839–45), 3:95–96 (hereafter cited as EW); A. P. Martinich, *The Two Gods of Leviathan: Thomas Hobbes on Religion and Politics* (Cambridge: Cambridge University Press, 1992), 62. Hobbes asserts that curiosity is the cause of religion. EW 3:94; see also Martinich, *Two Gods,* 51.
3. Hobbes believes this view is represented in Hesiod. *Leviathan,* ed. Edwin Curley (Indianapolis: Hackett, 1994), 473.
4. Humanism came to England through Poliziano rather than Ficino, Pico, or Machiavelli. William Gilbert, *Renaissance and Reformation* (Lawrence: University Press of Kansas, 1998), 169–70.
5. Nicholas Tyacke, *Anti-Calvinists: The Rise of English Arminianism, c. 1590–1640* (Oxford: Clarendon, 1987), 6.
6. Ibid., 7. He was following Richard Hooker.
7. Ibid., 74.
8. Ibid., 77.
9. Ibid., 185–86.
10. Presbyterians saw no biblical warrant for Episcopalianism. Eldon Eisenach, "Hobbes on Church, State, and Religion," in *Thomas Hobbes: Critical Assessments,* ed. Preston King, 4 vols. (New York: Routledge, 1993), 4:302.
11. Noel Malcolm, "A Summary Biography of Hobbes," in *The Cambridge Companion to Hobbes,* ed. Tom Sorell (Cambridge: Cambridge University Press, 1996), 13.
12. John Aubrey, "A Brief Life of Thomas Hobbes, 1588–1679," in *Aubrey's Brief Lives,* ed. Oliver Lawson Dick (London: Secker and Warburg, 1950), 149.
13. Martinich, *Two Gods,* 4; EW 2:xv–xvi. According to Aubrey, Hobbes also had a low view of human nature: "He said that if it were not for the gallows, some men are of so cruel a nature as to take a delight in killing men more than I should to kill a bird. I have heard him inveigh much against the cruelty of Moses for putting so many thousands to the sword for bowing to the golden calf." Aubrey, "A Brief Life," 157. See also Malcolm, "Hobbes," 16.
14. Ibid., 17. Martinich suggests that while Hobbes read Suarez both on metaphysics and politics, his influence was predominately negative. Martinich, *Two Gods,* 379.
15. Miriam M. Reik, *The Golden Lands of Thomas Hobbes* (Detroit: Wayne State University Press, 1977), 27.
16. Cavendish became a baron in 1605 and Earl of Devonshire in 1618.
17. Karl Schuhmann suggests that Hobbes' disgust with the scholastics led him to poetry and history rather than to Renaissance science. "Hobbes and Renaissance Philosophy," in *Hobbes Oggi,* ed. Andrea Napoli (Milan: Angeli, 1990), 332.
18. The Chatsworth library contained over 400 volumes on Hermeticism, including texts by Bruno and Fludd. Ibid., 336, 339. Hobbes also knew Dee's work. Ibid.,

337–38. He found biblical warrant for Hermeticism in the references in Exodus to the Egyptian priests' powers of transmutation. *Leviathan*, 297.

19. This essay, included in *Horae Subsecivae*, is one of three that Reynolds and Saxonhouse have demonstrated were written by Hobbes. *Three Discourses: A Critical Edition of Newly Identified Work of the Young Hobbes*, ed. Noel Reynolds and Arlene Saxonhouse (Chicago: University of Chicago Press, 1995), 71–102.

20. David Wootton, *Paolo Sarpi: Between Renaissance and Enlightenment* (Cambridge: Cambridge University Press, 1983), 3, 134. Hobbes corresponded with Sarpi's assistant Micanzo for years. Martinich, *Hobbes*, 39.

21. William Cavendish and Hobbes also composed essays modeled on those of Bacon. On this point see Arlene Saxonhouse, "The Origins of Hobbes' Pre-Scientific Thought: An Interpretation of the *Horae Subsecivae*," Ph.D. diss., Yale University, 1973.

22. Martinich, *Hobbes*, 66.

23. Noel Reynolds and John Hilton , "Who Wrote Bacon," unpublished essay, 17.

24. This long-withheld edition was published in 1629 as a critique of republicanism and particularly of parliament's extortion of the Petition of Right the year before. Reik, *Golden Lands,* 37. Hobbes criticized those who believed that because they had read Tully and Seneca they were fit to manage the state. Hobbes, *Behemoth or The Long Parliament,* ed. Ferdinand Tönnies, 2d ed. (New York: Barnes and Noble, 1969), 155–56.

25. Aubrey, "A Brief Life,"150.

26. Malcolm, "Hobbes," 21.

27. Ibid., 22.

28. Ibid.

29. Martinich, *Hobbes,* 108.

30. Ibid., 107.

31. Richard Tuck, "Hobbes and Descartes," in *Perspectives on Thomas Hobbes,* ed. G. A. J. Rogers and Alan Ryan (Oxford: Clarendon Press, 1988), 30.

32. Donald Hanson, "The Meaning of 'Demonstration' in Hobbes' Science," *The History of Political Thought* 9 (1990): 587–626. For an alternative view see Douglas Jesseph, "Galileo, Hobbes, and the Book of Nature," *Perspectives on Science* 12, no. 2 (2004): 191–211.

33. Malcolm, "Hobbes," 24.

34. Ibid., 25.

35. Ted Miller and Tracy Strong, "Meanings and Contexts: Mr. Skinner's Hobbes and the English Mode of Political Theory," *Inquiry* 40 (Fall, 1997): 339.

36. Malcolm, "Hobbes," 29.

37. Ibid., 30.

38. Tom Sorell, "Hobbes' Objections and Hobbes' System," in *Descartes and His Contemporaries: Meditations, Objections, and Replies* (Chicago: University of Chicago Press, 1995), 83.

39. Patricia Springborg, "Leviathan and the Problem of Ecclesiastical Authority," in *Thomas Hobbes: Critical Assessments,* 4:145.

40. Richard Tuck, "The 'Christian Atheism' of Thomas Hobbes," in *Atheism from the Reformation to the Enlightenment,* ed. Michael Hunter and David Wootton (Oxford: Clarendon Press, 1992), 112–13.

41. Martinich, *Hobbes,* 256.

42. According to Leopold Damrosch, Hobbes' theology is upsetting not because he parodies the Christian God but because like Milton he brings out the contradictions others leave obscure. Damrosch, "Hobbes as Reformation Theologian: Implications of the Free-Will Controversy," *Journal of the History of Ideas* 30, no. 3 (July-Sept. 1979): 340.

43. Malcolm, "Hobbes," 33.

44. Martinich, *Hobbes,* 195.

45. Bramhall like Erasmus defends human dignity and moral responsibility. On this point see, Damrosch, "Hobbes as Reformation Theologian," 343.

46. Martinich, *Hobbes,* 269.

47. Ibid., 196.

48. Ibid., 197.

49. Ibid., 279. Malcolm, "Hobbes," 35. Wallis had served Cromwell as a cryptographer. Samuel I. Mintz, *The Hunting of Leviathan: Seventeenth-Century Reactions to the Materialism and Moral Philosophy of Thomas Hobbes* (Cambridge: Cambridge University Pres, 1962), 13.

50. Reik, *Golden Lands,* 178, 180. Martinich, *Two Gods,* 354

51. The Royal Academy was predominately Arminian and was considered by some radical Protestants to be crypto-Catholic, or papist. Reik, *Golden Lands,* 184.

52. Malcolm, "Hobbes," 35.

53. Reik, *Golden Lands,* 165.

54. Ibid., 129.

55. Mintz, *Hunting of Leviathan,* 12.

56. Many members of parliament were Arminians opposed to Hobbes' Calvinism. Martinich, *Two Gods,* 37.

57. For Hobbes as for Mersenne all forms of science were forms of ballistics. On this point, see Richard Tuck, "Optics and Sceptics: the Philosophical Foundations of Hobbes' Political Thought," in *Conscience and Casuistry in Early Modern Europe,* ed. Edmund Leites (Cambridge: Cambridge University Press, 1988), 254–56.

58. Thomas Spragens, *The Politics of Motion: The World of Thomas Hobbes* (Lexington: University of Kentucky Press, 1973), 59.

59. Leo Strauss discusses Hobbes most fully in *The Political Philosophy of Hobbes: Its Basis and Its Genesis* (Chicago: University of Chicago Press, 1963). On Strauss's interpretation, see R. Gray, "Hobbes' System and His Early Philosophical Views," in *Thomas Hobbes: Critical Assessments,* 1:273–74. Strauss's interpretation of Hobbes draws upon Kojeve's account of Hegel's conception of the life-and-death struggle. Kojeve himself was deeply impacted in his interpretation of Hegel by Heidegger's emphasis on death as the entry to the question of being. Strauss thus reads Hobbes through Kojeve, Hegel, and Heidegger in a remarkably existential manner.

60. Quentin Skinner, *Reason and Rhetoric in the Philosophy of Hobbes* (Cambridge: Cambridge University Press, 1996), and his "Hobbes and the Renaissance *studia humanitatis*," in *Writing and Political Engagement in Seventeenth-Century England*, ed. Derek Hurst and Richard Strier (Cambridge: Cambridge University Press, 1999), 71. For a more convincing discussion of Hobbes relation to rhetoric see David Johnston, *The Rhetoric of the Leviathan: Thomas Hobbes and the Politics of Cultural Transformation* (Princeton: Princeton University Press, 1986).

61. Skinner, "Hobbes and the Renaissance *studia humanitatis*," 69.

62. Noel Malcolm, "Hobbes' Science of Politics," 153. Focusing on the watch analogy, Tom Sorell argues that natural science puts nature back together while political science constructs it anew. "Hobbes' Science of Politics and his Theory of Science," in *Hobbes Oggi*, 20–21.

63. Reik, *Golden Lands*, 15.

64. Martinich, *Two Gods*, 5. In recent years scholars have begun to recognize that Reformation theology was particularly hospitable to the development of modern science. On this point see Kenneth J. Howell, *God's Two Books: Copernican and Biblical Interpretation in Early Modern Science* (Notre Dame, Ind.: University of Notre Dame Press, 2002); and R. Hooykaas, *Religion and the Rise of Modern Science* (Grand Rapid, Mich.: Eerdmans, 1972). Calvin in particular emphasized the orderliness of God's will, which gave a new religious sanction for the study of nature. Equally important was his assertion that the account of creation in Genesis was thus not necessarily literal. L. S. Koetsier, *Natural Law and Calvinist Political Theory* (Victoria, B.C.: Trafford , 2003), 138–39. Calvin's emphasis on the mediating role of spirit also played an important role. As we saw, Luther put great weight on incarnation as a divine act that Satan could not duplicate. Calvin accepted this notion but emphasized the importance of the spirit in mediating not merely between God and Christ, or even Christ and humanity, but also between humanity and all the rest of God's creation. Luther did not believe that this order of nature was accessible to human reason after the Fall. Calvin, by contrast, was convinced that while Adam's sin had perverted nature, creation was still good and reflected the character of God. Humans thus could come to understand the nature of God by examining his creation. Since the movements of nature are governed by divine providence, humans thus could come to know God's will through an investigation of the natural world. Moreover, such an investigation might aid man in re-sanctifying the world, in preparation for the end of time, which he believed would include a restoration of the garden lost by Adam's sin. On this point, see Susan Schreiner, *In the Theater of His Glory: Nature and Natural Order in the Thought of John Calvin* (Durham, N.C.: Labyrinth Press, 1991), and Jason Foster, "The Ecology of John Calvin," *Reformed Perspectives Magazine* 7, no. 51 (Dec. 18–24, 2005). The natural world was thus pictured no longer as a vale of tears that we might eventually transcend but as a divine gift that can regained by the elect through a process of sanctification. Reformation thought and Calvinism in particular promoted modern science and gave it a theological justification.

65. Joshua Mitchell, "Luther and Hobbes on the Question: Who Was Moses, Who Was Christ?" *Journal of Politics* 53, no. 3 (Aug. 1991): 677–80. Within this general perspective one might also include Carl Schmitt. Schmitt is distinguished, however, by his conviction that liberalism, as we understand it, is not a form of Protestantism but a form of Judaism, indeed is a kind of Jewish conspiracy. On this point see his *Political Theology: Four Chapters on the Concept of Sovereignty*, trans. George Schwab (Cambridge, Mass.: MIT Press, 1985); Miguel Vatter, "Strauss and Schmitt as Readers of Hobbes and Spinoza: On the Relation between Political Theology and Liberalism, *New Centennial Review* 4, no. 3 (2004): 161–214; and Heinrich Meier, *Die Lehre Carl Schmitts: Vier Kapitel zur Unterscheidung Politischer Theologie und Politisher Philosophie*, 2d ed. (Stuttgart: Metzler, 2004).

66. See, for example, Thomas Hobbes, *Thomas White's De Mundo Examined*, trans. Harold Whitmore Hones (London: Bradford University Press, 1976), 393, 405, 416.

67. For Hobbes space is merely an abstraction from body formed in the imagination. Ibid., 40–41.

68. Hobbes to William Cavendish July 29/August 8, 1636 in *Correspondence*, ed. Noel Malcolm, 2 vols. (Oxford: Clarendon Press, 1994), 1:33.

69. *De corpore*, EW 1: 76.

70. Hobbes, *White's De Mundo*, 321.

71. Hobbes develops a negative theology in *Leviathan*, his critique of White, and *De corpore*. Pacchi Arrigo, "Hobbes and the Problem of God," in *Perspectives on Thomas Hobbes*, ed. Rogers and Ryan, 175–77.

72. For Hobbes creation has no beginning in time, since time is merely a phantasm of the mind. *Elements of Law Natural and Political*, 22, 48.

73. *De cive*, 298. Hobbes thought Catholics made God a mere spectator of fortune. Hobbes, *Behemoth*, 42.

74. 'Eternity' in Hobbes' view can only mean 'infinity.'

75. Arrigo, "Hobbes and the Problem of God, " 184. Hobbes rejects the notion that nature precedes God or is distinct from art. Martinich, *Two Gods*, 46. While this might seem to render God irrelevant such a conclusion would be a mistake. While God's will is indifferent in Hobbes' view, that fact does not mean that it is chaotic or unintentional. Nature may have an artificial end and precisely the one spelled out in Scripture. The divine will of nature's artificer is thus not superfluous in Hobbes' cosmos.

76. *De corpore*, EW 1:77, 121.

77. *De corpore*, EW 1:132. Even here, as we will see, they are disguised efficient causes.

78. This position is reminiscent of Bradwardine's assertion that "the divine will is the efficient cause of everything whatsoever." *De causa Dei contra Pelagium* 1.9.190D. See Anneliese Maier, *Metaphysische Hintergründe der spätscholastischen Naturphilosophie* (Rome: Edizioni di storia, 1955), 273–99. Martinich points out that Hobbes' doctrine of causality renders body superfluous. It is not bodies that matter but the accidental motions imparted to them by a capricious divine will.

Martinich, *Hobbes,* 191. Damrosch argues in a related vein that Hobbes' God is a *deus absconditus* with a vengeance. The Reformation in his view stressed God's ever-present power, Hobbes his divine remoteness. "Hobbes as Reformation Theologian," 346.

79. On this point see Tuck, "Hobbes and Descartes," in *Perspectives on Thomas Hobbes,* 13–40; as well as Amos Funkenstein, *Theology and the Scientific Imagination from the Middle Ages to the Seventeenth Century* (Princeton, N.J.: Princeton University Press, 1986), 80–86. As we will see, Hobbes also believes that we are directed toward this science by the insight God gives us.

80. *EW,* 1:17.

81. For Hobbes, theory that cannot be practiced has no value. Martinich, *Hobbes,* 91.

82. Tuck, "Hobbes and Descartes," 30.

83. Ibid., 31.

84. According to Ted Miller, Hobbes believes we reason by true fictions, but the purpose of reasoning is to make the fictions come true. "Thomas Hobbes and the Constraints that Enable the Imitation of God," *Inquiry* 42, no. 2 (June, 1999): 160.

85. Elizabeth Brient has argued that theological voluntarism humbled human epistemological pretension, so that *hypothesis* rather than *theoria* emerged as the appropriate attitude when faced with the mute facticity of nature. "From *Vita Contemplativa* to *Vita Activa:* Modern Instrumentalization of Theory and the Problem of Measurement," *International Journal of Philosophical Studies* 9, no. 1 (2001): 23.

86. Like the natural world, this new one is created by the word. Hobbes, *Leviathan,* 280. Hobbes urges readers to imitate God, but he also suggests we can become more dignified by creating something new. Miller, "Thomas Hobbes and the Constraints," 163.

87. Mersenne, "Ballistica," in *Thomas Hobbes Malmesburiensis opera philosophica quae latine scripsit omnia,* ed. Guliemi Molesworth, 5 vols. (London: Bohn, 1839–45), 5:309. The summary of Hobbes' work in the Meresenne essay was almost certainly composed by Hobbes himself.

88. Ibid., 5:315.

89. EW, 1:91–92.

90. *De Corpore,* EW 1: 91–92.

91. Ibid., 1:1.

92. Ibid., 1:66.

93. Martinich points out that Hobbes is unwilling to subordinate geometry to arithmetic, because he believes knowledge must be reducible to sensation. Thus numbers have no independent reality and are merely names of points. Martinich, *Hobbes,* 284.

94. Hobbes' truths thus take a hypothetical form, but the connections they specify are necessary. Hobbes believes, for example, that, "If x occurs, then y *necessarily* follows." This differs from the claim that the historian makes, which takes the form, "When x occurred, y followed." Obviously, the same event may occur in the future under similar circumstances, but a great deal depends on how similar

the circumstances are. In the preface to his translation of Thucydides, Hobbes wrote that the proper work of history was to instruct and enable men by knowledge of the past to bear themselves prudently in the present and providentially toward the future. EW 8:3. For a thoughtful discussion of Hobbes' notion of history see Robert Kraynak, *History and Modernity in the Thought of Thomas Hobbes* (Ithaca, N.Y.: Cornell University Press, 1990).

95. Hobbes knew there were some exceptions. *Man and Citizen (De Homine and De Cive)*, ed. Bernard Gert (Garden City, N.J.: Anchor Books, 1972), 52.

96. It may be hard to understand how something constantly in motion can have an identity, but Hobbes suggests "that man will be always the same, whose actions and thoughts proceed from the same beginning of motion, namely, that which was in his generation." EW 1:137. This solution, of course, has many problems of its own.

97. *Leviathan,* 41.

98. Hobbes in this regard is often thought to be closer to the Epicureans. While Hobbes certainly drew on Epicurean sources, his doctrine differs in important ways from theirs. The Epicureans were convinced that happiness could only be obtained by avoiding pain, limiting desires, and cultivating *ataraxia,* the absence of passions. In the end this involves accommodating oneself to nature, not, as Hobbes desired, mastering it.

99. It is impossible according to Hobbes to go beyond a syllogism or two without memory. EW 1:38, 48, 79, 95.

100. Unlike ants and bees, "men aim at dominion, superiority, and private wealth, which are distinct in every man, and breed contention." *Elements of Law,* 105.

101. Thus, he apologized in *De cive* for the absence of the preceding sections. *De cive,* 103.

102. Spragens, *The Politics of Motion,* 48, 55.

103. *On Man and Citizen,* 42.

104. Without a physics that demonstrates that all motion is determined by external causes, I might falsely imagine that I freely choose my own path. Spragens, *The Politics of Motion,* 56.

105. *Leviathan,* 498. Scholars have long noted that *De cive* and the *Leviathan* do not adequately explain the relation of the natural and the human and suggest this is an indication of a contradiction or discontinuity in Hobbes' thought. Hobbes himself recognized that these accounts were insufficient, but he attributed this insufficiency to the fact that he had not yet finished his foundational works. *De corpore* was only finished in 1654 and *De homine* in 1658. In the dedicatory letter to *De homine* he remarks that he has now finally fulfilled the promise he made in the *Elements of Law* of grounding his political science in an anthropology.

106. What is missing in the political thought of antiquity for Hobbes "is a true and certain rule of our actions, by which we might know whether that we undertake be just or unjust." *De corpore,* EW 1: 9. Ancient visions of the city may be eloquent or beautiful, but in Hobbes' view they are not valid and therefore not useful. Escher's paintings are delightful and perhaps true of some world, but not of the one we

inhabit. Similarly, Hobbes' construction may be valid for our world, but without a justification of the starting points we cannot know this to be the case. The self-reading of a madman might be consistent but not valid or generalizable.

107. EW 1:8.

108. *Leviathan,* 58. While Hobbes might agree with Machiavelli that most people want to be left alone, he does not agree that it is only a few oppressors that upset the apple cart.

109. The similarity to Luther's argument that we need to pass through despair to find grace is palpable and striking.

110. In the end for Hobbes all sane men will run just as Hector, despite his courage, does in the *Iliad*. Only the suicidally insane will follow the path of Achilles.

111. Hobbes, *Elements of Law,* 87. See also Martinich, *Two Gods,* 80.

112. God thus cannot be relegated to the background in the way Martinich suggests. *Two Gods,* 98.

113. Hobbes in many ways is simply reaffirming the position of James I: "The state of monarchy is the supremest thing upon earth; for kings are not only God's lieutenants upon earth, and sit upon God's throne, but even by God himself are called gods . . . for that they exercise a manner or resemblance of divine power upon earth." King James VI and I, "A Speech to the Lords and Commons of the Parliament at *White-Hall,* on Wednesday The XXI. Of March, Anno 1609," *Political Writings,* ed. Johann Sommerville (Cambridge: Cambridge University Press, 1994), 181. See also A. P. Martinich, *Hobbes: A Biography* (Cambridge: Cambridge University Press, 1999), 15.

114. Building on Kojeve's account of the warrior developed in his Hegel lectures, Strauss argued in his 1936 Hobbes book that the Leviathan is meant to restrain such men. Hobbes' Leviathan, however, could never have restrained such men since their chief characteristic (according to Kojeve and Hegel) is their willingness to die rather than submit. The Leviathan might simply kill them all, but who would do the killing if not other warriors? Hobbes' argument, in contrast to that of Hegel, Kojeve, and Strauss, seems to depend upon the *universal* fear of violent death, the strength of the sovereign in meting it out, and the continuing fear of a terrifying God in fostering obedience when the sovereign is distant or asleep. Although to be fair to the more liberal reading of Hobbes, the continued rule of the sovereign over a long period of time would inevitably routinize human motion in pathways that minimized conflict and fostered cooperation. Indeed, the rules regulating human motion and thus minimizing human collisions could over time become so well established that the visible force of the sovereign and the overarching terror of the omnipotent God could retreat into the background in favor of the rule of law. The operative word here, however, is 'retreat' not 'disappear.' In Hobbes' view even in a settled society with a population habituated to act in self-interested but cooperative ways, the absolute power of the sovereign is essential to peace and prosperity.

115. MacDuff makes this point in *Macbeth* 4.3.50–100.

116. While Hobbes' sovereign must enforce a uniform religious practice, there is much greater space for freedom of conscience or belief. On this question see Joshua Mitchell, "Thomas Hobbes: On Religious Liberty and Sovereignty," in *Religious Liberty in Western Thought,* ed. Noel Reynolds and W. Cole Durham Jr (Atlanta: Scholars Press, 1996). In his political theological reading of Hobbes, Schmitt saw liberty of conscience as the defect that brought the mighty Leviathan down. Carl Schmitt, *The Leviathan in the State Theory of Thomas Hobbes* (London: Greenwood, 1996), 56. See also Vatter, "Strauss and Schmitt," 189–90.

117. Martinich, *Two Gods,* 306.

118. *Leviathan,* 272; see also 464.

119. According to Martinich, the power of God is absent from the primary state of nature and therefore there is no law and no injustice, but they do exist in the secondary state of nature in which the law of God is the law of nature. *Two Gods,* 76.

120. The source of human misery for Hobbes is pride in the biblical sense as the refusal to subordinate oneself to authority. Martinich, *Two Gods,* 74. Like Luther Hobbes sees pride as the principal form of sin. His concern with pride, however, has more to do with relations among human beings than relations with God. As Alan Ryan points out, pride for Hobbes is incurable. Abundance cannot choke it, it demands the abasement of others, and it must therefore be crushed. "Hobbes and Individualism," in *Perspectives on Thomas Hobbes,* 103.

121. *Leviathan,* 275.

122. Thus, while Hobbes favors a Christian commonwealth, it is not inconceivable that he would accept other forms of religious states as legitimate.

123. *Elements of Law,* 97. See also EW 3:346; and Martinich, *Two Gods,* 97. Martinich suggests that for Hobbes the law of nature is both a divine command and deducible from self-preservation. He also suggests that he may have derived this view from Suarez. *Two Gods,* 134.

124. It is thus not the quantity of power but inequality in power that generates an obligation. Martinich, *Two Gods,* 94. This is a voluntarist position similar to that of Ockham.

125. Mitchell points out that while reason can work to preserve us in this life, it cannot help us win eternal life, which depends on Scripture. A full account of sovereignty must thus rely on both. "Luther and Hobbes," 691.

126. Martinich asserts that Hobbes had a strong emotional and intellectual attachment to Calvinism and the Anglican Church. *Two Gods,* 1.

127. Willis Glover, "God and Thomas Hobbes," in *Hobbes Studies,* ed. Keith C. Brown (Cambridge, Mass.: Harvard University Press, 1965), 148. Mintz, *Hunting of Leviathan,* 44. P. Geach, "The Religion of Thomas Hobbes," in *Thomas Hobbes: Critical Assessments,* 4:283.

128. Anecdotal evidence confirms Hobbes' religiosity. See Martinich, *Two Gods,* 24. While there are fideistic elements in Hobbes' thought, he relies more on Scripture than most fideists. See ibid., 347; Glover, "God and Thomas Hobbes," 159; and Tuck, "Christian Atheism," 114.

129. *Leviathan,* 347, 375.
130. See "On the Nicean Creed," an appendix to the Latin edition of the *Leviathan.* See also, Martinich, *Two Gods,* 2; and Eisenach, "Hobbes on Church, State, and Religion," 4:296.
131. *Behemoth,* 63.
132. Springborg, "Hobbes, Heresy, and the *Historia Ecclesiastica,*" *Journal of the History of Ideas* 55, no. 4 (1994): 554, 566.
133. For Hobbes the most frequent pretext for sedition and civil war is contradiction of laws and divine command. This was certainly true in England, where the pious wrongly concluded that it is legitimate to kill another out of religious zeal. *Leviathan,* 397, 493.
134. Hobbes, *White's De Mundo,* 306; *De corpore,* EW 1:10.
135. Spragens, *The Politics of Motion,* 46. See also Eisenach, "Hobbes on Church, State, and Religion," 4:290.
136. Arrigo, "Hobbes and the Problem of God," 172–75. See also Martinich, *Hobbes,* 214.
137. The question of the relationship of his theology and science has long been crucial to the interpretation of Hobbes' thought. We see this reflected in the contrasting interpretations of Hobbes by Leo Strauss and Carl Schmitt. On their agreements and disagreements, see *inter alia* Heinrich Meier's *Carl Schmitt, Leo Strauss und "Der Begriff des Politischens": Zu einem Dialog unter Abwesenden* (Stuttgart: Metzler, 1988); also his *Die Lehre Carl Schmitts;* John McCormick's "Fear, Technology, and the State: Carl Schmitt, Leo Strauss, and the Revival of Hobbes in Weimar and National Socialist Germany," *Political Theory* 22, no. 4 (Nov. 1994): 619–652; and Vatter, "Strauss and Schmitt." Schmitt saw Hobbes as a Christian thinker who was concerned not with philosophy or science but with political theology, that is, with establishing a state that aimed not merely at maintaining or improving life in this world but at realizing man's eternal destiny. Schmitt argued that Hobbes' science and his political science in particular were in the service of this theological vision. Such a Christian state, Schmitt believed, could only be established and maintained in opposition to its theologically determined enemy. This "enemy" in his view was the Antichrist that always hides behind a mask, in this case the mask of the liberal state that claims to be theologically neutral and concerned merely with the preservation and happiness of human beings in this world. This state in Schmitt's view merely concealed the identity of the real enemy of Christianity, Judaism. For Schmitt it was not Hobbes but Spinoza, a Jew, who was the true founder of this neutral liberalism and it was thus Judaism that ruined the best chance modern European humanity had to ground itself politically in Christianity.

 In opposition to Schmitt's anti-Semitic reading of the origins of liberalism (which was also at the heart of his attachment to National Socialism), Strauss tried to show that modern liberalism originated as the result of a turn away from religion to a kind of practical reasoning supported by the new science. The forefather of liberalism in his view was thus not Spinoza but Hobbes (and behind him Machiavelli). (For a contemporary discussion of the relationship of Hobbes and Spinoza on this question that in most respects supports Strauss's position, see Edwin Curley, "Hobbes and the Cause of Religious Toleration," in *A Critical Companion to Hobbes' Leviathan,* ed. Patricia Springborg [Cambridge: Cambridge University Press, 2007].) Strauss thus denied that religion and theology were ultimately important for Hobbes. This denial was in part certainly a reflection of his conviction (derived from Nietzsche and Heidegger) that there was a fundamental divide between religion and philosophy or what he often called Jerusalem and Athens. However, his denial of Hobbes' religiosity may also have been closely connected to his rejection of Schmitt's interpretation, since to admit the importance of religion for Hobbes would have meant giving credence to Schmitt's anti-Semitic critique of contemporary liberalism as a kind of Jewish conspiracy. Strauss may have had his doubts about liberalism, but he certainly did not think that it was a Jewish conspiracy.

Strauss recognized that Hobbes devoted a great deal of attention to religion, but he argued that Hobbes' interpretation of Christianity was an effort to turn his readers away from a scripturally based religion toward a more naturalistic understanding of religion, devoid of miracles and all of the other superstitions that first the Enlightenment and then Nietzsche attacked as the intellectual swindle of Christianity. In Strauss's view Hobbes made an unequivocal choice for science and technology and rejected revelation. Strauss thus saw Hobbes as the forefather of the liberalism that comes to full flower in the Enlightenment. From this point of view, Hobbes' use of Scripture was then merely an attempt to camouflage the atheism that was at the core of this vision of political life. On this point, see Leo Strauss, "The Mutual Influence of Theology and Philosophy," in *Faith and Political Philosophy: The Correspondence of Leo Strauss and Eric Voegelin, 1934–1964,* trans. and ed. Peter Emberly and Barry Cooper (University Park: Pennsylvania University Press, 1993), 230.

Strauss thus saw Hobbes as a progenitor of the Enlightenment, while Schmitt saw him as closer to the conservative nineteenth-century religious critics of the Enlightenment. The argument presented here suggests that the concept of religion that Schmitt and Strauss employ is distinctly different than that of Hobbes and his contemporaries. As a result, neither Schmitt nor Strauss sees how deeply religion and science are intertwined for Hobbes. Hobbes does turn toward nature, as Strauss suggests, but he does not therefore turn away *from* Scripture or Christianity because the nature he turns *to* is not an Epicurean conception of nature devoid of gods but a natural world that is itself a product of divine will. Schmitt appreciated Hobbes' religiosity but interpreted it in such a Manichean manner that he turned Hobbes, the broadly recognized proponent of religious peace, into an agent of religious war.

138. Glover, "God and Thomas Hobbes," 153.
139. While anticipated by Valla and others in some ways, Hobbes was one of the first to employ a historical/critical methodology to determine the authenticity of biblical texts.
140. Martinich, *Two Gods,* 230.

141. Springborg, "Leviathan and the Problem of Ecclesiastical Authority," 136. Hobbes' emphasis on reasonable interpretation favored broad access to Scripture. He criticized Puritans for using obscure language to ensnare people. *White's De Mundo,* 478.

142. See Ockham, I *Sent.* d. 2 q. 10, in *Opera philosophica et theologica,* ed. Stephen Brown (New York: Bonaventure Press, 1967), 355–56.

143. On this point, see Martinich, *Two Gods,* 196.

144. Damrosch, "Hobbes as Reformation Theologian," 345. Martinich notes the nominalist connection: since God is self-sufficient, nothing humans can do benefits him. *Two Gods,* 128.

145. Mintz, *Hunting the Leviathan,* 42. As Ronald Hepburn points out, discourse intended to honor God in Hobbes' view is neither true nor false. "Hobbes on the Knowledge of God," in *Hobbes and Rousseau: A Collection of Critical Essays,* ed. Maurice Cranston and Richard S. Peters (Garden City, N.Y.: Doubleday, 1972), 99.

146. Martinich points out that Hobbes' insistence that God is corporeal has led some to think that he was a pantheist like Spinoza. *Two Gods,* 248. Hobbes does admit that Spinoza spoke more frankly than he did. See Edwin Curley, "'I Durst Not Write So Boldly' or, How to Read Hobbes' Theological-Political Treatise," in *Hobbes e Spinoza: Atti del Convegno Internazionale, Urbino 14–17 ottobre, 1988,* ed. Daniela Bostrengi (Napels: Biblipolis, 1992): 497–593. However, Hobbes cannot be a pantheist because his God who acts and commands is not identical with the world. As Glover points out, Hobbes not only distinguished them but asserted that to identify them was to deny God's existence. "God and Thomas Hobbes," 166. It is often asserted that while Hobbes himself may not have been an atheist, his teaching led to atheism. This argument, however, would seem to apply to most Reformation theologians.

147. Such a claim would, of course, have left Hobbes open to the charge of occultism, which would itself certainly have led to his condemnation and probably to his death. Hobbes believed that the idea of an incorporeal God was not in Scripture but was due to the impact of Platonism on Christianity during the Patristic period. Such Platonism was anathema to Hobbes, who believed it was used by the church to undermine sovereignty.

148. Hobbes probably does not explicitly develop this explanation because it would seem to vitiate his claim that we can only conceive of a cause as the action of one body on another. The deep problem that Hobbes leaves unexplained is how bodies can be both inaccessible to us and yet essential to our conceptualization of causality. This perplexity could be resolved by admitting that bodies are merely imaginary entities, that is, merely arbitrary signs for demarcating and understanding motion.

149. Geach sees Hobbes as a Socinian, but this is unlikely. While Hobbes shared some of their beliefs, he did not share their ardent attachment to free will. "The Religion of Thomas Hobbes," 285–87.

150. It also props up his notion of the sovereign. On the political implications of this reading of the trinity see Joshua Mitchell's thoughtful "Luther and Hobbes," 676–700.

151. Martinich, *Hobbes,* 327. One might believe that this alteration reveals that Hobbes was ultimately not wedded to any doctrine, but it is important to remember than the Latin *Leviathan* was published in 1668, well after the restoration of political and religious authority in England. While Hobbes was willing to argue about controversial issues in 1651 when there was no established authority, he could not do so in 1668 because by his own argument he was required to submit to established authority. For this reason the 1668 edition is also less trustworthy as a source of his true opinions.

152. Timothy Fuller, "Hobbes on Christianity in a Skeptical Individualist World," paper delivered at the American Political Science Association Annual Meeting, Atlanta, September 1999, 20.

153. Strauss claims nature for Hobbes is disorder, but Hobbes himself is more on the side of design. K. C. Brown, "Hobbes' Grounds for Belief in a Deity," in *Thomas Hobbes: Critical Assessments,* 4:46. Damrosch points out that in the *Leviathan* Hobbes emphasizes the unbroken coherence of the causal chain rather than its origin in God. "Hobbes as Reformation Theologian," 339. But, as Brown suggests, Hobbes' argument for a first mover slides over into an argument for design since the mere motion of world cannot create its own matter. "Hobbes' Grounds," 4:44. Joshua Mitchell has made what is perhaps the strongest argument for the importance of God's guidance of history for Hobbes. *Not by Reason Alone: Religion, History, and Identity in Early Modern Political Thought* (Chicago: The University of Chicago Press, 1993), 46–72.

154. Fuller, "Hobbes on Christianity," 13.

155. Springborg, "Leviathan," 138.

156. This was the position of Beza and William Perkins. Martinich, *Two Gods,* 274.

157. EW 3:335. See also Martinich, *Two Gods,* 101. In the debate with Bramhall he asserts that the man predestined for election will examine his life to see if the path he follows is godly, while those who "reason erroneously, saying with themselves, *if I shall be saved, I shall be saved whether I walk uprightly or no:* and consequently there unto, shall behave themselves negligently, and pursue the pleasant way of the sins they are in love with," shall be damned, but good and bad action in this account are the consequence and not the source of salvation and damnation. EW 4:232. See also Reik, *Golden Lands,* 128.

158. In this respect the comparison to Lucretius is merited.

159. Martinich, *Two Gods,* 337, 345.

CHAPTER EIGHT

1. The plight of the large Tory population who fled to Canada and England went largely unnoticed in the popular imagination of European intellectuals.

2. The term 'Enlightenment' was apparently first used in English in 1865 by James Hutchinson Stirling in his *Secret of Hegel* (London: Longmans, 1865), xxvii, attributing deism, atheism, pantheism, and all manner of *isms* to the Enlightenment. Ibid., xxviii. It was, however, only in 1889 that Edward Caird referred to the age of the Enlightenment. *The Critical Philosophy of Kant*, 2 vols. (New York: Macmillan, 1889), 1:69.

3. Milton, *Paradise Lost*, 11.113–15.

4. Addison, *Spectator*, no. 419, July 1, 1712, paragraph 5.

5. Francis Bacon, *The New Organon and Related Writings*, ed. F. H. Anderson (New York: Macmillan, 1960), 5–6.

6. Thomas Hobbes, *Leviathan*, ed. Edwin Curley (Indianapolis: Hackett, 1994), 26 .

7. G. W. F. Hegel, *Sämmtliche Werke*, ed. Eva Moldenhauer and Karl Markus Michel, 20 vols. (Frankfurt a. M.: Suhrkamp, 1970), 12:521.

8. Jean d'Alembert, *Mélanges de Littérature, d'Histoire, et de Philosophie*, 6 vols. (Amsterdam: Zacharie Chatelain et fils, 1759), 4:3.

9. Immanuel Kant, *Was heisst Aufklärung?*, in *Gesammelte Schriften*, ed. Königliche Preussischen Akademie der Wissenschaften (Berlin: Reimer, 1900–),8:3.

10. Ibid., 8:36.

11. Ibid., 8:40.

12. Kant, *Gesammelte Schriften*, 12:257–58. His letter to Marcus Herz, after May 11, 1781, is also illuminating: "Above all the entirety of this sort of knowledge had to be placed before the eye in all of its articulation; otherwise I might have begun with that which I discussed under the title of the antinomy of p[ure] r[eason], which could have occurred in very florid discussions and would have made it a joy for the reader to investigate behind the sources of this conflict." Ibid., 10:252. Kant's footnote in the *Prolegomena* reemphasizes this point: "I wish that the critical reader would concern himself primarily with this antinomy, because nature itself seems to have established it in order to make reason in its most audacious presumptions perplexed and to require of it a self-examination." *Prolegomena zu einer jeden künftigen Metaphysik*, in *Gesammelte Schriften*, 4:341n; see also ibid., 338; *Kant's Reflections* 5015 and 5016, ibid., 18:60–62; and Feist's discussion of Kant's own estimation of the antinomy in Hans Feist, *Der Antinomiegedanke bei Kant und seine Entwicklung in den vorkritischen Schriften* (Borna-Leipzig: Noske, 1932; dissertation, Berlin, 1932), esp. 3–17. In his pre-Critical writing, Kant also uses the word 'labyrinth' in place of 'antinomy.' See Norbert Hinske, "Kants Begriff der Antinomie und die Etappen seiner Ausarbeitung," *Kant Studien* 56 (1965): 486. Kant does not begin, as is often claimed, with the epistemological problem of the Transcendental Aesthetic. For a comprehensive examination of the origins of Kant's thought that points to the importance of the antinomy, see Immanuel Kant, *Kants Prolegomena*, ed. Benno Erdmann (Leipzig: L. Voss, 1878). This point has often been reiterated; see Carl Siegel, "Kants Antinomielehre im Lichte der Inaugural Dissertation," *Kant Studien* 30 (1925); Hinske, "Kants Begriff der Antinomie"; and Heinz Heimsoeth, "Zum Kosmotheologischen Ursprung der Kantischen Freiheitsantinomie," *Kant Studien* 57 (1966), and his *Atom, Seele,*

Monad (Wiesbaden: Steiner, 1960). The problem that Hume posed for Kant was not epistemological: "Hume, whose *Enquiry* had strongly affected Kant, in the eighth chapter ('Liberty and Necessity') brings forth, with all 'skeptical' reservations, a radical determinism and indeed one-sidedly in favor of the causality according to natural necessity." Heimsoeth, "Kosmotheologischen," 218. Kant's consideration of the antinomy is a critique of the concepts of the whole or cosmos as a critique of the mathematical conception of the whole qua world and the dynamic conception of the whole qua nature. Immanuel Kant, *Kritik der reinen Vernunft*, ed. R. Schmidt (Hamburg: Meiner, 1956), A418/B446. In the Third Antinomy Kant considers the possibility of the dynamic or causal structure or synthesis of the whole.

13. Ibid., A410/B437–A411/B438.

14. There were a number of traditional ways that Cicero had enumerated in which this might be achieved. Cicero points to ten different means of resolving antinomies. *De inventione* 2.49.145–47. Kant neglects these solutions and pursues a dialectical path. On this point see my "Philosophy and Rhetoric in Kant's Third Antinomy," *Political Science Reviewer* 30 (2001): 7–33.

15. For an extended discussion of Kant's reception and critique in the next generation of German thinkers, see Frederick C. Beiser, *The Fate of Reason: German Philosophy from Kant to Fichte* (Cambridge, Mass.: Harvard University Press, 1987).

16. On this register their thought thus seems to be philosophic rather than theological, as Strauss and others argue. Or to put it in other words, their thought is not theological in the way scholastic and Reformation thought was. At a different level, however, their understanding of nature was itself fundamentally theological in the broader sense we discussed above.

17. On this point see my "Descartes and the Question of Toleration," in *Early Modern Skepticism and the Origins of Toleration*, ed. Alan Levine (Lanthan, Md.: Rowman and Littlefield, 1999).

18. Richard Tuck, "Hobbes and Descartes," in *Perspectives on Thomas Hobbes,* ed. G. A. J. Rogers and Alan Ryan (Oxford: Clarendon Press, 1988), 15–30.

19. The manner of presentation on both sides of this debate was shaped in some measure by the interlocutors' sense of the external audiences of the work. Descartes, whose position on human freedom was akin to that of the Arminians, had to walk a careful line between his Catholic audience in France and his Calvinist audience in Holland. Hobbes, whose position on freedom placed him nearer the Calvinists and in opposition to the Catholics and the Arminians, was in an even more difficult position since he was living in exile in Catholic France, among the Arminians and Catholics of the court, and with royalist sympathies that put him at odds with the confessionally similar Calvinists in England.

20. Descartes almost certainly was relieved to avoid an explicit debate about his claim that God was a deceiver since it put him most seriously at odds with the Catholic Church.

21. AT 7:57; CSM 2:40 (for abbreviations, see chap. 1, n. 58).

22. *Replies,* AT 7:367–68; CSM 2:253.

23. Indeed, as we have seen, even Hobbes had already ceased to consider theology a part of science.

24. In 1896 George Jacob Holyoake asserted: "Secularism is a code of duty pertaining to this life, founded on considerations purely human, and intended mainly for those who find theology indefinite or inadequate, unreliable or unbelievable." *English Secularism: A Confession of Belief* (Chicago: Open Court, 1896), 60.

25. On this point see Alexander Koyré, *From Closed World to Infinite Universe* (Baltimore: Johns Hopkins University Press, 1957).

26. This notion of secularization has been repeatedly defended. See, for example, Peter Berger, *The Sacred Canopy* (Garden City, N.Y.: Doubleday, 1967); Brian R. Wilson, *Religion and Secular Society* (London: Watts, 1966); David Martin, *A General Theory of Secularization* (Oxford: Blackwell, 1978); and Steve Bruce, *God Is Dead: Secularization in the West* (Oxford: Blackwell, 2002).

27. This was the conclusion of A. P. Martinich, who is as sensitive to the importance of religion in Hobbes as anyone. *The Two Gods of Leviathan: Thomas Hobbes on Religion and Politics* (Cambridge: Cambridge University Press, 1992), 337–48.

28. This issue is at the heart of the debate about the nature of secularization between Karl Löwith and Hans Blumenberg. In his *Reason in History* (Chicago: University of Chicago Press, 1949), Löwith portrays the modern world as an essentially Christian project that attempts to realize the millennium through secular means Blumenberg, by contrast, argues that while many elements in modernity appear to have Christian roots, these similarities are only formal, the result of modernity "reoccupying" abandoned Christian positions. Modernity in his view is not the result of an attempt to attain Christian ends by non-Christian means but the consequence of a new attitude of "self-assertion." In part their differing assessments arise from their different conceptions of the nature and extent of modernity. Löwith sees modernity culminating in the chiliastic projects of totalitarianism, while Blumenberg sees the essence of modernity in the Enlightenment. The argument presented in the preceding chapters is sympathetic to Blumenberg's formulation of the nominalist crisis of the late Middle Ages but sees the continued importance of theological elements in modernity as more than merely formal. In that respect, it shares Löwith's concern that the theological radicalism that played such an important role in the Wars of Religion was not expurgated by the modern turn toward nature and remains a hidden, and at times not so hidden, danger for the modern world. On this point, see also Eric Voegelin, *The New Science of Politics* (Chicago: University of Chicago Press, 1952). In contrast to Blumenberg, Voegelin sees modernity not as the solution to the Gnostic impulse but as the embodiment of it. He argues that it is crucial to distinguish this Gnostic impulse, which is responsible for the horrors of modernity, from authentic Christianity which can still serve as at least part of a solution. Löwith, by contrast, is convinced that no Christian solution is possible and thus believes the problems of modernity can only be solved by a return to a non-Christian natural law theory like that of Stoicism.

29. This has a number of pernicious consequences, as I have shown in my *Nihilism Before Nietzsche* (Chicago: University of Chicago Press, 1995).

30. Alexander Pope, *Essay on Man*, 2.1. On this point see, Ernst Cassirer, *The Philosophy of the Enlightenment*, trans. Fritz Koelln and James Pettegrove (Princeton: Princeton University Press, 1951), 5.

31. Patrick Riley, *The General Will Before Rousseau* (Princeton: Princeton University Press, 1986).

32. There is no naturalistic fallacy for those who see a divine will behind nature, and even as this will fades into obscurity the patina of divine goodness remains. This is nowhere so evident as in the modern environmental movement that moves from an anthropocentric and utilitarian justification to a pantheistic account of the independent value of the natural world.

33. Cassirer, *Philosophy of Enlightenment*, 134.

34. This secular Pelagianism, of course, does not realize or remember its own origins. Modernity, at least in its Cartesian form, imagines that it creates itself. It was as a result of such claims that Blumenberg was misled into imagining that modernity is grounded by its own self-assertion or autonomy rather than in its Christian inheritance. It is true that many moderns believe this to be the case, but what we have tried to show in the foregoing argument is that such a belief is only conceivable as the result of a long development within Christianity.

35. For an account of what this can mean, see Michael Oakeshott, *Rationalism and Politics and Other Essays* (Indianapolis: Liberty Press, 1991), 5–42.

36. On this point see also Denis Diderot, *Jack the Fatalist and His Master*, trans. Wesley D. Camp (New York: Peter Lang, 1984).

37. For a broad and comprehensive account of the importance of the fear of conspiracy throughout the French Revolution, see François Furet, *Penser la Révolution française* (Paris: Gallimard, 1978); Lynne Hunt, *Politics, Culture and Class in the French Revolution* (Berkeley and Los Angeles: University of California Press, 1984); Marisa Linton, *Conspiracy in the French Revolution* (Manchester: Manchester University Press, 2007).

38. The Baroness de Staël, *Considerations on the Principal Events of the French Revolution*, 3 vols. (London: Baldwin, Cradock, and Joy, 1818), 1:122. . Rousseau believed that all moral action was in harmony with the general will, but he understood that there was a great deal of human action that was neither moral nor immoral. His Jacobin successors became convinced that all action that was not in harmony with the general will was immoral. This is an extension of Rousseau's argument that he himself would certainly have rejected.

39. On this point see Albert Camus, *The Rebel: An Essay on Man in Revolt*, trans. Anthony Bower (New York, Random House, 1956), 112–32. There were, of course, a multitude of such examples during the Wars of Religion. However, it is important to distinguish between those who imagined themselves to be inspired by God or to be acting as his agents on earth, and those who imagine themselves to be divine or to possess divine capacities.

40. For a more extensive discussion of these matters, see my *Nihilism Before Nietzsche* and *Hegel, Heidegger, and the Ground of History,* and "The Search for Immediacy and the Problem of the Political in Existentialism and Phenomenology," in *The Blackwell Companion to Existentialism and Phenomenology,* ed. Hubert Dreyfus and Mark Wrathall (Oxford: Blackwell, 2006). I will discuss these matters only briefly here.

41. Nietzsche recognized this development of science as such a metaphysical transformation: "The faith in the dignity and uniqueness of man, in his irreplaceability in the great chain of being, is a thing of the past—he has become an *animal,* literally and without reservation or qualification, he who was, according to his old faith, almost God ('child of God,' 'God-man')." Friedrich Nietzsche, *Kritische Gesamtausgabe,* ed. Giorgio Colli und Mazzino Montinari (Berlin: de Gruyter, 1967–), VI 2:242.

42. Obviously, a defense of this claim would require a great deal more by way of argument and justification than can be given here. In lieu of such an argument, let me give just one example. Natural scientific accounts face the difficulty Kant points to in the third antinomy, since explanations that rely on an infinite series of causes violate the principle of sufficient reason, that is, they admit there is no ultimate cause and therefore no ultimate explanation. We find such an account satisfying only because we imagine that somehow this series will end or be complete, when in fact it simply disappears in the mists of time. In an effort to ameliorate this problem, contemporary cosmology pursues a theory of origins with its notion of an initial spectacular explosion or Big Bang. While this account is plausible (and explains much of the available data) as far as it goes, it cannot go far enough, because it cannot explain the reason for the "Bang" itself. Drawing on quantum theory, cosmologists have attempted to account for this primal event as a "quantum anomaly." While the possibility of such an anomaly is consistent with quantum theory, its explanatory force is essentially equivalent to the claim that "things happen" or that "miracles occur." The shadow of transcendental freedom (to use Kant's term) or God's incomprehensible power (to use the terminology of Christianity) thus shrouds all such accounts of beginnings. The continuing impact of such theological and metaphysical assumptions, however, remains concealed from science itself.

43. The extent of the dependence of this notion of prior determination on the notion of predestination becomes clear when one compares the modern account of the unfolding of events in time to that of nominalism or, as I will discuss briefly below, occasionalist theories in Islamic thought. In its cosmology, for example, modern science relies upon the connection of a series of secondary causes but denies the primary cause that makes such a connection not only possible but necessary. That there is such a connection and thus a unity or identity to the series is simply an assumption, but an assumption that is so deeply buried that we have forgotten its theological origin.

44. *Republic* 546a.

45. History in this way came in many people's mind to replace philosophy as an account of the whole. In the following discussion, I only consider those efforts to use

history to give a comprehensive account of the whole. There are obviously many other forms of historiography.

46. Thus even neo-Hegelians such as Benedeto Croce began with the assumption that his philosophy of nature was untenable. *What is Living and what is Dead of the Philosophy of Hegel,* trans. Douglas Ainslie (London: Macmillan, 1915). On the turn away from Hegel, see Karl Löwith, *From Hegel to Nietzsche: The Revolution in Nineteenth Century Thought* (New York: Columbia University Press, 1991); and Terry Pinkard, *German Philosophy, 1760–1860: The Legacy of Idealism* (Cambridge: Cambridge University Press, 2002).

47. This nightmarish vision of globalization is rooted in post-structuralism, which is itself deeply enmeshed in the concealed theology of modernity. Building on Saussure, structuralists such as Lévi-Strauss, Althusser, and Lacan argued that culture, economic life, and the psyche have to be understood on a linguistic model as self-contained social systems. Rejecting both functionalist explanations that focused on ends and purposes and causal explanations that looked at individual desire and choice, they focused instead on the structures, practices, and orders of social life. This approach left no room for individual freedom. In contrast to Sartre's emphasis on human freedom, they emphasized the ways in which social, cultural, and economic structures reproduced themselves by habituating human beings into social roles. Their work in this sense was antihumanist. They also abandoned the notion of historical development. Whereas earlier Marxists had imagined the evolving structures of socio-economic life to be the result of a universal historical process, structuralists imagined that each culture was particular and autonomous.

The successor generation of post-structuralists moved in a more radical direction. They rejected universalism, rationalism, the Enlightenment, and all grand narratives whether they promoted progress, the nation, the people, or the working class. In their view these notions were part and parcel of Western imperialism that sought to dominate and subordinate less developed cultures of the world by bringing them within the circuit of global capitalism. Derrida, Foucault, Deleuze, Lyotard, Baudrillard, Badiou, Žižek, and others decried Eurocentrism, logocentrism, phallocentrism, and all forms of liberal authority as essentially totalitarian structures of control. In opposition to the domination of Western culture and global capital, they promoted the cultures of the Third World and the marginalized subcultures within the First World.

Insofar as human beings are decisively shaped by linguistic and social structures, however, it was difficult for them to find reason to advocate political change. Post-structuralism thus seemed to end in quietism. This stance, however, was deeply at odds with their commitment to justice. In pursuit of a remedy to this contradiction, they turned to political theology.

From the beginning, structuralism had recognized that there must be something that transcended mere structures since it was not possible for such structures to have produced themselves. Whatever this transcendent element was, in their view it resisted symbolization and thus could not be captured or represented in language. Building on Heidegger's notion of the radical alterity of Being, and the work of Levinas and Benjamin, this transcendent element was conceived as the Real (Lacan), the Impossible (Derrida), and the Sublime (Žižek), to take only three examples. Post-structuralists in this way found their way back to something like the Christian or Jewish notion of transcendence, back to a hidden God. This hidden God was the basis for their political theology, which draws heavily on Carl Schmitt and is essentially Gnostic.

Within the symbolic realm of language and social structures, everything is determined by its difference from something else. The transcendent itself, however, is not subject to contradiction and division. As Lacan argued, it is not differentiated, or, as Derrida put it, it is infinite justice. It is "knowable," however, only by means of revelation. Humans cannot discover, intuit, or deduce it, but only wait on its arrival. In this way, almost all post-structuralists accept Heidegger's claim that only a "god" can save us. It is their task to find the magical word that can conjure up this "god." Thus Lacan hoped that his texts would give the reader a mystical experience that would open up a way to experience of the transcendent. Žižek similarly hopes that his work will call the sublime forth into the symbolic realm and thus provide the basis for a transformation of the existing totalitarian social order. The Gnostic impulse at work here is clear.

Whenever the transcendent appears within the symbolic realm, however, it is subject to the laws of binary opposition that govern this realm. In this context, Schmitt's notion of the necessity of opposition and the role of the enemy is crucial. For Žižek, for example, a new leader who will be able to transform the existing order can only come to be in opposition to a new "Jew" (or the structural equivalent) who remains the inimical other that must be repressed. The political theology of post-structuralism in this way becomes not merely Gnostic but Manichean. In this way the current opposition of liberalism and postmodernism recapitulates the opposition of Pelagianism and Manicheanism that we saw first in Erasmus and Luther and that has remained salient at the heart of modernity. For a brief introduction to the development of post-structuralism, see Mark Lilla, "The Politics of Jacques Derrida," *The New York Review of Books*, June 25, 1998, 36–41. For a more extensive account see François Dosse, *History of Structuralism*, trans. Deborah Glassman, 2 vols. (Minneapolis: University of Minnesota Press, 1997). See also Claudia Breger, "The Leader's Two Bodies: Slavoj Žižek's Postmodern Political Theology," *Diacritics* 31, no. 1 (2001): 73–90.

48. Matthew Arnold, "Dover Beach."

EPILOGUE

1. On Ghazali, see Ebrahim Moosa, *Ghazali and the Poetics of Imagination (Islamic Civilization and Muslim Networks)* (Chapel Hill: University of North Carolina Press, 2005).

2. The Mu'tazilite view was defended most prominently by perhaps the best-known and most influential member of this school, Averroes (Ibn Rushd, 1126–98). His

greatest work, *The Incoherence of the Incoherence*, was a defense of Aristotelianism against Ghazali's attack in his *Incoherence of the Philosophers*. For a general introduction to Islamic philosophy see *The History of Islamic Philosophy*, ed. Seyyed Hossein Nasr and Oliver Leaman (New York: Routledge, 1996).

3. There is some speculation that Ghazali directly or indirectly may have had an impact on Ockham's thought. It is certain that he had an impact on later nominalist thinkers. It is obvious that the debate between the realists and the nominalist parallels the debate between the Mu'tazilites and the Ash'arites. The impact of Mu'talzilite thought on scholastic realism is indisputable. It would not be surprising if nominalist thought was similarly indebted to earlier Islamic thinking. For a brief but excellent introduction to this question see Charles Burnett, "Islamic Philosophy: Transmission into Western Europe," in *Routledge Encyclopedia of Philosophy*, ed. E. Craig (London: Routledge, 1998), 21–25.

4. On the similarities of philosophical and theological problems faced by Christianity and Islam, see Harry Wolfson, *The Philosophy of Kalam* (Cambridge, Mass.: Harvard University Press, 1976).

5. I do not mean to assert that there is no possibility for the development of humanism within Islam. For a fuller discussion of the way humanism develops in the Islamic world, see Lenn E. Goodman, *Islamic Humanism* (New York: Oxford University Press, 2003). My goal here is rather to briefly highlight the theological/metaphysical differences between Christianity and Islam to help us understand the power of the ideas behind *radical* Islam, to allow us a greater purchase on our own concealed theological commitments, and to enable us to begin to discern the kinship between Islam and Christianity. I also hope that this comparison will highlight the theological elements that underpin, empower, and at times divinize Western humanism.

6. For a generally sympathetic account of Qutb, see Roxanne Euben, *The Enemy in the Mirror: Islamic Fundamentalism and the Limits of Modern Rationalism* (Princeton: Princeton University Press, 1999). On Mawdudi, see Seyyed Vali Reza Nasr, *Mawdudi and the Making of Islamic Revivalism* (New York: Oxford University Press, 1996).

INDEX

Abelard, Peter, 22, 26, 321n40
Academics, 140–41, 146, 148, 151, 265
accidents, 229
Adam, Charles, 175, 194, 303n58
Adams, Marilyn McCord, 299n5, 300n7,
  300n11, 300n16, 300n22
Addison, Joseph, 257
Adorno, Theodor, 9
Adrian VI, 97
afterlife, Hobbes on, 42, 248, 252–53, 272
Agrippa, Henricus Cornelius, 175, 176, 181,
  333n25, 333n29
Ailly, Peter d', 27, 103, 174
Åkerman, Susanna, 333n22
Albigensians, 102
alchemy, Descartes and, 174, 175, 182
Alexander the Great, 296n4
Alexander VI, 88, 96
Alfarabi, 291
Allen, M. M., 319n102, 326n23
Allen, Michael J. B., 315n41
Allen, P. S., 319n102, 326n23
Althusser, Louis, 359n47
American Revolution, 256, 353n1
Anabaptists, 111, 112, 139, 172, 321n37
'ancient', 3, 4. See also antiquity
Anderson, F. H., 297n13, 302n40, 354n5
Andreas of Newcastle, 174
Anglicanism, 213, 220, 247, 254, 349n126
Annibaldo, Cardinal, 50
Anselm of Canterbury, 113, 143; Descartes
  and, 174, 201, 202, 339n133
anthropology, 270. See also Hobbes,
  Thomas: anthropology of

antinomians, 139, 147
antinomies: Cicero on, 355n14; of Kant, 7,
  17, 43, 259–61, 262, 263, 276–77, 278, 284,
  340n156, 354n12, 358n42
antiquity: Bacon on, 37; church fathers
  and, 14, 298n28; cyclical view of time
  in, 3, 5, 280; Erasmus and, 98, 99,
  165–66; freedom as concept in, 139–41,
  146; Hobbes and, 214, 225; humanism
  and, 4, 5–6, 31, 32, 72–73, 75, 168, 227,
  297n10; Justinian's antipagan initiative and, 82; Luther and, 120; medieval
  Christian view of, 3, 296n4; modernity
  and, 3, 4, 5, 8–9, 227; Petrarch and, 4,
  30–31, 48–49, 51, 53–57, 66, 70–71, 75–76,
  88, 304n11, 306nn49–50, 306nn55–56,
  306nn60–62, 308n91; quarrel of
  ancients and moderns, 5–7, 256
apodictic knowledge: Descartes and, 40,
  183, 192, 194, 195, 201, 222, 231, 257, 267;
  Hobbes and, 232, 257, 269; Hume and,
  256; skeptical humanism and, 88; Stoics
  and, 140. See also Descartes: certainty
  and; Descartes' new science
Apuleius, 82
Aquinas, Thomas: Descartes and, 174;
  on divine and human will, 27, 143;
  Enlightenment reason and, 258; four-
  teenth- and fifteenth-century critics of,
  15; on nature of God, 133; ontological
  argument and, 201; skepticism and,
  317n64; Suarez as defender of, 30; on
  universals, 20. See also Thomism
Arendt, Hannah, 8–9

Arians, 87, 133, 134, 148, 250, 316n47
Ariew, Roger, 336n89
Aristophanes, 3, 296n2
Aristotelianism: Descartes' attack on, 190; Franciscans' opposition to, 25; in Hobbes' education, 214; humanist rejection of scholasticism and, 77; Islamic, 290, 360n2; Luther and, 119, 125, 126; of Marcello Virgilio, 89; Ockham's distrust of, 24; Petrarch on, 66; scholastic synthesis and, 21, 50, 133, 299n4; Valla's opposition to, 79
Aristotle: on causality, 229–30; Descartes and, 174, 182, 184, 186–87, 188, 335n68; Erasmus's God and, 160; Hobbes and, 217, 224, 228; on intuition of first principles, 336n80; Luther's ontology and, 321n40; Petrarch on, 53, 305n42; Pico on, 86; on political nature of man, 44–45; on practical vs. theoretical knowledge, 186–87; rediscovery of, 20, 21, 57; universals and, 4, 20; on voluntary and involuntary actions, 140; White on atomism and, 219; on wonder as source of knowledge, 209
Arminianism, 211–13; Descartes and, 253, 332n16, 340n155, 355n19; Erasmus and, 139, 211, 212, 217; Hobbes and, 217, 219, 220, 251–52, 254, 343n51, 343n56
Arminius, Jacobus, 211
Arnauld, Antoine, 195, 278
Arnold, Matthew, 360n48
Arnold, Paul, 334n41
Arnoldi, Bartholomaeus, 103, 107
Arrigo, Pacchi, 345n71, 345n75, 350n136
arts: concepts of the modern and, 4, 5–6, 297nn8–9; humanism and, 31, 32, 79–80, 81
Asclepius, 82
Ash'arites, 290, 291, 361n3
Athanasius, 83
atheism: Descartes' doubt and, 196; fideism and, 114; Hobbes and, 220, 221, 227–28, 247, 351n137, 352n146; humanism and, 72; Luther's debate with Erasmus and, 151, 152; materialism and, 36, 302n39; modernity and, xii; of Paolo Sarpi, 215;

post-Enlightenment thought and, 280; in Rome of Luther's visit, 106
atomism, 36, 219, 228–29
Aubrey, John, 214, 215, 216, 221, 224, 341nn12–13, 342n25
Auden, W. H., 295n2
Augustijn, Cornelis, 328n58, 330n133
Augustine: Against the Academics, 141, 146; city of God and, 45; Descartes and, 174, 265, 338n126; Enlightenment and, 257; Erasmus and, 97, 150, 151, 164; evil and, 114, 142, 159; Ficino and, 84; freedom of the will and, 114, 133, 137, 142–43, 146–47; Gnosticism and, 156; grace and, 116, 127, 143, 150, 164; humanism and, 57, 75, 77, 87, 88, 308n85; Luther and, 113, 119, 127, 151, 152–53, 154, 155, 159; Manicheanism and, 84, 142, 315n37; modern society and, 308n79; nominalism and, 57, 75; Pelagianism and, 28, 84, 142; Petrarch and, 47, 48, 56–59, 67, 76, 307n77, 308nn85–86, 308n88, 308n90, 309n101, 309n104, 310n138; Platonism of, 80, 141, 315n40; Plotinus and, 84, 141, 315n40; Salutati and, 77; scholastic realists and, 20; self-consciousness and, 198; Seneca and, 141; Trinity and, 133
Augustinians: on authority, 314n26; Luther in monastery of, 104, 105, 143; Petrarch and, 74–75, 314n25
Ausonius, 180
autonomy, 6, 7
Autrecourt, Nicholas d', 27, 131
Averroës, 21, 77, 360n2
Averroism: at Bologna, 313n17; Christian suspicion of Islam and, 21, 77; Condemnation of 1277 and, 299n4; Petrarch's attack on, 50; Pico and, 85; scholastic theology and, 133; Valla's opposition to, 79
Avicenna, 21, 291
Avignon: Eckhart at, 35; papacy at, 1, 30, 50; Petrarch at, 35, 43, 47, 74; three thinkers crossing paths in, 1, 35, 43; William of Ockham in, 22, 26, 30, 35, 43

Bacon, Francis, 37–39; on causality, 229, 232; Descartes and, 181, 184, 263,

334n45, 335n67; Enlightenment and,
257; Hermeticism and, 83, 210, 333n32,
334n42; Hobbes and, 215–16, 221, 223,
229, 234, 235, 263, 342n21; modernity
and, 5, 8, 19; nature and, 37, 38–39, 40,
262; *New Atlantis*, 39, 210, 215, 334n42;
Petrarch and, 311n145
Baillet, Adrien, 170, 175, 178, 334n39, 335n55
Bainton, Roland H., 126, 321n28, 324n115
Balzac, Jean-Louis Guez de, 183, 335n65
Baron, Hans, 73–74, 297n11, 306n49,
306n56, 309n97, 313n12
Basil, 78
Bates, B. W., 297n12
Battle of the Books. *See* quarrel of ancients
and moderns
Baudrillard, Jean, 359n47
Becker, Marvin, 313n19
becoming, 35–37
Beeckman, Isaac, 170, 171, 174–75, 176, 177,
178, 183, 223, 332nn19–20, 333n25
being: Averroism and, 50; Heidegger on,
13, 16, 360n47; Luther's ontology and,
113, 127, 321n40; metaphysics and, 16;
modernity and, 4, 14, 18, 19; Plato and,
36. *See also* individualism, ontological
Beiser, Frederick C., 355n15
Bentley, Richard, 6
Berger, Peter, 356n26
Berlin Wall, fall of, ix, 9–10, 285
Berman, Marshall, 298n19
Bernard of Clairvaux, 110, 115, 143, 321n40
Bernhard of Chartres, 3–4
Bérulle, Pierre de, 182–83, 335n56
Bessarion, John, 81, 82
Beyssade, Jean Marie, 339n135
Beza, Theodore, 211, 353n156
Biel, Gabriel, 27; Descartes and, 174;
devotio moderna and, 318n78, 320n16;
Erasmus and, 328n61; human freedom
and, 103; Luther and, 105, 113, 131, 144,
327n35; Pelagianism and, 28, 143
Bielfeldt, Dennis, 323n86
Bin Laden, Osama, 293
Biondo, Flavio, 78–79, 297n10
Bizer, Ernst, 322n69
Black Death: impact on lifespan, 301n28;
nominalist vision and, 15, 29; Petrarch's

loss of friends in, 46, 47–48; resurgent
Islam and, 315n39
Blumenberg, Hans, xi, 11–12, 156, 226,
296n6, 298n25, 299n6, 300n15, 300n17,
300n19, 302n34, 329n88, 356n28, 357n34
Boccaccio, Giovanni, 94, 102, 301n30,
304n23, 311n1
Boccolini, Traiano, 334n42
Boehner, Philotheus, 300n14
Boethius, 20
Boileau, Nicholas, 5
Bonaventure, 27, 143, 174, 203, 314n25,
339n134
Bostrengi, Daniela, 352n146
Bousma, O. K., 337n90
Bouwsma, William J., 307n78, 308n79,
308n85, 308n90, 311n169, 314n26
Boyle, Marjorie O'Rourke, 303n8, 326n24,
327n45, 327nn47–48, 328n68, 328n71,
328n73, 329n74, 329n86
Braaten, Carl E., 323n86
Bracciolini, Francesco, 73, 74
Bradwardine, Thomas, 27, 116, 131, 345n78
Bramhall, John, 220, 221, 228, 247, 343n45,
353n157
Braun, G., 328n66
Brecht, Martin, 319n87, 325n6, 326n14,
326nn19–20
Breger, Claudia, 360n47
Brethren of the Common Life, 93, 94,
102, 103
Brient, Elizabeth, 346n85
Brown, Keith C., 349n127, 353n153
Brown, Stephen, 299n6, 352n142
Bruce, Steve, 356n26
Bruni, Leonardo, 73, 78–79, 297n10
Bruno, Giordano, 83, 175, 179, 181, 317n63,
341n18
Burckhardt, Jacob, 72, 297n14, 313n12
Buridan, John, 27
Burnet, Thomas, 6
Burnett, Charles, 361n3
Burroughs, Charles, 331n154
Busson, Henri, 320n1
Butler, R. J., 338n119

Caesar, Julius: Hobbes and, 215; Petrarch
and, 53, 54, 65, 306nn55–56

Caird, Edward, 354n2
Cajetan, 109
Calvin, John: bourgeois revolution and, 111; development of Reformation and, 172; on divine election, 209; on God of nominalists, 25; incarnation and, 321n41; modern science and, 344n64; Neoplatonism in thought of, 127
Calvinism: Descartes and, 181, 253; English, 211, 212; of Hobbes' background, 213, 220, 228, 349n126; Hobbes' belief in, 208, 209–10, 216, 220, 247, 251–52, 254, 273, 355n19; Hobbes' science and, 225
Camus, Albert, 357n39
capitalism, 286, 359n47. See also globalization
Carneades, 148, 162
Cartesianism: humanism and, 5–6, 256, 312n4. See also dualism, Cartesian
Cassiodorus, 2
Cassirer, Ernst, 74, 303n7, 305n27, 307n77, 309n102, 312n4, 314n24, 317n63, 357n30, 357n33
Cathars, 25, 102
Catholic Church: Hobbes on, 252–53; in Luther's time, 102–3, 130–31; secularization and, 271. See also corruption in the church
Cato, 75, 78
Caton, Hiram, 194, 337n102
causality: Aristotle on, 229–30; Ash'arite view of, 290; divine attributes transferred to, 273; Enlightenment view of, 276; Hobbes' anthropology and, 235, 268; Hobbes' physics and, 229–30, 231–32, 233, 234, 345nn77–78, 352n148; Hobbes' theology and, 216, 220, 225, 249, 250–51, 254, 273, 275, 353n153; Hume on, 256, 355n11; Kant on, 259, 260, 355n11; Luther/Erasmus debate and, 262; in modern science, 280, 358nn42–43
Cavanaugh, William, 325n2
Cavendish, Charles, 217, 219, 220
Cavendish, William, 214, 216, 217, 341n16, 342n21
Cellarius, Christophus, 4–5, 297n10
Chaldean Oracles, 82
Chandoux, 182

change: modernity and, 36–37, 298n18; Petrarch on, 49, 305n35. See also progress
Chanut, 178
Charles I of England, 212, 213, 219
Charles II of England, 213, 219, 221
Charles IV (emperor), 49
Charles V (emperor), 95, 111
Charlet, Etienne, 174, 332n8
Charron, Pierre, 174, 181, 217
Christiana, Queen, 206
Christian humanism, 32, 73–79; English, 210; of Erasmus, 74, 95–97, 139, 163, 167, 319n87; Islam and, 292; Luther's rejection of, 131–32; of Machiavelli, 91; modernity and, 226–27; Reformation and, 32, 132–35
Christianity: early doctrinal consolidation in, 19–20; evangelical, xi, 71, 138, 139, 302n37; fundamentalist, 293; metaphysical/theological crisis in, 14; modernity and, 11–12, 14, 226–27, 357n34; primitivist movements in, 25, 102; secularization and, 11, 272, 356n28; seventeenth-century science and, 227. See also Catholic Church; incarnation; Protestantism
Chrysippus, 141
Cicero: Augustine and, 56, 142; on Cataline conspiracy, 277; Descartes and, 178; Erasmus and, 99, 166; Hobbes' approach to history and, 216; human freedom and, 146, 327n44; humanism and, 32, 77, 78; Luther and, 104, 166; Machiavelli and, 90; Petrarch and, 47, 48, 53, 55, 62, 66, 67, 68, 70, 76, 304n10, 305n42, 306n49, 310n138, 313n9; on resolving antinomies, 355n14; skepticism and, 88; on the will, 141
city of God, 45
civic republicanism, 73–74, 77, 214, 225. See also republicanism
Clark, David, 300n18
clash of civilizations, 10
classicism. See antiquity
Clement of Alexandria, 83
Clement VII, 96
Clersellier, 337n97, 339n136

Clifton, Gervase, 216
cogito ergo sum, 40, 189, 196–97, 200–201, 233
Cohn, Norman, 296n5
Cold War, ix, 8, 10
Cole, John R., 178, 331n1, 331n6, 332n8, 332nn19–20, 333n23, 334n38, 334nn43–44, 335n59
Coleridge, Samuel Taylor, 135
Colet, John, 93, 94, 95, 210
Coligny, Gaspard II de, 130
Colli, Giorgio, 298nn26–27, 358n41
Colonna family, 47, 48, 304n19
Columbus, Christopher, 5
Condemnation of 1277, 21, 79, 134, 299n4
Cooper, Barry, 351n137
Copernican Revolution, 167
Copernicus, Nicolaus, xi, 5, 83, 337n101
Corpus hermeticum, 82, 83
corruption in the church, 102–3; Boccacio on, 102; Christian humanism and, 132, 227; Enlightenment secularization and, 271; Erasmus and, 96, 135; hierarchy and, 131; Hobbes on, 214, 247, 252–53; Luther and, 33, 106, 131, 135; Machiavelli and, 90; Petrarch on, 49–50, 75, 102, 304n23; Savonarola and, 88. *See also* indulgences
cosmology, contemporary, 358nn42–43
Council of Ferrara, 80–81
Council of Nicea, 20, 133
Council of Trent, 172
Counter-reformation: Aristotelianism of, 188, 190; beginning of, 172; Erasmus's project and, 167; Hermeticism and, 179; Hobbes and, 208; Sorbonne and, 181
Courtenay, William, 299n5
Cowper, Samuel, 220
Craig, E., 361n3
Cranston, Maurice, 352n145
creationism, xii
Croce, Benedeto, 359n46
Crombie, A. C., 302n34
Cromwell, Oliver, 130, 213, 219, 343n49
Crusades, 15, 21, 29, 45, 69, 315n39
cunning of reason, 273, 282, 284
Curley, Edwin, 303n59, 341n3, 351n137, 352n146, 354n6

d'Alembert, Jean, 258, 275, 354n8
D'Amico, John F., 314n29, 315n31, 317n64
Damrosch, Leopold, 343n42, 343n45, 345n78, 352n144, 353n153
Daniel: prophecy in, 3, 296n3. *See also* four empire theory
Dante: city of God and, 45; infinite God of, 15; *moderno* used by, 3; Petrarch and, 46, 47, 52, 56, 69, 303n8; Socrates in limbo of, 78
Dantine, Wilhelm, 114, 157
dark age, Petrarch on, 4, 79
Daston, Lorraine, 336n87
death of God, xi, 13, 227, 272, 273, 274. *See also* secularization
Debus, Allen, 316n46
deduction: Aristotle on, 336n80; Descartes on, 191. *See also* logic
Dee, John, 210, 341n18
De Grazia, Sebastian, 90, 317nn68–70, 318nn71–73, 318n76
deism, 182, 271
Deleuze, Gilles, 9, 359n47
democracy, 8–9, 39, 286, 298n21
Derrida, Jacques, 9, 359n47
Descartes, René, 170–206; Beeckman and, 170, 171, 174–75, 176, 177, 178, 183, 223, 332n20, 333n25; Bérulle and, 182–83, 335n56; certainty and, 40, 190–91, 192, 194, 199, 200–201, 202, 336n87, 339n131 (*see also* apodictic knowledge); on clear and distinct ideas, 182, 183, 201, 202, 203; *cogito* of, 40, 189, 196–97, 200–201, 233; *Dioptrics*, 218, 264; *Discourse on Method*, 176, 179, 181, 184–89, 192–93, 196, 200, 218, 246, 253, 264, 265, 335n67; dream of, 177–78, 179–81, 185, 192, 205, 334n39, 334n46; early life and education, 173–75, 177, 185, 332nn8–9; Enlightenment and, 257, 258; expropriation of world by, 200; on fear of the Lord, 170–71, 205; fears about reception of his ideas, 183, 188, 336n70, 355n20; Hermeticism and, 83, 171, 174, 175, 177, 178, 179, 180–81, 185, 206, 333n25, 334n42; heterodox theology of, 183, 184, 202, 335n59; Hobbes and, 194, 217, 222–23, 254; Hobbes' debate with, 42, 218, 220, 221,

Descartes, René (*continued*)
228, 261, 264–70, 276, 355nn19–20; *Little Notebook*, 176, 178–80, 183, 185, 194, 204, 334n42, 335n59; mathematics and (*see* mathematics in Descartes' thought); *Meditations*, 177, 193–95, 196–97, 202, 336n89 (*see also* Hobbes, Thomas: Descartes' debate with); modernity and, xi, 5, 8, 17, 19, 39, 40–41, 42, 262–63, 273–74; ontological argument of, 201–5, 339n130, 339n144; *Passions of the Soul*, 222, 223, 338n127; Petrarch compared to, 177, 185, 187, 309n99; religion's role and, 271–72; religious beliefs of, 174, 332n16; religious conflicts of the time and, 173, 174, 175, 177, 186, 332n17; Rosicrucianism and, 175–76, 177, 179, 180–81, 182, 183, 185, 333n23, 333n35, 334nn41–42, 335n57; *Rules for the Regulation of the Mind*, 179, 183, 190–91, 197; on sense-perception, 217, 263, 265; skepticism and, 182, 184, 192, 193–96, 200, 265, 337n92, 338n126; on the will, 40–41, 171, 197–98, 199–200, 204, 205, 267, 338n119, 338n127, 339n139; *The World*, 184. *See also* Cartesianism; dualism, Cartesian
Descartes' new science: beginnings of, 170, 176–77, 179, 181, 185; certainty and, 190–92; existing political order and, 253; fundamental principle of, 189; Hobbes compared to, 222, 263–64; mastery of nature and, 40–41, 204–5, 206; method of doubt and, 193–94, 200; nominalism and, 40–41, 171, 183–84, 190
determinism: Hume on, 355n11; idea of history and, 285; Luther and, 145–46; modernity's deep divide and, 17; of nominalists, 29. *See also* freedom; necessity
deus absconditus (hidden God): Descartes and, 171, 204; Erasmus's response on, 165; Heidegger and, 272, 273; Hobbes and, 248, 345n78; Luther and, 114, 115, 127, 156–59; post-structuralism and, 360n47; Protestantism and, 226, 227
devil (Satan): Erasmus and, 148; Hobbes and, 250; Milton on, 329n95; Staupitz on, 106, 116

devil, in Luther's theology, 106, 115, 122, 126–27; church corruption and, 109, 110, 131; debate with Erasmus and, 151, 155, 156, 159, 163, 165; end of days and, 112; Scripture and, 117, 118; the will and, 119–20, 144, 146, 154–55
devotio moderna, 93, 94, 95, 97, 99, 318n78, 320n16
Dick, Oliver Lawson, 341n12
Dickens, A. G., 325n5
dictatores, 71–72
Diderot, Denis, 275, 276, 357n36
Diet of Worms, 110
dignity, human, 71, 77, 78, 84, 85, 164, 315n31
Dillenberger, John, 320n3, 322n59, 322nn61–62, 322n66, 322n70, 323n75, 323n78, 323nn80–82, 323n88
Dionysii, Sugurus Abbas S., 296n1
divine right of kings, 211, 213
Dominici, Giovanni, 77
Donation of Constantine, 79, 110
Dorey, T. A., 330n142
Dosse, François, 360n47
Dostoevsky, Fyodor, 330n131
Dreyfus, Hubert, 358n40
Dryden, John, 6
dualism, Cartesian, 191, 263; Hobbes' attack on, 218, 249, 265, 266
dualism, Platonic, 308n91
Dunn, Kevin, 335n67, 336n88
Dupré, Louis, 301n23
Dürer, Albrecht, 81, 82, 136
Durham, W. Cole, Jr., 349n116

Ebeling, Gerhard, 322n53, 324n95
Eck, Johann, 109, 127, 144
Eckhart, Meister, 35–36, 43, 81, 249, 302n38, 339n142
Eco, Umberto, 299n1, 316n46
Edict of Nantes, 172, 173
Edward VI, 211
Eisenach, Eldon, 226, 341n10, 350n130, 350n135
Elea del Medigo, 85
Eliade, Mircea, 296n2
Elizabeth, Princess, 188, 206
Elizabeth I, 211
Emberly, Peter, 351n137

Emerson, Ralph Waldo, 278
end of days: Erasmus and, 151; Hobbes
    and, 251; Luther and, 110, 112, 122, 124,
    328n66; Michelangelo's Last Judg-
    ment and, 168–69; Müntzer and, 112;
    twelfth-century vision of, 4. *See also*
    eschatology
end of history, 10, 298n21
Engels, Friedrich, 283, 298n19
English Civil War, 173, 213, 219, 221, 222,
    224, 243–44, 245, 253, 350n133
English Reformation, 210–13
Enlightenment: antinomy at end of, 263,
    270; Blumenberg on modernity and,
    356n28; concept of, 257–59, 354n2;
    Descartes and, 189, 340n156; Hobbes
    and, 351n137; idea of history and, 285;
    inferior position of religion and, xi,
    10; post-structuralism and, 359n47;
    problem of modernity and, 42; radical
    Hegelians and, 283; Romantic reaction
    against, 278–79; secularization and,
    271; transfer of divine attributes in,
    274–78
Epicureanism: freedom and, 140, 141,
    146; Hobbes and, 347n98, 351n137;
    humanism seen as, 72–73; Luther's
    debate with Erasmus and, 151, 152, 163;
    nominalism and, 36; Petrarch and, 62,
    63, 64–65, 66, 67, 310n143; Valla and,
    315n33
Episcopalianism, 211, 213, 341n10
Erasmus, 94–100; Arminianism and, 139,
    211, 212, 217; Christian humanism
    and, 74, 95–97, 139, 163, 167, 319n87;
    Education of a Christian Prince, 95, 167,
    306n62; *On the Freedom of the Will*, 138;
    on heresy, 148, 149, 327n49; long-term
    success of, 139; Luther's impact on
    hopes of, 97; Luther's scriptural inter-
    pretations and, 119; Neoplatonism and,
    88, 97, 98, 147, 150–51; Nicholas of Cusa
    and, 93; pacifism of, 95, 97, 319n91; pes-
    simism about humanist project, 167–68;
    Petrarch's influence on, 94, 97, 306n62;
    quasi-divine status of humans and, 292;
    rhetoric and, 96, 98, 319n88; salvation
    and, 96, 150, 319n103

Erasmus's debate with Luther, 34, 128,
    134–39; background of, 146–47, 327n45;
    Calvinists' struggle with Arminians
    and, 211; Descartes and, 199; Erasmus's
    diatribe in, 147–51, 162, 164, 327nn47–
    48; Erasmus's response to Luther,
    161–67; Hobbes/Bramhall debate and,
    220; Hobbes/Descartes debate and, 42,
    270; Kant's third antinomy and, 261–62,
    276; Luther's response in, 151–61; skepti-
    cism and, 153, 196; tone of, 326n22
Erastianism, 246–47, 252
Erdmann, Benno, 354n12
Erigena, John Scotus, 174
Erikson, Erik, 126
eschatology: city of God and, 45; Luther
    and, 110; in medieval Christianity, 3, 4,
    296n4. *See also* end of days
Espinas, Alfred, 194
Euben, Roxanne, 361n6
Eucharist. *See* transubstantiation
Euclid, influence on Hobbes, 216, 224–25,
    233
evangelical Christianity, xi, 71, 138, 139,
    302n37
Evans, Peter B., 331n4
evil: Augustine and, 114, 142, 159;
    Descartes' dreams and, 180, 334n46;
    divine omnipotence and, 114; Erasmus
    on, 150; Hobbes and, 236–37, 243–44,
    245, 246, 252, 254; Karlstadt on, 150;
    Luther on, 114–15, 120, 122, 144; Luther's
    debate with Erasmus and, 152, 156, 159,
    163, 165; Machiavelli on, 91; Maniche-
    anism and, 99, 142, 315n37; nominalist
    God and, 274; predestination and, 29;
    Reformation antihumanism and,
    34; Staupitz and, 116. *See also* devil
    (Satan)

Facientibus principle, 28, 105, 143–44,
    327n35
faith: Augustine on, 141, 152, 196; Descartes
    and, 199; *devotio moderna* and, 93;
    Enlightenment impasse and, 276;
    Erasmus and, 96; Hobbes on, 248, 249;
    modern, 270; Reformation and, 227;
    secularization and, 272

faith, in Luther's theology, 109, 111, 116–19, 120–21, 125, 144, 322n63, 322n70, 323n86; debate with Erasmus and, 152, 153, 158, 159–60; nominalism and, 33, 106–8, 113, 127, 131

Fall: free will and, 142, 144, 149, 150, 159; Hobbes and, 244; humanism and, 64, 70, 71, 76, 78, 104; Islam and, 290; Luther vs. Calvin on, 344n64; modern idea of progress and, 281; Poverty Dispute and, 26. See also original sin

Fascism, 9, 279, 283

Faulhaber, Johannes, 175, 333n27

Feist, Hans, 354n12

Ferdinand II, 172, 175, 185

Fichte, Johann Gottlieb, 39, 278, 339n144

Ficino, Marsilio, 74, 81–82, 83–85, 316n45, 316n49, 316n51, 316nn54–55; Erasmus and, 99, 150, 163; Luther and, 325n120; Machiavelli and, 89, 91; Mersenne's attack on, 181; Pico and, 85, 86; Rosicrucians and, 175

fideism, 114, 181, 220, 349n128

Fisher, John, 326n19

Fleming, Noel, 337n90

Fludd, Robert, 175, 181, 210, 341n18

Flynn, Bernard C., 319n94, 340n147

Fontenelle, Bernard, 5

fortune: Descartes' God as, 204; diminished role of religion and, 271; Hobbesian universe and, 225, 251, 345n73; humanist idea of, 31–32, 87, 281; Machiavelli and, 92; Petrarch on, 48, 51, 54, 55, 76, 305n35

Foster, Jason, 344n64

Foster, Kenelm, 303n6, 304n10, 304n25, 305n26, 305n31, 305n43, 306n50, 306n55, 306n58, 307nn67–68, 307n70, 307n74, 307n77, 308nn80–81, 308n86, 308nn88–89, 308nn91–93, 309nn95–97, 309n103, 309n115, 311n166, 314n24

four empire theory, 3, 79. See also Daniel

Foxe, John, 325n1

Francis, St., 25, 26, 27, 50, 51

Franciscan order: Augustine and, 57; conflict with papacy, 25–27, 47, 102, 300nn21–22; killing of heretics and, 130; nominalism and, 27; Petrarch's rela-

tions with, 50–51, 305n32; as primitivist movement, 25

Frankfurt, Harry G., 339n131

Fraticelli, 25, 102

Frederick V, Elector of the Palatinate, 173, 175, 176, 212

Fredrick the Wise, Elector of Saxony, 110, 136

freedom: in antiquity, 139–41, 146; Cold War and, ix; Descartes and, 17, 171, 263, 355n19; Enlightenment and, 258–59, 277; Erasmus on, 99, 261; French Revolution and, 281; globalization and, ix, 285, 286; Hegel on, 282, 283; Hobbes on, 17, 236, 355n19; Islamic theology and, 291; Kant on, 7, 259, 260–61, 277; Luther/Erasmus debate and, 262; Luther on, 111, 114, 119, 123, 326n19; Marx and Engels on, 298n19; modern idea of history and, 284, 285; modernity and, xi, 2, 5, 7, 8, 42, 277, 293; modern metaphysics and, 262; new antimodernists and, x; Nietzsche on, 13; nominalism and, 24, 28, 29, 103; of omnipotent God, 21, 22–25, 26, 27–28; Petrarch on, 49, 304n19; Pico on, 85–86; radical Hegelians and, 283; Romantics and idealists on, 7, 278–79; science and, 279–80; structuralism and, 359n47

free will: Arminianism and, 211; Augustine on, 114, 133, 137, 142–43, 146–47; Descartes and, 200, 205, 234, 268–69, 338n124, 340n151; early church and, 142; Enlightenment and, 276; Ficino and, 84; Hobbes' denial of, 41–42, 220–21, 235, 236, 252, 268, 352n149; humanism and, 31, 34, 71, 137–38; Luther on, 144–46, 327n39; nominalism and, 108; Pico on, 86; post-Enlightenment thinkers and, 278; Reformation theology and, 34; Salutati and, 77; Valla on, 80; in Western thought, 139–44. See also determinism; Erasmus's debate with Luther; freedom; will, human

French Revolution, 7, 43, 255, 260, 277–78, 281, 283

Freud, Sigmund: on Descartes, 177–78; on Luther, 126; secularization and, 271

Friedman, Thomas L., 295n1
Fukuyama, Francis, 298n21
Fuller, Timothy, 353n152, 353n154
Funkenstein, Amos, xii, 225, 296n6,
    298n23, 300n9, 301n33, 302n34, 302n48,
    314n23, 315n34, 340n146, 346n79
Furet, François, 357n37

Gabbey, Alan, 334n41
Galileo: critique of modern project and,
    8; Descartes and, 174, 181, 184, 194, 263;
    Hermeticism and, 83; Hobbes and,
    217–18, 224, 263; origin of modernity
    and, xi, 19; science of motion, 39,
    314n23; on sense-perception, 217
Garrod, H. W., 319n102
Gassendi, Pierre, 217, 219, 268
Gaukroger, Stephen, 331n5, 331n7, 332n14,
    332n17, 334n52, 335nn53–54, 335n57,
    335n64
Geach, P., 349n127, 352n149
Gemistus Pletho, George, 81, 82
general will, 273, 275, 277, 357n38
Gerrish, B. A., 327n39, 328n62, 330n133
Gerson, Jean, 27, 174
Gert, Bernard, 347n95
Ghazali, Abu Hamid al-, 290, 291, 292, 293,
    360nn1–2, 361n3
Gibieuf, Guillaume, 182–83
Gilbert, Neal W., 326n30, 326n33
Gilbert, William, 341n4
Gillespie, Michael Allen, 298n20, 299n5,
    340n155, 355n13, 355n17, 357n29, 358n40
Gilson, Etienne, 11, 72–73, 194, 298n22,
    313n10, 332nn10–11, 340nn148–49
globalization, ix, xi, 10, 43, 285–87, 295n1,
    359n47
Gloclenius, Rudolph, 332n11
Glover, Willis, 349nn127–28, 351n138,
    352n146
Gnosticism: Blumenberg on, 11, 156,
    300n19, 356n28; Ficino and, 85; free will
    and, 142; Manicheanism and, 315n37;
    post-structuralists and, 360n47; Voege-
    lin on, 356n28
God: Blumenberg on modernity and, 11,
    12; of Descartes, 171, 268, 269, 273, 275;
    Descartes' ontological argument and,

201–5, 339n130, 339n144; Eckhart's view
    of, 35; of Enlightenment, 275; Hobbes
    on, 209, 230–31, 248–52, 254, 268,
    352nn144–47; as human construct, 272;
    Italian humanists and, 71; Luther's un-
    derstanding of, 114–16, 321n45, 321n47,
    322n53; nominalist, 15, 24–25, 29, 274,
    300nn8–11, 300n17. See also death of
    God; deus absconditus; Holy Spirit;
    omnipotence, divine; pantheism; Trin-
    ity; will, divine
God, man, and nature: Descartes vs.
    Hobbes on, 39–42, 265–66; Enlighten-
    ment and, 42, 274–75; Hegel's recon-
    ciliation of, 282; Hobbes' priority of
    nature, 17, 248, 249, 262n63, 271, 355–16;
    humanism vs. Reformation and, 16–17,
    34–35, 261–62; Kant's antinomy and, 7,
    17, 43, 262; Luther on, 127, 128; medieval
    disintegration and, 45; modernity and,
    xi, xii, 14, 17, 35, 39–40, 42–43, 262, 270,
    273–74; nominalist revolution and, 16.
    See also metaphysica specialis
Goddu, André, 300n9
Godman, Peter, 317nn65–67
Goethe, Johann Wolfgang von, 278, 279
Goldblatt, David, 295n1
Goodman, Lenn E., 361n5
Gordon, G., 296n2
"Gothic," 3, 297n8
Gottschalk, 116
Gouhier, Henri, 178, 194
grace: Augustine on, 116, 127, 143, 150, 164;
    church's position on, 108; Erasmus
    on, 149, 150–51, 163–64, 167, 328n59,
    328n67; Ficino on nature as, 85, 150,
    328n67; Gregory of Rimini and, 301n26;
    Hobbes' debate with Bramhall and,
    220; Karlstadt on, 150; nominalism and,
    24, 28, 105; original sin and, 64; Pela-
    gianism and, 56, 143, 150, 301n25
grace, in Luther's theology: Christ and,
    120–21; church and, 124–25, 131; debate
    with Erasmus and, 152, 153, 155, 163;
    distinguished from his predecessors,
    116–17; humanism and, 136; indul-
    gences and, 109; love and, 325n120;
    nominalism and, 131; Paul and, 127–28;

grace, in Luther's theology (*continued*)
Scripture and, 106, 107; the will and,
144, 150, 161
Grant, Edward, 299n4
Gray, R., 343n59
Great Schism, 15, 29
Gregory of Rimini, 103, 131, 301n26
Gregory the Great, 301n29
Gregory XIII, 130
Grene, Marjorie, 336n89
Groote, Gerard, 93
Grotius, Hugo, 217
Guicciardini, Francesco, 73, 90, 301n30

Hacking, Ian, 336n87
Hakewill, George, 297n11
Hancock, Ralph, 298n20
Hankins, James, 313n12, 315n38
Hannibal, Petrarch on, 53, 54, 55, 90
Hanson, Donald, 217, 342n32
Harvey, William, 220
Hawlitschek, Kurt, 333n27
Hegel, G. W. F.: Descartes and, 189, 190,
339n144; on Enlightenment, 258; on
history, 281–82, 284, 285; modernity
and, 6, 10, 39; philosophy of nature, 282,
283, 359n46; postmodernists and, 9;
Strauss's interpretation of Hobbes and,
343n59, 348n114
Heidegger, Martin, 338n123; on Descartes,
190; on fundamental questions, 12–13;
on God's withdrawal, 272, 273; on
metaphysics, 16; pessimism about
modernity, 8, 285; post-structuralism
and, 360n47; Strauss's interpretation of
Hobbes and, 343n59, 351n137
Heimsoeth, Heinz, 302n34, 302n38,
354n12
Held, David, 295n1
Hellenistic thought: freedom in, 140;
institutionalized Christianity and, 19
Henry IV, 172, 173, 174
Henry of Ghent, 22, 143
Henry VII, 210
Henry VIII, 95, 97, 137, 172, 210–11
Hepburn, Ronald, 352n145
Heraclitus, 49
Herder, Johann Gottfried von, 6, 281

Hermes Trimegistus, 82
Hermeticism, 82–83, 85, 316nn45–46;
Bacon and, 83, 210, 333n32, 334n42;
Descartes and, 83, 171, 174, 175, 177, 178,
179, 180–81, 185, 206, 333n25, 334n42;
English humanists and, 210; Hobbes
and, 214, 341n18; libertines and, 182; of
Rosicrucians, 175–76
Hertling, Georg Freiherr von, 332n11,
332n14
Herz, Marcus, 354n12
Hesiod, 296n3, 341n3
hidden God. See *deus absconditus*
Hilton, John, 215, 342n23
Hinske, Norbert, 354n12
Hintikka, Jaakko, 338n108
historicism, 278
history: divine attributes transferred to,
273; modern conceptions of, 281–85,
358n45; structuralism and, 359n47;
tripartite division of, 79
Hobbes, Thomas, 207–54; achievement
of, 254; anthropology of, 222, 223, 228,
234–38, 239, 263, 266, 347n96; *Behemoth*,
221–22; *De cive*, 218–19, 220, 224, 238,
242, 247, 347n101, 347n105; *De corpore*,
201, 231, 345n71, 347n105; *De homine*,
347n105; Descartes and, 194, 217, 222–23,
254; Descartes' debate with, 42, 218, 220,
221, 228, 261, 264–70, 276, 355nn19–20;
Elements of Law, 218–19, 238, 347n105;
Enlightenment and, 257; epistemology
of, 233; on establishment of religion,
243–47, 349n122; fear and, 207–9, 231,
235, 237, 238, 239–40, 241, 348n114;
historical background of, 210–13;
Leviathan (see *Leviathan*); life of, 207,
213–22; low opinion of human nature,
341n13; mathematics and, 216, 219, 221,
224–25, 233–34, 267, 346n93; modernity
and, xi, 8, 19, 39, 40, 41–42; nominalism
and, 209–10, 215, 228–29, 231–34, 242,
249, 252, 254, 352n144; on obligation,
246, 349n124; physics of, 228–34, 345n67,
347n104; political science of, 222–24,
238–46, 247, 249, 252, 347nn105–6,
350n137; on practical goal of science,
231, 232, 234, 346n81, 346n86; on pride,

244, 349n120; priority of nature and, 17, 248, 249, 262–63, 271, 355n16; project of, 222–26; religion's role and, 271–72, 356n27; religion's source and, 209, 341n2; republicanism and, 214, 216, 225, 342n24; on Scriptural interpretation, 248, 351n139, 352n141; theology of, 219–20, 225, 227–28, 246–54, 343n42, 345n71, 350n137, 352nn144–49, 356n23; on three false doctrines, 208; on war of all against all, 237, 239, 240–41, 245

Hoffman, Manfred, 319n96, 319nn99–101, 327n46

Hogeland, Cornelius van, 333n35

Holbach, Paul-Henri d', 275, 276

Holcot, Robert, 27, 131, 174, 301n26

Holly, Robert, 334n41

Holocaust, 8, 130, 283

Holyoake, George Jacob, 356n24

Holy Roman Empire, 102

Holy Spirit: Catholicism and, 130; Hobbes on, 250; Luther and, 126, 131, 153, 155, 196; scholastic theology and, 134

Hooker, Richard, 217, 341n6

Hooykass, R., 344n64

Horn, Georg, 4–5

Howell, Kenneth J., 344n64

Huguenots, 130, 172, 173

Huizinga, J., 297n9

humanism: antiquity and, 4, 5–6, 31, 32, 72–73, 75, 168, 227, 297n10; Augustine and, 57, 75, 77, 87, 88, 308n85; Bacon and, 38, 39; Cartesianism and, 5–6, 256, 312n4; Christianity and (see Christian humanism); conflicting interpretations of, 72–74; contradictions faced by, 86–88; as cultural movement, 71; Descartes and, 41, 171, 180, 183, 185, 192, 199, 200, 206, 335n66; English, 210, 212, 341n4; freedom of the will and, 31, 34, 71, 137–38; Hermetic thought and, 83, 210; Hobbes and, 42, 208, 214, 215–17, 223–24, 225, 236, 247, 254; individual human being and, 31, 32, 41, 71, 75, 76, 81, 85; Islam and, 81, 292, 293, 361n5; Italian, 71–72, 74–75, 77–92 (see also Bruni, Leonardo; Ficino, Marsilio; Machiavelli, Niccolò; Petrarch, Fran-

cesco; Pico de la Mirandola, Giovanni; Salutati, Coluccio; Valla, Lorenzo); logic and, 75, 314n23; Luther and, 103, 113–14, 119, 122, 128, 131–32, 135–36, 168; Michelangelo and, 168; modernity and, 226–27; nature and, 31–32, 85; as nineteenth-century term, 71; nominalism and, 32, 74–75, 261; Northern, 71, 74, 92–100 (see also Erasmus); origins of, 69–77; Pelagianism and, 32, 34, 76, 78, 226; Petrarch as model for, 49, 68, 70, 309n102; as philosophical position, 72, 312n4; Plato's Symposium and, 309n95; in quarrel of ancients and moderns, 256; Reformation and, 16–17, 32, 34–35, 93, 128, 132–35, 167, 261–62; Renaissance and, 71, 297n14; Savonarola's attack on, 88; secular, 72, 73, 227, 293; sense-perception and, 217; the will and, 31, 32, 37, 73, 75, 79, 85, 122, 314n25

Hume, David, 40, 256, 259, 340n156, 355n11

Humiliati, 25

Hundred Years War, 15, 29

Hunt, Lynne, 357n37

Hunter, Michael, 343n40

Hurst, Derek, 344n60

Hus, Jan, 102, 103, 144, 145, 148, 210

Husserl, Edmund, 8, 285

Hutten, Ulrich von, 137

Hyperaspistes (Erasmus), 138, 161–67, 326n24

Hypognosticon, 155

idealism, 7, 17, 41, 278–79, 340n156

Ignatius Loyola, 177, 334n39

imagination: Descartes on, 191–92, 197–98, 200, 206, 267; Hobbes on, 232, 233, 267

imago dei: Augustine and, 133; Ficino and, 82, 84, 316n55; humanism and, 71, 76, 87; Neoplatonism and, 76, 104; Pico and, 86; scholasticism and, 14; Valla and, 80

imperialism, 10, 286, 292, 359n47

Incandela, Joseph Michael, 299n2

incarnation: humanism and, 291–92; Islam and, 290, 291; Luther on, 113, 115, 116, 125–27, 321n41; tension within Christianity about, 132–33 individual, human: Enlightenment and, 275; Erasmus and, 97; Hobbes and, 239, 242; humanism and, 31, 32, 41, 71, 75, 76, 81, 85; Islam and, 292; Luther and, 119, 158, 323n83; modernity and, xi, 9; Petrarch and, 31, 46–47, 60–61, 62, 64, 65, 66, 67–68, 70, 305n47, 307n77, 310n127; Salutati and, 77. *See also* man

individualism, ontological, 4, 14, 16; Bacon's agreement with, 37; Erasmus and, 98, 135; Ficino on love and, 84; Hobbes and, 228, 233, 249–50; humanism and, 31, 32, 75, 99, 261; Luther and, 135; nominalists' fearsome God and, 29; of Ockham, 22–23, 27, 300n9, 300n11; Petrarch and, 50, 52, 60–61; Reformation and, 261; science and, 35, 36. *See also* nominalism

indulgences: Erasmus and, 96; faculty at Erfurt and, 103; history and system of, 96, 108–9, 301n29, 321n28; Hobbes and, 252–53; Luther and, 33, 109, 110, 131, 136

infinite God: of Dante and Aquinas, 15; Descartes on, 202–4, 267–68, 273, 339n134; Hobbes on, 233, 248, 249, 267, 268; of Islam, 290; of nominalism, 274

infinite human will: Descartes on, 41, 171, 205, 273, 339n139

infinite time, 5

invisible hand, 273, 275, 284, 285

Islam, 286–87, 289–93; humanism and, 81, 292, 293, 361n5; medieval Christian fear of, 21, 69–70, 299n3, 315n39; rediscovery of Aristotle and, 20, 21, 24

Jacob, Margaret, 325n5
James I, 211–12, 348n113
Jenson, Robert W., 323n86, 329n80
Jerome, 97, 113, 147
Jesseph, Douglas, 342n32
Jesuits, 139, 172, 173–74, 175, 177, 188
Joachim of Fiore, 4, 296n5
John of Mirecourt, 27, 29
John of Ruysbroeck, 81
Johnson, E., 330n141
Johnston, David, 344n60
John XXII, 25–26, 47
Jonas, Justus, 138

Jonson, Ben, 220
Josephus, 316n48
Julius II, 168
Justinian, 82

Kabbalah, 82, 85
Kant, Immanuel: antinomies of, 7, 17, 43, 259–61, 262, 263, 276–77, 278, 284, 340n156, 354n12, 358n42; on humans as ends in themselves, 275, 292; on modern reason, 256–57, 258–59; on morality, 257, 259, 260–61, 277, 282; on relationship of man and God, 39–40; on religion within bounds of reason, xi
Karlstadt, Bodenstein von, 150
kataleptic impressions, 140, 152, 159, 328n73
Keefer, Michael H., 333n24, 333n26, 333nn30–31, 333n36, 334nn50–51
Kennington, Richard, 180, 194, 334nn45–48
Kenny, Antony, 338n119, 340n149
Kepler, Johannes, 83, 337n101
Kilwardby, Robert, 21
King, Preston, 341n10
King, Ross, 331n153
Klein, Jacob, 336n84
Kleineidam, F., 320n8
Koetsier, L. S., 344n64
Kojève, Alexandre, 343n59, 348n114
Körting, Gustav, 61, 310n116
Köselleck, Reinhardt, 296n4, 328n66
Koyré, Alexander, 194, 298n22, 302n34, 314n23, 332nn11–12, 339n134, 340n149, 340n152, 356n25
Kraynak, Robert, 347n94
Kretzmann, Norman, 299n4, 300n7
Kristeller, Paul Oskar, 297n11, 301n32, 305n30, 310n138, 311n149, 312n2, 312n4, 313n5, 313nn7–8, 313nn16–17, 315n32, 315nn43–44, 316n52, 316nn54–55, 317n58, 317nn60–61
Kruger, Gerhard, 338n121

Laberthonnière, Lucien, 194
Lacan, Jacques, 359n47
Lachterman, David, 335nn66–67, 336n69, 338n127
Lahne, Werner, 325n1
Laird, Louis, 194

Lamettrie, Julien Offroy de, 275, 276
Landino, Christoforo, 82, 89
language: Erasmus and, 98–99; Hobbes on, 237; Luther and, 113, 119; post-structuralism and, 359n47. *See also* rhetoric; signs
Laport, Jean, 194
Largeault, Jean, 300n11
Larmore, Charles, 302n39
last days. *See* end of days
Latimer, Robert, 213
Latitudinarians, 254
Latomus, Jacobus, 137
Laud, William, 212, 220
laws of nature: Bacon and, 39; Descartes on, 195; divine will and, 36; Hobbes and, 41, 239, 240–41, 245–46, 251, 252, 349n119, 349n123; nominalism and, 29; Ockham and, 26; scholasticism and, 20. *See also* natural law
Leaman, Oliver, 360n2
LeClerc, Jean, 327n49
Lefèvre, Roger, 333n22, 335n64
Lefèvre d'Étaples, Jacques, 93, 333n30
Leibniz, Gottfried Wilhelm, 39, 170, 275, 303n57, 340n156
Leites, Edmund, 343n57
Leonardo da Vinci, 295n4, 314n23
Leo X, 94, 109, 110, 144, 321n28
Lessius, Leonardus, 174
Levi, Anthony, 27, 301n24, 301nn26–27, 301n29, 314n30, 316nn47–50, 317n64, 318n77, 318n82, 318n86, 319n89, 330n142
Leviathan (Hobbes): end of the world and, 251; freedom of conscience and, 349n116; goal of, 219; nominalist God and, 228, 229; passions and, 235; reception of, 219–20, 353n151; religious opposition to ruler and, 245; rhetoric and, 224, 243; ruler as mortal god in, 42, 241–43, 348n114; scientific foundation for, 238, 347n105, 353n153; theology in, 247, 250, 253, 345n71
Levine, Alan, 340n155, 355n17
liberalism: Anglo-American, civic humanism and, 73; Christianity and, 226–27; fall of Berlin Wall and, ix, 9, 10; Fukuyama on, 298n21; globalization and, 285, 359n47; Hegel and, 282–83; modernity and, xi; post-structuralism and, 359n47; Schmitt on, 345n65, 350n137; Strauss on, 350n137; theological provenance of, 293; World Trade Center attack and, x
libertines, 182, 183
Lilla, Mark, 360n47
Linton, Marisa, 357n37
Little Ice Age, 15, 29, 301n28
Livy, 48, 53, 89, 216
Locke, John, 40, 254, 258, 275, 292
logic: Erasmus and, 98; humanism and, 75, 314n23; nominalism and, 16, 29, 75. *See also* deduction; syllogistic logic
Lombard, Peter, 57, 80
Loos, Erich, 61, 308n86, 309n101, 310n117
lost generation, 8, 295n2
Louis XVI, 255
love: Augustine's God and, 133; Ficino on, 84, 91, 316nn54–55, 325n120; Luther on, 121–22, 325n120; nominalist God and, 25, 300n17; Petrarch on, 52–55, 58, 66–67, 306n48, 307nn67–68, 308n81; Plato's ladder of, 236, 309n95, 315n33
Löwith, Karl, 11, 226, 298n24, 356n28, 359n46
Loys le Roy, 297n12
Lucian, 96, 104
Lucretius, 141, 251, 310n126, 353n158
Ludwig IV, 49
Luther, Martin, 101–28; *Bondage of the Will*, 138, 147, 151–61; call on princes to maintain order, 139, 245; on church's proper role, 124–25; Descartes and, 41, 199, 205–6; early life and education, 103–4; English Reformation and, 210; Erasmus and, 97, 119 (*see also* Erasmus's debate with Luther); Finnish school and, 323n86; on government, 122–24, 324n97, 324n99, 324nn102–3, 324n109; historical context of, 101–3; Hobbes and, 216, 254, 348n109; on human being, 119–25; on the law, 120, 122, 123, 136, 166; metaphysics of, 112–19, 274; as monk, 104–6, 320n15; on nature, 125–27, 325n119, 344n64; nominalism and, 27, 32–34, 103–8, 113–14, 117, 119, 125, 127, 131,

Luther, Martin (*continued*)
157–59; Reformation and, 106, 108–12, 115, 139; on Romans, 116, 136, 144, 158; Scriptural interpretation and, 117–19, 127, 135, 157, 323nn76–77; spiritual crisis of, 101, 104, 106, 108; summary of his thought, 127–28; Tower Experience of, 106, 116, 125–26; the will and, 33, 41, 106, 110, 120, 124, 135, 144–46, 158. *See also* devil, in Luther's theology; faith, in Luther's theology; grace, in Luther's theology; Reformation
Lutheranism: Erasmus and, 137; National Socialism and, 9
Lyotard, Jean-François, 359n47

Machiavelli, Niccolò, 89–92; Descartes and, 188; Erasmus and, 306n62; Hobbes and, 223–24, 225, 242, 251, 348n108, 350n137; humanism and, 73, 88, 89–90, 92; human limitations and, 31, 87, 91, 92; human will and, 37; libertines and, 182; Luther and, 122, 126, 324n97; modernity and, 295n4; ontic priority of man and, 100; Petrarch and, 54, 90, 91–92, 311n145; religious beliefs of, 90–91, 317n68, 318n74; Roman republicanism and, 216; Savonarola and, 89; Wars of Religion and, 130
MacIntyre, Alasdair, 226
Mack, Phyllis, 325n5
MacPherson, C. B., 226
Magdeburg, 129, 242, 325n1
Magnus, Bernd, 336n85
Maier, Anneliese, 345n78
Maier, Michael, 334n42
Malcolm, Noel, 224, 341n11, 341nn13–14, 342nn26–28, 342nn33–34, 342nn36–37, 343n43, 343n49, 343n52, 344n62, 345n68
Malebranche, Nicolas de, 39, 275, 278, 340n156
man: Enlightenment view of, 274–76; modern scientific view of, 279, 358n41; nominalists' view of, 29; political identity of, 44–45; as rational animal, 14, 31, 44, 275; replacing God as center, xi; scholastics' view of, 20; transference

of divinity to, 274–76, 277. *See also* God, man, and nature; *imago dei*; individual, human; will, human
Manetti, Giannozzo, 315n31
Manicheanism: Augustine and, 84, 142, 315n37; Erasmus and, 99; globalization and, 286; Luther and, 115, 147, 149, 155–56, 159; pessimism about history and, 284, 285; post-structuralism and, 360n47; Trinity and, 133, 134; Valla and, 80
Mannermaa, Tuomo, 323n86
Manns, Peter, 329n91
Manutius, Aldus, 94
Mariani, Ugo, 314n25
Marion, Jean-Luc, 194, 202, 336n89, 339n132, 339n135
Marius, Richard C., 126, 317n59, 320nn1–2, 320nn9–10, 320n14, 320n17, 321n32, 321nn35–38, 321n40, 321nn42–43, 321nn46–47, 322n53, 322n55, 322n65, 322n67, 322n69, 323n76, 323n83, 324n96, 324n98, 324n102, 324n109, 325n118, 325n122, 329n91, 331n152
Marlowe, Christopher, 210
Marsilius of Padua, 26, 314n26
Marsilius von Inghen, 27, 103, 174
Martin, David, 356n26
Martinich, A. P., 341n2, 341nn13–14, 342n20, 342n22, 342nn29–30, 343n41, 343n44, 343nn46–50, 343n56, 344n64, 345n75, 345n78, 346n81, 346n93, 348nn111–13, 349n117, 349nn119–20, 349nn123–24, 349n126, 349n128, 350n130, 350n136, 351n140, 352nn143–44, 352n146, 353n151, 353nn156–57, 353n159, 356n27
Marx, Karl, 7, 271, 283, 298n19, 359n47
Mary Stuart, Queen of Scots, 211
Mary Tudor, 211
Masters, Roger, 295n4
mastery of nature: Bacon on, 38–39; Descartes on, 40–41, 200, 204–5, 206; Enlightenment and, 258; enslavement by technology and, 285; Hobbes on, 42; humanist pessimism about, 32, 37; Kant on, 259, 260–61; modern historical notion of, 281; modernity and, xi,

5, 42; modern science and, 5, 35, 37; nominalist revolution and, 280; radical Hegelians and, 283

materialism: Descartes' doubt and, 196, 337n102; God's relationship with creation and, 36, 302n39; of Hobbes, 220, 248, 249, 252, 266; scientific, 280

mathematics: in Galileo's analysis of motion, 263; Hermeticism and, 176; Hobbes and, 216, 219, 221, 224–25, 233–34, 267, 346n93; modern world and, 169

mathematics in Descartes' thought: doubt and, 193–94, 200, 201, 202; Hobbes and, 234, 267; science and, 40, 180–81, 183, 184, 187, 191, 192, 204–5, 206, 263

mathesis universalis, 187, 205, 222, 234, 259, 267, 269

Maurice, Prince of Orange, 174, 332n17

Mawdudi, Mawlana, 293, 361n6

Mazzotta, Giuseppe, 304n12, 305nn36–37, 305nn46–47, 306nn52–53, 307nn67–68, 310n117, 314n26

McCormick, John, 350n137

McGrath, Alister, 320n9, 321n44

McGrew, Anthony, 295n1

McIntosh, Christopher, 333n22

McNeill, John, 300n19

McSorley, Harry J., 145, 155, 166, 325n7, 326n32, 326n34, 327n35, 327nn40–42, 328n61, 328n65, 329n83, 329n85, 329n94, 331n145

Medici, 82, 83, 88, 89

medieval world: modern world and, 11, 12, 14, 46; origins of, 19–20; passing of, 4, 45. *See also* Middle Ages

Meier, Heinrich, 345n65, 350n137

Melanchthon, Philipp, 96, 135, 136, 137, 138, 167, 322n60, 328n66

mendicant orders, 102, 136

Mersenne, Marin: Descartes and, 177, 181, 183, 184, 187, 194–95, 198; Hobbes and, 217, 218, 219, 264, 343n57, 346n87

Mésland, 195

metaphysica generalis, 16, 113, 132

metaphysica specialis, 16, 113–14, 132, 270, 271, 273–74, 280, 282. *See also* God, man, and nature

metaphysics and modernity, 15–18, 262, 270, 273–74, 279–80. *See also* ontology

Michael of Cesena, 26, 47

Michael Psellos, 82

Michel, Karl Markus, 336n73, 354n7

Michelangelo, 82, 168–69, 331n154

Middle Ages, 3, 5, 297n10. *See also* medieval world

Miethke, Jürgen, 299nn5–6, 300n15

Mill, John Stuart, 40

Miller, Ted, 218, 342n35, 346n84, 346n86

Milton, John, v, 257, 316n53, 329n95

Mintz, Samuel I., 343n49, 343n55, 349n127, 352n145

miracles: Erasmus on, 330n122; Hobbes on, 248, 250–51

Mitchell, Joshua, 226–27, 345n65, 349n116, 349n125, 353n150, 353n153

modernity: antiquity and, 3, 4, 5, 8–9, 227; change and, 36–37, 298n18; Christianity and, 11–12, 14, 226–27, 357n34; chronological extent of, 295nn3–4; concept of, 1–5; contradictions intrinsic to, 17–18, 42, 263, 284, 285; conventional story of, x–xi, 10–11; crisis of, ix–x, 7–10, 17, 283–84; early critique of, 256; Enlightenment and, 42, 257; humanism and, 226–27; Islam and, 292, 293; metaphysics and, 14, 15–18, 262, 270, 273–74, 279–80; progress and, 5, 6, 281, 293, 297n11; religion and, xi–xii (*see also* secularization); science and, xi, 35, 227, 270; self-consciousness of, 36; transference of divine attributes in, 273–76, 277; two goals of, 42

Moglio, 77

Moldenhauer, Eva, 336n73, 354n7

Molesworth, Guliemi, 346n87

Molesworth, William, 341n2

Mommsen, Theodore, 296n6

Montaigne, Michel de: Descartes and, 174, 177, 184, 187, 335n66; Hobbes and, 217; humanism and, 99, 181–82, 189; Petrarch and, 311n151

Montinari, Mazzino, 298nn26–27, 358n41

Moosa, Ebrahim, 360n1

More, Thomas: Christian humanism and, 74, 210, 212; Erasmus and, 94, 96, 97, 319n102; human freedom and, 320n10; Utopia of, 238

Morney, Michael, 312n2, 312n4

Moyal, Georges, 340n149

Müntzer, Thomas, 111–12, 130

Mu'tazilites, 290–91, 360n2, 361n3

mysticism: of Bernard of Clairvaux, 115; Islam and, 291, 292; Luther and, 105, 114, 118; of Müntzer, 111; nominalism and, 14

Nadler, Stephen, 337n97

Napoli, Andrea, 341n17

Nasr, Seyyed Hossein, 360n2

Nasr, Seyyed Vali Reza, 361n6

Nathen, Johannes, 104–5

nationalism, Romantic, 279, 283

National Socialism, 8, 9, 350n137. See also Nazism

natural law: Hobbes and, 253, 272; modernity's struggle against, xii; Stoicism and, 356n28; Strauss's defense of, 8. See also laws of nature

natural theology, 20, 24, 114, 248

nature: Bacon on, 37, 38–39, 40, 262; Calvin on, 344n64; Descartes and, 180, 184, 185, 200, 204–5, 206, 262–63, 339nn142–43, 355n16; Erasmus on, 150, 164, 328n67, 330n122; grace and, 85, 150, 164, 328n67; Hegel on, 282, 283, 359n46; Hobbes and, 41, 42, 209, 222, 229, 231, 238, 248, 249, 254, 262–63, 345n75, 351n137, 353n153; humanism and, 31–32, 85; Kant and, 7, 277; Luther on, 125–27, 325n119, 344n64; mastery of (see mastery of nature); Ockham on understanding of, 23; ontic priority of, 17; Paul on, 78; realist ontology and, 20; Romantics and idealists on, 278–79; scholastic understanding of, 24; science and, 279–80; transference of divinity to, 273, 274, 275, 276, 357n32. See also God, man, and nature

Nazism, 279, 283. See also National Socialism

necessity: Hobbes and, 263; Kant on, 277; Luther and, 145–46; modern idea of history and, 284; in modern metaphysics, 262. See also determinism

Neoplatonism: Calvinism and, 127; church fathers and, 82; Eckhart and, 35; Erasmus and, 88, 97, 98, 147, 150–51; Ficino and, 82, 83, 84, 85, 150, 163; Hellenistic world and, 19; Hermeticism and, 82–83; humanism and, 32, 70–71, 76, 81, 104, 168, 169; Islam and, 290; Luther and, 113, 125, 126; Pico and, 86; recovery of, 80–81, 82; scholasticism and, 20; self-consciousness and, 198; trinitarianism and, 133, 316n47; Valla and, 79, 80, 81–82, 315n33

Newcastle, earl of, 217, 218

Newton, Isaac, 6, 83, 275, 297n15, 303n57

Nicholas of Cusa, 36, 74, 93, 174, 312n4, 314n23, 317n63

Nicholas of Oresme, 3, 174

Niebuhr, Reinhold, 73, 313n11

Nietzsche, Friedrich: Blumenberg on, 11; on death of God, 13, 227, 273; Fukuyama on, 298n21; on history as decline, 285; on humanism, 72, 73; on man as animal, 358n41; on nihilism, 13; secularization and, 254

nihilism, 13, 14, 283

Ninety-Five Theses, 109

nominalism: atheistic materialism and, 36; Augustine and, 57, 75; Bacon's science and, 39, 215; catastrophes of Middle Ages and, 29, 301n29; cohesive system of, 103; defined, 14; Descartes and, 40–41, 171, 174, 183–84, 190, 192, 201, 204, 273, 337n97, 338n119; Erasmus and, 94, 95, 97, 99; as Franciscan theology, 27; Gnosticism and, 11; God of, 15, 24–25, 29, 274, 300nn8–11, 300n17; Hobbes and, 209–10, 215, 228–29, 231–34, 242, 249, 252, 254, 352n144; humanism and, 32, 74–75, 261; Islamic thought and, 291, 299n3, 361n3; Luther and, 27, 32–34, 103–8, 113–14, 117, 119, 125, 127, 131, 157–59; Machiavelli and, 92; modernity and, 39–40, 261, 270, 273–74; Ockham and, 21–24, 300n10; Pelagianism and, 28–29; Petrarch and, 30, 31, 50, 52, 60, 66, 67, 69, 74–75; Plato's *Parmenides* and, 43; Salutati and, 77; science and, 35, 36, 227; spread of, 27; teleology and, 14, 24; Trinity and, 249–50; triumph of, 29–30; *via moderna* and, 4; will and, 27–29, 31, 280. *See also* individualism, ontological

nominalist revolution, 14–15, 16, 27; Augustine and, 57; church's power and, 131, 252; mastery of nature and, 280; modernity and, 261; Petrarch and, 69; seventeenth-century science and, 227

Oakeshott, Michael, 226, 357n35
Oberman, Heiko, 299n5, 313n12, 314n22, 320nn3–8, 320nn11–12, 320nn15–16, 320nn18–21, 321nn25–26, 321n31, 321n49, 322n54, 322n58, 322n63, 323n79, 323n91, 324n111, 324nn113–14, 325nn119–21, 328n66, 328n69
Observant movements, 102
Ockham, William of, 21–24, 26–27, 300nn8–13, 300nn16–17; on authority, 314n26; at Avignon, 22, 26, 30, 35, 43; Descartes and, 174; on divine omnipotence, 22–24, 134, 300n9; English Reformation and, 210; free will and, 143; Ghazali and, 361n3; on gulf between God and creation, 35, 36, 274; Hobbes and, 248, 254; Luther and, 33, 104, 113; Petrarch and, 50, 74; Poverty Dispute and, 26, 47; Renaissance and, 302n34; salvation and, 104; scholasticism and, 22, 24, 299nn5, 313n17; on the will, 31
Ockham's razor, 23, 233, 300n12
Oedingen, Karlo, 337n91, 339n131
Oedipus, 19, 293–94
omnipotence, divine: Blumenberg on, 156; Condemnation of 1277 and, 21, 134; Descartes and, 40–41, 183–84, 192, 193, 194–96, 199, 204, 265, 272, 337n90, 337n97, 337n102, 340n156; Enlightenment and, 276; Erasmus and, 150, 261; free will and, 143; Hermeticism and, 83; Hobbes and, 210, 220, 228, 229, 230, 249, 254; humanism and, 31, 32, 34, 71, 75, 85, 292, 314n24; in Islam, 290–91, 292; Luther and, 108, 114–15, 116, 131, 144, 146; Luther's debate with Erasmus

and, 153–54, 156, 158–59, 160, 161, 167; Manicheanism and, 142; modernity and, 273–74; nominalism and, 14, 22, 28, 75, 131, 134, 143, 274; Ockham on, 22–24, 134, 300n9; Petrarch on, 66; Reformation and, 34; Salutati on, 77; scholasticism and, 14. *See also* will, divine
omnipotence, human, Descartes and, 206
ontic questions: defined, 16; divine power and, 274; Enlightenment and, 280; humanism and, 16–17, 70, 99–100, 132, 134, 261; priority of nature and, 262–63, 264, 270, 355n16; Reformation and, 16–17, 132, 134, 261
ontological argument, 201–5, 339n130, 339n144
ontology, 16; of Luther, 113, 127, 321n40. *See also* being; individualism, ontological
Oratorians, 182–83
Origen, 83, 97, 113, 147, 155
original sin: Erasmus and, 163–64; humanism and, 75, 76, 78, 85, 104; Luther and, 149; medieval Christianity and, 64; Ockham and, 300n16; Pelagianism and, 301n25; Petrarchian individuality and, 70. *See also* Fall
Osler, Margaret, 337n99

Pace, Richard, 319n91
Pagel, Walter, 316n46
Panofsky, Erwin, 297nn8–9
pantheism: environmental movement and, 357n32; Erasmus and, 164; Hobbes and, 249, 352n146; rationalism and, 36; of Romantics and idealists, 278; of Spinoza, 275
Paul: city of God and, 45; Erasmus and, 164, 166; Ficino's Platonism and, 316n54; grace and, 116, 127, 164; humanists and, 78; Luther and, 119, 121, 127–28
Paul III, 168
Paul IV, 139
Payne, Robert, 217, 220
peace: crisis of modernity and, 8, 10; Enlightenment and, 258; Erasmus and, 95, 97, 161, 319n91; globalization and, ix, 285, 286; Hobbes on, 42, 239, 240, 241,

peace (*continued*)
242, 243, 244–45; Kant on, 260; Luther on, 122, 124, 324n103; modern conception of history and, 281; Petrarch on, 49, 304n19

Peace of Augsburg, 172

Peasants' Rebellion, 111, 112, 130, 138, 161, 167

Pelagianism: Augustine and, 28, 84, 142; Biel and, 143; defined, 301n25; Descartes and, 340n155; Erasmus and, 99, 150, 151, 166, 328n67; Ficino and, 85, 317n57; humanism and, 32, 34, 71, 76, 78, 226; idea of history and, 285; Luther and, 131, 143–44, 147, 149; Machiavelli and, 90; modern notion of progress and, 281, 284; modern secular version of, 275, 357n34, 360n47; nominalism and, 28–29; Petrarch and, 56, 64, 66; Trinity and, 133, 134; Valla and, 80

Pelczynski, Z. A., 297n16

Perkins, William, 353n156

Perraton, Jonathan, 295n1

Perrault, Charles, 5

Pesch, Otto Hermann, 319n99, 327n46

Peters, Albrecht, 329n91

Peters, Richard S., 352n145

Petrarch, Francesco, 30–31, 46–68; *Africa*, 48, 53–55, 59, 306n48, 306n56, 306nn60–62, 307n65, 307n67; ancient world and, 4, 30–31, 48–49, 51, 53–57, 66, 70–71, 75–76, 88, 304n11, 306nn49–50, 306nn55–56, 306nn60–62, 308n91; ascent of Mount Ventoux, 57, 308n82; at Avignon, 35, 43, 47, 74; Boccaccio and, 301n31, 304n23; brother Gherardo, 47, 56, 57, 60, 63, 304n9, 304n20, 309n109, 314n24; Christianity of, 55–57, 64–68, 69–71, 75–76, 88, 308n91; on dark age, 4, 79; decay as theme for, 55, 307n65; Descartes compared to, 177, 185, 187, 309n99; *dictatores* tradition and, 71–72; divine power and, 66, 274; Erasmus and, 94, 97, 306n62; on human condition, 49–52, 304nn17–20, 305n35; human individuality and, 31, 46–47, 60–61, 62, 64, 65, 66, 67–68, 70, 305n47, 307n77, 310n127; *Illustrative Lives*, 48, 53, 55; impact in his time,
69, 311n1; Italian politics and, 48–49; Laura and, 47, 58, 303n8, 307n68, 309n96; letters of, 48, 63, 304n10; life of, 46, 47–49, 303n8, 304n9; on love, 52–55, 58, 66–67, 306n48, 307nn67–68, 308n81; Machiavelli and, 54, 90, 91–92, 311n145; *Memorable Things*, 55; as model for humanism, 49, 68, 70, 309n102; modern neglect of, 69; *My Secret*, 48, 57–59, 61, 62, 67, 308nn86–92, 309nn94–95, 309n101; nominalism and, 30, 31, 50, 52, 60, 66, 67, 69, 74–75; "Of Our Own Ignorance," 66–67; ontic priority of man and, 70, 100; on periods of European history, 50; Platonism and, 50, 57, 59, 68, 70, 76, 80; *Religious Leisure*, 63, 311n145; *Remedies for Fortune Fair and Foul*, 48, 49, 59, 61, 65, 75, 304nn18–20, 308n81, 309n94, 310n125, 311n144; Salutati and, 77; scholasticism and, 30, 50, 52, 301n30; *The Solitary Life*, 48, 50–51, 59–60, 62, 64, 67, 309nn106–7, 309n112, 310n118, 310nn123–26, 310n138, 310n143, 311n151; *Songbook*, 48, 52, 58, 61, 305n45; *Triumphs*, 307n68

Pfeiffer, Rudolph, 297n7

Phillips, M. M., 330n142

Philo, 83

Pico de la Mirandola, Giovanni, 85–87; Descartes and, 334n45; Erasmus and, 97, 151; Ficino and, 82; Luther and, 136; Machiavelli and, 91; Mersenne's attack on, 181; quasi-divine status of humans and, 292; on the will, 85–86, 314n25

Pinkard, Terry, 359n46

Pintard, René, 334n52

Pippin, Robert, 6, 297n17, 298n19

Plato: Augustine and, 56, 57, 80, 308n91; Bruni's translations of, 79; change and, 36; Descartes and, 265; Ficino's translations of, 83; human creation and, 79–80; Kallipolis of, 238; *Parmenides*, 43; Petrarch and, 70, 80; Pico on, 86; postmodernists and, 9; self-consciousness and, 198; *Symposium*, 84, 309n95, 316n54; *Timaeus*, 36, 83; on time, 280; virtue and, 56

Platonism: Enlightenment and, 257; of
Ficino, 83–85, 316n54; Hermeticism
and, 82, 83; Hobbes' rejection of, 214,
229, 250, 352n147; of humanists, 70–71,
76, 77, 81–82, 89; Petrarch and, 50, 57,
59, 68, 70, 76, 80; recovered in fifteenth
century, 80–81; Voegelin on Christianity and, 9. See also Neoplatonism
Pletho. See Gemistus Pletho, George
Plotinus: Augustine and, 84, 133, 141,
315n40; Ficino and, 84; Hermeticism
and, 83; mystical tradition and, 81;
Petrarch on, 65
Pocock, J. G. A., 313n13
Poe, Edgar Allan, 297n16
Poliziano, Angelo, 82, 89, 341n4
Pope, Alexander, 6, 274, 297n15
Popkin, Richard, 332n13, 334n52, 337n91
postmodernism, 9, 10, 17, 190, 296n5,
360n47
post-structuralism, 9, 359n47
Poverty Dispute, 26, 47, 102
predestination: Anselm and, 143; Church
of England and, 211; double, 252,
Enlightenment and, 276; Hobbes and,
42, 216, 220, 225, 236, 252, 254, 268–69,
272, 273, 353n157; Luther and, 117, 127;
modern science and, 358n43; nominalism and, 29, 143
Presbyterianism, 211, 213, 218, 221, 254,
341n10
Proclus, 83, 84
progress: Christian millennarianism
and, 11, 12; crisis of faith in, 7–8; divine
attributes transferred to, 273, 275; globalization and, ix, 295n1; history
as, 281–84; Kant on, 260; modernity
and, 5, 6, 37, 281, 293, 297n11; post-
structuralism and, 359n47; and quarrel
of ancients and moderns, 5–6. See also
change
Promethean perspective: Enlightenment,
276; of humanist individualism, 71, 76,
81, 86, 91, 95–96, 99, 189; modern, 281
prosperity, x, 8, 10, 42, 51, 283, 285, 286
Protestantism: liberalism and, 226–27;
secularization and, 271. See also
Anglicanism; Calvinism; Episcopalian-

ism; Lutheranism; Presbyterianism;
Reformation
Pseudo-Dionysus, 84
purgatory, 252–53
Puritans, 211, 213, 245, 352n141
purpose: humanism and, 31–32. See also
teleology
Pyrrhonian skepticism, 181, 192, 265,
327n44, 334n50, 338n126

quarrel of ancients and moderns, 5–7, 256
Qutb, Sayyid, 293

Rabil, Albert, 313n14, 314n29, 318nn79–81,
318n83, 318n85, 319n88, 319n91, 319n93,
319n98, 326n8, 326n15, 328n60, 330n142
Raphael, 82, 297n8
rationalism, 8, 20, 36, 41, 291
Rawski, Conrad H., 304n12
realism: Bacon's rejection of, 37; divine
omnipotence and, 22–23, 300n8; Erasmus and Luther on, 135; Hobbes and,
228; Islamic theology and, 291, 361n3;
Petrarch and, 50; Plato's Parmenides
and, 43; rejected by nominalism and
humanism, 75; of scholastics, 14, 20, 30;
tenth-century distinction about, 4. See
also universals
reason: crisis of modernity and, 8–9, 10;
cunning of, 273, 282, 284; Descartes
and, 170, 171, 191, 200, 205; early
critiques of modernity and, 256–57;
Enlightenment and, 257, 258; Erasmus
and, 135, 165; free will and, 142, 143;
French Revolution and, 7, 281; Hegel on
history and, 281–82; Hobbes and, 208,
209, 232, 234, 236, 237, 239, 248, 346n84;
Kant on, 258–59, 260, 354n12; Luther
on, 119, 120, 124, 135; metaphysics and,
16; modern displacement of religion
and, x, 11; nominalist revolution and,
14; origin of modernity and, 11, 12, 14,
18; Petrarch on, 50; scholasticism and,
20, 21, 133–34. See also logic
Reformation: development of, 171–73; English, 210–13; Erasmus and, 95; Hobbes
and, 42, 208, 209, 236, 247; humanism
and, 16–17, 32, 34–35, 93, 128, 132–35,

Reformation (*continued*)
167, 261–62; Luther and, 106, 108–12, 115, 139; modernity as consequence of, 189; nominalism and, 15, 29, 33, 261; Ockham and, 299n5; radical, 112, 139; sectarian diversity arising from, 227. *See also* Calvin, John; Luther, Martin; Protestantism

Reign of Terror, 255–56, 277–78, 281

Reik, Miriam M., 224, 341n15, 342n24, 343nn50–51, 343nn53–54, 344n63, 353n157

Renaissance: English, 210; Ficino's influence on, 81–82, 84; Gilson on, 313n10; humanism and, 32, 37, 71, 234; idealization of antiquity in, 5; as modern, 313n12; as nineteenth-century concept, 297n14; Ockham and, 302n34; Petrarch and, 69, 70

republicanism, 75, 216, 226, 342n24. *See also* civic republicanism

resurrection: of the body, Hobbes on, 251, 253; of Christ, 116, 120

Reuchlin, Johannes, 93–94, 96, 135, 318n79

Reuss, Timothy J., 331n3, 340nn153–54

Reventlow, Henning Graf, 226, 300n20

Reynolds, Noel, 215, 342n19, 342n23, 349n116

rhetoric: Erasmus on, 96, 98, 319n88; Hobbes and, 217, 224, 243; humanism and, 75, 132; Luther and, 113, 118, 125, 126, 138, 325n119; modern theology as, 270; Reformation and, 132

Riedl, Matthais, 296n5

Rienzo, Cola di, 49, 54

Riley, Patrick, 275, 357n31

Roberto da Mileto, 305n32

Robespierre, Maximilien, 277

Rochmonteix, Camille de, 331n7, 332n10

Rodis-Lewis, Geneviève, 332n14

Rogers, G. A. J., 342n31, 345n71, 355n18

Rogge, Joachim, 321n33

Romantics, 7, 9, 278–79, 280, 283, 297n16

Rorty, Amélie Oksenberg, 303n58, 339n132

Rosen, Stanley, 194, 336n85

Rosicrucianism, 175–76, 177, 179, 180–81, 182, 183, 185, 333nn22–23, 333nn34–35, 334nn41–42, 335n57

Rossi, Paolo, 316n46

Rousseau, Jean-Jacques, 6, 8, 256, 275, 277, 281, 284, 357n38

Rueschemeyer, Dietrich, 331n4

Rupp, Gordon, 318n84, 319n92, 325nn3–4, 326n11, 326n16, 326n19, 326nn21–22, 326n26, 328n61, 329n80, 329n87, 329n94, 329n97

Ryan, Alan, 342n31, 345n71, 349n120, 355n18

Salafism, 292

Salutati, Coluccio, 72, 73, 74–75, 77, 78, 80, 94, 314n25

salvation: Arminianism and, 211; Augustine on, 142–43; Descartes' silence on, 336n75; earthly, Hobbes on, 239, 240; Erasmus and, 96, 150, 319n103; Gregory of Rimini and, 301n26; Hobbes and, 42, 208, 209–10, 228, 234, 248, 252, 353n157; humanism and, 73, 78, 104, 138; Luther and, 33, 104–9, 111–12, 115–18, 120, 122, 124–25, 131, 144, 155, 161, 166–67, 323n83; Machiavelli and, 90, 318n74; medieval eschatology and, 3; nominalism and, 25, 28–29, 104, 109; Pelagianism and, 142, 150, 301n25; Petrarch and, 56, 64, 75. *See also* grace

Sanchez, Francisco, 174

Sarpi, Paolo, 215, 342n20

Sartre, Jean-Paul, 338n124, 359n47

Satan. *See* devil (Satan)

Savonarola, 86, 88–89, 90, 317n65

Saxonhouse, Arlene, 342n19, 342n21

Scala, Bartolomeo, 89

Schearer, S., 309n106, 314n24

Schell, James V., 340n154

Schelling, Friedrich, 278

Schiller, Johann, 6

Schlegel, Friedrich, 6

Schmidt, R., 354n12

Schmitt, Carl, 345n65, 349n116, 350n137, 360n47

Schneider, Ivo, 333n27

scholasticism: Augustinianism compared to, 308n79; collapse of, 29–30; Descartes and, 174, 189–90, 201, 263; Enlightenment and, 257, 258; Erasmus and, 95, 97,

135, 136; evil and, 159; Ficino's Platonic
Christianity and, 83; free will and, 143;
Hobbes and, 208, 214, 228, 263, 341n17;
humanism and, 72, 74, 77, 312n4; individual human being and, 60; instability
of, 20–21; Islamic influence on, 361n3;
in Italy, 74, 313n17; Luther and, 107, 112,
113, 119, 127, 135, 321n39; natural law
teachings of, xii; nominalism and, 11,
12, 14–15, 16, 27; Ockham and, 22, 24,
299n5, 313n17; Petrarch's dissatisfaction with, 30, 50, 52, 301n30; rise of, 20;
seventeenth-century rejection of, xi;
trinitarian theology of, 133–34; the will
and, 27–28
Scholtz, Heinrich, 338n105
Schopenhauer, Arthur, 39, 278
Schouls, Peter, 338n119
Schreiner, Susan, 344n64
Schuhmann, Karl, 341nn17–18
science: Bacon on, 37–39; contradictions
of modernity and, 277; of Descartes
(see Descartes' new science); displacement of religion and, x, xi; Eckhart's
theology and, 36; Hegelians and, 283;
Hermeticism and, 83, 316n46; Hobbes
and, 41, 209–10, 216–19, 221–26, 228–34,
248–49, 252–54, 263–64, 346n79,
346nn93–94, 350n137; humanist logic
and, 314n23; humanist project and, 167;
industrial civilization and, 7; Islam
and, 293; Kant on, 256–57, 259, 260–61;
Marx and Engels on, 298n19; mastery
of nature and, 5, 35, 37; modernity and,
xi, 35, 227, 270; nominalism and, 35,
36; Ockham's individualism and, 23;
post-Enlightenment, 271, 278, 279–80;
progress and, ix; and quarrel of ancients and moderns, 5, 6, 7; Reformation theology and, 344n64; theology
incorporated into, 274
Scipio Africanus: Machiavelli and, 90, 91,
318n72; Petrarch and, 48, 53–55, 60, 63,
65, 70, 75, 306n55, 306nn60–62
Scotus, Duns: divine omnipotence and,
21, 134, 143; divine will and, 27, 143, 154;
English Reformation and, 210; Erasmus
and, 94, 150, 328n61; Ockham and, 22;

Petrarch and, 50, 314n25; reception at
Bologna, 313n17
Sebba, Georg, 334n49
second coming: Hobbes and, 251, 253. See
also end of days
secular humanism, 72, 73, 227, 293
secularization, x–xi, 9, 11–12, 227, 254,
270–78, 281, 356n24, 356n28. See also
death of God
Seigel, Jerrold, 74, 306n51, 308n93, 310n123,
313n6, 313n9, 313n15
Seldon, John, 220
self-assertion: Blumenberg on, 11–12,
357n34; Descartes' new science and, 200
self-consciousness: Hegel on, 282; Kant on,
260; of modernity, 36
self-knowledge: Petrarch on, 52, 57, 58–59,
309n96, 309n99
Seneca: humanists and, 77; Petrarch and,
50, 53, 57, 59, 62, 67, 305n42; on the will,
141, 142
sense-perception: Descartes on, 217, 263,
265; Galileo on, 217; Hobbes on, 217,
231–32, 263, 265, 346n93
Sepper, Dennis, 336n84
September 11, 2001, attacks, ix–x, 10, 286
Sesonske, Alexander, 337n90
Sextus Empiricus, 192, 317n64, 334n50
Shakespeare, William, 32, 210, 243, 311n1,
348n115
Shklar, Judith, 297n16
Siegel, Carl, 354n12
signs: Hobbes on, 232–33, 234, 237, 266;
nominalism and, 14, 132, 232
Simon, Gérard, 337n101, 338n122
Sistine Chapel, 168–69
skepticism: Academic, 140–41, 146, 148, 151,
265; Arminianism as, 212; Augustine
and, 152, 196; Descartes and, 182, 184,
192, 193–96, 200, 265, 337n92, 338n126;
Erasmus and, 149, 151, 152, 153, 162,
163, 196; fideism and, 114, 182; Hobbes
and, 219; humanism and, 88, 104, 182,
317n64; Humean, 256, 259, 340n156,
355n11; Luther and, 106, 153, 196; Pyrrhonian, 181, 192, 265, 327n44, 334n50,
338n126; sixteenth-century, religious,
320n1

Skinner, Quentin, 223, 224, 313n13, 344nn60–61
Skocpol, Theda, 331n4
Smalley, Beryl, 313n20, 314n22
Socinians, 250, 352n149
Socrates, 44–45, 46; Erasmus and, 96, 99, 148, 163, 165–66, 319n88; Ficino on, 316n49; humanism and, 78; Luther and, 165; Petrarch and, 67, 70
Soderini, Piero, 89
Soffer, Walter, 337n102, 339n143
Sommerville, Johann, 348n113
Sorell, Tom, 341n11, 342n38, 344n62
soul: Ficino on, 84, 85, 316n51, 316n55; Hobbes on immortality and, 252
Spalatin, Georg, 136
Spengler, Ostwald, 8, 285, 298n20
Spinoza, Baruch, 39, 249, 275, 339n144, 350n137, 352n146
Spitz, Lewis, 325n5, 331n143
Spragens, Thomas, 303n55, 343n58, 347n102, 347n104, 350n135
Springborg, Patricia, 342n39, 350n132, 351n137, 352n141, 353n155
St. Bartholomew's Day Massacre, 130, 172, 211
Staël, the Baroness de, 357n38
state, xi, 42, 102, 139, 173, 325n2
Staupitz, Johannes von, 105, 106, 115–16
Steinmetz, David C., 322n51
Stherna, Kirsi, 323n86
Stirling, James Hutchinson, 354n2
Stoicism: Augustine and, 58, 308n91; divine logos and, 152, 155, 156, 157, 158, 328n73; Erasmus's diatribe and, 148, 149; freedom and, 140, 141, 142, 146, 147; Löwith on return to, 356n28; Luther and, 151, 152, 153, 155, 156, 157, 158, 159, 162–63; Petrarch and, 50, 58, 59, 61–62, 65–66, 67–68, 308n85, 308n91; political nature of man and, 45; Salutati and, 77; Valla and, 79, 315n33; virtue and, 56
Strauss, Leo, 8, 223–24, 226, 343n59, 348n114, 350n137, 353n153, 355n16
Strier, Richard, 344n60
Strong, Tracy, 218, 342n35
structuralism, 359n47

Stuart, Elizabeth, 175, 176
Suarez, Francisco, 30, 174, 190, 341n14, 349n123
subjectivity: Descartes and, 41, 189–90, 198, 305n47; modernity as, xi
substance, 229, 266, 275
substantial forms, 190
swerve, 141, 228–29
Swift, Jonathan, 6
syllogistic logic: Hobbes and, 228, 233, 347n99; humanism and, 75; Luther and, 113–14; nominalism and, 23, 75; realism and, 14, 20. See also logic

Tacitus, 89, 215, 277, 296n2
Tannery, Paul, 303n58
Tasso, Tarquato, 81
Tawney, R. H., 226
technology, ix, xi, 7, 283, 285, 286, 298n19
teleology, xii, 14, 24, 251, 282, 283, 353n153. See also purpose
Tempier, Etienne, 21
Temple, William, 6
Tertullian, 249
Thirty-Nine Articles, 211, 247, 249, 250
Thirty Years War, 172–73, 175, 185–86
Thomas à Kempis, 93
Thomism: at Bologna, 313n17; of Gilson, 72; vs. neo-Thomism, 189, 190. See also Aquinas, Thomas; scholasticism
Thucydides: Hobbes and, 215–16, 222, 224, 242, 346n94
Tilly, Charles, 173, 331n4
Tilly, Count von, 129, 325n1
time: ancient cyclical view of, 3, 5, 280; Hobbes on, 345n72, 345n74; humanist idea of fortune and, 31–32; medieval eschatology and, 3, 4, 296nn3–4; modernity and, 2, 4, 5, 18, 19, 37; nominalist revolution and, 280–81; Petrarch and, 56, 307n68. See also end of days
Tocqueville, Alexis de, 284
Tönnies, Ferdinand, 342n24
totalitarianism, ix, 9, 283, 356n28, 359n47
Tracy, James D., 326n13, 328nn63–64, 328n67, 328n69, 330n121
transubstantiation, 102, 125, 324n112

Trapp, Joseph, 311n1

Trinity: Arianism and, 87; as church doctrine, 133; Hobbes on, 249–50, 353n150; Neoplatonism and, 84, 133, 316n47; Petrarch on, 66; scholastic theology and, 133–34. *See also* Holy Spirit

Trinkaus, Charles, 74, 80, 299n5, 301n32, 305n29, 305n31, 305n35, 305n45, 306n54, 307n76, 309nn100–101, 309n104, 310n127, 311n145, 313n12, 313nn14–15, 313n18, 313n20, 314nn21–22, 314nn24–25, 314n27, 315n33, 315nn35–36, 319n87, 319n90, 319nn95–96, 326n10, 328n59

Tritheists, 250

Trutfetter, Jodokus, 103, 107

truth: Descartes on, 177, 179, 180, 181, 184, 185, 186, 189, 190–91, 201, 206, 263; Enlightenment and, 257; Hobbes and, 263, 266, 269; Kant on, 260; skeptical humanism and, 88

Tuck, Richard, 217, 264, 342n31, 343n40, 343n57, 346n79, 346nn82–83, 349n128, 355n18

Tunstall, Cuthbert, 326n19

Tweedale, Martin, 300n10, 300n15

Tyacke, Nicholas, 341nn5–9

Unitarianism, 250, 271

universals, 4, 14, 133, 230, 233, 300n8, 300n11. *See also* realism

Urban, W., 320n11

Usingen, 143, 144

utilitarianism, 279

Valla, Lorenzo, 4, 79–80, 81; biblical interpretation and, 351n139; Erasmus and, 94, 97, 98, 163; Luther and, 119, 136, 148; *On Pleasure*, 311n154, 315n33

Vatter, Miguel, 345n65, 349n116, 350n137

Vaughan, John, 220

Verbeek, Theo, 340n155

Veron, François, 174

via antiqua, 4, 107, 230, 299n5

via moderna, 4; Biel and, 318n78, 320n16; Erasmus and, 319n89; Erfurt as stronghold of, 320n8; Hobbes and, 230; Luther and, 105, 107, 108, 131

viator, 275, 301n29

Victorinus, 83, 316n47

violence: Hobbes and, 207, 208–9, 222, 235, 237–40, 241, 243, 246, 348n114; radical Hegelians and, 283. *See also* war

Virgil: Luther and, 104, 135, 145; Petrarch and, 47, 48, 53, 70

Virgilio, Marcello, 89

virtue: Erasmus and, 88, 99, 163, 166; humanist project and, 88; Petrarch on, 51, 53–55, 56, 59–60, 61–62, 64–65, 66–67, 76, 88, 306n50; Salutati and, 77

Voegelin, Eric, 9, 356n28

Voetius, 206, 340n155

Voigt, Georg, 56, 307n71

Voltaire, xi, 6, 258, 273, 281

voluntarism, 11, 17, 158, 291, 346n85, 349n124

Wahhab, Muhammad ibn Abd-al-, 292

Waldensians, 25, 102

Wallis, John, 221, 343n49

war: globalization and, 286; Hobbes on, 41, 225, 237, 239, 240, 248; Luther and, 123, 161; Petrarch on, 49

Wars of Religion, 17, 34, 129n31, 139, 167, 169, 325nn1–2; Descartes and, 171, 175, 185, 206; divine vs. human will and, 274, 357n39; historical chronology of, 172–73; Hobbes and, 246, 269; Kant's third antinomy and, 262; modern theological radicalism and, 356n28

Watain, Philip, 327n35

Watson, Richard, 175, 178, 331n5, 332n9, 332nn15–19, 333n21, 333n28, 333n33, 333n35, 334n37, 334nn39–40, 334n42, 335nn55–57, 335n62, 335n65

Weber, Max, 226, 271

Wells, Norman, 332n10

Wesel, Johannes, 103

White, Thomas, 219, 220, 228, 229, 247, 345n71

Whitfield, J. H., 64–65, 305nn38–39, 306n50, 307nn72–73, 311n145, 311n150, 311nn152–53, 311n155

Wiener, P. P., 297n11, 301n32

Wilbur, James B., 336n85

Wilkins, Ernest Hatch, 303nn5–6, 304n11, 304n23, 305n32, 305n40, 306n62, 307n69
Wilkinson, John, 214
will, divine: Bradwardine on, 345n78; Calvin on, 344n64; Descartes and, 171, 195, 199, 204, 205, 267, 271, 337n99; Eckhart and, 35–36; Erasmus and, 135, 147; Erasmus's debate with Luther and, 153, 154, 158, 262; Ficino and, 84, 85, 316n55; Hobbes and, 209, 216, 220, 225, 229, 230, 236, 251, 252, 271, 273, 275, 345n75, 345n78; humanism and, 79; in Islam, 291; Luther and, 41, 111, 120, 121, 122, 125, 131, 135, 144, 146; medieval eschatology and, 3; Petrarch on, 66; scholastics and, 133–34, 143; scientific turn and, 274; transferred to man and nature, 273, 275, 276, 277–78, 357n32; Valla and, 80. *See also* omnipotence, divine
will, general, 273, 275, 277, 357n38
will, human: ancient philosophers and, 139–41; Descartes and, 40–41, 171, 197–98, 199–200, 204, 205, 267, 338n119, 338n127, 339n139; divine attributes transferred to, 273, 275; divine omnipotence and, 141–42; Erasmus and, 135, 147, 167; Hobbes and, 269; humanism and, 31, 32, 37, 73, 75, 79, 85, 122, 314n25; Luther and, 33, 41, 106, 110, 120, 124, 135, 144–46, 158; nominalism and, 27–29, 31, 280; Petrarch on, 52, 58, 59, 64, 65, 66, 67, 79, 305n42, 308n88, 308n90, 314n25;

Pico on, 85–86, 314n25; Romantics and idealists on, 279; Rousseau on, 275; Salutati and, 77; scholastics and, 133–34, 143; scientific turn and, 274; Valla and, 80. *See also* free will
will, primordial, 278
Wills, Bernard, 326n27, 328n73
Wilson, Brian R., 356n26
Wilson, Margaret, 303n58, 339n139, 340n149
Winckelmann, Johann, 6
Wolfson, Harry, 361n4
Wolin, Sheldon, 226
Wolter, A. B., 299n6
Woodham, Adam, 27
Wootton, David, 215, 317n62, 342n20, 343n40
world-soul, 84, 278
world-spirit, 278, 280
World Trade Center. *See* September 11, 2001, attacks
World Wars, 7–8, 130, 283
Wotten, William, 6
Wrathall, Mark, 358n40
Wycliff, John, 102–3, 116, 145, 148, 210

Yates, Frances, 316n46, 333n22

Zeitlin, Jacob, 62, 305n33, 309n106, 310n143, 311n151
ŽiŽek, Slavoj, 359n47
Zoroastrianism, 82, 315n37, 316n45
Zwingli, Huldrych, 111, 172